Chaucer

Chaucer

AN OXFORD GUIDE

Edited by

Steve Ellis

OXFORD
UNIVERSITY PRESS

OXFORD
UNIVERSITY PRESS

Great Clarendon Street, Oxford OX2 6DP

Oxford University Press is a department of the University of Oxford.
It furthers the University's objective of excellence in research, scholarship,
and education by publishing worldwide in

Oxford New York

Auckland Cape Town Dar es Salaam Hong Kong Karachi
Kuala Lumpur Madrid Melbourne Mexico City Nairobi
New Delhi Shanghai Taipei Toronto

With offices in

Argentina Austria Brazil Chile Czech Republic France Greece
Guatemala Hungary Italy Japan South Korea Poland Portugal
Singapore Switzerland Thailand Turkey Ukraine Vietnam

Oxford is a registered trade mark of Oxford University Press
in the UK and in certain other countries

Published in the United States
by Oxford University Press Inc., New York

Database right Oxford University Press (maker)

First published 2005

A catalogue record for this book is available from the British Library

Library of Congress Cataloging in Publication Data

Chaucer: an Oxford guide/edited by Steve Ellis.
    p. cm.
  Includes bibliographical references and index.
  ISBN 0–19–925912–7 (alk. paper)
1. Chaucer, Geoffrey, d. 1440—Criticism and interpretation—Handbooks,
manuals, etc.   I. Ellis, Steve, 1952–
PR1924.C39 2005
821'.1—dc22   2004025110
ISBN 0–19–925912–7 (Pbk)

10 9 8 7 6 5 4 3 2 1

Typeset by RefineCatch Limited, Bungay, Suffolk
Printed in Great Britain by
Antony Rowe Ltd, Chippenham, Wiltshire

Acknowledgements

I should like to thank my team of wonderfully patient and responsive contributors to this volume, and all those academic colleagues who helped me assemble such a team. I should also like to thank the staff at Oxford University Press who have worked with me on the project, in particular Ruth Anderson, Laurien Berkeley, Alexandra Buckle, Matthew Cotton, and Fiona Kinnear.

S.E.

Outline contents

Detailed contents   ix
List of illustrations   xix
List of contributors   xxi
Abbreviations and note on references   xxiii

Introduction: Chaucer today *Steve Ellis*   1

Part I Historical contexts   **7**

1 Chaucer's life *Ruth Evans*   9

2 Society and politics *S. H. Rigby*   26

3 Nationhood *Ardis Butterfield*   50

4 London *C. David Benson*   66

5 Religion *Jim Rhodes*   81

6 Chivalry *Mark Sherman*   97

7 Literacy and literary production *Stephen Penn*   113

8 Chaucer's language: pronunciation, morphology, metre *Donka Minkova*   130

9 Philosophy *Richard Utz*   158

10 Science *J. A. Tasioulas*   174

11 Visual culture *David Griffith*   190

12 Sexuality *Alcuin Blamires*   208

13 Identity and subjecthood *John M. Ganim*   224

14 Love and marriage *Bernard O'Donoghue*   239

Part II Literary contexts   **253**

   15 The classical background *Helen Cooper*   255

   16 The English background *Wendy Scase*   272

   17 The French background *Helen Phillips*   292

   18 The Italian background *Nick Havely*   313

   19 The Bible *Valerie Edden*   332

Part III Readings   **353**

   20 Modern Chaucer criticism *Elizabeth Robertson*   355

   21 Feminisms *Gail Ashton*   369

   22 The carnivalesque *Marion Turner*   384

   23 Postmodernism *Barry Windeatt*   400

   24 New historicism *Sylvia Federico*   416

   25 Queer theory *Glenn Burger*   432

   26 Postcolonialism *Jeffrey J. Cohen*   448

   27 Psychoanalytic criticism *Patricia Clare Ingham*   463

Part IV Afterlife   **479**

   28 Editing Chaucer *Elizabeth Scala*   481

   29 Reception: fifteenth to seventeenth centuries *John J. Thompson*   497

   30 Reception: eighteenth and nineteenth centuries *David Matthews*   512

   31 Reception: twentieth and twenty-first centuries *Stephanie Trigg*   528

   32 Translations *Malcolm Andrew*   544

   33 Chaucer in performance *Kevin J. Harty*   560

   34 Chaucer and his guides *Peter Brown*   576

Part V Study resources   **593**

   35 Printed resources *Mark Allen*   595

   36 Electronic resources *Philippa Semper*   607

      Postscript *Julian Wasserman* †   621
      Chronology   625
      Index   627

Detailed contents

Detailed contents   ix
List of illustrations   xix
List of contributors   xxi
Abbreviations and note on references   xxiii

Introduction: Chaucer today *Steve Ellis*   1

Part I Historical contexts   **7**

1 **Chaucer's life** *Ruth Evans*   9

The life   12

Social Chaucer   16

Scandal?   17

Biography as narrative   19

The absent author and the author-function   20

The future of biography?   23

Further reading   23

2 **Society and politics** *S. H. Rigby*   26

Society   26

Social ideology: the three orders   26

Social reality: status, class, and gender   27

Plague, population, and economic change   29

Social conflict   32

Chaucer and the social order   35

Politics   38

Edward III, the Hundred Years War, and the deposition of Richard II 38

The descending concept of political authority   40

The ascending concept of political authority   44

Chaucer and politics   45

Conclusion   47
Further reading   48

3 **Nationhood** *Ardis Butterfield*   50
England and France: the Hundred Years War   52
Cultural identity: people   56
Cultural identity: language   58
Cultural identity: writing   60
Chaucer's Englishness   63
Further reading   64

4 **London** *C. David Benson*   66
London in the late fourteenth century   66
Chaucer's London   70
Chaucer's early poetry   71
Troilus and Criseyde and the 'Knight's Tale'   72
The 'General Prologue' of the *Canterbury Tales*   74
Chaucer's London tales: 'Canon's Yeoman's Tale' and 'Cook's Tale'   76
Further reading   79

5 **Religion** *Jim Rhodes*   81
'What man artow?'   82
'For soothly the lawe of God is the love of God'   83
The Virgin Mary and the communion of saints   89
The forgiveness of sins   91
'The naked text in English to declare'   92
Conclusion   94
Further reading   94

6 **Chivalry** *Mark Sherman*   97
The problem of definition   97
Historical origins   98
Imaginary origins   99
Chaucer's problematic chevalier   101
Antiquity and history: the 'Knight's Tale' and *Troilus and Criseyde*   102
Chivalry and Chaucer's modernity   105
Conclusion   110
Further reading   111

7 **Literacy and literary production** *Stephen Penn*   113
Literacy   115

Chaucer's medieval audience   119
The 'Chaucer circle'   121
Manuscript production   124
Further reading   127

8 **Chaucer's language: pronunciation, morphology, metre**
  Donka Minkova   130
  Sound–spelling correspondences   131
  Stress   138
  Morphology   141
  Metre   149
  Further reading   156

9 **Philosophy** *Richard Utz*   158
  Education and reading   158
  Boethius' *Consolation of Philosophy*   159
  Chaucer and the *Consolation of Philosophy*   160
  Non-Boethian contexts   164
  Augustinianism   165
  Late medieval literalism   167
  Late medieval nominalism   168
  Conclusion   171
  Further reading   171

10 **Science** *J. A. Tasioulas*   174
  Astronomy   174
  Astrology and horoscopes   176
  Planetary influence   179
  Medicine   181
  Magic   185
  Alchemy   186
  Conclusion   188
  Further reading   188

11 **Visual culture** *David Griffith*   190
  Iconographic traditions   191
  The garden in the 'Merchant's Tale'   196
  Marginal images   198
  Text and image   201

Portraits and textual authority   203
Further reading   205

12 **Sexuality** *Alcuin Blamires*   208
    Sexuality by any other name?   209
    Sexuality or sexualities?   212
    Active and passive   214
    Ownership of sexuality   216
    Sexualities and nature   218
    The burden of sexuality   220
    Further reading   222

13 **Identity and subjecthood** *John M. Ganim*   224
    Individual, self, and subject   224
    Mentality, affinity, and association   226
    Performance and negotiation   229
    Interiority and consciousness   233
    Personae and authorial subjecthood   235
    Conclusion   237
    Further reading   237

14 **Love and marriage** *Bernard O'Donoghue*   239
    The language of love   239
    Chaucer as love-poet   242
    Society and marriage   245
    Sexuality, marriage, and actual lovers   247
    Love, marriage, and Chaucer's texts   249
    Further reading   251

Part II Literary contexts   **253**

15 **The classical background** *Helen Cooper*   255
    Chaucer's classics   256
    Ovid without metamorphosis   260
    Classical settings   261
    The nature of authority   264
    Chaucer's poetic claims   267
    Further reading   269

16 **The English background** *Wendy Scase*   272
    Theories and practices of vernacular authorship   273

	Versification	275
	Manuscript culture	276
	Preaching, pardoners, and friars	277
	Religious plays and the 'Miller's Tale'	279
	Theological and devotional literature	280
	Lollardy and the lay reader	282
	Religion, vernacularity, the Wife, and the Prioress	283
	English romance	285
	'Verray lewednesse': 'Sir Thopas', the Franklin, and the Wife	287
	Critical traditions and future directions	289
	Further reading	290
17	**The French background** *Helen Phillips*	292
	Cosmopolitan England	293
	Chaucer and contemporary French poetry	295
	Dream poems: creative responses, interpretative independence	298
	Chaucer and French romance	300
	Fabliaux	302
	The Renart cycle and the 'Nun's Priest's Tale'	303
	French readings of Griselda and the 'Clerk's Tale'	303
	The 'Man of Law's Tale' and Nicholas Trevet's *Chronicle*	304
	French influence on style and versification	306
	Translations	307
	'Melibee'	308
	Chaucer and the *Roman de la Rose*	309
	Further reading	311
18	**The Italian background** *Nick Havely*	313
	Latin and Italian	313
	Lombards and Tuscans	315
	The English in Italy	317
	French connections	319
	Authors and authority: Dante, Boccaccio, Petrarch	320
	Poets and makers	324
	On the road and in the garden: the *Canterbury Tales* and the *Decameron*	325
	'Dante in English'? Six centuries of Chaucer's 'Italian background'	327
	Further reading	329
19	**The Bible** *Valerie Edden*	332
	The composition of the Bible	334

The interpretation of the Bible | 335

Biblical translation and the 'plain text': the Wycliffite controversy | 338

Chaucer's use of biblical allusions | 339

Chaucer and the 'glosing' debate | 343

Chaucer's 'biblical poetics' | 346

Further reading | 349

Part III Readings | 353

20 **Modern Chaucer criticism** *Elizabeth Robertson* | 355

Post-Victorian American criticism | 356

Post-Victorian English criticism | 361

Post-Second World War critics | 362

Later twentieth-century trends | 365

Further reading | 367

21 **Feminisms** *Gail Ashton* | 369

Chaucer and feminist readings | 371

The Wife as oral construction | 373

Departures | 375

Alison: noise and sound | 376

The repressed feminine | 378

Alison as monster | 379

Alison: a talking 'queynte' | 380

Asserting the feminine | 380

Further reading | 382

22 **The carnivalesque** *Marion Turner* | 384

Bakhtin and his readers | 384

The carnivalesque in medieval culture | 386

Chaucerian carnival | 389

The *Parliament of Fowls* | 391

Reading Bakhtin and Chaucer in the twenty-first century | 396

Further reading | 398

23 **Postmodernism** *Barry Windeatt* | 400

Cultural belatedness: Chaucer's postmodernity | 400

Chaucer and the themes of postmodernism | 401

Chaucer and postmodernist forms | 403

Magic, or realism, or magical realism? | 406

Post-romance		409
Postscript		413
Further reading		413
24 New historicism *Sylvia Federico*		416
Chaucer at Chancery		418
Representations of rape		420
Rape and revolt		424
The invisibility of rape		426
Rape and punishment		427
Rape and social position		429
Further reading		430
25 Queer theory *Glenn Burger*		432
Sexuality and Chaucer studies		432
Queer matters		435
Queering identity/historicizing modernity		437
Late medieval proto-capitalism and category confusion in the 'Shipman's Tale'		439
Money, exchange, and equality		442
Medieval conjugality and late medieval bourgeois identity formation		444
Further reading		446
26 Postcolonialism *Jeffrey J. Cohen*		448
Postcolonial practice		448
Canonical Chaucer		449
The medieval and the postcolonial		450
Postcolonial London		451
From English writer to island writer		452
Chaucer's orientalism		454
Remembrance and loss		458
Further reading		461
27 Psychoanalytic criticism *Patricia Clare Ingham*		463
Against common sense		463
An uncommon subject		464
Uncommon language and culture: the Symbolic Order		467
Uncommon histories		468
Considering the 'Knight's Tale'		471
Uncommon wisdom		476
Further reading		477

Part IV Afterlife — 479

28 Editing Chaucer *Elizabeth Scala* — 481
Textual notes ignored here — 481
The original Chaucer and Chaucer's 'originals' — 483
Chaucer in print — 486
Critical editions — 488
'Literary' complications and the order of the tales — 490
Hengwrt — 492
Chaucer in the age of computing — 493
Further reading — 494

29 Reception: fifteenth to seventeenth centuries *John J. Thompson* — 497
Premodern and early modern Chaucers — 497
Chaucer as author and canon formation — 499
Chaucer the father and England's laureate poet — 502
Reformation Chaucers and 'Canterbury Tales' — 505
Endings as beginnings: Chaucer absences — 507
Further reading — 509

30 Reception: eighteenth and nineteenth centuries *David Matthews* — 512
Chaucer at the end of the nineteenth century — 512
Chaucer and Dryden — 513
Thomas Warton and the Romantic revival — 517
Chaucer, nineteenth-century man of the world — 519
Further reading — 525

31 Reception: twentieth and twenty-first centuries *Stephanie Trigg* — 528
Chaucer and the general reader — 529
Virginia Woolf, G. K. Chesterton, and Harold Bloom — 531
Chaucer and the canon — 534
Rewriting Chaucer — 535
Australian Chaucer — 539
Conclusion — 541
Further reading — 542

32 Translations *Malcolm Andrew* — 544
The first translations — 544
Dryden — 545
Pope — 549
Other eighteenth-century translations — 550

Wordsworth 551

Other nineteenth-century translations 553

Developments in the twentieth century 555

Further reading 558

33 **Chaucer in performance** *Kevin J. Harty* 560

Chaucer on stage 560

Chaucer, Caryl Churchill, and John Guare 562

Canterbury Tales: the musicals 563

Chaucer as ballet 564

Chaucer as opera 564

Chaucer as choral piece: Dyson's *The Canterbury Pilgrims* 565

Chaucer on (and in) film: Pasolini's *I racconti di Canterbury* 566

Chaucer on (and in) film: Brian Helgeland's *A Knight's Tale* 568

Chaucer on film: minor appearances and allusions 570

Chaucer on television 572

Conclusion 573

Further reading 574

34 **Chaucer and his guides** *Peter Brown* 576

Academic guides to Chaucer 577

The common reader 581

The common non-reader 584

Homes and haunts 586

Conclusion 588

Further reading 590

Part V Study resources 593

35 **Printed resources** *Mark Allen* 595

Bibliographies 595

Dictionaries and reference works 598

Editions of Chaucer's works 600

Language and metre 601

Sources, analogues, and influences 603

Chaucer's life 605

Reception and reputation 606

36 **Electronic resources** *Philippa Semper* 607

Using web-based resources: searches 608

Using web-based resources: content   611

Non web-based electronic resources   616

Web links   617

Postscript *Julian Wasserman*†   621

Chronology   625

Index   627

List of illustrations

Figure I.1   Portrait of Chaucer. Illustration from Thomas Hoccleve, *Regement of Princes (1411–12). British Library, MS Harley 4866.* By permission of The British Library.   22

Figure I.2   The *Wilton Diptych* (anonymous), late 1390s: Richard II being presented to the Virgin and Child. By permission of The National Gallery, London.   42

Figure I.3   Map of Chaucer's Europe, 1360   53

Figure I.4   Map of Chaucer's London   68

Figure I.5   The poem being read before a court audience. Frontispiece to a manuscript of Chaucer's *Troilus and Criseyde*, early fifteenth century (Cambridge Corpus Christi College, MS 61). By permission of The Master and Fellows of Corpus Christi College, Cambridge.   114

Figure I.6   Creation of light and spheres. Illustration from a Book of Hours, mid-fourteenth Century (British Library, MS Egerton 2781). By permission of The British Library.   175

Figure I.7   Scenes from the 'Pardoner's Tale'. Fragment of wooden chest, early fifteenth Century (Museum of London). By permission of the Museum of London.   192

Figure I.8   King David, author of the Psalms, with marginal scene of a 'bawdy betrothal'. Page from the Ormesby Psalter, early fourteenth century (Bodleian Library, MS Douce 366, fol. 131). By permission of The Bodleian Library, University of Oxford.   200

Figure I.9   Pygmalion appeals to Venus; Venus' torch warms his statue to life. Manuscript illustration, late fourteenth century (British Library, MS Yates Thompson 21, fol. 138). By permission of The British Library.   210

Figure II.1   Christ carrying the cross, with typological scenes from the Old Testament. Illustration from the Eton Roundels, mid-thirteenth century (Eton College, MS 177). By permission of Eton College.   337

Figure III.1 Battle and inversion of the sexes. Misericord, early sixteenth century (Westminster Abbey). By permission of the Dean and Chapter of Westminster Abbey.   387

Figure IV.1   Ford Madox Brown, *Chaucer at the Court of Edward III*, 1847–1851, oil on canvas, 372x296cm. Purchased 1876. Collection: Art Gallery of NSW. Photograph: Ray Woodbury for AGNSW.   522

Figure IV.2   William (Heath Ledger, left) and Chaucer (Paul Bettany) in Brian
               Helgeland's *A Knight's Tale*. (Still courtesy of the collection of Kevin
               J. Harty and reproduced here solely for the purpose of critical analysis.)   569

Figure IV. 3   A bicycle ride along the pilgrims' route to Canterbury. Illustration
               by Joseph Pennell in Joseph and Elizabeth Robbins Pennell, *A
               Canterbury Pilgrimage (1885)*.   583

List of contributors

Mark Allen University of Texas at San Antonio

Malcolm Andrew Queen's University, Belfast

Gail Ashton University of Manchester

C. David Benson University of Connecticut

Alcuin Blamires Goldsmiths College, London

Peter Brown University of Kent

Glenn Burger Queens College, City University of New York

Ardis Butterfield University College London

Jeffrey J. Cohen George Washington University

Helen Cooper University College, Oxford

Valerie Edden University of Birmingham

Steve Ellis University of Birmingham

Ruth Evans University of Stirling

Sylvia Federico Bates College

John M. Ganim University of California, Riverside

David Griffith University of Birmingham

Kevin J. Harty LaSalle University

Nick Havely University of York

Patricia Clare Ingham Indiana University

David Matthews University of Newcastle, Australia

Donka Minkova University of California, Los Angeles

Bernard O'Donoghue Wadham College, Oxford

Stephen Penn University of Stirling

Helen Phillips Cardiff University

Jim Rhodes Southern Connecticut State University

S. H. Rigby University of Manchester

Elizabeth Robertson University of Colorado

Elizabeth Scala University of Texas at Austin

Wendy Scase University of Birmingham

Philippa Semper University of Birmingham

Mark Sherman Rhode Island School of Design

J. A. Tasioulas Clare College, Cambridge

John J. Thompson Queen's University, Belfast

Stephanie Trigg University of Melbourne

Marion Turner King's College London

Richard Utz University of Northern Iowa

Julian Wasserman[†] Loyola University

Barry Windeatt Emmanuel College, Cambridge

Abbreviations and note on references

The following abbreviations are used in citations of Chaucer's works.

AA	*Anelida and Arcite*
B	*Boece*
BD	*Book of the Duchess*
CT	*Canterbury Tales*
HF	*House of Fame*
LGW	*Legend of Good Women*
LGW (F)	*Prologue, Legend of Good Women*, Text F
LGW (G)	*Prologue, Legend of Good Women*, Text G
PF	*Parliament of Fowls*
RR	*Romaunt of the Rose*
TA	*Treatise on the Astrolabe*
TC	*Troilus and Criseyde*

Canterbury Tales

'ClP'	'Clerk's Prologue'
'ClT'	'Clerk's Tale'
'CP'	'Cook's Prologue'
'CR'	'Chaucer's Retraction'
'CT'	'Cook's Tale'
'CYP'	'Canon's Yeoman's Prologue'
'CYT'	'Canon's Yeoman's Tale'
'FP'	'Friar's Prologue'
'FrP'	'Franklin's Prologue'
'FrT'	'Franklin's Tale'
'FT'	'Friar's Tale'
'GP'	'General Prologue'
'KT'	'Knight's Tale'
'ManP'	'Manciple's Prologue'
'ManT'	'Manciple's Tale'
'Mel'	'Melibee'
'MerE'	'Merchant's Epilogue'
'MerP'	'Merchant's Prologue'
'MerT'	'Merchant's Tale'

'MLE'	'Man of Law's Epilogue'
'MLI'	'Man of Law's Introduction'
'MLP'	'Man of Law's Prologue'
'MLT'	'Man of Law's Tale'
'MoP'	'Monk's Prologue'
'MoT'	'Monk's Tale'
'MP'	'Miller's Prologue'
'MT'	'Miller's Tale'
'NPE'	'Nun's Priest's Epilogue'
'NPP'	'Nun's Priest's Prologue'
'NPT'	'Nun's Priest's Tale'
'ParI'	'Pardoner's Introduction'
'ParP'	'Pardoner's Prologue'
'ParsP'	'Parson's Prologue'
'ParsT'	'Parson's Tale'
'ParT'	'Pardoner's Tale'
'PrP'	'Prioress's Prologue'
'PrT'	'Prioress's Tale'
'PST'	'Prologue to Sir Thopas'
'PT'	'Physician's Tale'
'RP'	'Reeve's Prologue'
'RT'	'Reeve's Tale'
'ShT'	'Shipman's Tale'
'SNP'	'Second Nun's Prologue'
'SNT'	'Second Nun's Tale'
'SP'	'Summoner's Prologue'
'SqI'	'Squire's Introduction'
'SqT'	'Squire's Tale'
'ST'	'Summoner's Tale'
'TST'	'Tale of Sir Thopas'
'WBP'	'Wife of Bath's Prologue'
'WBT'	'Wife of Bath's Tale'

All quotations from Chaucer are taken from the *Riverside Chaucer*, general editor Larry D. Benson, 3rd edn. (Boston: Houghton Mifflin, 1987; Oxford: Oxford University Press, 1988).

Introduction: Chaucer today

Steve Ellis

In September 2003 BBC Television launched a six-part series of *Canterbury Tales*, recast-ings of some of Chaucer's narratives set in contemporary Britain and described in more detail in Chapter 33 below. The *Radio Times*, the BBC's listings magazine, introduced the series with an editorial in which the writer recalled the experience of studying the 'Nun's Priest's Tale' at school, likening it to being dosed with castor oil, and noting that Chaucer 'bored the brains out of me and, as a result, remains one of the few works of classic literature I never touched again' (the inaccuracy of the editor's recollection of the tale indeed confesses to her boredom). The new series, however, is 'deserving of a medal' for having 'succeeded in making me want to dust down ye olde copy of the original for the first time since I wore a blazer and tie'.[1]

The editorial is telling in a number of ways. Not simply does it suggest that it is Chaucer himself who is 'boring', rather than attributing the experience to the way he has been presented in the school system (or to the editor's own endeavours), but even the promise of reparation, of dusting down 'ye olde copy', is insincerely patronizing and only conceivable thanks to a far more interesting ('fabulous') television series. But what is more telling is the ready and sympathetic audience the editor assumes for such confessions in *Radio Times*-reading Britain. No disgrace is involved in being bored out of one's brains by Chaucer—the public declaration of finding Chaucer a harmless and irrelevant old(e) joke automatically counts on being echoed widely, and with no risk of incurring embarrassing charges of philistinism. Chaucer is a safe object to kick. And while I have no quibble with the television series itself, which was humorous and entertaining, or with the availability of Chaucerian plots for adaptation and modern-ization, selling such things under the Chaucer 'brand' frequently and exasperatingly involves just such a passing swipe at Chaucer's work itself.[2]

This present Guide to Chaucer, written essentially with an undergraduate audience in mind (some of whom may perhaps have had similarly disheartening school experi-ences), draws on the enormous amount of scholarship produced in recent times to present a Chaucer who is anything but boring and irrelevant to present concerns. A series of chapters on historical context in Part I gives necessary information about the turbulent period, politically, socially, and intellectually, which informs Chaucer's work, and in Part III the questions we are asking about that work today come to the fore in a series of readings and interpretations. Critics are presently finding that Chaucer's writing raises questions of race and ethnicity, of gender and sexuality, of social class issues, of the signifying procedures of literature itself and of the ways it mediates history, and of the ways individuals are constructed as ideological subjects. Chaucer speaks to us today on all these concerns, and while this Guide provides an abundance of literary and historical information about factors specific to the Middle Ages, it also wishes to present a Chaucer who is just as available to today's intellectual lines of enquiry as any other text is, medieval or post-medieval. Chaucer, we might say, is not 'ye olde' author but, as with any major literary figure, always bang up to date. Indeed, as many contributors to this volume explain, the culture of postmodernism finds much that anticipates it in Chaucer.

One instance of this is the way in which Chaucer manipulates the author–narrator–text relationship. For example, by introducing himself into his own work as fellow pilgrim, and by giving himself one of the most 'boring' tales to tell, that of 'Sir Thopas', which the Host is so exasperated by that he interrupts 'Chaucer' with 'Thy drasty rymyng is nat worth a toord!' (930), the poet executes an extraordinarily sophisticated act of narrative play that chimes with the self-reflexive practices of authorship that feature in many modern texts. Indeed, one of Chaucer's most sophisticated comic procedures is in the recurring creation of the author–narrator as a kind of simpleton, be it in the *Book of the Duchess*, the *House of Fame*, or the *Canterbury Tales* itself. There is a tradition in approaching Chaucer of taking this creation at face value, and hence the image of quaint affability arises which has fed into the patronizing attitude noted above. But Chaucer the author stands outside his personae, including that of 'Chaucer' himself, deploying them and their interactions in a deeply knowing way, and staging the encounter between multiple discourses—social, philosophical, iconographical, religious—in a highly ambitious manner. To do this, as Part II of this Guide specifies, he draws on a wide range of reading and learning, indicating a writer profoundly interested in the classical tradition and in the European literature of his day, versed in philosophy and theological writing—the 'great translator' as the French poet Deschamps called him. Chaucer indeed is truly cosmopolitan, and not to recognize this, and to see him as merely the author of a few dismissible 'tales', says a great deal about our own parochialism rather than his.

The writer discussed in the following pages is then a complex and very various figure, and indeed part of the diversity he encompasses raises the possibility of a 'darker' and less tolerant Chaucer than is usually assumed (discussed, for example, in Chapters 3, 25, and 26). Likewise the gregarious author of the *Tales*, the celebrant of human brotherhood, is looked on with some scepticism, as in the concluding pages of Chapter 22, where a Chaucer more in keeping with our own fraught world of racial and religious tension is discussed. It is no surprise, further, that Chaucer's incrimination in the 1380 rape case of Cecily Chaumpaigne receives a noticeable amount of attention in these pages (see, for example, Chapters 1 and 24). Of course, any approach to Chaucer will highlight the concerns of its own day, and rather than attempting to conceal such 'presentism' the following pages frequently explore it and ask what it means. Nor has the editor imposed or expected any party line in presenting this 'darker' Chaucer: in what follows this figure coexists, as one contributor puts it, with the Chaucer still valued for 'the sweep of his comic vision and for his humanity'. This Guide to Chaucer—properly Guide to Chaucers—shows criticism and scholarship involved in a necessary and inevitable dialogue.

Today therefore we have a Chaucer who is very far from the figure commonly recognized, but even in the wider public domain, as Stephanie Trigg notes at the end of Chapter 31, there may be signs of 'a growing impatience and reluctance with the standard trajectories of Chaucerian reception', and 'the time may well be ripe for a new wave of Chaucerian reinvention'. A whole section of this Guide, Part IV, is given to the history of Chaucer reception, and several contributors not only speculate on this history but consider its future. The disjunction between the 'complex and various' Chaucer described above and the belittled figure who frequently inhabits and has inhabited the public domain is extremely striking, and is considered at different points below, where contributors seek to explain it from a variety of positions (see Chapters 1, 31, 32, 33). As Ruth Evans notes, the commercial marketing of Chaucer, whether via eBay or 'The "Canterbury Tales" Visitor Attraction' in Canterbury (see Chapter 34), has nothing in common with the 'cultured, cosmopolitan, elusive, and postmodern' figure who features on the academic syllabus.

If postmodernism signals the death of meta-narrative—the rejection of the idea that there is a fundamental, controlling 'truth' or omniscient viewpoint which can be used as a benchmark or framework to measure all partial truths, or individual voices, or limited perspectives—then Chaucer might indeed seem to be 'postmodern' (on this, see particularly Chapter 23). The *Canterbury Tales* is of course a signal mixing of voices representing different positions on the world, positions inflected by social class, gender, professional office, but the task of knowing whether the work promotes or demotes any of these voices, or suggests that they can be judged or ranged hierarchically according to some religious or social framework, is a matter for endless and unfinalizable debate. Here Chaucerian 'elusiveness', also seen in pre-*Tales* works that take a debate form, like the *Parliament of Fowls*, or in the several works that are literally unfinished, like the *House of Fame*, can be for students a source of both fascination and frustration. Chaucer is not a poet of 'answers'. In this, as Nick Havely (Chapter 18) and David Wallace remind us, Chaucer differs from his great fellow medieval poet Dante; in Wallace's words, he 'explicitly rejects the Dantean option of writing a text with pretensions to universal knowledge'.[3] If Dante's *Divine Comedy* is a vision of judgement on individuals, the *Canterbury Tales* is not a 'vision' (the word assumes a transcendental 'truth') but among other things a statement about the difficulties of judging. And yet even this relativistic assessment is open to contestation from critics who do find Chaucerian 'judgements' and prejudices—anti-feminist, homophobic, aristocratic—present in his work, a position equally strongly challenged by those who hold to a feminist and inclusive Chaucer. Perhaps it would be safer to say that the *Canterbury Tales* is a statement about the difficulties of judging whether judgement is possible.

At any rate, the mixture of discourses, the scepticism about final truths, and the self-reflexiveness that all feature in Chaucer's work should make him more 'at home' in a postmodern period than he was in the earlier twentieth century, when many writers, themselves ambitious for a totalizing synthesis (one thinks of Eliot's *Four Quartets*, Joyce's *Ulysses*, Pound's *Cantos*) precisely promoted the claims of the medieval synthesis available in Dante in a way that eclipsed what Chaucer had to offer. Today's more hospitable climate is perhaps instanced in the fact that a writer like Ian McEwan could canvass Chaucer as the 'person of the millennium' in a recent end-of-century radio poll.[4] At the same time McEwan's own novel *Amsterdam* (1998), in which the two protagonists inflict death on each other, shows the 'Pardoner's Tale' once more darkly resurfacing in the narrative tradition. If newer scholarly approaches have helped to 'reinvigorate' Chaucer studies, as Patricia Ingham argues at the beginning of her chapter (Chapter 27), there are signs that a reinvigorated Chaucer is also spreading beyond the academy, and, who knows, may one day land on the desk of the editor of the *Radio Times*.

The present Guide therefore offers a Chaucer for today, and witnesses to the inescapability of reading Chaucer with today's concerns in mind. But we are hardly likely to understand our own 'presentism' without some indication of the presentism of the past, and the volume as remarked gives a good deal of space, in Part IV, the 'Afterlife', to the history of Chaucer reception. One feature of today's situation is precisely the growth in the 'guide culture' that results in volumes like the present one, and it would be remiss of this Guide's editor not to have commissioned a final chapter in Part IV that seeks to contextualize the Guide itself within such a culture (Chapter 34). At other points in the volume the encouragement to be self-reflexive results in further comments on the value and function of the academic guidebook (Chapters 16 and 26).

We began with the boredom of studying Chaucer at school. After a section on study resources (Part V), the volume has a short Postscript by Julian Wasserman (whose early death, alas, prevented him from contributing a full-length piece) which considers differences in the UK and US educational systems that contribute to different responses to Chaucer. As the great majority of contributors to the Guide are from one of these two countries, it is salutary to be reminded of both kinship and divergence, and also to be assured of the present healthy state of Chaucer studies, which a generation ago looked to be under some threat. The Postscript also acts as a kind of preface to the web site accompanying this Guide, which looks in detail at teaching-related issues in connection with Chaucer, considering the history and practice of the classroom (and of examinations) at both university and pre-university level on both sides of the Atlantic. As Wasserman reminds us, our response to Chaucer is not only historically, but also geographically, determined; all Chaucer is to some degree 'local' Chaucer. Chaucer has been exported right across the globe to the antipodes of his point of origin (see Chapter 31), but it is true that he does not have the worldwide following of Shakespeare, though there is an important tradition of reading and studying Chaucer in continental Europe and in Japan. A future we can only speculate on for this cosmopolitan writer is the extension of his global status, and indeed on the contestation between locality and globalization that will surely accompany it.

NOTES

1. Gill Hudson, 'Trick of the Tales', *Radio Times*, 6–12 Sept. 2003, 7.
2. Plentiful examples of this are offered in my *Chaucer at Large: The Poet in the Modern Imagination* (Minneapolis: University of Minnesota Press, 2000).
3. *Chaucerian Polity: Absolutist Lineages and Associational Forms in England and Italy* (Stanford, Calif.: Stanford University Press, 1997), 163.
4. Interview with Ian McEwan, *Today* (BBC Radio 4), 18 Dec. 1998.

Part I

Historical contexts

1 | Chaucer's life

Ruth Evans

Contrary to received opinion, we do not possess a superabundance of information about Geoffrey Chaucer's life. The poet John Milton's life-records fill five large volumes, but Chaucer's fill only one: the indispensable *Chaucer Life-Records*, assembled in the 1960s by Martin Crow and Clair Olson.[1] By the standards of modern, truth-telling (often dirt-raking) biography, much of this material is curiously depersonalized. It consists largely of legal documents: records of expenses, exchequer writs, payments of annuities, appointments to office, witness statements, pleas of debt, house leases. This is the obscure public record of a royal servant, singularly lacking in the information that a modern biographer would consider essential to her project: childhood, education, personal foibles, love affairs, sources of inspiration, and all the humdrum details (getting one's shoes mended, attending evensong) that are thought to be so fascinating when juxtaposed with the supposedly more high-minded preoccupations of the writing subject. We do, however, have a whiff of scandal. But perhaps the most striking thing about the evidence is that there is no record whatsoever of Chaucer's life as a man of letters. Chaucer was not a career poet: while he lived he was not known primarily as an author of literary works. But from careful scrutiny of the life-records critics have been able to put together a reasonably authoritative picture of Chaucer's career, his circle of friends and associates, and his literary milieu. The established facts are by now rather well worn. But there have been two significant events since Crow and Olson's volume: the discovery of a new record by Christopher Cannon, and Paul Strohm's landmark book on Chaucer's political ties, *Social Chaucer*.

None of Chaucer's works (with the possible exception of three lines in the 'Nun's Priest's Tale' that refer to 'Jakke Straw', one of the leaders of the 1381 English rebellion or 'Peasants' Revolt', 3394–6) refers explicitly to historical events. But it is hard not to interpret some of the poems in the light of obvious historical referents. For example, the not-so-cryptic references to 'goode faire White' (948) and a 'long castel' (1318) in the *Book of the Duchess*, a poem written shortly after the death in 1368 of John of Gaunt's first wife, Blanche, Duchess of Lancaster, may hint at Gaunt's possible patronage of Chaucer—or at Chaucer's seeking of it. But if there is so little direct historical allusion in the poetry, then why look at Chaucer's life at all? In any case, isn't the *writing* what really matters?

In this context it is now obligatory to cite the critic Roland Barthes, who famously proclaimed in the 1970s that the Author is dead. Barthes's obituary was of course deliberately polemical, in order to draw attention to (and endorse) the emergence of a new set of cultural assumptions governing literary interpretation: a shift away from the author towards the reader.[2] Ten or fifteen years ago, in the wake of Barthes, biographical readings were almost considered a theoretical crime in literary criticism. Knowing the author's 'experiences' or 'mind' (if one could know them at all) could—or should—contribute nothing to a reading. Meaning resided in the reader's encounter with the text and in understanding the text's historical place within a much larger textual weave. These reader- and text-based approaches still hold good for readings of Chaucer's œuvre (and I would defend them in many circumstances as politically, ethically, and aesthetically vital), but this certainly does not mean that the author is irrelevant or that the project of examining the author's life is worthless—or that we can serenely contemplate Chaucer's texts as detached aesthetic objects.

In the words of the historian of written culture Roger Chartier, the meaning of the text is not only historically constructed but 'produced in the dialogue that exists between the propositions contained in the work (which are *in part* controlled by *the author's intentions*) and the readers' responses' (my italics).[3] This author is emphatically not the sovereign genius of traditional critical biography but a figure at once 'dependent and constrained'. Dependent in so far as his intentions do not wholly govern the way the work is read (in Chaucer's case, we have only to think about the role of copyists, annotators, and booksellers, and later, editors and publishers, in imposing meanings at odds with authorial intention); constrained in so far as the space of literary production is socially determined. Chartier's analysis stresses 'dialogue' between text, author, and reader, but the real challenge to the binary between 'life' and 'text' is that authors do not just produce texts but are themselves texts. The composite figure we call 'Geoffrey Chaucer' is made up not only of the poetry (and prose) that he left us, but also of a variety of other texts: the life-records, and all of the academic and popular supplements (biographies, portraits, scholarly articles and books, films, musicals, images, e-discussions, and even novels) that form the dense network of meanings and representations that we now recognize as 'Chaucer'. Chaucer *is* those texts, and our encounter with his poetry is inescapably conditioned by our awareness of them all. This is why there is more, not less, need to think critically about the relationship between Chaucer's life and works.

There is not space in this chapter to offer a thoroughgoing reassessment of this relationship. But I will sketch out a few caveats. Nothing is more irritating than the crude reduction of the intricate surface of Chaucer's poetry to the effects of his personal circumstances, real or imagined. Derek Pearsall's otherwise astute criticism of Chaucer's work in his critical biography is sometimes marred by this whimsical reductionism. He invites us to imagine, for instance, that we hear the 'complaining voice' of Chaucer's wife, Philippa, in the voice of the eagle in the *House of Fame*.[4] Not only is this unwarranted (we know nothing about Chaucer's home life) and sexist, but it ignores altogether the signifying structures of the text, structures that make the experience of reading the poetry an altogether more elusive and complex event than if it were simply a window on the author's life.

More problematic is the issue of how to respond to the evidence that Chaucer was accused—although the charge was dropped—of rape. It says a great deal about our modern fascination with the scandals of writers' lives that the rape accusation is the one biographical fact, according to the critic Carolyn Dinshaw, that everyone remembers about Chaucer.[5] It has featured in several novels (the earliest appeared in 1905) in which a fictionalized Chaucer attempts to exonerate himself from the rape charge.[6] The document containing this 'evidence' was first unearthed in 1873. It is a Latin legal deposition, made in 1380 by a certain Cecily Chaumpaigne, releasing Chaucer from the charge of *raptus* (rape? abduction? the term is ambiguous, though less so now in the light of Cannon's discovery[7]). For Dinshaw, the case reminds us that there are not only '*figurative* rapes' and '*fictional* rapes', but there are '*real* rapes as well'.[8] Reading and rape belong to two different orders of reality. But our awareness of the Chaumpaigne case necessarily affects our understanding of Chaucer's representations not just of actual and figurative rapes (the knight's rape of the maiden at the beginning of the 'Wife of Bath's Tale'; Criseyde's dream of an eagle violently tearing out her heart and substituting its own in book 2 of *Troilus and Criseyde*, 925–31) but of gendered power relations as a whole. Even at moments where we might need—for the sake of pressing our own political readings—to repudiate authorial intention, it is very difficult to dismiss this incident from our minds when we read. But should we have to? Knowledge of the Chaumpaigne case makes us wary, for example, of claiming for Chaucer an enlightened attitude towards women; it highlights the contradictions of *gentil* masculinity in late medieval England (contradictions that are anyway very much on show in Chaucer's work), and the contradictions of readings that would purge the author of any relevance. Though the Chaumpaigne accusation is not part of our recent cultural memory (and therefore felt as less of an outrage to national literary history) and its full meaning is obscure, it is not unlike the revelation of T. S. Eliot's antisemitism or Paul de Man's youthful Nazi sympathies, cases that have called forth the most delicate critical reappraisals of those writers' works and which make it clear that the question of how to read the works *responsibly* is always already a question of how to read the life.[9] (For more on how the rape case might inform Chaucer's work, see Chapter 24.)

The question still remains of what is at stake in writing Chaucer's biography. Some readers talk about Chaucer's life as if it were of interest in its own right, but we would not consider it worthy of such attention if we did not know him as an important poet. Moreover, the impulse to write his biography has to be more than that of finding him a 'decent sort of fellow', as Pearsall (somewhat groping for words) describes him.[10] The most compelling reason is the opportunity it affords us to understand the social, political, and intellectual world that shaped Chaucer the writer. Paul Strohm's study has been exemplary here in probing Chaucer's factional ties, providing a careful analysis of the changing structure of social relations in late fourteenth-century England and its impact on Chaucer's poetry. This chapter does not offer any new revelations or interpretations, but it will consider some of the assumptions that lie behind many standard accounts of the life and indicate some alternatives to what the cultural historian Michel Foucault calls 'the-man-and-his-work criticism'.[11]

The life

The broad outlines of Chaucer's life are well known. It is the almost unblemished life of a royal servant, a non-aristocratic *gentil*, rising steadily through the ranks by virtue, initially, of his father's wealth and influence, to become a royal esquire. This would have been very unusual before the mid-fourteenth century. Charged with important (often secret) national and international commissions on the part of both Edward III and then Richard II, Chaucer also enjoyed the favours of the powerful duke of Lancaster, John of Gaunt, and established ties of common interest within the king's 'affinity'. His close associates at Richard's court in the 1380s were influential and powerful men. In the early 1360s Chaucer was also the friend of the distinguished French poet and chronicler Jean Froissart, and later of the aristocratic Savoyard poet Oton de Graunson, who served under Gaunt. Chaucer's poetic career began in the late 1360s, with translations from French poetry and the fashionable, French-influenced *Book of the Duchess*, with its pleasing eulogy to John of Gaunt's recently deceased wife, Blanche. But he made his name with the courtly romance *Troilus and Criseyde* (1381–6). He is best remembered today for the work that he was writing (or completed?) at the end of his life: the *Canterbury Tales*. While an esquire Chaucer also held posts as controller of customs in the port of London, Clerk of the King's Works, and as a Justice of the Peace (and briefly Member of Parliament) for Kent. Despite some close brushes with the law (see below), his career is marked by circumspection: he avoided being drawn into various political conflicts during the 1370s and late 1380s. This caution may account for the conspicuous lack of historical references in his work. This brief account makes Chaucer sound time-serving, but we should remember that life at court, especially during Richard's reign, must have been nerve-racking. That Chaucer managed to out-manoeuvre the fearsome Lords Appellant when they challenged Richard's power in the 1380s, that he escaped death and still retained a position at court—and continued to write poetry—says something about his political instincts, and perhaps also about his determination to write.

Born some time in the early 1340s, Chaucer was the only child (as far as we know) of a prosperous London wine merchant, John Chaucer. His mother was Agnes de Copton. Brought up in London, Chaucer lived through the Black Death, which arrived in Britain in 1348: an estimated 1.5–2 million people died in England. The plague had considerable social effects. It strengthened the hand of those workers who survived, because their labour was at a premium, and it created new wealth for some, as it did for John Chaucer, through inheritance windfalls. We assume (although this, as with so much else in the received biography, is speculation) that John was able to buy his son entry into an aristocratic household and from there into the royal household. We know nothing about Chaucer's childhood or his education: whether he went to grammar school or to university, or if he was ever a student at any of the Inns of Court. He would have learned his alphabet and received an elementary Christian education at home when very young.

The first documentary evidence tells us that by 1357 Chaucer had entered the service of Elizabeth, Countess of Ulster, wife of Prince Lionel, Edward III's second surviving son, and that he was nicely kitted out in a paltock (the entry is in the Countess's household accounts[12]). He was probably a page, that is, a relatively menial servant. This was the beginning of his entry into a system of patronage that was to sustain him throughout his life. He was captured in France during the 1359–60 campaign in which Edward III reasserted his claim to the throne of France: the king paid his ransom of £16. In 1367 he transferred to the king's service as a *valettus*, or yeoman, and started to receive a life annuity: that is, a salary. No documents exist for the 'lost years' between 1360–7, except for the so-called 'Spanish record', discovered in 1955 in the royal archives of Navarre in Pamplona. This is a 'safe conduct' (passport) for Chaucer and three companions to go to Spain on an unspecified diplomatic mission. Several documents attest that Chaucer made various trips abroad on the king's business during 1368–70.

In 1368 Chaucer is recorded as one of forty *esquiers* in the royal household, which also at this time included a 'demoiselle' (lady-in-waiting) called Philippa Chaucer. Evidently she married Chaucer in 1366: records of their marriage appear in 1374 and 1381. Philippa's origins are obscure: if—and it is only 'if' (the suggestion appeared in the sixteenth century)—she is the daughter of Payne de Roet of Hainault, then her sister is Katherine de Roet (later Swynford) who became John of Gaunt's mistress and then married him. If so, then Chaucer's marriage to Philippa places him in an intriguingly close relationship to John of Gaunt. Philippa probably died in 1387. She and Chaucer had a son, Thomas (who was knighted), and may have had a daughter, Elizabeth, who became a nun (the evidence is very slight), and another son, the 10-year-old 'little Lewis', to whom Chaucer dedicated his *Treatise on the Astrolabe* in 1391. Chaucer's granddaughter Alice married the future duke of Suffolk. Within four generations, then, the Chaucer family progressed from merchant vintners to aristocrats: a textbook example of the upward social mobility that characterizes the later fourteenth century and which shapes the representation of social relations in Chaucer's poetry, especially in the *Canterbury Tales*.

In the absence of any evidence for how Chaucer honed his literary skills, we can only speculate. As a courtier he would have been exposed to the literature of the leisured classes (often read out loud): French courtly romances and love poetry; chronicles; the matter of Britain and of Troy. But Chaucer's Latin, French, and Italian sources are extensive, including Virgil, Ovid, Macrobius, Boethius, and Dante, and he used many English sources too (though he never owns up to using these). His trips to Genoa and Florence in 1372–3, to France in 1377–81, and to Lombardy in 1378—all on royal business—gave him contact with humanist culture: he may even have met Petrarch. In Lombardy he visited Bernabò Visconti, lord of Milan and owner of a huge library. Chaucer brought back from Italy copies of Boccaccio's two great Italian poems, the *Filostrato* (source for *Troilus and Criseyde*) and the *Teseida* (source for the 'Knight's Tale'). Although we lack any documentation of his writing apprenticeship, Chaucer's life as a public royal servant certainly determined in very particular ways what Chartier calls 'the categories and the experiences that are the very matrices of writing'.[13] These matrices were strikingly different from those experienced by, for instance, the female authors who were his contemporaries (Julian of Norwich) or who wrote soon after (Margery Kempe, Christine de Pizan). A world separates Chaucer from these authors, socially and intellectually—and in the light of Strohm's analysis of Chaucer's male, royalist connections it is not hard to understand why.

Because literary texts were bespoke, not speculatively marketed, writers often sought patrons. But there is no evidence that Chaucer ever had a patron, though Gaunt is often fingered as such, due partly to the fact that the *Book of the Duchess* was a response to the death of Gaunt's wife, Blanche, and partly to the favours he bestowed on Chaucer. Gaunt granted him an annuity in 1374 (as he had done to his wife, Philippa, in 1372), which probably continued to be paid until Gaunt's death in 1399. But, as Pearsall observes, by their nature the life-records are 'routine, official':[14] mention of 'nostre ame esquire Geffrey Chaucer' is not a sign of special affection. Yet there was definite royal interest in the development of his career as it progressed.

Chaucer did well (but not overly well) for favours. In 1374 Edward III granted him a daily pitcher of wine for life, which Chaucer commuted in 1378 for an exchequer annuity of 20 marks. By 1380 he had accumulated a number of perks: a post as controller of the wool custom and petty custom in the port of London (appointed in 1374), several substantial annuities, and rent-free accommodation above the city gate at Aldgate (he was granted the lease for life in 1374). The cliché that has Chaucer watching as the English rebels enter London through this gate in 1381 says more about the desires of modern readers to place him in relation to epochal moments than about any hard reality. And in any case, how would we then imagine him? Waving to the rebels? Hiding beneath a table?

Chaucer's circle included many of the king's men: the lawyer Ralph Strode, Sir Philip de la Vache, the so-called Lollard knight Sir Lewis Clifford, Sir Richard Stury, Sir John Montagu, the poet Sir John Clanvowe, Sir Simon Burley (tutor to young Richard II), Sir Peter Bukton, Henry Scogan, Thomas Hoccleve, Thomas Usk, and (with qualifications) the poet John Gower, but he was not close to the notoriously factionalist London merchant Nicholas Brembre. Throughout the 1380s Chaucer frequently stood as mainprize (surety) or mainpernor (guarantor) for his associates in legal actions, clear evidence of the horizontal social ties emphasized by Strohm. He also had what Pearsall calls 'some generally less creditable associations with the law', such as pleas of debt, but these were again routine.[15] I will discuss the Cecily Chaumpaigne rape accusation below, since this is far from routine. Chaucer's deposition in the Scrope–Grosvenor trial of 1386, a dispute over the rights to a personal logo (and a document that incidentally discloses Chaucer's approximate age), symbolizes his high status as a public man.

In 1386 Chaucer gave up the house at Aldgate and his job at the customs, probably because the opposition faction demanded control of king's advisers. Likewise, he gave up his annuities in 1388: the Merciless Parliament had begun to prosecute its campaign against the king's household and especially against those who had received annuities during the reign of Edward III. Chaucer remained an esquire of the king's household, enjoying at this time a certain reputation as a poet, and writing the *Legend of Good Women* between 1386–7. He was MP for Kent from 1386, holding the seat for one session only. He also became JP for Kent (1385–9), and moved there for a while. Chaucer was appointed Clerk of the King's Works from 1389 to 1391, with responsibility for Westminster Palace, the Tower of London, various royal manors, and the building of the lists for the Smithfield tournament of 1390, a detail that is customarily mentioned as evidence that Chaucer's descriptions of the lists in the 'Knight's Tale' are based on first-hand knowledge. As so often, the assumption in many standard accounts is that authors write directly from experience. But Chaucer's poetry is profoundly intertextual: its authority derives as much from texts as from experience, and we should guard against tracing one-to-one correspondences between the life and the works.

Chaucer was famously robbed three times between 3 and 6 September 1390, but we know little of the circumstances. In 1391 he left the office of the King's Works; he was without any regular income except Gaunt's annuity, until in 1394 he was granted an exchequer annuity of £20 for life. Some time in the 1390s he was appointed deputy forester for the forest of North Petherton in Somerset. During the last decade of his life Chaucer was almost entirely occupied with writing the *Canterbury Tales*, begun some time around 1387. Pearsall (and others) see this work as the 'general embodiment of Chaucer's maturer reflections upon the life of men and women in society and in the Christian faith', a view that again suggests a direct correspondence between life and works, and which assumes (as with the traditional estimation of Shakespeare's late plays) that 'lateness' coincides with an apotheosis of personal and literary ripeness.[16]

Chaucer's poetic career has often been seen in terms of a progression from youthful works of 'immaturity' (the *Book of the Duchess*) to the 'golden age' of the *Canterbury Tales*, or has been divided into three periods (rather like those of artists, such as Picasso's Blue Period): first French, then Italian, and finally English. The assumptions behind these now outmoded models are various: an obsession with evolutionary periodization, cultural stereotyping (French 'artifice' giving way to earthy English 'realism'), and the mapping of Chaucer's professional trajectory onto his literary one, from French-speaking courtier, to diplomatic courier in Italy, to civil servant traipsing the byways of London and Kent. But Chaucer's literary output does not easily fit this evolutionary model. He made extensive use of French and Italian sources throughout his career: in many ways they are the dominant influences in the *Canterbury Tales*, supposedly from his 'English' phase. The work that made his fourteenth-century reputation was *Troilus and Criseyde*, still considered by many critics to be his greatest work. Outside academia (and even within it) Chaucer is known almost exclusively as the author of the *Canterbury Tales*. The prominence that is now accorded this work is also reflected in the syllabuses of the British school examination boards, which now solely prescribe the *Canterbury Tales* (and only a select few of those) as A level texts in England, Wales, and Northern Ireland. Although the most currently fashionable academic Chaucer is arguably the Italian one, it is just as possible to see Chaucer as a predominantly French-inspired poet or as an English vernacular one.

After Richard's abdication in 1399 and death soon after, Chaucer duly had his annuities confirmed by the new king, Henry IV. There is no official record of Chaucer's death, but the date is customarily accepted as 25 October 1400. Unusually, he left no will. He was buried in Westminster Abbey at the entrance to St Benedict's Chapel, an area beginning to be used for graves of monastic officials. His remains were moved in 1556 to a new tomb in the area now known as Poets' Corner.

Social Chaucer

This rather bland narrative does scant justice to a far more piquant aspect of the records: the precise nature and extent of Chaucer's factional ties. There is no doubt that Chaucer was a king's man, both under Edward III and Richard II, but this can only be properly understood by teasing apart the changing structure of social relations in late fourteenth-century England. Within this structure, the issue of gentility—especially the shifting faultline between *gentils* and non-*gentils*—is a crucial factor. Royal service of the sort performed by Chaucer had only lately been established as a point of entry to the rank of esquire. This meant that Chaucer, who was not aristocratic by birth, enjoyed a newly acquired status of gentility, a status that was denied to other ranks, such as the *valetti* and franklins. But this status embodied contradiction: along with other esquires (and knights) of the time, he was commonly assessed as *gentil*—but non-aristocratic. Moreover, gentle esquires shared equivalent claims with non-gentle merchants to social honour and were also aligned with clerks and scribes (by virtue of their clerical duties)—but separated from them by their gentility. In Strohm's words, 'As an esquire, [Chaucer] was situated at a particularly volatile and ambiguous point in the social structure of his day.'[17]

The old hierarchic model of degree was giving way to a model based less on domination and subordination and more on ties of common interest and experience. And Chaucer was bound to Edward III and Richard II by ties that were different from traditional vassalage: not dependent on oath or land tenure or military service, but on mutual interest. This is clearly seen (in Strohm's analysis) in Chaucer's situation within a network of complexly overlapping circles that Strohm calls 'the King's affinity'. Chaucer was *not* apolitical: he participated in the politics of royal faction, but he managed that participation with prudence and careful manipulation during difficult and dangerous times. When the 1385 Parliament opposed royal patronage and household extravagance, Chaucer responded by resigning his customs post and strengthening his Kentish connections. When in 1388 Parliament called for a purge of royal annuities, Chaucer granted his exchequer annuities to one John Scalby.

For Strohm, this 'thoughtful' circumspection marks the writing in terms of its even-handedness and receptiveness to other points of view. But this is a somewhat troubling critical evaluation. Where, after all, are the peasants in Chaucer's work? And where are the women in this shifting social structure? What is significant is that the King's affinity was Chaucer's prime organizer of the social space of literary production. Most members of Chaucer's amicable circle (Sir William Beauchamp, Clifford, Vache, Clanvowe, Nevill, Stury, Strode, Gower, Scogan, and Bukton) were writers or owners of books or addressees of others' books, suggesting a further set of mutual horizontal ties: through literary interests and literary sympathies. Such ties militate against our seeing Chaucer's writing as a private compulsion. This was, however, emphatically a man's world. Tellingly, Strohm's discussion of the Chaumpaigne document never once touches on the gender politics of that case or its implications for a reading of Chaucer's work. With that limitation in mind, I now turn to discuss in more detail the rape accusation.

Scandal?

One of the pleasures of biography, for readers of all stripes, is the prospect of learning about scandal. But precious little scandal clings to the dry bones of Chaucer's life-records. One myth that has not gone away—it has recently been revived in a thread on the scholarly electronic CHAUCER List[18]—is that Philippa, Chaucer's wife, may have been John of Gaunt's mistress and that Thomas Chaucer may have been Gaunt's bastard son. Gaunt's payments to Chaucer may have been pay-offs; Thomas's failure to use Chaucer's arms looks like a calculated snub to the latter's claiming him as his son. But not a shred of real evidence exists. Sometimes we can trace very precisely the birth of such myths. For instance, on 7 January 2001 an article appeared in the *Sunday Telegraph* asserting that 'academics who have spent 10 years examining the two earliest known manuscripts of Geoffrey Chaucer's medieval masterpiece the *Canterbury Tales* believe that they were written on stolen government parchment'.[19] This was a fabrication. One of the academics in question, Peter Robinson of the Canterbury Tales Project at De Montfort University, explained on the CHAUCER List the following day how the rumour had arisen:

[the reporter] asked me if it were possible that these manuscripts were written on stolen vellum: I said it was possible, as indeed it is. It is certainly likely that the scribes were working on official documents as well as on copying Chaucer . . . but no responsible person is going to assert from this that Chaucer paid the scribes to steal the parchment! (or that he stole it himself).

Here academic cautiousness (and naivety) meets journalistic instinct for good copy. Result: a story that can also be seen to derive its plausibility both from Chaucer's popular reputation as an ebullient figure (though never a criminal) and from the enigmatic gaps in the historical record (what secret business was Chaucer engaged in on the king's behalf on his various trips abroad? was Thomas really Chaucer's son?) that have created a popular myth of Chaucer as a man with something to hide. My point is not so much that readers need to know the difference between historical witness and rumour (of course they do) but that *both* form part of the kaleidoscope of disparate texts that make up the textual figure we now call 'Chaucer'—and which inevitably affects the way we read his poetry.

But the Chancery document that was enrolled by Cecily Chaumpaigne on 4 May 1380, releasing Chaucer from 'omnimodas acciones tam de raptu meo tam [sic] de aliqua alia re vel causa' ('from all manner of actions relating as much to my *raptus* as to any other thing or cause'), is neither rumour nor fabrication.[20] In 1993 Christopher Cannon announced his discovery of a new record, the first to appear since the *Life-Records* was published. This document, an unpublished memorandum that also records the Chaumpaigne release, likewise contains the phrase *de raptu meo*. When this phrase occurs on its own—that is, without supplementary descriptions—it usually refers to forced coitus and not simply abduction. Where Pearsall saw the original document as 'enigmatic', only reluctantly concluding that *raptus* probably did mean 'rape', as opposed to abduction, and arguing that there was still 'not enough evidence to come to a conclusion',[21] Cannon's finding—and his reading of its significance—tips the balance rather more decisively towards the view that Chaucer was guilty of rape.

Yet Cannon, who knows this material better than anyone else, has recently revisited this case, arguing that the problem is not with the definition of *raptus* per se, but with the confusion that medieval law had in defining 'rape', a confusion that will always make it possible that it might have also meant 'abduction'. Such uncertainty does not mean that we can say nothing more about the release. 'We have not yet been fully schooled by this document', Cannon contends, '. . . because our worry that we will be wrongly certain has prevented us from realizing that uncertainty is itself something we may be certain about.'[22]

What are the implications of this certain uncertainty for a biographical reading of Chaucer's depictions of non-consensual sex? Cannon's strategy is to finesse critical biography and to read Chaucer's texts exactly as he reads the legal release: for what they can tell us about medieval attitudes towards *raptus*. This has the important advantage of reminding us that both life and works are textual. By reading all the texts with and against each other, Cannon is able to bring out some of their tensions, contradictions, and similarities. Neither the literary texts nor the legal documents can provide us with any interpretative certainties: 'all medieval law makes certain to us', he argues, 'is that we cannot know precisely what we need to know to categorize most of its mentions of *raptus*'—and so with the gaps concerning rape in the literary texts: 'all we know for certain is that we are uncertain'.[23] In what is his only biographical claim, Cannon asserts that Chaucer was well aware of medieval law's merging of 'rape' and 'abduction' and of the delicate legal problem of 'consent'. What we therefore find in his poetry is an especial attentiveness to the questions of consent 'that may attend acts of sexual intercourse', and indeed 'a consideration of the conditions of consent that attend all human acts'.[24] For some readers, this will be an uncomfortable—and limited—conclusion. Despite his proper refusal to reduce literary texts to biographical events, Cannon nevertheless treats the legal documents as if they constituted the implicit meaning of the literary works and to some extent he also resurrects the humanist Chaucer of 1970s criticism. But his rigorous historicist work will stimulate further archival searches and further readings of all of these texts with and against each other, even though these subsequent readings may be prompted by a different set of ethical and political concerns.

Biography as narrative

The kind of Chaucer we construct from the life-records will depend, then, on our own preconceptions, as much historical and cultural as individual. Unlike the case with some modern authors (Sylvia Plath, Iris Murdoch) accounts of Chaucer's life have never had to arbitrate between violently competing versions of events. Yet all biographies are to some extent fictions. Their writers select from the facts and interpret them. But this does not mean that they are free to speculate. Biographies of Chaucer start to appear in the sixteenth century (John Leland, Bishop Bale, Thomas Speght), but these are based upon popular traditions and speculation rather than historical sources. Speght, for example, is responsible for the colourful but apocryphal story that 'Geoffrye Chaucer was fined two shillings for beatinge a Franciscane Fryer in fletestreate.'[25] This reveals more about Speght and his English Protestant readers than it does about Chaucer: although Chaucer's poetry contains anti-fraternal satire (common enough in the late fourteenth century), in his work as a JP in Kent Chaucer would have been trying the men who beat up friars, not doing it himself. Speght's story has a long currency. The Victorian F. D. Maurice, one of the Cambridge Apostles, pontificates that Chaucer 'hates Friars, because they are not English and not manly'.[26] This is Chaucer as staunch defender of white, male, heterosexual values: the epitome of Victorian decency.

   In general, the Victorians saw Chaucer as courtly and childlike, an effect of their view of the Middle Ages as a period of lost innocence. William Morris (who produced a beautifully illustrated edition of Chaucer's works, the Kelmscott Chaucer) paints a very idealized picture of Chaucer in the 1380s, stepping out in 'the rose-hung lanes of Kent' (the phrase is taken from his poem *The Life and Death of Jason* (1867)). But during the time that he was in Kent as a JP (1385–9), as Kellie Robertson observes, Chaucer was dealing with felonies, assaults, and violations of the labour laws (the Statutes of

Labourers).[27] For Morris, it seems, as for Marx, there was no alienated wage labour before the nineteenth century. The most recent biographies of Chaucer (Howard, Pearsall) are also influenced by Morris's 'rosy' view. Pearsall downplays the serious nature of his job of law enforcement, representing Chaucer as having 'quietly decamped' to Kent 'to look for some quieter place to live'.[28]

The life-records continue to spark off pseudo-biographical enterprises. A recent scholarly book by ex-Monty Python Terry Jones and academics Robert Yeager, Terry Dolan, Alan Fletcher, and Juliette Dor, treats Chaucer's death—not at all in the spirit of spoof—as detective fiction. Questioning some of the curious facts (why did Chaucer take out a fifty-three-year lease on his Westminster dwelling in December 1399, just nine months before his death? why didn't he leave a will?), the authors hypothesize that Chaucer was murdered—because he was Richard's man and because he was a critic of the Church. *Who Murdered Chaucer?* registers two important things about the current state of play in Chaucerian critical biography. Firstly, it acknowledges (following Strohm) the tightrope Chaucer walked as a man who was factionally committed. Secondly, it accepts the increasingly pervasive belief that there was a general climate of intolerance in the very late fourteenth century towards dissident religious views—not that Chaucer's were that dissident, but they could be interpreted that way.[29]

The absent author and the author-function

If only we knew the truth about Chaucer's death—or life. Despite the absence of any writings by Chaucer that will allow us to reconstruct the 'lived life', there are several places in his poetry where the author appears to be insistently and seductively confiding in us. In a celebrated passage at the end of the *Canterbury Tales* 'Chaucer' makes an apparently pious confession to the reader: he repents of writing certain poems and revokes them. Their indiscretions, he says, are the fault of his 'unkonnynge' (lack of skill). 'Wherfore I biseke yow mekely', he declares, 'for the mercy of God, that ye preye for me that Crist have mercy on me and foryeve me my giltes.' These 'sinful' writings include some of his major poems—*Troilus and Criseyde*, the *House of Fame*, the *Parliament of Fowls*, the *Legend of Good Women*, those Canterbury tales that 'sownen into synne', and 'many a song and many a leccherous lay' ('CR' 1082–7). Did Chaucer really mean to repudiate some of his most important and engaging works?

The 'Retraction' provokes some crucial questions about the relationship between an author and his works. Who is behind this 'I'? Is the author really present? Given that these statements appear as part of a literary fiction—the *Canterbury Tales*—is this voice inside or outside the text? Is this fiction or literary criticism? Many readers have long imagined that they have direct access to Chaucer the author via his poetry. In the Prologue to 'Sir Thopas' (the tale told by Chaucer the pilgrim), the Host describes 'Chaucer', in visually memorable terms, as a 'popet in an arm t'enbrace' (701). Near the beginning of the *Legend of Good Women*, the narrator ('Chaucer'?) expresses his delight in abandoning his books to gaze at daisies in May. An amalgam of these fictional personae has led to the construction of what E. T. Donaldson ironically described in 1970 as 'a school of Chaucerian criticism . . . that pictured a single Chaucer under the guise of a wide-eyed, jolly, rolypoly little man who, on fine Spring mornings, used to get up early, while the dew was still on the grass, and go look at daisies'.[30] Today's academic Chaucer cuts a very different kind of figure: cultured, cosmopolitan, elusive, and postmodern, he is more likely to be catching a plane to Renaissance Italy than tripping through a medieval English meadow. But outside the academy he embodies something else altogether: a nostalgia for bawdy 'English' humour or 'olde worlde' charm. This popular, commercial Chaucer is often in diametric opposition to academic Chaucer: there are at the time of writing over 607 Chaucer items for sale on the electronic auction site eBay, ranging from mugs and collector's plates to pillboxes, board games, and trading cards (in a Shell series called 'Great Britons').

Disdain for the biographical enterprise and its assumption that writing is essentially an expression of its author's mind or personality has led to an almost wholesale neglect of the figure of the author in current literary criticism. But there is a very different way of thinking about the relationship between author and text: what Foucault calls the 'author-function'. This describes how texts are classified by having proper names attached to them: scientific texts, for example, 'were accepted in the Middle Ages, and accepted as "true", only when marked with the name of their author'.[31] For Foucault, literary texts only come to have authors at the end of the eighteenth and beginning of the nineteenth century, when their authors become subject to the law (for example, copyright). But, as Chartier observes, the author-function is inscribed in all kinds of manuscript books (not only in scientific texts) as early as the fourteenth and fifteenth centuries.[32] Chaucer is certainly an author by the sixteenth century, when the first biographies appeared: Chartier cites a French library catalogue of 1584 that 'sets up the writer's biography as the fundamental reference for writing'.[33] But the author-function is attached to Chaucer's works much earlier. A key instrument here is the author-picture, designed to reinforce the idea that the writing is the direct, individual, and authentic expression of its author, and already found in manuscripts in the vernacular of the late fourteenth and the fifteenth centuries (Christine de Pizan, Froissart, Machaut, Petrarch, Boccaccio). One of the earliest copies of the *Canterbury Tales*, the Ellesmere manuscript (*c*.1401), contains a vivid portrait of Chaucer, as does a manuscript of Thomas Hoccleve's *Regement of Princes* (1411–12), where the picture accompanies a eulogy of Chaucer and is described extraordinarily by Hoccleve as a 'lyknesse' that will serve to remind readers of what Chaucer looked like (see Figure I.1). Another major expression of the author-function is 'the possibility of deciphering in the forms of a book the intention that lay behind the creation of the text'.[34] Petrarch proposed an 'author's book', produced from an autograph copy (not a scribe's copy), and designed to defend the author's intentions from scribal miswriting. Although Chaucer's practice of having copies of a text professionally made and then correcting those copies when

How he þ þ quaunt was mayden marie
And siþ his loue floure and fructifie

Al þogh his lyfe be queynt þe resemblaunce
Of him hay in me so fressh lyflynesse
Þat to putte othir men in remembraunce
Of his persone z haue heere his lyknesse
Do make to þis ende in sothfastnesse
Þat þei þt haue of him left þought & mynde
By þis peynture may ageyn him fynde

The ymages þt in þe chirche been
Maken folk þenke on god z on his seyntes
Whan þe ymages þei be holden z seen
Were oft vnsyte of hem caussith restreyntes
Of þoughtes gode whan a þing depeynt is
Or entrailed if men take of it heede
Thoght of þe lyknesse it wil in hym brede

Yit some holden oppinyon and sey
Þat none ymages schuld z maked be
Þei erren foule z goon out of þe wey
Of trouth haue þei scant sensibilite
Passe ouer þt now blessid trinite
Vppon my maistres soule mercy haue
ffor him lady eke þ mercy z craue

Othir þing wolde z fayne speke z touche
Heere in þis booke but such is my dulnesse
ffor þt al voyde and empty is my pouche
Þat al my lust is queynt wit heuynesse
And heuy spirit comaundith stilnesse

Fig. I.1 Portrait of Chaucer. Illustration from Thomas Hoccleve, *Regement of Princes* (1411–12) (British Library, MS Harley 4866).

they were returned leads to more than one authorized text, his short comic poem 'Chaucers Wordes unto Adam, his Owne Scriveyn', with its threat of punishment to the hapless scribe unless he writes 'more trewe', is a manifestation of a Petrarch-inspired desire to protect authorial intention from faulty copying. What is extraordinary about the manuscripts of the *Canterbury Tales* that begin to appear soon after Chaucer's death (none from his lifetime survives) is how many of them form a unified whole—a 'work', as opposed to part of an anthology. Of the eighty-two manuscripts, fifty-five are complete or near-complete copies. The idea of 'the work' is underpinned by the idea of the author: the unity it manifests is a product of the author-function. Admittedly, for medieval works in the vernacular the author-function was only constituted around a few great 'literary' figures—Dante, Petrarch, and Boccaccio—but these are precisely the figures whom Chaucer admired and imitated. 'Italian' Chaucer may be most useful to us as a way of thinking about Chaucer's author-function.

The future of biography?

Rapid technological changes in Western culture have brought about a rethinking of our attitudes towards the past. Although the memory of the past is dispersed and fragmented, we seek to hold on to memories of that past, especially if they embody forms of national cultural memory. Chaucer may be receding from national memory in a way that Shakespeare is not, but we still attach memory to him, not only in his problematic incarnation as the 'father of English poetry' but also because the man and his work have often been co-opted to serve a national project. From this perspective an account of Chaucer as a historical figure would no longer be a traditional biographical one, certainly not one that is concerned with events *qua* events. Rather it might take the form of what Lucasta Miller calls 'metabiography': a study of the myriad different versions of Chaucer purveyed by biographers, critics, and popular culture.[35] But the traditional biographical enterprise will continue. There are documents to find in the archives; there is historical work to be done, particularly on Chaucer as a man of letters; and the life-records will be resifted and reread with different political agendas, generating new meanings and making new and unforeseeable connections.

FURTHER READING

Cannon, Christopher, '*Raptus* in the Chaumpaigne Release and a Newly Discovered Document concerning the Life of Geoffrey Chaucer', *Speculum*, 68 (1993), 74–94. Announces the discovery of a new life-record—a memorandum that also records the Chaumpaigne release—and draws on unpublished court documents in order to argue that the word *raptus* in the release must refer to forced coitus, despite the fact that there is a complex continuum of behaviour between abduction and rape.

Cannon, Christopher, 'Chaucer and Rape: Uncertainty's Certainties', *Studies in the Age of Chaucer*, 22 (2000), 67–92. Argues that 'clearer understanding of the role rape may play in Chaucer's poetics has not resulted from any clearer understanding of what precisely the Chaumpaigne release refers to', and revisits the word *raptus* in the release, now arguing that the only sure thing we can know about its meaning is that consent to human acts is always uncertain.

Crow, M. M., and C. C. Olson, *Chaucer Life-Records*, 2nd edn. (Oxford: Clarendon Press, 1966). Indispensable and strictly factual collection of extracts from contemporary documents in Latin, French, and (some) Middle English (from the Public Record Office, London, and other sources) that pertain to Chaucer's career, from 1357 until his death on 25 Oct. 1400. No translations provided, but there are valuable contextualizing annotations.

Dillon, Janette, *Geoffrey Chaucer* (Basingstoke : Macmillan, 1993). The chapter 'Chaucer's Life and Times' offers a standard, factual account of the life in relation to contemporary politics and literary history.

Ellis, Steve, *Geoffrey Chaucer*, Writers and their Work (Plymouth: Northcote House, 1996). The chapter 'Life, Works, Reputation' is the best brief outline of the life.

Gardner, John, *The Life and Times of Chaucer* (1977; repr. New York: Vintage, 1978). An egregious example of the old-fashioned 'fanciful' biography, but symptomatic of a view of Chaucer that still has much popular and academic currency: a 'compassionate observer of humanity'.

Howard, Donald, *Chaucer and the Medieval World* (London: Weidenfeld & Nicolson, 1987). Huge and scholarly biography that nevertheless indulges in a fair amount of speculation.

Jones, Terry, Robert Yeager, Terry Dolan, Alan Fletcher, and Juliette Dor, *Who Murdered Chaucer? A Medieval Mystery* (London: Methuen, 2002). A work of 'historical speculation' that argues that Chaucer may have been murdered because he had become a dangerous poet.

Pearsall, Derek, *The Life of Geoffrey Chaucer: A Critical Biography* (Oxford: Blackwell, 1992). This important book draws on the *Life-Records*, on fourteenth-century social history, and on literary history to construct a reliable linear narrative of Chaucer's life, interspersed with critical readings of the poetry. It makes some informed guesses about matters we know little about, such as Chaucer's education.

Strohm, Paul, *Social Chaucer* (Cambridge, Mass.: Harvard University Press, 1989). Not a life, but a landmark historico-literary study charting new forms of social relation in Chaucer's day, based on contemporary legal and parliamentary documents, as well as on careful scrutiny of the *Life-Records*. Reinterprets Chaucer's social ties in the light of a new estimation of the role of status groups in late medieval England.

NOTES

1. M. M. Crow and C. C. Olson, *Chaucer Life-Records*, 2nd edn. (Oxford: Clarendon Press, 1966).
2. Roland Barthes, 'The Death of the Author', in his *Image: Music: Text*, ed. and trans. Stephen Heath (London: Fontana, 1977), 142–8.
3. Roger Chartier, 'Figures of the Author', in his *The Order of Books: Readers, Authors, and Libraries in Europe between the Fourteenth and Eighteenth Centuries*, trans. Lydia G. Cochrane (Stanford, Calif.: Stanford University Press, 1992), 27.
4. Derek Pearsall, *The Life of Geoffrey Chaucer: A Critical Biography* (Oxford: Blackwell, 1992), 98.
5. Carolyn Dinshaw, *Chaucer's Sexual Poetics* (Madison: University of Wisconsin Press, 1989), 10.
6. C. E. D. Phelps, *The Accolade: Or the Canon and his Yeoman* (Philadelphia: Lippincott, 1905); Wallace B. Nichols, *Deputy for Youth* (London: Ward, Lock, 1935); see Steve Ellis, *Chaucer at Large:*

The Poet in the Modern Imagination (Minneapolis: University of Minnesota Press, 2000), 145–8. The latest, as yet unpublished, example is by Gary O'Connor (personal communication).

7. Christopher Cannon, '*Raptus* in the Chaumpaigne Release and a Newly Discovered Document concerning the Life of Geoffrey Chaucer', *Speculum*, 68 (1993), 74–94.

8. *Chaucer's Sexual Poetics*, 11.

9. See Christopher B. Ricks, *T. S. Eliot and Prejudice* (London: Faber, 1988); Jacques Derrida, 'Like the Sound of the Sea Deep within a Shell: Paul de Man's War', trans. Peggy Kamuf, in his *Memoires for Paul de Man* (New York: Columbia University Press, 1989), 157–263.

10. *Life*, 8.

11. Michel Foucault, 'What is an Author?', in his *Textual Strategies: Perspectives in Post-Structuralist Criticism*, ed. and trans. Josué Harari (Ithaca, NY: Cornell University Press, 1979), 141.

12. Crow and Olson, *Life-Records*, 13.

13. 'Figures of the Author', 29.

14. *Life*, 95.

15. Ibid. 134.

16. Ibid. 227.

17. Paul Strohm, *Social Chaucer* (Cambridge, Mass.: Harvard University Press, 1989), 10.

18. See <http://listserv.uic.edu/htbin/wa?SUBED1=chaucer&A=1.>

19. See <http://www.telegraph.co.uk:80/et?ac=004115286347884&rtmo=0xK2GJ0q&atmo=rrrrr rrq&pg=/et/01/1/7/nchau07.html.>

20. Crow and Olson, *Life-Records*, 343.

21. *Life*, 136–7.

22. Christopher Cannon, 'Chaucer and Rape: Uncertainty's Certainties', *Studies in the Age of Chaucer*, 22 (2000), 70.

23. Ibid. 82.

24. Ibid.

25. Thomas Speght, 'Chaucer's Life', in *The Works of our Antient and Lerned English Poet, Geffrey Chaucer, newly Printed*, ed. Thomas Speght (London, 1598), sign. b. ii. For a facsimile edition, see *Geoffrey Chaucer: The Works 1532*, ed. D. S. Brewer, with supplementary material from the editions of 1542, 1561, 1598, and 1602 (London: Scolar Press, 1969).

26. F. D. Maurice, *The Workman and the Franchise: Chapters from English History on the Representation and Education of the People* (1866), 58.

27. Kellie Robertson, 'Chaucer, Nineteenth-Century Anti-Capitalist?', paper delivered at the New Chaucer Congress, 2002, Boulder, Colorado.

28. *Life*, 205.

29. Terry Jones, Robert Yeager, Terry Dolan, Alan Fletcher, and Juliette Dor, *Who Murdered Chaucer? A Medieval Mystery* (London: Methuen, 2002), 356–8.

30. E. Talbot Donaldson, 'Chaucer the Pilgrim', in his *Speaking of Chaucer* (London: Athlone, 1970), 1–2.

31. 'What is an Author?', 149.

32. 'Figures of the Author', 58–9.

33. Ibid. 42.

34. Ibid. 55.

35. Lucasta Miller, *The Brontë Myth* (London: Jonathan Cape, 2001).

2 | **Society and politics**

S. H. Rigby *

Chaucer's lifetime constitutes one of the most dramatic periods in English history. This was the age of the Black Death, the Peasants' Revolt, the Hundred Years War, the deposition of Richard II, the papal schism (1378–1417), and the emergence of the heretical doctrines of John Wyclif and the Lollards. These social, political, and religious crises and conflicts posed ethical questions which were addressed by the preachers, theologians, philosophers—and poets—of the day. This chapter will focus on two of these issues: firstly, on the economic changes and social conflicts that followed the Black Death; secondly, on the political strife that culminated in the deposition of Richard II and usurpation of Henry IV in 1399. What then was the nature of England's social structure in this period? What were the causes of economic change and social conflict? How could the removal of an anointed king in 1399 be justified? How did the imaginative literature of the day address these questions?

Society

Social ideology: the three orders

Within the orthodoxy of late medieval thought, the entire universe was seen as a divinely ordained hierarchical order in which everything had its own proper place. It followed that human society should take the form of a hierarchy whose rightful ordering would benefit all of its members, rich and poor alike. When late fourteenth-century theologians and preachers, such as John of Ayton and Thomas of Wimbledon, or poets, such as Chaucer's friend John Gower, characterized this social hierarchy, they invariably fell back on the centuries-old 'tripartite' conception. Just as the Holy Trinity comprised three persons, so society was made up of three estates: the clergy, those who pray; the nobles and knights, those who fight; and the labourers, those who work.

* I would like to thank Rosalind Brown-Grant, Bruce Campbell, Richard Davies, and Steve Ellis for their detailed and perceptive comments on earlier drafts of this chapter.

Within Chaucer's own work, the enduring influence of the tripartite conception can be seen in the three ideal characters described in the 'General Prologue': the Parson, a good shepherd who sacrifices himself for his parishioners (477–528); the Knight, who has devoted his life to crusading (43–78); and the Plowman, who works hard, lives in neighbourly harmony, and always pays his tithes (529–41).

In many ways, the tripartite theory failed to provide an accurate picture of late medieval society. For instance, it had difficulties in placing women and townspeople and also in ranking members of the clergy relative to the laity. However, such discrepancies between theory and actuality did not really concern contemporaries since the prime purpose of the tripartite conception was not to provide an accurate description of society but rather to teach a moral lesson. As Wimbledon said in his 1389 sermon *Redde rationem villicationis tue* ('Give Account of your Stewardship'; lines 27–118), since each estate needed the services of others, all the members of society should live in mutual harmony and work faithfully at their calling. Thus knights should defend the poor and needy; judges do justice to all; priests patiently pray and preach; merchants trade honestly and fairly; labourers and craftsmen work truly; and servants and bondsmen be subject and low and in dread of displeasing their lords (1 Peter 2: 18). Instead of seeking to better themselves, each man should keep to the estate to which God had called him (1 Corinthians 7: 20). If this was the official ideology expounded by preachers and poets in late fourteenth-century England, what was the social reality?

Social reality: status, class, and gender

The actual structure of English society in Chaucer's day, as opposed to its ideological representation, can be seen as made up of two ladders or pyramids, one on which the laity were ranked, the other made up of the clergy. The laity were broadly divided into three. At the top was the peerage, which during this period was emerging as a group of around fifty dukes, marquesses, earls, and barons with an hereditary right to sit in the House of Lords when a parliament was summoned. Secondly, there was the lesser nobility, or gentry: men of the rank of knight (like Chaucer's Knight), esquires, and, by the early fifteenth century, 'gentlemen'. At most, even including those like Chaucer's Franklin who were on the cusp between the 'gentle' and those below, this group included no more than 4 per cent of the population. Finally, making up the vast bulk of the population, came the commons, ranging from substantial free landholders, through urban traders and craftsmen, such as Chaucer's Haberdasher and Tapicer, and peasants, like the Plowman, down to the labourers of town and country.

The laity were ranked not just by their social status (noble, gentle, and commoner) but also in terms of their income and property rights, i.e. by their economic class. Some, like Chaucer's Franklin, were dependent on the proceeds of land ownership. They drew their income from renting out land or from selling produce such as grain and wool from their demesnes (the land which had not been permanently leased out), as the Reeve does on behalf of his trusting lord ('GP' 593–605). They were also able to collect a variety of manorial dues, such as tallage (a private tax levied by lords) and mill-fees, owed to them by their tenants, particularly the unfree (villeins), who were especially subject to their lords' control. Others among the laity, especially in the towns, which contained up to 20 per cent of England's population, lived off the profits earned from buying and selling goods, as did Chaucer's Merchant. Some, such as the Host, the landlord of the Tabard Inn, derived their income from providing services. Others, like the Carpenter and the Dyer, earned a living by selling goods which they themselves had manufactured. Some, such as the Doctor, the Manciple, or the Sergeant of the Law, were supported by the salaries or fees paid for their professional services. Many, like the Plowman, lived by renting land from the others, usually paying a money rent but perhaps also owing some compulsory labour services on their land-lord's demesne. Finally, about half of the population were dependent upon wages, as the Yeoman, the Knight's servant, would have been.

Compared to the laity, those in the clerical hierarchy formed only a small proportion of England's inhabitants. In 1377 around 38,000 clerics, including up to 2,000 nuns, comprised less than 2 per cent of the national population. The clergy were themselves split into two wings: the secular and the regular. The seculars were, in theory, those who ministered to the laity, ranging from the pope, down through archbishops, bishops, archdeacons, and deans, to the parish priests, such as Chaucer's Parson, and stipendiary (salaried) chaplains such as the Nun's Priest. The regulars comprised those such as the Monk, Friar, Prioress, and Second Nun, who had taken a vow of chastity, poverty, and obedience and who were bound by some particular rule which regulated their dress and lifestyle. If, as has been suggested, the Pardoner was actually a member of the Order of Roncesvalles ('GP' 670), then, as an Austin canon, he too was a member of the regular clergy. Among the seculars, only those in major orders (that is, who had been ordained as a priest, deacon, or subdeacon) were required to be celibate, which clearly distinguished them from the laity, which explains why the Wife of Bath was able to take a 'clerk' in minor orders as her fifth husband ('WBP' 628–9).

The clergy drew their income from two main sources: temporalities, the property which the Church owned just like any other landlord; and spiritualities, income specif-ically linked with the clergy's ecclesiastical status and functions, such as the tithes owed to Chaucer's Parson ('GP' 486). In terms of their wealth, the clergy were thus far more significant than their numbers alone would suggest: ecclesiastical landlords owned a third or more of England, while the compulsory tithes to which they were entitled accounted, in theory, for 10 per cent of all forms of production and income. Moreover, everyone in medieval England was subject to the ecclesiastical courts, whose juris-diction included such important issues as marriage and wills, of the type which provided employment for Chaucer's Summoner. Finally, the clergy's prominence was evident in their capacity as royal officials and civil servants: Simon Sudbury and Sir Robert Hales, the chancellor and treasurer who were both killed during the Peasants' Revolt in London in 1381, also happened to be, respectively, the archbishop of Canterbury and the Grand Master of the Knights Hospitaller in England.

If status (noble, gentle, or common; lay or clerical) and class were two key axes of inequality, a third major aspect of medieval social stratification was gender. Indeed, an awareness of the significance of gender is probably the major change in our understanding of the medieval social hierarchy in recent years. Women are represented at the Tabard only by a lay woman (the Wife of Bath) and two female religious (the Prioress and the Second Nun), but within English society as a whole, gender was a key determinant of an individual's access to, or exclusion from, wealth, status, and power. As the mid-thirteenth-century *Laws and Customs of England* attributed to Henry Bracton had put it, 'women differ from men in many respects for their position is inferior to that of men'.[1] In terms of property rights, from the nobility down to the peasantry, daughters were merely residual heirs, inheriting only in the absence of sons. An heiress was unlikely to remain single for long and, once married, her lands passed into her husband's control and her movable goods into his outright possession, a situation which the Wife of Bath has to use all of her wiles to remedy ('WBP' 212, 630–1). Only unmarried women enjoyed property rights equivalent to those of men, which means that the economic activities of wealthy widows like Chaucer's Alison ('GP' 447–8) are particularly well documented. In general, however, women's paid work, in town and country, was unskilled, poorly rewarded, and of low status. Furthermore, though they played a crucial productive role within the economy, women lacked any formal role in law or politics at a national or a local level.

As we have seen, the official ideology of the day gave a moral gloss to this complex hierarchy of class, status, and gender, presenting contemporary social structure as divinely ordained and so as timeless and unchanging. Yet, in practice, this ideal was increasingly divorced from social reality. Instead of stability, deference, and harmony, there was now change, mobility, and conflict, trends which were bound up with the dramatic fall in population of the period.

Plague, population, and economic change

Although we can only guess at the numbers of people who lived in medieval England, the national population probably rose between 1086 and *c*.1300 from around 2 million to at least 4 million and perhaps to as much as 6 million. Whether England was overpopulated by 1300, resulting in famine and impoverishment, which then drove down the population in the first half of the fourteenth century, is an extremely contentious issue. What is clear is that even if the population was already past its peak by the time of Chaucer's birth, the arrival of a great epidemic in England in 1348 marked the onset of an entirely new demographic regime. Known since the nineteenth century as the Black Death, this great pestilence originated in central Asia, passing along the trade routes through China, India, and the Crimea before arriving in Italy and France. The wine trade with Gascony, carried out by those such as Chaucer's Shipman ('GP' 396–7), seems to have brought the disease to England in the summer of 1348 and by the end of 1349 the whole country had been affected. The exact identity of this disease provokes much debate, although the orthodox view sees it as a combination of bubonic and pneumonic plague. What is important here is its consequences, with at least a third, and perhaps almost a half, of England's population dying in this first great epidemic.

Disastrous in itself, this first mortality was followed by a whole succession of further epidemics, including those of 1361–2, 1369, and 1375. Chaucer's 'Pardoner's Tale' captures the rapidity and extent of the mortality caused by the 'pestilence' which struck down 'Bothe man and womman, child, and hyne, and page' (670–700). From around 5 million people at the time of Chaucer's birth, England's population may have fallen to around 2.75 million by the time of the survey of adult population provided by the first poll tax of 1377. This decline continued thereafter; only in the early sixteenth century, by which time the population was perhaps 2.25 million or less, did sustained demographic growth take off once more. All of these population totals are extremely approximate; what is clear is the overall trend of a sharp fall followed by a long period of stagnation.

Inevitably, mortality on this scale resulted in profound economic and social change. Firstly, demand for land shrank. Initially, landlords seem to have been able to find tenants for their land by increasing the size of holdings and by making land available to those who were previously landless. Yet, maintaining the numbers of tenants in this way necessarily exacerbated the labour shortage that had been created by the plague as it reduced the numbers of those with insufficient land for subsistence who had to offer their labour for hire. As a result, by the start of the fifteenth century, money wage rates were 60–100 per cent higher than they had been a century earlier. At first sight, much of this increase in money wages seems to have been offset by the high prices of the 1350s and 1360s (see below), but in practice workers were now also able to demand bonuses in the form of cash, food, drink, and clothing, which further boosted their incomes in terms of their real purchasing power.

Eventually, as the population continued to decline, land began to drop out of cultivation. Nevertheless, the reduction in the arable area (i.e. in the grain supply) was far less than the decline in population (i.e. in demand for grain), which should have resulted in falling grain prices. In fact, grain prices (along with the prices of other commodities) remained surprisingly high for over a quarter of a century after the Black Death. However, food prices did start to decline from the mid-1370s, which meant that the real purchasing power of wages now rose even faster than the increase in money wages; only with the renewed population growth of the early sixteenth century were these long-term trends reversed. In an era of rising real wages, consumers could shift their expenditure towards 'luxury' goods. Thus, Langland's *Piers Plowman* (B. 6. 303–11) and Gower's *Mirour de l'Omme* (26449–60) bemoaned the pride of beggars and labourers who would no longer be satisfied with bread containing beans, cheap ale, water, bacon, and yesterday's vegetables but instead insisted on fine wheat bread, the best ale, and fresh fish and meat. Nor was this mere literary stereotype as such claims are supported by the evidence of the improved food and drink supplied by the lords to agricultural workers at harvest time.

For the landlords, rising wages and (after 1376) falling grain prices reduced the profits which could be had from marketing their arable produce. An increasingly popular alternative for them was to lease out their demesnes, withdrawing from production for the market altogether and becoming rentiers. As a result, they no longer needed the remaining labour services of their unfree tenants, which were instead commuted into money rents. To retain their tenants in an age of falling demand for land, the landlords eventually had to reduce rents along with the entry fines paid for taking on holdings and the tallages and other charges levied from their unfree tenants, although, as we shall see, many lords were at first reluctant to accept the reality of their new situation.

Finally, not only was this an age of rising living standards and growing freedom; the high mortality rates of this period also encouraged upward social mobility as people rose to fill empty places higher up the social ladder. Within the village, the landless and middling peasants could acquire land while richer yeomen may have been particularly well placed to take advantage of the opportunities of this period. Many opted for migration from the countryside to the towns to take advantage of the buoyancy of urban manufactures and trade, areas of the economy that benefited from rising per capita spending power.

An area of particular growth within the towns was the manufacture of woollen textiles. England had long been Europe's main supplier of high-quality wool, exporting this raw material to the cloth manufacturers of Italy and Flanders. However, the second half of the fourteenth century saw the beginnings of a revolution in England's export trade. Shipments of raw wool fell by almost a half in this period, although English merchants (the members of the Staple Company) were at first cushioned against this decline by being granted a virtual monopoly of the trade. England's wool was now increasingly being exported in the form of manufactured woollen cloth. The heavy duties imposed on the export of raw wool to finance the Hundred Years War raised its cost to foreign producers, offering a welcome, if unintended, protection to domestic cloth-making. Exports of English cloth thus rose sevenfold between the 1350s and the 1390s, although much of the trade remained in the hands of foreign merchants and it was only in the first half of the fifteenth century that cloth replaced wool as England's chief export. The wool and cloth trade is represented among Chaucer's pilgrims by the Merchant, who traded with Middelburg ('GP' 277), a staple for English wool and a common destination for its cloth exports. The cloth industry itself is personified by the Weaver and the Dyer, as well as by the Wife of Bath, who hailed from one of England's principal cloth-making regions and who reputedly surpassed in skill the cloth-makers of Ypres and Ghent ('GP' 447–8).

If the post-plague period was one of increased social and economic opportunities, then some historians and literary critics see women as having been particularly able to take advantage of this situation. As Peggy Knapp argues, the depleted state of the labour market of this period 'allowed and even encouraged some women to enhance their own estates and follow their own callings', providing us with a social context in which to understand the Wife of Bath's assertiveness.[2] In an age of high mortality and low male replacement rates, women were more likely to acquire land as heiresses or, like widows such as the Wife of Bath, through their common law right of dower (the widow's share in her late husband's estate). Women, particularly widows like Alison, could even become entrepreneurs in their own right with their own servants and apprentices. As labourers, women shared in the general increase in real wages and, given the types of work in which they were employed, particularly benefited from the disproportionate rise in the wages of the unskilled that always occurs at times of labour shortage. With skilled labour also in short supply, women could now secure jobs that had formerly been the preserve of men, as smiths, tanners, carpenters, or tilers. In the post-1349 era of labour mobility, women may have been disproportionately attracted to the towns as workers in the expanding textile trades and in other industries whose products were now in increasing demand. If the later Middle Ages were a 'golden age of the bacillus' or a 'golden age of the labourer', were they also a 'golden age' for women?

The answer to this question remains controversial. Even at the height of the late medieval labour shortage, women, in general, remained in low-skilled, low-status, low-paid jobs. Within the towns they were far less likely than men to be formally apprenticed to a skilled occupation, while in the countryside women's employment was often irregular and usually low paid. Although women were now more likely to be heiresses, at marriage they still surrendered their property rights to their husbands. Indeed, widows may even have experienced a decline in their dower rights in this period through the growing practice of men avoiding the common law rules of inheritance by granting land to feoffees (trustees), which allowed them to dispose of it freely by will. Even where women did make economic gains in the period after 1349, these gains were not accompanied by a growth in their legal rights or political power which meant that they were ill-equipped to defend their position when it came under threat from the mid-fifteenth century onwards. Thus, any advances made by women in the late fourteenth century were marginal and short-lived and women's fundamental position remained unchanged.

Social conflict

In Chaucer's 'Knight's Tale', the malevolent influence of Saturn in human affairs is not only seen as the cause of 'pestilence' but is also said to bring about 'the cherles rebellyng' ('KT' 2469, 2459). Certainly, the economic changes consequent upon the Black Death and later epidemics seem to have resulted in an intensification of conflict within English society. If Chaucer's lifetime saw the balance of supply and demand for land and labour shift in favour of the peasants and labourers, then the landlords did not submit meekly to this new state of affairs; instead they turned to their legal and political powers to maintain their position. The most obvious example of this is the wage freeze introduced by the royal Ordinance of Labourers of 1349, which, in response to the 'excessive wages' demanded by the labourers, enacted that every able-bodied man and woman under the age of 60 and without an independent source of income 'shall be bound to serve him who shall require him', receiving only the wages current *before* the Black Death. Those who refused to serve or who withdrew before the end of their contract were to be imprisoned.[3] Since the 1349 Ordinance was soon said to be completely disregarded by the labourers, it was supplemented in 1351 by the Statute of Labourers, which specified maximum wage rates. Further legislation followed, including, in 1361, the introduction of imprisonment and branding for those who broke the labour laws, although this penalty was repealed in the following year.

In the decades after the Black Death the English upper classes seem to have been entertaining the fantasy of solving their problems by putting an end to the social and geographical mobility of the lower orders. In 1376 the House of Commons, made up mainly of gentry and richer townsmen, protested that, because of the scarcity of labour, masters 'now dare not challenge or offend their servants but give them whatever they ask'. Their solution to this nightmarish situation was for all wandering labourers to be 'placed in the stocks or sent to the nearest gaol' until they confessed where they came from and made surety to return there.[4] This requirement for migrant labourers to be forcibly repatriated became law in 1388, when it was also enacted that anyone who worked on the land until their twelfth birthday was to remain there rather than enter a craft. There were also repeated complaints about able-bodied beggars who were too idle to work. In 1349 it was ordained that no charity should be given to such 'sturdy beggars', so they would be 'compelled to labour for the necessaries of life', while from 1388 all vagrants were to carry official letters explaining their absence from their home village.

In response to upper-class fears that the social hierarchy was being overturned and all social distinctions blurred, there were even attempts to use the law to regulate lifestyles so as to keep each person in his or her proper place. Thus the sumptuary legislation of 1363, noting the 'outrageous and excessive apparel of many people' contrary to their estate and degree, sought to specify the food and clothing of each social class from esquires and gentlemen, who were not to wear any cloth of gold, silver, or silk, down to resident servants, who were to receive 'appropriate, not excessive, food and drink'.[5] At the local level, too, the landlords continued to assert their rights. They persisted in levying manorial dues, used fines in their manorial courts to maintain their incomes, opposed rent reductions, punished those who 'ungratefully' claimed that they were free, charged their tenants for permission to leave the manor, and forced individuals, groups, or village communities to take on responsibility for unoccupied lands so as to ensure that they continued to produce a return for their lords.

Yet, if the landlords defended their interests through 'seigneurial reaction', their tenants and employees were also seeking to take advantage of their improved bargaining position: the ambitions of the two sides were bound towards collision. Thus Langland's *Piers Plowman* criticized those labourers who, unless they received high wages, complained against God and against 'Reason' and grumbled against the king's council for passing laws to restrict them. No longer would they follow wise Cato's advice: 'Bear patiently the burden of poverty'. Langland wistfully recalled an era when food was less abundant and labour less scarce: 'When hunger was their master, none of them complained' (B. 6. 312–19). Certainly, the decades after the Black Death saw tens of thousands of prosecutions of those who demanded 'excessive' wages, broke their contracts of service, and refused to swear to obey the labour laws; there were even attacks on the justices who attempted to enforce the labour legislation.

Tenants, as well as labourers, seem to have been asserting themselves in the years after the Black Death, fleeing their manors in search of better land and more favourable terms of tenure, seeking rent reductions, and dragging their feet when performing labour services. Others claimed to be free of villeinage altogether, as in 1376–7, when tenants in over forty villages in the south and south-west of England appealed to Domesday Book to show that they were exempt from the rents and services owed to their lords. Indeed, complaints about villeins evading their obligations were made in parliament in 1376, 1377, 1385, 1391, 1397, and 1402. By *c.*1377 Gower's *Mirour de l'Omme* was predicting impending rural revolt: unless the lords awoke from their lethargy, the violent and impatient 'nettle' of the 'folly of the common people . . . will very suddenly sting us all' (26437–508).

The explosion that Gower had foreseen erupted in June 1381, when rebels from Kent, led by Wat Tyler and John Ball, and from Essex converged on the capital and, at two meetings with the young king Richard II at Mile End and Smithfield, demanded radical reforms. Elsewhere in the south and East Anglia rebels seized towns such as St Albans, Norwich, and Bury St Edmunds. The revolt had a number of causes, including political and fiscal issues such as the conduct of the war against France and the levying of new poll taxes to pay for it. Nevertheless, social and economic issues were to the fore when the rebels put their grievances to the king. They demanded that 'henceforward no man should be a serf', that rents should only be 4*d.* an acre, and that, contrary to the labour laws, 'no-one should serve any man except at his own will'.[6] Outside London the rebels' actions were also directed against the landlords' property and seigneurial rights as they destroyed court rolls and other manorial records and asserted, as at Wivenhoe in Essex, that they would henceforth hold their land 'at their own will forever, freely, and not at the will of the lord'.[7]

The 1381 revolt also involved urban society. Sometimes the townsmen joined forces with the rural rebels; at others, they simply took advantage of the general breakdown of central government to pursue their own demands. The high mortality, migration, and economic dislocation of the three decades before 1381 led to mounting social tensions in towns such as Canterbury where townsmen shared a common hostility with the rural rebels towards the propertied elite and Crown officials who dominated the city's government. Elsewhere, as at York and at London, existing factional conflicts within the ruling elite spilled over in 1381 into popular discontent and violence. At St Albans and Bury St Edmunds, where the townsmen had yet to win the chartered self-government of boroughs such as Canterbury, there were violent risings against the Benedictine abbeys that were the townsmen's overlords. Small wonder that Gower's *Confessio amantis* looked back nostalgically to an (unspecified) golden age where

> The citees knewen no debat,
> The poeple stood in obeissance
> Under the reule of governance.
> (Prologue, 106–8)

In the short term, the revolt of 1381 was crushed and the rebels failed to achieve the abolition of serfdom. However, if the English peasants did not succeed in winning their freedom by national revolt, they did, in the course of the late fourteenth and fifteenth centuries, manage to secure by their local actions an end to compulsory labour services, a reduction of manorial impositions and restrictions, and protection of their rights in the royal courts. By 1500 serfdom in England was virtually extinct and the peasants were free, copyhold and leasehold tenants paying low money rents. In other places and times, population decline has been the occasion for landlords to assert their rights, responding to low grain prices and high wages by tying the peasants to the soil and enforcing compulsory labour services. That the lords did not manage to bring about this outcome in late medieval England was not simply due to external economic circumstances but was also the result of the agency and initiative of the peasants and labourers themselves.

Chaucer and the social order

If the second half of the fourteenth century was a period of growing social tension and of increased social mobility, how did Chaucer himself react to these changes? The problem here is that whereas the poetry of a Gower is relentlessly didactic in tone, leaving us in no doubt about what he saw as the moral decline of contemporary society, Chaucer's style is ironic and his message often left implicit. Whereas Gower addresses us directly in his work, waxing eloquent about the evils of the 1381 revolt, an event he discussed at length in book I of his *Vox clamantis*, Chaucer speaks to us through his characters—including the fictional persona of Chaucer the pilgrim—which makes it much more difficult to establish Chaucer the poet's own values and attitudes.

As a result of these difficulties, modern critics have tended to be divided into two opposed camps in their assessments of the social ideology contained in Chaucer's work. On the one hand are those such as D. W. Robertson, B. F. Huppé, Sheila

Delany, P. A. Olson, and Alcuin Blamires who, despite wide differences of critical approach, are agreed in seeing Chaucer as essentially an orthodox, conservative or even reactionary writer (it should be stressed that this does not necessarily mean that these critics are themselves conservatives sympathetic to Chaucer's views).[8] For these critics, Chaucer differs from Gower not in his social outlook but rather in the literary techniques with which he chose to express it. In this view, we are meant to judge his characters in terms of their willingness to work faithfully at the duties traditionally expected of their order or profession. Those such as the Parson, Knight, and Plowman who labour for the common profit, live in harmony with their neighbours, and accept their assigned place in society are judged positively; those such as the Miller, the Monk, or the Wife of Bath who prey on their fellows, seek personal promotion and enrichment, or refuse to accept their allotted place in society are condemned.

These critics argue that although Chaucer does not explicitly praise or criticize the pilgrims of the 'General Prologue', he still manages to convey his judgements of them through his subtle use of literary irony. For instance, whereas Gower's *Vox clamantis* attacks those lowly people who illegitimately seek to rise to the top of urban society ('Nothing is more troublesome than a lowly person when he has risen to the top—at least when he was born a serf', v. 15), Chaucer's 'General Prologue' does not denounce the Five Guildsmen for their ambition to be aldermen seated 'on a deys' (370). Rather, using the techniques of literary description recommended in Geoffrey of Vinsauf's *Poetria nova*, in which 'the discretion of the wise man observes what is said through what is left unsaid',[9] Chaucer simply tells us that the Guildsmen wear their daggers 'chaped noght with bras | But al with silver' ('GP' 366–7). He thus assumes that his 'wise' readers will appreciate that this seemingly objective description is actually morally loaded since this kind of finery had been prohibited to men of the Guildsmen's class by the Sumptuary Act of 1363 and, more generally, was a symbol of excessive luxury that was conventionally invoked by contemporary social commentators as a sign of the pride and social pretension of the lower orders.

Yet, the fact that Chaucer does not explicitly condemn those who would refuse to accept their assigned place within society means that his text is also open to a very different reading. In this alternative interpretation, Chaucer is seen not as a conservative writer but rather as one who possesses a dissident or subversive voice, one that was sceptical about the official ideology of the day. For David Aers, Chaucer challenged the interdependence of the social orders claimed by the tripartite conception and recognized that the society of his day was made up of 'inevitably competing groups motivated by individualist forms of self-interest'. His work thus exposes all claims to be pursuing an alleged common profit 'to a sceptical examination' and so undermines all attempts 'to erect ideologically secure, impersonally authoritative discourses' with which to judge the pilgrims.[10] Just as for those who see Chaucer as an orthodox voice, so for critics such as W. E. Rogers and Larry Sklute, Chaucer's choice of literary form is itself ideologically loaded since, in Bakhtinian terms, his dialogic contest between multiple, contrary voices necessarily undermines all claims to monologic certainty (for more on Chaucer and Bakhtin, see Chapter 22). Thus, while Chaucer himself only ever made one passing reference to the rising of 1381 ('NPT' 3394–6), his 'Miller's Tale' has been seen by critics such as Peggy Knapp, Stephen Knight, and Lee Patterson as a peasants' revolt in literary form, one in which the Miller's bawdy fabliau, with its realm of plebeian, carnivalesque disorder, systematically overturns and parodies the ordered, hierarchical world-view of the Knight's chivalric epic which precedes it. Far from Chaucer simply rehearsing the official ideology of his day, his texts are, in Paul Strohm's words, sites of 'unresolved contention, of a struggle between hegemony and counter-hegemony' in which there is no single truth or authoritative position from which to judge the competing discourses which are presented to us.[11]

The *Canterbury Tales* certainly counterposes the dissident voices within late medieval society against the official ideology of the day, but whether this conflict remains 'unresolved' is a more controversial issue. While a sceptical Chaucer is one who would be attractive to many of us, the plausibility of this interpretation of Chaucer's work may be undermined by the 'Parson's Tale', the tale which Chaucer places at the end of the *Canterbury Tales*. In medieval rhetoric, the ending of a work was often presented as the position which should be reserved for, as Dante put it in the *Convivio* (2. 8. 2–3), that which a 'speaker is most intent upon conveying' (see also *TC* 2. 256–60). In the tale to which Chaucer ascribes this authoritative position, the Parson provides a comprehensive view of the universe, of society, and of the individual's place within it, one which is based upon the orthodox teaching that God created all things in their rightful order and nothing without order (Wisdom 11: 21; see also *HF* 730–64). Only in Hell is there no order since the damned 'been nothyng in ordre, ne holden noon ordre' (218). Sin itself is an inversion of rightful order since it involves the rebellion of sensuality against reason, which is its rightful superior, with the result that proper hierarchy is 'turned up-so-doun' (260–70). Within society, the 'reason' that underlies this divinely ordained order requires that there should be 'degree above degree': the common profit could not be had within society, nor peace on earth achieved, unless, as God himself had ordained, 'som men hadde hyer degree and som men lower' (763–5, 773). Inferiors should accept the decisions of 'hym that is in hyer degree' and not 'seyn harm, and grucche, and murmure prively' or envy the prosperity of others (483, 499, 505–7, 763–5), virtues embodied in the patient poverty of the 'povre wydwe' of the 'Nun's Priest's Tale' (2821–7). Similarly, within the family, the Parson teaches that wives should be subject and obedient to their husbands (1 Peter 3: 1) who were their 'lords' (921–36). Although each man, high or low, should be 'served in his estaat and in his degree', when those in authority did not practise the charity due to their inferiors the latter should remember the benefits which patient endurance brought in terms of eternal salvation (771, 1055, 1080).

Is the Parson's conservative voice given a privileged place within the *Tales*, making Chaucer's work the literary counterpart of the seigneurial reaction of the day, or are his views no more valid than those of any other pilgrim? Is his tale the ideological culmination of all that has gone before or does it actually constitute the literary neg-ation of Chaucer's own poetic achievement, straining, as Stephen Knight argues it does, to contain the polyphony of competing voices which gives the *Canterbury Tales* its veracity? These are the questions that all modern readers of the text must address if they are to come to their own assessment of Chaucer's social meaning.

Politics

Edward III, the Hundred Years War, and the deposition of Richard II

In the realm of English politics, as in society, the late fourteenth century saw a striking divergence between the dominant ideals of the day, ideals which stressed the need for hierarchy, order, and deference, and the reality, which involved conflict, change, and revolt. In his lifetime, from the 1340s to 1400, Chaucer witnessed the reigns of three kings of England: Edward III (1327–77), Richard II (1377–99), and Henry IV (1399–1413). It is impossible here to provide a detailed account of sixty years of English political, military, and diplomatic history. Our focus will be less on the events them-selves than on the conflicting political ideals and conceptions of kingship with which contemporaries tried to represent and to make sense of them. It is this clash of ideo-logies and values, particularly that around the deposition of Richard II, which, as in the realm of economic and social change, links the realm of historical events on the one hand with that of imaginative literature of the period on the other.

Edward III came to the throne in 1327 following the deposition of his father, Edward II (1307–27). His reign was dominated by the Hundred Years War with France, which began in 1337, in which Edward laid claim to the French throne by hereditary right (although this claim may have been simply a bargaining counter to force French con-cessions on other issues, particularly those arising from the king of England's position, as duke of Aquitaine, as a vassal of the French Crown). At first, Edward was successful with great victories, such as Crécy (1346), Nevilles Cross (1346), and Poitiers (1356), against the French and their Scottish allies. King and nobility were united through the shared purpose—and joint benefits—which the war brought. To encourage support for the war among the nobility and gentry, Edward, and his eldest son, Edward, the Black Prince, consciously promoted the aristocratic code of chivalry. By 1360, when a highly favourable settlement seemed to have been made and Chaucer himself had just been ransomed from French captivity, the English king's possessions in France were greater than at any time since 1204 (for more on the Hundred Years War, see Chapter 3).

Yet, while success in war brought short-term profit and glory, eventually it rebounded on England's rulers. The vast territories conceded to Edward in 1360 were difficult to defend and expensive to occupy. This meant heavy taxation, a burden which the English landed classes were unwilling to assume themselves and which, following the end of the experiment with poll taxes (the third poll tax having sparked off the Peasants' Revolt), they were unable to pass on to the rest of society. When war was renewed from 1369, Edward's gains were gradually eroded; the king was now aged and infirm, while the Black Prince was an invalid and died in 1376. Almost inevitably, military failure led to accusations of incompetence and corruption first against the so-called 'clerical ministry' of Bishop Wykeham of Winchester (the chancellor) and Bishop Brantingham of Exeter (the treasurer), which was removed in 1371, and then against the court party, including the king's mistress, Alice Perrers, and against the increasingly influential John of Gaunt, duke of Lancaster, the third son of Edward III. The latter's unpopularity reached a peak with the Good Parliament of 1376, when Perrers and officials within the royal household were accused of embezzlement and various men, including the royal chamberlain, were impeached.

The death of Edward III and the accession of his 10-year-old grandson Richard II on 22 June 1377 saw little change in the conduct of the war. A succession of campaigns, including Bishop Despenser of Norwich's so-called 'crusade', in which Chaucer's Squire fought ('GP' 85–6), achieved nothing until, by 1386, England itself was threatened by invasion from France and Scotland. These years saw a series of complaints in parliament about the extravagant expenditure of the royal household, the excessive influence on the young king of his tutor, Sir Simon Burley, and the favour shown to others such as Sir Aubrey de Vere, to his nephew Robert de Vere, earl of Oxford, whom Richard promoted to the hitherto unheard-of rank of 'marquess' in 1385, and to Sir Michael de la Pole, the controversial chancellor, who was made earl of Suffolk in the same year. This discontent erupted in the Wonderful Parliament of 1386, which refused to grant a tax for coastal defence until Suffolk had been impeached. The king was reminded of the deposition of his great-grandfather Edward II as the fate of a king who refused to rule according to the law and with the advice of his lords. He was forced to dismiss the chancellor and treasurer and to accept a commission of fourteen prelates and nobles, which was set up to reform the royal household, finances, and administration. These events may have had an impact on Chaucer's own career, perhaps bringing about his removal from his position as London customs' controller.

Richard sought to overthrow the decisions made in the Wonderful Parliament through a verdict from his leading judges that this parliament had infringed the royal prerogative and that its actions were treasonous. However, when the king's forces, commanded by Robert de Vere, were defeated at Radcot Bridge in 1387, his opponents, led by his uncle the duke of Gloucester, and the earls of Arundel and Warwick, along with Henry Bolingbroke, the earl of Derby and the son of John of Gaunt, and the earl of Nottingham, were left with a free hand. At the so-called Merciless Parliament of February 1388 these five lords made an 'appeal' (that is, an accusation) of treason against de Vere and others, some of whom were executed, including Burley, while others were expelled from court. However, splits soon appeared among the five Appellant lords and also between the Lords and Commons in parliament, allowing the king to reassert his personal rule as he declared himself of age in 1389, when Chaucer himself returned to office as Clerk of the King's Works. From 1389 to 1397 there was a period of relative peace at home and abroad. A truce with France was extended for a further twenty-eight years in 1396. Richard's beloved first wife, Anne of Bohemia, whom he had married in 1382 (and to whom Chaucer refers in the *Legend of Good Women*, F 496–7), had died in 1394, which meant that, like the peace between Thebes and Athens in the 'Knight's Tale', the Anglo-French truce could be sealed by marriage when Richard took the 6-year-old Princess Isabella of France as his second wife.

Then suddenly, in July 1397, for reasons that remain unclear and controversial, Richard launched his so-called 'tyranny'. Arundel, Gloucester, and Warwick, three of the Appellants of 1388, were arrested by Richard and, in a deliberate reprise of the Merciless Parliament, were appealed of treason. Arundel was condemned to death and Warwick exiled to the Isle of Man, while Gloucester was murdered in Calais. Thomas Arundel, archbishop of Canterbury and brother to the Appellant earl, was banished and replaced as archbishop by the treasurer, Roger Walden. In the following year a dispute between Bolingbroke (now duke of Hereford) and Nottingham (now duke of Norfolk) led to both being exiled by the king: all five of the Appellants of 1388 were now dead or in exile.

The king's victory seemed so complete that when Gaunt died, in February 1399, Richard was able to refuse Bolingbroke his promised inheritance, assigning the Lancastrian estates to his own supporters until Bolingbroke's son, the future Henry V, was of age. In May 1399 he even felt secure enough to leave for Ireland as head of a force to defend the settlement which had resulted from an earlier expedition in 1394–5. However, in the king's absence Bolingbroke landed at Ravenspur in Yorkshire in July and gathered a military force, both Henry Percy, earl of Northumberland, and Ralph Neville, earl of Westmorland, rallying to him. By the end of the month Richard had returned to Wales and, having been lured from Conwy Castle, was captured at Flint on 16 August. On 30 September 1399 an assembly in the great hall of Westminster of the lords spiritual and temporal and of 'the people of the realm gathered there for the holding of parliament' was told that Richard had abdicated. However, to be certain, the king was also adjudged to have been deposed. Bolingbroke was named as Richard's successor and was then crowned as Henry IV on 13 October. Richard was imprisoned at Pontefract Castle and conveniently died in February 1400.

The descending concept of political authority

It would be wrong to present the revolutionaries of 1399 as high-minded idealists. Men such as the Nevilles and Percys were chiefly motivated by immediate concerns about property and patronage such as the control of offices like the wardenships of the East and West Marches, the lieutenancy of the March, and the shrievalty of Westmorland. Nevertheless, in order to achieve their aims, to justify their acts to themselves and to others, and to legitimize the new regime, Bolingbroke and his supporters had to rally support from a much wider cross-section of England's political community. Accordingly, the conflict between Richard and those who deposed him was represented not simply as a matter of personal interest but as a conflict between competing political values and ideologies.

Richard's own idea of kingship can be characterized as a 'descending' concept in which power flowed downwards, all power being derived ultimately from God (John 19: 11; Romans 13: 1). He who holds power is responsible to those above him: a royal official to the king, the king to God. Indeed, like other medieval monarchs, the kings of England claimed to rule 'by God's grace', that is, by divine gift and favour. Of course, the king did have responsibilities to those beneath him: he should keep the peace, maintain the law, do justice to all, and protect the weak. But the king was separate from the rest of the community, which, like the people of the 'Clerk's Tale' who meekly beseech Walter to take a wife (85–142), could petition him for privileges, liberties, and benefits but could not force him to accede to its requests. If the king proved to be an evil ruler, a tyrant, the people had to endure him as a punishment for their sins sent by God. The king, bound by divine law, would one day have to answer to God for his actions, but he was, in effect, above human law since the king himself gave and created law.

That Richard II shared in this descending concept of kingship can be seen in 1387 when he had his judges assert that a statute of 1386, by which a commission had been set up in parliament to control his royal administration, was contrary to his will and so 'derogatory to the regality and prerogative of the lord king'. Those who had forced the king to assent to its creation should therefore be punished 'as traitors'. Richard, or his advisers, may have derived this theory of kingship from *De regimine principum* ('On the Government of Princes') of Giles of Rome (d. 1316), with its emphasis on the subject's obedience to the ruler as the means to prosperity, internal peace, and security against foreign enemies: the evils of tyranny were less than those of civil disobedience. The focus here was not on the subject's liberties but on the ruler's 'dignity' and the maintenance of his prerogative, as was stressed in the bishop of Exeter's opening speech as chancellor to parliament in 1397, and on the 'peace' and 'order' which flowed from his subjects' submission to the ruler's will.

Unfortunately, we have no programmatic statement of Richard's conception of kingship. What does survive is a representation of his views in artistic form, in the iconography of kingship of the *Wilton Diptych* (see Figure I.2). The two inner panels of the diptych depict Richard II being presented by three saints to the Virgin Mary and the infant Christ, who are accompanied by eleven angels. On the left is St Edmund, the last Anglo-Saxon king of East Anglia, who was martyred by the Danes in 870 for his refusal to abandon his Christian faith, a martyrdom symbolized by the arrow he carries. A royal saint who came to the throne when he was only 15, St Edmund may have had a

Fig. 1.2 The *Wilton Diptych* (anonymous), late 1390s (National Gallery).

particular appeal for Richard. The middle of the three saints is King Edward the Confessor, who holds up the ring which he gave to St John the Evangelist, who had appeared to him in the guise of a poor man, the ring having later been returned to the king as a sign that he would soon join St John in heaven. Finally, carrying the lamb of God, there is St John the Baptist, another saint to whom Richard had a particular devotion as the king's birthday, 6 January, coincides with the feast of the baptism of Christ by St John. This date was also that of the feast of the Epiphany, when the three kings arrived to see the infant Jesus—an event itself replicated in the diptych—a festival for which the royal courts of Europe had a particular fondness. The white banner with the red cross being held by one of the angels refers both to the resurrection of Jesus, the instruments of whose Passion are depicted in his halo, and to St George, who, along with Sts Edmund and Edward, is another of the patron saints of England. Above the banner, an orb depicts England with a white tower, probably representing the Tower of London, which, ironically, was to be Richard's place of captivity at the time of his deposition.

On one of the outer panels of the diptych are depicted the arms of England and France impaled with those of Edward the Confessor, which Richard II adopted in 1395. The broomcods (the seed pods of the broom plant), a badge of the French kings, which appear on Richard's gown and on the collars which he and the angels wear, seem to link the diptych to the period just before or after Richard's marriage with Princess Isabella in 1396. All this personal imagery, including Richard's white hart emblem, which is worn by the eleven angels and which also appears on one of the outer panels of the diptych, suggests that the painting was commissioned by Richard himself and that it dates from the last three years of his reign, when the king was aged 29–32. Yet, while other pictures of the king from around this time show him as a bearded, mature man, the *Wilton Diptych* portrays the king as a smooth-faced boy. This depiction of the king is a reminder that Richard had come to the throne in his eleventh year (perhaps symbolized by the eleven angels), that he had received his power from God (represented by Christ's blessing of the banner of St George with its depiction of England), and that he ruled with the backing of the Virgin and the saints. To resist the king was thus to resist the will of heaven. It has been suggested that the depictions of Sts Edmund, Edward, and John are meant to portray King Richard's immediate forefathers: Edward II, Edward III, and the Black Prince. If so, the diptych is also an affirmation that Richard was king by hereditary right.

Finally, in representing Richard as he was in 1377, the diptych also alludes to Richard's sacramental anointing as king of England at his coronation, which took place on 14 July 1377, at which he wore the slippers of St Edmund and the coat and crown of St Edward. The *Wilton Diptych* thus depicts Richard II as having obtained his royal power by hereditary right and by his anointing. He was a ruler who enjoyed the blessing of heaven since, as was said at his coronation, 'no man can happily reign upon earth who has not received his authority from heaven'.[12] The diptych was linked to Richard's personal religious devotion but it is also political propaganda for the descending conception of kingship, even if, like so much propaganda in the Middle Ages, it was directed at an audience, in the form of the king and his immediate circle, that was already convinced of its claims.

The ascending concept of political authority

Ironically, while the *Wilton Diptych* alluded to Richard II's coronation in support of the king's descending concept of power, the coronation was soon to be invoked by those who mounted the coup of 1399. It was Richard's alleged failure to maintain his coronation oath, in which he had sworn to maintain the peace, to do justice, and to rule according to the existing laws and customs of England and those that the community of the realm should determine in future, that was used to justify why the king was worthy of deposition. Yet this justification implies that an alternative conception of kingship to that of the *Wilton Diptych* was also current in late fourteenth-century England. Whereas the descending theory of kingship was expounded in clerical treatises, this alternative 'ascending' conception of authority was, as in 1399, more evident in the actual practice of political life. Here, the ruler was responsible to the political community of which he was a part and with which he was in a contractual relationship. A king who did not uphold the rightful contract between ruler and ruled was no longer a legitimate ruler but an illegitimate tyrant since, as Gower's *Tripartite Chronicle* concludes, 'He who is a sinner cannot be a ruler' (III. 486). Although they never use the term, the Articles of Deposition certainly amount to a systematic accusation of 'tyranny' against Richard, a charge explicitly laid against him by Gower and by the chronicler Thomas Walsingham.

Medieval political thought defined a tyrant in terms of five main criteria. Firstly, a tyrant would not be bound by law but rather saw his own will as equivalent to the law. As the Articles of Deposition claimed, Richard believed that 'the laws were in his mouth ... and that he alone could change or make the laws of his kingdom'.[13] Secondly, if the king was above the law then his subjects no longer enjoyed any security of life or property. As the Articles of Deposition said, Richard had publicly claimed that 'the lives of each of his subjects, together with their land, tenements, goods and chattels were his and subject to his will ... which is entirely contrary to the laws of the kingdom'.

Thirdly, as Aristotle had stressed, the tyrant does not rule for the common good but rather for his own personal gain and glory. As the Articles of Deposition put it, Richard had imposed a heavy burden of taxation on his subjects, oppressing and impoverishing them and lavishing the proceeds on his own 'ostentation, pomp and vainglory'. Fourthly, while, as the Parson teaches, a willingness to be guided by good counsel is a sign of humility (482), tyrants refuse to listen to the counsel of wise and learned men. Thus the Articles of Deposition claimed that those who had sought to advise the king had been so violently rebuked that they 'dared not speak the truth' to him. Finally, tyrants were seen in medieval thought as being personally vicious and immoral. As a result, they were often depicted as unable to control their own sexual appetites. The Articles of Deposition themselves do not accuse Richard II of sexual vice, although Walsingham did imply the existence of a homosexual relationship between Richard and Robert de Vere. Instead, they focus on his lack of trustworthiness. Whereas for Gower's *Confessio amantis*, truth and constancy were the chief virtues of a king (7. 1723–77), the Articles of Deposition claimed that Richard had been 'variable and dissimulating in both word and letter, and so inconstant in his behaviour. . . that virtually no living person who came to know him could or wished to trust him'.

The events of Richard II's reign had shown how difficult it was to restrain a king; the only alternative left for his opponents was his removal in the name of the political community. This is not to say that those who deposed Richard in 1399 were modern democrats in their call for the king to rule with the advice of the 'community of the realm' since this community excluded most of the population. Rather, the 'community of the realm' comprised England's propertied elite who regarded themselves as the spokesmen for the entire nation, a claim which had been contested by the rebels of 1381.

Chaucer and politics

In his 'Complaint of Chaucer to his Purse', written shortly before his death, Chaucer addressed Henry IV directly, requesting financial aid from the new king whom he hailed as 'conquerour of Brutes Albyon | Which that by lyne and free eleccion | Been verray kyng' (22–4), thereby rehearsing Henry's three claims to the throne (conquest, inheritance, and popular recognition) which were also set out in Gower's *Tripartite Chronicle* (3. 330–40). Perhaps Chaucer had reconciled himself to the Lancastrian regime with the reflection that while Richard II had readily followed the advice which Chaucer had offered him in his 'Lak of Stedfastnesse' to 'Shew forth thy swerd of castigacioun', he had unfortunately neglected the poet's wise counsel on the need to 'Cherish thy folk and hate extorcioun' (22–8). What then were Chaucer's own views on political community, kingship, and tyranny?

As David Wallace points out, the 'General Prologue' to the *Canterbury Tales* presents us with a voluntary association of adults from a wide range of social groups who 'form themselves into a corporative unity and regulate their affairs without reference to external authority'.[14] Yet, within the tales themselves, the populace at large tend to be regarded with suspicion. Thus, in the 'Clerk's Tale', the more sober citizens criticize the changeable people who first weep at the fate of poor Griselda but soon applaud Walter's choice of a new wife: 'O stormy peple! Unsad and evere untrewe! . . . A ful greet fool is he that on yow leeveth' (897, 995–1001). As Prudence says in the 'Tale of Melibee', 'the trouthe of thynges and the profit been rather founden in fewe folk that been wise and ful of resoun than by greet multitude of folk ther every man crieth and clatereth what that hym liketh. Soothly swich multitude is nat honest' (1069). As can be seen in the conflict between Chaucer's Miller and Reeve ('RP' 3859–920), the lower orders were considered to be quarrelsome, immoderate in their speech, and incapable of seeing beyond their own narrow interests.

Yet, if Chaucer regarded the 'unsad' populace with disdain, he seems more concerned about the dangers of tyranny. This is not to say, as some critics have been tempted to do, that Chaucer's works should be seen as *romans-à-clef* which allegorically refer to contemporary political events and characters so that, for instance, Palamon and Arcite of the 'Knight's Tale' are cast in the roles of Richard II and Gloucester. Rather, in politics as in his discussion of social mobility and conflict, Chaucer's works adopt the customary medieval practice of translating the issues of his day into questions of individual morality, as can be seen from his discussion of tyranny. For Chaucer, a tyrant was not a legitimate king but rather, as the 'Manciple's Tale' put it, a 'titlelees' ruler (223) who regards his own will as equivalent to the law of the land. As the 'Monk's Tale' says of the emperor Nero, he slew his senators simply so as 'To heere how that men wolde wepe and crie' and 'His lustes were al lawe in his decree' (2477–81). As a result, the tyrant's subjects have no security of property so that, as the 'Manciple's Tale' argues, there is no difference between a tyrant and a thief except that the tyrant has more power and does more harm (223–34). The tyrant rules for his own personal vainglory, as can be seen from Nebuchadnezzar in the 'Monk's Tale', who, on pain of death, has all men bow down before a huge gold statue of himself (2159–63). The tyrant ignores wise counsel, as Melibee is first tempted to do when his wife, Prudence, offers her sage warnings against taking revenge on those who offend against us (1455–60), advice which Richard II was to ignore with such disastrous consequences. The tyrant is personally vicious like Creon in the 'Knight's Tale', who, 'Fulfild of ire and of iniquitee', refuses to bury the bodies of his defeated enemies but instead 'maketh houndes ete hem in despit' (940–7). In particular, tyrants lack sexual self-control, like Bernabò Visconti in the 'Monk's Tale', the 'God of delit and scourge of Lumbardye' (2400), or Apius, the 'lecherus' governor of the 'Physician's Tale' (266), who abuses his power so as to possess the noble Virginia, abandoning his reason and surrendering to his own lower nature.

Perhaps Walter, the Lombard prince in the 'Clerk's Tale', who resembles the Lombard tyrants 'that usen wilfulhed' of the *Legend of Good Women* (G 354–5), is the supreme example in the *Canterbury Tales* of a ruler who demands unquestioning obedience to his will. Yet, the political meaning of this tale is obscured by its allegorization by the Clerk into a lesson about the need for humanity to submit absolutely to God's will and to 'lyve in vertuous suffraunce' (1142–62). Thus, while the Clerk himself tells the Host that he can be obedient to his commands only 'as fer as resoun axeth' (25), Griselda, whom the tale's narrative asks us to admire even though she acquiesces in the death of her own children, goes far beyond what reason requires. As a result, the tale never makes clear the rational limits of an earthly ruler's legitimate authority or his subjects' duty of obedience.

Duke Theseus in the 'Knight's Tale' might also, at first glance, seem to embody the descending conception of power when he presents himself to his subjects, 'Arrayed right as he were a god in trone' (2529). Indeed, some critics have even seen Theseus as a tyrant who, through military might and ideological hegemony, pursues his own imperial ambitions, ensuring his own personal and political power by subordinating Scithia and Thebes and by forcing Emelye to marry against her will. Yet, as Wallace stresses, whatever our assessment of the duke by the standards of modern morality, in medieval terms, 'Theseus is no tyrant'.[15] Rather, as the legendary founder of chivalry and of parliaments, Theseus embodied the medieval ideal of a strong ruler who keeps the peace, maintains the law, defeats foreign enemies, and protects the weak, yet who also rules in partnership with the political community. That this balance between the descending and ascending concepts of kingship was an ideal shared by Chaucer himself is particularly clear at the end of the tale, where Theseus arranges the alliance of Athens and Thebes and the marriage between Palamon and Emelye with the advice of his 'parlement' and with the agreement of 'al the conseil and the baronage' (2970, 3096). If the Parson ends the *Canterbury Tales* with a Christian vision of how to achieve salvation in the next world, then, in the form of the 'Knight's Tale', Chaucer begins the pilgrims' storytelling contest with a recommendation of how justice and order is to be attained in the here and now. The tales are thus framed by the visions of hierarchy, order, and virtue provided by the ideal representatives of the second and first estates; it is tempting to speculate what tale Chaucer would have assigned to the Plowman, the third of the traditional estate-ideals among the pilgrims.

Conclusion

As we have seen, poetry in late fourteenth-century England was not confined to exploring the realm of the individual's inner emotions. Rather, writers such as Geoffrey Chaucer, John Gower, and William Langland engaged with more general issues such as 'How can society best be organized for the common good?', 'How does legitimate kingship differ from illegitimate tyranny?', and 'How can salvation be obtained?' Appealing to the evidence of history cannot equip us with a ready-made key to Chaucer's own answers to these questions. However, what a knowledge of Chaucer's historical context can do is to make us aware of the social and political issues that the poet had to address if he was to engage with the questions that so sharply divided the inhabitants of England in his own day. In literary criticism, historical context can never provide us with a conclusion but, nevertheless, it remains the indispensable starting point of our analysis.

FURTHER READING

Blamires, Alcuin, 'Chaucer the Reactionary: Ideology and the "General Prologue" to the *Canterbury Tales*', *Review of English Studies*, 51 (2000), 523–39. Argues that Chaucer is 'committed to the "dominant" social view and categorically does not sympathize with political dissent'.

Dyer, Christopher, *Making a Living in the Middle Ages: The People of Britain, 850–1520* (New Haven: Yale University Press, 2002). The most up-to-date account of the medieval economy with useful bibliographical guidance.

Gordon, Dillian, *Making and Meaning: The 'Wilton Diptych'* (London: National Gallery Publications, 1991). The best introduction to the *Wilton Diptych*.

McKisack, May, *The Fourteenth Century, 1307–1399* (Oxford: Oxford University Press, 1959). Still extremely useful for its readable account of political events.

Owst, G. R., *Literature and Pulpit in Medieval England*, 2nd edn. (Oxford: Blackwell, 1961). A treasure-house of references to medieval ideas about class, status, and gender.

Rigby, S. H., *Chaucer in Context: Society, Allegory, and Gender* (Manchester: Manchester University Press, 1996). Assesses conflicting attempts to locate Chaucer's work in its historical context and provides bibliographical references to the critics discussed in this chapter.

Rigby, S. H., *English Society in the Later Middle Ages: Class, Status and Gender* (Basingstoke: Macmillan, 1995). Discusses social structure, change, and conflict in the later Middle Ages.

Rigby, S. H. (ed.), *A Companion to Britain in the Later Middle Ages* (Oxford: Blackwell, 2003). Includes chapters on the medieval English economy, society, religion, and culture, along with suggestions for further reading.

Saul, Nigel, *Richard II* (New Haven: Yale University Press, 1997). This excellent, detailed account is the standard work on the reign.

Wimbledon's Sermon 'Redde Rationem Villicationis Tue': A Middle English Sermon of the Fourteenth Century, ed. Ione Kemp Knight (Pittsburgh: Duquesne University Press, 1967). An edition of one of the most famous statements of the tripartite conception of society.

NOTES

1. *Bracton on the Laws and Customs of England*, ed. Samuel E. Thorne (Cambridge, Mass.: Belknap Press, 1968), ii. 31.
2. Peggy Knapp, *Chaucer and the Social Contest* (New York: Routledge, 1990), 117.
3. A. E. Bland, P. A. Brown, and R. H. Tawney (eds.), *English Economic History: Select Documents* (London: Bell, 1914), 164–7.
4. R. B. Dobson (ed.), *The Peasants' Revolt of 1381* (London: Macmillan, 1983), 72–4.
5. Rosemary Horrox (ed.), *The Black Death* (Manchester: Manchester University Press, 1994), 340–2.
6. Dobson, *Peasants' Revolt*, 6.
7. Christopher Dyer, 'The Social and Economic Background to the Rural Revolt of 1381', in R. H. Hilton and T. H. Aston (eds.), *The English Rising of 1381* (Cambridge: Cambridge University Press, 1984), 41.
8. For references to the work of the critics named in this section, see the notes and bibliography in S. H. Rigby, *Chaucer in Context: Society, Allegory, and Gender* (Manchester: Manchester University Press, 1996).
9. Ernest Gallo, *The 'Poetria Nova' and its Sources in Early Rhetorical Doctrine* (The Hague: Mouton, 1971), 51, 97–9.

10. David Aers, *Chaucer* (Brighton: Harvester, 1986), 24.

11. Paul Strohm, *Social Chaucer* (Cambridge, Mass.: Harvard University Press, 1989), pp. xii–xiii, 171–2.

12. Thomas Walsingham, *Historia Anglicana*, i: *A.D. 1272–1381*, ed. Henry Thomas Riley, Rolls Series (1863), 335.

13. All quotations from the Articles of Deposition given below come from Chris Given-Wilson (ed.), *Chronicles of the Revolution, 1397–1400: The Reign of Richard II* (Manchester: Manchester University Press, 1993), 169–89.

14. David Wallace, *Chaucerian Polity: Absolutist Lineages and Associational Forms in England and Italy* (Stanford, Calif.: Stanford University Press, 1997), 65.

15. Ibid. 108.

3 | Nationhood

Ardis Butterfield

To explore nationhood in the Middle Ages is less straightforward than it may appear. Although it is a current and indeed urgent modern preoccupation, the conditions in which we conceive of nation and nationhood now are manifestly different from those prevalent in the fourteenth century. Many would argue that the term 'nationhood' is not applicable to the Middle Ages. Scholars working in later periods of English literature generally assume that ideas of nation or nationhood came into existence much later, although how much later is also an issue. Most historians of the modern period would locate the beginnings of nation in the eighteenth century, and its full flowering in the nineteenth. Others have argued that the first important stages of national consciousness occur during the Renaissance, in the attempts by the Tudor monarchy to promote its dynastic claims, the explosion across Europe of vernacular Bible translation in the sixteenth century, and the encounters with the New World by Elizabethan seafarers. The one area of common ground for these scholars appears to be that the medieval period is necessarily prior and distinct: it serves as a point of contrast from which to measure new beginnings.

Yet the medieval period does raise vital and complex questions about what we have subsequently come to call 'national' identity. The most important reason for this in the later Middle Ages is the Hundred Years War: a time of intense diplomacy, periodic conflict, violent rifts, and sudden rapprochements between England and France that changed the relationship between the two peoples in fundamental and far-reaching ways. Internal perceptions on either side of the Channel of 'English' and 'French' were transformed. The period between 1200 and 1500 has some claim to be one of the most absorbing of any in England's history as a nation, precisely because political, legal, and diplomatic formulations of statehood were thrown into such a state of flux. The prolonged tussle of possession between English and French kings and European landed aristocracy over areas of the Continent stimulated a re-examination of all kinds of issues of power and allegiance in medieval Europe. The story in the midst of this of how vernacular languages and literatures changed, and the impact of this change on the subsequent reputation of English, gains immeasurably from being placed in this context.

It follows that if we are to look for nationhood in the Middle Ages we might have to seek new terms and new approaches. Focusing on the latter half of the fourteenth century, the historical moment for Chaucer's writings, I shall be asking how a literate person in London might be capable of imagining himself or herself, not just as part of a local, or civic, or regional community, but, beyond that, as part of some larger set of identities. When we consider these identities we find that they were numerous, and intersected in rich and sometimes troubling ways. For example, people might see themselves as belonging to a community of subjects, ruled by a king. But, if they were from a noble lineage, they might also see themselves as part of a family whose members owed allegiance to different kings. If they were involved in finance or trade, then their professional loyalties with individuals and guilds or other fraternities in a variety of European cities might conflict with their feudal loyalty to a lord. An ordained priest, whether higher or lower on the social scale, would hold allegiance to the Church as well as to the king: but the medieval Church itself was a far from stable and coherent structure, and contained many rival networks of power across the Continent.

Concepts and structures of identity in the Middle Ages depended not on some single, overarching idea of the state, but rather on a variety of often competing allegiances. A single individual might have several conflicting loyalties, and the nature of these commitments would depend on his or her social status, occupation, and linguistic habits and competencies. We can further see this from the range of words in medieval English (and other languages) that articulate larger structures of belonging: these include *nation* itself (spelled *nacioun* in Chaucer (where it occurs eight times), *nascion* in French, *natio* in Latin), *folk, contree, kynde, comonalte*. 'Nacioun' here does not mean a sovereign, political 'state' but birth, family, or lineage. I will be looking at some examples in detail later in the chapter, but here we can perhaps already conclude that such terms show less of an abstract interest in community and more of a personal one. The perception of self and the community radiates outward from the condition of one's birth and family, and involves a fluid idea of the public domain in which one might see oneself. It is also worth commenting at the outset that language is crucial: it is not just that a word might have a different meaning in one language than in another, but that one language might depend on another for its meaning. Part of the fascination of the process is observing the extent to which 'nation' in English might be disengaging itself from Latin and French meanings, having originally identified itself with those meanings.

Would a literate Londoner, such as Chaucer, have a sense of being 'English'? To put it another way, what does it mean to call Chaucer an 'English' poet? And what are the implications for our understanding of his writings? In the context of the Hundred Years War, 'English' turns out to be as potentially complex and problematic a term as 'nation'. This chapter will explore some answers to these questions about 'Englishness' by choosing a range of approaches to Chaucer and his immediate social, political, and literary context.

Beginning with a brief account of the structure, conditions, and cross-cultural configurations of war between England and the Continent, and between England and the other insular peoples, this chapter will then focus on more specific examples of social and literary contacts. Through such figures as John of Gaunt, Froissart, and Edward III's queen, Philippa, as well as Chaucer himself, I shall attempt to convey a sense of the cultural atmosphere inhabited by each of them: their spheres of influence, the people they encountered, the linguistic environments in which they worked and lived. The effort will be to gain a sense of how people with some degree of political and literary influence viewed their own cultural identity: how they formed relationships and antagonisms across various European networks.

The latter part of the chapter will consider further how ideas of nationhood were articulated through writing, how Chaucer's poetry relates to discussions of identity and cultural difference, to cultural assertions and negations. This may help to provide a sharper sense of how Chaucer perceived himself as a writer, bound as he was by so many links of language, marriage, and career to Europe.

England and France: the Hundred Years War

The spark that lit the smouldering conflict between England and France in the thirteenth and fourteenth centuries was ostensibly generated in Aquitaine, the large region of south-west France that came into English royal possession with the marriage of Henry II and Eleanor of Aquitaine in the twelfth century (see Figure I.3). The impetus to war came from a complex of factors. In 1259 Henry III was made a peer of France. This apparently generous gesture created a profound feudal awkwardness. Henry, and English kings after him, were required, as dukes of Aquitaine, to pay liege homage to the French king. This subtly transferred power to the French kingdom over land that the English royalty regarded as theirs by right. Once Edward III came to the throne, he decided, through his mother's line, to secure Aquitaine once and for all by claiming the throne of France. The start of the war proper is usually described as the moment in 1337 when Philip of Valois declared the duchy of Aquitaine as confiscated to the French Crown, thereby provoking Edward's counter-claim.

It is interesting to consider how differently this narrative reads if we take a Continental perspective. From this point of view, the Hundred Years War is not so much about two countries warring over territory but something more like a civil war between two contrasting models of exercising power. The assertion of right to the French throne by Edward III looks less like a modern-style annexing of a rival state, and more like a family conflict, a means of seizing back control from a rival sibling.[1]

The duchy of Aquitaine has a pivotal role in the story on several counts. It reminds us that 'France' was not a single entity. On the contrary, until the end of the fifteenth century the various regions of 'France' were ruled by a variety of more or less powerful lords, some of whom were 'English'. Moreover, the history of Aquitaine and in particular the longevity of its association with the 'English' shows us how broad a definition of Englishness we need to understand the political realities of this period.[2] Being English

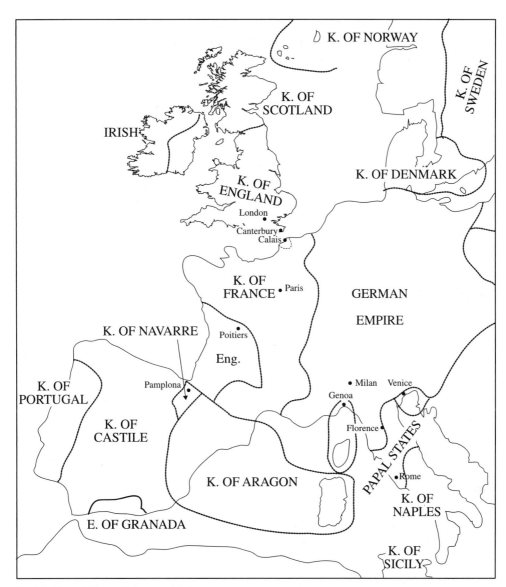

Fig. I.3 Map of Chaucer's Europe, 1360.

for the Gascons (Gascon was the language spoken widely in this south-west region) did not mean acquiring alien stereotypes, customs, or language, but rather protecting their own character and customs. When they fought for the English they did so, paradoxically, to assert their own independence, to maintain that distance between their way of life and the centralizing desires of northern French kings that being 'English' had enabled for many generations.

There is an irony, then, in the way that Aquitaine proved to be so fundamental to English interests in France. It further reminds us that we need a double perspective: what seems 'English' or 'French' from one side of the sea may not look the same from the opposite shore. Just as 'English' is a broad category, so is 'French'. The Gascons felt no more 'French' than they felt 'Norman' or 'Burgundian'.

If on the French side of nationhood we need to consider the fluidity of territorial acquisition and loss on the Continent, on the English side we need to take account of the relations between England and the rest of the peoples of Britain, the Scottish, Irish, and Welsh. Again, the two histories are connected: one of the most strongly defined features of Edward III's rule was his attempt to alternate campaigns against the Scots and campaigns within France throughout the active part of his reign. Several histories collide here: from the point of view of the Scots, the thirteenth and fourteenth centuries were an intense drive towards independence, marked by seemingly endless war. The complexity of Norman descent among the Scots, Irish, and Welsh worked in significantly different ways: whereas the Anglo-Irish and the Anglo-Welsh were subject to the English Crown, the Anglo-Scots were subject to the Scottish Crown. Their aristocratic descendants therefore became much more effective leaders in the cause of independence than the Welsh or Irish. Also, by the fourteenth century, they sought alliances with the French, and the French Crown with them, in ways that greatly complicated and occasionally destabilized English campaigns in France.[3]

Fourteenth-century relationships between England and the Continent, though dominated by the Hundred Years War, thus involved more than the 'local' squabble between the English and French kings. In the 1380s war involving English troops took place in Flanders, Castile, and Portugal as well as Scotland. Yet in this decade, one in which Chaucer was producing a succession of major works, the course of war dissipated and faltered. Richard II (at the age of 10) had inherited the war from his grandfather, Edward III. He also inherited a carefully fashioned narrative image of war, which has been handed on almost intact to the present day (and is gleefully resurrected by our sports feature writers at any French–English contest). In this narrative, the English faced huge French armies and through matchless bravery, regard for honour, and superior skill cut down the flower of French aristocracy, first at Crécy (26 August 1346), Calais (4 August 1347), and then Poitiers (19 September 1356). These were highly significant victories: Calais became a crucial English port for several centuries, and the most visible result of Poitiers was that the French king, Jean II, was taken prisoner and kept intermittently as a hostage over a period of some eight years as security for the payment of a huge ransom. It would be hard to find a more extravagant symbol of victory than that of a French king languishing in England for so extended a period, humiliatingly required to forfeit most of the wealth of his kingdom and many of his claims to territorial power (although in fact, Jean was permitted many luxuries and courtesies, and returned to France in 1360, his place taken by forty further hostages).

Yet by the time of Richard II's maturity, these glorious victories had lost some of their shine: a prolonged period of attrition following the peace treaty of Brétigny in 1360, and complex domestic and economic troubles, partly caused by plague outbreaks, led to a profound change of atmosphere. Triumphalism, and the heady glamour of Arthurian mythology, was replaced by a fragile relationship between king and commons, and a desire, through a variety of initiatives, to broker negotiated peace. On the French side, the capture of Jean II had created a severe crisis, leaving large areas of land vulnerable to the attacks of rioters, looting mercenaries, and rival factions for the Crown.

In trying to understand the wider (rather than merely the domestic) political climate of the 1380s and 1390s, it seems important to be sensitive to the near memory of English hauteur that was so dominant in the 1350s. Yet clearly, for both sides there was also a sense that this time was past, and that the current climate was less about clinging to certainties and asserting claims and more about surviving confusing and at times overwhelming bids for change. Whatever Edward III had achieved, it was not a continuing feeling of nationalism. In the treaty of Brétigny he renounced his claim to the French Crown in return for acknowledgement of his sovereignty over the lands originally ceded by Henry III. The negotiation was complex and parts left unresolved; nonetheless, the treaty does seem to have been about feudal power and its extent, and not about nationhood. It may be hard for us to grasp but kingship does not appear to have been synonymous with nationhood for either Edward III or Jean II.

In this respect, Richard's efforts to finish the unresolved business seem to rest on the same assumptions. The same old problem of Aquitaine remained, and he tried to solve it in the same terms in which it had arisen several centuries earlier.[4] In 1390, in what must have seemed like a brilliant escape from the dilemma, he devolved his own title of duke of Aquitaine onto John of Gaunt. The idea was that Aquitaine would remain under the same conditions of English control, yet there would no longer be any need for an English king to do homage to the French Crown. Ironically, it was not the French king who raised violent objections to this, but the Gascons. They were very wary of any arrangement that appeared to weaken English rights over the land: an absent English Crown was far preferable to a present 'French' duke in the person of Gaunt.[5]

After Richard II was deposed in 1399, Henry IV's son Henry V showed a quite different ambition from his predecessors. Like Edward III he proclaimed himself king of France, but this time his sense of what was involved included not only making good ancient English rights, but also seizing land, and conquering it through settlement as well as force of arms. Once again, the glamour and enduring mythology of Henry V's actions are misleading, particularly as a context for the climate of Chaucer's lifetime. It is tempting to link, retrospectively, the aims of Henry V and those of Edward III. Yet the late fourteenth century was not a period of increasing, or even incipient, nationalism. It seems much closer to the truth to see the medieval history of English and French relations to be part of a fluctuating and broken sequence of events rather than points on a neatly defined upward curve towards modern views of nation. For Chaucer and his contemporaries, the French were still feudal cousins, bound by ancient family ties to the English, but also engaged in alliances and enmities with other relations: the Burgundians, the Flemish, Spanish, Castilians, Germans, Bohemians, Luxembourgeois, and Italians, to name but a few.

Cultural identity: people

Chaucer worked for three kings: Edward III, Richard II, and, just before he died, Henry IV. His part in the war is not usually made much of by modern biographers, largely because war is not a prominent or at least direct topic in his poetry. However, enough survives from the documentary records of his life to gain a sense of how closely he was involved in some of the political events and issues described above. In service to Edward III's second surviving son, Lionel, duke of Clarence, after 1359 he was directly involved in the post-Poitiers efforts by Edward III to force the French to carry out his demands. The Black Prince led a campaign in 1359–60 from Calais to Reims: Lionel's division, which included Chaucer, was part of it. Chaucer was captured and ransomed. A little later he was actually present at the treaty of Brétigny itself, which was formally ratified in Calais by the Black Prince, Lionel, and Henry, duke of Lancaster.

While it is hard to flesh out these bare facts with any knowledge of what Chaucer felt and thought, we nonetheless know that he had direct experience of one of the most significant periods of tough negotiation between the English and the French about their special relationship. Nothing is known of him between 1360 and 1366: it has recently been suggested that he was working for the Black Prince, quite possibly in Aquitaine.[6] His numerous and extensive journeys on the Continent would have made Chaucer familiar not just with the topography of 'English' access to and within many areas of northern and southern France but with the great variety of 'Frenchness' in these areas. He saw and heard at first hand not just the French language (Francien) of Paris, but Artois, Norman, and Picard, as well as Gascon; he also worked with Italian and Dutch speakers—such as Genoese and Flemish merchants and diplomats. Then, as now, London was an international community in which many languages would have been spoken: Chaucer, moreover, also encountered other peoples in their own communities abroad. He clearly had a sense of the diversity of their experience, and this is unlikely to have given him an impression of 'France' (or for that matter 'Italy') as a single or even cohesive country.

His marriage to Philippa de Roet, the daughter of a knight from Hainault, can only have contributed to his view of Continental diversity. Edward III's queen, Philippa, was herself the daughter of William I, count of Hainault, a region bordering northern France. She brought a considerable retinue of Hainaulters with her, and Philippa Chaucer was initially a lady in her household. The fourteenth-century English court is often now described as French-speaking, and while this must be broadly true, it tends to gloss over the perceived differences between the kingdom of France and the duchy of Hainault. Jean Froissart, also a Hainaulter, describes Count William as remarking to Edward III that 'Hainault is a small country compared to the kingdom of France.'[7] The English used their family connections with Hainault carefully and extensively right from the beginning of the war with France. Both this region and the nearby areas of Flanders and the duchy of Brabant were fundamental to English interests over several centuries.

The cultural complexity of Philippa's situation is further illuminated by turning for comparison to Froissart and also John of Gaunt. To take Gaunt first: for anyone interested in Chaucer he combines two attributes, an astonishing degree of power and prestige and the tantalizing role of being the closest we have to a patron for Chaucer. A third, and perhaps even more tantalizing, role was his long-standing sexual relationship with Chaucer's sister-in-law Katherine de Roet.[8] In due course, when Gaunt married Katherine in 1396 to legitimize their four children, Gaunt became for a short while Chaucer's brother-in-law. These disconcertingly close familial ties with Chaucer belie the huge disparity between their social backgrounds: one a wine merchant's son, the other a royal prince and, as a result of his first marriage to Blanche of Lancaster, the wealthiest noble in the country. Gaunt was just three years older than Chaucer; both Chaucer and his wife, Philippa, received annual payments from him from the early 1370s.

The immediate question here about Gaunt is not so much whether he was a direct patron (for which the evidence is slight) as the kind of cultural model he might have been for Chaucer. In other words, what kind of influence did his style of life, social and political assumptions, and international connections have on Chaucer's wider perceptions? Only one feature can be briefly singled out. This is the emphasis Gaunt placed on furthering his claims by marriage (his second, to Constanza of Castile) to the Spanish Crown. Gaunt assumed the title of king of Castile and León in 1372 and for the next sixteen years, supported intermittently by military expeditions to Spain, he maintained two roles simultaneously, that of English prince and (more in title than in practice) Spanish king. In between, he led many campaigns in France on behalf of his father and then his nephew Richard II. He also played a pivotal (and often deeply unpopular) part in governing English affairs. Gaunt was unusual in the extent to which he sought out international commitments. He seems to have had a remarkably strong desire to assert power in his own right on the Continent, yet, through his Castilian claims, he kept this separate from English interests as understood by his father. Once more, none of this adds up to anything like a modern idea of promoting nationalism. On the contrary, Gaunt's life looks like an innovatory effort to establish himself as a figure of more than merely domestic, or 'English', status. He had an exceptionally broad and influential career as an international figure somewhere between diplomat, general, prince, and king. This breadth of attitude and ambition did not always find support in London and the shires (his great Savoy Palace was burned down in the 1381 revolt), but it must have stood powerfully for a certain internationalism.

The same can be said of Froissart, although his place in society was rather different from Gaunt's. His writing career coincided almost exactly with Chaucer's and thus gives us a way of perceiving Chaucer within a European frame of comparison that includes literati as well as soldiers and magnates. There are many aspects to the comparison. The connections are striking: like Chaucer's wife, Froissart was from Hainault, and came to the English court in 1362 as a result of Queen Philippa of Hainault's marriage to Edward III. He stayed in her household for six to seven years, and also spent the winter of 1366–7 at the Black Prince's court in Aquitaine. Yet despite being in parallel royal households during this time, Chaucer and Froissart did not seem to have comparable roles. This may be deduced more from their subsequent careers than from any surviving documentation (of which there is very little). For after leaving England on the queen's death, Froissart spent a fairly peripatetic life moving from one noble household to another: Wenceslas de Brabant, Guy de Blois, and Gaston de Foix.

Froissart, in short, behaved much more like a modern writer in search of a living than Chaucer ever did: Chaucer was a full-time professional courtier and bureaucrat who also happened to write poetry. Froissart saw the writer's identity as expressed by his social relationships with magnates and their courtiers from all over Europe. Chaucer did not define himself overtly as a writer in this way; his professional life, although he did travel widely, as we have seen, was based firmly in London. Perhaps because of his Hainault (as opposed to English or French) background, Froissart was able to find a style of writing, especially in his *Chroniques*, that was able to modulate with ease between the different interests of the European aristocracy. The *Chroniques* create a world and tone that, while they do not omit differences and antagonisms, masterfully coordinate them in the interest of creating a vast, all-embracing narrative of and for high society.

In certain ways, Froissart's achievements as a writer point up the contrasting features of Chaucer's. Chaucer did not have so broad a vision of the European household and its collective social behaviour. Yet, in other respects, as a literate Londoner, Chaucer had greater personal freedom as a writer. More thoroughly engaged in the routine business of urban, merchant life than Froissart, he was able to write more privately. Ironically, though he did not share Froissart's sophisticated, public, Continental perception of the writer, he was able to explore the nature and extent of poetic authority without seemingly feeling the need to work so directly to feed the desires and fantasies of the super-rich.

Cultural identity: language

Although so far I have been stressing the open, cosmopolitan character of fourteenth-century London, there were other sides too. It is certainly possible to find examples of vitriolic writing about the French and about the English, and to find evidence of active racism, such as the attacks on the Flemings in the 1381 revolt. Chaucer alludes to this in a vivid but cryptic metaphor describing a crowd chasing a fox:

> So hydous was the noyse—a, benedicitee!—
> Certes, he Jakke Strawe and his meynee
> Ne made nevere shoutes half so shrille
> Whan that they wolden any Flemyng kille.
>
> ('NPT' 3393–6)

This may escape sounding anti-Flemish, but only just. In the following anonymous instance of direct anti-Flemish feeling, the author puns on the word 'flemmed' meaning banished:

> ffor flemmynges com of flemmed men, ye shal wel vndirstand,
> ffor fflemed men & banshid men enhabit first youre land.[9]

This tradition of invective was particularly marked in the mid-fifteenth century. In fact, it stretches back much earlier with examples from the Conquest onwards in French and Latin, and a few in English. The Welsh, Irish, and Scots were not exempt: the author of *The Libelle of Englyshe Polycye* remarks sternly:

> Beware of Walys, Criste Ihesu mutt us kepe,
> That it make not oure childes childe to wepe,
> Ne us also.[10]

Certain tropes keep surfacing in the opposite direction: the English were caricatured as perpetually drunk, indiscriminate lovers of ale, and, more bizarrely, afflicted with tails. According to Boccaccio, Englishmen were 'the laziest, most fearful and worthless of men'.[11] One of their most risible characteristics (and the joke has not lost its currency) was their inability to speak French properly.

It is commonly assumed that language is an important marker of difference between peoples. The situation gains in complexity, however, when we remember that England was a multilingual country throughout the Middle Ages. The differences perceived in different language use could have related to class, gender, social status, and education before they had any necessary connection with birth, region, or country. In London the linguistic mix was especially great, including as it did not only 'native' Londoners, like Chaucer, who were familiar with English, French (in several varieties), and Latin, but also many people who spoke Continental languages. New research on London language use has started to indicate more broadly that languages did not function in discrete cultural groups. The language of law was written, not in English, but, with one or two exceptions, exclusively in Latin and French, yet even here there was some cross-fertilization with the English vernacular. The language of business, on the other hand, survives in intriguingly multilingual forms, where Latin grammar forms a kind of framework for a mixture of Latin, French, and English words and phrases.[12]

Against sudden expressions of chauvinism we therefore need to see London as an environment where constant cultural abrasions and accommodations were made on a daily basis. Chaucer's poetic language is thoroughly permeated with French, as well as Latin: some of these French words and expressions are new imports from the Continent, but many are older words that had been in developing use in England for several generations. Others again are no doubt examples of contemporary London meanings of either old or new French: in this Chaucer is reflecting the embedded linguistic culture of his time. One or two Flemish words and phrases can be found, such as the word 'quaad' meaning bad or unlucky. In the introductory banter to the 'Cook's Tale', one of only two *Canterbury Tales* that are set in the city, the 'Cook of Londoun', as he is styled, is satirized by the Host for his reheated pies, 'specials' of leftovers and fly-infested parsley. Roger replies ruefully that these gibes have some point. But he turns the tables with a Flemish proverb:

> But 'sooth pley, quaad pley,' as the Flemyng seith. (4357)

'A true jest is a bad jest', and Roger goes on to say he hopes the Host will not be angry if he 'quits' him with a story about an innkeeper. It is difficult to tease out the resonance of this remark: for a Flemish saying to have become part of a Londoner's ironic conversation gives a strong impression of how much the Flemish were an accepted daily presence in urban life. At the same time the little phrase 'as the Flemyng seith' quietly marks the edge of that acceptance: it is a characterizable and not just an anonymous saying. By contrast, another use of 'quaad' is precisely anonymous and unremarkable. The Host is commenting indignantly on the cheating monk in the 'Shipman's Tale':

> God yeve the monk a thousand last quade yeer! (438)

In this context the Flemish word is subsumed into the Host's colloquial idiolect: it has become English.

Cultural identity: writing

Trying to decide what Chaucer's perceptions of other cultures and other peoples might have been is not easy. It would not be easy even if he were less indirect as a writer, since at this distance we are liable to misunderstand or are simply ignorant of contexts and circumstances that could be crucially explanatory. The two examples of Flemish just discussed show subtle differences between two kinds of cultural assimilation: the use of the proverb crackles with implicit comment about the distinctiveness of Flemish ways of thinking, whereas the silent appropriation of the same word by the Host shows an unthinking affinity. Their language has become his. I want to explore further these processes of cultural adoption and resistance in Chaucer's writings by turning back to the word 'nacioun'. As I observed at the start of this chapter, the primary meanings of 'nacioun' in the medieval period involve birth and family. For example, in the 'Wife of Bath's Tale', when the young knight realizes that he has no option but to go to bed with his ugly old hag of a wife, he exclaims bitterly:

> Allas, that any of my nacioun
> Sholde evere so foule disparaged be! (1068–9)

However, it is interesting to note that the other seven instances in Chaucer diverge from this. They all refer to a foreign country, usually somewhere pagan. There is an instance in the description of the Knight in the 'General Prologue' where the narrator remarks that

> Ful ofte tyme he hadde the bord bigonne
> Aboven alle nacions in Pruce. (52–4)

The reference is to the crusades, where many peoples from Western Christendom would combine to fight against the perceived threat of non-Christian peoples. Chaucer's Knight often took the highest seat among these crusaders. Other examples come from the 'Man of Law's Tale', where Custance dreads having to go to the 'Barbre nacioun' (pagan world) to marry the Sultan (281), and the *House of Fame*, where there is a reference to Troy as 'the Troian nacion' (207). The implication here is that Chaucer uses the word 'nacioun', not in the modern meaning, but as a way of registering foreignness.

The final three examples all come from his translation of Boethius' *Consolation of Philosophy*. This brilliant and moving sixth-century semi-Christian, semi-pagan work was deeply influential in the Middle Ages. Chaucer translated it from Latin into English, first in a prose version, and then (partially) into verse in his great love poem, *Troilus and Criseyde*. Boethius had a profound effect on Chaucer, and this influence can briefly be traced through both the prose translation and a passage from *Troilus*. Boethius wrote the *Consolation* while in prison, condemned unjustly to die under torture having previously been in high political esteem. In this work Lady Philosophy teaches the wretched prisoner not to trust in the changeable favours of this world, but through reason and self-control to look beyond worldly ambition and wealth to the true unchanging goodness of providence. The references to 'nacioun' occur in book 2. Here Lady Philosophy is trying to provide a rational corrective to the human desire for fame: earthly renown, she says, is after all very limited. There is so 'manye a nacioun, diverse of tonge and of maneris and ek of resoun of hir lyvynge' that the reputation of exceptional men, or even of famous cities, may not reach them:

to the whiche nacyons, what for difficulte of weyes, and what for diversite of langages, and what for defaute of unusage [of] entrecomunynge of marchandise, nat oonly the names of synguler men ne may nat strecchen, but eek the fame of citees ne may nat strecchen.

(2, pr. 7. 50–9)

I have deliberately quoted this rather awkwardly written passage (which is only a small part of a much longer section) because it seems to me to raise some important issues in its very awkwardness. Even without looking at the Latin it is possible to guess that it is a translation. The long, sometimes clumsy, Latinate words and phrases clog the syntax (note the modern editor's despairing use of square brackets), and one suspects that even a medieval reader would struggle slightly to make sense of it. What makes this piece of writing interesting in the present context is that it combines two things. It is a discussion of the foreignness of the strange customs of people who live far away, which is itself being conducted through the effort of translation from another tongue. The examples of 'translationese' ('defaute of unusage [of] entrecomunynge of marchandise') make us simultaneously aware that this is not plain English even though it is no longer Latin. The tension between the attempt to find a 'natural' language for these thoughts and the sense that they are too foreign to convey naturally haunts the passage. Interestingly it so happens that every single citation of the word 'forein' in Chaucer comes from his translation of the *Consolation*. It is as if Boethius gives Chaucer a direct apprehension of the foreign, through the act of translating him.

Perhaps the subtlest meditation on cultural difference in Chaucer's poetry occurs in book 2 of *Troilus*. It comes right at the start in the proem, or formal introduction to the book. The first book has shown Troilus in the depths of unrequited, indeed undeclared, love. Now in the second book the narrator promises us that there will be an upward swing, and love will take centre stage. Yet he is full of precautionary anticipation. As he has no experience of love himself, he is bound to speak of it 'unfelyngly'. All he can do is follow his author. The proem, however, does not stop there, but takes an unexpected turn. If the reader does find the account of love that is to come strange, then this is because it all happened long ago. We need to recognize the strangeness of the past as like any other experience of foreignness, a sign not just that others are strange to us, but that we may be strange to them:

> Ye knowe ek that in forme of speche is chaunge
> Withinne a thousand yeer, and wordes tho
> That hadden pris, now wonder nyce and straunge
> Us thinketh hem, and yet thei spake hem so,
> And spedde as wel in love as men now do;
> Ek for to wynnen love in sondry ages,
> In sondry londes, sondry ben usages . . .
>
> For every wight which that to Rome went
> Halt nat o path, or alwey o manere;
> Ek in som lond were al the game shent,
> If that they ferde in love as men don here,
> As thus, in opyn doyng or in chere,
> In visityng in forme, or seyde hire sawes;
> Forthi men seyn, 'Ecch contree hath his lawes.' (2. 22–8, 36–42)

On the surface Chaucer appears to be arguing for a tolerant and relative perspective on life: we all take different paths, but we may all yet end up at the same destination. Under the surface of this well-known proverbial cliché, however, lies the memory of book 2 of the *Consolation* (the five-book structure of *Troilus* closely parallels the five-book structure of the *Consolation*). There, Lady Philosophy's bleaker point was that the diversity of language and custom among the many peoples of the world causes misunderstanding and ignorance. We struggle, through 'defaute of unusage', to know of one another; our understanding of fame is solipsistic. By the end of *Troilus*, tolerance no longer seems to be the issue: the poem's emotional power has forced us to choose passionately between impossibly difficult alternatives. Do we judge Criseyde? How can we not judge Criseyde? Should we walk away from human love and its inadequacies? How can we?

Troilus and Criseyde, a pagan love story, becomes a means for Chaucer of investigating the fine, and often veiled, boundaries that divide people. Compared to his Continental contemporaries, he does not offer much direct observation on the cultural differences and alliances of his time. But he does, through language, through concentrated attention to the slippages of meaning between people, provide a profound meditation on the detailed operations of nationhood. Since the mid-twentieth century the prevailing tradition among readers of Chaucer has been liberal and humanist. From this perspective Chaucer has been seen as tolerant and benign. More recently, with growing attention to the place of religion in medieval society, including attitudes to Judaism and Islam, and to sexuality, harder questions have been asked about prejudice in his writing and that of his contemporaries (for more on these topics, see Chapters 25 and 26). Likewise, from the perspective of nationhood, Chaucer's writings can be seen as engaged not merely with issues of tolerance. They raise awkward issues about how people judge one another, often through the tactic of turning the readers' assumptions against them (most famously in the sly opinions of the 'General Prologue'). They also (like most writings of any period) contain questionable judgements, carelessly clever humour (as in the 'Nun's Priest's Tale'), and racial and sexual prejudice.

Chaucer's Englishness

We have become very used to applying the word 'English' to literature of the medieval period. One purpose of this chapter has been to call into question the untroubled character of this convention. In particular, I argue that to call Chaucer an English poet is to risk, at best, misunderstanding. 'English' is a retrospective term, just like 'nation'. When we use the word, we mean something different in each case when we are discussing politics, or culture, or language. Moreover, these separate meanings, and the relation between them, change again between the medieval period and our own. It is not until the mid-fifteenth century, at the earliest, that 'English' approaches anything like its modern meaning (although what it means now is changing so rapidly that it can hardly be regarded as a stable term even in a modern context). A strong nationalistic streak in modern criticism, perhaps especially visible in Victorian readers, has insisted on Chaucer's primacy as an English poet, as the father of English poetry. In fact, the process of borrowing from French and Latin and other romance languages had been characteristic of English ever since the Norman Conquest. Chaucer's use of English was not in itself new.

The argument of this chapter is that 'English' in the Middle Ages is a capacious category. From the perspective of the fourteenth century its relationship with other languages is intimate and extensive; Londoners, in particular, needed a highly flexible, malleable language for business (of all kinds) that could accommodate several linguistic models at once. Chaucer was deeply implicated in this process, through his domestic, marital, familial world, his professional life, and his wide-ranging social and diplomatic ties. But to describe Chaucer's English as capacious is not to describe a homogeneous linguistic or imaginative world. It is capable of registering sharp differences as well as careful appropriations, of articulating the experience of foreignness as well as of homeliness. Compared to earlier readers, we are perhaps more receptive to the possibility that Chaucer's Englishness does not have as settled a character as was previously claimed. This may enable us, in the next generation of worldwide readers of English, to debate Chaucer's role in creating an idea of 'Englishness' with greater openness, as 'English' becomes both more questioned and questionable, and yet, linguistically, ever more globally pervasive.

FURTHER READING

Allmand, Christopher, *The Hundred Years War: England and France at War c.1300–c.1450* (Cambridge: Cambridge University Press, 1988). A classic and concise account of the Hundred Years War.

Butterfield, Ardis, 'French Culture and the Ricardian Court', in Alistair Minnis, Charlotte C. Morse, and Thorlac Turville-Petre (eds.), *Essays on Ricardian Literature in Honour of J. A. Burrow* (Oxford: Clarendon Press, 1997), 82–121. Gives an account of the role of French culture in the Ricardian period, stressing linguistic and poetic interchange.

Calin, William, *The French Tradition and the Literature of Medieval England* (Toronto: University of Toronto Press, 1994). A very full synthesis of Anglo-Norman and Middle French literature and its relations with English writing throughout the medieval period, including useful sectionalized bibliographies of texts and criticism.

Crane, Susan, 'Anglo-Norman Cultures in England, 1066–1460', in David Wallace (ed.), *The Cambridge History of Medieval English Literature* (Cambridge: Cambridge University Press, 1999), 35–60. Provides an overview of the place of Anglo-Norman in the literary production of post-Conquest England.

Curry, Anne, *The Hundred Years War*, rev. edn. (Basingstoke: Palgrave, 2003). Presents a lucid narrative with interesting discussion of the historiography of the war.

Froissart, Jean, *Chronicles*, ed. and trans. John Joliffe (Harmondsworth: Penguin, 1967). A modern translation of selected extracts from Froissart's celebrated history of the war.

Goodman, Anthony, *John of Gaunt: The Exercise of Princely Power in Fourteenth-Century Europe* (London: Longman, 1992). A readable biography of Gaunt, including a wide-ranging account of his international connections.

Pearsall, Derek, *The Life of Geoffrey Chaucer: A Critical Biography* (Oxford: Blackwell, 1992). The most concise, lively, and sharply contoured recent biography of Chaucer.

Rothwell, W., 'The Trilingual England of Geoffrey Chaucer', *Studies in the Age of Chaucer*, 16 (1994), 45–67. An important essay on the multilingual character of Chaucer's England.

Saul, Nigel, *Richard II* (New Haven: Yale University Press, 1997). An elegant study of the king, which is also a reliable and interesting guide to the nature of political society in the later fourteenth century.

Watson, Nicholas, 'The Politics of Writing Middle English', in Jocelyn Wogan-Browne, Nicholas Watson, Andrew Taylor, and Ruth Evans (eds.), *The Idea of the Vernacular: An Anthology of Middle English Literary Theory, 1280–1520* (Exeter: University of Exeter Press, 1999), 331–53. An interesting and influential essay, in a highly useful anthology of writings in English on authorship, audiences, and readers.

NOTES

1. See Christopher Allmand, *The Hundred Years War: England and France at War c.1300–c.1450* (Cambridge: Cambridge University Press, 1988), 11.

2. Aquitaine was renamed the duchy of Guyenne in 1259. English possession of the area waxed and waned, sometimes including much larger surrounding territories, sometimes only the area around Bordeaux.

3. For further discussion, see *The New Cambridge Medieval History, vi: c.1300–c.1415*, ed. Michael Jones (Cambridge: Cambridge University Press, 2000), ch. 13: 'The British Isles', 273–387.

4. For further discussion of the earlier historical context, see Robin Studd, 'England and Gascony 1216–1337', in Nigel Saul (ed.), *England in Europe 1066–1453* (London: Collins & Brown, 1994), 97–107.

5. See Allmand, *Hundred Years War*, 23–6.

6. Derek Pearsall, *The Life of Geoffrey Chaucer: A Critical Biography* (Oxford: Blackwell, 1992), 53.

7. Jean Froissart, *Chronicles*, ed. and trans. John Joliffe (Harmondsworth: Penguin, 1967), 69.

8. See Pearsall, *Life*, 50.

9. R. H. Robbins, (ed.), *Historical Poems of the Fourteenth and Fifteenth Centuries* (New York: Columbia University Press, 1959), 29, lines 59–60.

10. *The Libelle of Englyshe Polycye*, 784–6, quoted in V. J. Scattergood, *Politics and Poetry in the Fifteenth Century* (London: Blandford Press, 1971), 37.

11. Giovanni Boccaccio, *De casibus virorum illustrium*, quoted in Scattergood, *Politics and Poetry*, 43.

12. See L. C. Wright, 'Trade between England and the Low Countries: Evidence from Historical Linguistics', in Caroline Barron and Nigel Saul (eds.), *England and the Low Countries in the Late Middle Ages* (Stroud: Alan Sutton, 1995), 169–79; W. Rothwell, 'The Trilingual England of Geoffrey Chaucer', *Studies in the Age of Chaucer*, 16 (1994), 45–67; and D. A. Trotter (ed.), *Multilingualism in Later Medieval Britain* (Cambridge: Brewer, 2000).

4 | London

C. David Benson

Although Chaucer was born in London, lived many years over one of its gates, and died just outside its walls in Westminster, literary critics have usually regarded him as a detached courtly poet rather than one engaged with the actuality of the city (in contrast to his contemporary William Langland, the author of *Piers Plowman*). There is much justification for this view. Chaucer's early works are dream visions set in fantastic landscapes; the long romances of his middle period, *Troilus and Criseyde* and the 'Knight's Tale', occur in the legendary chivalric past; and even his last, most realistic and most English work, the *Canterbury Tales*, begins outside London and contains very few pilgrims or stories from the city itself. Recently, however, as part of a larger movement to understand Chaucer in his particular historical contexts, some scholars have begun to look more carefully at the political and social elements in his work, including his relationship to his native city. Most of these studies acknowledge that Chaucer rarely describes London directly or for long, but they nevertheless see the city's influence in his work, especially in his experiments with inclusive literary forms and multiple voices. The various ways in which Chaucer is, and is not, a London poet is a rich subject for future work, as the following chapter attempts to suggest.

London in the late fourteenth century

The London of Chaucer's time was far smaller than the modern metropolis. In 1300 it may have had as many as 100,000 residents, but by Chaucer's death a hundred years later that number had shrunk to about 50,000, chiefly due to periodic outbreaks of the plague. Despite disease and a low birth rate, the population of the city was constantly renewed from the provinces. Geoffrey Chaucer's grandfather Robert, for example, moved there from Ipswich. London was by far the most populous and important city in England—only a few other municipalities boasted as many as 10,000 residents. Less than a tenth of the population of the city were citizens with full political and commercial rights, however. Women, young males, aliens, and clergy were excluded from citizenship and only one in three or four of the remaining men was a freeman of the city, a status usually achieved in Chaucer's day after serving an apprenticeship in a guild.

Medieval London also looked different from the modern city (see Figure I.4). It was an enclosed town (like a modern gated community) with stone walls on three sides (its south was protected by the river Thames). Entrance into the city was through fortified gates, which were locked relatively early in the evening and not opened again until the next morning. London also contained a remarkable number of parish churches, over one hundred, the steeples of which dominated the skyline. In Chaucer's time (and for long after) only one bridge, London Bridge, crossed the Thames, though water ferries were commonly used to cross and travel on the river. Southwark just across London Bridge and Westminster upriver were not parts of a single urban whole as they are today, but small, independent jurisdictions much more loosely regulated than the city itself.

Much of London life was lived in the streets. Small shops selling everything from food to gold ornaments lined major thoroughfares, especially the wide central routes of Cheapside and Cornhill, and there were specific market areas for both citizens and those from outside the city to sell their goods. The sounds of such urban traders are heard at the end of the prologue to *Piers Plowman*: 'Cokes and hire knaves cryden, "Hote pies, hote!"' London streets were used for processions of all kinds, including royal coronations, local celebrations of parishes and guilds, and the parading of criminals from prison to the pillory.

London lacked some of the major institutions of other medieval European cities. The king's properties were outside the city, though sometimes only just outside, such as the Tower to the east and Westminster Palace, which was becoming the permanent location of the great offices of state, to the west. Universities were farther away at Oxford and Cambridge (though major scholars such as William Ockham worked and lived in London for substantial periods and the Inns of Court were developing into law schools), and the seats of the two English archbishops were at Canterbury and York. Nevertheless, London's growing importance as the economic, cultural, and (with Westminster) political capital of England meant that bishops, abbots, and aristocrats like Chaucer's patron John of Gaunt increasingly maintained town houses within or near the city. The lay and ecclesiastical clerks in these often enormous households, along with their civic and royal counterparts in the surrounding area, probably made up much of Chaucer's first audience. London was an intellectual, as well as a political and economic, crossroads.

From Roman times London was known primarily as a marketplace and trading centre. In addition to supplying the daily needs of its large population, the city was the primary source in England for luxury goods. The most ambitious London trade was the large-scale importing and exporting of commodities (including wool, wine, and spices) by rich merchants. One such was Chaucer's associate John Philipot, who was rich enough to lend the king money and finance a private navy to eliminate pirates who were preying on local shipping.

In the late fourteenth century the government of London and especially its local courts were run by twenty-four aldermen, usually merchants like Philipot, who also

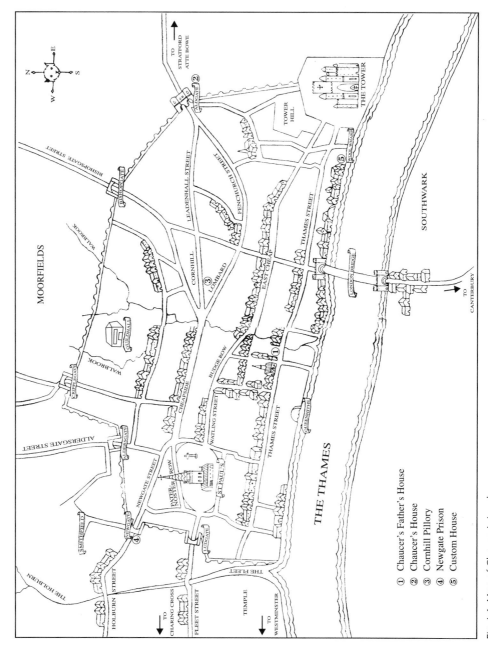

Fig. 1.4 Map of Chaucer's London.

① Chaucer's Father's House
② Chaucer's House
③ Cornhill Pillory
④ Newgate Prison
⑤ Custom House

administered their individual wards. From these aldermen a mayor was elected annually. A larger Common Council of prominent citizens also made decisions, especially about financial matters, and there was a growing municipal bureaucracy. The London authorities attempted (not always successfully) to regulate most aspects of social and commercial life in the city, including being abroad at night after curfew, the clothing to be worn by particular classes, and the price that could be charged for a variety of goods and services. Those convicted of violating the city's regulations were subject to a range of punishments, including fines or even exile. One of the most common civic penalties was exposure to public ridicule (or worse) on the pillory. A major collection of medieval London documents, the *Liber albus* ('White Book'), announces that in addition to punishing personal immorality (such as pimping or gambling), the pillory was the discipline for crimes of dishonesty, especially deceits involving the city's food supply (such as selling rotten meat). Despite London's long tradition of corporate rights, its officials acted in the name of the king (the mayor was often portrayed as a mediator between citizens and sovereign), who had the power to suspend the city's government, as Richard II did in the 1390s.

If control of late medieval London was largely in the hands of a small merchant oligarchy, there were other, more horizontal institutions in the city, such as citizen juries and guilds. Guilds took at least three related forms in medieval London. In addition to the powerful merchant guilds that supplied most of the city's aldermen, there were also more modest, and more numerous, craft guilds involved with manufacture and retail sales, as well as the fraternities associated with individual parish churches. The fraternities were primarily social and religious associations, providing their members (which might include women and clerics) with feasts and fellowship during their lives and prayers and memorial masses after their deaths. Guilds of all kinds helped to regulate the moral and social behaviour of their members and provided opportunities for collective decision-making. The mixture of both communal and hierarchical tendencies in medieval London is demonstrated by guild initiation ceremonies, which stressed equality (with other members) but also subordination (to the authority of guild officers).

Historians have often stressed the discord of London during Chaucer's lifetime. Guilds and groups of guilds battled, sometimes violently, over how the city should be governed and by whom, especially during the fierce mayoralty contests between Nicholas Brembre and John of Northampton. In the 1381 Peasants' Revolt, rebels from without and within actually took over the city (some aldermen were accused of aiding them), causing much death and destruction and challenging the existing social order. But the turbulence of late medieval London can be exaggerated: cities are always chaotic and contentious, as fractious, even dangerous, as they are exciting. More than any other city in England, London's size and centrality encouraged constant exchanges of all kinds. It was a marketplace of voices and ideas as well as of goods.

Chaucer's London

Chaucer's connections to London went deep. He was born there, lived over the city gate of Aldgate for more than a decade while controller of the wool customs in the city, and died and was buried in nearby Westminster. Despite royal service abroad and a period in Kent, he never seems to have gone far from London for long. Some of Chaucer's closest ties were with its civic elite. His father was a prominent city vintner, and at the customs he worked under three of London's richest and most powerful merchants, each of whom served as mayor: Philipot (who also witnessed legal documents for Chaucer), Brembre, and William Walworth. *Troilus and Criseyde* is dedicated to Ralph Strode (and John Gower, another poet with London associations), once an Oxford philosopher and later probably the important London lawyer who was the city's prosecutor as its Common Sergeant.

Recent scholarly interest in Chaucer's social and political interests has had to confront the extreme circumspection with which he treats London and other contemporary affairs in his writing. Chaucer probably knew more about how the city was actually run than any poet who has ever lived, but he reveals almost nothing about its governmental and economic elite and little about its daily life. Chaucer shows us London only fleetingly and from a distance. Yet even though he provides nothing like a full description of contemporary London, aspects of the city seem to have shaped his poetry in less obvious and more literary ways. The dynamic energy and variety of the city's voices, for example, seems paralleled in the poet's open structures and contrasting kinds of narrative. Furthermore, London gave Chaucer a unique access to international culture. Like the prominent merchants among whom he lived, Chaucer was a foreign trader, who imported into England luxury goods like Dante, Petrarch, and Boccaccio. London was essential to Chaucer's urbanity.

The 'Nun's Priest's Tale' suggests something of Chaucer's complex relationship to his native city. The tale contains the most direct reference in the poet's work to the 1381 capture of London by rebels—a comparison of the noise of those trying to rescue Chauntecleer from the fox to that made by Jack Straw, one of the leaders of the rebellion, and his men when 'that they wolden any Flemyng kille' (3396). The unprecedented takeover of London, which was hysterically denounced by Gower and contemporary chroniclers as a danger to civilization itself, is presented in the tale as just a little ethnic bloodletting. Chaucer must have known a great deal about the events of 1381 (some of the rebels entered the city through the gate over which he was living) and probably shared the fears of his class about the danger to established power, yet here he refuses to take it seriously. Chaucer's energies in the 'Nun's Priest's Tale' are not political but artistic; an insurrection becomes one item in the midst of an array of allusions that results in perhaps the most dazzling, demanding, and comic ending in medieval narrative.

Chaucer's early poetry

In Chaucer's early works, whose subjects are love and poetry and which are set in visionary landscapes, London is either conspicuously absent or briefly and indirectly glimpsed. One of his first dream poems, the *Book of the Duchess*, demonstrates Chaucer's tendency to sidestep London. The narrator finds a man in black complaining about a lost love. Later puns identify the man as John of Gaunt, who, as earl of Richmond and duke of Lancaster, was one of the richest and most powerful magnates in fourteenth-century England and a major player in national and London affairs. His actions in the capital earned him the hatred of its citizens and during the revolt of 1381 his great palace by the Thames, the Savoy, was burned to the ground. Chaucer had more reason than most to know about Gaunt's political manoeuvres because the duke was an occasional benefactor (perhaps securing the poet his post at the London customs) and later an in-law. But in the *Book of the Duchess* the man in black is a pastoral not an urban figure (the narrator comes across him during a hunt), an aristocratic lover rather than a politician or patron. The poem is absolutely silent about any aspect of Gaunt's London life.

The *House of Fame* is more promising as a London poem. In book 2 the eagle who snatches up the dreamer calls him 'Geffrey' (729) and seems to refer to Chaucer's customs job when he says, 'For when thy labour doon al ys, | And hast mad alle thy rekenynges . . .' (652–3). Students of medieval London can only wish they were told more, including the exact nature of Chaucer's work, his relations with his merchant supervisors, and what he learned about the governance of the city. No such details are forthcoming, however, for the eagle flies Chaucer away from London and even from the earth itself. The reason he gives is that the poet's life in the city has provided him with no literary material. Because Geoffrey spends his days at the customs office and his nights at home poring, 'domb as any stoon', over 'another book', he has been able to receive no 'tydynges' about love or anything else, no current news about foreign events or even his next-door 'neyghebores' (644–60). The Geoffrey Chaucer portrayed here is very different from one of his poetic disciples, Thomas Hoccleve, who learned much about London life as a Chancery clerk, which he then used in his poetry.

Or does the *House of Fame* leave behind the historical London only to discover a phantasmagoric version of the city? The wicker house at the end of the poem looks nothing like medieval London: it is made of twigs and is 60 miles long. But then dreams transform, exaggerate, and intensify. If *Piers Plowman* concludes its prologue with commercial street cries, the whirling house of twigs is full of 'tydynges' about every conceivable subject, including (among a few score others) war, peace, marriage, and good and bad government (1956–76). The same urgent tidings that the poet had been deaf to in the real London are heard in this dream space. The crowded cacophony of the twig house, in which honest statements mix with lies and the authority figure mentioned in the poem's final line never arrives, would have been a nightmare to the officials of medieval London, but it is a liberating vision for a bookish, reclusive poet. The discursive plenty of London, with its multitude of contentious voices, seems dramatized in this concluding scene.

The *Parliament of Fowls* opens more quietly than the *House of Fame* ends, and its action moves in the opposite direction. Whereas the latter poem abandons London (and the earth) for the heavens, the *Parliament* begins with Scipio's observing our planet from 'a sterry place' (43) before returning to an idealized world of nature. The second half of the poem includes a version of a major London area institution, the English parliament, whose usual location by Chaucer's day was Westminster. Because it is a dream vision, this parliament takes place in a flowery glade, and its members are birds who debate not war and taxes but love: which male eagle deserves the female eagle on Nature's hand. The clamour near the end of the *House of Fame*, which I suggested may echo the diverse voices of London, is replaced in the *Parliament* by individual speeches by spokesmen for the various classes of birds, which express a range of different views. The falcon advises the lady to choose according to the suitors' chivalry and gentility, for instance, whereas the representative of the waterfowls suggests a more pragmatic approach: any rejected suitor should simply 'love another' (567). Although this position is scorned by a hawk, 'Lo, here a parfit resoun of a goos!' (568), it obviously has merit as well as parallels in real life.

Although the bird parliament suggests its human model at Westminster, it is finally more inclusive. The House of Commons excluded both the top and bottom of English society (its members were the prosperous middle classes), but Chaucer's parliament embraces all kinds of fowl. And none is shown to be wholly right or wrong. Although the eagles are noble in their devotion, other birds note that they miss the point and pleasure of the occasion (to secure a mate). In contrast, the turtle-dove, who represents the lowly seed-eaters, utters one of the most delicate and honourable speeches of the day against infidelity in love (582–8). Although the sylvan assembly of birds has even less of the appearance of medieval London than the wicker building in the *House of Fame*, Chaucer uses it to create a kind of ideal urban forum in which vertical and horizontal forces coexist: all classes have their say and are given respect, at least by the poet. Such an open, welcoming discursive space did not exist in Westminster Hall or on the streets of medieval London, but Chaucer was able to dream it.

Troilus and Criseyde and the 'Knight's Tale'

In his two great romances, *Troilus and Criseyde* and the 'Knight's Tale' (although the latter is now one of the *Canterbury Tales*, it was apparently first written to stand alone), Chaucer leaves the world of dreams for classical history. We no longer have to search for urban echoes in nature or in the heavens, for these works unfold in three great cities: Troy, Thebes, and Athens. London itself is not explicitly mentioned in either romance, yet its influence is noticeable, especially in the Troy of *Troilus*, which many scholars argue resembles Chaucer's London. As stated at the beginning of *Sir Gawain and the Green Knight*, it was a widespread medieval belief that London, like Rome, was founded by descendants of Aeneas fleeing from the Trojan War and that its original name was Troynovant (New Troy). Some critics have even claimed that Chaucer's principal motive for writing *Troilus* was a desire to warn contemporary England (and especially its capital) against the pride and lust that brought low its ancient predecessor.

Certainly Chaucer's description of Troy consistently suggests the contemporary city. The palaces of Criseyde, Troilus, Pandarus, and Deiphebus contain spaces and activities that resemble those we know existed in the mansions of lords, prelates, and rich merchants in fourteenth-century London. Like many another courtly lady, Criseyde, when we first see her at home surrounded by her ladies, is being read to from a book that is decorated like a medieval manuscript. Her subsequent walk to discuss love with her niece Antigone occurs in the kind of urban garden with railed pathways and turf benches well known to Chaucer and his readers (2. 819–22; compare the poet's description of his own 'herber' in the Prologue to the *Legend of Good Women*, (G) 97–8). A specifically London institution at Troy is the parliament in book 4, a scene that Chaucer greatly expanded from his source.

If Chaucer's Troy is in many ways his most detailed depiction of medieval London, it is nevertheless a limited and far from positive portrait. The only society we see is that of the royal family and its friends. Ordinary citizens are only rarely glimpsed, as when they cheer Troilus' return from battle (2. 643–4), and the everyday life of the city, its crafts and markets, for example, go unmentioned. But as we have seen with Chaucer's early poetry, London may appear in disguise. Thus the expanded parliamentary debate over the exchange of Criseyde for the captured Trojan warrior Antenor suggests not only political Westminster but also mercantile London. The magnanimous Hector argues against giving up Criseyde, insisting that 'We usen here no wommen for to selle' (4. 182), but he is overcome by those who want just such a bargain. Like hard-headed business men, they know a great deal for the city when they see it, and they regard not trading a useless woman for a great fighter as simply one of Hector's courtly 'fantasies' (4. 187–93). In contrast to the respect granted to non-aristocratic views in the *Parliament of Fowls*, the voices that dominate the parliament in *Troilus* are as foolish as they are ignoble. Far from saving the city, Antenor, as medieval readers knew, will bring about its destruction through treason. That Chaucer presents the Trojan parliament more negatively than the bird parliament may relate to the difference between writing a knightly romance and a dream vision, or be because he had now served in the English assembly (as a representative for Kent in 1386, though *Troilus* may have been written before this).

The commercial ethos that so dominated medieval London may also have influenced Chaucer's characterization of Pandarus. Despite his high birth and royal connections, Pandarus' ceaseless activity, skill at arranging things, and manipulation of others make him resemble a merchant more than a knight. But he, too, ultimately fails despite his clever gamesmanship, ending up hating Criseyde for her betrayal and scorning Troilus for his loyalty. Perhaps Chaucer's conception of Pandarus reveals, among other things, some of his views about the London mercantile culture; if so, it was not a wholly positive view.

To the extent that Troy is a warning to London, it is a dire one. The love that distracts Troilus from his royal duties may be a criticism of the affair between Edward III and Alice Perrers, as some have suggested, but the failures we see are more general. For all his knightly nobility, Hector is unable to protect Criseyde, himself, or his city. Troy is marked by betrayal throughout, and among its few happy moments are the friendly royal dinner party at Deiphebus' palace (itself based on a series of deceptions) and the private joys of Troilus and Criseyde in a hidden room at the heart of the city. But instead of being secure in that amorous space, the lovers are encircled and doomed: one will leave the city by exile, the other by death.

Chaucer's other ancient romance, the 'Knight's Tale', offers a less pessimistic view of the urban experience. Arcite's death is indeed cruel and unjust, but the tale ends with moments of reconciliation between the two rivals, between Palamon and Emelye, and between Thebes and Athens. Yet Chaucer's Athens does not resemble medieval London as closely as does his Troy. Its exotic pagannness is repeatedly stressed, and its most prominent architectural feature, the amphitheatre with its temples, has no London parallel. Some readers have thought that one scene (2491–522) may reflect medieval London: the account of the preparations in Athens for the tournament, which perhaps derives from Chaucer's supervision of the lists for jousts at Smithfield when he was Clerk of the King's Works. Here we see a diverse city population, including armourers and 'Yemen on foote, and communes many oon' (2507–10). We also hear the various opinions of people who have crowded the palace about the outcome of the battle, the only time that someone other than members of the royal families of Athens or Thebes speaks in the poem. Nevertheless, these are rare urban scenes in a tale whose principal action takes place outdoors or in prison.

The 'General Prologue' of the *Canterbury Tales*

The *Canterbury Tales* is Chaucer's most English and most London work. Leaving behind both dreams and ancient history, it begins at the contemporary Tabard Inn across London Bridge in Southwark (a real establishment in the Middle Ages whose location can still be visited today). Yet even here London is rarely seen directly or extensively. David Wallace has argued that the city is 'absent' in the *Canterbury Tales*, as shown especially in the 'Cook's Tale', because instead of the coherent Florence found in Boccaccio's writing, Chaucer's London is a 'discourse of fragments, discontinuities, and contradictions' whose ideological and group conflicts are mirrored by disputes in the *Tales* themselves.[1] This argument has been influential, though it perhaps makes

Chaucer's view of London too exceptional, given that cities at all times are fragmentary and in conflict, whatever their claims to unity. But Wallace's position that London is an 'absent city' is provocative, especially if we broaden it beyond the question of the coherence of Chaucer's idea of the city to the ways that London inhabits and influences his work even when not described directly or at length. As I have already suggested with regard to Chaucer's early works, in the *Canterbury Tales* London is a more important theme than the few lines actually devoted to it would seem to justify.

The elusive presence of London is hinted at throughout the portraits in the 'General Prologue'. Although many critics have assumed that several pilgrims are residents of the city, almost all the examples they cite actually dwell outside the walls or may not be from the area at all. The Host of the Tabard, Harry Bailly (the name of a contemporary Southwark innkeeper), is one such who lives near but not in the city itself, and the Prioress and the Pardoner are two other suburbanites, though reference to their domiciles is characteristically indirect. The former's French is famously not Parisian but follows that of 'the scole of Stratford atte Bowe' (125), which most scholars understand to mean that she was from the Benedictine nunnery of St Leonard's near Stratford about 2 miles east of London. The Pardoner is said be 'of Rouncivale' (670), almost certainly a reference to a local cell of the Augustinian hospital at Charing Cross, an area now part of London's West End but then very much in the fields outside the city. The Manciple is also placed outside London's walls, but not its jurisdiction, at 'a temple' (567), one of the Inns of Court (near the modern Strand) at which some have thought Chaucer received legal training.

In addition to these extramural pilgrims, others have a much more uncertain relation to the city. The Sergeant of the Law, the Merchant, and the Guildsmen, who each suggest important London groups, may not be permanent residents at all. Chaucer appears to tease us about the home base of the pilgrim Sergeant. Said to have been often at 'the Parvys' (310), usually taken as a reference to the porch of St Paul's where lawyers met their clients, his work in the assize courts and extensive land purchases suggest rural activity outside the capital. The pilgrim Merchant certainly bears himself with the haughtiness and engages in the international trade of a London oligarch, but he is never specifically identified with the city, and we know that other English towns (such as Orwell in East Anglia, mentioned at line 277) also contained major importers and exporters. Chaucer lived and worked with London lawyers and merchants, including Strode and Philipot, but the portraits in the 'General Prologue' reveal no special knowledge of these occupations, being principally derived from traditional descriptions.

Chaucer's five Guildsmen are from a 'solempne and a greet fraternitee' (364), apparently a parish rather than a craft guild because of their diverse occupations. Although guilds were among the most important London institutions in the late fourteenth century, as noted above, we cannot be sure these pilgrims are citizens of the capital. Although many scholars assume so, they are never identified as such and the statement that each is a 'fair burgeys' worthy to sit on the dais of a guildhall (369–70) suggests, though does not prove, otherwise, for during Chaucer's lifetime no member of any of these trades ever became an alderman in London. In any case, Chaucer again provides not a searching study of guild members from his own experience, but a conventional literary satire of the social pretensions of bourgeois wives.

Only two pilgrims in the 'General Prologue' are definitely Londoners. The first is the ulcerous Cook. His residence is only implied in his portrait, 'Wel koude he knowe a draughte of Londoun ale' (382), but the first line of the Prologue to his own tale calls him the 'Cook of Londoun' ('CP' 4325). His nickname, Hogge of Ware (4336), however, indicates that like so many other medieval London residents, he was an immigrant from the provinces. The only other unmistakable London pilgrim is, of course, Chaucer himself. But we know this only from his biography; nothing about him in the *Canterbury Tales* reveals any connection to the city.

The 'General Prologue' is not a celebration of London. The only definite inhabitant, the Cook, fails to complete his first tale and is too drunk to begin a second (as described in the 'Manciple's Prologue'). Even if we include the suburbanites (the Host, Prioress, Pardoner, and Manciple) and the possibles (Merchant, Sergeant of the Law, and Guildsmen), we are left with an unprepossessing group of residents. The most admirable portrait in the 'General Prologue' is that of the Parson, who is specifically praised for not moving to London for the easy money he could earn as a chantry or guild priest (507–11).

When urban life appears positively in the *Canterbury Tales*, it is in the guise of its literary implications. Thus for all the importance of guilds in late medieval London, the five Guildsmen, who may not even be citizens of the city, are mocked with something like aristocratic disdain. Yet Paul Strohm argues that although none ever utters a word on the pilgrimage, theirs is the ethic of the Canterbury tale-telling: 'fraternity, expressed through vital and egalitarian social interchange', social values that Wallace also sees expressed in the 'associational form' of the *Tales*.[2] A striking example of Chaucer's being radical in art in a way that he may not have been in life is the Miller's interruption of the Host and his insistence that he, not the Monk, tell the second tale ('MP' 3120–7). The poet would undoubtedly have found the drunken, aggressive churl Robin as appalling in reality as associates such as Philpot and Gower found the London rebels of 1381. In the fictional arena of the *Canterbury Tales*, however, the Miller's quick, witty, wholly unexpected tale opens up the stylistic and ideological range of the work and first demonstrates the astonishing potential of its artistry.

Chaucer's London tales: 'Canon's Yeoman's Tale' and 'Cook's Tale'

We have seen that the few times when London appears in Chaucer's writing it is usually glimpsed briefly and from a distance or perhaps takes another shape altogether (the wicker house in the *House of Fame*, Troy in *Troilus*). The poet repeatedly declines to share his own experience of the city, even when he refers to his job at the customs or includes pilgrims from the mercantile world he knew so well. It is in the variety, energy, and openness of Chaucer's literary forms and diverse voices that London may have had its most profound effect. Nevertheless, there are two tales, or rather parts of tales, that are explicitly set in the city: the unfinished 'Cook's Tale' and the second part of the 'Canon's Yeoman's Tale'. No source or close analogue has been identified for either, and in the former Chaucer may for once be describing London from experience.

The second part of the 'Canon's Yeoman's Tale' is just barely a London tale. The Canon and his Yeoman join the pilgrimage a few miles before Canterbury and soon the servant has exposed the abject failure of his master to achieve any success whatsoever in their many alchemical experiments. In the second part, the Yeoman tells of another canon who wins rather than loses money at alchemy; instead of the sincere (if misguided) faith of the teller and his master, this canon is a con artist. With a series of clever substitutions, he produces the illusion of having changed base metals into precious ones and then sells his victims the 'secret'. Although this narrative begins with 'In Londoun was a preest' (1012), nothing is seen of the city itself, for the deceptions take place indoors.

The most significant London element in the second part of the 'Canon's Yeoman's Tale' is the resemblance to the frauds that the city authorities and courts were so keen to root out. As already noted, surviving London records show a special concern with a range of crimes of fraud, from selling rotten food to practising magic. Juries were charged to discover and punish such deceptions, whose perpetrators were publicly censured, often by being displayed on the pillory. The canon in Chaucer's story earns the trust of the priest by quickly returning a loan and then declares: 'Trouthe is a thyng that I wol evere kepe' (1044). The London records are full of similar tricks played on gullible victims that depend on the relative anonymity of the city. Thus, in 1376 two brothers testified that a man had lured them into playing a board game called 'quek' at which they repeatedly lost. The brothers accused the man of rigging the game, and a jury ordered that he be displayed on the pillory along with his false board and that his offence be proclaimed. Another instance seems even more like the false canon's trick because it too involves a clandestine substitution. In 1414 a soldier offered a Southwark pelterer a box with 16 gold nobles and a necklace as a pledge for furs worth 100 shillings. The box actually exchanged, however, contained only sand and stones and so the soldier was sentenced to the pillory.[3] The reason that Chaucer needed no literary source for his narrative of the defrauding of the priest may be that he, like his fellow London citizens, would have known of many comparable cases.

For all its brevity (just over fifty lines), the 'Cook's Tale' tells us the most about London life of any Chaucerian work, though it stops just when things get most interesting. The Prologue to the tale introduces the last teller of the first fragment of the *Canterbury Tales* as the 'Cook of Londoun' (4325). His verbal sparring with the Host in the rest of the Prologue immediately evokes the rivalries between different trades (here innkeepers and food-preparers) that frequently roiled London in the late fourteenth century, even to the point of armed conflict. The Host's taunt about the Cook's having sold many pies that 'hath been twies hoot and twies coold' (4348) also suggests a larger civic problem: the deceitful marketing of spoiled or rotten food that was one of the communal crimes most vigorously pursued by the London authorities.

But it is the abbreviated 'Cook's Tale' itself that shows us the street life of late fourteenth-century London with an immediacy and energy without parallel elsewhere in the *Canterbury Tales*. The tale concerns an apprentice to a 'craft of vitailliers' (4366), who is known as Perkyn Revelour (4371) because he would rather dance, sing, and chase women than learn his trade: 'He loved bet the taverne than the shoppe' (4376). Instead of working, Perkyn watches passing processions, plays dice, and even steals from the shop, and his master eventually decides to dismiss him so as not to taint others. Unrepentant, 'this joly prentys' (4413) moves in with a friend who 'lovede dys, and revel, and disport' (4420) and whose wife makes her living as a prostitute.

In these few lines, which contain little actual narrative, Chaucer succeeds in touching on many aspects of contemporary London society. The centrality of the craft guild in the fabric of the city, for example, is stressed throughout. Apprenticeship was the principal way to become one of the privileged citizens of London: Perkyn fails to achieve this and instead falls back into the netherworld of casual work and crime inhabited by so many of the city's residents. Perkyn's guild, unspecified here, was one of the victualling trades. This is undoubtedly because a cook is telling the tale, but, as in the Prologue, the mention of victuallers evokes the fierce mayoralty contests between Nicholas Brembre and John of Northampton in the late fourteenth century, which have often been interpreted as the latter's reforming attempts to control the monopoly of the food guilds, especially the Fishmongers.

Perkyn's refusal to show obedience to his master, even to the extent of robbing him, is a violation not only of guild regulations but also of the civic law. London, like all medieval society, was a deference culture and to disobey a parent, master, or city official was considered both a crime and a sin. Perkyn's disporting with his 'meynee' (4381), presumably a group of other apprentices, suggests a potentially more serious threat to civic order: the London oligarchy frequently expressed the worry that journeymen or other subordinates might be conspiring together in covens or cabals to take power. Perkyn and his gang seem primarily interested in fun, however, and Chaucer, as with his treatment of Jack Straw in the 'Nun's Priest's Tale', ignores the possibility of political insurrection. The apprentice's failings are limited to the kinds of vices (gambling, drinking, whoring, vagrancy, theft) that the fraternities in particular tried to control among their members and that the municipal law disciplined with the pillory. That the city authorities were especially worried about the corrupting effect of riotous behaviour among its subservient population is suggested by a summary couplet: 'Revel and trouthe, as in a lowe degree, | They been ful wrothe al day, as men may see' (4397–8).

In addition to evoking the occupational and judicial worlds of late fourteenth-century London, the 'Cook's Tale' also shows us some of its public life. Two of the many shops that distinguished the city are mentioned (Perkyn avoids doing much work in one and another is used by his friend's wife as a cover for her prostitution), as well as the wine, women, dicing, male companionship, and song available in the streets. We are also reminded of the frequent communal processions that were such a feature of medieval London. The ceremonial 'ridyng' of mounted men through Cheapside (the commercial centre of London and one of its widest streets) draws Perkyn out of his shop (4377–80) and echoes the riding of the nobles through Athens on their way to Theseus' tournament in the first tale of the fragment ('KT' 2569–75). Perkyn is himself a participant in another kind of London procession, for we are told that he was 'somtyme lad with revel to Newegate' (4402). The reference here is to an event often mentioned in the medieval London records: the parading of a prisoner through the city with accompanying 'revel' (music) to attract public attention and increase the shame of the miscreant. A route frequently mentioned in the records was from the prison at Newgate, where such miscreants were commonly held, through the centre of London, including Cheapside, to a session on the Cornhill pillory and back.

Chaucer's great achievement in including so much of London life in the brief compass of the 'Cook's Tale' prompts two additional observations. One is that despite the clear condemnation here of apprentice misbehaviour from the perspective of guild masters and the city establishment, which most critics stress, the beginning of the tale, as V. A. Kolve has observed, is 'celebratory in tone', presenting an attractive, graceful Perkyn, who resembles the Squire of the Canterbury pilgrimage in his youthful exuberance: for a while at least, he has a wonderful time enjoying the delights of London.[4] Once again, whatever Chaucer's personal views on masters versus servants, his poetry includes multiple perspectives: the contesting voices of urban experience. A second point that should be stressed about the 'Cook's Tale' is that Chaucer's one convincing and original account of London does not describe the higher political and mercantile circles in which he lived, but a much seedier world of shops, apprentices, and petty crime. How Chaucer came by his knowledge of the underside of London is unclear, but his representation of it again shows his reluctance to deal with the higher end of society he knew best. Chaucer is forthcoming (and remarkably balanced) only about this other London, which was close at hand but hardly his own habitat. And although the 'Cook's Tale' suggests much about London life in the late fourteenth century, it comes to a quick and abrupt end. Its provocative last words—'and swyved for hir sustenance' (4422)—tease us about the fate of Perkyn and his friends even as they make us wonder how much else Chaucer might have told us about medieval London.

FURTHER READING

Barron, Caroline M., *London in the Later Middle Ages: Government and People 1200–1500* (Oxford: Oxford University Press, 2004). A masterful and up-to-date historical, social, and cultural survey of medieval London.

Benson, C. David, '*Piers Plowman* as a Poetry Pillory: The Pillory and the Cross', in David Aers (ed.), *Medieval Literature and Historical Inquiry: Essays in Honour of Derek Pearsall* (Cambridge: Brewer, 2000), 31–54. An investigation of the commercial and judicial life of late medieval London in relation to Langland's *Piers Plowman*, with particular attention to city records.

Bird, Ruth, *The Turbulent London of Richard II* (London: Longman, 1949). The classic study of the political conflicts of Chaucer's time, including disputes involving the government of London, the power of its various guilds, and its relations with the Crown.

Liber albus: The White Book of the City of London, trans. Henry Thomas Riley (1861). A translation of an important early fifteenth-century compilation of documents from the London archives originally intended as a guide for those governing the city.

Pearsall, Derek, *The Life of Geoffrey Chaucer: A Critical Biography* (Oxford: Blackwell, 1992). The best biography of Chaucer, especially notable for its learning, wit, and literary perception, as well as for its less than reverent attitude towards its subject.

Riley, Henry Thomas (ed.), *Memorials of London and London Life, in the* XIIIth, *xivth, and* xvth *Centuries* (1868). A translation of a lively selection of London documents and municipal court decisions that illustrate the life of medieval London, especially its transgressive life.

Robertson, D. W., Jr., *Chaucer's London* (New York: Wiley, 1968). A learned but readable introduction to late medieval London that stresses its differences from modern cities.

Strohm, Paul, *Social Chaucer* (Cambridge, Mass: Harvard University Press, 1989). A ground-breaking study that examines Chaucer's complex relationship with his society, especially his place as a royal servant, and its influence on his poetry.

Wallace, David, 'Chaucer and the Absent City', in Barbara A. Hanawalt (ed.), *Chaucer's England: Literature in Historical Context* (Minneapolis: University of Minnesota Press, 1992), 59–90. A major study of the 'Cook's Tale', in particular, and of Chaucer's concept of London in contrast to Boccaccio's concept of Florence.

NOTES

1. David Wallace, 'Chaucer and the Absent City', in Barbara A. Hanawalt (ed.), *Chaucer's England: Literature in Historical Context* (Minneapolis: University of Minnesota Press, 1992), esp. 82–4.
2. Paul Strohm, 'The Social and Literary Scene in England', in Piero Boitani and Jill Mann (eds.), *The Cambridge Chaucer Companion* (Cambridge: Cambridge University Press, 1986), 14; David Wallace, *Chaucerian Polity: Absolutist Lineages and Associational Forms in England and Italy* (Stanford, Calif.: Stanford University Press, 1997); compare Paul Strohm, *Social Chaucer* (Cambridge, Mass: Harvard University Press, 1989).
3. For the two tricks, see Henry Thomas Riley (ed.), *Memorials of London and London Life, in the* XIIIth, *xivth, and* xvth *Centuries* (1868), 395–6, 599–600.
4. V. A. Kolve, *Chaucer and the Imagery of Narrative: The First Five Canterbury Tales* (Stanford, Calif.: Stanford University Press, 1984), 267.

5 | Religion

Jim Rhodes

Any attempt to introduce students to the rich and varied religious culture of the late Middle Ages in England, the age in which Chaucer lived and the context in which his poetry was written, is beset by three formidable problems: the first is the difficulty, in a brief account, of reducing the vast body of complex material that constitutes late medieval Christianity without omitting or slighting something that is vital or substantial to one's understanding of the subject. The second problem involves gauging the relationship between the sacred and the secular. It is clear that what characterizes religion in the fourteenth century, and what distinguishes it most from our present era, is the omnipresence of ecclesiastical rites and institutions in the rhythms of everyday life. Religion was not an activity set aside for worship on a single day of the week; it was an integral part of work, play, and significant events in the calendar year. Etymologically, 'religion' is derived from the Latin *ligo* or *lego*, and more directly from *religo*, which has the sense of 'to bind or to tie securely'.[1] In the late Middle Ages, the Church did everything in its power to bind, contain, or tie securely everyone who adhered to its system into a single moral community. Accordingly, religious rituals attended the most commonplace of events: birthdays, marriages, anniversaries, celebrations of every imaginable kind, sicknesses, and burials. The liturgy (official or approved forms of prayer and worship as distinct from private acts and devotions) structured the calendar year, just as the canonical hours structured the hours of the day.[2] Nearly every day was a saint's day and the stories associated with the particular saint made the events in the liturgy more meaningful to the laity and enabled them to link religious activity more fully with the social and the communal. The Church and religion, moreover, infused the vocabulary of the people with a level of referentiality that, alongside the sermons, verse treatises, and images in stained glass windows (sometimes called the Scriptures of the people) that surrounded their daily life, coalesced to shape a religious consciousness that led, ideally, to an internalization of various religious themes and patterns.

The third problem is the modern tendency to assume that the masses of people, especially those who lacked a formal education or were in the lower echelons of society, were naive, superstitious, and unquestioning in their faith. In actuality, the fourteenth century in England was a vibrant period for lay people, filled with controversy and ferocious debates, particularly in the area of religion. The era witnessed the rise of a vernacular theology that transformed the face of religion and the role of the laity within it. To be sure, the Church exercised considerable power and authority over the laity and had control over many instruments of culture, but in the fourteenth century it lacked the homogeneity associated with it today. In an age lacking in mass communication it was technically impossible to expect or to enforce a uniformity of belief or practice. Besides, at that time the Church had hundreds of divisions and subdivisions, ranging from the Church of the Lateran in Rome (the Church in which the pope was the presiding cleric) to the remote village parishes of rural England, which meant that a wide variety of beliefs and practices was able to flourish, and dissent and calls for reform were commonplace. As a result, although the people shared a core set of beliefs, English spirituality tended to be local and varied.[3]

'What man artow?' ('PST' 695)

Chaucer has always been regarded as a moral, if not a religious, poet even if there has been little agreement about how these terms should be applied to his poetry. In the past fifty years several schools of thought have contributed to the way Chaucer's relationship to religion has been conceived. Some readers, by no means a majority, regard Chaucer as a devout Christian whose faith undergirds his poetry. In this approach, his poems are a form of theology, and even the tales not explicitly religious in content promote the Augustinian doctrine of charity.[4] To these 'exegetical' critics, poems are vehicles for moral truths. The poem itself is like a shell that contains a kernel of truth inside. Once the moral truth is uncovered, the shell can be discarded (for more on exegetical criticism, see Chapters 9 and 19). Other readers, less convinced of Chaucer's orthodoxy, look at him as a sceptic who eschews didacticism and does not subscribe to any particular religious point of view. In this reading Chaucer uses his poetry to test religious institutions and ideas in the same way that he interrogates other systems of belief. Still other readers view Chaucer as disinterested, an objective observer and master ironist whose poems are not a reliable index to his personal (religious) beliefs. In this analysis Chaucer is free to address and to assess a wide variety of moral and ethical issues, but he allows his poems to speak for themselves without predisposing the reader in any way. Some recent critical approaches attempt to place his poetry on the side of the reformers, arguing that it strongly suggests at least sympathy with Wyclif's programme of reforms, even if Chaucer did not embrace Lollardy in any comprehensive way.

A telling passage is Chaucer's 'Retraction', which appears at the end of the *Canterbury Tales*, and which, if taken literally, cancels much of what readers cherish in his poetry. For those who read the 'Retraction' literally, Chaucer intended his poetry to be read from a specifically religious standpoint. The reader, however, should not feel compelled to respond in this way. The 'Retraction' may be regarded as a conventional gesture, one not uncommon at the conclusion of many medieval poems. In any case, it is not the starting point of the *Tales* and its perspective does not obtain throughout the body of the work. Perhaps the best advice is not to adopt an all-or-nothing approach to Chaucer's intent, but to treat the 'Retraction' as one of those delicious ambiguities that flavour the *Tales*, leaving it as a problem to grapple with in one's own experience with the poem (the 'Retraction' is further specifically discussed in Chapter 27).

Here it would be best to dispose of the assumption held by many students that Chaucer wrote his 'Retraction' out of fear of excommunication or fear of 'getting in trouble' with authorities in the Church, especially on account of his sometimes virulent anticlerical satire. This impression is a product of the belief that the Church was fundamentally an oppressive institution in the fourteenth century controlled by medieval thought-police. Yet much of the drama of the period, some of which was surely written by clergy, contains an even greater degree of satire and irreligious behaviour, bordering at times on the blasphemous. Audiences in Chaucer's day tolerated levels of irreligious behaviour that may seem shocking to us today.

It might be said of Chaucer that religion is both nowhere and everywhere in his poetry. It is nowhere if we look for a sustained or coherent religious vision of the kind we find in several of his contemporaries. But that does not mean that Chaucer is any less committed to engaging contemporary religious issues and problems. Even a casual review of his poetry reveals that Chaucer appreciates how religion is tightly woven into the fabric of everyday life. Nearly all of the *Canterbury Tales* deals directly or indirectly with a religious issue. The Reeve and the Shipman, for example, give stinging accounts of Church corruption at the local level. The Wife of Bath challenges the sexual politics of the Church and exposes how deeply misogyny is embedded in clerkly discourse. Chaucer may be as reform-minded as Langland but is not as programmatic about it. Like Langland, he seems most concerned with religious issues that impinge on one's everyday existence, and he shares with Langland the conviction that ethics is the foundation of a religious life. By enabling or empowering the voices of all of his pilgrims to participate in the discussion of religious issues and matters of doctrine, voices that are generally excluded from such a conversation, Chaucer's poetry reflects how religious thought and teaching were received and applied in his period. What we learn when we look closely is that Chaucer's poetry does indeed take us 'deep into the practice of religion among the common people', some instances of which we shall now turn to.[5]

'For soothly the lawe of God is the love of God' ('ParsT' 125)

A good place to start is with the portraits of the Parson and the Plowman in the 'General Prologue'. Although their portraits are highly idealized, they do represent the vast majority of ordinary Christians who in Chaucer's time lived and worked in parishes throughout England. Individually, each leads us to think about what kinds of things ordinary Christians were expected to know and how they were to learn it. Together they reflect some of the conceptual changes that were taking place in religion and society, especially the greater consciousness of social morality and the new emphasis on charity, or *caritas*, that resulted in the formation of a new kind of layperson.

Although the parish was the smallest unit in the ecclesiastical structure, it was the site within which Christians were expected to practise their faith and have their spiritual needs satisfied. The parish church also served as a meeting place for many secular activities, which meant that a parson and a ploughman would have regular contact. Perhaps Chaucer makes his Parson and Plowman brothers to suggest the kind of mutuality and interdependence that could and should exist between the laity and its priests (both place the welfare of others and of the community ahead of themselves), whereas the ideal nature of their portraits may indicate how much reform would be needed if a true Christian society were to be formed.

Simply put, the ultimate aim of all medieval Christians was to attain salvation, and the parish priest played an instrumental role in helping the laity attain that goal. Every ecclesiastical position in the Church had two aspects, office and benefice. The former entailed the duties and functions a parson was expected to perform, such as administration of the sacraments, preaching, teaching, and ministering to the spiritual needs of the people. Benefice referred to a body of rights and benefits in the way of fees, tithes, and rents as recompense for the duties performed. Chaucer's Parson obviously sets a high standard in the fulfilment of his office. He visits the sick and needy in his parish, and his refusal to overreact to those who did not pay their tithes ('GP' 486) coincides with his Christ-like poverty and sensitivity to the limited means of his parishioners. Abuse of tithes and taxes was an issue that aroused the ire and resentment of the laity towards venal priests in Chaucer's day (a situation that was exacerbated by the Great Schism, 1378–1417, in which the papacy was divided in two with a papal palace in Rome and another pope installed in Avignon, a scandal that drained the resources of the laity). This priest shares with his parishioners what he receives in the way of goods and rents. The Parson also refuses to hire out his benefice to some other priest in order that he might become a chaplain for a guild, a post that often rewarded the holder handsomely. The Parson's primary goal is one appropriate to his station: to teach Christ's lessons, to preach the Word (after first practising it himself), and to lead his people to heaven by his own good example.

In reality, many parsons were unable to serve their parishioners as well as Chaucer's Parson does; indeed, the Church had been failing the people, parson and ploughman alike, especially at the parish level. Many of the laity were illiterate and ignorant of the rudiments of their faith, and a number of secular clergy (those not in monastic or fraternal orders) who dealt directly with the laity were themselves poorly educated or lacked formal religious training. Catechisms were not yet available and all major Christian documents, including the Bible, were written in Latin and thus inaccessible to most lay people. To address this problem, the Church had initiated an ambitious programme of education and reform, beginning with the Fourth Lateran Council, convened in 1215, and followed in England by a series of measures instituted to ensure that the laity were educated in the faith and the parish priests were properly prepared to fulfil their pastoral function. These measures affected every aspect of public worship and private prayer. The programme was retarded or delayed in its effect by the mid-fourteenth-century plagues that devastated the countryside and claimed the lives of many lay people and a good many of the parish clergy who ministered to the sick. Guidebooks were prepared for priests that treated common doctrinal problems in an agreed-upon language in order to offer a coherent programme of religious instruction. One of the more popular and effective of these manuals was William of Pagula's *Oculus sacerdotis* ('Priest's Eye'), which stipulated that the priest was to expound to the people four times a year in the vulgar tongue, or vernacular (in England, English and Anglo-Norman), such fundamentals of the faith as the seven sacraments (baptism, confirmation, penance, the Eucharist, marriage, holy orders, and extreme unction), the Ten Commandments, the two commandments of the gospel (love of God and love of one's neighbour), and the seven deadly sins (the subject of Chaucer's 'Parson's Tale'). Archbishop Thoresby commissioned a similar manual of instruction for priests, based on a scheme of instruction devised at the Council of Lambeth in 1281. These instructions were rendered into a translation known as the *Lay Folks' Catechism*, for distribution in the diocese of York. The instructions called for all Christians to go to confession once a year and to receive the Eucharist or consecrated host (the body and blood of Christ) at Easter. More likely, the laity made confession at regular intervals during the year. Confession proved an especially effective means of educating the laity and instilling within them a moral conscience because it was conducted in the form of an interrogation on such things as the deadly sins and the Ten Commandments. To enhance the instructional value, examination of the penitent was adapted to address the layperson's social rank and vocation, thereby constituting an effort to add a moral dimension to his or her social and vocational activity. The emphasis placed on confession also opened the door to abuse, as enterprising and itinerant friars journeyed throughout the countryside hearing confessions, sometimes at the home of the penitent, and often offering absolution of sins for a fee. Chaucer's Friar well illustrates this practice:

> Ful swetely herde he confessioun,
> And plesaunt was his absolucioun:
> He was an esy man to yeve penaunce,
> Ther as he wiste to have a good pitaunce.
>
> ('GP' 221–4)

Another effective and informative mode of instruction was the medieval sermon. Through sermons, and preaching in general, which was widespread and very popular, the laity were able to become familiar with excerpts from the Bible—translated or summarized by the preachers—and learn about other aspects of their faith. Most people would have occasion to attend other churches than their local one and would in that way be exposed to a variety of preachers. First and foremost were the friars (from the Latin *frater* for 'brother') whose livelihood often depended on their preaching, usually in urban areas. There were four fraternal or mendicant orders in Chaucer's day: Franciscans, Dominicans, Carmelites, and Augustinians. They took vows of poverty and generally formed a convent of thirteen in imitation of Christ and his Apostles. A second kind of visiting preacher might be a figure like Chaucer's Pardoner, so named because he was empowered to dispense pardons in exchange for donations. Like the friars, pardoners were commissioned to work a 'limit', or district, and had to display credentials. Pardoners were generally forbidden to preach, but Chaucer's Pardoner evidently violated that ban weekly.

Since friars were well schooled in formal theology, they were able to acquaint the laity with some of the finer points of doctrine and were able to make difficult theological issues, such as those pertaining to justification, free will, and predestination, and God's relationship to his creatures, relevant and accessible to a non-professional audience. Many sermons and sermon collections survive and give us a clear picture of how well they were geared to a lay audience and how topical the subjects were in general. Most were linked to penitential themes, not unlike Chaucer's 'Parson's Tale', or to moral problems, salvation, the nature of the redemption, and the poverty of Christ. Chaucer's 'Pardoner's Tale' provides us with an excellent example of a medieval sermon, including the use of an *exemplum*, which is a story or allegory that illustrates the moral lesson of the sermon. In this instance the Pardoner tells a story of three rioters who join together to conquer death and instead find it in a pile of gold. The treachery and deaths that follow serve to illustrate the preacher's one and only theme, that money or avarice is the root of all evil.

A further word about the Friar and the Pardoner. Neither one seems especially interested in improving the moral life of the laypeople who come in contact with him, nor in aiding them in their quest for salvation. Many students come away from Chaucer's poetry with the impression that the Friar and Pardoner are representative of what the Church had become in the fourteenth century. The abuses and venality they embody were real and they make for lively reading, but they are no more representative of the Church than the Parson is. Anticlerical sentiment ran very high, and with good reason, but most clergy were of neither extreme, neither Parson nor Pardoner. What the corruption of the Church and some of its clergy did do was create an appetite for reform and move the laity to adopt private devotions independent of Church auspices. For a discussion of this development we need to turn to the Plowman.

The Plowman sets an excellent example for all laypeople. To achieve salvation laypeople were obliged to attend Mass, receive the sacraments, and pay tithes. They were also expected to avoid sin and to lead a moral existence; that is, they were expected to practise charity. Charity, or *caritas*, was a medieval imperative, fundamental to defining one's Christianity. The programme of instruction discussed above brought pressure on the laity to adopt an active Christianity and to acquire a sense of social responsibility, transforming *caritas* from a spiritual obligation to an act of social consciousness. R. N. Swanson neatly summarizes the place of charity in the whole Christian scheme of the late Middle Ages:

The emphasis on *caritas* is crucial, for while Christianity focused on Christ, it could be argued that it centred on Mankind. It was, essentially, an attempt to provide the means whereby a defective creature could achieve perfection. Man was defiled by the Fall, and by the Original Sin incurred when Adam succumbed to temptation. Eve may have been responsible for the Fall by allowing herself to be beguiled by the serpent, and beguiling Adam in her turn; but according to some, Adam's sin was greater than Eve's, for he had refused to accept responsibility for his actions in tasting the forbidden fruit, and sought to transfer the blame to Eve. Whoever was to blame, Mankind had fallen, had lost Eden. Christianity held out the prospect of its recovery, but not in this world. To that end, the penalties of original sin, latently expunged by Christ's Incarnation and Crucifixion, were actually expunged by baptism. Thereafter, it was for individuals, following the precepts of Christ and the church, to live out the pilgrimage of this earthly life, hoping to merit eternal presence with God after the final judgement. Human existence was thus only part of a lengthier life of the soul, which continued after bodily death, and might lead to eternal felicity in participation in the timelessness of God. But that felicity had to be earned, or at least merited. Life, then, was but a pilgrimage in search of salvation, with an unworldly goal. Thanks to the Incarnation, Redemption had become possible; but only the final judgement would clarify whether it had been granted.[6]

In keeping with this ideal, Chaucer's Plowman is described as loving God best with his whole heart and then his neighbour as himself, thus honouring Christ's two commandments. He also pays his tithes without complaint and he lends his labour to the poor ('He wolde thresshe, and thereto dyke and delve, | For Cristes sake, for every povre wight, | Withouten hire, if it lay in his myght', 'GP' 536–8). His charity is a sign of the inwardness of his faith, and is linked to his community and to attaining salvation by action. The opposite of the Plowman's *caritas* is the Pardoner's *cupiditas*, which connotes self-love or simply avarice. The Pardoner offers a short cut to salvation, through the monetary purchase of pardons, indulgences, and the miraculous power of relics. Indulgences were closely connected to the doctrine of purgatory. They were of two kinds, plenary and partial. A person earned an indulgence by prayer, pilgrimages, or works of charity, all of which led to remission of sin and its punishment in purgatory by drawing on the 'treasury of merits' accrued by Christ, the Virgin Mary, and the saints. The Pardoner also promises his clients the prospect of attaining salvation without having first to go to purgatory, an important omission because the theology of purgatory, as we shall see below, was one of the more powerful inducements to perform charitable works.

What ordinary laypersons like the Plowman needed to enhance the interiority of their religious devotions and activities, especially during the Mass, which was celebrated in Latin, were written materials like those afforded the parish priests which would allow them to become participants in the ceremony and be able to express their prayers to God in their own language. In the course of the fourteenth century, manuals and devotional texts were produced that taught them how to conduct themselves in church, how to adore the Eucharist, and how to recite the appropriate prayers during the Mass. Everyone was expected to be able to recite the Lord's Prayer, the Hail Mary, and the Creed. These prayers were often memorized first in Latin, but vernacular versions emerged in manuals like the *Lay Folks' Massbook*. The Creed was especially important because it contained nearly all the essential articles of faith promulgated by the Church; the following version is taken from the *Lay Folks' Massbook* and has been modernized by R. N. Swanson:

I believe in God, the powerful Father, who has made everything: Heaven and earth, day and night, and all from nothing. And in Jesus, who is God's only son, both God and man, endlessly Lord. I believe in him, who through the meekness of the Holy Ghost, that was so mild, settled in Mary, the chaste maiden, and became a child. Under Pontius Pilate he suffered pain in order to save us, he was put on the cross, and died, laid in his grave. His soul went into Hell, to tell the truth; he rose up in flesh and feeling on the third day; he went up to Heaven with open wounds, through his power. Now he sits at his Father's right side in majesty; from thence he shall come to judge us all in his manhood, the living and the dead, all who have been of Adam's seed. I believe well in the Holy Ghost, and the Holy Church which is so good; and so I believe that the eucharist is both flesh and blood, in the forgiveness of my sins if I repent, also the resurrection of my flesh, and life everlasting.[7]

The Creed calls attention to the Creation *ex nihilo*, to confirm that God created heaven and earth out of the void in order to dispel any notion of the eternity of matter, which had come under debate in theological circles in the wake of the recovery of texts of Aristotle. The prayer emphasizes that Christ is both fully God and fully a human being. He is the Son of the Father but not his inferior; that is, Christ does not proceed from nor is he created by the Father (a position known as the Arian heresy) but is eternal with him. The Trinity is one God with three divine persons, Father, Son, and Spirit. A very important development in late medieval Christology is the emphasis placed on Christ's humanness or complete human nature, which includes stress on his physical suffering and his very real human death. In the three days when Christ is dead and buried, he descends into hell (the Harrowing of Hell) to complete the redemption. Christ 'buys back' all human souls since the sin of Adam and, following his ascension into heaven, he will become the (merciful) judge of the living and the dead.

The Creed also calls attention to Christ's wounds. Adoration of the body and blood of Christ became something of a cult in the late Middle Ages, which led to the foundation of a special feast called Corpus Christi, the day on which many of the cycle plays were performed. The Passion of Christ (his suffering, death, and resurrection) emerged as the main focus of meditation in the Church and the activities and ceremonies of Holy Week (celebration of the events leading up to Easter) promoted all kinds of devotions to the body of Christ. The celebration of the Mass makes Christ present on the altar and the redemption of the world is renewed. The Mass was the sign of unity or the bond of love between human beings and God, and the language of Eucharistic belief was, as Duffy points out, saturated with communitarian and corporate imagery.[8] Under the simple elements of bread and wine, the bloody sacrifice of the cross is re-enacted by the unbloody sacrifice of Christ's body (transubstantiation). The consecration of the Eucharist by the priest was the most sacred moment of the Mass and the laity was instructed to revere it, an event that occasioned great displays of emotion. The Mass is a communal act, but the adoration of Christ's blood and wounds also sparked many private devotions of an affective nature.

Affective spirituality and mystical contemplation, especially of the crucifixion of Christ and the sufferings of Mary, reached a high point in the fourteenth century. The impetus behind this devotion was the belief that to suffer with Christ was a means to affective union with Christ, and that the religious elements found in faith can be experienced directly, without a priest as intermediary. What the mystic seeks is to be transported out of the physical world in the ecstasy of contemplation in order to enter into communion with Christ. Affective spirituality and mystical devotions are part of the democratization and laicization of religion, but true mystics were few in number because the mystical or the affective experience involves an intense degree of interiority most people may not be able to meet.

The problem with all of the devotions that sprouted in the fourteenth century, from pilgrimages to veneration of relics, worship of Mary, Christ's body, and devotion to saints, is the difficulty of distinguishing between outward gestures and rehearsed responses as opposed to a response that originates within the person and involves an internalization of the experience. Nevertheless, affective spirituality did bring attention to several themes of great importance to late medieval religion, namely the Incarnation, the humanity of Christ, and deification. Deification is the idea that human beings are made in the image and likeness of Christ and they are capable of union with him directly. Salvation as deification means not that human beings can become God, as some form of pantheism, but that they enter into a personal, affective relationship with Christ. In the Incarnation human nature is deified in Christ and deification restores human nature to the communion intended for human beings and God at the creation.

The Virgin Mary and the communion of saints

Less than a God but more than a saint, Mary occupies a pivotal position in late medieval devotion and spirituality. The Creed stresses her virginity and the miraculous nature of her conception of Christ by the Holy Spirit. In art she is sometimes depicted as having conceived of Christ through her ear, which preserves her virginity and shows her receiving the Word of God and it passing into her very being. The emphasis on the Incarnation indicates that Mary was not merely a passive agent through whom Christ passed to enter the world; she confers on him his human nature. Besides the Incarnation there are two features that distinguish her: the Immaculate Conception and the Assumption. Some students (and scholars) confuse or use interchangeably the events of the Incarnation and the Immaculate Conception. The Incarnation refers to Christ becoming flesh in Mary's womb. The Immaculate Conception is Mary being conceived immaculately, that is, without original sin, in her mother's (St Anne's) womb. The Assumption is the belief that Mary did not die but was assumed bodily into heaven.

Mary was easily the most important focus of veneration in the Middle Ages, with the possible exception of Christ. This devotion was especially intense in England, where an enormous number of shrines were dedicated to her. Some of the most inspired and affecting images of art in the period centre on Mary and so vast a literature of songs, poems, hymns, meditations, and devotions grew up in regard to her that here it is only possible to scratch the surface of her importance to the religious life and imagination of the people. Mary was such a multifarious figure in the fourteenth century that, for the sake of convenience, I have identified two main concepts or traditional ways of depicting her. The first concept portrays Mary as the semi-divine mother of Christ whose virginity is stressed as her most salient feature and who becomes a symbol for religious asceticism, monasticism, and mysticism. Here, Mary and her perpetual virginity are treated as the antithesis of Eve and the ills that are supposed to have emanated from Eve's capitulation to the flesh. The image of Mary standing on the head of the serpent became one of the most popular manifestations of this theme. This Mary became known as the Virgo Immaculata and her eternal purity was cultivated to sponsor various moral doctrines. Her perpetual virginity elevated her to the station of Queen of Heaven.

In contrast to this transcendent idea is the image of Mary in her earthly naturalness, as the mother of Christ whose humanity is stressed and who serves Christianity with a more this-worldly orientation. In this image the Queen of Heaven is replaced by the Mother tenderly fondling or nursing her child, which quickly established itself as the dominant expression of Mary's love of humanity. In this role she became identified as the figure most closely associated with forgiveness; she was regarded as the supreme mediatrix, or well of mercy. For a recitation of her many attributes one need only consult Chaucer's devotional poem to Mary, entitled 'An ABC'. Each of its twenty-three stanzas begins with a different letter of the alphabet, and each expands on Mary's various attributes, particularly her joys and sorrows. The Second Nun prefaces her tale, as does the Prioress, with a hymn to the Virgin Mary. In both cases the lines are adapted from St Bernard's hymn to the Virgin in canto 33 (1–51) of Dante's *Paradiso*.

The communion of saints is not mentioned in the medieval version of the Creed but the saints had a very important place in the devotional practices of the fourteenth century and deserve some comment here. Their images abounded in churches—many named after them—and ceremonies were conducted in their honour on appropriate days of the year. Although one of the functions of the saint's legend was to teach—the stories and deeds of their lives (hagiography) were held up as models of virtue for laypeople to imitate and bits of doctrine were sprinkled in to fortify their faith—the zeal with which the saints were embraced and the cults that grew up surrounding many of them suggest that they met the need for a personal connection to the sacred, in the same way that journeys to a shrine and veneration of relics did. Saints were regarded as the earthly representatives of God. They were valued because they were assumed already to be in heaven, where they could petition God directly to bestow blessings on their devotees.

Most saints belonged to the whole of Christendom, but local saints evoked the fiercest loyalty. They were hailed as helpers and healers, miracle-workers and intercessors who were expected to protect individuals and whole cities from plagues and misfortune in exchange for their devotion. Local saints were credited with strengthening bonds to the Church and the social order, keeping peace among rival groups in a city, and helping to regulate communal life. In the fourteenth century a new kind of saint began to emerge that reflected the growing independence of the laity and the need for social and moral leadership. Unlike the traditional saints, who had been singled out for their chastity and austerity, these new figures were valued for their active engagement with the world, for their service on behalf of the poor, and their dedication to ecclesiastical and civic reform. The emphasis on civic virtue suggests a greater consciousness of civic activity as a social and religious issue, expanding the idea of *caritas* into an existential ethic in pursuit of the common good.

Chaucer's 'Second Nun's Tale' illustrates the type. St Cecilia is a layperson but one who is active in the world. She advocates for the poor and is dedicated to ecclesiastical reform, holding up the example of the early, or apostolic, Church as a model of *communitas* and of *caritas*. Cecilia is said to burn with charity and at the end of her ordeal, a suffering which imitates the Passion of Christ, she gives away all her goods to the people and converts her house into a church open to everyone.

The forgiveness of sins

Christians in the late Middle Ages had a very strong concept of the afterlife, and a soul could go to heaven, hell, or purgatory. Souls in hell suffered physical torment, but the greater torment was the loss of the beatific vision, or sight of God. Souls in purgatory also underwent arduous but purifying punishments and would eventually enter heaven and enjoy the sight of God. Souls in hell were lost for eternity. Purgatory was thus the mainspring for a great deal of pious behaviour.[9] Although the Church did not formally institute purgatory until 1439, it existed in the popular imagination for centuries beforehand and was informally a part of Church teaching. The key points were that purgatory was a place where remission of sin could occur after death and that penance and charitable works performed here on earth, by oneself during life or on one's behalf following death, shortened one's stay. Psychologically, purgatory dissolved the binary structure of heaven and hell and promoted a strain of forgiveness and humanism, creating a stronger bond between the living and the dead and spawning a new attitude towards this world and towards the efficacy of good works. One of the more salutary effects of purgatory theology was the pressure it put on the rich to make some accommodation for the less fortunate in society. Another of its effects was the promotion of widespread penitential behaviour, which led to a new appreciation for human virtue, or *caritas*. Purgatory theology thus allowed lay-people to play a greater role in their own redemption. They still needed the sacraments and the Church, but the concept of *caritas* put some measure of control in their own hands.

The doctrine of purgatory also gave impetus to several of the devotions most popular among the laity, specifically pilgrimage, and thus the frame Chaucer uses for his great poem. In the fourteenth century a pilgrimage is a journey to a shrine, usually that of a saint or a martyr, or to a site where some miracle or sacred event had occurred, based on the early Christian practice of visiting places sanctified by the life of Christ. Such shrines existed in abundance all over England, but Canterbury was its most cherished shrine because of the tomb of Thomas Becket and because Augustine of Canterbury, who brought Christianity to England, was buried there. The journey to a shrine gave life to what it meant to be a pilgrim to God, and each pilgrimage was linked to the recovery of paradise. By Chaucer's day, pilgrimages were less of a private, ascetic act and more of a mass movement, often lacking apparent spiritual decorum, which made them the focus of much complaint, especially from the Lollards. Chaucer uses the pilgrimage as a convenient device to gather together a diverse group of people from various classes, regions, vocations, and genders. At the same time, he does suggest a redemptive or spiritual design as vital to the poem by keeping the pilgrimage motif before us, mainly in the links, and culminating in the 'Parson's Prologue' where the Parson likens the Canterbury pilgrimage to 'thilke parfit glorious pilgrymage | That highte Jerusalem celestial' (50–1), thus attaching a symbolic meaning to the journey. Pilgrims in the fourteenth century still pursued the same ideals as religious travellers of an earlier era and were motivated by some of the same impulses. Some went for miracles and relics, some out of fear of hell, some for cures from illnesses, some were sent as a penitential act, and others went voluntarily for spiritual renewal.

'The naked text in English to declare' (*LGW* (G) 86)

Near the end of the Creed comes the affirmation of one's belief in 'Holy Church'. What was happening in the Church in the fourteenth century was a greater accommodation of lay needs and interests, especially the rise of writing on theology in the vernacular. It would be difficult to overstate the value of the vernacular movement to the social and religious change that occurred in Chaucer's day. The appearance of writing in the vernacular languages encouraged the people to become literate and, as literacy increased, a demand rose for more materials to be read. The ready reception given by the laity to manuals and books of devotion indicates a voracious appetite for such texts and a desire to take a more active part in religious devotions. By the second half of the fourteenth century vernacular writings had begun to reproduce stories from the Bible, giving the laity direct access to the word of God and personal knowledge of the law of Christ, what Wyclif declared as the fundamental right of every Christian. This litera-ture cut across class lines and included such forms as pastoral and devotional works, religious polemics, and meditations on the life of Christ. As literacy increased, so did religious exchange between lay readers and the clergy, suggesting that the new role of lay activism contributed positively to the growth of official religion. The vernacu-larization of religion thus did not simply mediate the formal theology of the theo-logians 'downward' to the people; it reflected the spiritual and religious interests of the people 'upward' as well. This is most evident in the concomitant rise of private devo-tions sponsored by guilds and confraternities, those lay organizations that served as a bridge between the social order and the churches. These lay organizations assumed some of the duties previously under clerical control and provided services that the parish often did not, such as the establishment of hospitals and almshouses and making provisions for the aged, the poor, and the sick.

No account of religion in Chaucer's day would be complete without a discussion of dissent, which was percolating throughout the fourteenth century and boiled over before its close. The most clamorous voices of dissent were those of the Lollards. There is no agreement on the origin of the term but it now refers, in the words of Richard Rex, to 'the distinct, if still somewhat broad, band of dissident beliefs and practices which flourished in England at that time, and which owed its inspiration to Wyclif'.[10] Many of the issues raised by Lollardy, especially its anticlericalism, won widespread approval, although a good many of the criticisms levelled against the Church and popular devo-tions, among them the veneration of saints and relics, the excesses of pilgrimages, adoration of images, the wealth and simony of the Church, and papal authority, did not originate with Lollardy and attracted the support of many who were not Lollards. Its main appeal may have been its emphasis on the Bible and its encouragement of lay activism, areas that were advocated by Wyclif.

Other contributors to this volume discuss Wyclif's impact on religious developments in the fourteenth century (see Chapters 7, 16, and 19). What I wish to emphasize here is that all of the preaching and teaching of the Lollards and the views of Wyclif need to be seen as contributing meaningfully to the growth of lay spirituality, to Church reform, and to an attenuation of clerical authority. As interest in Lollardy has intensified in Chaucer studies, however, a few caveats are in order. As important as Lollardy is to understanding the nature of the Church and religion in the fourteenth century, there is a tendency to allot too much credit to Lollardy for change. Lollardy is only one dimension in a complex and diverse religious scene in the fourteenth century, and evidence is mounting that shows that neither the Church nor the clergy were resistant to change, and were, in fact, supportive of much lay activity and lay independence.

Conclusion

It is not clear what the exact nature of Chaucer's relation to Lollardy is, even though some of his friends and associates were known Lollards, and several of the pilgrims in the *Tales* express sentiments that can readily be construed as sympathetic to Lollard concerns. Chaucer's personal view of Lollardy and dissent is as elusive and ambiguous as his approach to religion in general in his poetry; we do not know what his personal religious beliefs are, and that is perhaps just as well. The most we can do is to make inferences from the poetry, which leads me to the following summation: the *Canterbury Tales* deals both directly and indirectly with many of the important religious practices and controversies of Chaucer's time. The traditional question about the relative value of faith and works, for example, is resolved by the Second Nun's insistence that 'feith is deed withouten werkis' ('SNP' 64). In a less spectacular, more muted fashion than the Second Nun, many of the Canterbury pilgrims are shown as concerned with linking their religious belief to social, moral, or ethical conduct and ideals. That this linkage does not always succeed and at times is based on 'bad faith' does not, perhaps, negate the centrality of this theme in the general structure or 'redemptive design' of the *Tales*, which, as I have recently argued elsewhere, allies Chaucer's poem with a major strand in late fourteenth-century theology, an optimism about the human capacity for salvation through an ethical 'imitation of Christ'.[11]

Finally, what strikes this reader after years of reading, teaching, and discussing Chaucer's poetry is how well the *Canterbury Tales* endures as Chaucer's work in progress towards a moral community. Throughout the work his pilgrims display a remarkable tolerance and generosity of spirit towards one another. No one is expelled from the group despite the reprehensible content of some tales, such as the Prioress's, and the worst that happens to anyone is the humiliation the Pardoner brings down upon himself—in the form of corrective laughter—for his lack of charity towards others. Inclusiveness emerges as the hallmark of the *Tales*. Perhaps there is a lesson for us all in this. We, as readers, can honour that spirit when we open Chaucer's book and invoke at the beginning the words Harry Bailly extends to the Parson at the end: 'Sey what yow list, and we wol gladly heere' ('ParsP' 73).

FURTHER READING

Brown, Andrew, *Church and Society in England, 1000–1500* (Basingstoke: Palgrave-Macmillan, 2003). Closely examines the relationship between the late medieval Church and society with special attention to the role played by the laity in Church teaching and practices. Other topics of special interest to students are the relationship between royal power and the Church, forms of orthodoxy and heresy in English religious life, and the emphasis placed on the inner life in late medieval religious devotions. Concludes with a brief but incisive review of the impact of Wyclif and Lollardy.

Brown, Andrew, *Popular Piety in Late Medieval England: The Diocese of Salisbury 1250–1550* (Oxford: Clarendon Press, 1995). Detailed discussion of the wide variety of pious practices displayed by the people, showing the similarity of these practices between the learned and the popular. Explains the roles played by the guilds and fraternities in parish life in what is described as the 'honeycomb of interlinking devotional structures' (p. 179). Useful discussions of penance, Lollardy, heresy, and dissent. Augments but also challenges some of Duffy's claims.

Catto, Jeremy, 'Currents of Religious Thought and Expression', in *The New Cambridge Medieval History, vi: 1300–c.1415*, ed. Michael Jones (Cambridge: Cambridge University Press, 2000), 42–65. Provides a general but insightful overview of the main issues discussed and debated by theologians in the era. Also discusses what and by what means the laity were taught. Incisive comments on the cult of saints, cult of the Eucharist, and varieties of spiritual experience. Pays special attention to the topic of God's omnipotence and how it relates to views on predestination and free will.

Duffy, Eamon, *The Stripping of the Altars: Traditional Religion in England 1400–1580* (New Haven: Yale University Press, 1992). A learned, informative, and extensive description of the Church in the late Middle Ages and an impassioned delineation of its practices, rituals, ceremonies, and prayers. Well written and carefully documented. Essential reading.

Kieckhefer, Richard, 'Major Currents in Late Medieval Devotion', in Jill Raitt (ed.), *Christian Spirituality: High Middle Ages and Reformation* (New York: Crossroads, 1987), 75–108. Highly focused discussion of late medieval devotional practices and themes, ranging from the Passion of Christ, Marian devotions, pilgrimages to the feast of Corpus Christi, and other devotions related to the Eucharist. Useful comments on the art and drama of the period.

Pantin, W. A., *The English Church in the Fourteenth Century* (Cambridge: Cambridge University Press, 1955). A seminal study of the English Church. Highly accessible and an excellent place to begin before more recent studies by Duffy and Swanson. Is especially strong in the discussion of the impact of the Fourth Lateran Council on religious practices and offers the best introduction to the way the manuals of instruction for secular clergy and the laity developed.

Schofield, Phillipp R., *Peasant and Community in Medieval England, 1200–1500* (New York: Palgrave, 2003). Has an excellent chapter on the experience of religion among the rural laity. Discusses in detail the role of the parish priest, the parish guild, and the modes of spirituality embraced by the laity.

Shinners, John, *Medieval Popular Religion 1000–1500: A Reader* (Peterborough, Ont.: Broadview Press, 1997). A collection (in translation) of various forms of daily religious practices and beliefs. Contains chapters with materials on faith, God, Mary, saints, and doctrine, augmented by a chapter on demons, spirits, and types of error. Excellent opening introduction and helpful comments at the head of each chapter.

Swanson, R. N., *Catholic England: Faith, Religion, and Observance before the Reformation* (Manchester: Manchester University Press, 1993). A collection of source materials (mainly in translation) that affords readers access to excerpts from instructional and devotional texts, sermons, pilgrim accounts, miracles, and rituals that accompanied deaths, burials, anniversaries, and the like. The introduction is also very informative.

Swanson, R. N., *Religion and Devotion in Europe c.1215–c.1515* (Cambridge: Cambridge University Press, 1995). A thoroughgoing examination of religious devotion and spirituality in the later Middle Ages. Designed and written with students in mind (the author states that he assumes an ignorance about much of Christianity among readers), it introduces readers to the foundations of the Christian faith and the way it was practised in the era. Discusses in detail the role and power of the Church and its clergy, as well as the spiritual experiences of the laity at all levels of society. One of the better studies of its kind. Essential reading.

NOTES

1. See Gavin I. Langmuir, *History, Religion, and Antisemitism* (Berkeley: University of California Press, 1990), 69–70.

2. See Eamon Duffy, *The Stripping of the Altars: Traditional Religion in England, 1400–1580* (New Haven: Yale University Press, 1992), 2.

3. See R. N. Swanson, *Catholic England: Faith, Religion and Observance before the Reformation* (Manchester: Manchester University Press, 1993), 40.

4. For an extended comparison of the exegetical and humanist approaches, see S. H. Rigby, *Chaucer in Context: Society, Allegory, and Gender* (Manchester: Manchester University Press, 1996), 78–115.

5. See Derek Pearsall, *The Life of Geoffrey Chaucer: A Critical Biography* (Oxford: Blackwell, 1992), 262.

6. R. N. Swanson, *Religion and Devotion in Europe c.1215–c.1515* (Cambridge: Cambridge University Press, 1995), 19.

7. Swanson, *Catholic England*, 86.

8. *Stripping of the Altars*, 91–130.

9. See Clive Burgess, ' "A fond thing vainly invented": An Essay on Purgatory and Pious Motive in Late Medieval England', in S. J. Wright (ed.), *Parish, Church and People: Local Studies in Lay Religion 1350–1750* (London: Hutchinson, 1988), 56–84.

10. Richard Rex, *The Lollards* (New York: Palgrave, 2002), p. xii. See also Margaret Aston, *Lollards and Reformers: Images and Literacy in Late Medieval Religion* (London: Hambledon, 1984); Anne Hudson, *The Premature Reformation: Wycliffite Texts and Lollard History* (Oxford: Clarendon Press, 1988); Peter Heath, *Church and Realm 1272–1461* (London: Fontana, 1988).

11. See Jim Rhodes, *Poetry Does Theology: Chaucer, Grosseteste, and the 'Pearl'-Poet* (Notre Dame, Ind: University of Notre Dame Press, 2001).

6 | Chivalry

Mark Sherman

The problem of definition

One of the most enduring legends associated with chivalry comes from the late six-teenth century when Sir Walter Ralegh spread his cloak across a muddy path at Greenwich Palace so that Queen Elizabeth I might pass unsullied. Historically true or not, this anecdote conveys much of what modernity inherited as the idea of the gentleman. Even though Ralegh's elegant cloak besmirched for the sake of his queen is an icon of a decidedly *courtly* mode of behaviour typical of the Renaissance, his gesture conveys certain essential qualities of chivalry—a great man's loyalty to his sovereign, dedication to his lady, and his willingness to sacrifice his own well-being for the sake of another or his group. It was expedient for Ralegh's reputation that the lady and the sovereign were the same person; nevertheless, the courtiers of that era, in order to maintain or improve their positions, were expected to behave in a refined manner and display their gentility—what Chaucer called *gentilesse*. The ideals of chivalry had become fused with those of courtesy by 1516, when Baldesar Castiglione defined the perfect courtier in *The Book of the Courtier*. But to focus exclusively on courtly gentility is misleading. Even Castiglione held that the courtier should serve his prince on the battlefield as well as he practised artful manners in court. And Ralegh was no stranger to the harsher side of life. In addition to being a poet, philosopher, historian, and politician, he was a soldier and adventurer. Earlier in his career he had fought for the Protestant cause in France and then in Ireland suppressing a rebellion against English authority. So Ralegh's sword, infrequently mentioned in his myth, was an important prerequisite to his fame.

As illuminating an example as the Renaissance courtier might be in the history of manners, the origins of chivalry as a cultural institution reside in a more remote corner of the past. Like so many terms current during the later Middle Ages, 'chivalry' comes down to us with connotations that have changed quite a bit. In modern English the word 'cavalry' comes closest to what 'chivalry' meant in Chaucer's day. Ultimately derived from the Latin *caballus*, which referred specifically to a packhorse or hackney, 'chivalry' eventually appeared in English alongside cognates in the Romance languages, most notably its immediate source in the French *chevalerie*. In Chaucer's poetry the term is virtually unchanged from the Anglo-Norman that introduced this military term to Britain, denoting armed men on horseback and their standards of conduct. The French and Middle English *chevalier* was the practical equivalent of 'knight'. Old English *cniht* possessed a range of definition to include the warrior or retainer, but most uses of the term invoked youth or boyhood.

Historical origins

The knight and the land-dependent feudal economy, driven almost exclusively by agricultural production, were inextricably linked. Under Charlemagne (742–814) the system by which kings exchanged land for loyalty and service from their nobles made western Europe a relatively cohesive administrative unit. But after the emperor's death, political control fragmented and couldn't extend beyond the micro-unit of the seigniorial estate, which was relatively independent economically and saw services and goods exchanged in kind between lord and peasant.

Vulnerable to invasion, the smaller demesnes in France organized into groups of fortresses under a single authority, a move which eventually formed the basis of larger regional powers under counts and dukes. Peter Haidu demonstrates how significant this reconsolidation of powers was for the rise of chivalry because it precipitated the use of money and transformed the relations between peasant and lord since the peasant's payment was no longer made exclusively through work or goods. In order to collect his due, the lord would invoke 'the *ban*, the right to command, to constrain, and to punish'.[1] The knightly class was born when the lords discovered that the expropriation of surplus profits could be accomplished only by means of 'a thoroughly institutionalized form of violence'. Moreover, taxes had to be extracted frequently to ensure both the continuity of production and the fiscal solvency of the ruling class. The lord, therefore, needed 'a major "police" presence' which was permanent and mobile, a need met by the lord's chevaliers. 'Their original function may well have been defensive, as claimed by the ideology of the three orders [on this, see Chapter 2]; during the eleventh and twelfth centuries, they were the source of violence rather than its control. Above all, they policed the countryside'. Their main duty was 'the *chevauchée* . . . in which part of the fortress's garrison rode out to reassert its presence and . . . the presence of the banal lord to the subject peasant population'.[2] The members of this policing force themselves came mostly from the subjugated class, but their service to the lords made them a separate group with higher status and greater allegiance to their employers than to their kin.

If feudalism prompted the social rise of the knight for reasons of internal government, knighthood had an enormous impact on the medieval world far beyond western Europe. Feudalism's land dependence imposed severe restrictions on the prospects of a young nobleman's wealth, and the rule of primogeniture ensured that the eldest son, who was presumed to be best able to defend it, inherited his father's estate. The heir's younger brothers were therefore at an economic disadvantage unless they or the family could acquire additional territory. These younger sons received timely technological assistance from the introduction of the stirrup and subsequent improvements to saddles and lances that made the cavalry charge a devastating military advantage. The French became particularly adept in such techniques, and the younger sons from Normandy, who began leaving home in order to hire out their cavalry expertise to ambitious or needy magnates, were soon prominent in the European military scene, first taking control of southern Italy and Sicily in the early to mid-eleventh century and then of England beginning in 1066. None of this would have been possible without a highly skilled, well-trained cadre of horse-borne warriors.

When Pope Urban II called for the first crusade in 1095, it was to prove a boon for this class of would-be lords who eventually established themselves in the eastern Mediterranean. The crusades were, in the words of Norbert Elias, 'the first great movement of expansion and colonization by the Christian West'.[3] With the crusades, also, the first orders of knighthood formed as Christian fraternities, and so the chevaliers established themselves as a comparatively independent, elite segment of society.

Imaginary origins

If the crusades created territorial, economic, and political opportunities for knights, this also gave them a new story to tell about themselves. Even if the crusaders' motives were a response to economic pressures, the crusades made religion a significant factor in the subsequent mythologization of knighthood. The crusades were wars promulgated in the name of the Christian godhead, with the expressed objective of liberating the holy city of Jerusalem from Muslim control. The crusaders' campaigning was therefore characterized as an act of devotion. Crusading had two effects for chivalry: it served to spread throughout most of the known world what had been a localized culture, and 'it brought the church authorities . . . to terms with war and the warrior's place in society'.[4] The pacifistic teachings of Jesus were at odds with the essential work of knighthood. If the gospels blessed the peacemakers and bade the Christian to love his enemies, insisting that he turn the other cheek, then knights did little that conformed to their Saviour's dictum. There was, therefore, a fundamental antagonism between the chevalier and the cleric concerning the matter of violence.

The clergy objected to knighthood on more than ethical grounds. Having a class of men whose primary function is to fight contributes to the proliferation of armed conflict, and even chivalric training activities spawned strife. The early tournament, for example, which differed little from a pitched battle, had deadly consequences. These tournaments were typically staged between towns, and proved to be just as hazardous to the non-combatants as to the knights. Furthermore, tournaments were thought to encourage a host of personal sins (pride, anger, dejection), were wasteful beyond the inevitable destruction of expensive equipment, and frequently brought about the financial ruin of those knights who lost. The damage wrought by real warfare was even greater.

When the time came to muster soldiers for the crusades, though, the pope dispensed indulgences for anyone who undertook the journey to wage war in the Holy Land. The upshot of the Church's accommodation was that violence became a path to salvation. Eventually, as Richard Kaeuper observes, 'Promises of heavenly rewards for crusaders . . . became a blessing on all knightly life.'[5] The crusades, then, were mutually beneficial for the Latin Church and knighthood. They expanded the sphere of the Church's influence by establishing European colonies in the eastern Mediterranean, and brought the chivalric class within the Church's purview. For their part, the knights made good use of Christianity by embracing the notion that their mission was divinely sanctioned and forging a collective identity as a Christian fraternity that transcended geopolitical boundaries.

Advocating that its followers love one another, Christianity contributed yet another dimension to the cult of knighthood when the twelfth-century troubadours from the south of France grafted the language of feudal vassalage onto heterosexual relationships and 'invented' Western romantic love. 'Courtly love', as it was labelled in the nineteenth century, was codified most famously by Andreas Capellanus, who served at the court of Champagne, a centre for arts and learning in the north of the country where the poet Chrétien de Troyes also resided. If force of strength was considered a virtue in battle or tournament, a knight's ability to please, to sing, and to speak well was valued just as highly in court. The demands upon knighthood became more complex as the knight was expected to behave according to a more subtle and refined code when at court, and especially in the company of women. Attending these changes was an increasing elitism among knights as the nobility itself adopted the ideals of the chevalier. When Chrétien wrote the first Arthurian romances around 1170, he joined the sensibilities of the troubadours with the heroics found in the medieval French epics, or *chansons de geste*, and chronicle histories to produce a version of knighthood that reflected its enhanced status and enlarged its reputation. In the fourteenth century this movement towards an elite class of chevalier among the nobility led to the formation of the Order of the Garter in England and the Order of the Star in France.

Whenever it told new stories about itself, chivalry tended to reinvent its origins. Chrétien's retelling of the Arthurian legend embraced what was called the Matter of Britain, which comprised part of chivalric history alongside stories concerning the Matter of France, about the reign of Charlemagne, and that of Rome, which plotted the translation of imperial power from mythical Troy to historical Rome. The Nine Worthies provided chivalric mythographers a grand genealogy and knighthood historical legitimacy. The Nine were a mixture of mythological and historical figures: King David, Joshua, and Judas Maccabeus represented the biblical past; Alexander, Hector, and Julius Caesar, the classical; Arthur, Charlemagne, and the crusader Godfroi de Bouillon came from the Christian world. The Nine Worthies granted knights considerable authority as a class by pushing the beginnings of chivalry back to a point far before its actual origins, thereby delineating a continuum that was virtually synonymous with human civilization. Conspiratorial as this scheme might sound, it didn't come out of the blue but was in fact typical of medieval Christianity's programme to make itself the culmination of all history. The way exegetes read the Hebrew Bible as an incomplete text that required the New Testament for fulfilment offers a relevant example of how Christianity sought to turn the past into occupied territory, not only in the case of Old Testament prophecies but also, for example, in seeing Noah's ark as an allegorical prefiguration of the Church and its role in salvation. When it sought to place itself in history, then, knighthood worked quite naturally within the models provided by its own culture to see itself prefigured in antiquity.

Alongside programmatic fictions like the Nine Worthies, Keen notes the inception of a new mode of secular history when individual families commissioned private historiographers to create a record of events that monastic chroniclers ignored. Consequently, aristocratic paternal lineage became valued to the point where 'true' nobility required at least four generations of 'pure' chivalric breeding behind it. Therefore, in order to meet the standards for such a pedigree it was not unusual for family historians to invent a mythical figure, a kind of private Worthy, who was the 'founder of the dynasty in the heroic past, with whose glory the whole line becomes associated'.[6]

Chaucer's problematic chevalier

Chaucer's pilgrim Knight from the *Canterbury Tales* is perhaps the poet's most prominent chivalric character and has been the focus of much scholarly attention. The last century saw seismic shifts in critical opinion concerning the Knight, much of it centred on his portrait as historically and ideologically representative of his class. Orthodox opinion held that the Knight was a paradigmatic, idealized figure, a nearly transcendent vision of the medieval knight as soldier of the faith. There was nothing to question in the narrator's observation that 'He was a verray, parfit gentil knyght' ('GP' 72).

Critics writing later in the century, however, undertook a profound reassessment of the Knight. Among these, Terry Jones's *Chaucer's Knight: The Portrait of a Medieval Mercenary*, whose title succinctly conveys his thesis, presents a substantive challenge to conservative orthodoxy. Jones follows the network of historical allusion in the Knight's portrait and tale to conclude that Chaucer's Knight was actually a professional soldier of the sort who terrorized Europe in the infamous free companies that formed in the late fourteenth century as a result of the Hundred Years War. Though the Knight's career took him farther afield than the typical free-company soldier, Jones considers him to be the type of elite mercenary epitomized in the Englishman John Hawkwood, who gained wealth and fame as a *condottiere*, or contract soldier, in Italy.

Whatever the inspiration for the Knight, his entourage on the Canterbury pilgrimage offers a profile of the basic mounted battle unit. Because his profession required a sizeable investment in equipment, a knight needed practical assistance, beyond the common practice of elite persons to be accompanied by retainers. A squire, therefore, would serve as an attendant while continuing his professional training to become a knight. The Yeoman, yet another attendant, a free servant, rounds out the group by representing the English archer, who provided a marked advantage in mobility and firepower during the Hundred Years War.

Antiquity and history: the 'Knight's Tale' and *Troilus and Criseyde*

As we have seen, antitheses of idealism and demystification establish the boundaries for critical reception of the Knight. Jones's critique pits the pilgrim and his tale against historical knowledge about fourteenth-century warfare. Other critics see in the tale Chaucer's concern with chivalry as a dominant discourse, and consider the tale to represent the poet's interrogation of the political and social operations of chivalric idealization per se. Two perceptive readers of Chaucer have noted problems in the way that Theseus, the duke of Athens, asserts his rule in the tale. Lee Patterson sees there a display of 'the chivalric mind engaged in an act of self-legitimization that simultaneously and secretly undoes itself.'[7] And Paul Strohm questions the voice of chivalric authority in the tale by explaining, 'Chaucer takes care that his audience understands Theseus to be wrong'.[8]

The tale opens with Theseus returning home from a military campaign on which he has conquered 'al the regne of Femenye' ('KT' 866) and married the Amazon queen. But the grieving widows of generals who died in the recent war against Thebes interrupt his triumphant march into Athens and implore him to enforce their right to bury their husbands, which Creon had denied. Theseus razes Thebes, and here Chaucer affords a glimpse of what the aftermath of a fourteenth-century battle might have looked like:

> To ransake in the taas of bodyes dede,
> Hem for to strepe of harneys and of wede,
> The pilours diden bisynesse and cure
> After the bataille and disconfiture. (1005–8)

The duke departs from convention, though, when he refuses to accept ransom for Palamon and Arcite, two young Theban knights pulled barely alive from a pile of corpses. Ransom was one of the chief sources of profit from medieval warfare, and the fact that Theseus refuses to consider them for exchange suggests that there is more at stake in this campaign than money could represent—and that is the image of knighthood itself.

Once revived, Palamon and Arcite fall to fighting for love of the Amazon princess Emelye. In order to control their violence, Theseus stages an elaborate tournament to determine who will marry her, but the tournament serves also to promulgate his vision of the world. His ultimate goal is territorial, to 'have fully of Thebans obeisaunce' (2974), and to establish his authority he assumes various rhetorical postures—from indignant conquistador to benevolent philosopher–king. He is, as many critics have noted, the voice of the Knight in the tale and the means by which the Knight attempts to establish his own pre-eminence among the group of Canterbury pilgrims. To assert Theseus' authority, the Knight is constantly shutting down potentially dangerous sections of his story, censoring it for his audience by saying that a potentially contradictory aspect in one of his *auctores* is 'to long to heere' (875). But his strategy ultimately fails, and results in an ideological backlash when various pilgrims, the Miller foremost, find his vision unconscionable and attack the Knight in their own tales. As Patterson concludes, 'the severity of control the Knight imposes upon his narrative is in fact the unwilling agent of control's subversion; and the harder he tries to civilize his materials and make them exemplify chivalry's belief in progress, the more evidently he produces formal stasis and moral incoherence'.[9]

Chaucer's other great narrative of chivalry also takes place in the mythic past. *Troilus and Criseyde* is the story of a love affair set during the Trojan War. A strong element driving it is the tension between the chivalric and the courtly, which the poem relates to the spatial poles of exteriority and interiority respectively. Outside the city walls are the Greeks, inhabiting the world of chivalric action, inside is the civic sphere of Priam's court, and the secret domestic recesses of a courtly love affair. The poem explores even more extended spatial extremes than these—the apprehensive psychological interiors of the main characters at one end, and the eighth sphere of the cosmos, and beyond, at the other—but the majority of its narrative concerns the immediate chivalric threat to civic and domestic stability.

The distinct values of these poles, however, are not so stable as their opposition would suggest. Troy might be besieged by Greeks, but it is also, in a way, at the mercy of the very warrior class that defends it, and on whom the attention of the entire population is understandably focused. A consequence of this focus is that the fate of any civic or personal activity is determined ultimately by the political sovereignty of the chevalier. The effect of this force can be seen in Criseyde herself, who first appears in the poem as a defiant, independent character. When she first encounters the haughty young warrior Troilus in the Palladium,

> she let falle
> Hire look a lite aside in swich manere,
> Ascaunces, 'What, may I nat stonden here?' (1. 290–2)

But when she finally succumbs to the spectacle of Troilus, fresh from battle and the object of public adoration, she is overcome, as if drugged: 'Who yaf me drynke?' (2. 651). While Criseyde's swooning is the effect of a powerful personal emotion, we cannot dismiss the influence exerted over her imagination by the public spectacle and adulation combined with Pandarus' promotion of Troilus as the city's saviour. The scene of her enamourment is dominated by the chivalric ethos that the war privileges.

If *Troilus and Criseyde* is a poem of 'double sorwe' (1. 1), it is also a poem that sharply contrasts bifurcated perspectives on violence and the heroic ethos. Despite Pandarus' hyperbole, we should recognize that Troilus is a junior member of the knightly class—even his name carries the diminutive form, meaning 'little Troy'. He might be a second Hector, but he is also naive, sexually inexperienced, and most likely enjoying at some level an adolescent thrill at the violence of combat, the consequences of which he has yet to appreciate fully. Criseyde, on the other hand, is vulnerable through her father's defection and undeniably terrorized by the violence just beyond the city walls. If Troilus rides out with enthusiasm, she trembles in fear of what might happen next. Commenting on this polarity in the poem, Louise O. Fradenburg notes, 'those who commit violence rarely remind us of what it is like to suffer', unless it is to remind us of 'their own capacity to suffer gloriously "*for*" lord, king, nation. Such a heroization of suffering *for*, in the history of the West, typically devalorizes actual suffering . . . For the heroic ideal, survival is a non-noble goal.'[10] The poem is thus in part about the education of Troilus, the making of the chivalric subject, and the cultural authority that would so value violence. If Troilus suffers, it is because he is confronted with these opposing perspectives, similar to the choice Achilles has in the *Iliad* between heroization and survival.

Towards the end of the poem, in despair at his loss of Criseyde, Troilus rides furiously into battle, seeking combat with his rival Diomede and his own death. In a burst of martial hyperbole he is slain 'despitously' by Achilles, but not before he makes the Greeks pay dearly: 'For thousandes his hondes maden deye' (5. 1802–6). To the last he is 'worthi Ector the secounde' (2. 158), but this noble epithet has a double edge. Since the same man who kills his brother kills him, it is possible that Troilus dies in a similar way. We never actually see the demise of Troilus, but with Hector Chaucer shows us how mundanely even the most noble of the ancients dies. And he offers it as something every knight should lament:

> For which me thynketh every manere wight
> That haunteth armes oughte to biwaille
> The deth of hym that was so noble a knyght;
> For as he drough a kyng by th'aventaille,
> Unwar of this, Achilles thorugh the maille
> And thorugh the body gan hym for to ryve;
> And thus this worthi knyght was brought of lyve. (5. 1555–61)

This stanza stages the meeting of two modes of militarism. When he drags down a king by his chain mail, Hector is subduing his adversary by non-lethal means. The Trojan prince and the anonymous Greek king are aristocrats; therefore, it is entirely possible that Hector has chivalric fraternity and the ransom of his captive in mind. But while Hector is so engaged, Achilles kills him from behind. We could say that here a true knight is killed by a false one, which would be to note the death of idealistic chivalry by upstart, violent opportunists. And this is a common observation among scholars of late medieval chivalry, particularly where a person like the mercenary Hawkwood is concerned. It is also an opinion behind Jones's reading of Chaucer when he invokes frequently the 'true spirit of chivalry' as something for which Chaucer and his contemporaries held a nostalgic longing.[11] However, whenever Chaucer probes the past for an era of exemplary chivalry he casts it to work remarkably like his own age, offering a disturbing continuum of violence that links heroisms past and present. Chaucer's writing never fully or openly embraces any of the nostalgic ideals that would legitimize the warrior class, but is dedicated instead to their intense scrutiny. In other words, no amount of aristocratic pageantry, rhetorical refinement, anatomization of honour, or the invocation of antique precedent can obliterate the fact that violence is an integral element of chivalric culture which could not be expunged lest chivalry itself should cease to be. As Kaeuper puts it, 'the bloody-minded side of the code . . . was of the essence of chivalry'.[12]

Chivalry and Chaucer's modernity

In the *Canterbury Tales* a distinction between old chivalry and new courtliness is evident in the pilgrim Knight's own entourage. The Knight is an old campaigner who seems to step onto English soil and into the present of the pilgrimage as if from a different era, 'wholly unconnected to the public life of late fourteenth-century England'.[13] His son the Squire, however, who is more courtier than chevalier, could not be more current. Even so, he participated in the controversial 'chyvachie' of the Despenser crusade 'In hope to stonden in his lady grace' ('GP' 85–8). Even with the new generation, then, the courtly has a military prerequisite. And the *chevauchée* in which the Squire took part was typical of the cavalry raids that wreaked havoc on the countryside throughout the Hundred Years War, when peasants and townspeople became the primary victims of military violence as chivalry took a 'decisive step toward the *jouissance* of massacre as the only way to make war'.[14] The courtly scene of Chaucer's day therefore couldn't help but be infected by the military ethos, however much *fin'amor* might improve the manners of the chevalier.

The Wife of Bath tells a courtly romance, and reveals something of the nefarious undercurrent of chivalric love when she depicts the primal scene of heterosexual relations as inherently violent. Her tale is set 'In th'olde dayes of the Kyng Arthour, | Of which that Britons speken greet honour' ('WBT' 857–8), but it opens on a dishonourable note when a young knight from Arthur's court,

> on a day cam ridynge fro ryver,
> And happed that, allone as he was born,
> He saugh a mayde walkynge hym biforn,

> Of which mayde anon, maugree hir heed,
> By verray force, he rafte hire maydenhed. (884–8)

The episode unfolds quickly and suggests there is little question in the knight's mind about what to do when one comes upon a maiden outside the context of the court. We have no idea who this maiden is—she disappears from the poem with the rape—but she is most likely a peasant. (Kaeuper illustrates well how rape of the lower classes was routinely rationalized by the chivalric imagination.[15]) Arthur sentences the 'lusty bacheler' to death for this rape, but Queen Guinevere intervenes to send him on a year-long quest to discover 'What thyng is it that wommen moost desiren' (905). Only an old woman can tell him the answer, and in return for the information that saves his life, the young knight has to marry the old woman, whom he despises for being 'so loothly, and so oold also, | And therto comen of so lough a kynde' (1100–1). Not only is she old, she also comes from the lower class—'so lough a kynde'. Since *kynde* can also mean nature, it seems her very femaleness, made utterly repulsive to him by her age and combined with her class, makes her despicable.

On their wedding night, however, the old woman delivers a lecture on *gentilesse* (1109–76) that challenges the fundamental principles of gentility to which chevaliers typically lay claim:

> But, for ye speken of swich gentillesse
> As is descended out of old richesse,
> That therfore sholden ye be gentil men,
> Swich arrogance is nat worth an hen. (1109–12)

She contradicts every presumption about lineage and rank that 'true chivalry' valued. Possessions mean nothing, nor do accidents of fortunate birth or titles. Instead, gentility is purely performative: 'he is gentil that dooth gentil dedis' (1170).

In the middle of her speech there is a curiously anachronistic moment when she quotes the poet Dante as an authority on *gentilesse* and stages a radical disruption of the chivalric world of the tale. This allusion would of course be impossible for anyone actually living in the days of Arthur, and is a startling citation to come from the Wife of Bath's narration, despite her demonstrated ability to quote *auctores* at length.

> Wel kan the wise poete of Florence,
> That highte Dant, speken in this sentence.
> Lo, in swich maner rym is Dantes tale:
> 'Ful selde up riseth by his branches smale
> Prowesse of man, for God, of his goodnesse,
> Wole that of hym we clayme oure gentillesse';
> For of our eldres may we no thyng clayme
> But temporel thyng, that man may hurte and mayme. (1125–32)

True *gentilesse* comes from God, not one's ancestors. Dante had reversed the logic of gentility when he wrote in his *Convivio*, 'the stock does not ennoble individuals but individuals ennoble the stock'.[16] Chaucer's old woman is quoting above from the seventh canto of *Purgatorio* in which the shade of the troubadour Sordello describes the Valley of the Rulers, where famous princes wait to ascend the mountain of Purgatory. The text contradicts the old ideas of noble lineage and primogeniture, since Sordello is commenting on the youngest son of the Aragonese King Pedro II, who would have made a better ruler than either of his two older brothers.[17]

By redefining *gentilesse*, the old woman also disentangles the chivalric virtue of prowess that clung to it. Dante says *l'umana probitate*, human worth, does not rise through the branches of a dynasty, and Chaucer translates *probitate* as 'prowesse', which according to Kaeuper 'was truly the demi-god in the quasi-religion of chivalric honour' and made knights 'the privileged practitioners of violence in their society'.[18] Elevated to the status of a virtue, prowess legitimizes violence by attributing moral cause to the effects of sheer force. For a knight, prowess is martial dominance moralized. Asserting that right by necessity stands behind might, the ideology of prowess, too, writes a model of heroic history, working from an effect of power to posit its imagined cause. Through her anachronistic quoting of Dante, the old woman effectively refutes this logic and puts the historic justification of chivalric superiority in a critical context for Chaucer's fourteenth-century readers.

Late medieval chivalric culture was deeply involved in self-representation; hence its indulgence in the elaborate display of signs, like heraldry, and ritualized performances like the tournament to maintain its dominance. But signifiers, as poets have always known, are unstable, even volatile, things. For the Wife of Bath as pilgrim–narrator, as for the old woman of her tale, prowess no longer resides in feats of arms. Hers is a decidedly 'feminine' language, dismissing essentialized class distinctions and the dominance of any man who would embrace such a philosophy. By appropriating the language of the court and chivalry—giving new meanings to *gentilesse* and *prowesse*, and a new definition of wealth—the Wife, through the medium of her fiction, mounts a concerted reformist attack on chivalry and all it engenders.

The 'Franklin's Tale' is also forthrightly concerned with the definition of *gentilesse*, and tells how a knight, a squire, and a lady negotiate the dangerous terrain of gentility. But while the 'Franklin's Tale' is about a chevalier and a courtier, its narrator, though like Chaucer himself a knight of the shire ('GP' 356), is hardly a member of the knightly class. It is therefore appropriate that class tensions over the status of knighthood and its claims to *gentilesse* are apparent from the very beginning of the Franklin's performance.[19]

The tale is set in Brittany, where the English *chevalerie* was very active in the late fourteenth century, but the ambience of the tale is courtly. Indeed, the only properly chivalric military adventure takes place to the north-west, beyond the horizon in England 'that cleped was *eek* Briteyne' (my italics), and thus cast as a homophonous chivalric otherworld where the knight Arveragus goes 'To seke in armes worshipe and honour' ('FrT' 810–1). A lot rests on this *eek* in so far as it implies that all the distance and difference associated with Britain cannot suppress the *also*, which joins the two realms together in more than name. In other words, Britain as the scene of chivalric violence—arms and honour—though beyond the horizon and out of sight, haunts the tale's courtly Brittany like an allegorical spectre, an eerie version of itself. The tale's audience has to imagine what Arveragus is doing over there and cannot escape the suggestion that the two realms share more than a name, and furthermore that gentility between men in civil society can work as a medium of chivalric violence when its end is the generation of 'honour' and when a woman has to suffer the brunt of masculine ambition. This convergence of interests is precisely what the tale offers when Arveragus returns home to find Dorigen in the difficult situation of having to break either her word to the squire or her fidelity to her marriage vows.

Being true to one's word was a central element in the chevalier's code, and Arveragus upholds this principle, much to Dorigen's dismay, by requiring her to fulfil her agreement to sleep with Aurelius when she believes he has fulfilled her rash, impossible request to remove all the rocks from the coastline. When Aurelius learns of the knight's gentility, he releases her from her promise, and then attempts to arrange an easier payment plan with the philosopher who generated the illusion. When the philosopher wipes out the squire's debt, the narrator closes the story by asking the audience, 'Which was the mooste fre, as thynketh yow?' (1622). The story thus ends on a profoundly inconclusive note, despite its seemingly happy ending. Who really was the most generous? And does the question even begin to consider Dorigen's perspective?

At this point it might behove us to read the tale 'backwards' through the lens the philosopher provides, because the question of who was the most 'free' is perhaps misleading. Reading the story from the perspective of the philosopher, a figure utterly outside the courtly circle of the story and uninvested in its social exchanges, casts the courtly economy of magnanimity in a different light. The loss of payment for services rendered is inconsequential to the philosopher, who in fact turns the sequence of debt back on itself by expunging Aurelius' account, leaving him both grateful and financially solvent. The philosopher's role as learned producer of illusions casts the entire aristocratic social economy, and especially the tenets of chivalric honour behind it, as a greater illusion than anything he could conjure.

The mercurial qualities of courtly currency are in fact apparent from the outset. If we examine the marriage agreement Dorigen and Arveragus strike within the tale's first thirty lines, we see that the latter is acutely cognizant of the subtle relationship between power and public performance. The tale opens by introducing us to

> a knyght that loved and dide his payne
> To serve a lady in his beste wise;
> And many a labour, many a greet emprise,
> He for his lady wroghte er she were wonne. (730–3)

The Franklin gives us a portrait of the lover as Hercules, undertaking great labours for the sake of his beloved. Dorigen's beauty and lineage, however, place her in a superior social position to Arveragus. His labours are undertaken in duress because class status determines he cannot broach the subject of love with her:

> wel unnethes dorste this knyght, for drede,
> Telle hire his wo, his peyne, and his distresse.
> But atte laste she, for his worthynesse,
> And namely for his meke obeysaunce,
> Hath swich a pitee caught of his penaunce
> That pryvely she fil of his accord
> To take hym for hir housbonde and hir lord,
> Of swich lordshipe as men han over hir wyves. (736–43)

This world of prohibited speech necessitates the performance of desire, 'peyne', and 'distresse' through alternate means. The courtly world thus becomes a zone of discursive doubleness where what is said and what is done cannot possibly match up. Should we think the ground rules are any different once Dorigen and Arveragus finally speak? Arveragus proposes a comparatively egalitarian marriage in which

> nevere in al his lyf he, day ne nyght,
> Ne sholde upon hym take no maistrie
> Agayn hir wyl. (746–8)

The marriage proposal concludes quickly when Arveragus introduces the exception that he would retain 'the *name* of soveraynetee, | . . . for shame of his degree' (751–2, my italics). As long as he can appear to be her master in public, in the arena of speech where he was heretofore subservient, he will be happy. Their marriage is thus founded on the possibility of a decisive split between public performance and private reality.

The narrator then praises the egalitarian qualities of love, only to close on a curious note:

> Heere may men seen an humble, wys accord;
> Thus hath she take hir servant and hir lord—
> Servant in love, and lord in mariage.
> Thanne was he bothe in lordshipe and servage.
> Servage? Nay, but in lordshipe above,
> Sith he hath bothe his lady and his love. (791–6)

This passage plays off several courtly conventions; for example, that love is distinct from marriage, and that the lover is the 'free thrall' who willingly enters into bondage for the sake of his beloved. But the Franklin pauses, wondering at the accuracy of servitude as a way to describe Arveragus' position: 'Servage? Nay, but in lordshipe above'. The knight has actually gained the upper hand through a discourse of submission, and the effective distinction between private and public relations, the potency and essential validity of the former over the latter, is obliterated. Moreover, this is the first step in a shift that sees Dorigen change from an independent, discerning woman into a 'thing' when she becomes a token of fraternity and 'freedom' exchanged in the chivalric economy.

By demonstrating that servitude functions as lordship, the Franklin has identified what Slavoj Žižek calls the 'masochistic theatre of courtly love'. Dismissing as fallacious the symmetry of sadism to masochism, where dominance and submission supposedly complement one another, Žižek illustrates how the dramatic narrative of the masochistic contract works to assert the power of the masochist over the scene of his submission. 'It is the servant', he says, 'who writes the screenplay . . . he stages his own servitude.'[20] In the 'Franklin's Tale', Arveragus' private submission to Dorigen is the first move in a sequence of exchanges that will put her under the thumb of the chevalier's code.

The 'Franklin's Tale' operates as if it were taking place in a theatrical otherworld, where a field of unimaginable power relations requires that one execute an inverted strategy in order to win the game. The progress of negotiations reveals to us that the characters are in a place similar to Chaucer's Troy, where the gaze of power is external to the spheres of courtly *politesse* and private desire. Through its inversion of space and social protocols, the tale lets slip that however much emphasis the knightly class might put on *gentilesse*, the source of its power and its very identity ultimately reside just over the horizon in that deadly otherworld where knights seek worship and honour in arms.

Conclusion

Between the late 1370s and early 1380s, before *Troilus and Criseyde* and well before the *Canterbury Tales*, Chaucer wrote the *Parliament of Fowls*, a dream vision about a hierarchical avian congress whose primary order of business is to ratify the natural order by choosing mates. Nature privileges the aristocratic 'foules of ravyne' (323), three tercel eagles who have their eyes on a single female, who has all the attributes of a courtly lady (372–8). When none of the tercels will relinquish his claim, the young tercelet remarks,

> '. . . I can not se that argumentes avayle:
> Thanne semeth it there moste be batayle.'
> 'Al redy!' quod these egles tercels tho. (538–40)

Political negotiations can accomplish nothing. Battle is the only solution, and the eagles respond with an emphatic 'Ay'. The *Parliament* shows, however, that the eagles can be brought to accept a more 'civilized' and less brutal form of proceeding, in line with the female's refusal to mate at present: clearly martial prowess, experience, status, and lineage are insufficient for her. But the old ideals died hard, and the first and most 'senior' of the yet-to-be-written *Tales* would return to the idealization of chivalric combat, to the passive woman who is won by it, and to the utility of martial slaughter.

FURTHER READING

Fradenburg, Louise O. Aranye, *Sacrifice your Love: Psychoanalysis, Historicism, Chaucer* (Minneapolis: University of Minnesota Press, 2002). Chivalric group identity and its relation to the principle of sacrifice are examined in this book, which wields psychoanalytical theory to present an innovative model of historicist inquiry.

Haidu, Peter, *The Subject of Violence: The 'Song of Roland' and the Birth of the State* (Bloomington: Indiana University Press, 1993). A sophisticated treatment of the *Song of Roland* that establishes the role of violence in feudal society as an important force in the formation of the nation-state.

Jones, Terry, *Chaucer's Knight: The Portrait of a Medieval Mercenary*, rev. edn. (London: Methuen, 1994). The two parts of this book detail the historical evidence in the 'General Prologue' portrait of the Knight and in his tale. Jones argues that the Knight is a professional soldier whose career presents a critique of fourteenth-century militarism.

Kaeuper, Richard W., *Chivalry and Violence in Medieval Europe* (Oxford: Oxford University Press, 1999). Using numerous literary sources, Kaeuper outlines the problem of chivalric violence and a number of responses to it. He argues that chivalry was as much a part of the problem as of the solution.

Keen, Maurice, *Chivalry* (New Haven: Yale University Press, 1984). This study offers a comprehensive overview of chivalry in the Middle Ages. It presents a review of major chivalric activity and informative discussions on such topics as heraldry, pageantry, and rituals.

Leicester, H. Marshall, Jr., *The Disenchanted Self: Representing the Subject in the 'Canterbury Tales'* (Berkeley and Los Angeles: University of California Press, 1990). Part 3, 'The Institution of the Subject: A Reading of the "Knight's Tale"' (pp. 219–382), offers an extensive investigation of the Knight as a character 'disenchanted' with chivalry and the epistemological order it entails.

Patterson, Lee, *Chaucer and the Subject of History* (Madison: University of Wisconsin Press, 1991). The topic of this book is the tension in Chaucer's poetry between history and subjectivity. The chapter on the 'Knight's Tale' argues chivalry's inability to rethink itself in the face of social and economic changes.

Sumption, Jonathan, *The Hundred Years War, ii: Trial by Fire* (Philadelphia: University of Pennsylvania Press, 1999). This volume is the second of a projected three-volume history of the Hundred Years War. It presents a thorough treatment of Anglo-French relations during the later fourteenth century.

Zeikowitz, Richard E., *Homoeroticism and Chivalry: Discourses in Male Same-Sex Desire in the Fourteenth Century* (New York: Palgrave-Macmillan, 2003). Zeikowitz draws on queer and psychoanalytic theories to read homoeroticism in representations of chivalric society, where he argues for fluidity between homoerotic and heterosexual desires.

NOTES

1. Peter Haidu, *The Subject of Violence: The 'Song of Roland' and the Birth of the State* (Bloomington: Indiana University Press, 1993), 50.
2. Ibid. 51–2.
3. Norbert Elias, *The Civilizing Process*, trans. Edmund Jephcott (Oxford: Blackwell, 1994), 294.
4. Maurice Keen, *Chivalry* (New Haven: Yale University Press, 1984), 44.

5. Richard W. Kaeuper, *Chivalry and Violence in Medieval Europe* (Oxford: Oxford University Press, 1999), 48.

6. Keen, *Chivalry*, 32–3.

7. Lee Patterson, *Chaucer and the Subject of History* (Madison: University of Wisconsin Press, 1991), 169.

8. Paul Strohm, *Social Chaucer* (Cambridge, Mass.: Harvard University Press, 1989), 133.

9. *Chaucer and the Subject of History*, 169.

10. Louise O. Fradenburg, ' "Our owen wo to drynke": Loss, Gender and Chivalry in *Troilus and Criseyde*', in R. A. Shoaf (ed.) with Catherine S. Cox, *Chaucer's 'Troilus and Criseyde': 'Subgit to alle Poesye'* (Binghamton: Medieval and Renaissance Texts and Studies, 1992), 89.

11. Terry Jones, *Chaucer's Knight: The Portrait of a Medieval Mercenary*, rev. edn. (London: Methuen, 1994), *passim*, but see esp. pp. 8–13 and 179–86.

12. *Chivalry and Violence*, 15.

13. Patterson, *Chaucer and the Subject of History*, 179.

14. Louise O. Aranye Fradenburg, *Sacrifice your Love: Psychoanalysis, Historicism, Chaucer* (Minneapolis: University of Minnesota Press, 2002), 216.

15. *Chivalry and Violence*, 225.

16. Dante Alighieri, *Dante's Convivio*, trans. William Walrond Jackson (Oxford: Clarendon Press, 1909), 4. 20. 5.

17. Dante Alighieri, *The Divine Comedy* ii: *Purgatorio*, trans. Charles S. Singleton (Princeton: Princeton University Press, 1972), 7. 121–3.

18. *Chivalry and Violence*, 130.

19. This Franklin, it is worth noting, demonstrates his aspirations towards the social status of a knight when he expresses his wish that his own son were more like the pilgrim Squire ('SqT' 673 ff.).

20. Slavoj Žižek, 'Courtly Love, or, Woman as Thing', in his *The Metastases of Enjoyment: Six Essays on Women and Causality* (London: Verso, 1994), 89.

7 | Literacy and literary production

Stephen Penn

> So whan I saw I might not slepe
> Til now late this other night,
> Upon my bed I sat upright
> And bad oon reche me a book,
> A romaunce, and he it me tok
> To rede and drive the night away;
> For me thoughte it better play
> Then playe either at ches or tables.
>
> (*BD* 44–51)

References to the act of reading are widespread in Chaucer's poetry. Narrators frequently present themselves as private or public readers, and there are literary depictions of a wide variety of readerly activities: the delivery of sermons or lectures, the recital of poetry, and the perusal of codices, manuscripts, and inscriptions. The distinction between a private and a public readership is an important one, as it rests on the broader distinction between literacy and illiteracy. Written texts will obviously not be produced for an illiterate audience, and Latin texts will not be read by a community of readers who are literate only in their native vernacular. The majority of manuscripts produced in England before the thirteenth century were composed for an educated ecclesiastical audience (a tiny, but immensely powerful, proportion of the population), rather than for a lay readership. The relatively large number of vernacular manuscripts surviving from the fourteenth century, many of which contain secular, rather than theological or religious, material, suggests that, as the century progressed, an increasing number of these would have been prepared with a literate lay readership in mind.

If Chaucer was writing in a period when an ability to read English was becoming more widespread, however, it would be a mistake simply to assume that all of his poems were written for, and consumed by, a private audience; the way in which his work was published, and the social composition of his audience, are known to have changed significantly from the time at which he began writing (*c*.1368) until his death at the end of the century. The famous illustration on the frontispiece to the Cambridge Corpus Christi *Troilus* manuscript (MS 61)—see Figure I.5—seems to depict Chaucer reading before an assembled courtly audience, and there are many invocations within his work to what would seem to be an imaginary auditor, rather than a reader. Though

Fig. I.5 The poem being read before a court audience. Frontispiece to a manuscript of Chaucer's *Troilus and Criseyde*, early fifteenth century (Cambridge Corpus Christi College, MS 61).

it is no longer fashionable to regard the illustration as a reliable guide to the composition of Chaucer's audience, or even as an indication of the way in which his texts might typically have reached an audience, speculation about the reception of Chaucer's poetry continues to fuel critical debate. This impressive work of art, therefore, if it can tell us relatively little about the context of reception of Chaucer's poetry, can at least serve to remind us that literary production and reception in late medieval England extended beyond the boundaries of the development of literacy.

Literacy

The question of literacy in medieval Europe is one that has occupied a relatively marginal place within the academy until recently. Popular perceptions of the Middle Ages as a benighted period of cultural decline and intellectual torpor have not been easy to alter, and there has been a tendency to regard literacy—however this broad and potentially confusing term is construed—as something which did not flower until the Renaissance, or even the eighteenth century. Part of the difficulty, as Michael Clanchy has observed, has been the primacy accorded to 'print culture' within the academy; the arrival of print in early modern Europe has been seen to have marked a revolution, 'the starting point of a new age'.[1] But cultures of writing existed for several thousands of years before the development of print, and manuscripts, no less than printed documents, required literate minds if they were to be understood. Any transition between a predominantly oral, or 'pre-literate' society, and one in which reading could be practised by a proportion of the population, must be seen to have been at least as monumental as the evolution of print, if not more so. To bring literacy properly into focus, Clanchy argues, we need to understand the history of printing differently, and to see the book as a product not of early modern *print* culture, but of medieval *literate* culture. The development of printing should be construed not as a departure point, but as the emergence of a technology which responded to the demands of an increasingly literate population. The transition between pre-literate and literate culture in England was, of course, very gradual, but the growth of literacy in late medieval England placed Chaucer and his contemporaries at what is arguably the most significant point in its history.

Modern conceptions of literacy differ quite markedly from those that existed in late medieval educational theory. Today we might describe as 'literate' people who can read and write in their native language, or, more generally, those who have been educated. The Latin term *litteratus* (or *litterata*), by contrast, would normally designate an individual who was able to read Latin (or, by extension, one who had acquired knowledge, through reading Latin texts, of a particular field of learning). Latin, which, alongside Greek and Hebrew, was regarded in the Middle Ages as a 'holy' language, was the principal vehicle of European philosophical, theological, and legal discourse. An ability to *read* the language gave access to a vast range of authoritative documents, and to the most important text of the medieval Christian world: the Bible. After the Norman Conquest of 1066 French became the language of the court in England, and its status was correspondingly magnified. It never acquired the prestige of Latin, however, and its uses beyond the court were relatively limited. Reading English was a poor substitute for reading Latin, whatever the text, and no reader of English alone would normally have been regarded as 'literate'. The situation in respect of the other European vernaculars had initially been very similar, but both French and Italian had begun to be used more regularly as literary and administrative languages in their respective territories by the twelfth century. English, which did not flourish as a literary language until the second half of the fourteenth century, was rather out of step with this tradition. Nevertheless, it is still possible to argue that Chaucer was writing at a time in which the production of vernacular literature throughout Europe was gaining momentum.

The most famous literary apologist for the vernacular is probably the Italian poet Dante Alighieri, whose important treatise on vernacular writing, *De vulgari eloquentia* ('On Eloquence in the Vernacular'), was written in the first decade of the fourteenth century, some years before Chaucer's birth. It is rather telling that, like the theologian and heresiarch John Wyclif at the end of the century, who presented compelling and controversial arguments about the need for an English vernacular Bible,[2] Dante felt the need to defend the vernacular through the medium of Latin. In the treatise he stresses the importance not merely of writing effectively in the vernacular, but also of the need to recognize the *primacy* of the vernacular European languages over Latin:

Harum quoque duarum nobilior est vulgaris: tum quia prima fuit humano generi usitata; tum quia totus orbis ipsa perfruitur, licet in diversas prolationes et vocabula sit divisa; tum quia naturalis est nobis, cum illa potius artificialis existat.

(Of these two kinds of language, the more noble is the vernacular: first, because it was the language originally used by the human race; second, because the whole world employs it, though with different pronunciations and using different words; and third, because it is natural to us, while the other is, in contrast, artificial.)[3]

Chaucer is unlikely to have been familiar with these words, but was a great admirer of the Italian poet. Like Dante, he was actively seeking to promote the vernacular through his own writing, even if, as Piero Boitani has argued, he felt that he would never be worthy to emulate Dante's great poem the *Divine Comedy*.[4] His translation of Boethius' *De consolatione philosophiae* ('On the Consolation of Philosophy')—a text on which he relied heavily in both *Troilus and Criseyde* and the *Canterbury Tales*—is an implicit acknowledgement of the need to bring Latin texts to a vernacular readership, and of the potential of the English vernacular to serve as a literary and philosophical language. In the proem to *Anelida and Arcite* he is more explicit, suggesting that his purpose is 'in Englyssh to endyte' an 'olde storie' which he originally read in Latin (8–10). But Chaucer also translated into English the massive thirteenth-century *Roman de la Rose* of the French poets Guillaume de Lorris and Jeun de Meun, and used Guillaume de

Deguilleville's *La pèlerinage de la vie humaine* ('The Pilgrimage of Human Life') as the basis for his short devotional lyric 'An ABC' (possibly his earliest poem, normally classified as a 'translation').

Chaucer's contemporaries John Gower, William Langland, and the *Pearl*-poet shared his faith in the English vernacular: Gower wrote in English, French, and Latin (the volume of vernacular writing by far exceeding that of the Latin, and the volume of English that of the French), and Langland and the *Pearl*-poet brought issues of theological and political importance into their English works (as did the many 'vernacular theologians' of the fourteenth and fifteenth centuries). We cannot, of course, be sure how often these works were read privately rather than in public, but the quantity of manuscripts surviving attests to their popularity (all poets except the *Pearl*-poet have works surviving in more than twenty copies), and can only increase the likelihood that they would often have been circulated among private readers. That a significant minority of the population of fourteenth- and fifteenth-century England would indeed have been able to read English is suggested by the political disturbances that arose out of the publication of the Wycliffite Bible (probably late in the 1380s). Vernacular literacy posed an obvious threat to the literate elite of churchmen and ecclesiastical administrators, since it offered the laity the opportunity to read and interpret the Bible for themselves. The desire to read in the vernacular was clearly felt by a good number of laymen and women, as the following passage illustrates:

Siþen þat þe trouþe of God stondiþ not in oo langage more þan in anoþer, but who so lyueþ best and techiþ best plesiþ moost God, of what langage þat euer it be, þerfore þe lawe of God writen and tauȝt in Englisch may edifie þe commen pepel, as it doiþ clerkis in Latyn, siþen it is þe sustynance to soulis þat shulden be saued.

(Since God's truth is conveyed no more in one language than in another, and since the person who lives and teaches in the best way pleases God most, whatever his or her language, therefore the law of God written and taught in English may guide the common people, as it does scholars in Latin, since it provides food for those souls that will be saved.)[5]

The author of this text, a fifteenth-century Wycliffite, apparently identifies himself with the 'commen pepel', a group more numerous, if less privileged, than the 'clerkis' who read Latin. The possibility that laymen and women should be equipped to read the Bible for themselves, without the mediation of a priest or other Church minister (an ideal of which John Wyclif had probably only dreamed), was perceived by many ecclesiasts as undesirable at best. This is clear from the fact that so many vernacular Wycliffite tracts circulated anonymously, and from the emergence, in the early fifteenth century, of legislation which sought to extinguish the flame of vernacular religious writing altogether. The Constitutions, instituted by Archbishop Thomas Arundel between 1407 and 1409, forbade the ownership of vernacular translations of Scripture, and severely limited the extent to which vernacular theological texts could be circulated. Nicholas Watson, who has perhaps done most to highlight the literary-historical significance of the Constitutions, has gone as far as to suggest that this piece of legislation was responsible for the perceived limitations, or aesthetic poverty, of much fifteenth-century literature (as opposed to that of Chaucer and his contemporaries).[6] (For more on Wyclif, see Chapters 16 and 19.)

The Constitutions are likely to have had a negligible impact on the circulation of Chaucer's poetry, whose secular focus placed it beyond the immediate concerns of the ecclesiastical administration. However, the fact that this legislation was deemed to be necessary can, at the very least, act as an index of the growth in vernacular literacy in the late fourteenth and early fifteenth centuries. This is only confirmed by Chaucer's own remarks and authorial practice. Though his fictional portrayals of the act of reading are often highly conventional, they would clearly be meaningless to a culture for whom reading was an entirely foreign activity. There can be no doubt that his imagination was stimulated by the idea of reading, and of the literate audience, from the beginning of his literary career. There is little to separate the dreamer of the *Book of the Duchess*, who reads to pass the night away, from the bookish narrator of the *Legend of Good Women*, who tells his audience, proudly, that 'ther is game noon | That fro my bokes maketh me to goon' (*LGW* (F) 33–4), even though these poems were written more than a decade apart. This point aside, it is certainly true that the narratorial voices of *Troilus* and the *Canterbury Tales* often seem to acknowledge that they may be addressing themselves both to an audience of listeners and to a private reader. At the end of the *Troilus*, immediately after his remarks on the variety of English dialects, Chaucer declares that the poem may be 'red' or 'elles songe', in apparent recognition of the fact that his audience would include literate readers as well as auditors (*TC* 5. 1797). Likewise, in the opening lines of his famous Retraction (at the end of the *Canterbury Tales*), he is very clear about his distinction between reading and listening; there can be no doubt that here he makes a deliberate opposition between the experience of reading privately, and of being read to:

Now preye I to hem alle that herkne this litel tretys or rede, that if ther be any thyng in it that liketh hem, that therof they thanken oure Lord Jhesu Crist, of whom procedeth al wit and al goodnesse. (1081)

These parting words supply one of the few unambiguous indications that the *Canterbury Tales* was devised with two modes of reception in mind. The pilgrim–narrator, throughout the main body of the text, is apparently inconsistent in his invocations to his audience, sometimes addressing the reader of a manuscript ('Turne over the leef and chese another tale', 'MP' 3177), and at others, members of an assembled company of auditors ('as ye shuln heere', 'NPE' 4652). To add to the confusion, the verbs 'heren', 'speken' and 'tellen' are all used loosely, often apparently to address a reader rather than a listener, or possibly to describe the reader's position as one who, in effect, *overhears* the pilgrims' tales. If we are able to draw a conclusion from these apparently conflicting pieces of evidence, it must surely be that Chaucer's medieval audience consisted neither exclusively of readers, nor exclusively of auditors, but of a mixture of the two whose relative proportions changed over time (the readers gradually displacing the auditors).

This broad inference is supported by the manuscript evidence. The Ellesmere manuscript of the *Canterbury Tales*, with its extravagant, costly decorations and marginal illustrations, cannot have been prepared simply as a prompt book for a public reader. It contains frequent Latin glosses in the margins, sometimes identifying literary and biblical sources, section headings, verse paragraph breaks (identified by the term *pausacio*) and the names of topics and literary characters. Each of these features would seem to indicate that its editor and prospective users or owners must have been educated to a relatively advanced level. Latin glosses in the manuscripts of the *Tales* are not unusual; they occur in more than twenty of the earlier manuscripts. Some are superficial instructions or headings ('nota', 'nota bene', 'quaestio', and so on), whereas others are relatively lengthy citations from sources (mainly biblical), with occasional observations on the text. Whether any of the Latin glosses which occur in Ellesmere and elsewhere are authorial must remain a matter for speculation (many obviously cannot have been), but whatever their origin, it was clearly believed that they would be helpful to the fifteenth-century readers of the text. Some are sufficiently extensive to suggest that the *Tales* must have prompted sophisticated debate and analysis. Graham Caie has argued persuasively that the 'Wife of Bath's Prologue', for example, which is heavily glossed in many manuscripts, serves an *interpretative* function in Ellesmere, rather than a purely mnemonic one.[7] This is not the place to attempt a detailed analysis either of the manuscripts themselves, or of their circulation. But we can, at the very least, be sure that Chaucer's readers grew steadily in number as the fifteenth century progressed, and that the steady rise in literacy was to continue to be accommodated by the developing technologies of textual production (for more on the Chaucer manuscripts, see Chapter 28).

Chaucer's medieval audience

Considered in its historical entirety, Chaucer's medieval audience of readers and listeners is likely to have been more socially diverse than the illustration in the *Troilus* manuscript suggests. Even if there can be little doubt that the audience depicted in the frontispiece is a courtly audience, it would be a mistake to assume that the scene bore a close relation to any recognizable 'reality'. The picture is, as Derek Pearsall has remarked, nothing if not 'highly stylized', and draws upon a host of recognizable conventions, few of which are directly representational (despite the fact that the figures of Richard II and Chaucer himself are readily identifiable).[8] The auditors are all elegantly dressed, sitting among flowers and trees, with intricately decorated castles and skyline in the background. However, critics have been puzzled by the fact that the figure standing before a lectern in the centre of the picture, if he is addressing the audience, is not obviously reading, and does not have a manuscript in front of him. This point aside, it is quite likely that Chaucer would have had opportunities to read publicly from his work, and, on occasion, to speak before a courtly audience. Nevertheless, it would be rash to assume that all, or even most, of his poetry would have been delivered formally in this way.

Though the audiences which are inscribed into Chaucer's texts—such as the Canterbury pilgrims and the listeners addressed by the narrator of *Troilus and Criseyde*—can offer us an insight into medieval storytelling and narrative convention, these audiences are clearly not to be confused with what we might identify as the 'implied reader' of those texts. The term 'implied reader' was introduced by Wayne C. Booth in the early 1960s, and was first used in a Chaucerian context by Paul Strohm. Such a reader might be identified as the one who is most obviously *anticipated* by the text, in such a way as to represent 'the sum of all the author's assumptions about the persons he or she is addressing'.[9] Although the aristocracy owned and used a large number of manuscript books, many of which contained romances and other similar narratives (Chaucer the pilgrim's suggestion that the 'Knight's Tale' would have appealed to 'the gentils everichon' is not a mistaken claim, 'MP' 3113), it would be wrong to assume that the implied reader of Chaucer's texts would have been exclusively aristocratic (an assumption which the texts themselves often seem to contradict), or that reading English was itself an activity confined to the top end of the social hierarchy. This is not true of the practice of reading, writing, or speaking French, which was indeed predominantly a courtly activity, though it also extended to some branches of civil administration and to the colleges of Oxford and Cambridge. This is not to say that it would have been impossible for members of the other social classes to learn French, given that grammatical treatises about the French language are known to have circulated quite widely throughout the late medieval period. Its aristocratic associations, nevertheless, were very clearly apparent to Chaucer himself; his depiction of the Prioress, whose social pretensions are betrayed by her use of Anglo-Norman, demonstrates a very acute awareness of the values associated with the language of the court, which modelled itself—often unsuccessfully—on Parisian French.

It is quite possible that Chaucer may have experimented with French early in his career, but in the absence of firm evidence we can only speculate. The very fact that only his English vernacular works survive would seem to suggest that any desire to write in the language of the court had forsaken him early, if it had existed at all. Nevertheless, if the desire to regard Chaucer as a court poet has waned in recent years, it has certainly not disappeared. It would be wrong, moreover, to seek to claim that his connections with the court were without significance. He is known to have worked as a squire for both Edward III and the duke of Lancaster, John of Gaunt. Some of his poems were, with varying degrees of explicitness, dedicated to royal patrons (Richard II, Queen Anne, and John of Gaunt), and he was clearly conscious of his debt to the court. Nevertheless, we cannot regard the fourteenth-century royal household as the equivalent of the court of Charlemagne (747–814), which has long been renowned as one of the key centres of literary and artistic patronage in medieval Europe.

If John of Gaunt and Richard II were supportive of Chaucer's poetic efforts, neither was engaged directly with the processes of literary production. Though it would be wrong to dismiss the court from our analysis of Chaucer's audience altogether, it would clearly be equally unwise to suppose that it occupied a focal role throughout his career. More important, as Pearsall has suggested in his influential biography of Chaucer, was the expansion of Chaucer's influence in the latter stages of his career.

The 'Chaucer circle'

Strohm has argued that Chaucer's 'core audience' would have consisted principally of 'social equals or near-equals', but he is careful to stress that the label itself should not be used to designate a uniform and invariable social group.[10] Chaucer himself was born into a mercantile London family, and would only mix with the aristocracy later in life. However, he apparently enjoyed the same educational privileges (to judge, at least, from his knowledge of Latin, French, and Italian) as the typical aristocrat or ecclesiast.[11] The mercantile classes represented a powerful social group, both as consumers and as producers, and acted as a necessary component of the increasingly commercialized publishing industry. Since Chaucer did not dwell solely among the emergent middle classes of London, however, we cannot rashly assume that they would have constituted his 'core' audience, even if many among such an audience would have been equipped to purchase and read from manuscript copies of his work. This, of course, leaves a significant problem: if Chaucer's audience is likely to have been neither exclusively aristocratic, nor predominantly mercantile, then where else might it be located?

Pearsall was not the first to draw attention to the possibility that Chaucer, at the height of his literary career, would have been addressing a wider audience than that of the court which he had enjoyed in his youth, and that his later audience would have extended beyond the immediate households of Richard II and Henry IV. R. T. Lenaghan introduced the term 'circle' to describe the group of friends and associates with which the poet would habitually have mixed in the royal households, in a deliberate attempt to look beyond the upper echelons of the court.[12] If these friends were indeed members of his audience, then it is clear that Chaucer might have been directing his poetic efforts to a group which was neither straightforwardly aristocratic nor mercantile. Sir Peter Bukton, Henry Scogan, and Sir Philip de la Vache are seen as key members of this circle, as each of them is addressed, directly or indirectly, in one or more of Chaucer's short poems (key among them, of course, being 'Lenvoy de Chaucer a Scogan' and 'Lenvoy de Chaucer a Bukton'). These individuals were all lay administrators in royal households, members of what Lenaghan identifies as a 'nascent civil service'.[13] Relations among them, he suggests, were defined not simply by their common allegiance to the king (which he describes as a 'vertical' relation), but also by their membership of a self-contained social circle (a 'lateral' relation among social equals on the outer fringes of the court).[14] This is a compelling argument, but it needs to be examined carefully. Of the three men, only Henry Scogan, a squire in the household of Henry IV, can be identified unproblematically with the addressee of the respective text by Chaucer. The poem is clearly addressed to a close friend, and not merely to a casual professional associate. The concluding section lavishes praise upon Scogan in a way which is typical of the poem as a whole:

> Scogan, that knelest at the stremes hed
> Of grace, of alle honour and worthynesse,
> In th'ende of which strem I am dul as ded,
> Forgete in solytarie wildernesse—
> Yet, Scogan, thenke on Tullius kyndenesse;
> Mynne thy frend, there it may fructyfye!
> Far-wel, and loke thow never eft Love dyffye.
>
> ('Lenvoy de Chaucer a Scogan', 43–9)

Peter Bukton and Philip de la Vache are also attractive candidates for membership of the 'Chaucer circle', but are not known for certain to have been the addressees of poems and verse-epistles. Nevertheless, the theory of the court circle, or what Lenaghan chooses to describe as 'Chaucer's circle of gentlemen and clerks',[15] cannot be dismissed. There can be no doubt that Chaucer mixed with a large number of people in his position as a court official, and it seems likely that, at the very least, his experiences within the royal households would have brought new members to his literary audience. The fact that he addresses his short poems not merely to members of the high aristocracy (Richard II, Queen Anne, and Henry IV), but to friends and associates, seems to suggest that it is indeed quite likely that his 'courtly' audience would have consisted of 'gentlemen' and 'clerks', as well as princes, kings, and queens.

Beyond the three names highlighted by Lenaghan, there are a host of other groups who might have formed part of the Chaucer circle. Among the most significant of these are a group of individuals who are normally identified as 'Lollard knights', a label first coined by W. T. Waugh, and redefined by K. B. McFarlane in his influential study *Lancastrian Kings and Lollard Knights*.[16] The Lollard knights, on McFarlane's definition (and that of virtually all subsequent commentators), were members of the lay nobility who may have harboured, but were not defined by their subscription to, Lollard beliefs and opinions, and who certainly enjoyed the protection of the royal household. Their political and theological convictions aside, the majority of these men are known to have been acquaintances of Chaucer, and to have been familiar with his work. Sir John Clanvowe, perhaps the most distinguished among them, was himself a poet, and his *Boke of Cupide*, a dream poem which tells of a contest between the Cuckoo and the Nightingale, was written in the tradition of Chaucer's *Parliament of Fowls* (to which it is certainly indebted). A possible allusion to Queen Anne's visit to Woodstock in 1389 has led John Scattergood to regard it as an occasional courtly poem,[17] but it seems likely that, like Chaucer's own poetry, it would have circulated among Clanvowe's peers within the wider court circle.

Thus far, it has been necessary to dismiss many of the conclusions about Chaucer's audience to which a superficial examination of the *Troilus* frontispiece might lead us. One of the most striking observations we might make about the people depicted in the illustration, however, is that they are not merely aristocrats, but that a good number of them are women. Some women—generally from the mercantile and aristocratic classes—are known to have owned books, and some, of course, produced books of their own. Moreover, lay piety was flourishing in the fourteenth and fifteenth centuries, and women played a very active role in its development. Though literacy was in no sense a prerequisite for a devotional existence, it clearly played an important role in the lives of many religious women. The historian Henrietta Leyser has gone so far as to proclaim that 'women's piety of the fifteenth century was . . bookish in unaccustomed ways'.[18] If educational opportunities for women were limited, therefore, it would be a mistake to suggest that literacy and learning in the late fourteenth century were the preserve of men alone. Many women who were not themselves able to read would have had the opportunity to listen to texts being read aloud (often from within the confines of their own homes). Though this would not have allowed them the freedom to explore written texts for themselves, it would nevertheless have represented a significant means of empowerment. This much is clear from the activities of the fifteenth-century mystic Margery Kempe, whose knowledge of an impressive range of written texts is acquired through the words of others. Margery also discovers about the lives of mystics and saints in this way, rather than from written accounts of their lives. A typical example of this occurs in chapter 39 of her book (which, she tells us, survives as a record of her life that she dictated to an amanuensis), in which she learns of some of St Bridget of Sweden's spiritual experiences from a German priest:

Sche was in þe chawmbre þat Seynt Brigypte deyd in, & herde a Dewche presete prechyn of hir þerin & of hir reuelacyonys & of hir maner of leuyng. & sche knelyd also on þe ston on þe whech owr Lord aperyd to Seynte Brigypte and teld hir what day sche xuld deyn on.

(She was in the chamber that St Bridget died in, and heard a German priest preach of her there, and of her revelations and of her manner of life. She knelt also on the stone on which our Lord appeared to St Bridget and told her what day she should die on.)[19]

It seems that Chaucer's Wife of Bath, who quotes regularly from a wide selection of textual authorities, both sacred and secular, must have learned of these in a similar way. We are frequently told of the almost obsessive reading habits of her fifth husband, Jankyn, but we also learn that he habitually read aloud to her ('read he me' is a phrase that occurs frequently in her Prologue). Though she is very clearly a literary invention, whose appearance and behaviour owe as much to popular anti-feminist stereotypes as to realistic observations, the Wife is nonetheless valuable as a guide to some of the likely characteristics of Chaucer's female audience. Like Margery, she is a member of the mercantile class, and draws an income from her cloth-making. Her portrait highlights the relative wealth which she enjoys (and abuses), and her dominant, garrulous, exploitative nature, but it also illustrates her fundamental desire to challenge patriarchal textual authority. If the realization of this challenge consists in satisfying a host of patriarchal stereotypes, it nevertheless highlights the threat which a knowledge of the written word (whether achieved through reading or being read to) might pose to a community in which the male reader had traditionally ruled.

Chaucer's audience, as recent scholarship has suggested, was a more complex phenomenon than early critics had recognized. It represented a dynamic cluster of social, political, and gendered types, which evolved and expanded as Chaucer's career progressed. The illustration on the *Troilus* frontispiece, by contrast, represents a static and socially exclusive group. Though we cannot easily dismiss the possibility that such a group may once have existed, the practice of imposing totalizing assumptions on the text is clearly highly problematic. In other words, we can accept that the audience may have *included* aristocrats, members of the wider court circle, merchants, academics, and churchmen, but we clearly cannot be content to assume that Chaucer wrote *principally* for the aristocracy, the middle classes, or the academic community.

Manuscript production

Chaucer was writing less than a century before William Caxton assembled the first English printing press, at a time when manuscript production was becoming an increasingly commercialized operation, often operating independently of the monasteries and universities that had been the traditional centres of manuscript culture (and major repositories of manuscripts and codices). Indeed, ecclesiastical institutions became themselves progressively more reliant upon the developing manuscript market, and less significant as scriptoria, as the end of the fourteenth century approached. The most fundamental material required by any manuscript guild would have been parchment (prepared by washing and stretching the skin of an adult animal, usually a sheep), or the more expensive and more refined alternative, vellum (produced in the same way, but with the skin of a calf or lamb). Both were costly to prepare, and manuscripts and codices, even when produced in greater volumes by the emergent private guilds of scribes and copyists, were expensive commodities (the purchase of the raw materials, and the cost of employing copyists and illustrators, were considerable). Secular manuscript production tended to be concentrated around the urban centres of late medieval England, and chiefly within the capital. Manuscripts were prepared according to the specifications of the client, as publishing was not yet a sufficiently large industry to allow documents to be copied in the absence of a contractual agreement. The quality of late medieval manuscripts is correspondingly variable, but even relatively modest manuscripts, lacking significant decoration or illumination, often represented a substantial investment on the part of the customer.

In the age before print, documents had to be copied painstakingly onto ruled parchment sheets by hand, using an inked quill. The sheets were sewn together and folded into quires, which would then have been bound together to form codices. The text would have been produced either by a single scribe or by a company of copyists, who would share the labour of copying the text, often drawing simultaneously on sections of a divided document. Words which were frequently used were often abbreviated, largely in an effort to keep costs down. A system of elaborate conventions governed the interpretation of scribal abbreviations, which might stand either for a syllable or for a whole word. The word 'that', for example, might be represented by the runic thorn character and a superscript 't' (the text would thus read 'þᵗ'). More costly manuscripts were often intricately decorated, with marginal flourishes, stylized capitals at the beginning of paragraphs and chapters, and illustrations of various kinds. Normally, the manuscript would be illustrated by a professional illustrator, who would work on it after the scribe had copied the text onto the parchment. The Ellesmere manuscript of the *Canterbury Tales*, on which the majority of modern editions are based, is one such version. It is here that we find the familiar portraits of the Canterbury pilgrims. This is likely to have been an expensive manuscript, whose text has been carefully copied, and which has then been decorated with intricate portraits of the Canterbury pilgrims. The text as it appears in the manuscript is very different from that which we would expect to find in a critical edition of the *Tales*. Typically, abbreviations are expanded in these editions, and textual variants are carefully listed (either in an appendix or at the foot of the page). Editions that seek to preserve manuscript abbreviations can bring us closer to the medieval experience of reading, but they are inevitably more difficult to decipher. Such editions are described as *diplomatic* editions.

Though scribes generally worked carefully, scribal errors were not uncommon, and could be magnified by later copyists. The text from which the scribe copied (referred to by textual scholars as an *exemplar*) may not itself have been of the highest quality, and would have been bound to deteriorate further as it went through several hands. Each exemplar normally served as the model for a number of manuscript copies (today described as *witnesses*). Few scribes would have had access to Chaucer's autograph text, and none of the manuscripts that survive was written in his own hand. Generally, it is possible to determine whether manuscripts were witnesses to a common exemplar, as they tend to preserve common features (whether deliberate revisions or inconspicuous errors). Scribes would not have felt any need to follow their author's text slavishly, and while some may have been unfaithful to their exemplar through negligence, others would have modified the text deliberately. For the author, therefore, the scribe could represent either a means to an end, or a potential source of frustration. Longer texts such as the *Canterbury Tales* and *Troilus*, both of which survive in a large number of manuscripts, contain a higher number of scribal and editorial revisions and corrections than we might expect to find in a relatively short piece of writing. The text of the *Canterbury Tales* gave rise to the production of a series of non-authorial additions which modern editors have described as 'spurious links'. These are generally short passages added by a scribe or editor to ease the transition between one tale (and its narrator's Prologue) and another. Such an example occurs after the hostile exchange between the Host and the Pardoner, which arises when the Pardoner suggests that the Host should kiss his relics ('ParT' 941–59). In the Ellesmere manuscript the Knight intervenes, asking the Host and the Pardoner to lay aside their differences, and to kiss each other. The 'Shipman's Tale' begins immediately after the Knight has spoken and the two rivals have been reconciled. Some medieval editors clearly felt that such a transition was rather abrupt, and supplied a linking passage in which the Host addresses the Shipman. The text of one such link is reproduced below, after the familiar words of the knight:

> 'I pray yowe that ye kisse the Pardonere.
> And Pardoner, I praie the that thou drau the nere,
> And as we dide, now late us lauhe and pleie!'
> Anone thei kisse and reden forthe theire weye.
>
> EXPLICIT FABULA QUESTORIS | INCIPIT PROLOGUS
>
> [Here ends the Pardoner's tale | Here begins the Prologue]
>
> [Link:]
>
> Bot than spak oure Hoste unto Maister Schipman.
> 'Maister,' quod he, 'to us summe tale tel ye can,
> Wherewithe ye myht glad al this company,
> If it were youre pleseinge, I wote wele sekurlye.'
>   'Sertes,' quod this Schipman, 'a tale I can tell,
> And therfore, herkeneth hyderward how that I wil spell.'
>
> EXPLICIT PROLOGUS | INCIPIT FABULA NAUTE
>
> [Here ends the Prologue | Here begins the Shipman's tale][20]

Such relatively minor modifications to Chaucer's text were clearly felt to be necessary, and similar links occur elsewhere in this manuscript.

Some fifteenth-century scribes were quite ambitious. One devised a tale for Chaucer's Plowman, and another completed the unfinished 'Cook's Tale'. Chaucer was, like many late medieval writers, painfully conscious of the problems that could arise in the process of textual transmission. In both *Troilus and Criseyde* and the famous lyric addressed to his scribe Adam, he expresses his desire to have his work copied accurately, with due attention to the complexities of language, metre, and, of course, content. In the former, he is also very clearly conscious of the problems which could arise if poet and scribe did not share a common dialect:

> And for ther is so gret diversite
> In Englissh and in writyng of oure tonge,
> So prey I God that non myswrite the,
> Ne the mysmetre for defaute of tonge.
>
> (*TC* 5. 1793–6)

These lines appear to have been written in anticipation of a wide geographical—and, by implication, social—readership or audience. Whether his text was to be read aloud or in private, Chaucer needed to feel confident that it would be copied accurately. His words to Adam, 'his owne scriveyn', convey an even less optimistic view of the scribe's abilities, referring explicitly to the laborious process of erasure and correction (achieved by scraping the parchment clean and rewriting the text) which he anticipates having to perform on the manuscript. The responsibility for the errors is seen to lie exclusively with the scribe himself, whose 'negligence and rape' (7) are held to be the main cause of the problem. Chaucer's distrust of his scribe did not evolve in a vacuum; medieval writers and readers were very aware of the problems which scribal copying could give rise to, and the figure of the scribe had long been accorded a lowly position by biblical scholars and commentators. As the person who committed an author's work to manuscript, he was naturally regarded as the author's inferior. His task, if it was recognized as a skilled one, was certainly not perceived to be in any way creative. Modern editors have been no less reluctant than Chaucer and Wyclif to find fault with the medieval scribe, whose carelessness has been blamed for sections of Chaucer's verse which seem to be uncharacteristically clumsy or lacking in fluency.

Scribal activity, if it represented a source of concern for proprietorial authors, also contributed to the extraordinary richness of late medieval manuscript culture. Both private and public readers were dependent upon the scribe's fidelity to his exemplar, but any reader who had the opportunity to examine a manuscript could potentially benefit from a wealth of scribal glosses and annotations. Marginal notes and corrections could be of use to later editors, but for modern readers, their principal value must be seen to lie in the insights which they provide for us into the medieval production, circulation, and consumption of Middle English texts.

FURTHER READING

Biller, P., and Anne Hudson (eds.), *Heresy and Literacy, 1000–1530* (Cambridge: Cambridge University Press, 1994). A collection of essays that discuss the relationship between the growth of literacy in late medieval Europe and the spread of heretical doctrines such as those of the Wycliffites in England and Bohemia.

Carruthers, Mary, *The Book of Memory: A Study of Memory in Medieval Culture* (Cambridge: Cambridge University Press, 1990). This study of the role of memory in medieval literary culture challenges the traditional opposition between mnemonic 'oral' cultures and cultures of literacy.

Clanchy, M. T., *From Memory to Written Record: England 1066–1307*, 2nd edn. (Oxford: Blackwell, 1993). This is among the most extensive and influential studies of the transition between pre-literate and literate culture in late medieval England.

Clanchy, M. T., 'Looking Back from the Invention of Printing', in Daniel P. Resnick (ed.), *Literacy in Historical Perspective* (Washington: Library of Congress, 1983), 7–22. A study of the prehistory of printing in medieval Europe, which draws attention to the significance of literacy as an emergent 'technology'.

Green, Richard Firth, 'Women in Chaucer's Audience', *Chaucer Review*, 18 (1983), 146–54. Offers a provocative analysis of the role of women in Chaucer's audience, based largely on their likely function in the Ricardian court.

Greetham, D. C., *Textual Scholarship: An Introduction* (New York: Garland, 1992). Manuscript culture is discussed in chapter 2 of this valuable reference guide, which also contains material on the procedures of editing medieval and post-medieval texts.

Ong, W. J., *Orality and Literacy: The Technologizing of the Word* (London: Routledge, 1982). This remains the most authoritative introduction to the main issues surrounding the development of writing in Western societies.

Strohm, Paul, *Social Chaucer* (Cambridge, Mass.: Harvard University Press, 1989). An influential study of the conflicting ideologies which inform Chaucer's poetry, including a chapter on his audiences, both 'fictional' and 'real'.

Taylor, Andrew, 'Authors, Scribes, Patrons and Books', in Jocelyn Wogan-Browne, Nicholas Watson, Andrew Taylor, and Ruth Evans (eds.), *The Idea of the Vernacular: An Anthology of Middle English Literary Theory, 1280–1520* (Philadelphia: Pennsylvania State University Press, 1999), 353–65. An excellent introductory discussion of the medieval book trade, which addresses such issues as book production, ownership, and circulation, and the gradual emergence of 'speculative' publication. It usefully interrogates the popular identification of the late medieval growth of the book trade with the rise of the 'middle class'.

NOTES

1. 'Looking Back from the Invention of Printing', in Daniel P. Resnick (ed.), *Literacy in Historical Perspective* (Washington: Library of Congress, 1983), 7.

2. See esp. Wyclif, *De veritate sacrae scripturae*, ed. Rudolf Buddensieg (London: Wyclif Society, 1901). Selections from this text are translated in *John Wyclif: On the Truth of Holy Scripture*, trans. Ian Christopher Levy (Kalamazoo: Medieval Institute Publications, 2001).

3. *De vulgari eloquentia*, ed. and trans. Stephen Botterill (Cambridge: Cambridge University Press, 1996), 2–3.

4. 'What Dante Meant to Chaucer', in Piero Boitani (ed.), *Chaucer and the Italian Trecento* (Cambridge: Cambridge University Press, 1983), 136–7.

5. Anne Hudson (ed.), *Selections from English Wycliffite Writings* (Toronto: University of Toronto Press, 1997), 107 (my translation).

6. 'Censorship and Cultural Change in Late-Medieval England: Vernacular Theology, the Oxford Translation Debate, and Arundel's Constitutions of 1409', *Speculum*, 70 (1995), 822–64.

7. 'The Significance of the Early Chaucer Manuscript Glosses (with Special Reference to the "Wife of Bath's Prologue")', *Chaucer Review*, 10 (1976), 350–60.

8. 'The *Troilus* Frontispiece and Chaucer's Audience', *Yearbook of English Studies*, 7 (1977), 72.

9. Paul Strohm, 'Chaucer's Audience(s): Fictional, Implied, Intended, Actual', *Chaucer Review*, 18 (1983), 140. On the implied reader more generally conceived, see Wayne C. Booth, *The Rhetoric of Fiction* (Chicago: University of Chicago Press, 1961).

10. *Social Chaucer* (Cambridge, Mass.: Harvard University Press, 1989), 47–83 (the cited phrase occurs on p. 50).

11. The nature of Chaucer's schooling has remained a matter for speculation, given the lack of solid evidence. It is not clear that he attended either of the English universities, but he possessed a sound knowledge of Latin and some of the major European vernaculars. For a balanced account of the possibilities, see Derek Pearsall, *The Life of Geoffrey Chaucer: A Critical Biography* (Oxford: Blackwell, 1992), 29–34.

12. 'Chaucer's Circle of Gentlemen and Clerks', *Chaucer Review*, 18 (1983), 155–60.

13. Ibid. 155.

14. Ibid. 156.

15. Ibid. 155.

16. *Lancastrian Kings and Lollard Knights* (Oxford: Clarendon Press, 1972).

17. *The Works of Sir John Clanvowe: 'The Boke of Cupide' and 'The Two Ways'*, ed. V. J. Scattergood (Cambridge: Brewer, 1975), 9–10.

18. *Medieval Women: A Social History of Women in England 450–1500* (London: Butler & Tanner, 1999), 233.

19. *The Book of Margery Kempe*, ed. Sanford Meech and Hope Emily Allen (Oxford: Oxford University Press, 1940), 95, lines 22–7. The translation is taken from *The Book of Margery Kempe*, trans. and introd. Barry Windeatt (London: Penguin, 1985), 132.

20. John M. Bowers (ed.), *The Canterbury Tales: Fifteenth-Century Continuations and Additions* (Kalamazoo: Medieval Institute Publications, 1992), 45 (translations from the Latin are my own).

8 | Chaucer's language: pronunciation, morphology, metre

Donka Minkova

In the words of the great eighteenth-century French poet and philosopher Voltaire, 'Appreciation is a wonderful thing: It makes what is excellent in others belong to us as well'. This present Guide is an appreciation of Chaucer and a testimony to the relevance and *modernity* of his literary legacy. One aspect of that legacy is distinctly *unmodern*, however: his language. Chaucer learned to read and write English more than 650 years ago. Languages never stand still; for the modern reader, the pronunciation, grammar, and vocabulary of late fourteenth-century English can be a barrier to the understanding and appreciation of Chaucer's excellence. A single chapter cannot cover all the linguistic subtleties and complexities of his texts, but an introduction to the main features of Chaucerian English will help change a hurdle into a gate.

'Chaucerian' English is a subtype of Middle English (ME) spoken in and around London in the second half of the fourteenth century. Middle English itself is a period in the history of the language that started roughly after the Norman Conquest of 1066 and ended with the introduction of printing in England in 1476. Only classical or foreign languages, for example Latin, Greek, French, Italian, were systematically taught and studied in England during that time. Professional scribes were trained to write English, but there were no manuals, grammars, or dictionaries that would give a literate person a guide to what was 'correct' in spelling, pronunciation, or sentence structure. In the absence of a national 'standard', each geographical area developed its own local practices of speech and writing. The Middle English that we have inherited is therefore an aggregate of dialects: northern, east Midland, west Midland, and southern. In the south a separate dialect, Kentish, developed in the counties of Kent and Sussex. The boundaries between these 'constructed' divisions are blurred; in reality the transition from one variety to another represents a continuum. Moreover, when copying documents, scribes could alter them in accord with their local speech and writing habits. Against the backdrop of that diverse and unstable dialectal picture, Chaucer's English, synonymous with London English from the second half of the fourteenth century, can be characterized as a mixture of east Midlands and southern forms.

Sound–spelling correspondences

Stressed vowels

The southern dialects of fourteenth-century English, reconstructed on the basis of spelling and rhymes, used three types of stressed vowels: short, long, and diphthongal. Except in instances involving vowel shortenings in monosyllabic words, as in *good, flood, bread, ten, friend, said,* and some later lengthenings before fricatives and [r], as in *staff, bath, harm,* the quantity of the stressed vowels in Chaucer's English was the same as in Present-Day English (PDE).

The pronunciation of the short vowels is shown in the second column of Table 8.1, using the standard symbols of the International Phonetic Alphabet (IPA). The first column matches the symbols to the vowels in representative modern words, the third column matches them to the Middle English forms, and the fourth column lists the most frequent spellings for the respective vowels.

Table 8.1 Short vowels

Modern English	ME value	Middle English	ME spelling
WITH, SIN	ɪ	*with, synn*	*i, y*
SET, WENT	ɛ	*set, went*	*e*
SAT, THAT	a	*sat, that*	*a*
PAW, BOUGHT	ɔ	*God, strong*	*o*
BUSH, PUT	ʊ	*bush, cuppe*	*u, v, o*

The vowels in the top two rows are identical to the corresponding modern vowels. The short [a] was a front vowel, probably close to the pronunciation of the vowel of *sat, that* in the northern and western regions in England, a somewhat lower, 'flatter' version of the vowel [æ] found in south-eastern England or the United States today.[1] The short vowel written <o> was somewhat more rounded, sounding more like the Scots, Australian, or New Zealand variety of <o> in *God, strong.* The most noticeable difference in the quality of the short vowels in Chaucer's time and today is found in the vowel [ʊ]. It was always pronounced as a high back vowel; thus *skull* and *dull* in the following rhymes have the northern and north Midlands value [ʊ], as in *bush, full* in general American and southern British English:

> As piled as an ape was his *skulle.*
> He was a market-betere atte *fulle.*
>
> ('RT' 3935–6)

Another potentially confusing fact about this vowel is that in addition to being spelled with <u>, it can have a variant spelling with <o>. During the thirteenth century scribes began to use <o> instead of <u> in words in which the next letter was <m, n, u (= v)>, that is, letters that are also written with down-strokes (minims), as in *some, son, loue* (= love). This spelling has largely survived into modern English; this was merely a graphic, not a phonetic, change. A reference to the etymology of the word and its modern form helps. *Come* rhymes with *some*, but not with *Rome*; the pronunciation of the rhyme vowel in the 'General Prologue', 7–8 *sonne : yronne* or 265–6 *tonge : songe* is with [-ʊ-], exactly like *cuppe : uppe, curses : purses*, and so on.

The long vowels, their Modern and Middle English counterparts, and some typical spellings for these vowels are shown in Table 8.2; the colon after the IPA symbol marks vowel length.

Table 8.2 Long vowels

Modern English	ME value	Middle English	ME spelling
EAT, FIEND, BEE	i:	*rise, why, wyde*	*i, y, ij*
MAKE, MAID	e:	*see, grene, grief*	*e, ee*
SWEAR, THERE	ɛ:	*sweren, eten, sea*	*e, ee*
CALM, FATHER	ɑ:~æ:	*tale, maad*	*a, aa*
ROSE, COAT	o:	*boot, moon*	*o, oo*
AWNING, PAW	ɔ:	*bone, hooly 'holy'*	*o, oo*
DO, SOUP	u:	*loude, now*	*ou, ow*

The exact nature of the long vowels [i:] and [u:] in Chaucer's English is a controversial topic. The traditional position presupposes that none of the changes collectively described as the 'Great Vowel Shift', which lead to the current pronunciation of the vowels in *rise, loud* as the diphthongs [ai] and [au], had started before the end of the fourteenth century. There is convincing scribal evidence, however, that the historical [i:] in words like *rise, wyde* was treated as a diphthong, spelled <iy>, <ei>, <ey>, <ie>, <ye> in the first half of the fifteenth century; indeed the first signs of diphthongization date back to the end of the thirteenth century. It is highly unlikely that Chaucer used the undiphthongized vowels, though he might have been familiar with the old-fashioned pronunciation, which would remind him 'of the speech of his grandparents'.[2] Since the histories of [i:] and [u:] are parallel in every other way, a diphthongal value for [u:] in the fourteenth century is also a reasonable assumption, though in this case the scribal evidence is missing, the vowel being already represented by <ou> or <ow> since about 1300. Pronouncing *rise, loud*-type words with [i:] and [u:] should be understood as a conscious archaizing of Chaucer's language. The option of [əi] and [əu], a more 'modern' pronunciation, closer to the Canadian vowels in *bite, out*, than the pure [i:], [u:] vowels in PDE *bee, soup*, should be considered seriously by readers concerned with the authenticity of Chaucerian pronunciation.[3]

Another difficulty arises from the pronunciation of the vowels [e:], as in *queene, ysene*, and the lower and more open [ɛ:] as in *meene, clene*. In spite of their uninformative, identical spellings, and their coalescence in later English, these vowels have different histories; that they were still distinct in Chaucer's variety of Middle English is clear from the rarity of rhymes showing a genuine crossover between [e:] and [ɛ:].

The alternatives for the low vowels in *tale, maad*, namely [ɑ:]~[æ:], refer to two traditions in reconstructing Chaucer's pronunciation. The low back vowel [ɑ:], if it existed at all in the fourteenth century, would have been distinctly archaic. In Kentish the vowel had been raised and fronted especially early, and by the fifteenth century the pronunciation with [æ:] is confirmed by spellings such as <hest> 'haste', <mek> 'to make' in London English. This suggests that the closest 'authentic' Chaucerian pronunciation of this vowel would have been the Australian (Sydney) vowel in *sample, aunt*.

The two mid back vowels, the close [o:], the precursor of PDE [u:], and the open [ɔ:] were kept apart in rhyme. It is possible that the Great Vowel Shift raising of [o:], as well as the parallel front-row raising of [e:], had already started; Chaucer rhymes <dys> 'dice' < OF *dés* with *paradys* ('KT' 1237–8), and with *prentys* ('CT' 4385–6). Rhymes indicating raised [e:] appear also in the first half of the fifteenth century, in the *Castle of Perseverance* (*c*.1400–1425), and in Lydgate (*c*.1370–1450).

The diphthongs in fourteenth-century English were in many ways similar to the diphthongs of Present-Day English.

Table 8.3 Diphthongs

Modern English	ME value	Middle English	ME spelling
DAY, THEY	ɛi ~ ei	day, away, they	ay, ey
COY, OIL	oi	coy, oille	oy, oi
OUT, NOW	au	laude, drawen	au, aw
SOUL, KNOW	ou	bough, blowe	ou, ow
NEW, HEW	iu / ɛu	newe, shrewe, dure	ew, eu, u

The exact value of the diphthong spelled <ay, ey> is difficult to ascertain. Many traditional phonetic transcriptions of Chaucerian texts opt for two separate diphthongs: [ai] or [æi] for *day, May, lay*, and [ei] for *they, veil, prey*. The value [ai] is highly unlikely, however. The high front glide at the end-point of the vowel spelled <ai, ay> for words with etymological [-æ-] would have raised the onset of the diphthong; both [æi] and [ɛi] are possible outcomes. The realizations [ɛi] and [ei] took another 150 years to merge completely under [ei], yet Chaucer's rhyming practice suggests that for his variety of English the two diphthongs were already two phonetic variants of a single phoneme, allowing flexibility in the choice of rhymes:

Out of the harde bones knokke *they* [ei]
The mary, for they caste noght *awey*.

('ParT' 541–2)

The water shal aslake and goon *away*
Aboute pryme upon the nexte *day* [ɛi]
('MT' 3553–4)

What, how! What do ye, maister *Nicholay*? [æi]
How may ye slepen al the longe *day*?
('MT' 3437–8)

The two realizations are not kept apart in the spelling; for example, we find both
<away> and <awey>, <sayde> and <seyde>, <sayl> and <seyl>, <rayn> and <reyn>.
Attempting to keep them apart along etymological lines in reading Chaucer aloud is
unmotivated and likely to produce odd realizations; for this set of words the pronunciation of modern English *day*, *they*, that is, [ei] for American and British readers, and
[æi]/[ɛi] for Australian and New Zealand readers, is both easy and justified.

The diphthongs [oi], [au], and [ou] are straightforward; the only reminder to the
modern reader here would be that the spellings <ou, ow> can represent also etymological [u:] as in *loud*, *now*, that is, [u:~əu]. The reconstruction of the diphthongs
spelled <eu, ew> calls for two different pronunciations: [ɛu] for words such as *fewe*,
lewed, *shrewe*, and [iu] for *newe*, *trewe*, *knewe*. The division is drawn on etymological
lines.[4] Keeping the two sounds apart is very difficult for the modern reader, however,
since neither spelling nor subsequent history indicates the original sources. Only four
words with [ɛu] appear in rhyme position in the *Canterbury Tales*: *fewe*, *(dronke)lewe*,
shrewe, and *shewe*. They rhyme consistently with each other. The majority of words
with which [ɛu] subsequently merges have [iu]: *hewe*, *newe*, *knewe*, *trewe*, *rewe*. Unless
one takes special care to memorize the [ɛu] items, pronouncing these words with [iu]
is not a serious infraction of authenticity. The diphthong [iu] is also a plausible adaptation of the [ü] in words of French origin: *dure*, *cure*, *due*, *eschue*.

Unstressed vowels

The loss of distinctiveness of vowels in unstressed syllables was already in evidence in
early Middle English. The vowel resulting from this reduction is reconstructed as a
neutral mid-central vowel, a shwa [ə], normally spelled <-e->: *bones*, *justen*, *knoweth*,
fuller, *allone*, *dore*, *olde*. The realization of an unstressed vowel depends on its phonological environment, the type of word affected, the number of syllables in the word,
and its grammatical class and function. Of these, the most important one in the
context of Chaucer's verse is phonological environment.

When unstressed vowels were not protected by a following consonant, they could
be dropped, especially before vowel-initial words, in trisyllabic words, and in words of
low prosodic prominence. While the northern dialects of Middle English were 'leaders'
in this process, by the second half of the fourteenth century final unstressed vowels

were retained in speech only in some well-defined circumstances even in the more conservative southern dialects. As with the stressed vowel changes, the loss of the unstressed vowels was a lengthy process. Chaucer and his contemporaries must have been familiar with alternative forms of one and the same word in the same function; this allows metrically based choices, as is clear from the following examples, where the first use of each italicized pair of words must be realized as disyllabic, and the second as monosyllabic:

> Ne yet the *grete* strengthe of Ercules.
> ('KT' 1943)

> The *grete* effect, for which that I bygan.
> ('KT' 2482)

> Whan that Arcite to Thebes *comen* was.
> ('KT' 1355)

> The day was *come* that homward moste he tourne.
> ('WBT' 988)

Observing the alternation between stressed and unstressed syllables in verse is an important factor in the selection of forms, but it must be understood that all of the patterns found in verse are grounded in the phonology and grammar of the spoken language. The probability of dropping an unstressed final vowel is associated with the following processes and conditions:

1   *Elision* before another vowel or a weak [h-], the latter appearing in pronouns (*he, her, hem*), before forms of the verb *to have*, and before French borrowings with orthographic <h->. The italicized -*e* in the following lines is elided:

> His slep, his met*e*, his drynk*e*, is hym biraft,
> That len*e* he wex and dry*e* as is a shaft.
> ('KT' 1361–2)

> Wel may his hert*e* in joy and bliss*e* habounde.
> ('MerT' 1286)

Prevocalic elision of -*e* is practically the norm in Chaucer's verse. It is most common in words of more than one syllable, but occurs also at the juncture of a weakly stressed monosyllable, a *clitic*, followed by a vowel-initial word; in these cases, known also as instances of *apocope*, the consonant of the clitic becomes an onset of the following syllable:

> *Th'* estaat, *th'* array, the nombre, and eek the cause.
> ('GP' 716)

> *T'* espien where he myghte wedded be.
> ('MerT' 1257)

The apostrophes are an editorial reinterpretation of fused scribal forms, <*thestaat*>, <*tharray*>, and so forth. Like elision, apocope is not shown systematically by scribes, as in the following lines, in which apocope of <th*e* ende> and <th*e y*mage> must be assumed:

> In th*e e*nde of which an ounce, and namoore.
>
> ('CYT' 1266)

> And to th*e y*mage of Juppiter hem sente.
>
> ('SNT' 364)

2   *Synizesis*, or fusion of two syllables into one when an unstressed short [ɪ] or [ʊ] is followed by a vowel. The original vowel in such instances becomes consonantal [j] or [w] and forms the onset of the following syllable:

> Nowher so bis*y a* man as he ther nas,
> And yet he semed bis*ier* than he was.
>
> ('GP' 321–2)

> This Pardoner hadde heer as yel*ow a*s wex.
>
> ('GP' 675)

3   *Contraction*, or *syncope*, of unstressed vowels adjacent to the sonorants [r, l, m, n], as in PDE *imagery*, *summoner*, *asterisk*, *lingering*. In such cases the sonorant moves to the onset of the following syllable:

> And everemoore he hadde a sov(*e*)reyn prys.
>
> ('GP' 67)

> And writen in the tabl(*e*) of atthamaunt.
>
> ('KT' 1305)

> That ev(*e*)re in oon was drawynge to that place.
>
> ('ShT' 27)

The probability of dropping *-e* is also high in words of inherently low prosodic prominence, especially pronouns and auxiliaries:

> Our*e* suster deere—lo! Heere I write your*e* name—
>
> ('ST' 1752)

> I hav*e* to day been at your*e* chirche at messe.
>
> ('ST' 1788)

The final *-e* is also unstable in originally trisyllabic words:

> In al the parrissh*e* wif ne was ther noon.
>
> ('GP' 449)

> And after that hir lokyng*e* gan she lighte.
>
> (*TC* 1. 293)

Some grammatical constraints on the sounding of <*-e*> are also observable. Mono-syllabic adjectives in the plural or in the singular following determiners *the*, *this*, or possessive adjectives like *his*, *her* commonly preserve the *-e*:

> So wel they lovede, as *olde* bookes sayn.
>
> ('KT' 1198)

> For she koude of that art the *olde* daunce.
> ('GP' 476)

Similarly, the -*e*(*n*) in infinitives can occasionally be syncopated before a vowel-initial word, but most commonly the -*e*(*n*) is preserved, even in elision environments:

> To yelden Jhesu Crist his propre rente.
> ('ST' 1821)
>
> To lyven in delit was evere his wone.
> ('GP' 335)

A final question, which has exercised the minds of many philologists and readers, is whether orthographic <-*e*> in rhymes should be pronounced. As is clear from the discussion in this section, the sounding or suppression of <-*e*> is subject to a complex interplay of phonological and morphological constraints; its realization is a scale of probability rather than a clear-cut yes–no line: subject nouns, inflected verbs, singular adjectives, are more likely to be -*e*-less than nouns after a preposition, infinitives, and plural adjectives; trisyllabic words are more likely to lose the -*e* than disyllabic words, and so on. In the absence of a complete record of preservation or elision in the entire corpus, however, no firm recommendation can be offered; the modern reader has the option of both masculine and feminine rhymes.

Consonants

Compared to the vowels, the pronunciation of consonants in Chaucer's time was much closer to PDE. The modern pronunciation is a reliable guide in many instances where the orthography has subsequently changed. Table 8.4 summarizes the differences between the realization of the consonants in relation to spelling in Chaucer's time, and their realization today. The zero symbols indicate that the letter in the right-hand column was, or is, silent. In the case of <h->, it is likely that in addition to Latinate/French words, in which the <h-> had been lost, pronouns such as *he, hem, her* and the verb *have* were also commonly pronounced as vowel-initial words in Chaucer's time, though the orthography does not reflect that. The degree of preservation of the initial [h-] in native nouns, verbs, and adjectives, *half, head, heaven, hear, hare, husband,* is uncertain. On the one hand, the form of the indefinite article with these words suggests silent <h->: *an* hat ('GP' 470), *an* hert ('KT' 1689), *an* heigh folye ('KT' 1798). On the other hand, the scribal evidence for loss of <h-> in fourteenth-century southern documents is not very strong. The dropping of initial [h-] in native words in Chaucer is therefore likely, but not provable. A further difference that should be noted is that the letters <c> and <t> in French loan-words still had the values [s] and [t] in front of [i, j], as in *pacient, nacioun, precius* with [-s-], and *vertue, creature, tortuous* with [t].

Table 8.4 Late Middle English consonants

ME spelling	Examples	ME value	PDE value
<-gg->	drogge 'drug'	[g]	[g]
	brigge 'bridge'	[dʒ]	[dʒ]
<-gh->	noght 'naught'	[x]	Ø
	knyght 'knight'	[ç]	
	ynogh 'enough'	[x]	[f]
<gn->	gnawynge 'gnawing'	[gn-]	[n-]
<kn->	knyght 'knight'	[kn-]	
<h->	helpen 'help'	[h-]	[h-]
	humour 'bodily fluid'	Ø	[h-/Ø]
<-l->	half, almesse 'alms'	[l]	Ø
<-ng>	song, yonge 'young'	[ŋg]	[-ŋ]
<-r->	ferther 'further'	[r]	[-r-/ Ø]
<wr->	wroght 'wrought'	[wr-]	[r-]
<-z>	tormentz 'torments'	[s]	[s]

A point that is still debated among linguists is the reconstruction of the pronunciation of orthographically double consonants, as in *wille, fulfille, inne, bigynne, cappe, happe*. It is sometimes asserted that the orthography represents genuine long consonants, and this carries over into modern recordings of Chaucer's poetry. The authenticity of consonantal length in Chaucer is questionable, however. PDE does not have long consonants word-internally, even if the orthography suggests otherwise: *dagger, pattern, drummer* have *short* [-g-, -t-, -m-]. For the modern reader, using the PDE single consonant values for words of the type *wille, fulfille, inne, bigynne* is both easier and philologically justifiable.

Stress

As in PDE, stress placement in Middle English depended on the word's composition and its etymological source. For simple, or *underived*, words, the dominant accentuation pattern in Chaucerian English was a continuation of the Old English model of stress on the first syllable of the root: *sómer, fóweles, máken, twénty*. This principle was applied widely also to the borrowed French vocabulary, especially in disyllabic words, as in *cóntree, fórtune, púrpos, sérgeant, séso(u)n*. A common assertion to the effect that such words can retain their stress on the final syllable should be treated with care.[5]

After the Norman Conquest, English gradually absorbed large numbers of words of Romance origin; the total number of French words adopted during the Middle English period has been estimated at slightly over 10,000.[6] The nature and frequency of a word, as well as the date of borrowing, can affect its accentuation. A common word like *season*, known in English since about 1300 and in popular use in the second half of the fourteenth century, was clearly pronounced with stress on the first syllable: eleven of the twelve uses of the word *seso(u)n* in the *Tales* and in *Troilus and Criseyde* are of the type attested in the 'Knight's Tale':

> The sésoun priketh every gentil herte.
> ('KT' 1043)

The single use of the word where stress on the second syllable is suggested is the rhyme *declinacion : seson* ('FrT' 1033–4). A similar distribution is shown by the noun *torment*, first recorded around 1290. In the *Tales* and in *Troilus* it requires end-stress only twice ('MLT' 845 and *TC* 1. 8), and in both cases the noun is in rhyme position. In all of the other twenty-one instances, the word has stress on the first syllable:

> With tórment and with shameful deeth echon.
> ('PrT' 628)

Such distribution suggests that final stress in *sesoun, torment* may be artificially forced by the rhyme. By way of comparison, for Chaucer and other poets 'tilting' of the stress in rhyme is a common practice with native words (compare 'ManT' 209–10 *thyng : werkyng*; 'MLT' 1100–2 *dresse : gladnesse*; 'MoP' 1915–6 *I : hardy*). Clearly, the requirement of the rhyme in verse overrides the 'natural' pronunciation that would have been current in contemporary speech. A blanket assumption of variable pronunciation for all French loan-words in Chaucer's language is therefore unwarranted; words that have final stress by virtue of appearing in rhyme position, while they have initial stress elsewhere, must be assumed to have the PDE stress contour, thus *béaute, cítee, mércy, pítous, préyere, sérvant, sésoun, tórment, vísage*. Only words that have final stress with some frequency line-internally can be reconstructed as items with variable pronunciation. Such is the distribution of, for example, *diverse, fortune, honour, roial*. At the other end of that scale are words that have stress on the first syllable today, but must still have had their foreign stress in Chaucer's language. Here belong words like *languáge*, always finally stressed in the verse portions of the *Tales* and in *Troilus*, or *mesúre, messáge*, both of which are avoided line-internally, but are freely used in rhyme position with stress on the second syllable.

Obviously, checking the distribution of each borrowed word before deciding where to put the stress is impractical and, indeed, impossible for present editions of Chaucer. In our digital age, however, we can probably look forward to editions that recognize that not all French loans had variable stress and that mark the stresses accordingly. The relevance of a detailed gradient picture of stress lies in an enhanced understanding and appreciation of Chaucer's metre. Knowing the behaviour of a word in the entire corpus affects the interpretation of the choices made mostly at the beginning of lines, but also further in the line, where inversion of the stresses is also possible. If a word is used regularly with word-initial stress elsewhere in the verse, keeping the initial stress is preferable in cases that allow both metrical options. Thus, the opening of the 'General Prologue' 314, 352 is trochaic, parallel to the inverted opening of lines 105, 532:

> Jústice he was ful often in assise.
> ('GP' 314)

> Póynaunt and sharp, and redy al his geere.
> ('GP' 352)

> Únder his belt he bar ful thriftily.
> ('GP' 105)

> Lývynge in pees and parfit charitee.
> ('GP' 532)

In both sets of lines the iambic pentameter ideal is abandoned in favour of a metrically more interesting pattern, opening a window into Chaucer's art of versification.

Words formed by combining two or more roots, namely compounds, have primary stress on the first syllable of the root, and secondary stress on the second root or the suffix: *hánde-brède, hérte-spòon, húndred-fòold, mílne-stòn, wódecràft*. In the verse secondary stresses behave like main stresses. Derivational suffixes: *-dom, -hod|-hed, -ere, -ing, -ly|-lich, -ness(e), -ish, -ship(e), -ward*, are realized with some degree of stress only when attached to a disyllabic base: *brótelnèsse, mártirdòm, wómmanhède*; if attached to a monosyllabic base, they are usually unstressed unless some prominence is required by the metre, for example at the end of the line where the rhyme triggers an inversion of the stress:

> And eek of martir*dóm* the ruby bright.
> ('PrT' 610)

> And eek, for she was somdel smoter*lích*.   (rhymes with *dich*)
> ('RT' 3963)

> Thou mayst, syn thou hast *wísdom* and man*héd*e.
> ('KT' 1285)

> Shewe now youre pacience in youre wer*kýng*.   (rhymes with *thyng*)
> ('ClT' 495)

The prosodic contour of derived words like *chapmanhod, martyrdom, smoterlich* in Chaucer's language was similar to that in words which were borrowed as trisyllabic: *appetit, mencioun, instrument, orisoun, patient, Samuel, violent*. Such words have two stresses too, only in them the primary prominence is on the final syllable, while the first syllable probably had secondary stress. This pattern can be generalized to all

French borrowings with suffixes such as *-ance/-ence*, *-esse*, *-(i)er*, *-io(u)n*, *-ité(e)*, *-y(e)*, *-ment*, *-ous*. These suffixes carried the main stress of the word in the source language. Within English they developed a second stress two syllables back from the main stress: *àrgumént*, *èloquénce*, *gèntilésse*, *iàlousýe*, *partìculér*, *humànitée*, *pàrlemént*. This phenomenon is known as 'countertonic accentuation', a term coined specifically for the accentuation of classical and Romance loan-words in English. The development of countertonic stress is based on the principle of rhythmic alternation which favours stresses occurring at regular intervals. The same principle governs the accentuation of proper names, whose stressed syllables are also separated by a buffer unstressed syllable: *Dányèl*, *Márciàn*, *Máchabèe*, *Mákomète*, *Pálamòn*, *Trámyssène*.

Morphology

Nouns

By the middle of the fourteenth century the noun forms were very similar to those in PDE. The loss of distinctive inflections for gender on adjectives and the replacement of the old gender-marked demonstrative pronouns by the single article form *the* had led to complete loss of grammatical gender in the noun system.

As in PDE, the noun had separate forms for number: singular and plural. The plural marker *-(e)s* differs from its PDE counterpart primarily in terms of pronunciation and spelling. A fully syllabic *-es* [-əs] was still the most common inflection after stems ending in any consonant, not just after [s, z, ʃ, ʒ, tʃ, dʒ]: *kynges*, *okes*, *stones*, *swerdes*, *thynges*, *wyves* were all disyllabic. Syncopation resulting in the loss of the vowel was a frequent option after the sonorants [r, l, m, n, w, j]; a simple [-s] could be added also to French nouns in *-er*, *-oun*, *-our*:

> With wilde *mares*, as faste as he may go.
> ('RT' 4081)

> Of queynte *mirours* and of perspectives.
> ('SqT' 234)

The probability of syncopation increases if the noun is disyllabic:

> With *buttokes* brode and brestes rounde and hye.
> ('RT' 3975)

Spellings with <-z> appear in the plural of some borrowed words whose stem ends in <-t->: *aduocatz*, *argumentz*, *dyamauntz*, *testamentz*. The spelling <-ys, -is> for the plural, regularly rhyming with the verb <is, ys>, as in *wyvys : alyve is* ('WBP' 39–40), *beryis : mery is* ('NPT' 2965–6), reflects the option of a higher unstressed vowel, probably [ɪ], like the unstressed vowel in PDE *business*, *fittest*, *duchess*. The class of mutated plurals (*teeth, feet, mys, wom(m)en, men*) was well preserved in Chaucer's English. Among other surviving irregularities are some unchanged plurals (*sheep, swyn, deer, hors*), and plurals in <-en>: *do(u)ghtren, sustren, hosen, yen, pesen, ashen*.

The normal form of the Genitive was also <-(e)s> [-əs]: *beddes heed, chirches blood, clerkes hors, milleres doghter, pigges bones*. The patterns of syncopation are similar to those for the plural inflection <-(e)s>:

> Swyved the *milleres* doghter bolt upright.
> ('RT' 4266)

The prepositional, or 'of', Genitive, for example *droghte of March* ('GP' 2), *reule of Seint Maure or of Seint Beneit* ('GP' 173), *the reynes of his brydel* ('KT' 904), was already well established. Some nouns such as *brother, fader, lady, hevene, herte, chirche* can remain uninflected in the Genitive: his *lady* grace, *brother* sone, *fader* soule, *chirche* reves, *herte* roote. The Genitive of measure can also be left uninflected: twenty *yeer*, a thousand *pound* of wighte. The possessive is also unmarked with proper nouns ending in <-s>: *Venus* heigh servyse, *kyng Priamus* sone, *Troilus* vnsely auenture.

It should be noted that unlike PDE, where the <-'s> form is no longer an inflection but rather a clitic which can be attached to whole phrases, in Chaucer's grammar the possessive marker is attached directly to the head noun in the phrase, not to its last word: *the Wyues tale of Bathe* (Ellesmere manuscript) for our *Wife of Bath's Tale*. The so-called 'his' Genitive, a phonetic echo of the inflection <-es>, is also found occasionally, thus *the Cook **his** tale* (Hengwrt manuscript) rather than *Cookes tale* (Ellesmere), *the Millere **his** tale* (Ellesmere) rather than *the Millerys tale* (Hengwrt). For more on the Chaucer manuscripts, see Chapter 28.

Pronouns

The personal pronouns in Chaucer maintained separate Subject and Object forms, except for the neuter pronoun *it*. Unlike PDE, second-person pronouns could be singular or plural. The full set of forms and some spelling variants of the personal pronouns are shown in Table 8.5. The distribution of the three variants for the first-person singular is uneven. The most common form is <I>, and that is the only form that can appear in rhyme position in the *Tales*. The form *ich* is extremely rare in the *Tales*, but in *Troilus* it is used over fifty times. In most cases the consonantal form avoids a potential hiatus between two vowels: *ich* assente ('MLI' 39), if *ich* al nyght (*TC* 3. 873), have *ich* eyen tweye (*TC* 4. 314); that the choice is phonological is illustrated by the pronoun use in the following lines:

> For ay thurst **I**, the more that *ich* it drynke.
> (*TC* 1. 406)
> For **I** loved ek, though *ich* unworthi were.
> (*TC* 4. 329)

Table 8.5 Personal pronouns

Person	Case	Singular			Plural
First	Subject	I, y, ich, ik			we, wee
	Object	me			us
Second	Subject	thou, thow			ye, yee
	Object	thee, the			you, yow
Third	Subject	he, hee	she, shee	it	they
	Object	him	here, hir(e)		hem

The northern form *ik* appears only in the *Tales*, in the words of Osewold the Reve, at 'Reeve's Prologue' 3867 and 3888.

The second-person singular pronoun appears as either <thou> or <thow>. In interrogative forms where the verb precedes the subject, the pronoun is frequently attached enclitically to the end of the verb, with accompanying assimilation of the [-θ] to the [(s)t-] of the verb inflection: art thou → *artow*, makest thou → *makestow*, shalt thou → *shaltow*, wost thou → *wostow*.

In Chaucer's language the selection of the singular or plural form of the pronoun was no longer grammatically determined when the addressee was a single person. The social and attitudinal nuances of addressing one person are both subtle and complex. In exchanges between equals of lower status, as well as in prayers and other religious contexts, the expected form is *thou*. The *thou* form is also used between friends, younger people, and in broad speech. In the courtly style of addressing an unfamiliar person, or a person of higher social status or of venerable age, the preferred form is the polite or distancing plural *ye/you*.[7]

The most notable difference between the third-person plural pronouns in PDE and their forms in Chaucer's time is the object pronoun *hem* 'them'. This is a typically southern form, corresponding to an earlier subject pronoun *hi, hy*; the latter had been gradually replaced by the Scandinavian loan-word *they* during the twelfth and the thirteenth centuries—a change which started in the northern dialects. While in Chaucer the replacement is complete for the subject pronoun *they*, the object pronoun *them*, as well as the possessive *thair/theyr(e)*, were still associated exclusively with northern speech. The pronoun *them* is not found in Chaucer's corpus, and *thair* appears in a single line ('RT' 4172), in the famous passage in which the students' language fits the description of their origins as 'Of o toun were they born . . . | Fer in the north' ('RT' 4014–15).

The Object forms of the personal pronouns were also used reflexively: we baren *us*, I shape *me*. The combination of the Object or possessive pronouns *my, youre, hym + self/selve(n)* was also used emphatically in conjunction with a subject pronoun, instead of the subject, and as a reflexive pronoun, as in the respective examples below:

> Crist spak *hymself* ful brode in hooly writ.
> ('GP' 739)

> And but *youreselven* telle us what it is.
> (*TC* 2. 131)

> That caused hym to sette *hymself* afyre.
> ('WBP' 726)

The possessive forms of the pronouns *min(e)*, *thin(e)*, when used adjectivally before a consonant-initial word, had already developed their shortened forms as in PDE: *my mayster and my lord, my lyve, my wit, thi frend, thi lady*. However, if the noun was vowel-initial, or <h-> initial, the *min(e)*, *thin(e)* forms were still used:

> As keepe me fro *thy* vengeaunce and *thyn* ire.
> ('KT' 2302)

> Fare wel, *my* sweete foo, *myn* Emelye!
> ('KT' 2780)

Another point on which PDE and Chaucerian English differ is the use of relative pronouns. The most frequent relative pronoun was *that*; unlike PDE, *that* could introduce restrictive clauses:

> And Palamon, *that* was his cosyn deere.
> ('KT' 2763)

The PDE equivalent of *that* would be 'Palamon *who* . . .', but in Chaucer's English this option was unavailable since *who* was only an interrogative or an indefinite pronoun. The relative *which* was used freely for both animate and inanimate antecedents:

> My fifthe housbonde—God his soule blesse!—
> *Which that* I took for love, and no richesse.
> ('WBP' 525–6)

> Crist, *which* that is to every harm triacle.
> ('MLT' 479)

The first example above illustrates yet another difference between Chaucer's language and PDE with respect to the relative pronouns: Chaucerian English used compound relatives. A compound relative is composed by an interrogative word followed by *that*: *which that* 'which, who', *when that* 'when', *whom that* 'whom', *whose that* 'whose'.

Adjectives

The difference between Chaucerian usage and PDE with respect to adjectives is restricted to the apparently different grammatical treatment of adjectives depending on their syllable structure and phonetic composition. Adjectives of two or more syllables (*devout, mortal, precious*) and all adjectives ending in a vowel (*fre, bysy, nedy*) have the same forms in all grammatical functions. However, monosyllabic adjectives whose stem ends in a consonant, *blak, long, white, fals, yong, first, fresh*, regularly have <-e> for the plural, thus 'smale tithes and . . . *smal* offrynge' ('FT' 1315), 'smale children' ('PrT' 501), 'smale thynges' ('ManP' 73). When such adjectives are preceded by a determiner—the definite article, a demonstrative pronoun (*this, that*), or a possessive noun or pronoun—they also take the inflection <-e>, thus 'this *yonge* mayden' ('ClT' 210), 'hir *olde* . . . fader' ('ClT' 222). This pattern continues the so-called definite or weak inflection of Old English.

The extent to which this pattern reflects the grammar of the spoken language in the second half of the fourteenth century is debatable. The majority of the adjectives in the language did not have separate forms for the definite and the indefinite inflections. The evidence we have for the survival of the definite inflection is overwhelmingly from syllable-counting stress-alternating verse where monosyllabic stems have to be followed by a weak syllable. It is also relevant that the definite inflection for monosyllabic adjectives is dropped if the following noun begins with an unstressed syllable or a vowel. Compare the following pairs of grammatically identical phrases, in which the choice of form is governed by the stress on the following noun:

> *That goode Arcite*, of chivalrie flour.
> ('KT' 3059)

> And so bifel how that *this goode man*.
> ('MerT' 1897)

> *This same accord* was sworn on eyther syde.
> ('MLT' 244)

> But in *the same ship* as he hire fond.
> ('MLT' 799)

The priority of rhythm over grammar is further corroborated by the behaviour of trisyllabic adjectives when they precede an initially stressed noun—they too tend to preserve the *-e* after determiners:

> Youre *excellente* doghter that is heere.
> ('SqT' 145)

The survival of the <-e> in these cases, both in speech and in verse, was evidently reinforced by rhythmic considerations; the archaic inflections surfaced only in mono- or trisyllabic adjectives. Avoidance of stress clash, or rhythmic alternation, as we saw in the previous section on stress, was a powerful factor in shaping the prosodic form of words in Chaucer's time; here the same principle affects the grammatical form of some adjectives.

Verbs

Recognizing the verb forms of fourteenth-century southern English is generally easy for the speaker of PDE. Weak verbs, that is, verbs that form their past tense with the help of the <-ed> suffix, had already become the dominant type. Borrowed French verbs followed the weak pattern: *assented, despised, empoisoned, obeyed*. The core vocabulary still had a good number of strong verbs, that is, verbs whose root vowel changes in the past tense and the past participle, as in *ride, choose, break, come, stand*. Some historically strong verbs, which subsequently developed weak past-tense forms, were still strong in Chaucer. Also, some strong verbs show distinctions between the past-tense form and the past participle that have been subsequently lost. Here is a small sample of strong verbs that differ from PDE with respect to their main forms:

Infinitive	Past tense	Past participle
fare(n)	ferde	fare(n)
helpe(n)	help(e)	holpe(n)
speke(n)	spak(e)	spoke(n)
stonde(n)	stood(e)	stonde(n)

The past participle is sometimes accompanied by the prefix *y-*. The forms preserving *y-* (*ybroght, ybounden, yfetered, ysworn*) are the expected southern forms, yet Chaucer must have been comfortable with the corresponding Midland forms without *y-*, because the unprefixed form appears commonly as the metre requires:

> That is so lowe *ybroght* by tirannye.
> ('KT' 1111)

> The bryde was *broght* abedde as stille as stoon.
> ('MerT' 1818)

The other verb form which allowed convenient flexibility with respect to the number of syllables was the form of the infinitive, see the section above on sound–spelling correspondences. Moreover, the infinitive can appear alone, or following the prepositions *to* and *for to*. The choice of *for to* can foreground the goal-oriented nature of the verb, but more often there is no meaningful difference between the two options, and the selection is metrically based.[8]

Other notable differences in the verb appear in the inflections for person, number, and mood. Table 8.6 summarizes the forms for the Indicative for two verbs, *bere(n)* 'to bear', and *lyve(n)* 'to live', representing the strong and weak paradigms respectively. The typical inflections are in boldface. Parentheses indicate that the form is orthographically variable. Medial unstressed vowels can be syncopated and the final unstressed syllables are subject to the processes described above in the subsection on unstressed vowels. The southern third-person-singular present tense *-eth* is by far the most frequent form used by Chaucer, but occasionally, as in the *House of Fame* (426) and the *Book of the Duchess* (73, 257), the northern *-es* (or *-is* variant) is also used. The *-es* forms in the lines spoken by Aleyn the clerk in the 'Reeve's Tale', *tydes* at line 4175, *says* at line 4180, are part of a concentration of northern forms in the students' speech, including *wha, swa, ham, raa* for *who, so, home, roe*, or *slyk* and

Table 8.6 Verb inflections (*Indicative*)

| Person | Type | Present tense | | Past tense | |
		Singular	Plural (all persons)	Singular	Plural (all persons)
First	Strong	bere	bere(n)~	barØ	beren lyv(e)den
	Weak	lyve		lyved(e)	
Second	Strong	berest	bereth	barØ	
	Weak	lyvest	lyve(n)~	lyv(e)**dest**	
Third	Strong	bereth	lyveth	barØ	
	Weak	lyveth		lyved(e)	

Table 8.7 Verb inflections (*Subjunctive* and *Imperative*)

| Type | Subjunctive | | Imperative | |
	Singular (all persons)	Plural (all persons)	Singular	Plural
Strong	bere	bere(n)	berØ	bereth
Weak	lyve	lyve(n)	lyve	lyveth

swilk for *swich*. This appears to be a deliberate and remarkably accurate representation of a dialect whose features would have been easily identifiable by Chaucer's contemporaries.

The subjunctive mood is opposed to the indicative in that it can express condition, possibility, desirability, concession, suggestion, and a number of other subtle shifts away from the statement of a mere testable fact. In PDE the most common form of the subjunctive is the *analytical* form, which requires an auxiliary followed by the main verb: *would see, should go, might take,* and so on. Rarely, more so in American English than in British English, we still use the subjunctive forms which are a continuation of the subjunctive inflections in Table 8.7: I urge that she *submit* the proposal. In Chaucer's language the latter form, the *synthetic subjunctive*, was used much more frequently than it is used in PDE:

> That if gold *ruste*, what shal iren do?
> ('GP' 500)

> And, goode lemman, God thee *save* and *kepe*!
> ('RT' 4247)

Another characteristic of the verb forms in Chaucer is the widespread use of the so-called 'impersonal' verbs, that is, verbs that in PDE would take a 'dummy' subject *it*, as in *it seems to me*. In Chaucer's English the grammatical subject of these verbs was in what was historically the Dative, but had merged with the Accusative into a single Object case. The verbs *neden*, *listen* 'to be pleased', and *thinken* 'to appear' below are used in that way:

> Ther nas na moore—*hem nedede* no dwale.
> ('RT' 4161)

> And wher *hym lest*, best felawshipe kan
> To swich as *hym thynketh* able for to thryve.
> (*TC* 2. 206–7)

Other verbs that are used in such impersonal constructions are *bihoven*, *happen*, *befallen*.

Although this chapter will not deal with syntax, semantics, and pragmatics, it might be helpful to note that multiple negation in Chaucer is a syntactic feature which was not associated with a particular social variety of English. A verb preceded by the negative adverb *ne* (pronounced [nə]) could be followed by a negated complement; notice that *ne* can be reduced to *n-* when attached to some verbs and adverbs, so *nas* < *ne was*, *nere* < *ne were*, *nys* < *ne ys*, *nolde* < *ne wolde*, *nyste* < *ne wiste*, *nevere* < *ne evere*. This is illustrated by the following examples:

> Ther *nas no* good day, ne *no* saluyng.
> ('KT' 1649)

> Ther *nere no* prescience of thyng comynge.
> (*TC* 4. 987)

Another form of double negation that might seem strange to the modern reader is the historically emphatic structure in which the verb is flanked by negatives: the *ne* to the left, and *noght* 'naught', or its variant *nat*, to the right:

> But he *ne* lefte *nat*, for reyn ne thonder.
> ('GP' 492)

> That *noon* of us *ne* speke *nat* a word.
> ('MT' 3586)

In addition to negation on both the verb and its object, and the historically emphatic *ne* + verb + *noght/nat* construction, multiple negation can extend over other sentence elements:

> And of this cry they *nolde nevere* stenten.
> ('KT' 903)

> I *ne* loved *nevere* by *no* discrecioun.
> ('WBP' 622)

As will be seen from the above examples, Chaucer's English did not require the auxiliary *do* for negating the main verb. Similarly, interrogative sentences were formed by simple inversion of the main verb and the subject:

And *wostow* why? For they were used weel.
('WBP' 562)

Knowe ich hire aught? For my love, telle me this.
(*TC* 1. 864)

The verb *don* was still a full verb meaning 'to make, to perform, to complete, to cause'. Although *do* was not used as an auxiliary for the interrogative and for negation, it paired with another verb, *gan*, etymologically the shortened past tense of *begin*, in providing a metrically useful extra syllable in the verse. The metrical use of *gan* is especially frequent. It can be simply a signal that the following verb is in the past tense, or in some contexts it can be equivalent to 'begin', that is, the combination of *gan* + *infinitive* has an inchoative (inceptive) meaning.

Metre

The term *metre* here will be used in its linguistic sense. The metrical organization of a line is projected from an abstract template, which encodes the idealized alternation and grouping of stressed and unstressed syllables in the line. *Metre* and *metrical* can also refer to the rhythmic realization of verse in recitation, that is, to the performance of verse. The template and its allowable variations are defined on the basis of the great majority of lines in a given body of verse, so that ideally the metre and its realization overlap completely. There are, however, in any form of verse, instances where the abstract design must, or can, be disregarded in performance. In the huge scholarly literature on Chaucer's metre this tension between abstract design and realization has led to arguments about the validity of classifying Chaucer's poetry as tightly organized tetrameter and pentameter. The position taken here is that Chaucer composed in a clearly defined metrical scheme, the deviations from which in performance were also clearly defined and limited.

The two metrical forms that Chaucer uses in his verse are the *iambic tetrameter* and the *iambic pentameter*. These terms imply that in addition to the fixed syllable count eight and ten, the lines are divided further into four and five measures respectively, that is, the verse is *footed*. Ideally, each measure, or foot, is iambic, which means that an unstressed syllable is followed by a stressed one, *The droghte of March, this king, thy wo*. The foot divisions do not have to coincide with word boundaries, as, for example, in the first three feet of 'General Prologue' 17: 'The hoo // ly blis // ful mar // tir for to seke'.

End-rhyme is another important element of Chaucer's verse. An ideal rhyme presupposes identity of the stressed vowels of the rhyming words as well as identity of the following sounds, including a fully unstressed syllable. Rhymes in which the stressed vowel is final or is followed only by consonants are called masculine rhymes, thus (all from the 'General Prologue') *she : thre, he : contree, wight : knyght, men : hen, hond : lond*. When the rhyming syllable is followed by an unstressed syllable, the rhyme is called feminine: *strondes* : *londes*, *berye* : *merye*, *cloystre* : *oystre*, *digestible* : *Bible*. The rhyme can have only one unstressed syllable; that extra syllable at the line-end is optional and has no bearing on the metrical design.

Chaucer's tetrameter verse

The tetrameter had been a familiar form in English long before Chaucer's time; he must have been acquainted with it both from native models and from the octosyllabic Continental tradition. Chaucer's early translation of the *Romaunt of the Rose*, and his early poems the *Book of the Duchess* and the *House of Fame*, are in tetrameter form. These poems are metrically smooth, the syllable count is regular, allowing for a feminine rhyme, or an extra ninth syllable at the end of the line. Even at this early stage, however, Chaucer approached the familiar template with originality. While in previous English tetrameter compositions the lines were end-stopped, meaning that the end of the line coincided with a major syntactic break, Chaucer diversified the rhythm by introducing a large number of run-on lines, or lines with *enjambment*, in which single syntactic units straddle two lines:

> And whider thou shalt, and why I *cam*
> *To do* thys, so that thou *take*
> *Good herte*, and not for fere quake.
>
> (*HF* 602–5)

After Chaucer turned to the pentameter as his metre of choice, he must have regarded the tetrameter as an inferior metrical scheme. Echoes of the tetrameter are heard in 'Sir Thopas', a parody described by the Chaucer-pilgrim himself as being in 'a rym I lerned longe agoon' ('PST' 709). The Host's rude interruption of the tale, dismissing it as 'rym dogerel' and 'drasty rymyng', and his disparaging 'Thou doost noght elles but despendest tyme' ('TST' 925, 930–1), suggest that, like his fictional mirror-image of a rhymester, the mature Chaucer considered the previously popular form a waste of time. Instead, Chaucer turned to the Continent for a decasyllabic model.

The iambic pentameter

In the introduction to the 'Man of Law's Tale', Chaucer holds up the mirror to his metrical skills, obliquely recognizing his own success as a storyteller:

> I kan right now no thrifty tale seyn
> That Chaucer, thogh he kan but lewedly
> On metres and on rymyng craftily,
> Hath seyd hem in swich Englissh as he kan
> Of olde tyme, as knoweth many a man.
>
> ('MLI' 46–50)

The obligatory modesty forces Chaucer to play down his verse-craft, of which in his words *he kan but lewedly*, 'he knows little about'. His protestations notwithstanding, his superior command of metre and rhyme, as well as his pioneering approach to the Continental model, have made him one of the major innovators in the history of English verse. Chaucer was indeed the inventor of the English iambic pentameter.

There is no known body of iambic pentameter verse in English prior to Chaucer. The individual components of the iambic pentameter were not original with him: iambic verse had been composed in English since the end of the twelfth century, but the earlier iambic feet were used in either eight- or fourteen-syllable lines. Decasyllabic lines were known in France, Portugal, and Spain, and were a popular form in fourteenth-century Italian verse, though the rhythmic contour of the Continental models was not strictly iambic. Chaucer's metrical innovation, then, consisted in combining the iambic rhythm of the English tradition with the decasyllabic line borrowed from the Continent.

The two main features that define the template of Chaucer's pentameter verse line are a fixed number of syllables per line and iambic feet. The number of feet corresponds to the number of strong syllables. Ideally, each foot includes a weak syllable followed by a strong syllable. The line is often split in two parts by a *caesura*. The caesura is a syntactic break which occurs commonly after the second foot, but also (with diminishing frequency) after the third foot, the fourth and the first foot, and, occasionally, even within the third and the fourth foot.

Syllabic count

The typical pentameter line has ten syllables, each one of which corresponds to a single metrical position.[9] Metrical positions can be weak (W) or strong (S); in iambic metres the weaks and the strongs alternate in strict succession.

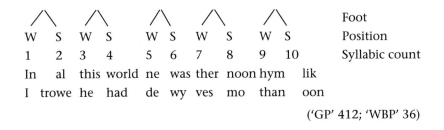

										Foot
W	S	W	S	W	S	W	S	W	S	Position
1	2	3	4	5	6	7	8	9	10	Syllabic count
In	al	this	world	ne	was	ther	noon	hym	lik	
I	trowe	he	had	de	wy	ves	mo	than	oon	

('GP' 412; 'WBP' 36)

The treatment of unstressed syllables follows the patterns discussed in the subsection on unstressed vowels above; loss of -*e* in hiatus, synizesis, and all the various contractions have to be taken into consideration when scanning the line. There are two well-known deviations from the basic syllabic count. One involves the possibility of an additional weak syllable at the end of the line, that is, the use of a feminine rhyme:

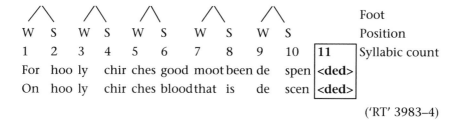

											Foot
W	S	W	S	W	S	W	S	W	S		Position
1	2	3	4	5	6	7	8	9	10	11	Syllabic count
For	hoo	ly	chir	ches	good	moot	been	de	spen	\<ded\>	
On	hoo	ly	chir	ches	blood	that	is	de	scen	\<ded\>	

('RT' 3983–4)

As noted earlier, the presence of an unstressed syllable as part of the end-rhyme is a frequent option in any kind of iambic syllable-counting verse. The syllable to the right of the last foot is outside the metrical scheme; it is *extrametrical*.[10] Extrametricality has a tightly limited application: only a single unstressed syllable can follow the last stressed position in the line. Any other prosodic arrangement would make the line unmetrical.

The second deviation from the ten-syllable count occurs when the initial foot is incomplete, that is, when it is missing its weak syllable. Again, this variation of the metre is shared with other types of iambic verse, resulting in seven syllables for the tetrameter line, or nine syllables for the pentameter. Lines in which the first position is unfilled are known as *headless* lines. Headless lines must start with a stressed syllable.

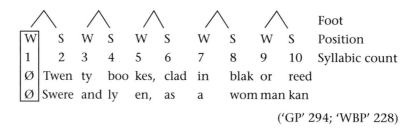

										Foot
W	S	W	S	W	S	W	S	W	S	Position
1	2	3	4	5	6	7	8	9	10	Syllabic count
Ø	Twen	ty	boo	kes,	clad	in	blak	or	reed	
Ø	Swere	and	ly	en,	as	a	wom	man	kan	

('GP' 294; 'WBP' 228)

Extrametricality and headlessness can be combined in a single line. If a line is headless, it can never have more than ten syllables, and if a tenth syllable is present, it is extrametrical. This is shown in the scansion of the lines below:

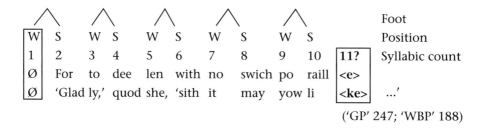

											Foot
W	S	W	S	W	S	W	S	W	S		Position
1	2	3	4	5	6	7	8	9	10	11?	Syllabic count
Ø	For	to	dee	len	with	no	swich	po	raill	\<e\>	
Ø	'Glad	ly,'	quod	she,	'sith	it	may	yow	li	\<ke\>	…'

('GP' 247; 'WBP' 188)

In such cases the appearance of ten syllables is deceptive: only nine of the basic metrical positions are filled, and the lines are headless; any other scansion would result in unnatural stressing within the line, for example, *deelén*, *gladlý*, and a strange placement of an unstressed -e in the strong tenth position. From this follows a very important observation which should guide the reader in the scansion: whether the leftmost position is filled or empty, the tenth position must always be filled by a stressed syllable.

Stress alternation

The basic stress alternation in the realization of iambic verse is that of unstressed syllables placed in the odd, or weak, positions, and stressed syllables placed in the even, or strong, positions. This type of fit between the abstract template and the actual line is by far the most frequent pattern found in Chaucer's verse. Once again, however, we can expect some variation in the realization of the basic scheme; after all, an unrelenting regularity of metre weakens the artistic effect of the composition and can degenerate into the burlesque. The most common type of variation which breaks the monotony and produces a more interesting prosodic contour is the reversal of the strength relations in the first foot: *iambic reversal*, or *trochaic substitution*, which places an unambiguously stressed syllable at the left edge of the line, followed by two unstressed syllables—a rhythmic *triple*:

> *Líggyng* abedde, and make hem for to grone.
> (*TC* 1. 915)

> *Áfter* thy text, ne after thy rubriche.
> ('WBP' 346)

> *Slépynge* agayn the sonne upon a day.
> ('ManT' 110)

The first foot is the most amenable metrical site for iambic reversal. As noted in the section on stress above, trochaic substitution in the first foot must be considered a valid prosodic option even in the case of French loan-words:

> *Jústice* he was ful often in assise.
> ('GP' 314)

> *Póynaunt* and sharp, and redy al his geere.
> ('GP' 352)

Trochaic substitutions resulting in a rhythmic triple occur also line-internally, but the likelihood of that decreases from left to right in the line. Occasionally there will be more than one reversed foot in a line, creating a strikingly different prosodic contour of the line in an otherwise fully iambic metrical context:

> As alle trouthe and alle gentilesse,
> *Wísdom, hónour, frédom,* and worthinesse.
> (*TC* 2. 160–1)

> To riden out, he loved chivalrie,
> *Tróuthe and hónour, frédom* and *cúrteisíe.*
> ('GP' 45–6)

The fifth foot in the verse disallows reversal; it can accommodate only iambic sequences. In that position compounds can shift the main stress from the first to the second element, and derived words may be stressed on the suffix:

Right so a wyf destroyeth hire *housbónde*.
('WBP' 377)

And al was fals, but that I took *witnésse*.
('WBP' 382)

The metrical template for Chaucer's iambic pentameter, as presented here, mandates that at least four weak and exactly five strong metrical positions in the line must be filled. If weak positions are filled by unstressed, and strong positions, by stressed syllables, the fit between metre and language is perfect. In speech, however, in present-day English, as well as in Chaucer's time, weak and strong syllables do not alternate at absolutely regular intervals: we produce strings of unstressed syllables, as well as stress-clashes between two or more stressed syllables. This inevitable discrepancy between the rhythm of speech and the abstract metrical scheme is sometimes taken as an argument against the metrical regularity of Chaucer's iambic pentameter. One of the hotly debated issues in Chaucerian metrical studies is whether Chaucer's ten-syllable line can legitimately be described as a five-stress line. It is indeed the case that Chaucer's narrative verse naturally reflects the imperfect stress alternation found in the spoken language, so that the number of full stresses in a line realized in recitation can be four or even three:

For of góod náme and wísdom and ma*nére*.
(*TC* 1. 880)

Póynaunt and shárp, and ré*dy al his* géere.
('GP' 352)

Thanne wolde he spéke and críe *as he were* wóod.
('GP' 636)

No one would want to *read* the first line here as 'For *óf* good náme and wísdom *ánd* manére', matching pedantically the surface string of syllables to the abstract metre. This does not mean that the lines above are not perfect instantiations of the iambic pentameter. In metre, as in language in general, the underlying categories and their surface realization can differ within some well-defined limits. In this case, the limits are set by the syllabic composition of the words and by their grammatical function. Monosyllabic words are free to occupy both strong and weak positions, though in practice nouns, verbs, and adjectives gravitate towards the strong positions, while function words are placed in the weak positions. However, if two full lexical monosyllables appear next to each other, one of them will be matched to a weak/odd position, and can therefore be pronounced with reduced stress, as is the case with the nouns *swerd* and *month* in the following lines:

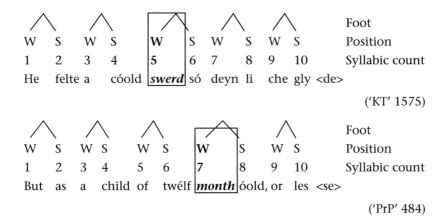

('KT' 1575)

('PrP' 484)

Similarly, within a string of unstressed syllables, including monosyllabic function words such as prepositions, auxiliaries, and pronouns, the syllable matched to a strong/even metrical position can be prosodically slightly more prominent:

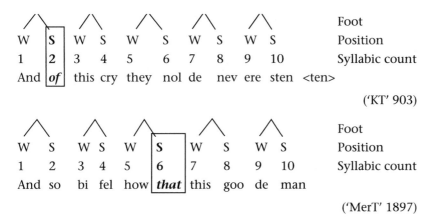

('KT' 903)

('MerT' 1897)

The degree of promotion of weak syllables filling strong positions in the line is largely a function of the grammatical nature of the syllable. Inflections cannot be promoted; a mismatch there would trigger iambic reversal. Determiners (*a*, *some*, *any*, *the*) are very rarely promoted. Prepositions and pronouns, as well as auxiliaries (*be*, *have*, *wol*) and conjunctions (*and*, *or*) are more promotable.

The adjustments to the syllable count described in the subsection on unstressed vowels and the metrical accommodations covered in this section account for over 98 per cent of the lines in Chaucer's pentameter verse. Bad lines do occur, but those are genuinely rare and attributing them to the poet or to one of his later scribes remains speculative if it cannot be decided on the basis of comparing manuscripts in each individual case.

This concludes our survey of three aspects of Chaucer's language: pronunciation, morphology, and metre. A full treatment of Chaucer's syntax, word-formation, semantics, and pragmatics will be found in the sources cited in Further Reading and the references there. As noted at the outset, the first step to understanding Chaucer's excellence is familiarity with the sounds and forms of fourteenth-century London English. I hope that this chapter will take the modern reader beyond the language barrier to a better appreciation of Chaucer's literary legacy.

FURTHER READING

Barney, Stephen, *Studies in 'Troilus': Chaucer's Text, Meter, and Diction* (East Lansing, Mich.: Colleagues Press, 1993). An indispensable companion to the editorial and philological intricacies of the manuscripts and early printed editions of Chaucer's *Troilus*.

Blake, Norman (ed.), *The Cambridge History of the English Language, ii: 1066–1476* (Cambridge: Cambridge University Press, 1992). The best in-depth and most comprehensive linguistic survey of Middle English.

Burnley, David, *A Guide to Chaucer's Language* (Norman: University of Oklahoma Press, 1983). The book offers original interpretations of the poet's grammar, syntax, and style.

Cannon, Christopher, *The Making of Chaucer's English: A Study of Words* (Cambridge: Cambridge University Press, 1998). An innovative interpretation of Chaucer's contribution to the formation of literary English. The book includes a very useful etymological index of Chaucer's lexicon.

Davis, Norman, 'Language and Versification', in *The Riverside Chaucer*, ed. Larry Benson, 3rd edn. (Boston: Houghton Mifflin, 1987), pp. xxix–xlv; (Oxford: Oxford University Press, 1988), pp. xxv–xli.

Fries, Udo, *Einführung in die Sprache Chaucers. Phonologie, Metrik und Morphologie* (Tübingen: Max Niemeyer Verlag, 1985). A comprehensive structuralist account of Chaucer's language and metre—the best single reference source for readers of German.

Horobin, Simon, *The Language of the Chaucer Tradition* (Cambridge: Brewer, 2003). The book concentrates on the manuscript evidence for reconstructing Chaucer's language, tracing the scribal and editorial transmission of Chaucer's work in the fifteenth century.

Kökeritz, Helge, *A Guide to Chaucer's Pronunciation* (New York: Holt, Rinehart, and Winston, 1953). A concise philologically sophisticated reconstruction of Chaucer's sounds; contains useful phonetic transcriptions of various passages from the *Tales* and *Troilus*.

Ten Brink, Bernhard, *Chaucers Sprache und Verskunst* (1884). A pioneering philological survey of Chaucer's language and metre, a classic work which has provided the foundation for all subsequent research in these areas. An English translation entitled *The Language and Metre of Chaucer* by M. Bentinck Smith appeared in 1901 (London: Macmillan).

NOTES

1. Square brackets enclose pronunciation; angle brackets enclose spelling.
2. See Helge Kökeritz, *A Guide to Chaucer's Pronunciation* (New York: Holt, Rinehart, and Winston, 1953), 9.
3. See further A. J. Bliss, 'Three Middle English Studies', *English and Germanic Studies*, 2 (1948–9), 40–54; D. Minkova and R. Stockwell, 'Chaucerian Phonemics: Evidence and Interpretation', in

Raymond Hickey and Stanislaw Puppel (eds.), *Language History and Linguistic Modelling* (Berlin: Mouton de Gruyter, 1997), 29–59.

4. See Kökeritz, *A Guide*, 15, and Norman Davis, 'Language and Versification', in *The Riverside Chaucer*, ed. Larry Benson, 3rd edn. (Boston: Houghton Mifflin, 1987), p. xxxii.

5. See Kökeritz, *A Guide*, 19; Davis, 'Language and Versification', p. xxx.

6. The estimate is based on a word's first appearance as recorded by the *Oxford English Dictionary*; see Albert C. Baugh and Thomas Cable, *A History of the English Language* (Englewood Cliffs, NJ: Prentice-Hall, 1993), 174.

7. For more details on this stylistic point, see David Burnley, *A Guide to Chaucer's Language* (Norman: University of Oklahoma Press, 1983), 17–23, and Norman Blake (ed.), *The Cambridge History of the English Language, ii: 1066–1476* (Cambridge: Cambridge University Press, 1992), 538–9.

8. See Burnley, *A Guide to Chaucer's Language*, 28–31, 122–3.

9. The discussion is based on R. Stockwell and D. Minkova, 'On the Partial-Contact Origins of English Pentameter Verse', in Dieter Kastovsky and Arthur Mettinger (eds.), *Language Contact in the History of English* (Frankfurt: Peter Lang, 2001), 337–63, and D. Minkova and Robert Stockwell, 'Editorial Emendation and the Chaucerian Metrical Template', in D. Minkova and T. Tinkle (eds.), *Chaucer and the Challenges of Medievalism: Essays in Honor of H. A. Kelly* (Frankfurt: Peter Lang, 2003), 129–40.

10. Here angle brackets enclose extrametrical syllables, following a common notational practice in the metrical literature.

9 | Philosophy

Richard Utz

One of the fascinating features of Chaucer's poetry is its richness in philosophical thought. So impressed was his contemporary, the French poet Eustache Deschamps (1346–1407), that he not only honoured Chaucer with the epithet of 'great translator', but also called him a 'Socrates filled with philosophy'.[1] In the nineteenth and the first half of the twentieth century, readers and critics of Chaucerian texts assumed that the two abilities praised by Deschamps were intimately related. Consequently, Chaucer's *Boece* (*c*.1380), an English translation of Boethius' *De consolatione philosophiae* (*c*.524), one of the most famous works in the history of medieval philosophy, was regarded as one of his prime achievements as a writer. Indeed, the existence of the *Boece* and the poet's ample use of material from it in many of his poems were seen as irrefutable evidence of his wholehearted support of Boethius' philosophical convictions. More recently this narrow view of direct textual and philosophical dependence has been revised by approaches which also take into consideration the specific late medieval character of Chaucer's philosophical leanings. Based on such contextualizing approaches, this chapter will discuss what Chaucer knew about philosophy, how he came in contact with philosophical thought, and how he included philosophical subject matter in his work.

Education and reading

Perhaps the biggest obstacle to gauging the philosophical content of Chaucer's poems and his philosophical convictions is the long and contested history of the term 'philosophy'. Twenty-first-century readers tend to associate philosophy with a clearly defined subject area taught in school and at university and comprising the study of ultimate reality, the most general causes and principles underlying conduct, thought, knowledge, and the nature of the universe. In the fourteenth century the term was far from denoting an autonomous discipline, and much philosophical speculation was still accomplished by theologians intending to find rational proof whereby to plumb the mysteries of the Christian God. Accordingly, any debate over Chaucer's knowledge and use of philosophy will need to take into account the foundational role of religious belief and theological doctrine. Moreover, late medieval non-academic uses of 'philosophy' were so undefined as to include any interest in general wisdom or the knowledge of things and their causes. Thus, even Pandarus, the verbose go-between of *Troilus and Criseyde*, whose speech is replete with abstract proverbial sayings, would have qualified as a philosophical thinker.[2] Similarly, the *Canterbury Tales* extends the definition of 'philosopher' to mean 'astrologer' ('MLT' 310) and 'magician' ('FrT' 1561).

We should imagine much of Chaucer's direct contact with learning in general and with all kinds of specific philosophical teachings as occurring within this medieval cultural framework. Like the Prioress's 7-year old 'litel clergeon' ('PrT' 503), Chaucer would have attended a 'grammar school' to gain access to Latin, the language of the theological, scientific, and philosophical discourses. In the absence of modern means of record-keeping, he would have committed to memory hundreds of short selections from student anthologies (for example, *Cato's Distichs*), including many of the pithy moral sayings and illustrative anecdotes (*exempla*) with which as adult poet he would later sprinkle his texts. Even as an adult, after refining his knowledge of Latin and French (and learning Italian) during his service in noble households and as soldier and minor diplomat, most of Chaucer's surface acquaintance with classical and medieval philosophical thought would have originated from easily available intermediary sources (anthologies, miscellanies, moral and homiletic compilations, and encyclopedias) and only in exceptional cases from the scarcely accessible original versions. The simpler syntax of such digested versions of otherwise forbidding texts and subjects rendered the poet's task of remembering, or Englishing and medievalizing, these selections a much less daunting task. He even preferred to follow a twelfth-century French translation and a fourteenth-century Latin commentary when translating the prose parts of Boethius' *Consolation of Philosophy* from Latin into Middle English. It is mainly upon this translation of the *Consolation* that Chaucer's reputation as a more than superficially philosophical poet rests.

Boethius' *Consolation of Philosophy*

Few texts have had such a profound influence on the history of Western thought as the *Consolation of Philosophy*. Its Roman author, Anicius Manlius Severinus Boethius (*c.*475–525), was a veritable polymath and remained through his various treatises, textbooks, commentaries, and translations the principal source of Aristotelian philosophy and the most widely known music theorist until the advent of the Renaissance. During the semi-Roman regime of the Ostrogothic king Theodoric, he rose to the highest ranks of statesmanship, but was later suspected of treason, imprisoned, and finally executed. He apparently produced the *Consolation* around the year 524, while in prison and awaiting his trial and execution, which convinced some medieval readers that his tragic death was brought about by his adherence to the Christian faith. As a historically true testament of Boethius' own fall, the *Consolation* was recognized as a philosophical statement applicable to various other sudden and undeserved desperate circumstances and consequently became, throughout the Middle Ages, the most widely circulated of all early medieval writings. As a piece of applied philosophy providing solace in the face of the vagaries of statesmanship, it became essential reading for many a monarch, and it is quite possible that Chaucer's own translation was commissioned to serve in the education of the young Richard II. The treatise had already been chosen by Alfred the Great as one of the seminal works he translated (or had translated) from Latin into Old English (*c.*887–892) as part of his ambitious educational reforms. Seven hundred years later, in 1593, when distraught about Henry IV of France's conversion from Protestantism to Catholicism, Elizabeth I similarly sought the consolations of philosophy by translating Boethius' work into Early Modern English.

The *Consolation of Philosophy* is an analytical 'prosimetrum' (sometimes referred to as a 'Menippean satire', its Roman precursor genre), in which passages of philosophical prose dialogue between a Boethius-like persona and a personified (Lady) Philosophy alternate with meditative 'meters' (poems) in a variety of stanzaic patterns. From this pioneering example of pre-modern literary psychotherapy emerges what the German philosopher Gottfried Wilhelm von Leibniz (1646–1716) termed 'theodicy', the justification of God's omnipotence, omniscience, and eternal benevolence in the face of the evil and sufferings endured by human beings on earth. The Boethian persona, who complains bitterly about the unjust adversities originating from a fickle goddess named Fortuna, is instructed by Lady Philosophy that Fortune only seems like chance from a human vantage point, but that from God's timeless perspective it is part of the divine order of things (providence) and all her workings are just and right. Thus, bad things happen to good people only when they fall for the false attractions Fortune offers. Instead of trusting in the mutability inherent in all of Fortune's gifts, Lady Philosophy recommends indifference to or downright contempt of the world (*contemptus mundi*) as an assured remedy against Fortune's disappointments.

Chaucer and the *Consolation of Philosophy*

If Boethius' *Consolation* presented an attractive solution to a serious theological question, it had an added appeal to Chaucer the poet. Chaucer and his contemporaries were strongly oriented towards the past and thought of themselves as augmenting (in the etymological sense of the word 'author') familiar storylines by expanding upon or abbreviating the versions of some of the most famous literary models, 'Virgile, Ovide, Omer, Lucan, and Stace' (*TC* 5. 1792). Chaucer would tacitly have considered these models' stories as unfinished, but would have thought their pre-Christian philosophical and religious foundations raised difficult issues for the Christian adapter.

The *Consolation of Philosophy*, which offers a rational philosophical statement of the providence of God without ever making direct reference to Christ, the clergy, or religious institutions, must have appeared to him as the perfect link between the pagan classical tradition and his medieval Christian present. Thus, Chaucer recognized and used for his own poetry the formidable synthetic quality Boethius' work had for medieval readers in general: while it provides a secure foundation for a Christian belief in an all-benevolent Creator–God, it does so with the help of natural reason and is based on the thought systems of 'pagan' philosophers such as Plato and Seneca.

Chaucer realized this specific mediating potential of Boethian thought between pagan and Christian materials in his 'Knight's Tale'. The Knight, who not only knows about the ups and downs of courtly love but also has experienced the dangerous powers of Fortune by participating in wars all over the known medieval world, regales the Canterbury pilgrims with a story from classical antiquity that is replete with sudden and undeserved reversals of chance: the two protagonists, Palamon and Arcite, represent what is left of the proverbially fate-stricken city of Thebes and the family of Oedipus, the man who killed his own father and married his own mother. To explain his resolution of urging Palamon and Emelye to marry after Arcite's death, Duke Theseus delivers the so-called 'First Mover speech', containing material based on Chaucer's *Boece* ('KT' 2987–3016, 3035–40; *B* 2, met. 8; 4, pr. 6; 3, pr. 10). Here, Theseus repeats Lady Philosophy's position, namely that a 'faire cheyne of love' (2991), created by 'thilke Moevere stable ... and eterne' (3004), perfectly regulates the universe and the earth. Since humans cannot understand the creator's 'wise purveiaunce' (3011) and since they may not escape his eternal order, in which everything and everybody has a foreseen specific beginning and end, they might as well make 'vertu of necessitee, | And take it weel that we may nat eschue' (3042–3). Such a philosophy of life, one in which the existing social and political order cannot be challenged since it has been ordained by a divine creator, perfectly pleases the Knight, who would have identified with Theseus' principles of authoritarian governance. The privileged position of his social class, which is guaranteed by a God-given, and thus unchangeable, idealized social order consisting of three estates (nobility, clergy, and peasants), had been under continued attack by an increasingly influential middle class since the twelfth century. By identifying the Boethian 'First Mover' with a pagan deity, 'Juppiter' (3035), the Knight establishes for the pre-Christian protagonists of Thebes and Athens a kind of proto-Christian mindset. This connection between the medieval Christian social order and its classical precursor societies, a great chain of historical 'successiouns' and 'progressiouns' (3013–14) all emanating from the same divine creator, exists since time immemorial and should not be changed.

Another famous Boethian passage is Troilus' speech on predestination (*TC* 4. 953–1085; compare *B* 5, prs. 2–3). When his love relationship with Criseyde is in grave danger, Troilus, an irrational and impulsive character rather than a philosophical thinker, surprises readers by entering into a lengthy consideration of the antagonism between predestination and free will. Specifically, he complains about the two irreconcilable positions held by thinkers who debate the issue:

> But natheles, allas, whom shal I leeve?
> For ther ben grete clerkes many oon
> That destyne thorugh argumentes preve;
> And som men seyn that nedely ther is noon,
> But that fre chois is yeven us everychon.
> O, welaway! So sleighe arn clerkes olde
> That I not whos opynyoun I may holde. (4. 967–73)

What follows is almost verbatim Boethius' argument in the *Consolation*: Troilus disputes with himself the existing opinions for twenty-odd stanzas and concludes that God's foreknowledge of events predestines them to happen. Since 'thynges . . . | mowe nat ben eschued' (4. 1077–8), he has no ability to determine his own course of action, abandons all hope to keep Criseyde, and prays to the gods to deliver both lovers from this earth as quickly as possible. In the *Consolation*, Boethius' long-winded argument is followed by Lady Philosophy's rational explanation of 'the olde questioun of the purveaunce of God' (*B* 5, pr. 4). She distinguishes between two natures of knowing: unlike human beings, who live in history and perceive events in past, present, and future time, the nature of the divine being is eternal, and God's knowledge transcends all movement of time, perceiving all things in an immediate present. From the perspective of divine knowledge functioning in a never-changing present, future events and acts of free will are necessary only because of the *condition* of their being known by God (conditional necessity). Considered in themselves, however, acts of free will are not necessary (simple necessity); before they happened, they were able not to happen. Troilus, of course, does not have a Lady Philosophy as an adviser, but simply his pedestrian and practically minded friend Pandarus, who dismisses Troilus' entire philosophical 'disputyng with hymself' (4. 1084) as a foolish endeavour.

Although Troilus' reflections happen at the time of a tragic reversal in his love relationship with Criseyde, there is an element of situation comedy in the young knight's long digression into scholastic thought. Chaucer may have thought the distinction between conditional and simple necessity a particularly funny example of the high-flown philosophical discussions regarding free will when applied to a real-life situation.

In the 'Nun's Priest's Tale' he has the narrator insert a passage which even more obviously pokes fun at misguided philosophical sophistication. When Chauntecleer leaves the security of the hen house and descends into the yard despite a dream that had warned him to watch out for danger on that day, the narrator waxes philosophical, only to acknowledge that there is little need for such an intellectual digression since his tale is, after all, about chickens:

> in scole is greet altercacioun
> In this mateere, and greet disputisoun,
> And hath been of an hundred thousand men.

But I ne kan nat bulte it to the bren
As kan the hooly doctour Augustyn,
Or Boece, or the Bisshop Bradwardyn,
Wheither that Goddes worthy forwityng
Streyneth me nedely for to doon a thyng—
'Nedely' clepe I symple necessitee—
Or elles, if free choys be graunted me
To do that same thyng, or do it noght,
Though God forwoot it er that I was wroght;
Or if his wityng streyneth never a deel
But by necessitee condicioneel.
I wol nat han to do of swich mateere;
My tale is of a cok, as ye may heere. (3237–52)

Of course, the Nun's Priest might have felt the need to balance the Monk's tediously repetitious and simplistic medieval tragedies in the tale that precedes his. All the Monk has retained from Boethius' *Consolation* is its advice that orientation towards the worldly goods proffered by Fortune will engender unhappiness. The central image of his stories is the ever-turning wheel of Fortune, upon which figures from Satan, Hercules, Julius Caesar, through to Bernabò Visconti have climbed and from which they have all been hurled down to destruction and death. There is no mention of Lady Philosophy's explanation—given in book 5 of the *Consolation*—that all Creation is fundamentally ordered and benevolent and that in loving the Good, that is, God, we may reach a substantial degree of happiness even while on earth. As a result, fate, not individual responsibility, causes these men's downfall, and the Monk's world appears unjust and meaningless, a solution that resembles Pope Innocent III's *De contemptu mundi*, which Chaucer claims to have translated as the 'Wreched Engendrynge of Mankynde' in the Prologue to the *Legend of Good Women* (G 414). Like Innocent III's treatise, the Monk's *exempla* hope to scare the audience into contempt of all things mundane. The Nun's Priest mocks this one-sided view of human tragedy by telling a story of the fall (and subsequent miraculous rise) of a cock, and Chaucer may have ascribed to him the section on simple and conditional necessity to demonstrate how unrefined the Monk's views are.

While these examples demonstrate Chaucer's direct borrowing of Boethian passages for a variety of specific narrative purposes, the *Consolation* may also have suggested to him the designing of the particular relationship between narrator and author emerging from several of his works. He may have found Boethius' own masked presence as a naïf who is slowly progressing in wisdom during the course of a given story a particularly helpful device when speaking to a courtly, hence socially superior, audience. In *Troilus and Criseyde*, for example, the narrator–author might be seen to live through such a personal spiritual growth process. In the beginning, he simply is a 'sorwful instrument' (1. 10) who intends to advance his own soul towards salvation by serving the 'God of Loves servantz' (1. 15). By the time the lovers spend their first night of love together, he is ready to sell his own soul for the 'leeste joie' Troilus and Criseyde are experiencing

(3. 1319–20). And finally, he moves on to offer a religious resolution of his story that ends in Troilus' contemptuous look down on all earthly pleasures and a prayer to the 'sothfast Crist, that starf on rode' (5. 1860). Advancing in perspective together with such a humble and ignorant, but slowly evolving, voice would have inclined a courtly audience to receive instruction even on 'Love', their own social class's preferred topic. The never fully resolved ambiguity about the source of the audience's information, narrator or author, would have offered Chaucer the opportunity to interweave elements of realism and fiction and to experiment with the creative tension between the authority of his sources and his own poetic freedom. This freedom is palpable when he attaches a few stanzas advocating contempt of the world to a poem which, until its Boethian 'epilogue', seemed to celebrate, as much as it might question, the secular love the 'yonge, fresshe folkes' (5. 1835) in his audience desired to hear and read about.

Chaucer's varied and often playful adaptation of the structural and philosophical aspects of the *Consolation* to his own poetry offers little evidence of the poet's own views. Even his short moral ballad 'Truth', a straightforward literary exemplification of the Boethian *contemptus mundi* and the biblical 'Truth shall set you free' (John 8: 22), may be less a sign of Chaucer's wholehearted agreement with the early medieval philosopher than a writer's finger exercise with a popular genre. One of the manuscript versions of the poem incorporates a dispatching stanza, or 'envoi', addressed to Sir Philip de la Vache (1346–1408), who, like Chaucer, was out of favour with the Lords Appellant, a group of powerful barons who either influenced or controlled the English government between 1386 and 1389. It seems that the poet may have added the 'envoi' to encourage his friend to remain true to his word, that is, remain supportive of the young Richard II, whose powers the Lords Appellant had weakened but whom they never deposed. However, even this rather sombre-sounding advice to remain stoically indifferent to all the 'wrecchednesse' of this world (22), and stay his political course, is delivered in a humorous and playful tone. When Chaucer admonishes de la Vache with the words 'Forth, beste, out of thy stal!' (18), he puns on his friend's French family name, which means 'cow'.

Non-Boethian contexts

The notorious playfulness of Chaucer's writing noted above has not kept readers from claiming that his translating of the *Consolation*, as well as the extensive borrowings from it for his poetry, mean that Chaucer thought of Boethius as a congenial spirit or that he even agreed with Boethius on the meaning of life and the way in which life should be conducted. The predominance of scientistic methodology in language and literature study in the nineteenth and first part of the twentieth century (then usually called 'philology') made scholars hunt exclusively for direct textual evidence of Boethian influence in Chaucer's works. Scholars thinking and researching within this methodological paradigm drew up impressive lists documenting these examples of unimpeachable evidence, but they concomitantly silenced readings that would have contextualized the poet's use of a late classical or early medieval text within late medieval philosophical and theological debates.

There are two main considerations why such contexts should be included in readings of Chaucer's philosophy. First, when working on his translation of the *Consolation*, Chaucer consulted sources that had already managed to bring Boethius closer to his own times. In the absence of a Middle English translation, he used *Li Livres de confort*, a thirteenth-century French translation by Jean de Meun. Of even greater impact may have been the most popular and widely influential of the many medieval commentaries on the *Consolation*, composed by the English Dominican Nicholas Trevet late in the thirteenth or very early in the fourteenth century (before 1304). De Meun's French translation and Trevet's Latin glosses clearly assisted Chaucer in acquiring a practical understanding of Boethius' original. They were exactly the kind of intermediaries the poet needed for his own interpretative translation, the *Boece*, in which he expounds the meaning of the sixth-century text for himself and his fourteenth-century readership.

Secondly, when looking for the typically late medieval mindset that might have guided Chaucer in his adaptations of early medieval philosophical thought, we shall need to include the general intellectual and cultural climate of the fourteenth century in addition to direct influences through texts and personal acquaintances. While students of literature in the early twenty-first century may not have read Sigmund Freud or Jacques Lacan in the original, they may still have a general understanding of both psychoanalytic thinkers because their theories—be it the Oedipal complex or the 'mirror stage' respectively—have trickled down into mainstream academic or even popular culture. Similarly, some of the major late medieval philosophical and theological debates will have been known to Chaucer as part of what scholars representing different critical methodologies have termed 'Zeitgeist' (spirit of the age), 'mentalité' (mentality), or 'milieu' (environment, setting). Thus, while the *Consolation* may have supplied Chaucer with numerous building blocks for becoming a philosophical poet, it would have been his own century that provided him with a specifically late medieval understanding of those building blocks and shaped his conception of the value of philosophical reflection.

Augustinianism

In Chaucer studies, the search for the general medieval Zeitgeist that would have surrounded the poet is often associated with the name of D. W. Robertson, Jr., and the movement of criticism he established. Robertson, dismayed by interpretations of medieval literature that disregarded its specifically medieval nature, postulated the radical alterity of medieval texts. He claimed that all medieval artists and writers were immersed in the system of seeing and interpreting developed by the early Church fathers, especially Augustine of Hippo's *De doctrina christiana*. This multi-layered system of expounding the Bible (exegesis) assumed that God, the 'real' author of the Bible, had established in his text a hierarchical structure that would help readers to be guided from the world of visible phenomena to that of invisible ones, from a 'literal' or 'historical' level of understanding (*sensus literalis*) to a spiritual one (*sensus mysticus/spiritualis*). A common medieval example was 'Jerusalem', which, on the literal level, simply meant a series of letters making up the word, and on the historical level, the actual city. The spiritual level could have up to three semantic distinctions: on an allegorical level, which relates words to salvation history, 'Jerusalem' represents the Church; on a tropological level, which relates words to an edifying moral or to advice on conducting one's life, it symbolizes the soul of the believer; and on an anagogical level, which relates words to ultimate things (death, salvation), it stands for the heavenly City of God.

Robertson did not expect that artists and writers without the direct divine inspiration of the four evangelists would include all four of these levels. However, their thorough training in seeing in every object, picture, or story a symbol that might serve as a disguised representation for meanings beyond those indicated on the surface would have made it almost a natural effort to produce art that should be understood as functioning on more than one level. Applied to the frame of the *Canterbury Tales*, few readers would deny that the literal level of the actual pilgrimage might invoke the universal Christian pilgrimage to the heavenly Jerusalem. However, the dangers of Robertsonian–Augustinian readings become obvious when we would reduce the psychologically intricate *Troilus and Criseyde* into a simple admonition against the dangers of carnal desire: Troilus would then figure as a misguided Adam, Criseyde as an eternally fickle Eve, and Pandarus as the tempter and evil incarnate. According to this system of interpretation, Chaucer's entire writerly craft would have served an exclusively didactic function: to camouflage Christian lore within popular classical stories in order to guide his audiences towards spiritual salvation (for more on Robertsonian criticism, see Chapter 19).

The crucial deficiency of this approach is its postulating the totalizing idea of a uniform Christian Middle Ages in which all artists, from the end of the Roman through to the end of the Byzantine empire, were following the same system of textual encoding and decoding. Chaucer appears to have begun with texts that invite readings on at least a second referential plane: the *Book of the Duchess* is without doubt an attempt at consoling John of Gaunt for the death of his wife, Blanche, duchess of Lancaster; and the *Parliament of Fowls* is perhaps commenting on the negotiations in 1380 for the betrothal of Richard II to Anne of Bohemia. However, the allegorical levels in these two texts are personal and political. In general, Chaucer avoided any sustained use of religious allegory, which means that there is little cause for forcing extended exegetical readings upon his texts. The possible causes for the poet's avoidance can be seen in some late medieval views on how human beings know and believe.

Late medieval literalism

One reason why a homogenized idea of medieval culture cannot do justice to explaining Chaucer's thoughts on philosophical issues is the existence of a movement of religious dissent like the one begun by the Oxford theologian John Wyclif (c.1328–1384). Among a host of issues Wyclif and his followers, the so-called Lollards, had with the late medieval Church was its jealously guarded control over the text and interpretation of Holy Scripture. A forerunner of the Protestant Reformation, Wyclif demanded that all Christians receive direct access to the Bible, and he himself achieved the first complete translation of the Vulgate into (Middle) English to help his propositions become reality. The reformer thought that parish priests should cease performing services in Latin and that friars should be taken to task for embellishing, and thereby falsifying, the biblical stories. Instead of the expounding of three or four levels of meaning, he trusted that the literal meaning and a literalistic understanding of the actual words in the Bible conveyed higher authority than a trained specialist's learned exegesis. The consequences of his literalism became especially apparent when applied to the doctrine of transubstantiation. The Church claimed that during the central moment of mass, the ritual of consecration, bread and wine, without changing their external appearance, miraculously changed their material substance and became the body and blood of Jesus. Wyclif's position was that mere words, even when spoken by a priest, could not possibly change the material substance of the elements, a position supported by the growing empirical attitude among late medieval thinkers and exemplified, albeit humorously, by the Wife of Bath in her Prologue.

What Wyclif's literalist position might mean to Chaucer, the poet, becomes obvious in the 'General Prologue' to the *Canterbury Tales*, where the narrator authenticates the tales as his word-by-word record of what every pilgrim said:

> Whoso shal telle a tale after a man,
> He moot reherce as ny as evere he kan
> Everich a word, if it be in his charge,
> Al speke he never so rudeliche and large,
> Or ellis he moot telle his tale untrewe,
> Or feyne thyng, or fynde wordes newe.
> He may nat spare, althogh he were his brother;
> He moot as wel seye o word as another.
> Crist spak hymself ful brode in hooly writ,
> And wel ye woot no vileynye is it.
> Eek Plato seith, whoso kan hym rede,
> The wordes moote be cosyn to the dede. (731–42)

While the claim to adhere to the very letter of one's source is a well-known motif in classical and medieval literature, the poet's particular insistence on making the relationship between 'words' and 'things' such a central topic may be indicative of his awareness of (Christian) literalism in his immediate surroundings.[3] Chaucer, who may have known Wyclif personally while both men shared John of Gaunt as their royal patron, and who was associated with a group of Richard II's chamber knights who displayed Wycliffite sympathies, shows some indication in his poetry that he thought of literalism as a helpful epistemological principle. In the *Book of the Duchess*, for example, the literalistic and incompetent naivety of the poet–dreamer and the sophisticated metaphoricity of the mournful 'man in blak' (445) allow for a situation in which Chaucer, the social inferior, can communicate with his patron, the powerful John of Gaunt, about the loss of his wife, Duchess Blanche. As their at times hilarious (mis)communication continues, it is the dreamer's obstinate inability to understand the knight's protective symbolic speech that helps the knight acknowledge the reality of his loss. Exhausted by his own hyperbolic attempts to shield himself from the awful truth, the knight finally yields to the dreamer's therapeutic insouciance and cries out, 'She ys ded!', to which the dreamer laconically replies, 'Be God, hyt ys routhe!' (1309–10). The inevitable material reality of the knight's loss has found an apt expression in these short, literalistic lines, and the poem ends soon thereafter.[4]

We find the same kind of literalistic attitude throughout Chaucer's poetry. It serves to produce situation comedy as when the naive carpenter in the 'Miller's Tale' misinterprets the burned Nicholas's cry for 'Water!' as the onset of 'Nowelis flood' (3815–18); or it can reflect a serious critique of medieval double standards about an adulterous woman who, depending on her social class, could be praised as a man's 'lady, as in love' or scorned as 'his wenche or his lemman' ('ManT' 218–20). It may be this tendency to point to the chasm between the primary meanings of words and their figurative, metaphorical, or allegorical implications that has rendered Chaucer's texts so attractive to modern readers who hold, in opposition to dominant medieval epistemology, that ultimate reality rests with the secular material world.

Late medieval nominalism

There is a second movement of thought, late medieval nominalism, which could also have strengthened what appears to most contemporary readers as Chaucer's more empirical or naturalistic mentality. The rise of this movement is usually associated with another Oxford theologian, the Franciscan William of Ockham (*c.*1285–1349), whom Umberto Eco memorialized as a fictional detective, William of Baskerville, in his medievalist bestseller *The Name of the Rose* (1980).

Late medieval nominalism began as a conservative movement whose adherents intended to defend God's power against the increasingly rationalistic attempts to explain away the mystery of his omnipotence. Plato's theory of knowledge had postulated that our world and everything in it was framed in the likeness of unchanging 'forms', ungenerated and indestructible. Medieval Neoplatonic theology Christianized

Plato's 'forms' into the 'ideas' in the divine mind, a principle that offered the foundation for an endless series of analogical relationships between cause and effect, that is, between the Creator's ideas and all Creation. Among these were the cosmological theory that all planetary movement is caused by certain eternal and innate principles of motion, the political theory that society is an organic body with a precise and necessary structure, the epistemological theory that all abstractions or universal concepts have real existence, the theory of physiognomics that certain bodily traits always reveal the state of a person's soul, and the artistic theory that an abstract form of behaviour may be properly represented through an allegorical figure (or, conversely, that a literary protagonist would necessarily imply spiritual concepts in addition to a literal one on the level of a specific story).

Nominalist thinkers challenged the foundations of this system because the eternal validity of these relational conditions implicitly limited the immediacy and free will of God's power. They stressed the distinction between two aspects of God's power, the *potentia absoluta* (all the possibilities open to God, absolutely and hypothetically speaking) and the *potentia ordinata* (those possibilities he has chosen and which are visible in the existing order of Creation). According to his absolute power, he could have chosen to create a different world, to incarnate himself as an ass or a stone, or to cause someone to see something that did not really exist. The only limitation to this power is the principle of non-contradiction—that is, God cannot do something logically contradictory. Of course, God has promised that he will follow his chosen order, so in fact God will not suddenly and arbitrarily exercise his absolute power to compromise the goodness and reliability of the divine legislator.[5] However, even the hypothetical possibility of God's exercise of his *potentia absoluta* became a tool for advancing theoretical speculation among scholastic thinkers, and the concentration on the nature of God's absolute power led to a systematic critique of all analogical thought. Without the validity of analogy, gaining knowledge about God by linking his eternal ideas and intentions to their visible consequences in the cosmic and human order no longer made sense and rendered the world a potentially contingent place, one in which the complex motivations of human agency replace God's determining and eternally reliable master plan. Parallel with this theological and philosophical critique of the systemic limitations of analogy, various other late medieval condemnations of analogical thought by scientific and political theorists can be seen as coeval phenomena originating from the same cultural conditions. It appears that the complex nature of fourteenth-century reality—the Black Death (after 1347), the Hundred Years War (1337–1453), the revolts of the French Jacquerie (1357) and the English peasants (1381), the rise of the middle class, and the violent dissension in the Church (culminating in the Great Schism, 1378–1417)—presented a radical contingency and uncertainty that questioned the existing order of things and the analogical relationality constructed to keep it in place.

Chaucer could have had direct knowledge of nominalist thought through sermons, public university disputations, popularized versions of nominalist views such as in

Robert Holcot's widely known *Wisdom Commentary* (*Super libros sapientiae*), or through his friend the philosopher Ralph Strode, whose treatises on logic had nominalist leanings and to whom Chaucer dedicated (together with John Gower) his *Troilus and Criseyde*. But even without direct nominalist influence, the broad fourteenth-century opposition to epistemological analogy would have interested him as a poet. If he intended to portray the contingency of his fourteenth-century life, there was little reason to resort to allegorical personae (universals) which, speaking nominalistically, did not correspond to anything knowable outside poetry, but were only 'names' (hence, 'nominalism'). Similarly, since allegorical characters are limited to one-dimensional motivations such as 'charity' or 'lust', a poet would deprive himself of depicting paradox, ambiguity, or wilful decision-making. Furthermore, allegorical writing may be a fine tool for writers interested in teaching a specific lesson: Prudentius' early medieval *Psychomachia* instructs Christian readers how to fight humanity's eternal battle against evil, and Jean de Meun's *Roman de la Rose* successfully inculcates behavioural patterns for those in the process of becoming knights and courtly lovers. Both texts generate symbols and provide in advance the accurate reading of these symbols, so that, epistemologically, meaning precedes narrative in allegorical texts. However, if a writer was either not on a didactic mission or thought it preferable—for reasons of social position or aesthetic pleasure—to leave his texts open to the judgement of his audiences, he would perhaps reject the allegorical mode.

The nominalist concentration on God's absolute power separated theological assertions about God and about nature and led to the rise of two distinct levels of truth: a religious truth of revelation, which was the only secure truth and which could only be reached by faith alone; or a contingent, secular truth that could be gained through human rational thinking. This separation of truth resulted in a shift of interest from transcendence to immanence or, more simply put, it encouraged humans to speculate on the world as though God were non-existent. This induced a restless taking stock of the world of visible phenomena. Nominalist philosophers and scientists, when following their new secular logic, would arrive at theses contradicting Christian doctrine and consequently had to recant and take a leap of faith. Indeed, leaving certain treatises unfinished or deciding in favour of the orthodox teachings of the Church after amassing evidence to the contrary became almost habitual for nominalist thinkers. Nicholas Oresme (1320–82), who used logic and mathematics to prove the possibility of a heliocentric universe, abandoned his theory when challenged for the fideistic assertion that God had made the existing geocentric one.

Could a similar feeling of caution explain the chasm readers have observed between the questions raised and the answers given (or withheld) by some of Chaucer's poems or the fact that he left so many of his poems unfinished? The *House of Fame* stops short when 'A man of gret auctorite' (2158) might have sorted out the dreamer–narrator's abundance of volatile sense impressions; the *Legend of Good Women* contains two prologues and breaks off just as the narrator relates that his 'Legend of Hypermnestra' was all 'seyd for this conclusioun—' (2723); the tales of the Cook, the Squire, and Chaucer the pilgrim remain without closure, and the *Canterbury Tales* as a whole is fragmentary and ends in a highly ambiguous 'Retraction'. The *Parliament of Fowls* raises questions about value, but never resolves them; and *Troilus and Criseyde* ends in a leap of faith incommensurate with the force of the issues and emotions raised throughout the poem. It appears that the poet was unable or unwilling to adapt his sources to unified and orthodox interpretations of human reality. Like some of his contemporaries at late medieval universities, Chaucer may have made a structural virtue of a cultural necessity.[6]

Finally, a nominalist mentality may also help explain why Chaucer applied practically all his substantial Boethian passages either in a humorous fashion and/or without Lady Philosophy's solutions to the Boethian persona's plaintive questions. If the visible world no longer had analogical signifying power to point towards the invisible ideas of the Creator, then the 'faire cheyne of love' ('KT' 2991), the symbolic cord thought to link every being and thing in the universe to 'thilke Moevere stable . . . and eterne' ('KT' 3004), had been cut. In such a contingent, nominalistic world, the cause and effect of all things would have to be attributed to human action, and it would appear more fitting that the befuddled proverbialist Pandarus attempt to answer Troilus' soliloquy on predestination and free will than an omniscient personified allegory like Lady Philosophy.

Conclusion

As new generations of readers ponder the question of Chaucer's philosophical leanings, we should bear in mind that the view of a nominalist Chaucer developed coevally with postmodern notions of the twentieth century's own radically contingent character, and that earlier positions about Chaucer's direct textual and personal dependence on Boethius' *Consolation* were advanced by several generations of committed textual scholars. If the main theories on this topic seem to depend on which kind of author representatives of certain scholarly paradigms project into their particular image of Chaucer, it is all the more crucial to read and investigate each philosophical statement in his texts from a variety of perspectives. Thus, any responsible approach to the elusive medieval and contemporary term 'philosophy' and the philosophical content in Chaucer's writing should include questions about direct textual influence, specific literary context, the general medieval tradition, the specific late medieval Zeitgeist, and an awareness of our own scholarly desires and intentions.

FURTHER READING

Delaney, Sheila, 'Undoing Substantial Connection: The Late Medieval Attack on Analogical Thought', *Mosaic*, 5/4 (1972), 33–52; repr. in her *Medieval Literary Politics: Shapes of Ideology*

(Manchester: Manchester University Press, 1990). Surveys the relationship between analogy, allegory, and their fourteenth-century discontents.

Eldredge, Laurence, 'Chaucer's *Hous of Fame* and the *Via Moderna*', *Neuphilologische Mitteilungen*, 71 (1970), 105–19. Reads Chaucer's poem as a parody of the search for transcendental truth, and thus as lending literary support to late medieval philosophical mentalities.

Jefferson, Bernard L., *Chaucer and the 'Consolation of Philosophy' of Boethius* (Princeton: Princeton University Press, 1917). The classic account of direct Boethian influence on Chaucer's poetry and mindset.

Lynch, Kathryn L., *Chaucer's Philosophical Visions* (Cambridge: Brewer, 2000). An illuminating discussion of the late medieval philosophical background of Chaucer's *Book of the Duchess, Parliament of Fowls, House of Fame*, and the Prologue to the *Legend of Good Women*.

Marenbon, John, *Boethius* (Oxford: Oxford University Press, 2003). A concise and accessible introduction to Boethian thought and its reception.

Minnis, A. J. (ed.), *Chaucer's 'Boece' and the Medieval Tradition of Boethius* (Cambridge: Brewer, 1993). Studies demonstrating Chaucer's dependence on Nicholas Trevet and Jean de Meun and discussing the *Boece* as a typically late medieval translation.

Peck, Russel A., 'Chaucer and the Nominalist Questions', *Speculum*, 53 (1978), 745–60. The single most influential essay considering Chaucer's potential leanings towards nominalist thought.

Robertson, D. W., Jr., *A Preface to Chaucer* (Princeton: Princeton University Press, 1962). One of the founding documents of Augustinianism in Chaucer studies.

Shepherd, Geoffrey, 'Religion and Philosophy in Chaucer', in Derek Brewer (ed.), *Geoffrey Chaucer* (Athens: Ohio University Press, 1975), 262–89. Surveys the late medieval English background for Chaucer's poetry with regard to both religion and philosophy.

Watts, William H., and Richard J. Utz, 'Nominalist Perspectives on Chaucer's Poetry: A Bibliographical Essay', *Medievalia et Humanistica*, NS 20 (1993), 147–73. A comprehensive critical survey of nominalist readings of Chaucer's poetry.

WEB LINK

Medieval Nominalism and the Literary Questions: Selected Studies: <http://www.perspicuitas.uni-essen.de/aufsatz.htm>>.

NOTES

1. *Œuvres complètes d'Eustache Deschamps*, ed. le marquis de Queux de Saint-Hilaire and Gaston Raynaud, Société des Anciens Textes Français, 11 vols. (Paris: Champion, 1878–1904), ii. 138–40, no. 138 (my translations).

2. See the entry 'philosopher' in Hans Kurath *et al.* (eds.), *Middle English Dictionary* (Ann Arbor: University of Michigan Press, 1956–), which includes 'proverbialist' among its semantic possibilities.

3. Another centrally placed discussion of the correspondence between words and things is contained in the 'Tale of Melibee' (940–64), and the entire 'Friar's Tale' can be read as negotiating the literalistic intention of curses.

4. This reading of the *Book of the Duchess* and its links to literalism has been advanced by Derek Brewer, *A New Introduction to Chaucer* (London: Longman, 1998), 98–9.

5. Elizabeth Kirk, in 'Nominalism and the Dynamics of the "Clerk's Tale": *Homo Viator* as Woman', in C. David Benson and Elizabeth Robertson (eds.), *Chaucer's Religious Tales* (Cambridge: Brewer, 1990), 111–20, has discussed the correspondences between Griselda's predicament as a woman under the constraints of Walter, her dictatorial husband, and the predicament of human beings living under the constraints of an omnipotent and wilful God. Kirk argues that Griselda's passive endurance becomes a means by which she asserts her autonomy and selfhood.

6. For readings examining these conspicuous structural features of Chaucer's poetry, see Larry Sklute, *Virtue of Necessity: Inconclusiveness and Narrative Form in Chaucer's Poetry* (Columbus: Ohio State University Press, 1985), and Richard Utz, 'Negotiating the Paradigm: Literary Nominalism and the Theory of Rereading Late Medieval Texts', in Utz (ed.), *Literary Nominalism and the Theory of Rereading Late Medieval Texts* (Lewiston, NY: Edwin Mellen, 1995), 1–30.

10 | Science

J. A. Tasioulas

It was believed in the Middle Ages that the earth was the fixed centre of the universe. The sun, the moon, and the five other known planets circled it, each one enclosed in its own transparent sphere, each sphere sitting inside the next like concentric balls of glass. The eighth sphere was that of the fixed stars and the ninth that of the *primum mobile*, the First Movable that sets the universe in motion. Beyond this, according to most accounts, is heaven itself, and God, whose love brings everything into being (see Figure I.6). For, even though the universe is in constant motion, it was clear to all medieval scientists that movement could not be infinite. There had to be a beginning, a point in the chain when something itself unmoved caused motion in everything else. From one point of view, therefore, it is a geocentric universe, with earth being the focus of the cosmos; and yet, it is also a God-centred universe: 'The engendrynge of alle thinges . . . and alle the progressiouns of muable nature, and al that moeveth in any manere, taketh hise causes, his ordre, and his formes, of the stablenesse of the devyne thought' (*B* 4, pr. 6. 42–7). All stability is derived from God and he is the cause of all harmony. The earth, on the other hand, being the furthest planet from the stable heavenly realm, is a place 'dissevable and ful of harde grace' (*PF* 65); so insignificant that mankind exists upon a mere pinprick on a pinprick in the universe (*B* 2, pr. 7. 43–4). Everything about this tiny planet was held to be mutable, consisting as it did of four unstable elements—water, air, fire, and earth—that were capable of changing into one another. Heaven was incorruptible and eternal but the earthly sphere was viewed as one of growth, decay, and change. Chaucer is working, therefore, within a cosmological system that views an imperfect earth as the heart of a perfect universe, and this belief pervades his scientific world-view. His interests encompass many of the nascent sciences and, indeed, the distinction between one branch of the subject and another is often blurred. However, we can discern three main areas that particularly engrossed Chaucer: astronomy, medicine, and magic.

Astronomy

Astronomy formed an essential part of the curriculum followed by all university students in the Middle Ages, largely, though not exclusively, because this highly

Fig. I.6 Creation of light and the spheres. Illustration from a Book of Hours, mid-fourteenth century (British Library, MS Egerton 2781).

mathematical science allowed the calculation of time. That Chaucer had a serious interest in astronomy is evident throughout his work but strikingly so in his translation of a scientific treatise on the use of one of the most important astronomical instruments. The astrolabe (from the Greek for 'star-catcher') was invaluable to medieval astronomers, allowing them to do everything from telling the time at night to calculating the position of the sun and stars for any required date. Chaucer's *Treatise on the Astrolabe*, ostensibly written (as it declares at the outset) for his son 'little Lewis', is a step-by-step guide to using one of these objects, straightforward enough to have been written for a child, though clearly produced by someone with a great deal of scientific knowledge. There are occasional poetic details, but it is essentially an instructional text intended to teach its reader how to manipulate the brass plates of the astrolabe to calculate time and astrological influence.[1]

Elsewhere in Chaucer's work, only the crafty student Nicholas of the 'Miller's Tale' explicitly owns an astrolabe, proudly displayed on a shelf above his bed, but other characters exhibit the sort of scientific knowledge the instrument would provide. It is never clear exactly how the clerk of the 'Franklin's Tale' manages to rid the coast of Brittany of rocks, but in spite of the Franklin's use of the word 'magik' (1295), what he gives is actually a list of astrological terms, tables, and machinery (1273–91). Indeed, the final section of Chaucer's *Treatise on the Astrolabe* is given over to just the kind of calculation of high tides the clerk may have required, and while the Franklin may justly claim that he knows 'no termes of astrologye' ('FrT' 1266), the passage has evidently been composed by someone who does. The poetry is suffused with astronomical references, always more than mere colourful details, and on many occasions Chaucer holds up his narrative in order to provide specific, often perplexing, accounts of planetary activity. The reference to Libra in the 'Parson's Prologue' may merely be a symbolic allusion to the balanced scales of divine justice, or it may be an indication of a specific date or event. As for the extremely rare conjunction of Saturn, Jupiter, and the moon in Cancer in *Troilus and Criseyde* (3. 624–5), it may allow Pandarus to predict some amatorily convenient rain but it also sets the consummation scene against a backdrop of portentous disaster linked to Noah's flood.[2]

Astrology and horoscopes

A further use for the medieval astrolabe was, of course, in the casting of horoscopes, the Middle Ages blurring the distinction between the science of astronomy and astrology. Chaucer claims in all seriousness in the *Treatise* that such matters are the 'rytes of payens, in whiche my spirit hath no feith, ne knowing of her *horoscopum*' (2. 4. 58–60), but he is still very much interested in the idea of planetary influence on human actions in his poetry. With so many tempting references, and even where there are none, critics have attempted to provide horoscopes for everyone from Harry Bailly to the chicken Pertelote (a Taurean, incidentally, and an astral sister of the Wife of Bath).[3] Nor is it simply a matter of ascertaining star signs, for medieval horoscopes were endlessly complicated, with further rarefications proliferating, such as fortune treatises that predicted the likely life—and time and manner of death—of those born in each 'nativity'; and 'election' treatises similarly offering each sign advice on the best times to undertake any enterprise.[4] A glance at the very popular medieval representations of 'zodiac man' reveals that the whole body was believed to be directly influenced by the planets. So, Pertelote's magnificent throat is no more than we would expect of a chicken born in the sign of the Bull ('NPT' 2869–70). The Wife of Bath has a birthmark on her face and 'also in another privee place' ('WBP' 619–20) that identify her as the splendid product of Mars and Venus and therefore, according to the ancient astrologer Ptolemy, 'ardent, impetuous and adulterous'.[5]

These are amusing details, but Chaucer occasionally provides us with horoscopes that are intended to dominate the narrative, notably those of Hypermnestra in the *Legend of Good Women*, and of Custance in the 'Man of Law's Tale'. Hypermnestra is a fittingly passive heroine for the final surviving tale in the *Legend*'s series of increasingly passive victims. As a group they tremble, shake, collapse, and faint through several thousand lines, culminating with Hypermnestra, who, faced with a father who demands that she murder her bridegroom or die, and unable to follow her husband as he flees through the window, finally 'sat hire doun ryght tho' to await her fate (2721). Indeed, Chaucer takes pains to ensure that any autonomy is taken, literally, out of her hands, as he ranks not just a vicious father and a fleet-footed husband against her, but also the whole cosmic machinery. Her entire future is charted in the detailed horoscope Chaucer provides for her at the beginning of her legend. We are told that the conjunction of Venus and Jupiter gives her conscience, fidelity, and fear of shame; her beauty is a natal gift from Venus; and Venus also manages to suppress the influence of Mars to such an extent 'That Ypermystra dar nat handle a knyf | In malyce, thogh she shulde lese hire lyf' (2594–5). The malign influence of Saturn finally predicts her death in prison.

This horoscope is one of Chaucer's most significant additions to a story found in Ovid, and in providing and explaining his character's astral destiny so clearly, he makes Hypermnestra's powerlessness complete. Her one possible act of autonomy in this tale would have been to *choose* not to wield the knife and so allow her husband to live, but the nativity outlined for her robs her even of this active choice. Nowhere does she state that she abhors the idea of murder; instead we hear, as her horoscope predicted, that her hands 'ben nat shapen for a knyf' (2692). There is much more a sense that she *cannot* kill than that she *will not* kill, and though she concludes with a reference to her wifely fidelity, this is again only what her horoscope predicted.

But Hypermnestra's tale need not have ended this way. Indeed, her whole tragedy is brought about precisely because her father intends to change what is apparently preordained for him. In spite of his references to the Furies spinning out his destiny, he will not wait to be murdered by his son-in-law, and the son-in-law does not wait to be apprehended either. Only Hypermnestra, like countless women before her, waits.

She sits down right there until she is caught and imprisoned, just as the stars had foretold, and in so doing she becomes the ultimate victim of the *Legend of Good Women*, effectively choosing a helpless passivity.

For while the Middle Ages believed in the influence of the stars, it was not thought that the future was determined by them. They could, it was thought, affect people's daily lives, causing the events around them to occur, and their influence could similarly affect the reason and will of the unwary. But, in the end, it was believed that each individual made his or her own choices, dealing freely with whatever befell them. Medieval astrological treatises were peppered with aphorisms such as: 'the wise man dominates the stars because through his wisdom he can avoid that which the stars dispose'.[6] The Wife of Bath, therefore, cannot really excuse her behaviour as being entirely 'Venerian' and 'Marcien', much as her horoscope and, indeed, her body, bears all the hallmarks of a zodiacal good-time girl. With a nudge and a wink and a few well-known references to Ptolemaic science she may assert that 'I folwed ay myn inclinacioun [astrologically determined path] | By vertu of my constellacioun' ('WBP' 615–16), but it is clear that she is in fact following her wilful inclination plain and simple. Similarly, Hypermnestra is free to make her own choices, although her pagan viewpoint may make this less apparent to her.

Chaucer's clearest exposition of the power of reason and faith over astral determinism can be found in his account of the life of Custance, the long-suffering heroine of the 'Man of Law's Tale'. Indeed, 'long-suffering' scarcely describes a woman who endures the murder of her first husband, apparent abandonment by the second, the slaying of her companion, a false trial for murder, two homicidal mothers-in-law, attempted rape, and many years drifting in a rudderless boat. Such tragedies are, however, hinted at in the astrological references that Chaucer has, once again, added to his source. For, the Man of Law stresses:

> in the sterres, clerer than is glas,
> Is writen, God woot, whoso koude it rede,
> The deeth of every man, withouten drede.

('MLT' 194–6)

Custance's horoscope is, however, a notoriously difficult passage to decipher (295–315), though it is clear even without any knowledge of astrology that the negative tone of 'crueel Mars', 'infortunat', 'tortuous', 'helplees', and 'fieble' all indicate misfortune.[7]

The two heroines also share an essential passivity, though Custance's endurance remains a little more active. While Hypermnestra cannot shin down the drainpipe after her husband, Custance can throw a potential rapist overboard when she chooses, with only a little heavenly intervention (921–3), and equally chooses not to reveal her identity at crucial points in the narrative when she could have altered her fate. However, as her countless prayers show (and she rarely opens her mouth without uttering a prayer), Custance is not surrendering to the stars as Hypermnestra had done, but rather placing her faith in divine providence. Unlike the pagan Hypermnestra, Custance is a Christian heroine whose submissive faith in God sustains her through even the most disastrous horoscope. In the end, her trust is rewarded and she is reunited with her faithful second husband, though only for a year before his death.

The harshness of life is everywhere emphasized in the 'Man of Law's Tale', which stresses the ubiquity of misery by its cyclical pattern of horrors, and we cannot expect a 'happy ending' in a universe where even the planets appear to be suffering. Indeed, that the innocent do suffer is one of the fundamental problems of Christianity, and Chaucer here presents the universe for a moment as a place of cruelty on a cosmic scale with disaster preordained. It is the position of Boethius before his enlightenment, doubting the goodness of a God who can either cause or allow such terrible things to happen. We do not, however, have a Lady Philosophy to guide us as Boethius had. Consequently, as Mann has argued, there is in the 'Man of Law's Tale', 'no final answer to the "why" of suffering on a metaphysical level, and Chaucer does not try to give one. Faith in the "purveiaunce" of God does nothing to dispel or deny the darkness of man's "ignorance".'[8] And astrology is no help either. The Man of Law is astonished that no one consulted the stars as Custance set out on her first voyage:

> Imprudent Emperour of Rome, allas!
> Was ther no philosophre in al thy toun?
> Is no tyme bet than oother in swich cas?
> Of viage is ther noon eleccioun,
> Namely to folk of heigh condicioun?
> Noght whan a roote is of a burthe yknowe?
> Allas, we been to lewed or to slowe! (309–15)

It is, therefore, ironic that the source of this exasperated incredulity should be one of the most confusing astrological passages in Chaucer's work. Chaucer never gives a full horoscope in any of his poems, but Custance's appears to be a particularly imprecise example, set against a wilfully misconstrued picture of the universe. The cry that 'we been to lewed or to slowe' may well be apt but not for the reasons the Man of Law thinks. There simply is not enough information in the stars, ever, to provide us with a blueprint of how things must be. Stargazing cannot account for human free will, for as Custance proves, no matter what disasters the stars may seem to predict, no one is bound by astral destiny. We are indeed too ignorant and too slow-witted to understand the workings of this universe and its apparent cruelties, but what is clear is that our fates are not written in the stars.

Planetary influence

Armed with this idea, we can now turn to one of the most overtly astrological of all Chaucer's works, the 'Knight's Tale', for this is a tale in which we see the whole planetary machinery at work as the lives of mortals hang in the balance. Two knights, Palamon and Arcite, are captured in battle and imprisoned in a high tower, a fate which they feel was preordained from birth:

> Som wikke aspect or disposicioun
> Of Saturne, by som constellacioun,
> Hath yeven us this, although we hadde it sworn;
> So stood the hevene when that we were born. (1087–90)

They both fall in love with Emelye and eventually fight one another in a tournament for her, each character offering prayers to a different god to influence the outcome. Palamon, the first to fall in love, prays to Venus; the more hasty Arcite sides with Mars; and the rather blank Emelye chooses Diana, virgin goddess of the moon.

Chaucer makes it clear, however, that we are dealing not with Olympian deities but with planets, and constructs an amphitheatre for the tournament along zodiacal principles. The circular arena has an oratory for Venus on the east wall, one for Mars on the west wall, with Diana's temple situated in the north. A glance at any chart of the zodiac shows that this placing of the temples is in keeping with traditional planetary positions and so what we have in this amphitheatre is a symbolic cosmos: the planets are going to do battle before our eyes for these knights, whose destinies will thus be decided by the stars. Further, Chaucer's care over the date and timing of the tournament is significant. For, as North summarizes it, while the protagonists pray, 'they are unaware that . . . the corresponding planets are in unhappy situations, with Venus in the house of brothers, falling from her angle, the Moon in the house of prison and enemies, and falling likewise, and Mars in the eighth house, of death and inheritance'.[9] It looks as though all three characters are victims of forces beyond their control, the planets themselves bickering as each attempts to emerge triumphant from the conflict and claim victory for their supplicant. It is Mars' knight Arcite, in the end, who appropriately wins the battle and Emelye. But he has not even finished his victory lap when disaster strikes and he is fatally injured in a fall from his horse. There are, however, no such things as 'accidents' and this one was orchestrated by Saturn, ascendant in the sign of Leo and therefore associated with violence, suffering, and cruelty. Another glance at the figure of zodiac man reveals that the Saturnian Leo influences the chest and this is the very part of the body that proves fatal to Arcite as his lungs fill with blood. His death means that Palamon, Venus' knight, is permitted to marry Emelye; and Emelye, child of the moon that she is, is happy enough to reflect the desires of others.

It would appear, therefore, that we are indeed the stars' tennis balls, if it were not for the fact that what Palamon and Arcite get in the 'Knight's Tale' is exactly what they themselves ask for. Saturn interferes only to provide each of the protagonists with precisely the thing they choose of their own free will: Arcite asks only to win the tournament; Palamon asks only to win Emelye; and Emelye marries the man who, on the strength of the evidence, does indeed love her more, at least to the extent that she is paramount in his mind when it comes to naming his prize. The intricate cosmic machinery does not in the end determine anything of significance, no matter what the characters themselves may believe. It is a tale set in antiquity and while its pagan protagonists worship the planets as gods, Chaucer takes pains to remind us that they are in fact planets. At his moment of greatest malice, Saturn himself makes this clear:

> My cours, that hath so wyde for to turne,
> Hath moore power than woot any man . . .
> I do vengeance and pleyn correccioun,
> Whil I dwelle in the signe of the leoun. (2454–62)

And the fact that they are not all-powerful deities is one of the reasons that Duke Theseus' final speech of consolation fails to satisfy. As Arcite dies, Theseus is forced to consider the question earlier asked by Palamon:

> What governance is in this prescience,
> That giltelees tormenteth innocence? (1313–14)

It is the concern of the 'Man of Law's Tale' again, though without Custance and her rudderless boat to steer us towards faith in God. Instead, faith in these planetary gods leaves us as Palamon described, like 'the sheep that rouketh in the folde' (1308). Theseus gropes towards the idea of a benign First Mover creating a world of order and harmony, but he equates this force with Jupiter, already seen here to be powerless when faced with the opposition of Mars and Venus (2987–3040). We are not, however, mere lambs to the slaughter, even in this tale of suffering and death. For while the planets influence our lives, we are not their puppets, nor are we their passive victims. We are asked by Chaucer to dwell on the horror of Arcite's death, but the graphic nature of the description of his wounds may paradoxically contribute to the idea of free will that lies at the heart of the 'Knight's Tale'. For this, however, we must turn to another area of science that was evidently of interest to Chaucer: medicine.

Medicine

Medieval medicine was regarded very much as a sister science to astrology. As the highly popular pictures of 'zodiac man' show, the whole body was subject to the influence of the planets (the source of modern 'influenza'). Chaucer's Doctor of Physic, we are told:

> was grounded in astronomye.
> He kepte his pacient a ful greet deel
> In houres by his magyk natureel.
> Wel koude he fortunen the ascendent
> Of his ymages for his pacient.
>
> ('GP' 414–18)

And, wary as some critics are of the Physician, his practice here of calculating astronomical hours and planetary positions in order to make talismans or select the most propitious moment for treatment is borne out by the sober *Treatise on the Astrolabe*.[10] Chaucer states without irony that each of the signs of the zodiac 'hath respect to a certeyn parcel of the body of a man, and hath it in governaunce; as Aries hath thin heved, and Taurus thy nekke and thy throte, Gemini thin armholes and thin armes, and so furth' (*TA* 1. 21. 71–5)

The *Treatise* here also makes the connection between the planets and the four qualities—hot, cold, wet, and dry—that lie, the Doctor of Physic believes, at the root of every illness. In this he is in good company, for the so-called theory of the humours formed the basis of medieval physiology in the writings of almost every medieval scientist. Accordingly, the human body was assigned to one of four groups: the hot and wet body dominated by blood was termed sanguine; a predominance of phlegm in a cold and wet body produced a phlegmatic; hot, dry, and red or yellow bile meant choleric; and black bile, coldness, and dryness were predominant in a melancholic personality. It was imbalance in these humours that was believed to lead to illness, as that other great *Canterbury Tales* physician, the chicken Pertelote, makes clear. Her overly exuberant treatment of Chauntecleer's excessive choler and melancholy may well have killed him had she been allowed to proceed ('NPT' 2946), and her exasperated 'For Goddes love, as taak som laxatyf' (2943) implies a dubious bedside manner. Nevertheless, Chaucer's extensive pharmacological knowledge is apparent in the list of plants that Pertelote intended to gather from the chicken coop, and her prescription of 'wormes' (2962) is found in at least one well-known medical treatise as a cure for (human) fever.[11] There are countless similar examples of Chaucer's medical interests throughout his works from the 'sursanure' (1113) in the 'Franklin's Tale' (a wound that heals on the surface but continues to fester underneath) to the sanguine complexion of the Franklin himself ('GP' 333). Nowhere, however, are the workings of the human body scrutinized more carefully than in the 'Knight's Tale', and it is to this we must return for some of Chaucer's most sustained medical passages.

The full horror of a tournament injury that crushes the internal organs, leaving the victim to endure twenty-four hours of agony until he effectively suffocates, is not the usual stuff of chivalric romance, but this is what Chaucer gives us in his account of Arcite's death:

> The clothered blood, for any lechecraft,
> Corrupteth, and is in his bouk ylaft,
> That neither veyne-blood, ne ventusynge,
> Ne drynke of herbes may ben his helpynge.
> The vertu expulsif, or animal,
> Fro thilke vertu cleped natural
> Ne may the venym voyden ne expelle.
> The pipes of his longes gonne to swelle,

And every lacerte in his brest adoun
Is shent with venym and corrupcioun.

('KT' 2745–54)

One effect of this graphic description of human vulnerability and medical ineffectuality is to undermine Theseus' 'way of all flesh' speech (3027–34), for it is far easier to accept death in the abstract than it is to come to terms with the gradual paralysis of a young knight whose eyes are fixed on his beloved even when he can no longer see. This does not mean, however, that Arcite is the victim of universal malice, wriggling on the end of a celestial pin.

It is true that Saturn is in the sign of Leo as Arcite falls from his horse (2462), and that Leo governs the heart and lungs. It is also true, as Curry has observed, that Saturn was believed to govern the body's retentive capacity that prevents Arcite from expelling the corrupting blood.[12] There is also the matter of the Fury, summoned by Saturn to terrify the horse and cause Arcite's accident. As we have seen, however, none of this amounts to a preordained fate and Arcite would have done well to remember Aquinas' warning that 'the wise man is master of the stars in that he is the master of his own passions'.[13] Passion is, however, a rather tame term for Arcite's affliction, for he is, in fact, lovesick in a very literal sense.

References to the sickness of the lover, cured only by his lady's glance, are commonplace in medieval poetry to the extent that Pandarus wisely advises Troilus against using any such medical metaphors in his letter to Criseyde (TC 2. 1037–9). But in Arcite's case we are dealing with the real thing, not some tired convention. His wild mood swings, deathly pallor, and continual swooning are symptoms, Chaucer tells us, 'Nat oonly lik the loveris maladye | Of Hereos, but rather lyk manye' ('KT' 1373–4). In fact, as Lowes long ago pointed out, the lengthy description of Arcite's illness 'might almost be a paraphrase of a chapter on *hereos* from one of the medical treatises'.[14] A disease of the brain, *amor hereos* was a kind of melancholy caused by thinking so much about the beloved that her image becomes fixed in the mind. With the middle ventricle thus infected, the part of the brain that discerns and reasons receives only the image of the beloved and has no choice but to accept it as the greatest good. What follows is a mania, as Chaucer tells us, and a disease so all-consuming that it was sometimes referred to as *amor furiosus*, or simply *furia*. Schweitzer makes the link between this medical *furia* and the Fury that causes Arcite's fall, with the added detail that the horse and rider are traditionally a symbol of the passions being controlled by reason.[15] This lovers' melancholy is itself Saturnian in nature and so what springs from the earth need not be some malicious act of the wilful planets but rather the inevitable outcome of Arcite's illness. A man obsessed, in the clearest medical terms, he has surrendered all reason and given in to his passions. In the end, as Schweitzer says, 'the fury epitomizes the intervention of cosmic forces to determine events but epitomizes also the paradox that those forces determine only what the human protagonists have freely chosen'.[16]

The clinical description of Arcite's suffocating body shows the horrible consequences of that choice. The proper response may well be to clear the middle ventricle and ensure that we see and reason clearly, and realize that worldly suffering and misfortune are mere illusions in a scheme of benevolent Providence. However, Chaucer employs his scientific knowledge to ensure that this is, in fact, very difficult to do. In his source, Boccaccio's *Teseida*, we are told that the dead knight's soul ascends to the eighth sphere. Chaucer, however, steadfastly refuses to allow us this consolation. The distant view of the earth that might have allowed us to see death as part of the grand plan is denied us and replaced instead by so close a view that we feel Arcite's dying breath and see the blood swelling in his lungs. And the replacement of Boccaccio's telescopic lens with Chaucerian X-ray means that the real horror of death is impressed upon us. It may all be part of the divine plan, as Theseus asserts, but Chaucer here makes us confront exactly what this means.

By comparison, the 'Physician's Tale' is a remarkably bloodless affair, not a single drop being mentioned in the account of Virginia's beheading by her father as he attempts to 'save' her from the lustful judge Apius. Whether or not it is an appropriate tale for the Doctor of Physic has been much debated, but there are several elements in it that provide interesting comparison with his description in the 'General Prologue'. As we have seen, the emphasis on the Physician's astrological skill does not necessarily mark him out as a charlatan, and he is also learned in all the major medical authorities available in the period such as Hippocrates, Galen, and Avicenna. Indeed, the medical knowledge the medieval West inherited from the Greeks and Arabs should not be underestimated, though it should not, of course, be exaggerated either. Medieval doctors were frequently feared, both for the treatments they might suggest and for the fees they might charge. The worst that Chaucer's Physician can be accused of, however, is a rather too profitable arrangement with the local pharmacist, a tendency towards avarice, and the fact that 'His studie was but litel on the Bible' ('GP' 438). With fifteen major authors cited in his portrait as reading matter this is perhaps not surprising, and yet it is a failing that becomes very significant in his tale.

Like the 'Knight's Tale', the story of Virginius and his daughter is set in pagan antiquity, but unlike that tale, there are here no gods, First Movers, planets, or stars. The corrupt judge Apius simply comes up with a plan to abduct and rape Virginia, and her father beheads her rather than allow this to happen. It is a short tale with unusually few historical or literary allusions. Virginia's comparison of herself with Jephtha's daughter ('PT' 240), a biblical virgin sacrificed by her father, is therefore very striking. As Hoffman points out, most medieval commentators on the Bible interpreted Jephtha as Christ and the daughter as his flesh, sacrificed to save mankind.[17] Virginia's reference therefore emphasizes her own role as symbolic flesh, for this is, in fact, the story of a body: it is Virginia's body alone that Apius desires and her body that Virginius prevents him from taking. In spite of the assertion that 'As wel in goost as body chast was she' (43), it is her physical intactness alone that ultimately matters to everyone in the tale, not her spiritual state. Further, while Virginia utters a few prayers at the news of her imminent death, we hear no such appeals to heaven from Virginius. He simply ascertains that his daughter's body is under threat from corrupting forces and decides on a cure that will, in the process, kill her. He does not pray, nor does he ever think of her in anything other than physical terms. He is, in fact, a fitting protagonist for the tale of a minimally religious physician.

John of Salisbury, writing in the fourteenth century, complains of the godless doctors who think too highly of their own medical knowledge:

> But the physicians, while they attribute too much authority to Nature, cast aside the Author of Nature . . . 'As if earth-born giants were to attempt the stars' . . . such are dishonest in that they give themselves the credit for a recovery which is due to time, or rather to the gift of God; for it is due to God and to the natural power of his constitution that the sick man is raised up.[18]

Such contemporary statements shed some light on the opening section of the tale in which Nature is extolled. For while Nature describes herself as God's 'vicaire general' (20), the emphasis in this passage is very much on her own role as creator with everything under her jurisdiction. God may be the 'formere principal' (19) but he is sidelined in this speech in which Nature takes centre stage and is credited with creating the superlatively beautiful Virginia. In turn, bodies are no longer divine mysteries but rather 'erthely creaturis' (21), mere biological entities. The Physician ultimately aligns himself with a lesser god, concerned with the body alone, and no one can save Virginia.

Magic

There remains one final category of science that occupied the Middle Ages, and that is magic, not a modern science by any stretch of the imagination but to the medieval mind encompassing a great deal of what is now considered legitimately scientific. One of the areas of expertise of the Doctor of Physic, for example, is 'magyk natureel' ('GP' 416). Essentially this relates to the wonders of nature, observed but not fully understood by medieval man, such as the hardening effect of radish water on iron or the curative power of mould on wounds. We see in the *Parliament of Fowls* the narrator's delight in magnets (148–53), and the 'Squire's Tale' provides us with a group of enthusiastic amateur scientists who 'wondren somme on cause of thonder, | On ebbe, on flood, on gossomer, and on myst' (258–9). But such 'natural magic' was the acceptable side of a much larger subject that encompassed demonology and the black arts. Most medieval intellectuals were at least knowledgeable about magic, and while scholars such as Roger Bacon are dismissive of the hocus-pocus of 'jugglers' and 'cunning women', its possibilities as a science are treated with the utmost seriousness.[19] Indeed, many of the most popular scientific collections of the period have sections on magic together with those on medicine and astrology. Nevertheless, the Church was concerned about the curiosity that might prompt man to vie with God in terms of knowledge and power. Writing in the 1120s, Hugh of St Victor condemns magic as 'the mistress of every form of iniquity', though as the lines between natural and black magic were so blurred, many of the great scholars of the later Middle Ages were implicated in the forbidden arts.[20]

Alchemy

Of all the possibilities offered by this science, however, it was alchemy that proved the most seductive. Based once again on the theory of the four elements that formed the basis for medieval medicine, it was thought that by somehow isolating the qualities of heat, cold, dryness, and moisture, any imbalance in a substance could be rectified. Thus, a base metal could be transformed into a more perfect one such as gold. People too could be treated in this way, the balance in their humours restored, so that alchemists were essentially offering the elixir of life.

Given Chaucer's very serious interest in astrology and medicine, it is not surprising that he should also have been curious about alchemy. Indeed, in later centuries he came to be regarded as an expert in these mysteries on the strength of the knowledge exhibited in the 'Canon's Yeoman's Tale'.[21] Technical terms abound as the Canon's Yeoman, having caught up with the group of pilgrims in slightly suspicious circumstances, tells the assembled company about his seven years of tribulation in the service of his alchemist master. We hear of the countless tools of their trade, including

> Unslekked lym, chalk, and gleyre of an ey,
> Poudres diverse, asshes, donge, pisse, and cley,
> Cered pokkets, sal peter, vitriole,
> And diverse fires maad of wode and cole.
>
> ('CYT' 806–9)

As Cooper points out, this tumbling list suggests not only the impossibility of ever achieving their goal by these means, but also that a medieval audience would have 'fully understood only a handful of words, and those are the "wrong" ones'.[22] And yet, the impression of the Canon and Yeoman as misconceived dealers in such 'dung', 'piss', and 'clay' belies Chaucer's very extensive knowledge of the subject. A wealth of reading has gone into creating this jumble of jargon, and most of what is here has been adapted from the most renowned alchemical works of the time.

The Canon's Yeoman's account of his life as the sorcerer's apprentice, aware of his own 'madnesse' (959) and yet still driven, gives way to a tale of flagrant trickery in which another canon dupes a priest. Sleight of hand takes the place of any genuine attempt at alchemy, and the priest becomes another in the long line of the canon–alchemist's gulls, robbed of £40 and left with a useless formula for making silver. In both halves of the tale, the alchemy simply fails and the only chemical changes that occur are in the protagonists themselves. They become part of a bizarre anti-process, their faces dripping with so much sweat that they resemble an alchemical still (580), with complexions changing from the desired red to the leaden hue of the despised base metal (727–8). People, in the end, cannot transform matter, unless it is their own, in which case the transformation can be a terrible thing.

In spite of the potential comedy of exploding cauldrons and gullible priests the tale does not embrace its fabliau possibilities; there is too much greed and human desperation amid the alchemical paraphernalia. The Doctor of Physic had presented a universe in which God is almost forgotten; in the 'Canon's Yeoman's Tale' there is an attempt at usurping his power entirely. As has been apparent from the beginning of the tale, however, such forays into the realm of the divine cannot succeed, ultimately because these scientific secrets are to Christ 'so lief and deere' (1467) that he will not make them common knowledge. The Canon's Yeoman still clings to the possibilities of alchemy in the end though the power to create and transform, he acknowledges, is God's alone. The final message of the tale could have been the complacently dismissive one of John the Carpenter in the 'Miller's Tale':

> Men sholde nat knowe of Goddes pryvetee.
> Ye, blessed be alwey a lewed man
> That noght but oonly his bileve kan! (3454–6)

But significantly this is not the case. The 'lewed man' who appears in the Canon's Yeoman's final speech is not blessedly uneducated but rather foolishly ignorant, criticized not for attempting alchemy but for doing so without first making a careful study of the subject:

> Lat no man bisye hym this art for to seche,
> But if that he th'entencioun and speche
> Of philosophres understonde kan;
> And if he do, he is a lewed man.
>
> ('CYT'1442–5)

That, at least, appears to be his meaning, though the sentence, like much of the logic in the final speech, is difficult to follow. Those who attempt to arrogate to man the power to change the nature of things are God's adversaries. But this final admission of God's power is no simple declaration of faith, for it is derived from the Canon's Yeoman's alchemical reading. He ends by quoting Arnaldus of Villanova and Plato, both regarded as experts in the field. The limitations of human power are acknowledged, but alchemy itself is not completely condemned. In fact, the prohibition serves to glorify it as God himself becomes the Great Alchemist, withholding his secrets, but with the eternal promise of enlightenment to a chosen few, 'where it liketh to his deitee | Men for t'enspire' (1469–70). The tale has laid alchemy bare as the resource of charlatans and the destroyer of men. And yet, there remains a comprehension of the desire that compels someone onwards in the quest for knowledge.

Conclusion

Medieval scientific belief, then, was dependent upon the idea of a universal plan that gave shape and meaning to human life, and there has been a tendency among critics to view Chaucer's scientific interests as bolstering this ordered view of the cosmos. Such glimpses of celestial planning do, of course, occur, but they are not the whole picture and should not be overestimated. Chaucer himself certainly never blinds us with science. His impressive knowledge of astronomy, medicine, and popular magic is used instead to lay the problems bare, allowing us to see the workings of the body, the mind, and even the stars themselves. This potential friction between medieval science and established religious ideas requires further study by Chaucer critics. The immense scholarship of previous generations has provided an excellent tradition upon which to build, particularly in the area of medieval astronomy, but there has been in the last twenty years a surge of interest in medieval scientific texts, the outcome of which has not yet been fully reflected in literary criticism.

FURTHER READING

Curry, Walter Clyde, *Chaucer and the Mediaeval Sciences*, rev. edn. (New York: Barnes & Noble; London: Allen & Unwin, 1960). A fascinating account of Chaucer's interest in the medieval sciences and the inspiration for much further work.

Manzalaoui, Mahmoud A., 'Chaucer and Science', in Derek Brewer (ed.), *Geoffrey Chaucer* (London: Bell, 1974), 224–61. A comprehensive article that offers a challenge to some of the ideas of Curry and Wood.

North, J. D., *Chaucer's Universe* (Oxford: Oxford University Press, 1988). A deeply learned study of Chaucer's astronomy, the second half of which is given over to a detailed account of astronomical references in the poetry.

Schuler, Robert M., 'The Renaissance Chaucer as Alchemist', *Viator*, 15 (1984), 305–33. A revealing account of the Renaissance assessment of Chaucer's alchemical knowledge.

Siraisi, Nancy, *Medieval and Early Renaissance Medicine* (Chicago: University of Chicago Press, 1990). A good introduction to early medicine in its socio-historical context.

Ussery, Huling E., *Chaucer's Physician: Medicine and Literature in Fourteenth-Century England* (New Orleans: Tulane University Press, 1971). A detailed examination of Chaucer's Physician in the context of medieval medical practice.

Wood, Chauncey, *Chaucer and the Country of the Stars: Poetic Uses of Astrological Imagery* (Princeton: Princeton University Press, 1970). An in-depth study of Chaucer's astrological knowledge and imagery.

NOTES

1. For a complete description of the astrolabe and how it works, see J. D. North, *Chaucer's Universe* (Oxford: Oxford University Press, 1988). Critics have been tempted to assign a second scientific treatise, *The Equatorie of the Planetis*, to Chaucer. However, the most recent and extensive study of

the text has concluded that Chaucer's authorship must remain 'not proven'. See Kari Rand Schmidt, *The Authorship of the 'Equatorie of the Planetis'* (Cambridge: Brewer, 1993).

2. See Chauncey Wood, *Chaucer and the Country of the Stars: Poetic Uses of Astrological Imagery* (Princeton: Princeton University Press, 1970), 272–97.

3. See James Winny, 'Chaucer's Science', in Maurice Hussey, A. C. Spearing, and James Winny (eds.), *An Introduction to Chaucer* (Cambridge: Cambridge University Press, 1965), 153–84; Henning Standish, 'Chauntecleer and Taurus', *English Language Notes*, 3 (1965), 1–4; North, *Chaucer's Universe*, 289–304, 545–8.

4. For a detailed examination of these treatises as applied to the horoscope of the Wife of Bath, see John B. Friedman, 'Alice of Bath's Astral Destiny: A Re-appraisal', *Chaucer Review*, 35 (2000), 166–81.

5. North, *Chaucer's Universe*, 300.

6. Quoted in Friedman, 'Alice of Bath's Astral Destiny', 171.

7. There is a great deal of controversy over this passage, to the extent that critics learned in medieval astrology offer widely divergent interpretations. All are agreed on the negative tone of the lines but disagree as to the exact position and function of the planets. See e.g. Walter Clyde Curry, *Chaucer and the Mediaeval Sciences*, rev. edn. (New York: Barnes & Noble; London: Allen & Unwin, 1960), 174–88; Wood, *Chaucer and the Country of the Stars*, 200–34.

8. Jill Mann, *Feminizing Chaucer* (Cambridge: Brewer, 2002), 105.

9. *Chaucer's Universe*, 534.

10. For a negative interpretation of the portrait of the Doctor of Physic, see Muriel A. Bowden, *A Commentary on the 'General Prologue' to the 'Canterbury Tales'*, 2nd edn. (London: Souvenir Press, 1973). A far more positive view is offered in Huling E. Ussery, *Chaucer's Physician: Medicine and Literature in Fourteenth-Century England* (New Orleans: Tulane University Press, 1971).

11. See John Livingston Lowes, *Geoffrey Chaucer* (Oxford: Oxford University Press, 1934), 26–7 n.

12. *Chaucer and the Mediaeval Sciences*, 147.

13. St Thomas Aquinas, *Summa theologiae*, ed. M. J. Charlesworth (London: Blackfriars, Eyre & Spottiswoode; New York: McGraw-Hill, 1970), xv. 107, 1a. 115. 4.

14. John Livingston Lowes, 'The Loveres Maladye of Hereos', *Modern Philology*, 11 (1914), 525.

15. Edward C. Schweitzer, 'Fate and Freedom in the "Knight's Tale" ', *Studies in the Age of Chaucer*, 3 (1981), 21–4.

16. Ibid. 29.

17. Richard L. Hoffman, 'Jephthah's Daughter and Chaucer's Virginia', *Chaucer Review*, 2 (1967), 29.

18. Quoted in Curry, *Chaucer and the Mediaeval Sciences*, 30.

19. William Eamon, *Science and the Secrets of Nature: Books of Secrets in Medieval and Early Modern Culture* (Princeton: Princeton University Press, 1994), 49.

20. Ibid. 59–68.

21. Robert M. Schuler, 'The Renaissance Chaucer as Alchemist', *Viator*, 15 (1984), 305–33.

22. Helen Cooper, *Oxford Guides to Chaucer: The 'Canterbury Tales'* (Oxford: Oxford University Press, 1989), 379.

| **Visual culture**

| *David Griffith*

Chaucer is a visual poet. His habit of visualizing operates on all levels of his writing and is rooted in minute observation of people, places, and action. In the 'Miller's Tale' Absolon's foppishness is perfectly captured in the images of 'Poules wyndow' carved into his fancy shoes (3318); in Ariadne's tale in the *Legend of Good Women* the perils of the minotaur's labyrinth are graphically presented in the expression that it 'krynkeled to and fro' (2012); and the fantasy sequences of the dream visions, from the garden of love in the *Parliament of Fowls* to the Temple of Fame in the *House of Fame*, are crowded with substantiating images of naive dreamers, talking birds, and all manner of allegorical and classical figures. Beyond this there is a metaphorical practice that describes, for example, Virginius in the 'Physician's Tale' as having a 'fadres pitee stikynge thurgh his herte' (211) or that counsels equanimity in the ballad 'Truth' with the injunction 'Stryve not, as doth the crokke with the wal' (12). Even entire narrative structures, like the pilgrims' journey from Southwark to Thomas Becket's tomb at Canterbury, are mapped onto the realities of English topography.

Critics have generally understood this visual dimension in terms of either iconography, that is, the particular forms of iconic representation of any given subject or topic, or more generally as a stylistic feature. Importantly, both approaches actively seek to locate Chaucer within broader cultural and intellectual environments and are predicated on comparative analysis with other visual and textual sources. Some of the most influential writing in this regard derives from D. W. Robertson and B. F. Huppé and their method of reading Chaucer in terms of Christian iconography, as shown in an early article by Robertson on the 'Friar's Tale' in which he argues that the 'courtepy of grene' (1382) worn by the fiendish yeoman operates on both literal and symbolic levels.[1] This kind of understanding is common to patristic writing (the writings of the early Church fathers) and to later medieval Christian scholarship, and is ultimately sourced in St Augustine's statement in *De doctrina Christiana* ('On Christian Doctrine', book 2. 1) that 'a sign is a thing which of itself makes some other thing come to mind, besides the impression it presents to the senses'.[2] In this way green has moral significance deriving not from its traditional association with the Celtic otherworld but from the writings of the French scholar Pierre Bersuire (*c.*1290–1362), who identifies the devil as a hunter in green clothing. To view all of Chaucer's iconography through the lens of Augustinian sign theory has obvious pitfalls, and as new critical models have developed the practice has fallen out of fashion. Even so, it is important to acknowledge that apparently trivial visual detail can hold signification.

Other critics approach Chaucer as a 'Gothic' poet. In its narrowest sense 'Gothic' denotes an artistic and architectural style popular in England from the mid-thirteenth century through to the Reformation—one of pointed arches and a profusion of ornament and detail—but by extension Chaucer's literary vision has been seen as shaped by the underlying aesthetic principles of Gothic art and architecture. Chaucer's works are to be understood in relation to a notion of order and disorder, which is based upon the idea of God's Creation as the primary model of 'variety in unity'. As Robert Jordan argues, 'Chaucer's varieties of structural unity are many. But they follow the Gothic principle of juxtaposition . . . characteristically, the total form is determined by the accumulation of individually complete elements.'[3] Thus the elaborate, apparently untidy, frame of the *Canterbury Tales* corresponds to artistic and architectural forms in which a grand design is composed of numerous individual but interdependent components as in, say, the individual programmes of sculpture that adorn English cathedral façades like Exeter or the linked scenes of panel paintings such as the *Despenser Retable* (*c*.1369–1406).

Chaucer's description of character and setting also arguably accords with Gothic modes of representation. Naturalistic or realistic aspects, what we might call 'life sketches', coexist with conventional methods of identification. Thus in the devotional portrait commissioned by Richard II in the 1390s and known today as the *Wilton Diptych* (Figure I.2), Richard is identified as much by his regal crown and the Plantagenet emblems adorning his cloak as by any physical likeness. Similarly his patron saints, as flesh and blood as the king himself, are identified by their respective attributes or emblems—Edmund of East Anglia by an arrow, Edward the Confessor by a ring, John the Baptist by the lamb of God. On the opposite panel the youthful angelic host, clothed like the Virgin Mary in blue robes (symbolic of purity and virtue), announces its allegiance to the king by adopting his emblem of the white hart, a customary means of displaying political affinity. All fourteenth-century art, from panel painting to literary narrative, is characterized by this 'chequer-board of styles and approaches'.[4]

Iconographic traditions

The operation of Chaucer's iconographic and symbolic schemes is best understood within this contemporary artistic milieu. Sometime before 1420 the *exemplum* of the three young men in search of Death in the 'Pardoner's Tale' was carved onto the front panel of a domestic wooden chest (Figure I.7). Only one worm-eaten section survives, but this fragment reveals the artist's skill in isolating the most significant dramatic moments of the tale. Events are picked up where the youngest 'riotour' buys poison from an apothecary in a tall narrow house 'that he myghte his rattes quelle' (854). In

Fig. 1.7 Scenes from the 'Pardoner's Tale'. Fragment of wooden chest, early fifteenth century (Museum of London).

the next scene the youth is violently stabbed by his older partners in crime who 'hadde cast his deeth bifoore' (880). The final episode diverges from the textual narrative, which climaxes with the death of the two remaining revellers beneath the tree where the treasure has been found. Instead they are shown drinking the poisoned wine from flasks while seated at a table on which are strewn a knife, a die, and other items associated with loose living.

The tale embodies the biblical maxim that the wages of sin is Death (Romans 23), but Chaucer displaces the rioters' quest for the unknown murderer, that 'privee theef men clepeth Deeth' (675), into meetings with a series of unexplained 'signs'. The Old Man, the oak tree, and the gold all signal the impending presence, yet visual absence, of Death itself, but the purely literal significance is left unstated. This of course ironizes the rioters' misguided quest for a physical being, and more generally typifies Chaucer's avoidance of assigning explicit meaning to his symbols. In this way the iconography of the 'Pardoner's Tale' is a departure from the standard iconography of Death that had developed in the thirteenth and fourteenth centuries (the catastrophic effects of the Black Death in the late 1340s and early 1360s had given the tradition considerable impetus), as in the legend of 'The Three Living and the Three Dead'. A version of the story found in an English psalter manuscript owned by the De Lisle family is typical of its kind.[5] Here the French verse text (with English marginal gloss) is accompanied by a half-page miniature in which three princely figures are brought back to the path of righteousness by a chance meeting while out hunting with their dead royal fathers, imagined as talking corpses or medieval zombies. The traditional thematic associations of hunting as a pastime of the rich are inverted and, as in the 'Pardoner's Tale', the humans themselves become the quarry of Death. The starkness of its warning made the legend peculiarly appropriate for depiction in parish churches and many examples survive from c.1300 onwards, but its appearance as a visual *memento mori* in domestic buildings such as Longthorpe Tower (Cambridgeshire) shows that secular patrons were attracted by its message of the transience of life and vanity of worldly aspirations. Elsewhere Death is diversely imagined as the great leveller in images of anthropomorphized figures of skeletons or cadavers attacking or dragging away representative members of society. A more systematic representation of Death summoning members of every degree comes in the form of the *danse macabre*, or dance of death. The earliest English image dates from the early fifteenth century, when it was painted in the cloisters of Old St Paul's Cathedral in London. Chaucer's younger contemporary John Lydgate later composed a translation of the French text that accompanied the paintings, which amounts to a kind of macabre version of the estates scheme in the 'General Prologue'.[6]

The 'Pardoner's Tale' carving imitates the text's symbolic register, and the viewer is encouraged to engage with the multiple possibilities of the subject. We can see this in action in the fox at the bottom right-hand corner of the panel bounding away as if onto the adjoining panel. This detail is apparently unconnected with the human action, but the vulpine iconography has a relevance with which Chaucer's audiences would have been very familiar. Traditional attitudes to the wiliness of the fox gave rise to the fictional character of Reynard, hero of an immensely popular mock-epic narrative cycle and the model for the sly iniquitous 'daun Russell the fox' (3334), who snatches Chauntecleer in the 'Nun's Priest's Tale', as well as a related body of textual and visual materials. One popular incident from the Reynard stories has the eponymous hero–fox dressed in the cowl of a friar preaching from a pulpit to an unwary flock of geese. In this aspect Reynard embodies sin and duplicity. Wooden carvings of this scene from Ripon and Ely cathedrals and elsewhere all bear witness to his popularity as a warning against false sermonizing and corruption in the clergy. By including the fox in his version of the *exemplum* the artist alludes to this network of textual and visual Reynard materials and of course to the craftiness of the Pardoner himself. The potential for multiple readings of the 'Pardoner's Tale', rooted in its symbolic detail, could well have provided the inspiration for this domestic ornamentation. In a merchant's household the story may well have been read as an antidote to avarice or a warning against theft; the chest may even have been used to house a copy of Chaucer's text itself, a common practice at a time when even non-illuminated books were valuable commodities.[7]

Sinfulness that blinds to the reality of spiritual truths is an important theme in the 'Pardoner's Tale' as a whole, where it is extensively visualized for didactic purposes. The revellers' blasphemy in the opening tavern scene involves a figurative tearing of 'oure blissed Lordes body' (474, 651–4, 692, 695). In wall paintings an image known as the Warning to Sabbath Breakers targeted those who avoided attendance at mass either to work or to 'play'. The items that surround a bloodied and wounded image of Christ at Breage (Cornwall) include the equivalent of the dice, or 'bicched bones' (656), to which the Pardoner refers. The obvious message here is that failure to respect Christ's sacrifice inflicts new wounds on his body and will bring divine punishment. And of course the vision of the Last Judgement, known as the Doom, is a ubiquitous feature of the art of the parish church.

Parochial iconographic programmes are then of real significance for our deeper understanding of Chaucer's iconography. The use of art as what Michael Camille calls 'a universal medium of communication' goes back to the early Church and especially the teaching of Pope Gregory the Great (in office 590–604).[8] Visual materials proved so effective in leading the unlettered laity to the truth of the Scriptures that they remained a principal element of the Church's pastoral care until the Reformation, though the potential for their idolatrous use was a hotly disputed area of theology especially in Chaucer's time. This attitude is conveniently summarized by the clerical figure of Pauper in *Dives and Pauper*, a didactic prose treatise from around 1400, who states that images are 'ordeyned to been a tokene and a book to the lewyd [unlearned] peple, þat þey moun [may] redyn in ymagerye and peynture þat clerkys redyn in boke'.[9] The interior of any contemporary church demonstrates the truth of these words. Following the practice in Gothic art of blanket decoration of plain surfaces, devotional and moralizing imagery adorned the walls and windows of every religious building from the smallest parish church to the grandest cathedral. Ecclesiastical and secular patrons paid for depictions of Bible stories and hagiographic sequences as well as images of favourite individual saints, plus diverse other didactic and moral subjects.

A couple of examples will further show how Chaucerian iconography operates within this nexus of religious and biblical images. The treatment of symbols in the 'Pardoner's Tale' can be compared productively with the Parson's explication of the Seven Deadly Sins in terms of an image of a tree in the instructional 'Parson's Tale' ('And everich of thise chief synnes hath his braunches and his twigges', 389). To express in comprehensible form complex theological issues such as the Seven Deadly Sins and the Seven Corporal Works of Mercy, the Church authorities turned to diagrammatic and schematic representation. Extant examples survive in the wall paintings of the Tree of the Seven Deadly Sins at Hessett (Suffolk) and Crostwight (Norfolk), both roughly contemporary with Chaucer. Being familiar with such images in parochial contexts, Chaucer's pilgrims and readers would have instinctively visualized the Parson's procession through the worst examples of vice and wickedness.

Visual materials can also point towards the rationale for matching tellers with particular tales. The Prioress's pious legend of the young boy murdered by the Jews but saved by the Virgin Mary is not, as Helen Cooper notes, a 'comfortable' tale.[10] Certainly the Prioress's denunciations are in keeping with standard medieval antisemitism, and her 'cursed Jewes' ('PrT' 570, 685) match the type of the violent Christ-killers seen in much Christian art of the period. What intrigues about Chaucer's version of the story is that, unlike many of the analogues, Mary does not restore the child to life at the end, and there is no recognition of the Christian God by the Jews. Indeed, despite the extensive praise of the Virgin in the 'Prioress's Prologue', the tale emphasizes the murderous qualities of the 'cursed folk of Herodes al newe' (574) as much as it promotes Marian devotion. There is no trace here of the conversions that resolve English pictorial narratives in which miracles of the Virgin are also conflated with legends of the unbelieving Jews. In the stained glass at Stanton St John and the wall painting at Chalgrove (both from fourteenth-century Oxfordshire) the apocryphal Funeral of the Virgin combines with the story of the Jew who, attempting to disrupt proceedings, finds his hands miraculously stuck to the bier. His conversion swiftly follows acknowledgement of Christ's power to release his grip. These images undoubtedly participate in the general antisemitic and Marian discourses of the day but the conversion of the Jew contrasts markedly with the tale's resolution. This manipulation of traditional iconography reveals Chaucer's attitudes to tale, teller, and genre. While the church images are designed to spur the pious spectator towards ever greater devotion to the Virgin, the primary impulse of the 'Prioress's Tale' seems geared towards revealing both the excessive sentimentality of the Prioress and the intellectual limitations of the devotional or miraculous narrative. Crude polarizations of religious difference are here fully exposed regardless of the sincerity of their inspiration.

The garden in the 'Merchant's Tale'

The most extended discussion of visual signification in Chaucer's poetry is by V. A. Kolve. In his readings of the first five Canterbury tales he argues that the extensive interaction between signs in Chaucerian texts encourages the reader to recognize the potential for multiple meanings at particular points within individual narratives. He suggests that at the same time Chaucer allows particular images to become the means of focusing and clarifying modes of interpretation for the narrative as a whole.[11]

This layering of meaning created by networks of images, following Kolve, can be seen in the topos of the garden in the 'Merchant's Tale'. The garden is both the literal place of the central action of the story and a sign for meanings beyond the fabliau genre. Scholars have long recognized the garden as a site of both innocence and sin, linking it figuratively or allegorically with the Garden of Eden, the enclosed garden of the Old Testament Song of Songs (4: 12), the place of romantic love in secular literature, and the earthly paradise of the afterlife.[12] All of these places share notions of a search for paradisal bliss and are explicitly related to the female body through either the curse of Eve, the Virgin Mary's chastity, or courtly love traditions referring to the male's sexual pursuit of the female.

From the outset of the tale the reader is introduced to issues that will bear fruit in the garden by means of a chain of iconographic details that foreshadow the moment of narrative climax. In the earlier sections the virtues of marriage are extolled (ironically and with a strong misogynist undertow) by the Merchant narrator and by January, who seeks a wife to be his 'paradys terrestre' (1332). At this point May is linked through the Edenic garden to the enclosure mentioned in Solomon's song for his queen ('My sister, my spouse, is a garden enclosed', Song of Songs 4: 12). In biblical exposition this song was understood as Christ calling to the Church or to the soul, and the garden was taken as a figure of the purity of the Virgin Mary, who had conceived without sin. The import of these references is spelt out clearly in the Merchant's injunction to 'Love wel thy wyf, as Crist loved his chirche' (1384). January's carnality, however, is at odds with such spiritual mysteries, and the space he creates is for the indulgence of his sexual appetites ('And thynges whiche that were nat doon abedde, | He in the gardyn parfourned hem and spedde', 2051–2). This disparity is underscored in his entreaty to May to come into the garden, which is a close verbal echo of Solomon's song:

> Rys up, my wyf, my love, my lady free!
> The turtles voys is herd, my dowve sweete;
> The wynter is goon with alle his reynes weete.
> Com forth now, with thyne eyen columbyn!
> How fairer been thy brestes than is wyn!
> The gardyn is enclosed al aboute;
> Com forth, my white spouse! (2138–44)

January's garden is 'walled al with stoon' (2029) and contains a well, a 'laurer alwey grene' (2037), and a pear tree at its centre. Both trees are suggestive of fecundity and virility, and the description of the garden as a whole aligns it with the recreational and often eroticized gardens of secular tradition, especially that of the *Romance of the Rose*. This work is expressly named as a source text in the tale (2032) and prompts the reader to contrast the seediness of the present fabliau with the courtly pursuit of the lover in the *Romance*. May, like the garden itself, is owned by January, who enjoys his pleasure at her expense. This view of patriarchal and mercantile control within marriage is exemplified by the 'smale wyket' to which only January has a 'clyket' (2045–6). In typical fabliau fashion the overturning of hierarchy and authority sees Damyan literally and metaphorically appropriate this ownership through the imprinting of the key in warm wax. Chaucer's audiences may also have remembered that the wall of the garden in the *Romance of the Rose* is adorned with images of those whom the God of Love has excluded from his presence. The *Romance*'s use of the garden as a metaphor for physical and emotional bliss is here inverted, and it becomes something more like a prison of envy, lust, and covetousness. The hell of May's marriage to January is reinforced by the appearance of their mythological equivalents Pluto and Proserpina. 'Blynd' January resembles Pluto, King of the Underworld; May is equated with Proserpina, abducted and raped by Pluto. For those familiar with the rest of the *Canterbury Tales* this configuration of garden and captivity parallels the relationship between Emelye, Palamon, and Arcite in the 'Knight's Tale', with its own associations of female confinement and aggressive male desire. Only the seasonal allegory embodied in their own names offers 'fresshe May' any hope of renewal or triumph over the wintry January.

Male obsession and vanity is also alluded to in the detail of the well. In the *Romance of the Rose* (1449–1538) the God of Love leads the lover to a well on which is written the legend 'Here starf the fayre Narcisus' (1468). In this ironic counterpoint to the gender relations in the fabliau Narcissus rejects the love of the nymph Echo, who pines away to death, but not before she curses that he

Myght on a day ben hampred so
For love, and ben so hoot for woo,
That never he myght to joye atteyne. (1493–5)

Narcissus' fate is to fall in love with his own reflection in the well's 'mirrour' and to die from unrequited love. At first the well might seem an inconsequential detail in the 'Merchant's Tale', but the implied reference to classical myth is part of a sequence of images that focus attention upon the issues of sight, deception, or 'fantasye', and moral and physical blindness. Chief among these is January's viewing the unmarried May through the distortions of a mirror (1582) and his sudden blindness, which is remedied by Pluto, and which leads to May's explanation, prompted by Proserpina, that the sole aim of having sex with Damyan up the tree was to restore his vision. As the misanthropic narrator observes, 'For as good is blynd deceyved be | As to be deceyved whan a man may se' (2109–10).

The zigzag course between this barrage of visual and textual allusions comes to rest with a travesty of the events in the Garden of Eden. January here is a sightless Adam, May a sinful Eve, who declares that she 'han to fruyt so greet an appetit | That she may dyen but she of it have' (2336–7), and Damyan is the 'famulier foo' and 'lyk to the naddre' (1784, 1786). For January the terrestrial paradise becomes a 'purgatorie' (1670) of deceit and shame, and for the young lovers it is a place of adultery and moral corruption. The presence of Pluto and Proserpina as traditional rulers of Hades reinforces the threat of damnation.

The post-coital events, however, offer a final flick of the interpretative tail. Typological readings saw the serpent's temptation of Eve as a prefiguring of the Crucifixion, and the actions in January's garden invite equally creative responses that see beyond an uncomplicated condemnation of vice and folly. When January raises his newly opened eyes to see her sin, May cries out:

> Sire, what eyleth yow?
> Have pacience and resoun in youre mynde.
> I have yow holpe on bothe youre eyen blynde.
> Up peril of my soule, I shal nat lyen,
> As me was taught, to heele with youre eyen,
> Was no thyng bet, to make yow to see,
> Than strugle with a man upon a tree. (2368–74)

In this intricate web of references the phrase 'a man upon a tree' inescapably leads to an image of Christ crucified. Medieval readers would also have known the popular apocryphal Bible stories that had the cross of Christ made from the wood of the Tree of Knowledge. This single image captures the history of mankind from original sin to the Redemption, but the implication is a blasphemous confusion of the sacred and secular. Damyan becomes a type of Christ and January the blind Longinus standing at the foot of the Cross, whose sight is restored by Christ's blood. As for May, she might be taken for the Virgin Mary, though the allegory need not be consistent. Indeed, the interpretative maze created by this interplay of signs is indicative of Chaucer's rhetorical strategy. Interpretation relies on mapping these proliferations and their competing claims to significance.

Marginal images

Kolve's analysis of symbols has proved influential in two particular ways. Most obviously it demonstrates the importance of treating iconographical details as parts of entire networks rather than as isolated motifs, while also emphasizing the processes by which meaning can emerge in Chaucer's writings. Equally important, it has contributed to the ongoing critical analysis of manifestations of cultural conflict in Chaucerian narrative. In these terms the iconographic diversity that generates sequences of juxtapositions—for example, sacred–profane, vice–virtue, spiritual–worldly, youth–age, male–female—relates particularly closely to the application of Bakhtin's theory of the carnivalesque and contested authority. (For more on the carnivalesque, see Chapter 22.)

Latterly, Michael Camille has argued that manuscript marginalia hold the key to understanding the impulse towards subversion, parody, and deviation in medieval culture.[13] Image-makers routinely illustrated manuscripts with crazily hybrid beasts, copulating clerics, and defecating knights. But far from 'systematic incoherence', these bizarre juxtapositions are a means of asserting religious and social norms through contrast with something 'less stable, more base and, in semiotic terms, even more illusory—the image on the edge'.[14] Thus marginal images 'add an extra dimension, a supplement, that is able to gloss, parody, modernise and problematize' the text they accompany while remaining essentially conservative and reinforcing conformity and the side of the law.[15]

Reference to manuscript art demonstrates the applicability of Camille's method to Chaucer's writings. The Latin text of Psalm 101 in the Ormesby Psalter (c.1310–20), beginning 'Domine exaudi orationem meam' ('Hear, O Lord, my prayer'), is accompanied by a marginal picture of a young couple exchanging a ring, with attendant animals—a scene commonly referred to as a 'bawdy betrothal' (Figure I.8). Dressed in virginal blue the damsel's veil flows out behind her as if in a stiff breeze, a movement picked up in the outstretched arms and in the man's erect sword–penis. The theme of sexual desire is quite explicit but is extended to the level of the predatory by the presence of the bird of prey, the hunting dog, and the squirrel (an emblem of female genitalia in the fabliau tradition) perched in the lady's hand. These conventional responses to expected gender roles are, however, complicated by the reversed positioning of the cat stalking a mouse beneath the couple. The scene can be read, among other things, as a parodic 'anti-illustration' of the verse 'I am smitten as grass, and my heart is withered' in the verse above,[16] a comment on the sexual passions of King David, the author of the Psalms, who is illustrated in the decorated initial above, or censure of sex and bodily desire in relation to the spiritual truth of the Word of God.

An obvious parallel for this vision of sexually vigorous youth appears in Chaucer's 'Miller's Tale', in which gesture and animal symbolism signify a complex erotic narrative enacted against a biblical text, in this case an allusion to Noah's flood. John's young wife, Alison, is sexually objectified through a sequence of images likening her to animals (weasel, colt, kid, calf, swallow) and consumables (money, apples, honeycomb). She is also the focus of unwanted attention from the effeminate Absolon, who 'if she hadde been a mous, | And he a cat, he wolde hire hente anon' (3346–7). Ironically it is Absolon who ends up practising reversed sex roles as he aims the coulter at her lover Nicholas's backside. All this is played out against an initial narratorial promise that the story is of 'a legende and a lyf | Bothe of a carpenter and of his wyf' (3141–2)—more Nazareth than Oxford—and an injunction that creates a vulgar parallelism between the sacred and the profane:

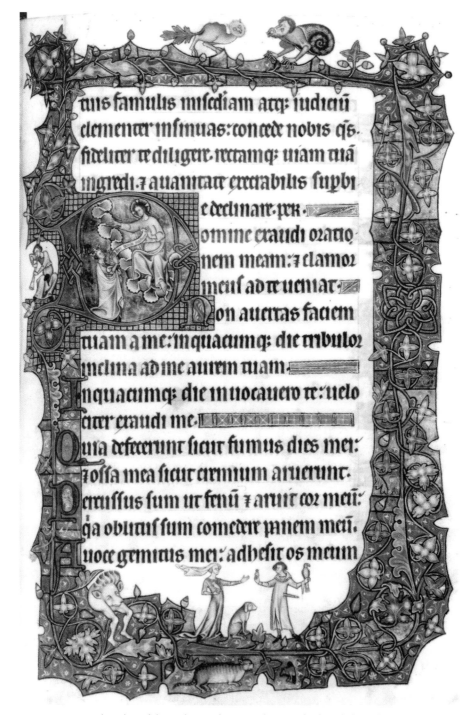

Fig. I.8 King David, author of the Psalms, with marginal scene of a 'bawdy betrothal'. Page from the Ormesby Psalter, early fourteenth century (Bodleian Library, MS Douce 366).

An housbonde shal nat been inquisityf
Of Goddes pryvetee, nor of his wyf.
So he may fynde Goddes foyson there,
Of the remenant nedeth nat enquere. (3163–6)

As with the Ormesby Psalter's visual performance of the Psalm, the fabliau sex scenes offer an irreverent perspective on sacred truth while ultimately leaving its authority intact.

In structural terms the margins of the manuscripts are also analogous to the links between the Canterbury tales. Images in the borders of manuscripts may play upon and question the authority and permanence of the central text but they can also be seen as in turn critiqued by that text and remain precisely in the marginal position. The gaps between the tales promote an exchange of voices and opinions that threatens to disrupt the tales themselves—the rolling dispute between the Miller and Reeve on the first day is a case in point—but they too are ultimately constrained and subordinated to the larger structural composition.

Text and image

Very recent scholarly approaches to the visual aspects of Chaucer's poetry emphasize this interest in iconography. These, in the context of the historical study of manuscripts, have led to the growth of what are termed text–image studies. Extant illustrated versions of Chaucer's major works are rare, and by far the most famous survivor is the Ellesmere manuscript,[17] a luxuriously illuminated copy of the *Canterbury Tales* made in London before 1420. As in many other high-status English manuscripts of the period, elegant decorated borders of floral patterns surround the pages of the Ellesmere text. But the manuscript's unique feature is the set of twenty-three equestrian portraits of the pilgrims.

These images, like any in illustrated medieval manuscripts, have various functions.[18] Most obviously they have an aesthetic appeal designed to impress upon the viewer the skill of representation and the overall beauty of the book. With each portrait positioned in the margin at the start of each narrator's tale they also provide a convenient visual index for the poem as a whole. They also offer a visual commentary on the text that helps us understand the original audience's responses.

The relations between the text and the images are complex.[19] The painted pilgrims are not mirror images of their textual portraits and there are varying degrees of artistic interpretation in the representations. Some replicate many of the details of the thumbnail sketches given in the 'General Prologue' and the links between the tales, revealing the artists or their patrons as close readers of the poem. Thus the red-bearded, 'short-sholdred' ('GP' 549), drunken miller, dressed in a white coat and blue hood, is shown hunched over his horse, clutching his bagpipe. Even his 'thombe of gold' ('GP' 563), a reference to the sharp practice of the proverbial miller, is clearly visible.

Others are less faithful illustrations, with emphasis often placed upon unspoken details of clothing or physiognomy or accessories, while still keeping a focus upon particular textual details. The Wife of Bath is 'ywympled wel' with a large hat ('GP' 470–1), but her 'hosen' here is blue rather than 'fyn scarlet reed', her complexion pale rather than 'reed of hewe' (456–8), and there is no sign of her famous gap teeth. She seems a younger, less ostentatious, less overtly sexual figure than the five-times married 'parisshe wif' (449), and is perhaps closer in appearance and temper to the enchanted maiden of her tale. In similar fashion the Pardoner's portrait renders certain textual details but also offers supplementary information that suggests a reading shaped by cultural responses to the figure of the pardoner.[20] He is clean-shaven with the same 'glarynge eyen' and hair 'as yelow as wex' hanging dishevelled about his shoulders (675–84). His relic pouch is as clearly visible as the badge of St Veronica's cloth on his cap, a mark of pilgrimage to Rome (685), but his oversized crucifix is an embellishment of Chaucer's 'croys of latoun ful of stones' (699). The Pardoner's declared intent is to fleece the pilgrims under the guise of pious concern ('I rekke nevere, whan that they been beryed, | Though that hir soules goon a-blakeberyed!', 'ParP' 405–6), and this portrait declares a heightened awareness of the tools of his trade and his insidious corruption.

If the pilgrim portraits help us appreciate Chaucer's meticulous use of detail to suggest credible emotional, psychological, and physical states, they also remind us that Chaucerian character is an amalgam of realism and the representative. In the Ellesmere portrait Roger the Cook is identified by his (non-textual) meat hook and by the 'mormal' on his shin ('GP' 386), which in terms of the standard medieval equation between outward appearance and inner moral worth implies both physical illness and moral corruption. The Prioress's delicate beauty—her 'eyen greye as glas', her 'mouth ful smal', and 'fair forheed' (152–4)—matches the idealized feminine beauty common to traditions of lyric and romance poetry. Taken on their own such details might confirm the Prioress as a type of worldly religious nun. But when keyed into the more personalized information of her cockney French and her brooch engraved with the ambiguous legend *Amor vincit omnia* ('Love conquers all', 162) we recognize the need to reassess these habitual responses. This combination of verisimilitude and the conventional signals the artifice of the 'General Prologue'. The informality of the groupings in the tavern and on the road to Canterbury masks the structural care with which Chaucer juxtaposes individually separate portraits in the manner, perhaps, of the static, formally posed figures of contemporary paintings such as those on the lower panels of church rood-screens and in stained glass.

The complexity of pictorial responses to textual materials also defines the only other significant manuscript illustration of Chaucer's poetry, the frontispiece of a copy of *Troilus and Criseyde* dated to *c*.1415–1425 (Figure I.5).[21] The layout of the manuscript indicates that an extensive programme of illustrations was planned but only the prefatory miniature, in effect a visual summary of the narrative, was actually executed. This dramatic full-page image is divided into upper and lower sections or registers, which are surrounded by a wide decorative frame; leaf and foliage decoration completely fill the rest of the page. In the lower register a youthful bearded man to be taken as the poet himself stands in a lectern addressing a mixed and vaguely attentive court audience. The upper scene, separated from the lower one by a shelf of stylized rocks and trees running diagonally across the page, shows Criseyde exchanged with the Greeks for the hero–traitor Antenor while her lover, Troilus, is left behind in Troy.

This image responds to the text on a number of levels. Immediately noticeable is the recasting of the opposing forces of Troy and Greece as warring city states and the lack of distinction between the courtiers and the classical characters. All the figures are dressed in the same luxurious garments and, if taken in isolation from the text that follows, we might imagine we are being offered two scenes from the same narrative set in some exaggerated vision of a fortified English landscape, typifying the ways in which legendary materials offered a means of playing out contemporary concerns. Of these the examination of the position and treatment of Criseyde is recognized by the artist as the central dynamic of Chaucer's story. The sense of a woman objectified, controlled, and passed between men is heightened by the presence of the milling crowd in the foreground of the composition. So too the framing towers of the rival cities capture the sense of enclosure and confinement that Chaucer exploits in the latter stages of the narrative, especially when he has Troilus looking on helplessly in book 5 to where he imagines Criseyde resides (with Diomede) in the Greek camp. The impulse shared by the poet and the artist—typical of medieval responses to complex narratives—is to concentrate their energies into the representation of highly significant dramatic moments. Had the rest of the commissioned illustrations been executed, we could have expected further attempts to distil intellectual and emotional processes into moments of heightened intensity. Criseyde's dream of the white eagle (2. 925–31) and Troilus' equivalent dream of the boar (5. 1233–43), the letters and the exchange of the love-tokens, and so forth, all show Chaucer's capacity and inclination to render conflicting desires and impulses in symbolic form within the psychologically realistic progression of the lovers' affair.

Portraits and textual authority

Both the Ellesmere and the Cambridge *Troilus* manuscripts show that contemporary readers used visual materials to enhance their enjoyment of Chaucerian texts. However, it is important to remember that the status of imaginative writing in English was at this time still relatively low. To some extent this helps explain the dearth of visuals directly associated with Chaucerian texts. Even by 1400 only a small proportion of literate society read vernacular fiction and those English patrons who were willing to pay for illuminated manuscripts invariably chose to spend their money on Latin religious texts such as books of hours or psalters. Where English readers did own recreational works even these were likely to be in the prestige languages of Latin or French and by classical authorities such as Virgil and Ovid. Such authoritative works, perceived to have greater intellectual, moral, and cultural worth than any in English, could more appropriately justify the expense of illustration. Texts such as the *Romance of the Rose* and some works by Boccaccio came to be routinely accompanied by a standard sequence of miniatures. In sharp contrast only three surviving manuscripts of English poetry from the period before Chaucer's death have any significant pictorial element and none is a particularly fine example of the illuminator's art. These are the voluminous Auchinleck manuscript from early fourteenth-century London with its small miniatures depicting romance heroes; the so-called *Gawain*-manuscript to which were added twelve rather crude illustrations at the instigation of an early fifteenth-century reader; and the Vernon manuscript, a large collection of hagiographic and biblical material produced around 1390 for a monastic house in the west Midlands, in which a number of gospel and hagiographic narratives carry illustrations. Expense and limited readership certainly constrained production, but it is also true that without a tradition of illustrating English texts the artists had few models to use as source material.

Seen from this angle the lavishness of the Ellesmere portraits and the *Troilus* frontispiece is a declaration of the perceived worth and importance of Chaucer's vernacular texts. The portraits of the poet make a significant statement about the elevated literary status of Chaucer and more generally of English poetic endeavour. It is a critical commonplace to say that Chaucer writes texts about texts. His entire body of work is profoundly self-conscious about creating an English literary tradition from the 'olde bokes' of his *auctours*, whether classical or contemporary Latin writers, Italians, or French. The clearest example of this comes at the end of *Troilus and Criseyde*, when the fictive distance between narrator and poet suddenly narrows and a voice more closely approximating Chaucer's own expresses paternal anxiety for his textual offspring as he bequeaths it to posterity:

> Go, litel bok, go, litel myn tragedye . . .
> And kis the steppes where as thow seest pace
> Virgile, Ovide, Omer, Lucan, and Stace. (5. 1786–92)

Even though the poet in the *Troilus* frontispiece is contemporized as an oral performer to Richard II's court—he does not read from a book and the iconography is that of the religious preacher—a definite link is forged between the narrative and its creator. Indeed, the portrait identifies him as the English-reading audience's own *auctour*, and of course aligns each successive viewer of the manuscript with that tradition.

The promotion of Chaucer was central to the activities of the generation of poets writing in the immediate aftermath of his death. By presenting Chaucer as the originator of a new tradition of English letters these poets conferred his posthumous blessing on themselves and thereby created textual space for their own writings. In an extended passage of praise in his *Regement of Princes*, Thomas Hoccleve, a clerk in the office of the

Privy Seal who claimed to have known Chaucer personally, describes him as the 'first findere of our fayre langage' (4978) and 'my worthy mayster' (4983).[22] At this point in the poem Hoccleve enshrines Chaucer's enduring literary presence by indicating that a marginal portrait should stand next to the stanza 'to put other men in remembraunce | Of his persone' (4994–5). The image appearing in a British Library manuscript of the poem (MS Harley 4866) bears a marked resemblance to the bearded, portly figure of Geoffrey that marks the opening of his 'Tale of Melibee' in the Ellesmere manuscript, and has become an iconic figure of the poet (see Figure I.1). Pictures of contemporary English authors are used elsewhere as a means of authenticating the English text, notably of John Gower in versions of his compendious English poem *Confessio amantis* and the (probably fictional) John Mandeville in his *Travels*, but the collectively imagined and personalized figure of Chaucer provides a forcible reminder of the pre-eminence of his reputation.

If the Harley manuscript portrait demonstrates how imagery can be enlisted to augment textual discourse, its iconographic, stylistic, and structural features—naturalistic detail fused with conventional gesture, the margins relating to and informing the centre—also return us to the visual culture in which Chaucer's own writings are firmly rooted. For Chaucer and his contemporaries visualization is a key to demonstrating the realities of the physical and spiritual worlds.

FURTHER READING

Alexander, J. J. G., and Paul Binski (eds.), *Age of Chivalry: Art in Plantagenet England 1200–1400* (London: Weidenfeld & Nicolson, 1987). Extensively illustrated catalogue of a major exhibition of English medieval art; includes introductory essays and detailed descriptions of more than 600 items.

Camille, Michael, *Image on the Edge: The Margins of Medieval Art* (London: Reaktion Books, 1992). Influential if controversial study of the role of marginal art in medieval religious and secular culture.

Coldstream, Nicola, *The Decorated Style: Architecture and Ornament 1240–1360* (London: British Museum Press, 1994). Overview of aesthetic principles and social and religious contexts of the English Decorated style of Gothic art; richly illustrated.

Cooper, Helen, *Oxford Guides to Chaucer: The 'Canterbury Tales'*, 2nd edn. (Oxford: Oxford University Press, 1996). Excellent discussion of all of the *Canterbury Tales* with extensive reference to iconography.

Hilmo, Maidie, *Medieval Images, Icons, and Illustrated English Literary Texts* (Aldershot: Ashgate, 2004). Survey of text–image relations in Anglo-Saxon and later medieval English art, including the Vernon and Ellesmere manuscripts.

Kolve, V. A., *Chaucer and the Imagery of Narrative: The First Five Canterbury Tales* (Stanford, Calif.: Stanford University Press, 1984). Study of medieval aesthetics, iconography, and iconographic traditions of the tales of the Knight, Miller, Reeve, Cook, and Man of Law.

Salter, Elizabeth, 'Medieval Poetry and the Visual Arts', *Essays and Studies*, NS 22 (1969), 16–32; repr. in Salter, *English and International: Studies in the Literature, Art and Patronage of Medieval*

England, ed. Derek Pearsall and Nicolette Zeeman (Cambridge: Cambridge University Press, 1988), 245–55, 339–40. Analysis of the relations between the visual arts and medieval English literature; numerous references to Chaucerian modes of representation.

Stevens, Martin, and Daniel Woodward (eds.), *The Ellesmere Chaucer: Essays in Interpretation* (San Marino, Calif.: Huntingdon Library, 1995). Essay collection exploring numerous aspects of the manuscript, including layout and illustrations.

WEB LINKS

<<http://www.paintedchurch.org> A developing web site devoted to English medieval wall paintings; organized by location and subject material; extensively illustrated with descriptive text.

<http//www.cvma.ac.uk.> A developing web site dedicated to the medieval stained glass of Great Britain; searchable picture archive.

NOTES

1. 'Why the Devil Wears Green', *Modern Language Notes*, 69 (1954), 470–2; D. W. Robertson, Jr., *A Preface to Chaucer* (London: Oxford University Press, 1963); and Bernard F. Huppé, *A Reading of the 'Canterbury Tales'* (Albany: State University of New York, 1964).
2. St Augustine of Hippo, *On Christian Teaching*, trans. R. P. H. Green (Oxford: Oxford University Press, 1997), 31.
3. Robert M. Jordan, *Chaucer and the Shape of Creation: The Aesthetic Possibilities of Inorganic Structure* (Cambridge, Mass.: Harvard University Press, 1967), 130.
4. Elizabeth Salter, 'Medieval Poetry and the Visual Arts', *Essays and Studies*, NS 22 (1969), 16.
5. British Library, MS Arundel 83 II, *c.*1330.
6. Derek Pearsall (ed.), *Chaucer to Spenser: An Anthology of Writings 1380–1560* (Oxford: Blackwell, 1999), 354.
7. See also Muriel Whitaker, 'The Chaucer Chest and the "Pardoner's Tale": Didacticism in Narrative Art', *Chaucer Review*, 34 (1999), 174–89.
8. Michael Camille, 'The Language of Images', in J. J. Alexander and Paul Binski (eds.), *Age of Chivalry: Plantagenet Art 1200–1400* (London: Weidenfeld & Nicolson, 1987), 33.
9. Priscilla Barnum (ed.), *Dives and Pauper*, i, Early English Text Society Original Series 275 (Oxford: Oxford University Press, 1976), 82. For an introduction to the contemporary debate about images, see Margaret Aston, *Lollards and Reformers: Images and Literacy in Late Medieval England* (London: Hambledon Press, 1984).
10. Helen Cooper, *Oxford Guides to Chaucer: The 'Canterbury Tales'*, 2nd edn. (Oxford: Oxford University Press, 1996), 292.
11. V. A. Kolve, *Chaucer and the Imagery of Narrative: The First Five Canterbury Tales* (Stanford, Calif.: Stanford University Press, 1984).
12. Derek Pearsall and Elizabeth Salter, *Landscapes and Seasons of the Medieval World* (London: Elek, 1973).
13. Michael Camille, *Image on the Edge: The Margins of Medieval Art* (London: Reaktion Books, 1992).
14. Ibid. 12, 26.
15. Ibid. 39–40.
16. Ibid. 41.
17. Huntingdon Library, San Marino, Calif., MS EL 26 C 9.

18. Lesley Lawton, 'The Illustration of Late Medieval Secular Texts, with Special Reference to Lydgate's *Troy Book*', in Derek Pearsall (ed.), *Manuscripts and Readers in Fifteenth Century England: The Literary Implications of Manuscript Study* (Cambridge: Brewer, 1983), 41–69.

19. Richard K. Emmerson, 'Text and Image in the Ellesmere Portraits of the Tale-Tellers', in Martin Stevens and Daniel Woodward (eds.), *The Ellesmere Chaucer: Essays in Interpretation* (San Marino, Calif.: Huntington Library, 1995), 143–70. This volume features colour reproductions of all of the pilgrim portraits.

20. Maidie Hilmo, *Medieval Images, Icons, and Illustrated English Literary Texts* (Aldershot: Ashgate, 2004), 162.

21. Corpus Christi College, Cambridge, MS 61.

22. *Selections from Hoccleve*, ed. M. C. Seymour (Oxford: Clarendon Press, 1981), 51, 124 n.

12 | Sexuality

Alcuin Blamires

Not much more than a generation ago the subject of 'sexuality' in Chaucer's writings would have been expected to focus either on the sexual libertarianism popularly discerned in his bawdy works (as opposed to the sublimation of sex discerned in his courtly works), or on the so-called 'marriage debate' in the *Canterbury Tales*. The first attempt to describe Chaucer's 'sexual poetics' was published by Carolyn Dinshaw in 1989 and rested somewhat tenuously on an analogy between the scribe's act of writing on parchment, and male sexual control of the female body. Subsequently much has been written about gender formations in Chaucer—and particularly about a 'feminizing' of the male that some have detected in the writings—but sexuality has not in itself been an explicit concern of critics except for those who controversially see the poet's works as susceptible to readings informed by contemporary psychoanalytical theories.

Sexuality is such a familiar concept to us now that it can be a shock to discover that no such word existed until quite recently. It is not present, for example, in Samuel Johnson's English dictionary published in 1755. Here is one explanation of how the innovation subsequently occurred:

> Something new happens to the various relations among sexual roles, sexual object-choices, sexual categories, sexual behaviors, and sexual identities in bourgeois Europe between the end of the seventeenth century and the beginning of the twentieth. Sex . . . assumes a new importance in defining and normalizing the modern self. The conception of the sexual instinct as an autonomous human function . . . appears for the first time in the nineteenth century, and without it our heavily psychologized model of sexual subjectivity—which knits up desire, its objects, sexual behavior, gender identity, reproductive function, mental health, erotic sensibility, personal style, and degrees of normality or deviance into an individuating normativizing feature of the personality called 'sexuality' or 'sexual orientation'—is inconceivable. Sexuality is indeed, as Foucault claimed, a distinctively modern production.[1]

Not surprisingly the argument that the concept of sexuality is 'distinctively modern' has been challenged. For instance, in a landmark issue of the medieval journal *Speculum* devoted to the study of sex and gender in the period, Nancy Partner champions the presence in medieval culture of sexuality 'in the complexly extended modern sense, the kernel of individual personality which leaves its signature on other, nonsexual behavior'.[2] She resists readings of sexualities that interpret them as the historically conditioned product of the interplay of power in a particular society. Hence she insists on recognizing a familiar impulse of sexuality in Heloise, a twelfth-century woman who in Partner's view was patently 'compounded of the drives we all share'.[3] What is historically strange about Heloise, her medievalness, resides not in her sexuality but in her socially conditioned gender, her *femininity*: 'Heloise's complex sexuality speaks to us intelligibly and powerfully: sexuality speaks to our common humanity. Her femininity, her particular twelfth-century European way of being a woman, living a woman's life, is what disconcerts us: gender [as opposed to sexuality] speaks of distance and difference'.[4]

Sexuality by any other name?

Amid such claims and counter-claims, how should we talk of sexuality in Chaucer? We have to begin by confirming that Chaucer knew no word for, and to that extent possibly had no emphatic concept of, 'sexuality'—as distinct from, say, 'difference of sex'—whether in vernacular English and French or in Latin. To be sure, his writings habitually refer to manhood and womanhood, though generally with a certain emotive vagueness. He had expressions for the sex drive (e.g. 'corage', 'appetit', 'lust voluptuous') but apparently no lexical means of expressing that kernel of individual personality of which Partner speaks. We shall risk anachronism in this chapter as we bring the concept, warily, into the reading of Chaucer's work; but it would be over-punctilious to banish the word from discussion altogether. For instance, Chaucer to some degree thought of and verbalized sexuality as an external force. In a pre-modern era when culture often externalized human passions and impulses and projected temptation as the agency of the devil, sexuality too (or aspects of it) could be expressed as an external agency—the tutelage of the planet–goddess Venus, or of Amor, the 'god' of love. Chaucer was extremely familiar with medieval Europe's favourite poem about the impact of erotic attraction on the young masculine psyche, the *Romance of the Rose* (completed *c.*1275). In that poem what we might want to define as sexuality is a phenomenon that seems to exist as the sum of the interplay among a large cast of personified figures such as Generosity, Fear, Modesty, Responsiveness. Dominant among them are the god Amor, who promotes the male youth's sexual development, and the goddess Venus, who mostly spreads desire and receptivity among women (see Figure I.9). While Amor and Venus are not male and female sexuality exactly, they are not far from filling those roles. In Chaucer's poetry their complex functions and interrelationship still admit of a sense that they are frequently invoked, whether separately or together, to objectify the power of sexuality—for instance, in *Troilus and Criseyde*, the 'Knight's Tale', and the *Parliament of Fowls*.

Venus is prominent in a famous passage about sexual preference in the 'Wife of Bath's Prologue'. Perhaps nowhere might the absence of a nameable concept of

Fig. I.9 Pygmalion appeals to Venus; Venus' torch warms his statue to life. Manuscript illustration, late fourteenth century (British Library, MS Yates Thompson 21).

sexuality be so keenly felt by Chaucer's readers as in the case of the Wife's monologue: critics can scarcely avoid supplying the deficiency by talking of her 'sexuality' in their analyses. But in lines 600–26 of her Prologue she makes her own concerted attempt to define, and to excuse, what sounds like her sexuality. Reflecting on her eventual fifth marriage to a man half her age, she explains how her youthful taste (her 'coltes tooth') continued sharp, how she was vigorous, pretty, and had a pussy men raved about. The traces of Venus upon her showed in a birthmark and also in her 'feelynge', her 'lust', and 'likerousnesse' (her emotions, desire, and randiness). The different traces of Mars showed in other birthmarks, and in her 'herte' and 'sturdy hardynesse' (her 'spirit' and 'bold strength'). All in all her 'appetit' was never to be constrained, so long as she found a partner pleasing.

Although it is often held that the planets of Venus and Mars together determine her appetites for love and marital strife respectively, the passage itself links the Wife's Martial 'hardynesse' not with marital strife but with the bold adventuring of her desire—never mind (she declares) whether her partner were 'short, or long, or blak, or whit' (624). In fact the passage tells us that Venus alone can't 'be' one's sexuality. A person's particular sexual stance will be a balance of other factors along with Venus. It is the passage's configuration of colt's tooth, Venus, 'feelynge', Mars, strong 'herte', and appetite that looks like a way of encapsulating the Wife's sexuality in the sense in which we have seen the concept defined—the individuating model of her sexual identity.

Perhaps Chaucer here takes his received structures remarkably far in this modern direction, but it would still be anachronistic to talk of 'individuation'. Scholarship has established that the text's planetary allusions are such as would signify female promiscuity in standard astrological science, and that the Wife's use of them to shuffle off moral responsibility for her sexual exploits consciously flouts theological doctrine. In a way the whole sketch is just a colourful pretext for revisiting a common medieval misogynous and morally loaded caricature of the insatiable, superstitious, assertive widow. Moreover, various other emphases in her Prologue make it difficult to accept this self-description at face value. We are too aware of the speaker's mischievously exaggerating self-dramatizing style playing with a conventional satire on female desire. Ultimately we would have to resort to identifying the individuated 'sexuality' projected by the passage, if it exists, as an elusive dramatization that conceals rather than reveals the underlying sexuality of the person ostensibly uttering it.

This discussion has raised the crucial question of the moral dimension of sexuality, which will be addressed in a moment. Meanwhile, faced with at least a residual impression of a selective version of sexuality in the case of the Wife of Bath, it is natural to ask how far sexualit(ies) might be present in Chaucer's work as a flexible range of options to be selected, rather than as segregated norms from which deviation was firmly discouraged.

Sexuality or sexualities?

There has been a concern in recent times to pluralize sexuality, to think in terms of 'sexualities' rather than sexuality, and this concern is not necessarily foreign to the medieval understanding. Sexual orientation was thought of as occurring within a continuum. Physiological and medical doctrine on the production of sexual identity can be found in writings that Chaucer seems to have known, such as Constantine the African's treatise *On Coitus*, mentioned in the 'Merchant's Tale' (1810–1). The doctrine was structured around standard medieval hierarchical binaries giving greater value to (male) heat and dryness in relation to (female) cold and moisture, and (male) right in relation to (female) left location. Variables in these predetermined the particular proportioning of male–female tendencies in the embryo produced by a procreating couple. For instance, a man with a bigger *right* testicle had a likelihood of fathering males: but if his semen was received in one of the *left* cells (the 'weaker' side) of the woman's womb, an 'effeminate male' would be the likely result. The permutations created a range of possibility encompassing also the virile woman, and the hermaphrodite.[5] Anyone born female could have what might now be called a male side to her identity, and vice versa. We should therefore be wary of imagining medieval culture's whole sexual paradigm only in terms of stereotypical absolutes. But was it, nevertheless, radically less flexible than our own?

There are certainly constructions in Chaucer's writing—for instance, a remark about no woman seeming 'less mannish' than Criseyde—that could imply a context of medieval sexual relativities. The verse that introduces Criseyde in this way is complimenting her, as if from Troilus' admiring, objectifying heterosexual point of view. She had limbs 'so wel answerynge . . . to wommanhod' that no person was 'lasse mannyssh in semynge' (*TC* 1. 282–4). Chaucer has taken off from a more conventional formulation in his Italian source, which says that her limbs were proportionate to her height and that her features displayed ladylike loftiness (*donnesca altezza*).[6] However, the logical corollary of complimenting a woman for being non-mannish is that a mannish woman will provoke suspicion. We are not in a world of benignly accepted variations of sexual orientation. Hence in the 'Man of Law's Tale' the villainous Donegild, a queen mother who conducts a malicious campaign against her son's new wife and child, is denounced for being mannish. Her mannishness attests a perverse hybridity, a devilish tyrannical spirit ('MLT' 782–3). In a tale that cultivates lurid polarities of all sorts, the reader is twice asked to recoil from the idea of any woman whose personality manifests allegedly male features. Earlier there has been the example of a Sultaness responsible for instigating the victimization of the heroine in the story. The Sultaness is unflatteringly hailed as a 'virago' and described in terms of fraudulent sexuality, to the extent that she is deemed not a woman but a *feigned* woman ('MLT' 359–62).

Perhaps, then, these configurations (both in *Troilus* and in the 'Man of Law's Tale') do not so much demonstrate the porosity of boundaries within sexuality as reinforce such boundaries by dwelling on destabilizations of them. To champion Chaucer's open-mindedness in the tale, the reader would have to decide that the negative representation of its mannish viragos betrays the Man of Law's patriarchal bigotry; but this tends to presuppose, controversially, that we interpret the tale's speaker as being subjected to pervasive irony. Does the tale mean to underline through irony its narrator's inability to tolerate flexibility in sexuality, to recognize *sexualities*; or does the tale unironically voice an anxious reaction to deviations from normative feminine standards?

The Pardoner is a test case in this regard, as we shall note later. Meanwhile, it is important to acknowledge that representation of what we would call sexuality in Chaucer is usually obscured behind a primary attention to gendered behaviour. This can be seen in those moments when someone's masculinity is ostensibly queried in his fictions. In the 'Nun's Priest's Tale', for instance, Pertelote the hen taunts Chauntecleer the cockerel for being scared by a dream of a fox. How can he fall so short of the model of a 'hardy' husband—'Have ye no mannes herte, and han a berd?' (2920). Not only do the canons of masculinity appear laughable when applied in the context of a cockerel's 'beard', but Chauntecleer's attempt to conform to them by strutting the garden like a grim lion (3179) merely exposes him to the jaws of the fox. Gender models are no very sure guide to successful living.

Masculine gendering comes under analogous scrutiny in the central episodes of *Troilus and Criseyde*. When Troilus the lover, overcome by the stress of acting out a pretext for being in Criseyde's bedroom, unexpectedly faints there and has to be cast inert on to her bed, Criseyde joins Pandarus in querying his manhood: 'Is this a mannes game?' (*TC* 3. 1098, 1126). Perhaps indeed the scene confusingly assimilates Troilus' role to that of a bride, in a subversion of the traditional ritual whereby kin and associates ceremoniously lay the bride in the nuptial bed, ready for the attentions of the groom.[7] Yet the poem generally makes abundantly clear that diffidence and emotional confusion in the male are not to be considered problematic in relation to gender or sexuality. Troilus has earlier been reduced to blushing speechlessness in his first private encounter with Criseyde. But we are told that her love for him was not diminished by the fact that he betrayed 'shame' (embarrassment, 3. 89) and that he was neither presumptuous nor 'made it tough' (was not sexually aggressive, 3. 87).[8] Here is an instance of a corrective emphasis widely noted in Chaucer's courtly narratives, termed by Jill Mann 'feminization', whereby some of his male characters are positively endowed with certain ethically resonant traits normally ascribed to femininity in medieval discourse—'shame' of tongue being one of them.[9] Troilus' diffidence has been part of his attraction for Criseyde from her first serious glimpse of him, when she has looked him up and down as he returns from battle along her street. In order to assess the balancing act that Chaucer sustains we should note, however, that the same scene loads Troilus with conventional signs of masculinity, summed up in the sexually suggestive adjective 'weldy'. Thus he also strikes Criseyde as a man of arms, full of prowess, who 'hadde a body and a myght | To don that thing' (2. 631–6: but what thing—combat or coitus?). The 'feminization' argument should not be allowed to obscure residual stereotype: the male body is active, it has power, it is for 'doing'. Because in the formation of sexuality inherited by Chaucer the active–passive gender binary is a major concept whose presence in his writing has sometimes been underestimated, we need to take further account of it here.

Active and passive

That male sexuality is essentially 'active' and female sexuality is essentially 'passive' was a keystone of medieval thinking. It was rehearsed unequivocally in contexts both academic and popular. It was underpinned by ideas on physiology, as shown by the proposition that in terms of natural human origin the father theoretically deserves more love from children than the mother: 'the father, as the active partner [in procreation], is a principle in a higher way than the mother, who supplies the passive or material element'.[10] The principle appears in Alan of Lille's homophobic *Complaint of Nature*, a twelfth-century text cited by Chaucer in the *Parliament of Fowls* (316). The narrator of the *Complaint* claims there is evidence of the collapse of Nature's law because 'the active sex shudders in disgrace as it sees itself degenerate into the passive sex'.[11] Elsewhere, the same distinction supports a brisk claim that in sexual matters a greater share of moral responsibility and thence culpability falls upon men:

> If it is as evil to do lechery as the Bible and the Lord Himself tells us, then who is the more blameworthy: the one who instigates it, or the one who doesn't so much do it as suffer what men do to her? You know very well that it is the male who *does* it, and whoever says otherwise is wrong and is lying through his teeth.[12]

How far Chaucer disrupts or critiques this binary model of sexual roles is a matter of debate. Like many writers of courtly narratives in the Middle Ages, but perhaps with unusual relish, he projects the courtly lover (for example, Troilus and the Man in Black in the *Book of the Duchess*) as self-abasing and submissive to the woman loved. However, this self-disciplinary male abasement is allowed for within conventional medieval discourse on love as a means of coercing a woman's (passive) feelings of compassion. 'Active' masculine competitiveness merely regroups, as it were, into a competition in levels of 'unworthiness' to capture the love-object.

Chaucer's poetry has been scoured for signs that he breaches the active–passive sexual paradigm. What, for instance, can we make of May's urgency to 'have' her lover Damyan in the 'Merchant's Tale'? It is tempting to credit May with autonomy. Certainly the story credits her with the initiative to organize a counterfeit key to the love-garden. She also signals her sexual interest in Damyan by twisting his hand with conspicuous force; her love for the squire becomes so keen that either she must die or else 'han hym as hir leste' ('MerT' 2094–5). However, this latent suggestion of sharp female desire is never actually realized. Rather, her letter to Damyan seems to articulate the sexual roles operative in the story: in it she grants her favour and communicates that there remain only a time and place to be found so that 'she myghte unto his lust suffise' (1999). In the event she is reduced to what that implies—a female body, receiving and satisfying the active male, as Damyan piles desperately into her in the branches of a tree (2352–3).

If May does little to upend the theory of female sexuality as 'passive', Alison in the 'Miller's Tale' seems more promising and has often been read as a sexually 'active' woman. This impression owes much to her initial description with its emphasis upon her animal energy and boisterous spirits. There is a deal of critical sentimentality about her role that really ought to be tempered by cooler assessment of her contribution to the subsequent narrative. Her main intervention is the jest of baring her bottom through the window to discomfit her unsuccessful admirer, Absolon, when her successful admirer, Nicholas, is enjoying a night with her. She places her bottom in a position to *be kissed* there, with the further result that she is lined up in our imaginations to be assaulted in the same place when Absolon returns to take vengeance for that insult with a ploughing implement. The basic passivity of her role as the males' plaything is not only summed up in the conclusion, 'Thus swyved was this carpenteris wyf' ('MT' 3850), but has also been made plain earlier, in the punning rhyme of the lines that herald Nicholas's 'wooing' of her. He accosts her with the alleged artfulness of his male profession—'As clerkes ben ful subtile and ful queynte'—whereas she is not 'artful' in that active mental sense but simply constitutes the bodily work of art to be grasped: 'And prively he caughte hire by the queynte' (3275–6).

It is not clear whether the 'Miller's Tale' asks any serious questions about active–passive sexuality in its comic culmination. Nicholas experiences the savage penetration from the rear by Absolon's red-hot ploughing implement that was in prospect for Alison. The implement is certainly a symbol for Absolon's phallus, whether or not implying his personal insufficiency in that department. Nicholas, by substituting his bottom for Alison's and consequently receiving that 'plough', emasculates himself; in the same moment he steps into the role of passive partner in a quasi-sodomitical act, replete with red-hot retribution. These implicit readings produce a farrago of sexual antics without, I believe, yielding a coherent statement on sexuality, though it may be that the figuring of sodomy in this violent way is an oblique means (Chaucer's, or the Miller's?) of demonizing it. In the event only the consequences for Absolon's sexuality are spelt out. He is healed of his fantasy of courtly love (3756–8), but this does not seem to confirm or deny what a modern reader might most want to know: namely, whether the tale has meant to present him as a gay person who by means of his discomfiture has (in our parlance) 'discovered his sexuality'.

Ownership of sexuality

Where we might talk thus of defining and 'owning' our sexuality, ownership of sexual-ity—especially female sexuality—was a matter for intense regulation in the Middle Ages. In general people were encouraged to believe that not they, but others, owned their sexuality. Legal and doctrinal ownership of one's sexuality were topics that espe-cially interested Chaucer. Legal, in the sense that law encouraged males to assert owner-ship of wives and daughters, and hence masculinities are implicated in upholding that ownership (Chaucer engages with this in the 'Reeve's Tale' and the 'Franklin's Tale', but I shall not pursue it here). Doctrinal ownership consisted in the affirmation by canonical law that although the basis for marriage was consent, the body of each spouse was sexually 'owed' to the other. This was grounded in St Paul's concept of the sexual 'debt' in 1 Corinthians 7: 4–5, a passage sonorously rendered thus in the King James Bible: 'The wife hath not power of her own body, but the husband: and likewise also the husband hath not power of his own body, but the wife. Defraud ye not one the other.' According to this Pauline formula, each spouse's sexual capacity was bound by a reciprocal obligation of sexual compliance to the other.

Ostensibly the dogma constituted a key area of marital equality. In the words of Pierre Payer, analyst of medieval doctrine on marital sex, 'the man, who in every other area of medieval life enjoyed superiority because of his maleness, was not considered to have any more rights or to be advantaged or superior in matters relating to the conjugal debt'.[13] Arguably, however, the dogma was in reality a façade for the regulation of women's sexual drives in submission to men. This may seem like a sur-prising assertion, given the way in which we see the theory of the 'mutuality' of the debt of intercourse trotted out in medieval writing. But it is instructive to take stock of the small print surrounding the doctrine in, for instance, a representative medieval English guide to morality known as the *Book of Vices and Virtues*.

In its discussion of chastity, this text offers conventional advice accumulated by the Church over centuries. Marital sex carries no sin when it is either performed for the sake of offspring, or 'when one yields to the other his debt when it is asked; and to this, justice prompts us, which yields to every person what is his own'.[14] This links recipro-cal marital sex to a laudable principle of natural justice inherited from antiquity. But when we come down to finer points, it is apparent that husbands have considerable latitude in deciding when it is necessary for a wife to receive the 'debt'. The moralist goes on to say that one must not refuse the 'right' when it is asked, whether asked for in words, or only 'by signs—as many women do who are embarrassed to ask outright for such a thing'.[15] Evidently the husband is imagined having to interpret, or intuit, times when the wife (envisaged as a shrinking violet in these matters) may actually desire an instalment of the sexual debt. No mention of the converse.

And the treatise pursues the point when it proceeds to discuss the validity of marital sexual intercourse under St Paul's other most influential heading, as a 'remedy for fornication' (curative outlet for sexual urges). The remedy proves unexpectedly gender-specific, something primarily enacted by the husband to service the *wife's* sex drive. Thus the 'remedy' is demonstrated

when a man requests such a thing from his wife in order to protect her from sin, particularly when he sees that she is so full of modesty that she would never ask her master for such a thing: and therefore he fears that she might fall easily into sin [presumably by masturbation or with another man] unless he makes that request of her himself.[16]

The 'remedy' argument, far from being offered here as an outlet for excesses of male testosterone, is tortuously predicated on thwarted female desire; a desire which wives are presumed too embarrassed or inhibited to express, and which husbands have to be specially on their guard to satisfy. This casuistry had an authoritative background, in the work of St Thomas Aquinas, who even goes so far as to discern a gender *disparity* underlying the theoretical parity:

the husband, because he has the more noble part in the conjugal act, is naturally more disposed than his wife not to be ashamed to ask for the debt. Consequently the wife is not bound to pay the debt to her husband when he does not seek it, in the way the husband is bound to pay it to his wife when she does not seek it.[17]

There is only a thin line to distinguish the teaching that husbands must anticipate and thus remedy their wives' desires from an open encouragement to husbands to suppose that their sexual advances upon outwardly unreceptive wives may *at any time* be justified as a 'remedy' for wives' hypothetically repressed sexual drives. We are not actually far from a justification of marital rape. The 'debt' can be construed as a doctrinal sophistry, purportedly egalitarian but in an ulterior way establishing an obligation for wives to resign their bodies to importunate husbands.

The usefulness of this investigation into the small print of the doctrine is that it helps us to understand ways in which Chaucer acknowledges the one-way traffic hidden there. He is aware of the hypothesis of equality ('MerT' 1451–2) but frequently and wryly registers how it generally reduces wives to resignation of their bodies in the marital bed. This is most blatant and most shocking to the modern sensibility in the case of Dorigen, declaring to her suitor Aurelius that her husband has her body whenever it pleases him ('FrT' 1005). Even if we infer that she puts it thus starkly as a ploy to quench an unwanted suitor's desire, the same phenomenon of wifely resignation is echoed elsewhere in the cases of Custance and Cecilia, both of whom, however holy they aspire to be, have to face the prospect of nuptial attentions like any wife ('MLT' 708–14; 'SNT' 141–2).

Chaucer's formulations of a counter-emphasis on husbands rendering the 'debt' to wives appear to be largely tongue-in-cheek. They steer towards the satirical stereotype of the worn-out husband with a sexually voracious wife. This observation would include the Wife of Bath, asserting her control over the sexual debt, to be paid by her husband when he 'comes forth'—as if reluctantly or from hiding ('WBP' 152–3). Where husbands are 'laboured' by wives exacting *their* due it is because the husbands are elderly cuckold-fodder, quaking in a corner like a hare terrorized by hounds, as a monk self-consciously jests in the 'Shipman's Tale' (100–5). The same monk wonders on the other hand whether his hostess in the story is looking pale because she has been 'laboured' all night by her spouse (106–9). Chaucer's exploration of these issues implies as a norm (though without endorsing it) that wives are expected to be 'laboured' by husbands who are exacting their due, like the odious January in the 'Merchant's Tale'.

It seems significant that, apart from the Parson, the most fulsome (though often misguided) champion of St Paul's doctrines on heterosexuality in Chaucer is that utterly unpalatable old lecher in the 'Merchant's Tale'. Our overview of the Pauline dogma as it is experienced in Chaucer's writings would suggest an uncomfortable awareness that the doctrines led to the control and exploitation of women's sexuality.

Sexualities and nature

Gay and lesbian sexual practices were generally deemed 'contrary to nature' in medieval writings. St Paul's teachings spoke darkly of such practices as a punishment that God visited on the ungodly who failed to acknowledge their Creator. God abandoned them to their 'vile' passions, whereby 'even their women did change the natural use into that which is against nature' while men, abandoning 'natural' intercourse with women, 'burned in their lust one toward another' (Romans 1: 26–7). The laity were reminded from the pulpit of the dire biblical example of Sodom and Gomorrah, cities engulfed in catastrophe as a divine retribution for sexual sin. The shocking detail of this biblical story was widely known, of how Lot offered his daughters as 'natural' sexual bait to deflect a crowd of lustful male citizens in Sodom from their predatory desire for the handsome male angels who were guests in his house (Genesis: 19: 1–10).

The category 'sodomy' itself was rather loosely applied in the period. Joan Cadden, a specialist in medieval medical and natural science, explains how even in a narrow definition it could encompass both gay and lesbian practice. Characteristic condemnation is expressed by the academic theologian Albertus Magnus in the late thirteenth century, declaring sodomy to be 'a sin against nature, male with male and female with female'. Arguing elsewhere as a natural philosopher he moderates his tone: sodomy (here specifically homosexual practice) is a problem, for which a homoeopathic remedy can be found—namely, application to the man's anus of ash of hyena fur mixed with pitch.[18]

Either way homosexuality represented an aberration that needed to be corrected. Sexualities, then, were clearly defined less capaciously in the Middle Ages than they would be in some modern societies, despite the theoretical inclusiveness we have noticed above. The understanding of permutations within the overall binary of male–female did not so much accommodate homosexuality and lesbianism as exclude them, by refusing to *name* them except as phenomena outside nature, or as subversions of gender norms. Cadden maintains that the language used to refer to same-sex erotic practices tends to imply an 'enforcement of gender roles' because descriptions of such practices 'were commonly put in terms of role reversals, bearing the implication that there is something inherently feminine about taking what was construed as a passive role in intercourse, and something inherently masculine about having sex with a woman'.[19]

Arguably it is the culture of enforcement of gender roles, much more than the culture of denigration of same-sex practices per se, that absorbs Chaucer's imagination. Modern criticism is in danger of mightily exaggerating the degree of engagement with homosexuality in the case of the Pardoner, perhaps to compensate for finding that the *Tales* generally sustains such a relentlessly heterosexual focus. It is true that the 'General Prologue' teases us with alternative sexual identities for the Pardoner when the narrator guesses that, with his beardlessness, his long yellow locks, and thin goatlike voice, he is 'a geldyng or a mare' ('GP' 688–91). This has been a wonderful spur to critics intent on sexual identification: castrated male? eunuch from birth? homosexual who takes the 'female' (the mare's) role? maybe even a hermaphrodite? There are stunning psychoanalytical readings that attempt to harness this 'General Prologue' description to the end of the 'Pardoner's Tale' in which the Host angrily threatens to cut off the Pardoner's testicles (952–5). While contradictions spice up this connection (notably, how can the testicles be cut off if they were already conjecturally absent?), there is at any rate a hint that something about the Pardoner's person draws not just attention to his sexual status but also suspicion and reprisal. But is this problematic sexual status a focus in itself, or is it introduced as a means of targeting his spiritual deficit? Moreover, one powerful medieval tradition associated 'effeminacy' with excessive lustfulness and womanizing (a factor that could equally inform the representation of Absolon, about whom we spoke earlier). So while some, drawing on psychoanalysis, would say that the Pardoner's boast ('ParP' 453) about having a 'joly wenche' in every town constitutes the defensive bravado or satirical intent of a consciously deviant personality, others, drawing on moral and physiological medieval comment on sexual activity, would say that it attests an obsessive heterosexual activity that actually *explains* his conspicuous 'effemination'.[20] For more on the sexuality of the Pardoner, see Chapter 25.

It has to be admitted that Chaucer is much less interested than, for example, his contemporary John Gower in exploring quasi-same-sex scenarios (though these scenarios in Gower either mask, or soon dissolve into, heterosexuality).[21] Chaucer's interest lay insistently in the ambivalence of the heterosexual drive endowed by Nature. What was Nature's—or God's or the gods'—responsibility for the powerful irrationalities of desire wrought by heterosexual love? His fascination with the doctrinal and philosophical ramifications of this, sometimes comic and sometimes tragic, was galvanized by his reading of Boethius and Jean de Meun. It is the most continuous thread in Chaucer's engagement with sexuality. As Hugh White has suggested, it leads in directions that can be very bleak: Troilus' fate (and, I would add, Criseyde's) as their bond slips inexorably away from them, 'suggests that sexual love does not urge human beings benignly along the path their nature should follow, but leads to painful entrapment within the ultimately unsatisfying'.[22]

The burden of sexuality

It should not be surprising that sexuality, so far as the concept was acknowledged in that era, prompted dark reflections. St Paul had declared sexual drives to be at best a necessary evil, insinuating that Christians should ideally be celibate like himself. Marriage was second best, a kind of safety net legitimizing sexual activity (1 Corinthians: 7: 7–9). As Christian doctrine developed, St Augustine—perhaps the greatest single influence on Western medieval thought—diagnosed sexual drives as typifying the body's threat to the soul. Augustine considered sexual arousal to be the defining feature of what went wrong with humanity after the Fall. The fact that sexual organs were no longer under the control of the mind and the will but responded autonomously to erotic stimuli seemed to him an entirely apt punishment for humanity's disobedience in Eden. The uncontrollability of sexual arousal epitomized the state of fallen humanity, always struggling to subdue the body to the rational will and the soul.[23]

In theory there was usually a taint of sin in the innate unruliness of sexuality. Medical authorities might take a different view, linking moderate heterosexual activity with the healthiness of both men and women. But the doctrine of the confessional and the pulpit gave a generally negative emphasis, resolutely sustaining the hypothesis that all expression of physical sexuality not consciously directed towards achieving procreation or towards rendering the conjugal 'debt' was in some way sinful. Chaucer's Parson subscribes to that hypothesis. Sexual intercourse 'oonly for amorous love', performed frequently, 'to accomplice . . . brennynge delit', is deadly sin ('ParsT' 943).

The shadow of guilt cast over demonstrative sexuality by this teaching makes itself felt explicitly in the Wife of Bath's exclamation 'Allas, allas! That evere love was synne!' ('WBP' 614). It is interesting that this sentiment is ascribed to a woman. Medieval moralists provocatively asserted that a woman, merely by expressing and enjoying her sexuality, in the end merely by being visible as a sexed female, became *responsible* for the mental sin of lust committed by males (this is never put in same-sex terms) who admired her. While the *Canterbury Tales* does not espouse such gross simplifications, it does repeatedly suggest how, for a woman who is uninterested in sexual relationships or who seeks to maintain a religious purity, her sexuality amounts to a particular impediment. As has been mentioned, Custance has to lay aside in the nuptial bed her developing sense of religious mission; Cecilia sustains her sense of mission only by exerting enormous resourcefulness and persuasion to avert marital intercourse. The Church recognized that for many women the social and gender imperative of marriage meant offering up their sexuality without resistance. Chaucer's Parson explains, in another interesting hint of the partisan reality of the conjugal debt, that 'she hath merite of chastitee that yeldeth to hire housbonde the dette of hir body, ye, though it be agayn hir likynge and the lust of hire herte' ('ParsT' 941).

Yet that is of course only part of the picture Chaucer creates. The way he draws attention to the insistent doctrine of the Church that even marital sex is not to be pursued purely for pleasure but for procreation, exposes this teaching to currents of humorous scepticism. On the one hand, it is comically disobeyed by a cockerel in the 'Nun's Priest's Tale' because he is ignorant of it (3342–5). On the other, the only character in the *Tales* who is found to adhere scrupulously to this teaching is an extraordinary Amazonian queen named Cenobia who should never have heard of it and who, besides, is stated to be resistant to the 'office' (functions or duties) of women ('MoT' 2255–6, 2279–94).

Chaucer's writings also communicate the passionate thrill and satisfaction of sexual activity, however transient. He exploits the morality-free zone of comic fabliau to project consummation as 'revel and melodye'. He also exploits the morally blurred zone of semi-pagan narratives to project this 'revel' more emotionally: the bliss of the lovers' union in *Troilus and Criseyde* (3. 1219 ff.) cannot be *cancelled out* by the separation that follows or even by the philosophical questioning that surrounds it.[24] Under Boccaccio's influence, Chaucer even exploits the liberation delivered by a part-pagan fictional context to imagine temporary independent female sexuality in an eerily 'modern' way. We overhear Criseyde contemplating her sense of sexual independence—of being 'her own woman', 'untied' in a lush pasture—as she ponders Troilus' interest in her (*TC* 2. 750–2).[25] Criseyde's meditation at this point perhaps constitutes a rare instance where Chaucer reaches some way towards a notion of an individual's sexuality in that modern sense we began with: 'the kernel of individual personality'.

Contemporary practitioners of both psychoanalytical and historical criticism would probably want to go further with such inquiry (for example, into Criseyde's sexual psyche and into the impact of civic Italian mores on ideas about sexual autonomy, respectively). Historically based criticism of one kind or another will continue to sharpen facets of our understanding of the subject, though the current insistence on *localized* historical context yields thin results in this instance. Where sexuality in Chaucer is concerned I foresee a resurgence of source study, an approach always capable of rewarding readers because it takes them through verbal and cultural experiences that distantly replicate Chaucer's own. But we can already see that, leaning on his readings in Boccaccio and others, Chaucer learned how to query doctrine: how to use pagan locale and other strategies to free sexual matters from a context of automatic spiritual opprobrium. Although this does not mean that he wished to free them from doctrinal and ethical constraint altogether, it does contribute to a sense of affinity within strangeness that we feel in reading Chaucer, despite what has been called 'the complexity, fragmentation, and difference of what we call "sexuality" in the Middle Ages'.[26]

FURTHER READING

Augustine, St, *City of God*, trans. Henry Bettenson (Harmondsworth: Penguin, 1972). Chapters 15–24 of book 14 argue a foundational dichotomy between 'fallen' sexuality and the rational human will, which was crucial in medieval thought.

Cadden, Joan, *Meanings of Sex Difference in the Middle Ages* (Cambridge: Cambridge University Press, 1993). A very authoritative and informative analysis of medieval medical and physiological accounts of sex difference.

de Lorris, Guillaume, and Jean de Meun, *The Romance of the Rose*, trans. Frances Horgan (Oxford: Oxford University Press, 1994). The classic medieval literary fictional analysis of sexual desire and courtship, mostly from a male point of view. Chaucer knew it inside out because he translated it.

Jacquart, Danielle, and Claude Thomasset, *Sexuality and Medicine in the Middle Ages*, trans. Matthew Adamson (Princeton: Princeton University Press; Cambridge: Polity Press, 1988). Another absorbing account of a range of medical theories about the production of sexuality and the role of sexuality in the maintenance of health.

Mann, Jill, *Feminizing Chaucer*, new edn. (Cambridge: Brewer, 2002). The particular argument is that Chaucer moves beyond inherited norms and antitheses of gender representation. The application of the argument to a range of Chaucer's texts gives food for thought on sexuality as well as gender.

Partner, Nancy F., 'No Sex, No Gender', *Speculum*, 68 (1993), 419–43. A vigorous argument for the psychoanalytical recognition of an essentially familiar phenomenon of sexuality in medieval culture despite historical difference.

Patterson, Lee, 'Chaucer's Pardoner on the Couch: Psyche and Clio in Medieval Literary Studies', *Speculum*, 76 (2001), 638–80. A critique of psychoanalytical interpretations of the Pardoner, by a critic more committed to historical study.

Payer, Pierre J., *The Bridling of Desire: Views of Sex in the Later Middle Ages* (Toronto: University of Toronto Press, 1993). An absorbing description and analysis of the medieval theologians' interpretations of subtleties of sexual morality, especially in marriage.

Sturges, Robert S., *Chaucer's Pardoner and Gender Theory* (New York: St Martin's Press, 1999). Uses a wide scatter of contemporary psychoanalytical and other theories to query the sexual identity of the Pardoner, with colourful results.

White, Hugh, *Nature, Sex, and Goodness in a Medieval Literary Tradition* (Oxford: Oxford University Press, 2000). Incorporates interesting sources from ecclesiastical law into a focused investigation of medieval literary questioning (especially Chaucer's and Gower's) as to whether 'naturalness' implied 'goodness' in human sexual drives.

NOTES

1. David Halperin, 'Forgetting Foucault: Acts, Identities, and the History of Sexuality', *Representations*, 63 (1998), 96–7.
2. Nancy F. Partner, 'No Sex, No Gender', *Speculum*, 68 (1993), 425.
3. Ibid. 436.
4. Ibid. 439.
5. Danielle Jacquart and Claude Thomasset, *Sexuality and Medicine in the Middle Ages*, trans. Matthew Adamson (Princeton: Princeton University Press; Cambridge: Polity Press, 1988), 117, 141.

6. *Troilus and Criseyde: A New Edition of 'The Book of Troilus'*, ed. B. A. Windeatt (London: Longman, 1984), 104–5.

7. The ritual is enacted in the case of May in the 'Merchant's Tale' 1817–18. See Alcuin Blamires, 'Questions of Gender in Chaucer, from *Anelida to Troilus*', *Leeds Studies in English*, 25 (1994), 83–110.

8. This translation, rather than 'was not arrogant' as usually suggested, is justified by analogy with the 'Shipman's Tale' (379).

9. Jill Mann, *Feminizing Chaucer*, new edn. (Cambridge: Brewer, 2002).

10. St Thomas Aquinas, *Summa theologiae*, xxxiv, trans. R. J. Batten (London: Blackfriars; New York: McGraw-Hill, 1975), 149, 2. 2. 26. 10. Aquinas envisages male seed as 'active' and female 'matter' as a 'passive' receiver. An alternative 'two-seed' theory inherited from the ancient medical authority Galen allowed for greater female agency in procreation.

11. Alan of Lille, *The Plaint of Nature*, trans. James J. Sheridan (Toronto: Pontifical Institute of Medieval Studies, 1980), 67–8.

12. From *The Southern Passion*, a thirteenth-century text translated in Alcuin Blamires (ed.) with Karen Pratt and C. W. Marx, *Woman Defamed and Woman Defended* (Oxford: Clarendon Press, 1992), 246.

13. Pierre J. Payer, *The Bridling of Desire: Views of Sex in the Later Middle Ages* (Toronto: University of Toronto Press, 1993), 92.

14. *The Book of Vices and Virtues*, ed. W. Nelson Francis, Early English Text Society Original Series 217 (Oxford: Oxford University Press, 1942), 246 (my modernization).

15. Ibid. 246–7.

16. Ibid. 247.

17. Payer, *Bridling of Desire*, 95, quoting Aquinas' discussions on 'Whether husband and wife are mutually bound to the payment of the marriage debt?' and on 'Whether husband and wife are equal in the marriage act?'

18. Joan Cadden, *Meanings of Sex Difference in the Middle Ages* (Cambridge: Cambridge University Press, 1993), 218–19.

19. Ibid. 220.

20. See Helen Cooper, *Oxford Guides to Chaucer: The 'Canterbury Tales'* (Oxford: Oxford University Press, 1989), 59, with references.

21. Achilles in the guise of a girl sleeps with Deidamia; Iphis, a girl brought up as a boy, is married to Iante but then miraculously transformed into a male: John Gower, *Confessio amantis*, 5. 2961–3201 and 4. 451–505 respectively, in *The English Works of John Gower*, ed. G. C. Macaulay, Early English Text Society Extra Series 81–2 (London: Oxford University Press, 1900–1).

22. Hugh White, *Nature, Sex, and Goodness in a Medieval Literary Tradition* (Oxford: Oxford University Press, 2000), 253.

23. St Augustine, *City of God*, trans. Henry Bettenson (Harmondsworth: Penguin, 1972), 522–3, 574–89.

24. Even so, Chaucer nowhere quite matches the unexpectedly absolute *approval* of heterosexual practice found in the alliterative poem *Cleanness*, written in the same period: see *Poems of the Pearl Manuscript*, ed. Malcolm Andrew and Ronald Waldron (London: Arnold, 1978), *Cleanness*, 697–708.

25. The association with an untethered horse definitely carries sexual innuendo: for its use as a metaphor for uninhibited sexuality, see the *Romance of the Rose*, trans. Frances Horgan (Oxford: Oxford University Press, 1994), 216–17, lines 14023 ff.

26. Cadden, *Meanings*, 7.

Identity and subjecthood

John M. Ganim

Part of the enduring appeal of Chaucer's poetry, especially in the *Canterbury Tales* and *Troilus and Criseyde*, is his apparent ability to create realistic individuals with believable and understandable interior lives. Generations of readers have felt as if they know Chaucer's characters, and Chaucer himself, the way they know their neighbours and acquaintances. Indeed, it is not uncommon for us to observe how modern Chaucer's characters sound, at least when we factor out his antiquated language. Over the past few decades, however, a number of critical approaches have converged to question this time-honoured response to Chaucer. Initially, scholars directed our attention to the conventions of medieval literature and the degree to which they represent abstract types rather than psychologically motivated human beings. Then, cultural theory replaced the commonly held idea of an integrated, autonomous self with the complex idea of a constructed subject. More recently, historically based interpretations of medieval identities have pointed to the ways in which traditional medieval social categories were beginning to unravel, with new formations and associations replacing older allegiances.

All of these new developments have implications for understanding Chaucer's work and characters, as well as for understanding his own representation of himself as an author or narrator. What seems to be a modernizing self-presentation on the part of Chaucer's most fully developed characters turns out to be a deeply enigmatic construction. At the moment in the history of European culture when the very conception of the modern individual seems to be articulating itself, Chaucer can be seen to be demonstrating the degree to which this apparent modernity is implicated in the discourses of the past. This chapter will describe these literary and historical contexts in relation to Chaucer's works.

Individual, self, and subject

Most readers instinctively understand literary characters as if they were real people. We even judge the success of fictional or dramatic works by holding their characters or narrators to the standard of 'real life', even if we demand more consistency from literature than we do from life itself. In a tradition stretching back many centuries, one of the apparent purposes of literature has been to show us what it means to be fully human, especially in terms of identifying with an autonomous, coherent, individual self. Chaucer's characters, especially some of the pilgrims in the *Canterbury Tales*, such as the Wife of Bath, have a special place in this tradition, appearing to be among the first characters to articulate their needs, desires, lives, and circumstances in a fully developed and unified vision. Seen from this perspective, Chaucer seems to predict what we have traditionally understood as the Renaissance discovery of the individual.

In recent decades, however, this traditional understanding of the self has come under attack. The great nineteenth-century deterministic models of Sigmund Freud, Karl Marx, and Charles Darwin initiated a rethinking of just how unique humans were as individuals by emphasizing how much we are shaped by biological and economic forces, but structuralist and poststructuralist thought has fully pursued the implications of this determinism. Freud's understanding of human consciousness as undergirded by layers beneath our comprehension, for instance, suggests that our awareness of motivations and patterns of thought and behaviour could only be partial at best. Still, Freud was concerned with helping the individual understand, and therefore master, the unconscious history that helped shape them. The postmodern theory of the subject, however, depends on another revolution, that in linguistics, especially the structuralist linguistics of the Swiss linguist Ferdinand de Saussure (1857–1913), who emphasized the system of language, which authorized individual expression, rather than individual expression itself. Taking the system of language as a model, structuralist and poststructuralist theories have questioned whether an autonomous self can exist in any society. These theories have attempted to replace the terminology of the 'self' with the terminology of the 'subject'. In so doing, we are made to confront the possibility that the coherent, autonomous, fully conscious self is an illusion. As with the notion of the subject in grammar, the subject is acted upon, even constituted, by other discourses. We are not the conscious centres of awareness we think we are, but are sites upon which various forces—psychological, sociological, economic, and political—act and intersect. Like the replicants and cyborgs in recent science fiction, our apparent awareness of ourselves as individuals, even our memories and desires, are invented, constructed, and implanted by forces beyond our control. From this point of view, the Wife of Bath is a creation of the many anti-feminist tracts and discourses that she argues against.

This extremely pessimistic view of the subject has been modified by some poststructuralist theorists to allow a certain modicum of manoeuvring room to the subject. In the psychological theories of the French psychoanalyst Jacques Lacan, the subject emerges from infancy with a concept of the self that is basically a fiction. The French poststructuralist philosopher Michel Foucault has argued that the discourses of authority that control behaviour are so various and contradictory that the individual subject can sometimes appropriate and manipulate these discourses. Power can circulate from system to individual and back again. Feminist theorists, drawing upon Lacan, have pointed to the ways in which identity, especially gender identity, can be 'performed', thereby subverting the binary categories of normal and deviant behaviour. New historicist interpretations of Early Modern (a term borrowed from linguistics and applied to what we used to call the Renaissance) literature and culture have employed some of these concepts to redefine Renaissance individualism as a 'self-fashioning', a fictional, almost literary, making of one's identity in the face of many conflicting social forces. As some of the other chapters in this volume demonstrate, these theories and ideas have important consequences for understanding Chaucer's work and characters, but they also resemble debates that have been carried on about, and within, the Middle Ages.

Mentality, affinity, and association

Recent theories of the subject have threatened the traditional humanist conception of the autonomous individual psyche. Interestingly, an earlier debate about the nature of the individual in medieval society had defined the issues surrounding identity and subjecthood in a surprisingly similar manner. On one side of this debate was an attitude towards the Middle Ages that dated back to the Renaissance, and that peaked during the Enlightenment of the eighteenth century. From this point of view, the Middle Ages were indeed the dark ages, controlled by an arrogantly oppressive feudal system that virtually enslaved its populace, and a coercive Church that encouraged superstition and blind obedience. The Renaissance began to overthrow this dark past by emphasizing the centrality of the human individual and by rediscovering the rational philosophy and science of classical Greece and Rome. The classic celebration of the Renaissance individual is a famous book by Jacob Burckhardt (1818–97) called *The Civilization of the Renaissance in Italy*. From this point of view, Chaucer represents a preview of Renaissance individualism, especially in his anticlerical satire and in his presentation of 'rounded' human characters who articulate their psychological states. A more complex and more recent variant on this stark distinction between the medieval and the modern argues for a radical difference between modern and medieval mentalities. Medieval people did not think of themselves as individuals, but rather as part of a group, and defined themselves through the complex network of loyalties developed under feudalism. Where we might think of society in terms of a conflict model, with opposing sides pitted against each other, medieval people thought in terms of an hierarchical model, in which one accepted one's place. Emotions, feelings, and reactions we would consider private and interiorized were for medieval people to be expressed publicly in authorized rituals. A largely oral culture emphasized shared experiences and memories, rather than the private meditation encouraged by silent reading in the later age of print. There may even have been, some psychologists speculate, a shift in the very neurological basis of consciousness itself, from one side of the brain to the other, so that premodern people literally thought differently. Hence, we may be indulging in an illusion when we attempt to identify emotionally with Chaucer's characters, who represent a very different way of thinking, even about emotions, than we do.[1]

The other side of this debate over medieval mentality rejected this picture of the Middle Ages as a stereotype, while at the same time agreeing with a general pattern of the evolution of individual human freedom.[2] From this less negative view of the individual in medieval society, changes were already occurring in the twelfth century, which had its own renaissance. Indeed, Charles Homer Haskins coined the term in a book called *The Renaissance of the Twelfth Century* (1927). The crusades and the opening of trade routes to the East ended the cultural isolation of western Europe. The establishment of early universities helped encourage new ideas and a certain rational scepticism. The rise of cities, especially in Italy and north-western Europe, resulted in nascent conceptions of citizenship and liberty and served as an incubator for an emerging middle class. Certain forms of religious practice, especially mysticism, emphasized individual piety and interiorized spirituality. Literature began concerning itself with inward states, and the new discourses of love in the troubadours and in medieval romance reflected a new interest in the hero as an individual and in private emotions as worthy of cultivation. The apparent emphasis we find on individual character and autobiographical explanation on the part of Chaucer's pilgrims, for instance, is from this point of view not an exception to medieval traditions, but a culmination of several centuries of emerging individualism.

Not surprisingly, recent scholarship on the medieval subject has suggested that neither of these two pictures of the medieval subjectivity, neither an incipient nor evolving modern self nor a consciousness entirely determined by group or institutional identity, is complete in itself. Medieval subjects negotiated a sense of themselves as individuals and also as members of larger defining groups such as the social estates that divided medieval society into aristocracy, peasantry, and clergy, and into higher and lower status within those estates (on this, see Chapter 2). They thought of themselves as members of religious fraternities and of guilds (which could often be similar in composition). But medieval individuals also negotiated their position as subjects, contesting the various overlapping and perhaps conflicting spheres of influence through which they were constituted.[3] In this regard, Chaucer's often conflicted characters, lashing out at the very structures which define them, such as the Monk mocking the counter-intuitive rules of monastic orders, or the Wife of Bath railing against a patriarchy that has in fact seeped into every crevice of her consciousness, are typical.

Chaucer and his characters were also heirs to a long tradition of thinking and writing about the self, even when that self was defined by subjection. One of the great classics of spirituality to this day remains St Augustine's *Confessions*. While we may read the *Confessions* as a proto-modern autobiography, it was probably read more in terms of its emphasis on conversion and submission in the Middle Ages; the generic soul was probably a more important marker than the unique Augustine. Later medieval writers also emphasized their personal relation to spiritual truth, such as Abelard and Hugh of St Victor. After the eleventh and twelfth centuries, poets such as the troubadours wove the details of their supposed personal experiences into a literature of love that has defined the discourse of love to the present day. Dante Alighieri, the author of the *Divine Comedy*, transformed this tradition by linking his spiritual and erotic autobiography, even linking his own life to the shape of creation itself. From the twelfth century on, a newly personalized and internalized piety, loosely defined as mysticism, emphasized a direct experience with an extremely humanized Jesus, one who took an interest in the subject as an individual.[4] As mysticism developed, it opened a particular window for female spirituality, which often involved erotic experience, sometimes in relation to Jesus himself, becoming a metaphor for spiritual transcendence. In the fourteenth and fifteenth centuries a widespread and considerable literature of spiritual autobiography is produced by female mystics, and one of the most famous, Julian of Norwich, recorded her *Showings* during and shortly after Chaucer's lifetime. Julian was visited by Margery Kempe, whose life, in *The Book of Margery Kempe*, has become part of the literary canon, and whose extravagant emotional displays and sometimes shocking frankness are often compared to the Wife of Bath by modern readers.

Of course, the lives of the medieval mystics (with perhaps the exception of Margery) were so similar that it is possible that they were producing a life history and a sense of themselves as an individual that was dictated by what had become an always already existing spiritual narrative. A similarly complex relation between an apparently modern self and the procedures of medieval subjection emerges from debates surrounding the impact of the institutionalization of confession. In response to a general sense that the quality of parish clergy had declined, to fears of heresy and heterodox movements, and to an anxiety about the competitive authority and power of the Church in relation to royal and aristocratic courts and to cities and towns newly empowered by economic changes, the Fourth Lateran Council was called by Pope Innocent III in 1215. It mandated a series of reforms, the most far-reaching of which was the requirement of annual aural confession by every Christian to his or her priest. Guides and handbooks were produced which detailed the nature of sin and the appropriate response of both penitent and priest. To an unprecedented degree, the interior life of the individual medieval Christian was now open to examination and definition.[5]

Some modern scholars have suggested that after the resurgence of individualism in the twelfth century, the Church was attempting to dampen what it feared to be secularizing and modernizing tendencies. Others have suggested that, for better or worse, the sense of the medieval subject as an individual emerged at this point, paradoxically in response to the authority and surveillance of the most powerful corporate social institution of the Middle Ages. What is interesting to note for our purposes in understanding how the subject and identity articulate themselves in Chaucer is how often Chaucer's characters define themselves through a sort of confession. The Wife of Bath, the Pardoner, the Merchant, and others detail their everyday lives and their desires and conflicts in ways that suggest an appeal to absolution or forgiveness (even while they dig themselves deeper in so doing). The 'Parson's Tale', with which the *Canterbury Tales* ends, is actually based on a tract that had its origins as a confessional manual. We would not want to suggest, as did some scholars a century ago, that we can understand the *Canterbury Tales* in terms of the Seven Deadly Sins, but it is interesting to note how Chaucer's characters test the boundaries of acceptable and forbidden behaviours, and articulate their actions and feelings in terms of fixed values and standards that all too frequently fail. Chaucer's great contemporary William Langland, for instance, in his *Piers Plowman*, envisions a scene in which the Seven Deadly Sins themselves, personified as allegorical characters, agree to go to confession, but never quite get there. Chaucer and Langland may seem to be very modern in their questioning of the discourses that define individual behaviour, but that questioning still takes place within a system of medieval practices and patterns of conduct.

Two important books, one largely historicist and the other largely phenomenological in approach, address precisely this negotiation between self and subject in their titles. Lee Patterson's *Chaucer and the Subject of History*[6] conflates the awareness of being a historical subject on the part of the critic with an argument for the acute self-consciousness of the medieval author and an analysis of the historically conditioned subjectivity of characters such as the Knight, the Pardoner, the Wife, and the Miller. Patterson's Chaucer, as it were, invents the ironic supra-historical artist of humanist interpretation as a response to a specific historical and social position, and this negotiation is enacted in the performances of many of his characters. In *The Disenchanted Self: Representing the Subject in the 'Canterbury Tales'*,[7] H. Marshall Leicester, Jr., asserts that Chaucer's most fully engaged narrators, the Pardoner, the Wife, and the Knight, are represented both as postmodern subjects, whose effective construction by social and historical conditions is made transparent, and as selves, autonomous consciousnesses who compose themselves in the performance of their own textuality.

Performance and negotiation

Contemporary theories of the subject have suggested that the subject can achieve a modicum of agency through the practice of performance. Somewhat earlier, the sociologist Erving Goffman proposed the idea of 'the presentation of the self in everyday life', noting how we follow dramatic scripts or even scenes in our interactions with others, particularly in social hierarchies or institutional settings.[8] Everyday life, that is, requires that we assume certain roles. Reacting to conflicting social demands, we, and literary characters, perform many different roles. Feminist theory has questioned the notion of an essential gender identity, noting that the appearance of gender difference is often the result of performing a series of culturally prescribed roles, which can then be parodied or subverted. The critical school called new historicism has described how the apparently heroic individuals of Renaissance drama and historical narrative engage in a process of 'self-fashioning', negotiating among the various centres of political and institutional authority, such as the rapidly transforming Church and royal state, changing themselves in response to these changes but also achieving some individual power in so doing.[9] What Chaucer does with the question of what we would call identity or subjecthood is to dramatize or theatricalize its operations, to show the struggle involved for his characters and himself in claiming a personal autonomy distinct from the literary, cultural, or textual contexts in which they are set.

Even if we employ Early Modern concepts, or postmodern concepts, with some caution in interpreting the Chaucerian subject, there is no doubt that performance pervades the *Canterbury Tales*, as well as many of Chaucer's other works. The fiction of the work is that it is a performance, wherein the various pilgrims actually tell their tales. The 'General Prologue' is structured much like one of the many processions and ridings that marked important occasions in late medieval cities. The pilgrims seem to ride out at the end of the 'General Prologue' to the tune of the Miller's bagpipe. This and other incidents locate the work in terms of the highly performative folk culture and marketplace entertainment of the late Middle Ages. The interaction between the various pilgrims forms a sort of sideshow within the work, and an earlier generation of critics took this 'dramatic principle' to be the main event. Some of the characters literally perform as part of their tale-telling, such as in the Prologue to the 'Prioress's Tale', with its prayer to the Virgin, and in the great sermon performance of the 'Pardoner's Prologue'.

Chaucer's descriptions of people pay a great deal of attention to what we would consider external details, including clothing, accessories, and comportment. Medieval rhetoric prescribed a certain procedure for describing people, but Chaucer takes some liberty with the conventions. The 'General Prologue' is a fashion show of sorts, with specific enumeration of clothing materials, jewellery, hairstyles, and the relative success of managing the total package as what we might call a personal style. Sometimes, as in the case of the Knight, with his appropriate disarmament, his rusty mail, and stained tunic, Chaucer seems to imply a certain authenticity. In other cases, such as in the description of the Prioress or the Monk, the loving picture of sartorial splendour, including fabric, texture, and workmanship, is clearly meant to alert us to a disjunction between their religious roles and their love of the things of this world. In the later Middle Ages, and particularly in the court circles Chaucer travelled in, clothing and livery were politically and socially significant, and an indicator of class or family identity. Personal and class appearances were 'branded', and legal redress could be sought for infractions. Chaucer, for instance, testified in the Scrope–Grosvenor trial concerning a dispute involving the right to a coat of arms. Sumptuary laws determined what kind of materials and fabrics could be worn by certain estates. The surplus of luxury goods caused by the population decline after the plague occasioned some anxiety about social inappropriateness, actually about social mobility. By this standard, the Merchant and the Man of Law might be regarded as social climbers, if not perpetrators of misdemeanours. Clothing could, as it can today, also be a personal statement by virtue of its outrageousness. The Wife of Bath's red outfit, for instance, could be understood symbolically (see Revelation 17: 4), but it could also be read as a call for attention, a lapse of taste for a woman of a certain age, or even as a defiance of taste and propriety.

The 'General Prologue' pays a great deal of attention to the faces as well as the clothing of the pilgrims. Such details have made the pilgrims memorable for many centuries of readers. Medieval tracts on physiognomy suggested that one's character was imprinted and readable on one's face. The coarse face of the Miller, the skin afflictions of the Summoner, the shapes of noses and the cast of eyes, are all detailed by the narrator. Such an emphasis suggests that Chaucer regarded character in terms of stereotypes. Modern readers are likely to think of such stereotyping as a form of prejudice, and to think of, say, nineteenth-century and early twentieth-century forensics that attempted to identify a 'criminal type', and pseudo-scientific theories that accorded relative intelligence to certain skin colours or sought to identify racial identity and characteristics through the shapes of noses. Physiognomy, like astrology, seems to suggest that character was fixed and immutable, determined by forces above and beyond our own ability to define ourselves. But, as with other medieval codes, Chaucer seems as interested in exposing the thought systems behind such assumptions as embracing them. Medieval science, for instance, could also suggest that we begin to resemble physically our behaviour patterns rather than the other way around. Chaucer seems alert to the possibility that we tend to act the way we are treated. A certain measure of defiance in the Pardoner's self-presentation, for instance, seems to derive from a satisfaction in acting the way people expect him to act based on his appearance. The Wife of Bath's personality is related to her birth sign or her physiognomy (especially her gap teeth), but in other areas of her self-presentation, she defies received wisdom, suggesting that she is willing to accept deterministic explanations when it suits her and reject them when it does not. That is, Chaucer seems to juxtapose situational and relative explanations for character on the one hand with deterministic and absolute explanations on the other. Chaucer's explanations, or his characters' explanations for why they are how they are, are often circular in ways that make us aware of how circular are our own assumptions about the relation between inner character and appearance.

How men or women 'carry themselves' impresses the narrator of the *Canterbury Tales*, and sometimes impresses other pilgrims. Medieval conduct books went into great detail about table manners, dress, social graces, and other forms of external social behaviour, but Chaucer seems to be especially interested in variances from type and in the nuances of gendered behaviour. Harry Bailly seems particularly sensitive to such matters of bearing and comportment. The Clerk appears to him to be as bashful as a newly-wed bride at a wedding reception: 'Ye ryde as coy and stille as dooth a mayde | Were newe spoused, sittynge at the bord' ('ClP' 2–3). This sense of the relation of comportment to gender is despite the fact that the narrator has earlier praised the Knight for his comportment—'of his port as meeke as is a mayde' ('GP' 69). Elsewhere

Harry notes the masculinity, wasted in his celibate role, of the Nun's Priest ('NPE' 3450–9), just as Chaucer in his role as narrator had praised the manliness of the Monk ('GP' 167, 204–5). Clearly defined gender roles can also fall into the sort of comic role-reversal found in medieval festive misrule, such as the charivari, which featured parodic cross-dressing (for more on such reversals, see Chapter 22).[10] Harry's portrait of his wife as a sort of incipient Lady Macbeth, urging him to beat his servants when they are remiss, is in this comic tradition ('MoP' 1897–1900).

Group identity is clearly important to the portraits of the individuals in the 'General Prologue', but even here that sense of group association is complicated. There is only a hint of emerging forms of national identity, except perhaps for the enthusiasm for the military adventures of the Knight and the Squire, and the concern for maritime policy alluded to in the Merchant's portrait ('GP' 276–7). Elsewhere in the *Canterbury Tales* there are suggestions that identity is associated with opposition to another group, or with belonging to a group that excludes others. For instance, in the 'Prioress's Tale' the Christian members of the town understand themselves by their difference from the ghettoized Jews, but this sense of belonging or not belonging could be ascribed to the simplistic understanding of the Prioress herself. In the 'Man of Law's Tale' some Muslim characters are stereotyped as evil, but others, especially those willing to convert to Christianity, are pictured as potentially good. Even in these cases, otherness, and therefore group identity, is not absolute, but provisional. The catastrophic events of the fourteenth century, including the recurring waves of the plague, the Peasants' Revolt of 1381, and the Dual Papacy, had called into question, at least for a time, traditional schemes of social and political organization. Chaucer is writing in the tradition of estates satire, which contrasted the ideal arrangement of medieval society into the three major groups of clergy, aristocracy, and commoners, against its apparent decline and decay. Chaucer, however, calls into question the validity of that grouping by the relatively small part played by the aristocracy (the Knight and, potentially, the Prioress may belong to the lower aristocracy) and the peasantry (only the Plowman represents what would have been the largest sector of the medieval population), and by populating his pilgrimage with members of society for whom there was no clearly prescribed or ordained estate. The Guildsmen, for instance, represent a new force in late medieval society. Some modern readers might expect them to be represented as a newly energetic and progressive force in the evolution of society towards individual enterprise, but Chaucer's portrait lumps them together anonymously, almost contemptuously, as if they lacked the subjectivity that arises from conflicts between old and new values ('GP' 361–78). In the case of the religious figures, Chaucer consistently emphasizes their private and personal negotiation of their roles as members of religious communities, roles which we might expect to render them less individual. The Monk, for instance, questions whether the rules for monastic behaviour apply to him, at least as paraphrased by the narrator: 'What sholde he studie and make hymselven wood, | Upon a book in cloystre alwey to poure . . .?' ('GP' 184–5). Obviously, here and elsewhere Chaucer may be pointing to the social shortcomings of his characters by contrasting the ideal to their actual behaviour, but the result is that what we consider literary character is produced by this conflict, as if subjectivity itself were the result of conflict.

Interiority and consciousness

Subjectivity is represented inconsistently across and within Chaucer's works, suggesting that at times subjectivity is specific to genre. The excruciating inner motivations of *Troilus and Criseyde*, for instance, which have reminded readers of the subtle psychology of much later literature, may also be regarded as specific to the genre of romance. Criseyde's awareness of her own plight, and her conversation with herself regarding whether or not she should engage in an affair with Troilus, is often cited as an example of one of the first and fullest expressions of consciousness in literature:

> Criseÿda gan al his chere aspien,
> And leet it so softe in hire herte synke,
> That to hireself she seyde, 'Who yaf me drynke?'
>
> For of hire owen thought she wex al reed,
> Remembryng hire right thus, 'Lo, this is he
> Which that myn uncle swerith he moot be deed,
> But I on hym have mercy and pitee.'
> And with that thought, for pure ashamed, she
> Gan in hire hed to pulle, and that as faste,
> Whil he and alle the peple forby paste,
>
> And gan to caste and rollen up and down
> Withinne hire thought his excellent prowesse,
> And his estat, and also his renown,
> His wit, his shap, and ek his gentilesse;
> But moost hire favour was, for his distresse
> Was al for hire, and thoughte it was a routhe
> To sleen swich oon, if that he mente trouthe. (2. 649–65)

Criseyde has just seen Troilus passing below her fresh from battle, modestly acknowledging the cheers of the crowd. Almost as if Chaucer were alluding to the famous scene in the legend of Tristan and Isolde when the two fall in love by quaffing a love potion, she asks rhetorically whether she has been given a magical drink. She then considers the various external attributes of Troilus, particularly his bearing, and considers whether this reflects the quality of his inner virtue. To do so requires that she reconstruct his image in her memory, and play it back as it were, to mull over the consequences of her decision. Several stanzas follow in which she adds up the pros and cons of an affair with Troilus. She almost convinces us, as she does herself, that 'I am myn owene womman, wel at ese' (2. 750). She deliberates at great length, attempting to look at the situation from many different angles, to consider her feelings, her precarious social situation, even her own attractiveness. It is one of the most extensive attempts by a male author of the Middle Ages to represent the consciousness of a woman. Certainly it is much beholden to earlier medieval traditions. She parses the grammar of her emotions in a procedure that gestures back to scholasticism, and to the institution of confession that in fact reflects a scholastic precision in its deliberations about what might or might not be a sin, and if so what kind. Her debate with herself is akin to the debates between personifications in love allegories such as the *Romance of the Rose*, which after all were meant to represent the thought processes of men and women in love. Her use of memory and mnemonic techniques is consistent with the importance of memory to the medieval understanding of human psychology.[11]

Yet by framing these philosophical and religious discourses in terms of the interiority of a female character who makes a claim to be an autonomous being, Chaucer's creation gestures as much forward as backward in terms of the history of consciousness. If she seems to calculate her odds and consider her economic and social status in ways that might strike us as inauthentically analytical, we must remember that the heroines of much later fiction consider themselves in terms of analogous categories. The heroines of Jane Austen and Edith Wharton, and Tolstoy's Anna Karenina and Flaubert's Emma Bovary, are also limited in their choices, and also attempt to convince themselves that their choices are their own, or that, on the other hand, there is no other choice than the one they have already decided on. As soon as we recognize her modernity, however, we find ourselves paradoxically back with the contradictions of subjectivity with which we began. For not only are Emma Bovary, Anna Karenina, and their literary sisters limited by the conventions of their local cultures and the economic dependency of women, they are limited, so to speak, by their own internalized literary genre. They read themselves as if characters in a novel, much as Criseyde reads herself as a heroine of romance. They are, of course, and she is, a figment of the text, but the literary self-reflexiveness of the way in which their and her consciousness is described and represented teaches us the extent to which subjectivity itself is prompted and conditioned by codes, genres, and scripts. The apparent freedom of Criseyde's consciousness at this point (and one would not want to minimize its momentarily liberating elation) must be read in conjunction with her similar thought processes in book 5. There she accepts the fate of her consignment to the Greeks and to Diomede. That is, Criseyde seems to imagine herself as free to choose that which has already been chosen for her. The very thought processes that allow her to plumb her desires and emotions, to consider her social and political situation, are the very same processes that result in her acceptance of the limits of her freedom. It is only in the momentary and provisional suspension of all that she must consider that she is able to imagine the possibility of agency, however fleetingly.

Personae and authorial subjecthood

How did Chaucer think of himself? With many later writers, we have reams of letters and interviews and personal accounts. In Chaucer's case, the very extensive documents of his life make virtually no mention of his literary career. The few comments made by his contemporaries are largely formulaic or honorific. Fifteenth-century writers who depended on the image of Chaucer to authorize their own literary careers offer us a very different Chaucer from the one we recognize. In their eyes, he is not only the 'father' of English poetry, but he sometimes assumes a somewhat forbidding patriarchal role as rhetorician and moralist. The Chaucer generations of readers have been more comfortable with is the one portrayed in the dream visions such as the *Book of the Duchess*, the *House of Fame*, and the *Parliament of Fowls*. These dream visions begin with the narrator complaining about his insomnia, and then finding himself in a magical, and usually beautiful, landscape. He then begins a dialogue with an interlocutor who functions as a guide. In the *House of Fame* the guide for part of the way is a giant and somewhat loquacious eagle, who answers the narrator's sometimes obvious questions as they ascend into the sky, while the narrator holds on fearfully. In the *Book of the Duchess* the interlocutor is a man dressed in black. After a long series of questions and answers, the narrator realizes that the interlocutor is a grieving widower, who has been speaking to him indirectly and metaphorically.

The portrait that emerges, as it does from the image of the narrator in the 'General Prologue', is of a somewhat obtuse, inquisitive, and vaguely inappropriate observer of supernatural events and personal crises that he is ill-equipped to understand. Since Chaucer himself, with his diplomatic, bureaucratic, and government experience, is highly unlikely to have been so naive, scholars have looked elsewhere for an explanation of his self-portrayal. Other late medieval poets writing in the tradition of dream visions, such as Chaucer's contemporary Machaut, also portrayed themselves in a less than flattering light, and also dramatized their incompetencies and failures. Chaucer may have fashioned this convention to suit his own situation as a poet and courtier of non-aristocratic origins writing for his social superiors, who may have been both charmed and flattered by an appeal to their greater sophistication. He may also have been distancing himself from potentially controversial content in his work. For instance, in the Prologue to the *Legend of Good Women*, he allows Alceste to characterize him as a fool who did not know what he was doing (G 340–5). That is, in the dream visions Chaucer seems to have been negotiating his identity as an author and his identity as a historical person in the service of the royal court. Chaucer seems outwardly respectful of traditional social distinctions, but his narratives and descriptions often undermine those distinctions, and his own success in life was testament to the new possibility of social mobility leveraged by personal ability and ambition as well as by birth or wealth.

Chaucer presents himself as a character in the *Canterbury Tales*, almost as if he were performing his own identity. His literal performance, at least on one attempt, is not so successful. After he attempts to tell the tale of 'Sir Thopas', he is silenced by Harry Bailly in a particularly insulting way: ' "By God," quod he, "for pleynly, at a word, | Thy drasty rymyng is nat worth a toord! . . ." ' ('TST' 929–30). Chaucer here is also assuming a series of poetic identities. By telling the tale of 'Sir Thopas', he is assuming the role of a popular romancer, which is roundly rejected. In telling the serious tale of 'Melibee', he takes on a more august role for a medieval author, that of an adviser and dispenser of wisdom. At the very end of the *Canterbury Tales*, in the 'Retraction', he asks to be remembered for his pious writings, and not for those tales that might lead us into sin.

Who is the 'real' Chaucer? Even Harry Bailly is not sure: 'What man artow?' ('PST' 695). The question conflates modern and medieval conceptions of identity, for it can mean 'Who are you?' in a modern existential sense as well as 'What kind of person are you?' in the medieval sense exemplified by the 'General Prologue' portraits. Chaucer has been lurking, as it were, in the corners of an event he has in fact created. He is in effect making an ironic comment about his own identity as an author, since he is being ordered around by figures of his own devising. Our immediate assumption is to identify Chaucer the author with his self-portrait, here in 'Sir Thopas' a puppet-like figure, perhaps overweight. Near the beginning of the *Legend of Good Women* he describes his pleasure in waking up early to enjoy the morning and the flowers, and in several of the dream visions he describes himself as insomniac, exhausted by his detailed work associated with his positions such as collector of customs during the day.

Medieval poets often employed an image of themselves, like architects and builders who include an image of their own faces in sculptural decorations, as a narrative device, even when the overall meaning of the work is not dependent on their status as an individual. Even so, compared to Dante in the *Divine Comedy* or Langland in *Piers Plowman*, Chaucer is actually rather reticent about his self-presentation in his major works. It is true that he offers the *Legend of Good Women* as penance for seemingly blaming women in his earlier works, but the tales themselves follow with little reference to that autobiographical frame. The narrator of *Troilus and Criseyde* occasionally interrupts the action to apologize for its tragic course, or to appeal to us as readers, but he does not make the action dependent on his perspective. That is, from a modern critical perspective, Chaucer is operating like one of Conrad's narrators, shaping the story with his own sometimes confused misunderstandings. We have had to learn to read his narrative persona as if he were a distinct fictional character, which criticism has come to call 'Chaucer the narrator' or 'Chaucer the pilgrim'. Yet the number of lines that present any of these Chaucers outside of the dream visions is relatively limited. In the *Canterbury Tales*, Chaucer disappears, like the sort of artist James Joyce celebrated, allowing his creations to interact almost as if they had lives of their own. It is this negative dramatic mode of presentation which so often leads us to forget that the characters exist only as words on a page, and that the Chaucer we feel so comfortable with as a guide is absent much of the time.

Conclusion

The notion of personal identity, subjecthood, and the idea of the self in Chaucer are illuminated by consideration of modern and postmodern theories of subjectivity. Yet a number of unique late medieval discourses and systems of signification, including the practice of confession, the tension between private and public forms of worship, the importance of estates and social classes in defining identity, and the elaborate deployment of visible signs of individuality such as sartorial array and physiognomy, remind us of the irreducible historicity of Chaucer's subjects. At the same time, he projects the subjectivity of his characters largely as a conflict between modernity and tradition, in such a way as to suggest that this conflict is part of the human condition rather than as a specifically late medieval quandary. As with his own understanding of language change in *Troilus and Criseyde*, where he demonstrates a deep understanding of how language can become obscure ('in forme of speche is chaunge', 2. 22) and a concomitant understanding of how social and aesthetic values can change with time and culture, Chaucer purposely conflates cultural alterity and apparent translatability in his arrangement of the signs and languages of subjecthood. In so doing, he appeals to our desire to reach out to and comprehend what seem to be complete and complex beings such as we imagine ourselves to be, at the same time that he demonstrates the difficulties and contradictions of that desire.

FURTHER READING

Cohen, Jeffrey, *Medieval Identity Machines* (Minneapolis: University of Minnesota Press, 2003). How awareness of ethnicity, race, gender, and class intersect in medieval literature.

Crane, Susan, *The Performance of Self: Ritual, Clothing and Identity during the Hundred Years War*, The Middle Ages (Philadelphia: University of Pennsylvania Press, 2002). A study of how English and French medieval culture marked identity during the age of Chaucer.

Greenblatt, Stephen, *Renaissance Self-Fashioning: From More to Shakespeare* (Chicago: University of Chicago Press, 1980). A new historicist reading of how the Early Modern self shapes itself.

Hanning, Robert W., *The Individual in Twelfth-Century Romance* (New Haven: Yale University Press, 1977). Classic study linking twelfth-century intellectual innovations with the rise of romance.

Kay, Sarah, *Subjectivity in Troubadour Poetry* (Cambridge: Cambridge University Press, 1990). How subjectivity in troubadour poetry is repeatedly negotiated anew.

Leicester, H. Marshall, Jr., *The Disenchanted Self: Representing the Subject in the 'Canterbury Tales'* (Berkeley: University of California Press, 1990). Emphasizes the radical textuality of Chaucer's literary characters.

Patterson, Lee, *Chaucer and the Subject of History* (Madison: University of Wisconsin Press, 1991). How the strategic pose of the Chaucerian narrator as above and beyond the historical is transformed into the humanist conception of Chaucer as a poet for all times and places, disguising the radical historicity of both poet and his characters.

Root, Jerry, *Space to Speke: The Confessional Subject in Medieval Literature* (New York: Peter Lang, 1997). Argues for a relation between confessional reform and a specifically late medieval conception of subjectivity in literature.

Spence, Sarah, *Texts and the Self in the Twelfth Century* (Cambridge: Cambridge University Press, 1996). Shows how transitions from Latin to vernacular languages and from visual to verbal signs impact the development of the high medieval subject.

Zink, Michel, *The Invention of Literary Subjectivity*, trans. David Sices (Baltimore: Johns Hopkins University Press, 1999). On subjectivity and interiority in French medieval literature.

NOTES

1. A widely discussed interpretation of Chaucer's work from this point of view was D. W. Robertson, Jr., *A Preface to Chaucer: A Study in Medieval Perspectives* (Princeton: Princeton University Press, 1962).

2. On the idea that the twelfth century developed a proto-modern notion of individuality, see Colin Morris, *The Discovery of the Individual, 1050–1200* (London: SPCK, 1972) and the classic study by Robert Hanning, *The Individual in Twelfth-Century Romance* (New Haven: Yale University Press, 1977).

3. For a wide-ranging discussion of how state formation and other forms of coercion shaped individual and group identities, and how individuals and groups resisted such coercion, see Peter Haidu, *The Subject Medieval/Modern: Text and Governance in the Middle Ages* (Stanford, Calif.: Stanford University Press, 2004).

4. On the relation of new forms of spiritual practice in the twelfth century to the idea of selfhood, especially in connection with women, see Linda Georgianna, *The Solitary Self: Individuality in the 'Ancrene Wisse'* (Cambridge, Mass.: Harvard University Press, 1981).

5. One of the most influential studies of the role of confession is Thomas N. Tentler, *Sin and Confession on the Eve of the Reformation* (Princeton: Princeton University Press, 1977).

6. (Madison: University of Wisconsin, 1991).

7. (Berkeley: University of California Press, 1990).

8. Erving Goffman, *The Presentation of the Self in Everyday Life* (Garden City, NY: Doubleday, 1959).

9. For a critique of new historicism's dismissal of medieval subjectivity, see David Aers, 'A Whisper in the Ear of Early Modernists; or, Reflections on Literary Critics Writing the "History of the Subject"', in Aers (ed.), *Culture and History, 1350–1600: Essays on English Communities, Identities and Writing* (Detroit: Wayne State University Press, 1992), 177–203.

10. On the uses of charivari, see Natalie Zemon Davis, *Society and Culture in Early Modern France: Eight Essays* (Stanford, Calif.: Stanford University Press, 1975).

11. The most influential recent discussion of the role of memory in medieval literature is Mary Carruthers, *The Book of Memory: A Study of Memory in Medieval Culture* (Cambridge: Cambridge University Press, 1992).

14 | **Love and marriage**

Bernard O'Donoghue

In a famous passage in *The Allegory of Love*, C. S. Lewis with characteristic decisiveness places Chaucer in context as 'a court poet of the age of Froissart', declaring that the poet's affiliation in the love-dispute between the courtly eagles and the reductive, worldly duck in the *Parliament of Fowls* cannot be with the latter.[1] To believe that Chaucer could have shared the crudely practical opinion of the duck ('But she wol love hym, lat hym love another!', *PF* 567) is to be guilty of 'square-headed vulgarity'.[2] The principal subject for 'a court poet of the age of Froissart' was love, and Lewis is writing of an age when love was the all-prevailing subject for poetry. The opposition Lewis is drawing was later given its clearest critical form in Charles Muscatine's *Chaucer and the French Tradition: A Study in Style and Meaning* (1957), in which a broad distinction is made between genteel views of love, associated with the character of Troilus and the *Parliament*'s noble eagles and founded in Guillaume de Lorris's early, courtly section of the *Romance of the Rose*, and what Muscatine called the 'bourgeois' view, associated with Pandarus, the duck of the *Parliament*, and a new mercantilism in the later Middle Ages, founded in Jean de Meun's continuation of the *Romance* in the late thirteenth century. It is an opposition that works well for Chaucer, even if it goes back a good deal before his time. And it is a characterization of a kind that needs to be made; all serious poets in Italian or French of the Middle Ages were scrutinized for their 'theory of love', evident as a definable ingredient in their work. Chaucer among English writers of his age was the most clearly a poet of love in the sense that his European predecessors were.

The language of love

I want to begin by considering the linguistic context of Chaucer's love-writings, before going on to describe where love is the main subject of his works, and finally considering the place of marriage in relation to love (something which has prompted a great deal of discussion over the past century: more, I will suggest, than its prominence in the works of Chaucer warrants). I am starting with some consideration of language to note ways in which it was not easy for an English writer of Chaucer's time to fill the role of courtly love-poet. But courtly love remains one of the most important Chaucerian contexts because it informs the cultural world of some of his greatest works—of *Troilus and Criseyde* and the 'Knight's Tale'—and it had been the central literary subject in Europe from the twelfth-century troubadours through to the poets of the *Romance of the Rose* and to Chaucer's great fourteenth-century predecessors Dante, Petrarch, and Boccaccio. I want also to suggest, with reference to marriage as well as to love, that the unease of the English language with the sophisticated European terminology of love was for Chaucer the occasion of a highly characteristic ambivalence.

To introduce this ambivalence, we might recall a luminous observation made by Derek Brewer about the criticism of writings of this period: 'perhaps "contradiction", especially "self-contradiction", and paradox, are due to take the place of the New Criticism's "irony" as the defining characteristic of poetry'.[3] Whether or not this is true of criticism as a whole, it applies enlighteningly to the writings of Chaucer especially and of his English contemporaries. The kind of self-contradiction identified here is partly a consequence of writing in a language and a literary culture which was not current in English. To illustrate the unease of English with both the terms and the concepts of European love-poetry we might consider the terms for love itself. The Old-English-derived word 'love' needed to serve as a term of far wider application than the various cognates of the Latin term *amor* in the European languages that developed the Latin-derived system of *fin'amor* from the twelfth century onwards. David Burnley suggests that such lexical deficiencies were successfully supplied by Chaucer and Gower by drawing on religious language: 'in poetry of Chaucer's time we find a characteristic extension of the use of the word *charite* from its theological and moral registers into the courtly discussions of secular love, and this is matched by the adoption of the terms of *curteisie* into homiletic discourse'.[4] We might recall here D. W. Rowe's contention about Troilus' famous imprecation 'O Love, O Charite!' (*TC* 3. 1254), that he is confusing *caritas* with *cupiditas*, in keeping with Rowe's overall reading of the poem as exemplifying a contradictory centre, a c*oncordia discors*.[5] Burnley's chapter on 'The Gentil Man' is an enlightening discussion of love in Chaucer, and it is supplemented by his 1998 book which is the most extensive modern discussion of love and courtliness in medieval English.[6] His general argument is that the lexical 'architecture' (a rather elusive term) of Chaucer and Gower's poetic usage—by contrast with the more theological bias in the language of Langland and the *Gawain*-poet—is more complex in connotative terms than has been suggested in traditional accounts of Chaucer's language because of its negotiations with the language of *curteisie*.

This is a suggestive idea, but linguistically it is stating the exception rather than the rule. It remains obvious than not even in Chaucer did the language of courtliness translate in its full semantic range into English. In the terminology of the courtly system—shared by Latin, Provençal, Northern French, and Italian, as well as German—a whole lexicon for love-poetry developed, which was translatable in full from one of these languages to another. A convenient example might be the terms for the morning-song at the lovers' awakening before parting: *alba, aube, aubade, tagelied*. Although the morning-song is familiar in English from *Troilus and Criseyde* to *Romeo and Juliet* and John Donne's 'The Sunne Rising', no native term in English developed for it; in the mid-twentieth century Sylvia Plath still had to devise a loan-translation for her poem 'Morning Song'. It is even truer for the more particular terminology of love-poetry and states of love: such things as *fin'amor* itself as opposed to *fals amor* (faithful love as against libidinous); *canso* for love-song; the cognates of the term *connoissensa* (love-insight); *mesura* (moderation); love which was *entier* (integral), as opposed to *frait* (fragmentary). These terms all still sound recondite in English, but they had become commonplace to the point of constituting the clichés of poetics in European love-poems. English failed to develop a corresponding series of terms because love-poetry in the English vernacular was a later development. Clearly it could partly borrow this terminology by translation, and Chaucer—saluted in 1386 by the French poet Eustache Deschamps as the *grant translateur*—did so to some extent. But it remains a striking fact that many of the French terms that have become commonplaces in the criticism of Chaucer (*fals semblant*, *courtoisie*, and so on) do not occur in the poet's works. It is salutary to remember that, if Chaucer was of the age of Froissart, he did not primarily write in Froissart's language. This means both that courtly love-language remained foreign, and perhaps rather old-fashioned, in English, and that the duck's 'bourgeois' view of love, in Muscatine's terms, even if it too originated in France, is not necessarily as 'vulgar' for Chaucer as Lewis suggests. A glance down any glossary of Chaucer shows a considerable proportion of borrowed Latin-derived language, but very little of it was the courtly terminology that was the most obvious romance language in the Middle Ages.

Indeed it is not immediately obvious what the connotative range of Chaucer's love-language was. As a first instance of his narrower love-lexicon, as well as his constructive use of it, we might consider the most famous occurrence in his writings of a slippery term for love, the Prioress's brooch bearing the inscription *Amor vincit omnia* ('Love conquers all', 'GP' 162), recalling among other things the *Carmina Burana*'s profane *Amor tenet omnia*. Of course in Italian, as in all Latin-derived languages of the era, despite the multiplicity of terms for states of mind, the term *amor* did indeed carry religious and sexual meanings. From the earliest Provençal troubadours onwards love had two very distinct areas of operation: the amorous–secular and the divine. In particular cases (most notoriously in some of those early troubadours) it is difficult to be certain which category a poem belonged to: whether the love described was purely amorous or a figure for the divine, or both. But could the Prioress's decidedly secular-sounding Latin formula stretch to cover divine love as the Italian cognate does in the last line of Dante's *Divine Comedy*: 'the love that moves the sun and the other stars'? It seems unlikely. What Chaucer appears to be doing is to exploit for satirical effect the way that the Latin term could occur in both secular and religious contexts. The Prioress is perhaps associated with an implicit blasphemy, of a kind that Chaucer turned to repeatedly; she may even be distantly connected to a similar tension and ambivalence in the troubadours. But the whole question of parody and blasphemy has been oddly under-explored in the criticism of medieval English literature.

Chaucer's writings are full of such ambivalences, particularly in the use of the English term 'love' itself. To illustrate not so much the ambivalence of the term as its range, we might consider some usages in the 'Man of Law's Tale'. The tale's introduction remarks that Chaucer, despite his failures in metre and rhyming (it is in the context of writing on love, that most competitive medieval literary field, that the Chaucer poet-persona most often declares his poetic inadequacies), has attempted to write about many lovers, including Jason 'that was of love so fals' (74). Jason's betrayal of Medea in love fits the general sense of attachment (or its betrayal) naturally enough; but we soon encounter a much more disturbing employment of the term (as a verb) in the tale of Custance that follows. One of the heroine's many trials is sexual assault by 'a yong knyght that dwelte in that toun' who was moved to

> Love hire so hoote, of foul affeccioun,
> That verraily hym thoughte he sholde spille,
> But he of hire myghte ones have his wille. (585–8)

This loving 'of foul affeccioun' is clearly a serious crime, and the king Alla has such compassion for Custance that 'This false knyght was slayn ... | By juggement of Alla hastifly' (687–8). We are a long way from the court poetry of the age of Froissart; 'love' in this sense is as remote from the exalted romantic love of Troilus for Criseyde as it is from the divine. It is a social crime and a mortal sin. (The missing term of course is 'lust' in its modern sense; but 'lust' in Chaucer means 'wish' or 'inclination' generally, and can even have a more positive uxorious sense, as when the Black Knight calls his 'swete wif' 'my lust, my lyf', *BD* 1037–8. The rare Chaucerian term 'luxure' never became fully naturalized in English as a term for the sin.) We find a similarly wide semantic range of the word 'love' in other contexts in Chaucer, extending well beyond such various kinds of natural or evil erotic attraction. Chaucer's translation of Boethius understandably has to cope in English terminology with a more philosophical range, representing the love-impulse in all creation: 'al this accordaunce ... of thynges is bounde with love, that governeth erthe and see, and hath also comandement to the hevene' (2, met. 8. 13–16), a passage familiar from Troilus' beautiful song of love, transferred to the context of his erotic response to Criseyde: 'Love, that of erthe and se hath governaunce' (*TC* 3. 1744). 'It was an hevene his wordes for to here', the narrator comments (1742). So secular 'love' can stretch to the Dantesque realm of the transcendent if necessary.

Chaucer as love-poet

I shall here be concerned with the various secular applications of the term 'love' in Chaucer, as they occur in his love-poetry and in wider social contexts. Turning to a more systematic examination of Chaucer's placing of himself as love-poet, we might start with a much-quoted passage which makes it clear that, ostensibly at least, he saw himself as such a poet, though one of somewhat uneasy aspirations. This is the point in the Prologue to the *Legend of Good Women* when the god of love accuses the poet of having written the 'draf' (chaff) of stories, leaving the corn, and of being guilty of 'reneying' (denying) love's law, 'As othere olde foles many a day' (G 312–15). Alceste, the god of love's queen, replies in Chaucer's defence that he has written assiduously about love, however bad he was at it. She lists the works that Chaucer has written in praise of love: the *House of Fame*, the *Book of the Duchess*, the *Parliament of Fowls*, and 'the love of Palamon and Arcite' (either the 'Knight's Tale' or an earlier version of Boccaccio's *Teseida*), as well as 'many an ympne' (hymn) of love. All these works cause 'lewed folk' (love's laity) to delight in love's service (G 402–10).

We recognize here of course the convention of the naive, self-effacing narrator. But the conventionality does not mean that we cannot infer from it an impression of what the concerns and treatments of Chaucerian love-poetry were. This important passage comes at a late point in Chaucer's career: only the *Canterbury Tales* of the major works remains to be written, apart perhaps from some of the 'Legends' themselves (though it is probable that the mature Prologue was written after several of them). It reminds us that from the *Book of the Duchess* onwards Chaucer's central subject has always been love: the courtly love of the Black Knight for his dead Duchess, or of the eagles in the *Parliament*, or the fated loves of women in stories like those of Dido in the *House of Fame* or the *Legend*, or of Ceyx in the *Book of the Duchess* or the 'Franklin's Tale', or above all the profound exploration of love in *Troilus and Criseyde*. To illustrate rapidly what the love-works itemized here are, we might start with the hymns of love among the 'Short Poems', which feature a parade of standard medieval love-themes. Against those critics who believe that courtly love was a dead issue by Chaucer's time, or in response to Robertson, who called it 'an impediment to the understanding of medieval texts',[7] it would be hard to find a more classically conventional courtly love-poem than the beautiful 'A Complaint to his Lady':

> This Love, that hath me set in such a place
> That my desir [he] nevere wol fulfille,
> For neither pitee, mercy, neither grace
> Can I nat fynde, and yit my sorwful herte
> For to be deed I can hit nought arace.
> The more I love, the more she doth me smerte. (15–20)

The Petrarchan structure of the last line here, reminiscent of the expert translation of one of the sonnets from Petrarch's *Rime* in the 'Canticus Troili' in book 1 of *Troilus and Criseyde* ('For ay thurst I, the more that ich it drynke', 406), should warn us not to dismiss this poem as dead convention. It is in the vanguard of the love-poetry that was to develop in the Renaissance, founded in the courtly love tradition as that poetry was. The further ambition towards originality in this poem, as with other apparently mysterious Chaucerian pieces like *Anelida and Arcite*, lies in the variety of stanza forms it employs as a setting for the entirely traditional love-poetry it enshrines. As with all the medieval love-lyricists, love-poetry for Chaucer was important as much for its form as for its substance.

This prominence of artistry as the principal quality in love-poetry is stated most familiarly in one of Chaucer's many great openings. The *Parliament of Fowls* starts with an elegant apostrophe which is a classic statement of this identification of love as an inseparable part of the poet's craft, as it had been for the troubadours in a tradition descending from Ovid:

> The lyf so short, the craft so long to lerne,
> Th'assay so hard, so sharp the conquerynge,
> The dredful joye alwey that slit so yerne:
> Al this mene I by Love.

> (*PF* 1–4)

The commonplaces agelessly associated with artistic achievement in the classical tradition—*ars longa, vita brevis*—are here adapted in application to love. It has often been said, though perhaps not often enough with reference to Chaucer, that the Petrarchan tradition of love-poetry was concerned with the poet rather than with the ostensible human object of his love. In the tradition descending from Ovid, the real *ars* is love, the art in which it was most essential to demonstrate expertise. What the development of the *Parliament* suggests is that the 'art' at the beginning is a matter of understanding and writing about love. Chaucer had said so before, in the words of the Black Knight in the *Book of the Duchess*: 'I ches love to my firste craft' (791). The *Parliament* fails to resolve a straightforward love-question, a *démande d'amour*: when two or more (here three) noble suitors of equal deserving fall in love with the same lady, how is she to choose, or the lord of love to pronounce? The matter is shelved for a year, and the poet ends with the rather resigned-sounding hope of reading

> so som day
> That I shal mete som thyng for to fare
> The bet. (697–9)

There is no doubt that this is Lewis's court poet for whom love is a decidedly textual matter. It does not matter—or even mean anything—which of three nameless male eagles the female chooses. The crucial art for the medieval poet—the craft it takes so long to learn—is the writing of a love-poetry that enshrines and promotes the attitudes of *fin'amor*.

Such a literary ambition is far from new with Chaucer, and we do not need to go back to Ovid through the troubadours to find the source of this *ars amatoria* in his era. The crucial influence was the *Roman de la Rose*, translated by Chaucer, where we encounter Guillaume de Lorris's project of producing a book in which 'l'art d'Amors est toute enclose' ('the whole art of love is included').[8] Jean de Meun's late thirteenth-century continuation of de Lorris's text was undertaken forty years later precisely, he claims, because the courtly elegance of de Lorris's allegory failed to deal with 'the whole art of love', defining it too narrowly in purely aesthetic terms. De Meun's extensive continuation shows the realm of love to extend into wider philosophical areas. But, as far as the Chaucer of the dream poems is concerned, it was de Lorris's courtly allegory that was crucial.

It is convenient, if somewhat facile, to see the more philosophical opening out of the field of love demanded by Jean de Meun as operative for the later, major works of Chaucer. French critics have often identified de Meun's continuation of the *Romance* as a founding text for the social emphasis (Muscatine's term 'bourgeois' might be invoked again) that French literature developed. I shall now look at the treatment of marriage in Chaucer, especially in the *Canterbury Tales*. In this work, as in *Troilus and Criseyde*, it can be claimed that Chaucer, like de Meun, is extending the realm of love in a social, rather than solely poetic, direction that bids to fulfil the ambition declared at the start of the *Roman de la Rose*, to enclose the whole of 'the art of love'.

Society and marriage

Turning to a consideration of marriage—an institution that has no meaning in the courtly de Lorris allegory—will give implicit prominence to de Meun's continuation. Particularly in reference to the *Canterbury Tales* the social contexts will require reflection on how love relates to marriage. We might begin by noting that the best-known passage in the whole of Chaucer ostensibly centres on the opposition and tensions between physical and spiritual love. At the same time as the spring with its sweet showers 'engenders' the flowers and sexually arouses the birds in the realm of physical nature, human beings—*homo sapiens*—are prompted towards spiritual renewal. But of course the end of this first sentence of the *Canterbury Tales* is open to a misconstruction that Chaucer exploits richly throughout the work: when the birds sing and cannot sleep

> (So priketh hem nature in hir corages),
> Thanne longen folk to goon on pilgrimages.

> ('GP' 11–12)

Human beings set off on pilgrimages—a decidedly social as well as spiritual journey. Here the opposing loves are all suggested with great economy: the spiritual love that the pilgrimage is officially concerned with; the natural physical love of the birds, reinforced by the strongly libidinous terms 'priketh' and 'corages'; and a contaminating association of the latter, sexual impulse which leaks into the world of the pilgrimage.

Of course the placing of this passage at the start of all editions of Chaucer's works is chronologically misleading. It makes it look like Chaucer's opening statement on the matter of love; but it is the start of his last, grandest work which comes as he is approaching the end of a writing lifetime as love-poet: a culmination, not a beginning. The treatment of love in the *Tales* is a complicated matter, nowhere more so than in the case of marriage. From the early Middle Ages it had been recognized that marriage was a vexed matter for the consideration of the various worlds of love: social, spiritual, and erotic. The title of this chapter suggests that 'Love and Marriage' go together inextricably. Twentieth-century Chaucer criticism mostly considered them in this way, joined by a curious (and I think misleading) kind of symbiotic opposition. Later some attempts were made to give a more systematic account of types of marriage—for example, by Rowe in his study *O Love, O Charite!* where a distinction is made between two Venuses: the wife of Hymen and of Antigamus, relating respectively to faithful marital love and love driven by passion.[9] But the critical tradition in the earlier part of the twentieth century, particularly in America (though also upheld by critics like Lewis), tended to propound a cruder opposition between views of the relations between love and marriage: first that love was 'courtly love' and was directly opposed to marital emotions, however deplorable this state of affairs was. The fullest statement of this opposition came in the early (and better) sections of a very notable work, Denis de Rougemont's *L'Amour et l'Occident* (1939), translated into English in 1940 under the influential title *Passion and Society*, a title that succinctly declares its theme. Love was a passion, similar to Lacan's 'desire', a wilful inclination to fulfil personal inclinations regardless of whether they undermined the good workings of society. Marriage was the perfect institutional building block of the well-ordered society. Not only did love have nothing to do with marriage; as social forces they were radically opposed. The classic case was the ungainsayable love of Tristan for Iseult, the wife of his uncle King Mark (the love of Lancelot and Guinevere represents the same dilemma).

Broadly speaking the literary consensus up to about the 1930s was to feel sympathy with the situation of the fated lovers whose anti-social passion ends up as a personal as well as political disaster. But since Lewis—who fumed about 'the revolting passages of irreligion' in Chrétien de Troyes's *Lancelot*[10]—the responsible worthiness of marital love has enjoyed majority support. This reaction against the imperatives of courtly love was stated with almost comic indignation by David Aers in 1980, when he railed against 'the disastrous separation of love from sex and marriage'.[11] There have also been gallant attempts to reconcile the two; van Hoecke and Welkenhuysen begin their *Love and Marriage in the Twelfth Century* by declaring its twin themes to be 'Love, the mightiest feeling that can inspire human beings, and Marriage, the institution which, if not animated by this feeling, loses its sense and its soul'.[12] A different positive view of love in relation to marriage is stated strongly in the course of a valuable anthology on the matter, *The Olde Daunce*. In an important essay in this volume, R. R. Edwards refers firmly to 'love and its subsidiary themes of marriage, sexuality and friendship'.[13] This is to give great centrality to the dominance of love.

A more familiar and now largely discredited view of the relations of love and marriage held that Chaucer has threshed the matter out fully and surprisingly conclusively in a section of the *Canterbury Tales*, the tales that G. L. Kittredge called 'the marriage group'.[14] This is now ancient critical history, but it is necessary to summarize it briefly in order to evaluate its relevance for positing a view of love and/or marriage held by Chaucer. According to this view the topic of marriage is effectively raised for debate at the start of a so-called 'group' of tales by the Wife of Bath, who says she needs no authoritative text 'To speke of wo that is in mariage' ('WBP' 3); her experience is enough. Her long Prologue, itemizing her woeful experiences of marriage, is followed by her disconcerting tale of a knight who rapes a maiden and is dubiously punished by discovering that what women most desire is 'sovereynetee' ('WBT' 1038). The argument for a marriage group within the *Canterbury Tales* claims that, after an extensive interruption by the altercating tales of the Friar and the Summoner (an interruption which Kittredge somewhat improbably called a dramatic master stroke), the Clerk resumes the debate by telling the tale of the trials of patient Griselda, whose experience of marriage was anything but sovereign. The Merchant continues the debate 'Of mariage, which we have on honde' ('MerT' 1686) by telling the grim story of the marriage of aged, repulsive January to young, betraying May. But finally peace is restored by the 'Franklin's Tale' which describes the perfect love-match of Arveragus—'Servant in love, and lord in mariage' (793)—and Dorigen, the wife urged by her husband to undergo extramarital sex because she has promised to. The Franklin concludes by marvelling at how 'fre' (noble) everyone's behaviour has been (1622).

Sexuality, marriage, and actual lovers

Although the idea of the 'marriage group' has proved depressingly tenacious in popular discussion of Chaucer, more scholarly explorations of marriage in the Middle Ages have produced a much more complex picture of Chaucer's representations of love and marriage. It has not proved difficult to produce evidence of the deplorable experiences of marriage suffered by women in the Middle Ages, mostly underwritten by canon and civil law; as Aers notes, marriage was 'primarily a transaction organized by males to serve economic and political ends with the woman treated as a useful child-bearing appendage to the lands and goods being exchanged'.[15] There is not space here to deal generally with the crucial relevance of the treatment of women in Chaucer; there is a substantial literature on this, inevitably in the case of the poet characterized by Gavin Douglas, in the Prologue to book 1 of his translation of the *Aeneid* (1553), as 'evir all womanis frend'. Here I deal with the issue solely within the context of marriage.

In the works of Chaucer, Aers's view of the exploitation of women in marriage arises principally from the 'Parson's Tale'. In his rightful indignation against the Parson's failure to allow for sexual love between marital partners, Aers quotes such passages as the orthodox pronouncement that if the husband and wife 'assemble oonly for amorous love . . . to accomplice thilke brennynge delit . . . it is deedly synne' ('ParsT' 943). This is consistent with the evidence adduced by H. A. Kelly that among the motives for marriage given by medieval Church canon lawyers 'mutual love between the spouses is notably absent'.[16] However repugnant we find such pro-hibitions, we might note the suggestion in Ariès and Béjin's volume that the idea of marital eroticism only emerged in the eighteenth century.[17] Aers makes much of J. T. Noonan's evidence that the Church failed 'to incorporate love into the purpose of marital intercourse'.[18] With other of Chaucer's tales, and tellers, however, surely it is deeply anachronistic, decent as it is, to find fault, as Aers does at the end of the Athenian epic–romance of the 'Knight's Tale', on the grounds that 'it is a hopelessly inadequate one for sustaining any thought about the nature of long-term, loving relationships and the many kinds of pressures they come under in two people's lives, then or today',[19] as if the question arises of whether Emelye or Palamon will take responsibility for childcare. Such reflections are surely bizarrely out of place in the world of romance.

Several studies since the 1970s have provided a context for examining marriage in Chaucer and his contemporaries in a more socio-historical framework, to escape the restrictions of discussing it only in the terms of its literary convention, or in terms of modern indignations. The most authoritative text is R. H. Bloch's *Medieval French Literature and Law*,[20] which makes a decisive distinction between literary marriage or love and real legal circumstances. Such studies might have prevented some of the more anachronistic readings which, interesting as they often are, are also far more historic-ally insensitive than is the supposedly anachronistic code of courtly love which we are so often triumphantly reminded was an invention of the nineteenth century. In fact what is most striking in looking at these detailed examinations is how little the situ-ations they deal with arise in Chaucer's writings, even when Chaucer is their ostensible subject. This is well demonstrated in Margaret Hallissy's fine study of Chaucer's women in relation to the laws of the time, showing how little the contemporary legal rulings have to do with the highly conventionalized conditions that apply in the *Tales*—the place where current historical circumstances would have relevance if any-where.[21] In Hallissy's chapter 'The Archwife' she shows how far the Wife of Bath (whom of course we know to be a literary stereotype) is from the condition of the wife or widow of that time. She ought not to be a trained speaker,[22] and her observation that 'conseillyng is no comandement' ('WBP' 67) is a lawyer's remark. What these studies establish, surprisingly at first glance in the light of traditional Chaucer criticism, is how little consideration of actual contemporary marriage there is in Chaucer. It is notori-ously and tantalizingly uncertain who the 'we' are who have 'mariage . . . on honde' in the 'Merchant's Tale' (1686); in the text it could be Justinus, the Merchant, Chaucer the pilgrim, or even Chaucer himself; but it is hard to see it as a serious contribution to the understanding of marriage in Chaucer's era. And it is surely strange that the nearest approaches to a mimetic account of the 'woes' in marriage come in the 'Merchant's Tale', which is halfway to allegory.

A good short recent account of the historical circumstances of marriage by Dyan Elliott shows how remote Chaucer's debates are from actual experiences of marriage.[23] Elliott's unsensational but horrifying itemizing of legal cases involving brutality towards wives, including the infamous twelfth-century account of Christina of Markyate, shows that even the 'Wife of Bath's Prologue' (still less of course her morally irresponsible tale) has nothing to do with actual marriage with its many legislative constraints. Of the other tales in the putative marriage group, the moral of the 'Clerk's Tale', most obviously, is hagiographic, not marital. Elliott says her purpose 'is to acquaint the reader with a wide array of primary sources while pointing to how these sources correspond to various analogues in literature'.[24] In practice the analogues remain distant. Another direction in which the exploration of actual circumstances has been taken is in Jean-Louis Flandrin's research, which suggests a surprisingly permissive, not to say explicit, discussion by the Church of sexual activity within marriage from St Augustine onwards.[25] Elizabeth Clark also offers an interesting explanation of the discontinuities between marital practices, Church rulings, and literary discussions, arguing that ambivalence was introduced into the debate by Augustine's 'failure to develop a fully-fledged theory of companionate marriage' as he attempted to steer a middle course between the ascetical excesses of St Jerome's opposition to Jovinian and the lusty sexuality of the Pelagians.[26] This is of course a familiar context for the Wife of Bath, but it is far removed from the specific conditions of medieval marriage, and it is salutary to be reminded of the often anachronistic historicist invocation of the repressions of canon and civil law, interesting as those are for the social historian.

Love, marriage, and Chaucer's texts

The representation of marriage in Chaucer is often little more than a setting for the events of a story. For example, we have little concern with the relations between the miller and his wife in the 'Reeve's Tale' or of the merchant with his wife in the 'Shipman's Tale' beyond the requirements of the plot. Chaucer, whether as bourgeois or courtly poet, is not specifically interested in marriage.

It is also striking, given how much critical discussion has stressed the opposition of the two terms in my chapter title, how similar the indeterminacies of both terms have been. We have seen how the word 'love' has been required both to cover the lustful designs of 'foul affeccioun' in the 'Man of Law's Tale' and to act as a kind of doublet with charity in 'O Love, O Charite!' for Troilus. Marriage has by contrast traditionally been represented as a fixed mark, opposed to the uncertainty of love, serving the interests of 'society' as opposed to the transgressiveness of 'passion'. Under examination though, marriage too proves a surprisingly unstable term in the medieval period. H. A. Kelly has argued (even if he has not found general assent) that the arrangements made by Troilus and Criseyde are recognizable as a kind of 'clandestine marriage' based on mutual consent which was recognized by canon lawyers, attempting to make their actions compatible with D. S. Brewer's view that 'Chaucer nowhere celebrates illicit love'.[27] There was more than one kind of marriage.

Similarly, it seems that the indeterminacy of love is even more extreme than is often recognized. This is not merely a lexical matter. Traditional objections to courtly love, such as Tatlock's characterization of it in 1940 as 'a rather silly outgrowth' by contrast with 'the expressed romantic love' in *Troilus*,[28] are often lacking in any sense of historical difference (in the easy use of the anachronistic term 'romantic love' here, for instance). A fascinating recent example of the recognition of extreme historical difference is Jaeger's study *Ennobling Love*, which describes a non-homosexual physical intimacy between male figures of nobility which we can hardly comprehend.[29] The more we examine the evidence for views of love and marriage in Chaucer, the more striking it is how anachronistic much of the modern discussion of both has been. I do not wish to take further issue with Aers, whose various interventions into medieval critical debate have brought a welcome vigour and seriousness to the field, but it is hard to accept his view that 'in the *Canterbury Tales* Chaucer's fascination with the interactions between individual being, predominant social practices and received ideas focussed on those living within the institution of marriage'.[30] This seems to be less revealing of Chaucer's time than of our own.

The modern connotations of the term 'love', or even the current practices of it, are not a safe guide to its senses in the Middle Ages (or, for that matter, the Renaissance—a poetic world with which Chaucer's views of love have much in common). Indeed, the most salutary warning against expecting the practices of love (or language or marriage) to be the same in all ages comes in Chaucer's own greatest love-text, in the Prologue to book 2 of *Troilus and Criseyde*. This warning, that people in different ages and places pursue love by different means (22–42), seemed to fall on deaf ears in the twentieth century, with reference to marriage as well as to love:

> Ye knowe ek that in forme of speche is chaunge
> Withinne a thousand yeer, and wordes tho
> That hadden pris, now wonder nyce and straunge
> Us thinketh hem, and yet thei spake hem so,
> And spedde as wel in love as men now do;
> Ek for to wynnen love in sondry ages,
> In sondry londes, sondry ben usages.
>
> And forthi if it happe in any wyse,
> That here be any lovere in this place
> That herkneth, as the storie wol devise,
> How Troilus com to his lady grace,
> And thenketh, 'So nold I nat love purchace,'
> Or wondreth on his speche or his doynge,
> I noot; but it is me no wonderynge. (2. 22–35)

This wise passage is important advice to modern Chaucerians who have found their views of love, and recently of marriage, borne out or disappointed in Chaucer's writing. Love was inevitably Chaucer's subject, given the literary milieu of romance, love-lyric, and epic that he inherited and translated. But it is not to be expected that he will have a unitary view of love, as this passage makes clear, given too the breadth of genre (romance, fabliau, parody, and sermon) that he wrote in. In those diverse literary worlds—the bourgeois and the courtly—Love itself (or himself) ranged from the gracious consort of Alceste in the Prologue to the *Legend of Good Women* to the 'village tyrant' identified by Burnley.[31] In the terms of Edwards and Spector's introduction, there is no 'petrified ideal of love but an essentially contested term'.[32]

FURTHER READING

Burnley, David, *Chaucer's Language and the Philosophers' Tradition* (Cambridge: Brewer, 1979). The best discussion of the language of love in Chaucer.

Burnley, David, *Courtliness and Literature in Medieval England* (London: Longman, 1998). A good introduction to the courtly tradition in which Chaucer's love-poetry is written.

Edwards, R. R., and S. Spector (eds.), *The Olde Daunce: Love, Friendship, Sex, and Marriage in the Medieval World* (Albany: State University of New York Press, 1991). The best anthology of discussions of love and marriage in Chaucer and later.

Kelly, H. A., *Love and Marriage in the Age of Chaucer* (Ithaca, NY: Cornell University Press, 1975). Sometimes eccentric, but for Chaucer in particular the most useful introduction to the two subjects.

Valency, Maurice, *In Praise of Love: An Introduction to the Love-Poetry of the Renaissance* (New York: Macmillan, 1958). Remains a useful discussion of courtly love, also relevant for Chaucer.

NOTES

1. C. S. Lewis, *The Allegory of Love: A Study in Medieval Tradition* (Oxford: Oxford University Press, 1936), 172.
2. Ibid.
3. See Brewer's introduction to D. Brewer and J. Gibson (eds.), *A Companion to the 'Gawain'-Poet* (Woodbridge: Brewer, 1997), 8.
4. David Burnley, *Chaucer's Language and the Philosophers' Tradition* (Cambridge: Brewer, 1979), 7–8.
5. Donald W. Rowe, *O Love, O Charite! Contraries Harmonized in Chaucer's 'Troilus'* (Carbondale: Southern Illinois University Press, 1976), 105.
6. 'The Gentil Man', in his *Chaucer's Language and the Philosophers' Tradition*, 151–70; and Burnley, *Courtliness and Literature in Medieval England* (London: Longman, 1998).
7. D. W. Robertson, Jr., 'The Concept of Courtly Love as an Impediment to the Understanding of Medieval Texts', repr. in his *Essays in Medieval Culture* (Princeton: Princeton University Press, 1980), 257–72.
8. *Le Roman de la Rose*, ed. Daniel Poirion (Paris: Garnier-Flammarion, 1974), 44, line 38.
9. *O Love, O Charite!*, 93. There is no extensive consideration of the two Venuses in English, to correspond, for example, to Robert Hollander's *Boccaccio's Two Venuses* (New York: Columbia University Press, 1977).
10. *Allegory of Love*, 29.
11. David Aers, *Chaucer, Langland and the Creative Imagination* (London: Routledge & Kegan Paul, 1980), 146.

12. W. van Hoecke and A. Welkenhuysen, *Love and Marriage in the Twelfth Century* (Leuven: Leuven University Press, 1981), p. vii.

13. 'Faithful Translations: Love and the Question of Poetry in Chaucer', in R. R. Edwards and S. Spector (eds.), *The Olde Daunce: Love, Friendship, Sex, and Marriage in the Medieval World* (Albany: State University of New York Press, 1991), 140.

14. G. L. Kittredge, *Chaucer and his Poetry* (Cambridge, Mass.: Harvard University Press, 1915), 185–211.

15. Aers, *Chaucer, Langland and the Creative Imagination*, 143.

16. H. A. Kelly, *Love and Marriage in the Age of Chaucer* (Ithaca, NY: Cornell University Press, 1975), 247.

17. P. Ariès and A. Béjin (eds.), *Western Sexuality: Practice and Precept in Past and Present Times*, trans A. Foster (Oxford: Blackwell, 1985), 114–39.

18. John T. Noonan, Jr., *Contraception: A History of its Treatment by the Catholic Theologians and Canonists* (Cambridge, Mass.: Harvard University Press, 1966), 256–7.

19. Aers, *Chaucer, Langland and the Creative Imagination*, 81.

20. (Berkeley: University of California Press, 1977.)

21. Margaret Hallissy, *Clean Maids, True Wives, Steadfast Widows: Chaucer's Women and Medieval Codes of Conduct* (Westport, Conn.: Greenwood Press, 1993).

22. Ibid. 171.

23. Dyan Elliott, 'Marriage', in Carolyn Dinshaw and David Wallace (eds.), *The Cambridge Companion to Medieval Women's Writing* (Cambridge: Cambridge University Press, 2003), 40–57.

24. Ibid. 41.

25. 'Sex in Married Life in the Early Middle Ages: The Church's Teaching and Behavioural Reality', in Ariès and Béjin (eds.), *Western Sexuality*, 114–29.

26. ' "Adam's only companion": Augustine and the Early Christian Debate on Marriage', in Edwards and Spector (eds.), *The Olde Daunce*, 15–31.

27. D. S. Brewer, 'Love and Marriage in Chaucer's Poetry', *Modern Language Review*, 49 (1954), 461–4; see Kelly, *Love and Marriage in the Age of Chaucer*, 217.

28. J. S. P. Tatlock, 'The People in Chaucer's *Troilus*', *PMLA* 56 (1941), 88.

29. C. Stephen Jaeger, *Ennobling Love: In Search of a Lost Sensibility* (Philadelphia: University of Pennsylvania Press, 1999).

30. Aers, *Chaucer, Langland and the Creative Imagination*, 143.

31. *Chaucer's Language and the Philosophers' Tradition*, 30.

32. *The Olde Daunce*, 1.

Part II

Literary Contexts

15 | The classical background

Helen Cooper

Medieval writers were very conscious of living in the shadow of the classical world, its literature, and its learning. 'The Philosopher' meant Aristotle; Virgil and Ovid were the greatest poets. The vernacular languages of Europe, the languages actually spoken by ordinary people, developed literary traditions of their own, but any writer of serious intent or ambition knew that the greatest poetic tradition was represented by the classics. Chaucer, for all his humour and self-deprecation, was a very serious poet.

The ancient world feeds into his poetry in three distinct ways. He uses it as a fictional or quasi-historical setting, for stories set in the pagan past. It offered him an abundance of narratives, information, and aphorisms on which he draws in his poetry. And thirdly, it helped him to define his own role and status as a poet, by providing a corpus of literature that carried authoritative status, but whose authority he increasingly challenged. There is inevitably some overlap between those three areas. Stories with classical settings may well also have classical sources; and one of the foremost ways in which Chaucer mounts his challenges to established authority is by retelling narratives deriving from Virgil or Ovid in new ways and from different angles. Originality of material was not highly valued in the Middle Ages; retelling stories was equivalent to our own adapting a book for a film, or to literary criticism—a way of making old material more immediately interesting, more expressive of the new author's and audience's concerns. Chaucer describes the composition of new works, in the *Parliament of Fowls*, as being like harvesting new crops from old fields (22–5), and you do not always need to sow the same crop. He does not take old stories on trust just because they carry the authority of the ancient world with them. He is often explicit about how different versions of the same story may undermine each other's authority, or about the nature of his own disagreements with his sources. These challenges cumulatively amount to a claim for his own status as a poet in the same great tradition as those poets with whom he engages, and as a poet carrying comparable authority. It is an extraordinary claim for any medieval writer to make, especially one working outside the learned discourses of Latin. English was a language that was marginal in every sense, spoken on the very edge of the known world and not understood beyond that, and even within England broken up into a variety of local dialects and subject to rapid temporal change. Yet Chaucer uses that medium of English to make direct contact with the great classical authors, and to create the first literature in English that can stand comparison with them.

Such an account probably seems counter-intuitive. This is not how Chaucer most often invites us to think of him. The self-image he propagates most lovingly develops out of the narrators of the early dream visions, who have to be presented as simple-minded in order that they may receive the larger message of the poem that he himself, as invisible author, wants to get across to his audience. From there he moves on to the inadequate narrator of *Troilus and Criseyde*, with no personal experience of loving and no privileged knowledge, who is at the mercy of what his source author does or does not record. The *Canterbury Tales* gives us the transcriber who can do no more than give a word-for-word repetition of what the other pilgrims say, and who writes himself definitively out of the competition for the prize for the best story with 'Sir Thopas' and 'Melibee'. A Chaucer who not only knows his Ovid (the favourite classical poet throughout the Middle Ages) and his Virgil (the acknowledged master-poet of the Western literary tradition), but who is prepared to question their authority and to compare his own role as poet to theirs, is radically at odds with the self-presentation that his works push to the fore. The evidence is nonetheless there, and is compelling; and it invites the reading of Chaucer's classical background in new, and more interesting, ways than has been customary.

The study of Chaucer and the classics has been marked over the past few decades by a greater concern to see what he himself was doing with what he knew, especially in the light of modern theory and its destabilizing of established critical categories. Earlier scholarship, much of which has been extended rather than superseded, sometimes offered broad parallels between Chaucer and ancient authors. It noted, for instance, the urbane mindset common to him and Ovid; it established the sources Chaucer was using; and nineteenth-century critics in particular, with their own rigorously classical training, would note how he misinterprets those sources or reads them in non-classical ways. It is certainly true that Chaucer does read them in non-classical ways, and especially as the Victorians understood the classics; but his reading of them is not typically medieval either. It is, for instance, marked by a distinct lack of piety towards them, a much more questioning attitude than is taken by most medieval authors, or indeed by most classical scholars. The increasing readiness among critics to admit both that Chaucer was quite exceptionally intelligent, and that scepticism may well be a better critical tool than a searching after truth (even a medieval version of truth), reveals a richness investing his use of the classics much greater than was for long suspected. Advances in critical theory, medieval as well as modern, have speeded this greater appreciation, not least work on the nature of authorship, and the rise of feminism. Both come into play extensively in understanding how Chaucer responds to classical authors.

Chaucer's classics

The canon of classical works familiar in the Middle Ages was rather different from what a modern scholar would define as important. Greek was almost unknown in western Europe in the Middle Ages, so it was Latin that dominated the classical tradition. The few Greek authors who were studied were read in Latin translation. The best known were a handful of philosophers, with Aristotle foremost among them; Plato came very much second. Even their writings were known only partially, and some works now thought of as being of key literary interest (such as Aristotle's *Poetics*) were in effect unknown. After those came some practical writers, notably Ptolemy, who wrote the standard work on astronomy, and the physician Galen, whose writings dominated medieval medicine. Chaucer knew enough about all these writers to cite them, but there is little evidence that he read their works extensively or in first-hand detail. Knowledge of Greek literary texts was almost non-existent, to Chaucer or anyone else in western Europe. Homer was a familiar name, but he was a name without a text.

The story of the Trojan War was nonetheless immensely popular, a popularity encouraged by the belief that it was the dispersal of the last surviving Trojans, led by Aeneas, from the burning city that had led to the founding, first of Rome, then of France and Britain and other Western nations. Although there was some keen interest in this account of the origins of Britain in fourteenth-century England, Chaucer makes almost no mention of it (just a passing allusion in the 'Complaint of Chaucer to his Purse', 22), but he was very interested in Troy itself. Medieval scholarship on the city was primarily grounded on two works that were believed to be eyewitness accounts of the war (and therefore more reliable than Homer) but which are in fact essentially historical novels. One, by 'Dictys the Cretan', was written from the Greek point of view; the other, by 'Dares the Phrygian', from the Trojan.[1] Latin versions of them appeared in the fourth and fifth centuries respectively, both claiming to be translations of Greek originals (apparently true in the case of Dictys, though without the antiquity to which it also laid claim), and both were widely known throughout the Middle Ages. Chaucer appears to have done his homework in these works before writing his *Troilus*, or at least in Dares, which he may have read in the better-known twelfth-century retelling by Joseph of Exeter. The story of Aeneas' founding of Rome was given its fullest development in Latin in Virgil's *Aeneid*,[2] a work that was not only read in the Middle Ages but that was provided with an allegorical commentary that made its stories of gods and heroes compatible with Christian ethics. Chaucer had at least some familiarity with the *Aeneid*, but what interests him about it is more the story itself and the status that Virgil carried—the nature of his authority—than the commentary or any allegorical meanings. As with almost all his encounters with classical literature, and indeed contemporary literature, he is much more attracted by narrative and its possibilities than by moral abstractions.

The same preference shows in his reading of Ovid, whose works he knew much better and uses more extensively. Virgil was the most admired of the classical poets in the Middle Ages (that is the main reason why Dante takes him for his guide in the earlier part of his *Divine Comedy*), but Ovid was the best loved. His *Metamorphoses* is a collection of all the best of the classical myths, and was therefore both a useful reference book and a wonderful quarry for good stories.[3] The title refers to the fact that each story tells of how someone or something turns into something else: the crow, originally white, acquires black feathers; Philomela and Procne turn respectively into a nightingale and a swallow; the blood of Pyramus and Thisbe for ever stains the fruit of the mulberry tree. The agent of change is most often a pagan god, and the work therefore presented something of a problem for the Christian Middle Ages. It was accordingly itself made the subject of metamorphosis by being given a series of Christian commentaries that transformed it into an allegorical compendium of moral and theological wisdom. Chaucer probably had access to at least two of these commentaries, one (the fourteenth-century commentary of Pierre Bersuire) in Latin, the other (the slightly earlier *Ovide moralisé*) in French, but he rarely lets them impinge on the stories he borrows. He has his own agendas to follow when he is retelling or alluding to Ovidian narratives, and those do not normally square with the agendas of the commentators. If he used the *Ovide moralisé*, it is because it made Ovid's stories more linguistically accessible, not for the sake of its allegories. His most extensive use of Bersuire draws not on his commentaries on the tales but on the preliminary chapter describing the pagan gods, which he adapts for the descriptions of the temples in the 'Knight's Tale' (1918–2088). These descriptions show that his interest in Ovidian narrative also extends to mythography, the branch of knowledge concerned with developing a Christian understanding of the basis of pagan myth, and the gods in particular. This was a highly developed art in the Middle Ages, and its influence is evident in Chaucer's work even though he never explores it in its more arcane detail.[4] It overlaps with astrology, the whole question of the influence of the stars and planets on the earth. Although there was no longer any belief in the pagan gods as divine beings in the Middle Ages, the planets carried their names (Venus, Mars, Saturn, Jupiter, Mercury), and were believed to have a powerful influence over the earth that could easily be personified back into figures of the gods themselves (for more on astrology, see Chapter 10).

In the *House of Fame*, Chaucer calls Ovid 'Venus clerk', Venus' secretary (1487), and the epithet would not have surprised anyone in the Middle Ages. Venus was still a personification to conjure with, representing the power of desire and the astrological force that impelled it. The *Ars amatoria* and *Remedia amoris*, Ovid's writings on love—or more properly, sex—were widely read, and seem on occasion to have been taken rather more seriously than they would be by most modern readers. It was also possible to read them as a warning about the wiles of women and how to circumvent them, and Chaucer's most direct citation of them is in that context, in the 'Wife of Bath's Prologue' (680)—a citation that could be based just on a knowledge of their existence rather than on familiarity with the texts themselves. Many of the stories Chaucer takes from Ovid touch on matters of love, but the two love-treatises contribute little or nothing directly to his own writings (their larger influence on medieval views on love is a contested topic beyond the scope of this chapter). The work of Chaucer's that draws most comprehensively on Ovid is the *Legend of Good Women*, a series of stories of classical heroines abandoned by their lovers. He took the idea and many of the stories from the *Heroides*, a similar series that Ovid wrote in the form of first-person letters from the abused women to the men who had mistreated them.

Apart from Virgil and Ovid, the Latin works and authors with whom Chaucer was most familiar are much less widely read now than they were in the Middle Ages. The 'Nine books of memorable deeds and sayings of the Romans', compiled around AD 35 by Valerius Maximus, provided him, as it provided many other medieval writers, with another good source of illustrative stories. Cicero, for Chaucer, meant just the ending of his *De re publica* (the only section of the work known in the Middle Ages), which recounts the dream of Scipio about the littleness of the world and how one should act in one's brief time within it; it was preserved for succeeding centuries in the fifth-century commentary on it by Macrobius, which contains a useful summary of classical dream theory. Chaucer summarizes the dream in the opening of the *Parliament of Fowls*, and he was clearly acquainted with Macrobius too, though he treats the original story and the commentary material as separate entities. Chaucer's other citations of Cicero usually come to him ready embedded in other texts, notably the thirteenth-century treatise on prudence (practical wisdom) by Albertanus of Brescia, which Chaucer translates as his tale of 'Melibee'. The same is true of Seneca, valued in the Middle Ages primarily for his moral wisdom, who is likewise generously quoted in the 'Melibee', though Chaucer may also have had some first-hand knowledge of his work. Also highly valued for practical wisdom was Cato—though we know, as Chaucer did not, that the *Distichs* of Cato that he cites so often is in fact not by Cato at all; it is a collection of moral aphorisms dating from around AD 200, which became a favourite medieval school text. Chaucer does seem to know the *Distichs* directly, probably from his own education.

The notes in many editions of Chaucer's works list numerous other classical authors, so many as to give the impression that he must have been immensely widely read— impossibly widely read, indeed, given the comparative scarcity of manuscripts of many of these writers, and Chaucer's own demanding employment schedule. A great many of these further references in fact came to him second-hand, through medieval retellings or compendia or encyclopedias, as is illustrated by the 'Melibee'. His knowledge of Livy and Suetonius seems likely to be entirely filtered through the French *Roman de la Rose*. Other references and allusions may well have come to him not through reading at all, but through conversation with friends and colleagues: men such as Ralph Strode, one of the dedicatees of *Troilus* (see *TC* 5. 1857), who was an eminent London lawyer and also (unless, as seems unlikely, there were two men of the same name) a fellow of Merton College, Oxford. Chaucer was nonetheless quite exceptionally well read for an Englishman who lacked, so far as we know, any formal academic training. He did not himself go to university, and despite the story current in the sixteenth century that he had been a student at one of the Inns of Court, there is no supporting evidence. It might be expected that someone who had acquired all his classical knowledge on no more than the basis of a grammar school education, if that was what he had, and his own personal reading, might show anxious deference towards the authors from whom he borrowed. In fact, Chaucer shows the exact opposite.

Ovid without metamorphosis

There have been hundreds of retellings of stories from the *Metamorphoses* over the course of English literature, from Spenser and Shakespeare to Ted Hughes. In any account of the reception of the work in England, Chaucer should figure large, for historical primacy, quantity, and quality. Yet in one respect he is deeply uncharacteristic: he avoids metamorphosis itself almost entirely.

The story of Ceyx and Alcione, retold in the *Book of the Duchess*, is typical. Ceyx is drowned when his ship founders; his wife, desperate for his return, prays to Juno to show her what has happened to him. Juno commands Morpheus, the god of sleep, to take up the drowned corpse and to present himself in that form in dream to the sleeping Alcione, to tell her that he is dead. She, overwhelmed with grief, dies 'within the thridde morwe' (214). And that is all: there is nothing of Ovid's coda, the coda that qualifies the story for inclusion in the *Metamorphoses*, about how the lovers are turned into waterbirds (the halcyon is the kingfisher) and have a kind of afterlife in altered form. The 'Legend of Philomel', in the *Legend of Good Women*, ends with the lament of Philomel and her sister Procne, but it says nothing about their transformation into the nightingale and the swallow. Pyramus and Thisbe, in Ovid, is an aetiological myth—a just-so story—about how the mulberry became red; in the *Legend* it stops at being a story of unhappy love. The only time Chaucer gives a full account of a metamorphosis, it concerns not a human being, but a bird: the 'Manciple's Tale' is the story of how a swan-white bird with a voice sweeter than the nightingale is condemned to becoming the raucous black creature familiar all over Europe as the crow.

The avoidance of human metamorphosis is so consistent as to indicate that Chaucer had some radical objection to the whole idea. It is always dangerous to try to read the mind of a great writer, but various possibilities suggest themselves. One is that his objections were rational: metamorphosis does not happen. It is over the edge of fantasy, and Chaucer is more interested in what is or could be true, in verisimilitude if not fact. Another is that it conflicted with his Christian faith, though he never hints at that in the way that he does when he invites questions as to the destination of the souls of the pagan. A third is humanist as well as Christian: that belief in the dignity of the human was an immovable principle for him. God had created Adam and Eve to be superior to the animals, with a soul as well as a body, and Chaucer is not going to accept the reduction of the human to beast, let alone to tree or flower. He may allow birds to speak, but degradation downwards on the scale of creation is a different matter.

It is impossible to adjudicate between those three motives, and any or all might be true. Ovid may be one of the most fertile of his source authors so far as stories are concerned, but Chaucer will follow his own judgement, or his own principles, concerning how much he takes over. He does, however, allow metamorphosis in one single area. This is the description of the temple of Diana in the 'Knight's Tale'. Diana is not only the goddess who is the direct agent of metamorphosis in a number of Ovid's tales; she is also, as the moon, the astrological body that presides over change. Her mutability is accordingly represented by a full set of Ovidian transformations:

> Ther saugh I how woful Calistopee [Callisto],
> Whan that Diane agreved was with here,
> Was turned from a womman til a bere . . .
> Ther saugh I Dane [Daphne], yturned til a tree . . .
> Ther saugh I Attheon [Actaeon] an hert ymaked. (2056–65)

The iconography of the temples represents one of Chaucer's most extensive engagements with medieval scholarship on the pagan gods and their adaptation into astrological learning, and he does not give them a good press. Emelye may pray to Diana as the goddess of chastity, as Palamon prays to the goddess of love and Arcite to the god of war; but the temples offer a different version of what they stand for. Venus presides over folly and rape and pimping; Mars over any irrational violence, the sow eating the baby, the carter run over by his own cart, 'The smylere with the knyf under the cloke' (1999). Diana might seem to offer less scope for such negative representation, but in fact she lays a claim to being the most sinister of them all: the goddess who can deprive humankind of its humanity. That may be the central motif of Ovid's greatest work, but it is not one that Chaucer will make central to his own poetry.

Classical settings

A number of Chaucer's works are set in the classical, pagan world, foremost among them being *Troilus and Criseyde* and the 'Knight's Tale'. A classical setting does not, however, mean that he is working from an ancient source. For all his research in Dares and Dictys as part of his preparation for the writing of *Troilus*, the work itself is an adaptation of a poem by his near-contemporary Boccaccio. The 'Knight's Tale' is headed in some manuscripts by a quotation from the Latin epic poet Statius, who had written about the war in Thebes that provides the starting point for the tale, but here too Boccaccio serves as its actual source.[5] Yet no study of Chaucer's sense of the classics would be complete without a consideration of how he uses the ancient world as a setting, even if he is not working directly from classical authors. The setting matters because in these poems he makes a striking attempt to re-create the mindset of his pre-Christian characters.[6] When other medieval writers tell stories from the pagan past, they usually give their characters thoughts and actions indistinguishable from Christian and contemporary ones (as Chaucer himself sometimes does elsewhere: the paganism of the Physician's or Franklin's Tales is much more half-hearted or occasional). No one had the archaeological knowledge to re-create the material world of ancient Troy or Athens, but the mentality of the ancient world could be accessed through its writings, and so re-created by those who made a concerned attempt to do so. For Chaucer, this is not just a matter of historical plausibility; it is much more urgent than that. He uses the pagan past as a point outside his own age of faith, from which to ask questions of a kind normally disallowed.

The most compelling process of questioning occurs within the 'Knight's Tale', and is put into the mouths of the imprisoned cousins, who fall in love with the same woman, and who are the victims of those gods portrayed in the temples. Although Arcite is readier to take the initiative than Palamon, and (fatally) looks to means more than to ends, the cousins are to all intents and purposes emotionally and ethically indistinguishable—much more so than in Boccaccio's *Teseida*. Apart from the legalistic point that one of them saw her first, there is no reason why one lover should succeed in winning Emelye and the other not. The way Chaucer sets up the story thus ensures that justice cannot be served—poetic justice or divine justice or any sense of a fair outcome. The sense of injustice is intensified when Arcite wins the tournament for her hand, but is then fatally wounded in a fall from his horse. Palamon gets the girl, and the happy ending of marriage; Arcite ends up in his 'colde grave | Allone, withouten any compaignye' (2778–9). His accident is described within the tale as being not fortuitous, but the result of the scheming of the pagan gods—the planetary gods Mars and Venus and Saturn, representing violence, desire, and devouring time. Chaucer's Christian readers believed that prayer could help to frustrate the influence of the planets, and that a virtuous life would help the soul to gain entry to heaven; but neither of those comforts is available to the characters within the tale. They see themselves as victims of a universe that is at best arbitrary and at worst malign, where the divine order does not promise any kind of just reward for the innocent or the good:

> What governance is in this prescience,
> That giltelees tormenteth innocence? (1313–14)

Everyone on earth wants to be happy—wants to engage in the pursuit of happiness, to use the language of the American Declaration of Independence— but there is no way to tell what the best way to happiness is, and every attempt to find it is thwarted:

> We faren as he that dronke is as a mous.
> A dronke man woot wel he hath an hous,
> But he noot which the righte wey is thider,
> And to a dronke man the wey is slider.
> And certes, in this world so faren we;
> We seken faste after felicitee,
> But we goon wrong ful often, trewely. (1261–7)

The early Christian writer Boethius (see Chapter 9) had set out to answer such problems through the exercise of reason and philosophy rather than revelation and faith; and because of that angling of his material away from Christian knowledge,

Chaucer can allow his pagans some of the same insights. Theseus, at the end of the 'Knight's Tale', accordingly insists that there is a benevolent order in the universe. It is, however, an assertion made in the teeth of the evidence so far as the story is concerned. Justice, whether poetic or cosmic, is not served. A Christian setting for, or treatment of, the story would have been able to predict heaven for its dying protagonist; but as a pagan, Arcite has nothing beyond the grave to look forward to, since active Christian faith, or, for those who lived before Christ, active hope in the future coming of Christ, was taken as a prerequisite of salvation. There was a debate in the fourteenth century as to what happened to the souls of righteous pagans, but it is far from clear that a love for Emelye so passionate as to override all considerations of friendship would count as virtue. Chaucer avoids saying what the final resting place for Arcite's soul might be—indeed he makes a point of not saying anything on the topic (2809–14)—and so the injustice of the world, the lack of any providential ordering, dominates the tone of the story to the end.

Very much the same thing happens in *Troilus and Criseyde*. Troilus' soul is allowed to ascend 'blisfully' to the outer edge of the physical cosmos (5. 1808–9), but then it is taken off to where Mercury, the god in charge of the dead, chooses to take it, and we are given no idea as to where that might be. Certainly no fourteenth-century reader could have imagined that it *necessarily* meant the eternal 'felicite | That is in hevene above' (5. 1818–9), even though Chaucer's phrasing is careful not to exclude such a possibility. The last insight we are given into Troilus' soul is his condemnation of earthly impercipience, in respect of both grief and love (5. 1821–4): an impercipience that prevents humankind, and especially pagan humankind (including, as the poem has shown, himself), from perceiving eternal truth from within this world. Chaucer concludes his poem by urging his Christian readers to do better, to love God above all else, since everything earthly 'passeth soone as floures faire' (5. 1841). But that is not an option that has been available to the pagan Troilus, who has loved Criseyde with a single-mindedness of heroic proportions, like Shakespeare's Romeo. It is easy, for a modern as for a medieval audience, to say that Troilus ought not to have loved her so intensely, though medieval readers would cite God or distrust of women as a reason where modern readers might cite common sense or a more general cynicism about ideals; but, as with Romeo, there would be no story worth telling without that intensity of passion. Chaucer exploits the implications of the classical setting of the story to a degree no previous medieval writer had done, to give the fullest space to his love. That generosity of treatment in turn opens up questions as to the status of human love in a pagan world in which God cannot be perceived, or in a Christian world where the wholehearted commitment that makes it so remarkable is condemned. Here too, Boethius is allowed space—and more space than in the 'Knight's Tale' is given to the perceptions of Philosophy about the love that binds the universe (3.1744–71)—but in many ways those insights only increase the bewilderment as to how those general principles operate in the individual case, or why they may fail to operate at all.

Christianity had an answer, though it was an answer that disallowed the question: God does, by definition, rule all things for the best, and it is an article of faith to believe that. Arcite and Troilus, with no access to that faith or obligation to its tenets, can question those principles. Chaucer, as an author writing from within an age of faith, can use classical settings to ask just such questions through the mouths of his characters. Given the weight of the works in which he does so, and the ways in which he adapts Boccaccio to express that questioning, it seems indeed that he actively chooses classical settings so as to enable him to pose the questions. The ancient world gives him a place to stand outside his own historical time and place, and it is not an altogether comfortable spot to choose.

The nature of authority

The great classical authors were 'auctors', authorities: writers who, for all their lack of Christianity, wrote with special insight and special ethical weight. The term carried with it an implication that they should be treated with deference. It had long been recognized, however, that authorities could be made to mean what you wanted them to mean—authority had a waxen nose, as the twelfth-century Latin writer Alan of Lille put it, so you could bend it whichever way you liked. Chaucer is much too intelligent a writer simply to reproduce authority on trust. Many of his most explicit citations of authorities call attention to how self-serving is the use to which they may be put. As a narrative poet, he is very conscious of the degree of fictionality in any retelling of a story, however authoritative it may be claimed to be, and of the kinds of agendas that even the most authoritative authors may be promoting. That perception cuts two ways: it reduces the authority inherent in *auctors*, but it enables him to claim an authority comparable with theirs.

Chaucer rarely cites authorities for what he is saying in his own voice. If he wants to speak authoritatively, as author, he normally lets such statements speak for themselves, without classical endorsement. The most notable exception is his use of Cicero's 'Dream of Scipio' at the opening of the *Parliament of Fowls*, where its representation of the ordering of the macrocosm—the place of the earth in the universe, the rewards for good and ill behaviour—serves to frame the microcosmic action that is to take place within the narrator's own dream, and which is concerned with the continuation of the created world through the natural processes of the birds' mating. Although the use of Cicero is much more direct and unmediated than is usual for Chaucer's borrowings from the classics, there is still debate as to quite what he meant by juxtaposing the two dreams, Scipio's and his own dreamer's; and elsewhere, classical authority is still less likely to be authoritative. It is exceptional for him to use it to confirm either the substance or the ethics of his own writing. The densest citation of classical and other maxims that come with their footnotes attached occurs in his tale ('treatise' would be a better word) of 'Melibee', and although he ascribes that to his pilgrim self, it is in fact a close translation of Albertanus' widely known Latin work, which comes complete with all its quotations already in place. They are spoken, moreover, by Prudence, who is as close as Chaucer ever comes in the *Tales* to a fully allegorical figure: what the 'Melibee' is saying is that action that is prudent should follow all the precepts that the treatise supplies. When other tellers or characters within the tales cite authorities, their bending of them for their own purposes, or their refusal to accept what they say, is often explicit. 'Straw for thy Senek . . .!' is January's response to his friend's quotation of Seneca (or, more accurately, the *Distichs* of Cato) as advice against marrying ('MerT' 1567). Jankyn, the Wife of Bath's fifth husband, has a fondness for lecturing his wife for misbehaviour with exemplary stories from Valerius Maximus ('WBP' 642). He also owns a 'Book of Wicked Wives' that contains some classical texts alongside patristic and medieval ones, and he reads them out to Alison in order to needle her. The book includes Ovid's *Ars*, but its major item is an intemperate condemnation of women by the Greek Theophrastus, transmitted to the Middle Ages in the Latin version embedded in a treatise against marriage by St Jerome. It is a text on which the Wife has very clear views, and they are not those of the saint. Chaucer's views are not so easy to fathom, but he is certainly not taking either classical or saintly authority on trust, and he delights in stirring the brew.

Perhaps the strangest of all Chaucer's uses of authority is the Lollius whom he names as a source for *Troilus*, since Lollius never in fact existed. There is some evidence that the name might have been thought to be that of a real classical author, but Chaucer certainly knew that he had no access to any such writings. He continually makes reference to his *auctor*, his authoritative source, throughout the work, and implies that this source was writing close to the events he recounts, as if he were a classical writer, even though his actual source was Boccaccio. Furthermore, he appeals to his *auctor* much the most often when he is making things up, when he has no source at all. Lollius is actually named only twice in the whole poem (1. 394, 5. 1653), and the first of those occasions is when Chaucer is translating an ultra-fashionable sonnet of Petrarch's, when there can be no question of his not knowing precisely what he was doing. By putting Petrarch's words into Troilus' mouth and so firmly ascribing them to Lollius, Chaucer dares his audience not to believe him. Here, classical authority becomes a rhetorical fiction, a strategy for making effects, to be called on for specific local purposes within the poem.

There is one work in which Chaucer does not just draw on classical authors, but discusses the nature of their authority; and that is the *House of Fame*—a work that may, contrary to its common dating in the 1370s, have been written in 1384, at around the time when Chaucer was completing *Troilus*.[7] The third and final book of the poem is set in the palace of the goddess Fame, and the *auctors* of the past are represented standing on pillars and supporting the fame of the people they wrote about—Virgil supports 'The fame of Pius Eneas', for instance (1485), 'pius', attentive to his duties, being Virgil's standard epithet for Aeneas. Yet Chaucer makes explicit that their accounts are not reliable: they record only what Fame allows to be put on record, and it is completely arbitrary whether or not that is true. A long succession of people come to the goddess asking for fame, and she gives them good or ill repute, or indeed condemns them to oblivion, quite regardless of whether they have done anything to deserve it. So it is perhaps not surprising that Lollius should figure among the writers bearing up the fame of Troy (1468), as a writer who has the credit for existing without actually having done so. Even the genuine writers have their authority undermined, since they are quarrelling among themselves: Homer is accused of lying on the grounds of his being too favourable to the Greeks (1476–80)—Britain, it will be remembered, having been founded by the descendants of the Trojans. The Trojans, in this particular dispute, are therefore 'us', the Greeks are 'them'.

The most extensive dispute between authorities, however, occurs between Virgil and Ovid. They stand side by side in the hall of pillars; but they have already figured as opposed in the first book of the work, which consists of a retelling of the *Aeneid*, and in particular the story of Dido. That it is Virgil's own poem that is at issue, and not just the story of Aeneas, is made explicit by Chaucer's paraphrase of its opening lines: Virgil's 'I sing of arms and the man' becomes

> I wol now synge, yif I kan,
> The armes and also the man . . . (143–4)

and carries on for a few lines in similarly recognizable vein. The story is engraved on the wall of the temple of Venus within the dream that constitutes the bulk of the *House of Fame*, and serves as the keynote for all that follows. This is a poem about the nature of poetic authority, as represented by the master-poet of the Latin tradition—the only authoritative tradition that Chaucer and his readers knew. That it is not going to be simply a repetition of Virgil emerges as soon as the story reaches Dido.[8] In his travels across the Mediterranean after fleeing from Troy, Aeneas had come to Carthage, where Dido was queen. She fell in love with him, they had an affair, and he abandoned her in order to seek his destiny in Italy. He did so, Virgil claimed, at the instruction of the gods—a self-serving male excuse for infidelity if ever there was one, as other writers noted. One of the first to do so was Ovid, in the *Heroides*, and Chaucer accordingly switches sources part-way through to remind his readers that the piety of 'pius Eneas' was perhaps not all that it was cracked up to be:

> Ther may be under godlyhed
> Kevered many a shrewed vice. (274–5)

By the end of his account of Dido, Chaucer is explicitly encouraging his reader to check out Ovid's account instead (379). The basic facts of the stories may be the same, but the interpretation given them by the two authorities is very different—and Chaucer is unquestionably on the side of Ovid, and Dido.

Exactly the same thing happens again when he tells the story of Dido in the *Legend of Good Women*. It begins with a resounding paean to Virgil:

> Glorye and honour, Virgil Mantoan,
> Be to thy name! and I shal, as I can,
> Folwe thy lanterne, as thow gost byforn . . . (924–6)

So far so good; but the next line blows the whole claim of following Virgil apart, as Aeneas is represented not as following the instructions of the gods but as breaking his vows to her:

> How Eneas to Dido was forsworn. (927)

That is not how his master-poet puts it, so it is perhaps no surprise that the final line of the legend urges us to 'rede Ovyde' as a supplement (1367), and to get Dido's own view on the matter. Such a lack of respect towards Virgil did not pass without attracting comment. Gavin Douglas, the great Scottish poet who translated the *Aeneid* some 130 years after Chaucer was writing, cites the 'forswearing' couplet in his prologue and scolds him for his lack of deference. He declares that Chaucer meant merely to reprove Aeneas, and the fact that the way he does it also impugns the 'prynce of poetis', Virgil himself, is a regrettable mistake, a consequence of Chaucer's being too much 'womanis frend'.[9] Chaucer's own formulations suggest that he meant exactly what he said, and that he thought Virgil to be too much women's enemy. But as a poet himself, he has reasons of his own for writing across Virgil rather than in line with him.

Chaucer's poetic claims

When Aeneas first betrays Dido in the *House of Fame*, and she realizes what he has done, Chaucer starts to recount the lament that she spoke; but after just a few lines, he interrupts himself, to cite his source. And it is not what we might expect:

> In suche wordes gan to pleyne
> Dydo of hir grete peyne,
> As me mette redely—
> Non other auctour alegge I. (311–14)

The statement in that last line, 'I claim no *other* authority', insists that he is himself an *auctour*, an authority in his own right, every bit as good as Virgil or Ovid. After all, this is a lament spoken in soliloquy, with no mention of any listeners—perhaps even spoken silently, in her own mind. There is no way that any authority can know what she said or thought, and so Chaucer's invention is just as truthful, or just as likely to be true, as anyone else's. Finally—and this too becomes one of the larger themes of the whole poem—he alone is responsible for what he writes:

> what I drye, or what I thynke,
> I wil myselven al hyt drynke,
> Certeyn, for the more part,
> As fer forth as I kan myn art. (1879–82)

Similarly, it is his own 'thought' that writes everything he claims to be dreaming (523)—even his rewriting of Virgil. He is, in other words, claiming a kind of equality with Virgil, as a writer who generates his own poetry. Chaucer may follow him, as Virgil himself drew on Homer, but they all equally follow their own poetic inspiration. It is no coincidence that Chaucer is the first writer in English to call on the Muses, and that he does so in this poem (520–2).

Chaucer seems to make a similar claim for his status as poet later in the work too, in his depiction of the Hall of Fame with the writers on the pillars. The writers who are listed as upholding the fame of Troy are Dares and Dictys; the medieval Latin writer Guido delle Colonne; the enigmatic Lollius and the lying Homer; and 'Englysshe Gaufride', 'Gaufride' being derived from *Galfridus*, the Latin form for Geoffrey (1466–70). Commentators are almost universal in identifying this last as Geoffrey of Monmouth, the twelfth-century writer who had largely invented the story of the founding of the nations of western Europe by the descendants of Aeneas. He does not, however, tell the story of Troy; and he is not 'English' in any identifiable sense—he was a Norman from Wales who wrote in Latin. A second possibility would be the rhetorical writer Geoffrey of Vinsauf, who was English, and whose works Chaucer knew; but those works, at least as they survive, contain even less about Troy than Geoffrey of Monmouth's. Furthermore, every single one of Chaucer's other usages of the word 'English' refers to the language. By 1384, if that dating is indeed right, there was just one Geoffrey who had written the story of Troy in English, and that was Chaucer himself. The *Troilus*, he seems to be suggesting, qualifies him for a place alongside Dares and Dictys and Homer, Ovid, and Virgil.

It was not a new idea to him that he might be a writer who could compare with the greatest of the classical authors. The first, very quiet, suggestion comes in his earliest original poem, the *Book of the Duchess*. This again gives a much more self-assured representation of himself as poet than has usually been assumed. In it, he makes himself the spokesman—the lament-speaker—for one of the very greatest princes in the land, John of Gaunt, duke of Lancaster, after the death of the wife he seems to have loved exceptionally dearly. Whether or not the duke commissioned the poem, writing on such a subject in such a way is a very tall order, and Chaucer fulfils it magnificently. He constructs the work as a series of frames—of narrator, of Ovidian narrative (it is here that he reads, and retells, the story of Ceyx and Alcione), of dream, of the reminiscences of the mourning knight as he re-creates in his mind the loveliness of the lady he has lost—so as to focus at the centre on an evocation of the woman as she lived. The immediate models for the poem are French, though Chaucer rethinks them radically. What is most interesting in the classical context is that John of Gaunt is personified twice over in the poem: once as the grieving lover, once as the emperor Octavian, the great lord whose possessions are the same as Gaunt's own (1314–19; the 'king' is the royal emperor, not the knight), and whose public life continues even through the devastation of his private emotions. And Octavian was the name of Virgil's patron, the man for whom the *Aeneid* was written, and indeed whom the *Metamorphoses* was ultimately designed to celebrate. It may be a very understated way for Chaucer to invite the duke to assume a comparable role as patron with regard to himself; but it also casts Chaucer himself as a second Virgil, a second Ovid.

The moment when Chaucer claims a role for himself most directly as a poet in the great Latin tradition comes at the end of *Troilus*. He sends his own 'litel bok' out into the world with an injunction to it to

> subgit be to alle poesye;
> And kis the steppes where as thow seest pace
> Virgile, Ovide, Omer, Lucan, and Stace. (5. 1790–2)

These are the great classical narrative poets, and Chaucer aligns his own work, his own great classical narrative, with theirs. It is phrased as an act of humility and homage, but it carries a strong suggestion that he himself can make the sixth in the line of poets. The idea is reinforced by the fact that the 'sixth of six' motif had already been used both by Dante, in the *Divine Comedy*, and by Boccaccio. For all the formulation of subjection, this is a very different self-representation from the inadequate narrator Chaucer has drawn in the rest of the poem. These lines serve as a reminder of how much his self-deprecation is rhetorically strategic—part indeed of the brilliance of the work. With *Troilus*, English poetry takes its place in the great tradition of European literature derived from the classics.[10]

It is a claim of astonishing self-assurance. Chaucer rapidly came to be regarded as the founding father of English literature, not because he was the first English poet (he comes almost halfway through English literary history), but because he was the first named poet to whom later writers could look up, and from whom later poetry and narrative springs in a continuing and unbroken tradition. At the time he was writing, however, and especially given his choice of such an out-of-the-way parochial language, the claim must have threatened to seem hubristic in the extreme: Virgil, Ovid, and me. Yet the very degree to which Chaucer reached back to the classics and touched hands with them made the claim plausible, even as he was writing it; and it has more than stood the test of time.

FURTHER READING

Baswell, Christopher, *Virgil in Medieval England: Figuring the 'Aeneid' from the Twelfth Century to Chaucer* (Cambridge: Cambridge University Press, 1995). A dense, scholarly account of the circulation and reception of the *Aeneid* in England, including a chapter on Chaucer.

Calabrese, Michael A., *Chaucer's Ovidian Arts of Love* (Gainesville: University Press of Florida, 1994). A survey of the whole of Ovid's works and life down to his exile in comparison with Chaucer's career down to the 'Retraction', with particular emphasis on *Troilus* and the Wife of Bath. Thought-provoking, even if its argument tends to exceed the evidence.

Comparetti, Domenico, *Virgil in the Middle Ages*, trans. E. F. M. Benecke (repr. Princeton: Princeton University Press, 1996). Although first published in 1872, this book remains the best single introduction to its subject. It includes not only the Virgil of the scholars, but the magician

Virgil of popular tradition. Its area of interest is continental Europe rather than England, but it is still a good way into understanding Chaucer's Virgil.

Fleming, John V., *Classical Imitation and Interpretation in Chaucer's 'Troilus'* (Lincoln, Nebr.: University of Nebraska University Press, 1990). Fleming argues that Chaucer goes to great lengths to imagine and reconstruct 'a spiritually foreign ancient culture' in order to condemn its idolatry.

Fyler, John, *Chaucer and Ovid* (New Haven: Yale University Press, 1979). A thoughtful extended comparison between Chaucer and Ovid in the light of their long-recognized affinities of temperament.

Martindale, Charles, (ed.), *Ovid Renewed: Ovidian Influences on Literature and Art from the Middle Ages to the Twentieth Century* (Cambridge: Cambridge University Press, 1988). Contains a number of essays on Ovid in the Middle Ages, including one by Helen Cooper specifically on Chaucer.

Minnis, A. J., *Chaucer and Pagan Antiquity* (Cambridge: Brewer, 1982). A study of Chaucer's engagement with the ancient world, as history, theology, and philosophy, primarily in *Troilus* and the 'Knight's Tale'.

Rand, Edward Kennard, *Ovid and his Influence* (New York: Cooper Square Publishers, 1964). A short and user-friendly introduction to the afterlife of Ovid.

Wetherbee, Winthrop P., *Chaucer and the Poets: An Essay on 'Troilus and Criseyde'* (Ithaca, NY: Cornell University Press, 1984). A study of how Chaucer responded to Ovid, Virgil, and Statius.

Windeatt, B. A. *Oxford Guides to Chaucer: 'Troilus and Criseyde'* (Oxford: Clarendon Press, 1992). A helpful and reliable guide to all aspects of the poem, including its relation to Dares and Dictys and the classical tradition.

NOTES

1. They are available in a translation by Richard M. Frazer, Jr., *The Trojan War: The Chronicles of Dictys of Crete and Dares the Phrygian* (Bloomington: Indiana University Press, 1966).

2. There are numerous translations; the prose ones are the most accurate, and some are very readable too (for instance, that by E. V. Rieu in Penguin Classics (1958 and repr.)), but there is much to be said for a verse translation, since prose alone cannot begin to give a sense of the poetry. C. Day Lewis's version is probably the very best of the twentieth-century translations (*The Eclogues, Georgics and Aeneid of Virgil* (Oxford: Oxford University Press, 1966 and repr.). On the medieval Virgil, see Baswell and Comparetti under Further Reading.

3. A good practicable prose translation of the *Metamorphoses* by Mary M. Innes is available in Penguin Classics (1955 and repr.). The work has attracted the attention of numerous later poets in addition to Chaucer. Ted Hughes, with his fascination for animals and their metaphorical relationship to humans, has made some of the finest creative adaptations, which transmit remarkably well the sheer oddness of metamorphosis: see his *Tales from Ovid* (London: Faber & Faber, 1997). For broad studies of Ovid's afterlife, see Martindale and Rand under Further Reading; for his relationship to Chaucer, see Calabrese and Fyler.

4. A fine introduction to Chaucer's mythography is John P. McCall's *Chaucer among the Gods: The Poetics of Classical Myth* (University Park: Pennsylvania State University Press, 1979). A more advanced work is Jane Chance's *The Mythographic Chaucer: The Fabulation of Sexual Politics* (Minneapolis: University of Minnesota Press, 1995).

5. On Boccaccio's mediation of Statius to Chaucer, see David Anderson, *Before the 'Knight's Tale': Imitation of Classical Epic in Boccaccio's 'Teseida'* (Philadelphia: University of Pennsylvania Press, 1988).

6. Minnis and Fleming offer very different accounts of this process (see Further Reading).

7. Thomas Usk alludes to *Troilus* in his *Testament of Love*, which may have been written early in 1385. See further Helen Cooper, 'The Four Last Things in Dante and Chaucer: Ugolino in the House of Rumour', *New Medieval Literatures*, 3 (1999), 39–66.

8. For contrasting readings of Chaucer's attitude to the Dido story, see A. J. Minnis, '*De vulgari auctoritate*: Chaucer, Gower, and the Men of Great Authority', in R. F. Yeager (ed.), *Chaucer and Gower: Difference, Mutuality, Exchange*, English Literary Studies, 8 (Victoria, BC: University of Victoria, 1991), 36–74, and Marilyn Desmond, *Reading Dido: Gender, Textuality and the Medieval 'Aeneid'* (Minneapolis: University of Minnesota Press, 1994).

9. Quoted from the prologue to his 1513 translation of the *Eneados* in Derek Brewer (ed.), *Chaucer: The Critical Heritage* (London: Routledge & Kegan Paul, 1978), i. 86.

10. See Fleming, Wetherbee, and Windeatt under Further Reading.

16 The English background

Wendy Scase

Chaucer's writings may be the best-known medieval English literary texts, but they comprise only part of the rich Middle English literature that survives from the period. In this chapter I shall explore some of the perspectives on Chaucer that knowledge of other medieval English literature can give us. Perhaps one of the liveliest topics in Middle English literary criticism currently is that of vernacularity: the status and properties of English as the common, everyday language in medieval England and its relationships with Latin (language of learning and record) and French (language of culture, law, and business). Chaucer long ago secured a place in literary history for having made English a language fit for literature. More recently, critics have been learning to read other medieval English texts as explorations of the possibilities of the vernacular for literary composition. Of course, English was not the only vernacular language to be gaining in cultural prestige at this time. An interest in vernacularity was Europe-wide; French and Italian, for example, had distinguished literatures that Chaucer knew well. In a related trend, critics are currently recognizing that in order to interpret and understand the achievement of Middle English texts it is necessary to consider the social dimensions and contexts of literature in late medieval England—literacy, education, and religion, for example—and also its material aspects—how Middle English texts were composed, copied, and disseminated in a manuscript culture. The purpose of this chapter is to examine Chaucer's writing in relation to the vernacular project in late medieval England.

In the first part of this chapter I shall examine how Chaucer positions himself and his writings in relation to some of the theories and practices of vernacular literature. Following sections will examine Chaucer's engagement with key areas of vernacular composition, focusing on the ways in which Chaucer explores the potentials, pitfalls, and problems of writing in English. In the closing section I shall outline the history, politics, and future of critical inquiry into Chaucer's relationship to the English literature of his day.

Theories and practices of vernacular authorship

Called upon to tell a tale, as he has agreed, the Man of Law objects that Chaucer has already told all of the suitable tales; in fact, he has told more stories in English than Ovid related in the *Heroides*:

> I kan right now no thrifty tale seyn
> That Chaucer, thogh he kan but lewedly
> On metres and on rymyng craftily,
> Hath seyd hem in swich Englissh as he kan
> Of olde tyme, as knoweth many a man;
> And if he have noght seyd hem, leve brother,
> In o book, he hath seyd hem in another.

('MLI' 46–52)

By means of such passages Chaucer engages with problems of his status as a vernacular writer. Here he creates a sense of vernacular precedent—but the precedent is his own works. In the estimation of the Man of Law, Chaucer has done everything already: 'What sholde I tellen hem, syn they been tolde?' ('MLI' 56). There is but one oblique, vague reference to alternatives ('cursed stories' (80) of incest—possibly the reference is to tales in John Gower's *Confessio amantis*, a work Chaucer echoes in the 'Wife of Bath's Tale'), but neither Chaucer, nor he, will relate such narratives. The Man of Law (Chaucer's own creation, of course), like 'many a man', is aware of a history of composition in the vernacular, but it is a history that largely comprises Chaucer's retellings of the classical stories of love. Here, it is as if Chaucer's writings constitute their own vernacular precedent.

In some ways this is typical of the ways in which medieval English writers saw themselves and their works. Middle English texts often speak eloquently of their relation with texts and literature of other languages (principally Latin, French, and Italian), but seem hardly aware of one another. It is only around the turn of the fifteenth century that we can recognize writers clearly acknowledging a debt to English-language models, precedents, and authors (for example, Thomas Hoccleve explicitly follows his 'master' Chaucer, and a group of texts allude intertextually to *Piers Plowman*). Before this, what we call medieval English literature is not a literature, if by that term we mean a body of writings self-consciously related through intertextuality, influence, and tradition.

Chaucer's interest in naming and identifying his œuvre is another of the ways in which he engages with a problematics of vernacular authorship. The Man of Law refers to the story of Ceyx and Alcione, and the stories of noble wives that comprise 'his large volume . . . | Cleped the Seintes Legende of Cupide' ('MLI' 57–61). Thus naming Chaucer here as the author of the *Book of the Duchess* and the *Legend of Good Women*, one of the functions of this passage is to identify a body of English writings and attribute it to a named author. A comparable passage, with a longer list of works, occurs in the dream vision Prologue to the *Legend of Good Women*, where Cupid indicts the dreaming poet for his translation of the *Romance of the Rose* and his telling in English of *Troilus and Criseyde* (G 248–66), claiming that these works have turned lovers against the service of love. The queen Alceste retorts that the dreamer has written in praise of love, listing a series of Chaucer's works as evidence (G 398–420). Another such list of his works occurs at the end of the *Canterbury Tales*, in the 'Retraction' (1086–8).

In identifying his writings as part of an œuvre attributable to a named writer, Chaucer differs from most other vernacular writers of his day. Most English writings from the period are anonymous. This is true of some of the most innovative texts from the period. Many texts are completely devoid of any authorial signature—not just because the names have been lost (although they have) but because attribution of works to named authors was usually associated with (and used to confer) prestige and authority. Somewhat disregarding the deliberate self-effacement of medieval vernacular writers, modern critics have sometimes coined names for them, such as the *Gawain*-poet, the *Pearl*-poet, the Wakefield Master, and the York Realist. Some texts conceal the writer behind riddles, ciphers, and pseudonyms in the text; several of what critics take for authors' names from this period (for example, John But, William Langland, and Julian of Norwich) really belong with this tradition.

However, despite differing in these ways from his contemporaries, Chaucer is like many other vernacular writers in hesitating to claim to be an *auctor*. Whereas in modern English *author* denotes any composer of an original work, however humble, the medieval word *auctor* was reserved for writers accepted as specially authoritative. Typically of many vernacular writers, Chaucer represents his works as having a derivative and dependent relationship with the writings of *auctores*. In her defence of Chaucer in the Prologue to the *Legend*, Alceste claims that he is merely the translator of the offending work:

> He ne hath not don so grevously amys
> To translate that olde clerkes wryte,
> As thogh that he of maleys wolde endyte
> Despit of love, and hadde hymself ywrought.

(G 349–52)

The claim that he is not an author, but only a translator, echoes *Troilus* itself. The narrator in *Troilus and Criseyde* explains that he is translating, sense for sense and word for word, from 'myn auctour called Lollius' (1. 393–9). Chaucer's ironic, obviously specious defences (Lollius is an invention, for example) problematize authority, sharing a problematic with much other vernacular composition in the period.

Elsewhere, Chaucer adopts another humble pose, that of the 'compiler'. *Compilatio* involved assembling authoritative material (*auctoritates*) and organizing it in ways most useful for the reader. The compiler differed from the *auctor* in adding nothing of his own to the work. The *Treatise on the Astrolabe* is aimed at the needs of 'Lyte Lowys my sone' (1), a 10-year old boy who as yet knows little Latin: 'But considre wel that I ne usurpe not to have founden this werk of my labour or of myn engyn. I n'am but a lewd compilator of the labour of olde astrologiens, and have it translatid in myn Englissh oonly for thy doctrine' (59–64). Describing himself here as a translator and as an unlearned compiler ('a lewd compilator') of the treatise, rather than attributing it to his own 'labour' or devising ('engyn'), Chaucer aligns his work with much vernacular composition in the period. The *Astrolabe* is largely a translation of a work by the eighth-century writer Messahala. Other examples of translation into Middle English range from anonymous homiletic and moral material (for example, the *Book of Vices and Virtues*) to John Trevisa's translations of Latin political and historical texts for Thomas, Lord Berkeley; and from English verse versions of Marie de France's *lais*, to the English prose *Brut*, a history of Britain compiled from Anglo-Norman and Latin sources.

Elsewhere, Chaucer refers to himself as a 'makere'. This is the term commonly used for the poet in Middle English (the French equivalent was *faiseur*), so it associates Chaucer with vernacular poets, and distinguishes him from *auctores*. The *Piers Plowman* dreamer is challenged, 'thow medlest the with makynges';[1] William Dunbar composed a 'Lament for the Makaris'. Likewise Chaucer is the 'makere' of *Troilus* (*TC* 5. 1787). In the Prologue to the *Legend of Good Women*, Alceste says the dreamer 'useth bokes for to make' (G 342); awakening from his dream, he begins 'making' poetry: 'And ryght thus on my Legende gan I make' (G 545).

Versification

Versification is another medium in which Chaucer expresses his relationship with (and difference from) English-language traditions. He suggests that his own metre is imitative of, and inferior to, that of French. In the 'Complaint of Venus' he blames the English language; his verse is inferior because it is hard to find rhyming words: 'Syth rym in Englissh hath such skarsete' (80). Middle English lyrics have their own varied, often quite complex, versification, with elaborate stanza forms, rhyme schemes, and alliteration. There are a few snatches of English lyrics and songs in Chaucer's poetry, but we lose the original versification. The Pardoner sings, 'Com hider, love, to me!' ('GP' 672), while the Summoner accompanies with a 'stif burdoun' ('GP' 673); Chauntecleer and Pertelote chorus, 'My lief is faren in londe!' ('NPT' 2879). But these snatches are filtered through Chaucer's pentameter, and irony.

Chaucer does refer to two English verse forms, but in each case he registers his own distance from them. The first-person narrator of the *Canterbury Tales*, when not simply reporting the words of the other pilgrims, uses what the Host condemns as 'rym dogerel' ('TST' 925). The six-line stanza of 'Sir Thopas' parodies the 'tail-rhyme' of romances such as *Emaré* and *Octavian*. The host suggests that a good alternative to his 'drasty rymyng' would be to tell a tale 'in geeste' ('TST' 930–3), meaning alliterative verse.

Alliterative verse went back to pre-Conquest poems such as the Old English *Beowulf*. The Middle English version (longer, looser lines, more flexibility of diction, theme, and register) was used in many earlier and contemporary poems (for example, *Winner and Waster*, the *Parliament of the Three Ages*, and *Sir Gawain and the Green Knight*). In Middle English alliterative verse several syllables begin with the same sound. The Parson's description evokes the effect: 'I kan nat geeste "rum, ram, ruf," by lettre' ('ParsP' 43). The Parson claims that he cannot compose alliterative verse because he is a 'Southren man' ('ParsP' 42). However, poems composed in alliterative verse circulated in all regions (the example par excellence is *Piers Plowman*) and could have southern origins (for example, *Sir Erkenwald*, associated with St Paul's in London). Nonetheless, there is only one unmistakable echo of the medium in Chaucer, in the passage where the Knight describes the inhospitable landscape painted on the temple of Mars ('KT' 1975–80, for example, 'knotty, knarry, bareyne trees olde, | Of stubbes sharpe and hidouse to biholde'). These lines resound with the sounds of landscape description in, for instance, the description of the Wirral in *Sir Gawain and the Green Knight*, although Chaucer conveys the effect of alliterative poetry rather than reproducing the alliterative long line exactly.

Manuscript culture

Chaucer associates his work with the modes of textual production and dissemination of vernacular texts. Vernacular texts were less stable—more subject to local and large-scale variation—than the texts of *auctores*. In part this may have been because the concepts of accuracy and correctness that applied to the transmission of Latin authors were not held to apply to vernacular texts (this means that the concept of a definitive text is probably not applicable either). John Gower was unusual among vernacular authors in (probably) supervising the copying of his own works and checking them against authoritative exemplars. In part it reflects the conditions of textual production. Error could creep in readily if there was no authoritative exemplar against which to check. Moreover, in the culture of authorlessness and anonymity, reading, copying, and writing were closely related activities that begot one another. Scribes clearly felt free to intervene: to adapt, rewrite, revise, update, and censor vernacular material.

Chaucer characterizes his work as suspended between these two divergent textual cultures of vernacular instability and Latin stability. In 'Chaucers Wordes unto Adam, his Owne Scriveyn', he complains about the risk to his 'makyng' from the carelessness of his scribe. Chaucer aims for his writing to attain the stability of the classical œuvre, but recognizes that it is subject to the vicissitudes of vernacular textual practice. In

Troilus he expresses the tension between his classical ambitions and the dissemination of vernacular texts:

> But litel book, no makyng thow n'envie,
> But subgit be to alle poesye;
> And kis the steppes where as thow seest pace
> Virgile, Ovide, Omer, Lucan, and Stace.

> And for ther is so gret diversite
> In Englissh and in writyng of oure tonge,
> So prey I God that non myswrite the,
> Ne the mysmetre for defaute of tonge;
> And red wherso thow be, or elles songe,
> That thow be understonde, God I biseche! (5. 1789–98)

Miscopying, corruption of the metre, and misunderstanding are linked with the 'gret diversite' and 'defaute of tonge' of English. With its regional dialects, and the absence of standard spellings and grammar, the English language (like the unfaithful Criseyde) was unstable and undependable.

Chaucer also associates his writings with some alternative modes of dissemination and performance. A significant section of the population could not read, and books were expensive and not easy to come by. In these circumstances, many people would be more likely to hear a text read aloud than to read for themselves. Chaucer explores the dynamics of aural dissemination by fictionalizing acts of performance and reception within his texts. In *Troilus and Criseyde* a courtly narrator addresses an audience of young lovers. In the *Canterbury Tales* the narrators and pilgrim audience come 'from every shires ende | Of Engelond' ('GP' 15–16), and from every social status ('degree', 'GP' 40). Extending the social range of his tale-tellers and audience, Chaucer gestures towards the potential of the vernacular to include in literary culture anyone who understands spoken English.

Preaching, pardoners, and friars

The medieval Church in England was quick to recognize and exploit the potential of English to reach a wide audience of all social classes. The Church claimed to be the channel of all salvation. All Christians were supposed to go to confession and attend mass at least once a year, and parish priests were obliged to instruct all of their parishioners in the basic tenets of the faith. Latin was the language of the texts, practices of interpretation, and learning that legitimized the claims of the Church. But where the 'lewed' people were concerned (that is, broadly, the large section of the population not literate in Latin), English was recognized to have a useful role. Later medieval England saw vigorous production of vernacular texts associated with the Church's pastoral mission. During the period in which Chaucer was writing, the authority claims of clerical, Latin learning and textual practice were reviewed and the assumption of the superiority of Latin to the vernacular was challenged.

Among the means open to the Church to educate and evangelize the unlearned were preaching and religious drama. Chaucer did not (as far as we know) write sermons or plays, nor does he refer to any identifiable vernacular sermons or specific plays in his work. But he does engage with the vernacular textual practices associated with these forms: he draws on the genres used by the preacher and the priest, such as the penitential, and the *exemplum*, and he engages with clerical practices of exegesis (biblical interpretation), glossing, and sermon rhetoric. This section and the next will offer examples of Chaucer's engagement with the popular sermon and the religious play, and will consider the ways in which his critique reflects back on his own vernacular art.

The art of vernacular preaching is a frequent point of reference in Chaucer's writing. The 'Pardoner's Prologue and Tale' is perhaps the most famous and extended example (the 'Parson's Tale', although considerably longer, is a religious handbook rather than a sermon). The 'Pardoner's Tale' is not simply a sermon, but a sermon framed by the Pardoner's account of his art. One of the key ways in which the Pardoner captures the attention of his audience is by using 'ensamples'. The *exemplum* (plural *exempla*) was a short narrative used to support or illustrate a point. For the Pardoner, it is one of a repertory of devices for preaching to 'lewed' people:

> Thanne telle I hem ensamples many oon
> Of olde stories longe tyme agoon.
> For lewed peple loven tales olde;
> Swiche thynges kan they wel reporte and holde.
>
> ('ParP' 435–8)

Preachers in search of sermon material could turn to handy compilations of *exempla*. For example, in *Handlynge Synne*, by Robert Mannyng, stories are organized for use in preaching about the Seven Deadly Sins. Some collections were written in the vernacular (*Handlynge Synne* was translated from a French source), while preachers would have made their own English adaptations of *exempla* written in Latin or French.

In the 'Summoner's Tale', Chaucer represents, and critiques, the use of *exempla* in a pastoral context. The friar, visiting the sick layman Thomas, and finding him lying 'ful of anger and of ire' (1981), delivers a homily on ire, illustrating the sin with three little stories about irate characters (2017–88). The friar's hypocrisy in asking for money— supposedly to support his preaching—ironically angers sick Thomas yet further:

> This sike man wax wel ny wood for ire;
> He wolde that the frere had been on-fire
> With his false dissymulacioun. (2121–3)

Another critique of using stories in sermons (associated with the followers of the late fourteenth-century theologian John Wyclif, and others) was that preaching should be based on Scripture. The debate on this issue is illustrated by two of Chaucer's tale-tellers. The Nun's Priest is an advocate of the moral value of secular stories, so long as the audience separates the 'fruyt' (the moral meaning) from the 'chaf' (the story) ('NPT' 3443). The Parson, however, takes the opposite view ('Why sholde I sowen draf out of my fest, | Whan I may sowen whete, if that me lest?', 'ParsP' 35–6), refusing to tell 'fables and swich wrecchednesse' (34).

Another criticism was that some vernacular preaching and teaching did not give the unlearned access to the text of the Bible, only a distorted or misleading interpretation. Chaucer engages too with this critique of clerical practices. The friar in the 'Summoner's Tale' justifies his mediation of Scripture to laypeople on the grounds of their intellectual and educational inferiority:

> I have to day been at youre chirche at messe,
> And seyd a sermon after my symple wit—
> Nat al after the text of hooly writ,
> For it is hard to yow, as I suppose,
> And therfore wole I teche yow al the glose. (1788–92)

Less defensible motives for the friar's practice are suggested when the friar defends his order's claims to poverty: 'I ne have no text of it, as I suppose, | But I shal fynde it in a maner glose' (1919–20). He admits that he cannot produce a biblical *text* to prove his point, only a *gloss*.

Chaucer's engagement with vernacular preaching is not simply a morally superior critique of abuse. Chaucer also explores the relation of his own art with these vernacular traditions, confronting the question of the extent to which he can claim that his own practices are any different. Chaucer raises this question throughout, but his depiction of the Pardoner is perhaps his most sustained exploration of it. What distinguishes the Pardoner and his vernacular tale-telling from Chaucer and his narrative art? Chaucer is able to raise this question by using sermon discourse (the corrupt preacher is an example of hypocrisy and greed), and at the same time acknowledging his own relation with it (Chaucer, like the Pardoner, is an ambitious vernacular tale-teller). Chaucer poses an insoluble conundrum: if *all* moral discourse must be suspect (as it must, if the Pardoner, so perfectly convincing, is a fraud), then how can critique, itself a form of moral discourse, *ever* have firm grounds? Exposing this terrifying abyss, Chaucer explores the relationships between vernacular preaching and his own art.

Religious plays and the 'Miller's Tale'

Religious drama was another genre through which religious teaching could be communicated to a vernacular audience. The Mystery cycles, the most ambitious and extensive form of religious drama, provided an annual performance of the story of salvation in the form of short vernacular pageants based on key biblical (and sometimes apocryphal) incidents. Although probably scripted by clerics, the plays were largely sponsored and performed by members of the guilds. Whereas for some people the plays' treatment of sublime matter sanctified vernacular culture, for Chaucer the plays provide a reference for the gestures, behaviour, and cultural horizons of lower-class characters in the *Canterbury Tales*.

The discourteous language and behaviour of the pilgrim Miller when he butts in front of the Monk are characterized with reference to the stage villain Pontius Pilate:

> The Millere, that for dronken was al pale,
> So that unnethe upon his hors he sat,
> He nolde avalen neither hood ne hat,
> Ne abyde no man for his curteisie,
> But in Pilates voys he gan to crie.
>
> ('MP' 3120–4)

In the 'Miller's Tale', in order to try to appear attractively masterful to Alison, Absolon ludicrously takes the part of Herod, another stage villain:

> Somtyme, to shewe his lightnesse and maistrye,
> He pleyeth Herodes upon a scaffold hye. (3383–4)

As well as exposing the shortcomings of the Miller and Absolon, these references ridicule the performance culture of the religious drama. The tale, moreover, suggests that this kind of biblical education makes possible outrageous mischief and deceit. In order to trick John into getting out of the way so that he can spend a night with Alison, John's wife, Nicholas refers him to the story of Noah. He uses the story to arouse in the carpenter penitential fear of the end of the world, predicting rain far more terrible than that of the Flood. If, like Noah, John listens to God's warning and follows similar advice (except that he may avoid Noah's problems of a recalcitrant wife by arranging for them to have separate vessels), he may be saved (3534–43).

Of course, this story of Noah's wife had no biblical basis. Its inclusion in the story of salvation was justified because Noah's wife echoed the figure of Eve (blamed for mankind's expulsion from paradise), and looked forward to the Virgin Mary (mother of Christ, channel of redemption), while the stereotypical representation of marital conflict was exploited for its appeal to a broad, lay audience. Nicholas quite clearly exploits the potential of the story to manipulate John. *Noah* was regularly performed by carpenters' guilds (the story of the making of the ark provided an opportunity for them to celebrate their craft).[2] In exploiting the Noah play in this way, the clerk Nicholas perfectly targets the carpenter John.

Theological and devotional literature

Although vernacular preaching, teaching, and drama continued to be important ways of communicating the faith to people who were not literate in Latin, increasingly during the period devotional, and sometimes theological, reading matter was provided as well. The audience for such material, though narrower than that of the vernacular sermon or religious play, was still quite diverse, including all kinds of people who could be categorized as 'lewed' *and* had some access to books. Many different kinds of texts were translated into, or composed in, English, in order to meet the diverse needs of this group. This vigorous literary production also led, from the closing decades of the fourteenth century, to questioning of the needs and abilities of such readers, and to debate about what kinds of vernacular texts it was appropriate, and legitimate, for them to read. Chaucer's literary career coincided with these decades, and the earliest surviving manuscripts of his work (none of which was produced during his lifetime) date from the years in which explicit censorship of vernacular writings began. Chaucer's writings engage in many ways with the flourishing of vernacular devotional and theological writing in this period. By positioning his own writing in relation to the theories and practices of vernacular devotional literacy, he was able to deepen his exploration of his status as a vernacular writer.

Many vernacular texts were designed to educate and support those living a religious—or semi-religious—life, such as recluses, or vowesses (widows who took vows of chastity after the death of their husbands). Such texts included prayers and devotional lyrics; material for contemplation and meditation; and practical advice on such matters as appropriate clothing and food (the *Ancrene Wisse*, a guide for female recluses, provides both of these latter kinds of material). Many such texts were narratives, such as saints' and other exemplary lives; narratives that reinforced faith, charitable giving, and liturgical practice (for example, miracle stories); and stories of divinely inspired revelations (for example, the *Revelation of Divine Love* by Julian of Norwich). Other texts, such as the works of Walter Hilton, Richard Rolle, and the *Cloud of Unknowing*, were aimed at a spiritual elite who were committed to a life of contemplation or even mysticism.

Some vernacular texts were aimed at clergy who were unable to read Latin or French materials adequately. However, once translated into English, texts originally intended, say, as manuals for confessors could and did find broader audiences. Chaucer's 'Parson's Tale' is an example of this kind of material. It combines an exposition of the sacrament of penance with an analysis of sin organized systematically according to 'chieftaynes' (the Deadly Sins, of which pride is the 'roote') and their 'braunches' and 'twigges' (387–9). The tale is organized, like many comparable penitential manuals, as a resource for priests. However, such material could also have other less formal literary uses and adaptations. The *Ayenbite of Inwit* adapts the French *Somme le roi* into English, targeting the penitent (the person going to confession) rather than (or as well as) the confessor (the title means 'Remorse of Conscience'). The confessional provides the framework for John Gower's vernacular story collection the *Confessio amantis* ('Confession of the Lover'). *Piers Plowman* exploits penitential material in a variety of ways, for example, including 'confessions' of the Seven Deadly Sins, while the penitential pilgrimage becomes a structuring metaphor: salvation is the goal of the 'pilgrimage of life'. Chaucer's use of the genre also engages with these ambiguities of the function, address, and purpose of penitential literature. The matter of the 'Parson's Tale' informs some of the representations of sin in the other tales (for example, the analysis of ire has parallels with that in the 'Summoner's Tale'), while the embedding of this 'tale' as one pilgrim's tale among many problematizes the relation of the penitential treatise with fictional and worldly vernacular writing.

Lollardy and the lay reader

At the same time that demand for material of this kind was growing, and while it was being met by a vigorous flood of new works, the issue of precisely what kind of material was appropriate for 'lewed' readers was being raised. This problem was closely connected with late medieval questioning of the authority of the Church, the clergy, and clerical literary practices. John Wyclif and his followers (known as Wycliffites, or (after their medieval nickname) as Lollards) argued vehemently that everyone should have access to Scripture, and took practical steps to bring this about. The Wycliffites prepared vernacular translations of the Bible, and also resources such as concordances and sermons, to help teachers and preachers to spread the word of the gospel in the vernacular. They issued vernacular (as well as Latin) treatises that marshalled biblical texts and other authoritative writings to challenge the authority of the Church and some of its doctrines. They opposed textual practices and genres that, in their view, got in the way of access to the Bible, such as self-interested glossing of Scripture of the kind practised by the friar in the 'Summoner's Tale', and fictions, fables, and saints' lives. The Church authorities identified some Wycliffite doctrines as heresies, and, after two or more decades of prosecutions and trials of those accused of heresy, Thomas Arundel, archbishop of Canterbury, sought in the first decade of the fifteenth century to contain the spread of Wycliffite doctrine by subjecting vernacular writing to censorship and restriction.

Many texts from Chaucer's period and later can be seen as aware of the dangers of promoting heresy. Some appear to have been carefully contrived to satisfy demands for reading matter without permitting the unlearned access to inappropriate material. The demand for biblical reading was met by gospel harmonies and synopses and other kinds of narrative paraphrase, such as Nicholas Love's *Mirror of the Life of Jesus Christ*, and *Patience*, a verse homily based on the biblical story of Jonah and the whale. Some texts dealt with basic matters of faith (for example, preparation for confession), or gave moral guidance on matters such as almsgiving, or preparation for death, while, with their broad, 'lewed' audience in mind, carefully omitting theological exposition.

Chaucer's relation with Lollardy is a vexed critical issue. After the Reformation many Protestant readers of Chaucer considered him to have been a follower of Wyclif. From most modern vantage points, however, Chaucer's relation to Lollardy is as ambiguous as the Parson's. The Parson's moral, intellectual, and literary preferences have much in common with those of the Wycliffites. He espouses clerical poverty, but not begging (or living on extorted tithes, 'GP' 486–90); refuses to 'glose'; scorns poetry and fiction; and, as we have seen, instead of a tale presents a prose 'meditacioun' of 'Moralitee and vertuous mateere' ('ParsP' 30–8). In the Prologue attributed in the *Riverside* edition to the Shipman (the manuscripts disagree at this point), the Host and the Shipman declare that they believe the Parson to be a Lollard. The Host wants to hear the Parson preach, but the Shipman objects that he will introduce 'cokkel in our clene corn', that is, heresy:

> 'Nay, by my fader soule, that schal he nat!'
> Seyde the Shipman, 'Heer schal he nat preche;
> He schal no gospel glosen here ne teche.
> We leven alle in the grete God,' quod he;
> 'He wolde sowen som difficulte,
> Or springen cokkel in our clene corn . . .'

('MLE' 1178–83)

At the end of the *Tales*, however, the Host and pilgrims defer to the Parson's authority, and the Parson defers to the authority of the Church ('clerkes', 'ParsP' 57) and Christ.

Chaucer uses the language associated with charges against Lollards in the Prologue to the *Legend of Good Women*, when depicting himself called to account for having written *Troilus* and for having translated the *Romance of the Rose* into English:

> Thow mayst it nat denye,
> For in pleyn text, it nedeth nat to glose,
> Thow hast translated the Romauns of the Rose,
> That is an heresye ageyns my lawe . . .
> Hast thow nat mad in Englysh ek the bok
> How that Crisseyde Troylus forsok,
> In shewynge how that wemen han don mis?

(G 253–6, 264–6)

Here Chaucer associates Lollard textual practices—translation of heretical matter into English; providing the 'pleyn text' not the 'glose'—with his own writings. But of course this 'heresy trial' takes place in the court of Cupid, not in an ecclesiastical court. Chaucer eroticizes the dangers associated with writing in the vernacular and exploits the scenario as a pretext for yet further composition. His 'penance' for having written 'heresy' about women is to compose the *Legend of Good Women*—the stories of secular 'saints'. The proximity of Chaucer's writing with Lollardy charges his work with danger, but it is danger managed, orchestrated, and exploited as part of his exploration of vernacular writing. (For more on Chaucer and Lollardy, see Chapters 5, 7, and 19.)

Religion, vernacularity, the Wife, and the Prioress

The two prologues and tales that Chaucer allocates unambiguously to women, those of the Prioress and the Wife of Bath (the 'Second Nun's Prologue' seems to envisage a male speaker), offer particularly interesting and sustained examples of Chaucer's engagement with lay devotional reading and the issues it raised. Medieval women were by definition excluded from clerical literary practice, since membership of the clergy was restricted to males. Not (usually) educated in Latin themselves, or given training in such matters as the interpretation of Scripture, women were placed in an unauthoritative position in textual culture. Very few women indeed became writers and (not surprisingly) the issue of authority is central to the work of those that did (such as Julian of Norwich and Margery Kempe). Both nuns and laywomen were dependent on vernacular texts, and male confessors, preachers, and spiritual guides, to mediate the faith and provide for their devotional reading. It is a striking fact that many of the surviving manuscripts of vernacular devotional texts are associated with nunneries, and it seems likely that much of the output of vernacular devotional material in the period was aimed at female audiences and readers. In his treatment of the Prioress and the Wife of Bath, Chaucer engages with the gendering of the theories and practices associated with lay devotional literature.

In her Prologue the Prioress alludes to contemporary theories about women's literacy to support her declaration of unworthiness. She declares that she has too little knowledge to praise the Virgin Mary properly ('my konnyng is so wayk'), and calls on the Virgin to guide her 'song' (481, 487). She compares herself with a 12-month-old child, and with a baby 'on the brest soukynge' (484, 458), using images of children unable to speak to represent her inadequacy to her literary task. The 'Prioress's Tale' is a miracle tale, a genre that spoke to the fears and educational limitations of unlearned people like the Prioress. A little boy, murdered by Jews who hear him singing a hymn to the Virgin, is granted the gift of song in death when the Virgin appears to him in a vision; once released from singing he goes to the Virgin's protection in heaven. The plot of this particular tale echoes the Prioress's fears and desires concerning her own lack of learning. The boy's educational attainment is similar to that of a medieval woman, perhaps particularly a nun—he learns to sing a Latin hymn by heart, without understanding its meaning. The intervention of the Virgin endorses and validates his humble devotion, just as the Prioress wishes for the Virgin to guide her own 'song'.

In view of the tale's cruelty, prejudice, and sentimentality, we might be tempted to conclude that Chaucer is aligning himself here with the critics of miracle stories and all such non-biblical religious narratives. From this point of view, we might read the 'Prioress's Prologue and Tale' as a critique both of the Prioress and of the vernacular textual practices that formed her. But the situation is more complicated than this, because Chaucer also engages with a more positive perspective on vernacular religion. At the beginning of her Prologue the Prioress claims that, when praising the Virgin Mary, the least learned child can equal 'men of dignitee':

> O Lord, oure Lord, thy name how merveillous
> Is in this large world ysprad—quod she—
> For noght oonly thy laude precious
> Parfourned is by men of dignitee,

But by the mouth of children thy bountee
Parfourned is, for on the brest soukynge
Somtyme shewen they thyn heriynge. (453–9)

The 'Prioress's Prologue' challenges the hierarchies of discourse. Her tale, a story in which the little boy's song is validated by a miracle, authorizes her claims that vernacularity may be as valid and powerful as clerical literate practice. In exploring the miracle tale in this conflicted way, Chaucer reflects on the status of vernacular narrative art.

The Wife of Bath, too, is portrayed both as the product of clerical textual theories and practices, and as the agent of their deconstruction. One important vernacular genre with which Chaucer engages here is that of virginity literature. Vernacular texts such as *Hali Meithhad* ('Holy Maidenhood') aimed to teach female readers the value and advantages of virginity over marriage. The Wife vigorously opposes the idealization of female virgins promoted by virginity literature, answering clerics' exegesis with her own:

Wher can ye seye, in any manere age,
That hye God defended mariage
By expres word? I pray yow, telleth me.
Or where comanded he virginitee?
I woot as wel as ye, it is no drede,
Th'apostel, whan he speketh of maydenhede,
He seyde that precept therof hadde he noon.

('WBP' 59–65)

By these means, the Wife refuses to be hailed by virginity literature: 'He [Christ] spak to hem that wolde lyve parfitly; | And lordynges, by youre leve, that am nat I' (111–12). And yet the 'Wife of Bath's Prologue' also reaffirms the power relations, and frustrations, of vernacular textual practice. Virginity texts, idealizing chaste women, were the counterpart of Latin anti-feminist, anti-marriage writings such as those read by the Wife's fifth husband, Jankyn. Night after night Jankyn (formerly a 'clerk' himself, 527) reads and expounds literature to the Wife, teaching her that she and her sex are the ruin of men. Jankyn is in control both of the text and of its interpretation; Alison can only intervene by tearing out three of its leaves. This confirms the traditional hierarchies: far from challenging Jankyn's anti-feminist interpretation of the text, her action exemplifies the stereotype of women as irrational, unintellectual creatures whose carnality, unbridled, brings about men's misery. As the Wife challenges the representation of women in literature, she confirms its truth. Like the Parson, Pardoner, and Prioress, the Wife provides Chaucer with a vehicle for exploring the possibilities, and paradoxes, of vernacular textuality.

English romance

Chaucer's exploration of the Wife's vernacular literary agency is completed, of course, by her tale. It is likely that originally Chaucer had a bawdy fabliau in mind for her (possibly the 'Shipman's Tale'). As he developed her character, though, he seems to have turned to the more complex and less obvious challenge of having her tell a romance. I shall now turn to Chaucer's awareness of, and exploitations of, English romance, and to the ways in which he uses that engagement with romance to position himself as a vernacular writer.

To talk of romance in medieval England is to talk, broadly, of a tradition of secular narrative that went back to the years after the Norman conquest of England in 1066. It is also to talk of vernacular culture. Romance was definitively vernacular. Before it came to be associated with secular narrative, the French word *romance* meant simply 'vernacular language'. In England the vernacular language of romance was at first the French spoken by the new Norman rulers (Anglo-Norman). The themes, plots, and value systems of romance reflected the interests and anxieties of a courtly class, providing a vehicle for the exploration of issues of identity, social relations, and order. The most vigorous period for the composition of romances in Anglo-Norman was over by the first half of the thirteenth century. From this period date the earliest romances composed in English, such as *King Horn* and *Havelock the Dane*, which are related to earlier Anglo-Norman narratives. By Chaucer's time English romances were plentiful: some sixty Middle English romances date from before Chaucer's death in 1400.[3]

English romance would have been available to Chaucer, as to others, in a variety of ways. Some specific suggestions have been made about the texts Chaucer may have known and how he might have come by them. It has been suggested that he may have used, or even owned, the Auchinleck manuscript, an early fourteenth-century London book that includes *Guy of Warwick* and *Bevis of Hampton*, two of the romances mentioned in 'Sir Thopas'.[4] It has also been suggested that he may have known the *Tale of Gamelyn*, a text which survives as a spurious tale in twenty-five manuscripts of the *Canterbury Tales*, where it is sometimes ascribed to the Cook.[5] Practically the only name of an author of English verse romance that has come down to us is that of Sir Thomas Chestre, author of *Lybeaus Desconus* ('The Fair Unknown'—'Sir Lybeux' in 'Sir Thopas') and also author of an English adaptation (possibly made from memory) of Marie de France's *lai Lanval*. Chaucer was ransomed with a Thomas Chestre in 1360, and it has been suggested that this Thomas—if he was indeed the romance poet—might have performed his work for Chaucer.[6]

It is hard to be precise about what kinds of people formed the audience for the English romance. Romance stories tell of knights, ladies, kings, and courts, but of course it does not follow that they were aimed exclusively (or at all) at the highest social groups. Romances encoded, in terms appropriate for the unlearned, the desires and anxieties of possession and dispossession, loss and attainment of social position, identity and lineage, the responsibilities of lords and their retainers, of kin, of husbands and wives, and of comrades-at-arms. Chaucer must have expected that his own readers would know enough about English romances to enjoy his parody of them, 'Sir Thopas'. Going by the ownership of manuscripts, we can say that romances were available to a range of lay readers, from urban merchants to country gentry. It is even harder to pin down quite who comprised the audience that may have *heard* these texts read aloud or recited from memory.

'Verray lewednesse': 'Sir Thopas', the Franklin, and the Wife

Chaucer's merciless—and highly entertaining—parody 'Sir Thopas' is his most sustained engagement with the practices of English romance. It foregrounds particular aspects of romance composition, especially its oral aspects. Formulaic addresses to a listening audience, 'Listeth, lordes', 'Yet listeth, lordes' (712, 833), echo the opening, for example, of *Havelock*. 'Now holde youre mouth, *par charitee*' (891) ridicules such phrases as (highly comic) pretensions to courtly discourse. The ballad-like rhythm of the tail-rhyme stanza comically points up the banality of the sense, while the Host complains that this 'drasty speche' makes his ears ache (923). The pilgrim Chaucer's statement that 'Sir Thopas' is a 'rym I lerned longe agoon' ('PST' 709) could suggest memorization rather than reading of the text in a written source.[7] These 'oral' features of 'Sir Thopas' are part of the way that Chaucer caricatures and critiques the 'lewednesse' of English romance. 'Sir Thopas' is offered as a typical, and the best, romance. Its hero is superior to those of other 'romances of prys':

> Of Horn child and of Ypotys,
>   Of Beves and sir Gy,
> Of sir Lybeux and Pleyndamour—
> But sir Thopas, he bereth the flour
>   Of roial chivalry! (897–902)

Just as the character Sir Thopas exceeds popular romance heroes such as those of the romances *Horn*, *Beves of Hampton*, and *Guy of Warwick*, so the tale is the 'beste rym' (928) that the pilgrim Chaucer is able to tell. But for the Host, it is 'verray lewednesse' (921), the definitively vernacular product, with all of its drawbacks.

Chaucer is here engaging with some of the anxieties and instabilities associated with this mode of vernacular literature. One of these anxieties was that vernacular entertainment of this kind diverted its audiences from the literature of moral and religious edification. The *Cursor mundi*, for example, a late thirteenth-century English verse narrative of world history, announces itself as an antidote to the romances about Alexander, Julius Caesar, the Trojan Wars, Arthur, Gawain and Kay of the Round Table, and suchlike that deal with the vanities of the world and lead people to misspend their lives on ephemeral fancies.[8] The *Cursor's* criticism of romance is echoed by the Host when he interrupts the telling of 'Sir Thopas': 'Thou doost noght elles but despendest tyme' (931). The pilgrim Chaucer's replacement of 'Sir Thopas' with the morally serious 'Tale of Melibee' gives a contemporary twist to this anxiety about romance. In the light of concerns about Lollardy, an ethical treatise was less potentially provocative than a text based on the Bible.

Another source of anxiety was the protean and unclassifiable nature of vernacular narrative. Romance deals with many different kinds of subject matter: it tells of exotic marvels (such as the horse of brass in the land of Tartary in the 'Squire's Tale') and the mundane (Havelock impresses as a kitchen-hand); its settings range from beyond Christendom (*Floris and Blancheflour*) to England and Wales (*Sir Gawain and the Green Knight*); its matter ranges from Arthurian (*Ywain and Gawain*) to classical (*The Seege of Troye*); its modes range from moral and didactic (Emaré converts a sultan to Christianity), to comic (*The Wedding of Sir Gawain and Dame Ragnell*). Medieval readers and writers inherited a theory of genre from classical literature. However, vernacular narrative was (and is) difficult to classify in such a way. In the late twelfth century Jean Bodel classified romances according to three 'matters': the matters of Britain, of France, and of Rome.[9] The *Cursor mundi* offers a rather different approach to the 'many maner' of romance, classifying first by subject matter, then by language.[10]

The 'Franklin's Prologue and Tale' engage with the desires and frustrations of attempting to categorize romance. In his Prologue the Franklin identifies his tale as a Breton *lai*. He introduces his audience to *lais*, describing them as narratives of adventure composed in rhyming verse, written originally in the vernacular language of the Bretons, and either sung with a musical accompaniment or read. The Prologue aligns the 'Franklin's Tale' with a number of Middle English romances that similarly include passages that claim they are Breton *lais*, and describe the genre, such as *Sir Orfeo*, *Lai le Freine*, and *Emaré*. But there are problems with this classification. The claim that some romances belong to an ancient British genre goes back at least to Marie de France, the twelfth-century author of twelve Anglo-Norman *lais*; some of the English tales, such as *Landevale* and *Lai le Freine*, are based on Marie's stories rather than actually coming from Celtic originals; and the classification is applied to several different kinds of English tale. We might read the 'Franklin's Tale' as a narrative that parallels the conflicted story of the English Breton *lai*. Just as the Breton *lai* prologue or epilogue tells how a Breton *tale* has been translated into English, so the 'Franklin's Tale' concerns the journey of a Breton *hero* to England, and the dangers and adventures that come about as a result of his journey.

Some of the *lais* of Marie de France focus on female protagonists and on issues concerning society's treatment of women. Their focus on women—and their female authorship—make them unusual; romance much more frequently focuses on male protagonists (famous examples include Lancelot, Gawain, and Tristan) and encodes male experiences and problems from a male point of view.[11] Chaucer, however, was clearly interested in women's experience of the genre. The Nun's Priest jokes about the appeal of the story of Lancelot to women:

> This storie is also trewe, I undertake,
> As is the book of Launcelot de Lake,
> That wommen holde in ful greet reverence.
>
> ('NPT' 3211–13)

When Pandarus visits his niece at home, he finds her with two other women, all of them listening to a maiden who is reading 'the geste | Of the siege of Thebes' (*TC* 2. 81–4).

With the 'Wife of Bath's Tale' Chaucer undertakes an extended exploration of romance in relation to a female point of view. In many ways the Wife's romance is a conventional tale of male 'disparagement' (loss of social standing) reversed. After facing the threats of death, and a humiliating marriage, at the end of the tale the knight finds himself married to a woman 'as fair to seene | As any lady, emperice, or queene' (1245–6). Again, typically of romance, the tale focuses on the experience of the knight; it has nothing to say directly of the viewpoint of the maiden who is raped by the knight, nor of the motives and identity of the old woman. Yet, by allocating the tale to a female teller, Chaucer is clearly encouraging a reading of the romance in relation to a female viewpoint. The knight's quest focuses on this; he has to find out what women most desire. After he has succeeded in this quest, he receives another insight into a woman's viewpoint. When forced to sleep with the old woman, he is put in a similar position to that in which he put the maiden whom he raped:

> 'My love?' quod he, 'nay, my dampnacioun!
> Allas, that any of my nacioun
> Sholde evere so foule disparaged be!'
> But al for noght; the ende is this, that he
> Constreyned was; he nedes moste hire wedde,
> And taketh his olde wyf, and gooth to bedde. (1067–72)

At the end of his adventure the knight receives romance teaching from the old woman. She teaches him that true gentility is not dependent on lineage, possession, or youth, explicitly challenging his version of 'the lawe of kyng Arthures hous' (1089). In exploring the ways in which romance excludes—and could include—the female viewpoint, Chaucer suggests new possibilities for English narrative.

Critical traditions and future directions

Ever since fifteenth-century poets extolled Chaucer as their 'master', readers and writers have seen Chaucer as the 'father' of English literature. Chaucer's sources have been recognized as French, Italian, and Latin, and his achievement seen as that of founding a comparable tradition in English. Chaucer continued to be read, at first in manuscript and later in print, while many of the other texts discussed in this chapter became neglected. By the sixteenth century the language of many of these texts had come to seem difficult and archaic, their style unsophisticated, their aesthetics crude, and their religious views unacceptable. They were not admitted to the new category of 'literature'.

Now that many of the English writings of the period have been rediscovered, readers today probably have access to more vernacular writing than any individual medieval reader could have known. Nonetheless, the conceptual division between Chaucer and other medieval English writing persists. Aside from Chaucer, much Middle English literature is still the preserve of the specialist reader, and scholars' interests in these writings have often been linguistic or editorial rather than critical. This way of approaching non-Chaucerian literature has perhaps sometimes affirmed and perpetuated the view that medieval English writing is unworthy of critical attention. The view that there is a great divide between the literary author Chaucer and 'the rest' has also perhaps sometimes been affirmed by pedagogy (medieval literature, where taught, is often mostly or all Chaucer), and by educational publishing (there are no 'companions' to the *Cursor mundi*). This view could be said to inform the structure and agenda of this Oxford Guide itself.

In this chapter I have attempted to show that our own interpretations of Chaucer may be enriched by knowledge of what his contemporaries were reading and writing in the English language. I have offered a reading of Chaucer in which awareness of the changing and diverse theories and practices of vernacular reading and writing can deepen our understanding and enjoyment of his own vernacular art. While we have many books on Chaucer, we still have a great deal to learn about other medieval English texts and textualities, and about how and why their pleasures have slipped out of view. Like other literatures currently being recovered (for example, women's writing), Middle English literature has much exciting potential. Future studies of medieval English writing will continue to offer us fresh ways to read Chaucer, and new perspectives on our own textual theories and practices.

FURTHER READING

Burrow, John, *Medieval Writers and their Work: Middle English Literature and its Background*, rev. edn. (Oxford: Oxford University Press, 1982). An extremely clear and accessible introduction to medieval English literature and its contexts; a little dated, inevitably, but still offering an excellent orientation for someone new to the field.

Burrow, John, and Thorlac Turville-Petre (eds.), *A Book of Middle English*, 2nd edn. (Oxford: Blackwell, 1996). Half an introduction to the grammar, sounds, and syntax of Middle English, half an anthology of texts edited with notes and a glossary. The two parts can be used independently.

Matthews, David, *The Making of Middle English 1765–1910* (Minneapolis: University of Minnesota Press, 1999). Traces the rediscovery of Middle English texts in the eighteenth and nineteenth centuries and the shifting ways in which they have been read.

Meale, Carol M. (ed.), *Women and Literature in Medieval Britain, c.1150–1500* (Cambridge: Cambridge University Press, 1993). Essays by specialists on women as readers, book-owners, patrons, etc. Contains a wealth of suggestive material on women's participation in literary culture.

Pearsall, Derek (ed.), *Chaucer to Spenser: An Anthology* (Oxford: Blackwell, 1999). A selection of extracts and shorter works in a reader-friendly edition. Especially useful for anyone new to reading medieval English texts in the original language.

Simpson, James, *The Oxford English Literary History, ii: 1350–1547: Reform and Cultural Revolution* (Oxford: Oxford University Press, 2002). A literary history organized by genre, mode, and theme, rather than observing conventional period boundaries. Challenges the view that medieval literature is inferior to that written after the Reformation and Renaissance, and that the 'medieval' and 'post-medieval' are monolithic blocks separated by a cultural watershed.

Treharne, Elaine (ed.), *Old English and Early Middle English: An Anthology* (Oxford: Blackwell, 2000). Provides texts and extracts up to about the time of Chaucer, in the original language with either parallel modern English translations or on-page glosses.

Wallace, David (ed.), *The Cambridge History of Medieval English Literature* (Cambridge: Cambridge University Press, 1999). Essays by specialists on the important genres and authors; considers medieval English alongside writings in Latin and the other vernacular languages of medieval Britain. Indispensable, though anyone new to the field might do well to consult a more basic orientation (for example, Burrow) first.

Wogan-Browne, Jocelyn, Nicholas Watson, Andrew Taylor, and Ruth Evans (eds.), *The Idea of the Vernacular: An Anthology of Middle English Literary Theory 1280–1520* (Exeter: University of Exeter Press, 1999). Assembles a wealth of primary texts illustrating the medieval literary theory embedded in vernacular texts. Also includes very useful short essays that put the material in context.

NOTES

1. William Langland, *The Vision of Piers Plowman*, ed. A. V. C. Schmidt (London: Dent, 1978), 13. 16.
2. Derek Brewer, *A New Introduction to Chaucer*, 2nd edn. (Harlow: Longman, 1988), 286.
3. Rosalind Field, 'Romance in Medieval England', in David Wallace (ed.), *The Cambridge History of Medieval English Literature* (Cambridge: Cambridge University Press, 1999), 169.
4. Laura H. Loomis, 'Chaucer and the Auchinleck Manuscript', in W. P. Long (ed.), *Essays and Studies in Honor of Carleton Brown* (New York: Columbia University Press, 1940), 111–28.
5. T. A. Shippey, '*The Tale of Gamelyn*: Class Warfare and the Embarrassments of Genre', in Ad Putter and Jane Gilbert (eds.), *The Spirit of English Popular Romance* (Harlow: Longman, 2000), 78–96.
6. Ad Putter, 'An Historical Introduction', in Putter and Gilbert (eds.), *The Spirit of English Popular Romance*, 13.
7. For 'oral versus written' debates on romance, see ibid. 3–15.
8. Jocelyn Wogan-Browne, Nicholas Watson, Andrew Taylor, and Ruth Evans (eds.), *The Idea of the Vernacular: An Anthology of Middle English Literary Theory 1280–1520* (Exeter: University of Exeter Press, 1999), 269, lines 1–55.
9. Field, 'Romance in Medieval England', 172 n. 70.
10. See Wogan-Browne *et al*, *The Idea of the Vernacular*, 268, lines 1–16.
11. Compare Felicity Riddy, 'Middle English Romance: Family, Marriage, Intimacy', in Roberta L. Kruger (ed.), *The Cambridge Companion to Medieval Romance* (Cambridge: Cambridge University Press, 2000), 235–52.

17 The French background

Helen Phillips

French influence was a major inspiration throughout Chaucer's literary career and in all areas of his writing. French culture was dominant in thirteenth- and fourteenth-century Europe. The great thirteenth-century *Roman de la Rose*, by Guillaume de Lorris and Jean de Meun, had more creative importance for Chaucer than any other single influence. Chaucer's dream poems are in the mode of the elegant, fashionable *dit amoureux*, in which contemporary French poets were making sophisticated experiments with fresh subjects and structures. *Dits amoureux*, a late medieval genre of narrative, often dream poems, focused on the sorrows of love and also frequently included philosophical and didactic themes relating to Fortune, Fame, and Nature, together with allegorical characters, debates, and lovers' complaints. They cross the boundaries between the worlds of narrative and lyric, both in their structures, which embed emotional laments and intellectual debates within narrative frames, and at a deeper level in their invention of narratives that express the customary lyric themes of despair, desire, and consolation. Several of the Canterbury tales (the Miller's, Reeve's, Friar's, Summoner's, Merchant's, and Shipman's) are in another familiar French genre, that of fabliau: farce-like tales with cynical, usually bawdy, subject matter, a fast pace, and often some slapstick or absurd physical indignities, all leading up to a hilarious denouement which brings a kind of justice.

A constant feature of Chaucer's response to previous writings is to combine genres, stylistic registers, and the often incompatible world-views that go with them. His fabliau tales, for example, also draw on the elegant short tales of his Italian contemporary Boccaccio, as well as on witty sermon-stories, sharp contemporary sociological observations, and intellectual speculations, to produce a cocktail of wit and entertainment on many different levels. The *Roman de la Rose* itself is a text of such multiple attitudes to life that it has excited anger, admiration, and debate, ever since its composition, about whether it is moral or immoral, frivolous or intellectually profound, misogynistic and obscene or an idealization of women and love. Chaucer used it for some of the most cynical and materialistic comments in the 'Wife of Bath's Prologue' yet it also underlies the delicate love-vision in the *Book of the Duchess*.

Influences never come singly for a great author, especially one, like Chaucer, intensely interested in setting different approaches to human experience in challenging interface with one another. Christianity and the Latin classics were the greatest influences on medieval thought, and French writers, such as Jean de Meun and Machaut, were key inspirations in demonstrating how modern writing could include and discuss certain classical concepts of great importance for medieval thinking about human life: the concepts of Nature, Fortune, Venus, and Amor, and the philosophy of Boethius. These writers also, like Chaucer, juxtapose the worlds of Christian morality, philosophy, and sexual passion. The romance, a genre born in twelfth-century French literature, evolved in many different directions over three centuries, and Chaucer's work shows how much he learnt from French and English romances, while *Troilus* and the 'Knight's Tale' show his engagement with the new directions in which Boccaccio had taken two important French legacies to European literature: the imagery of 'courtly love', and the *roman antique*—that is, the reworking of classical myth and epic themes in the style and with the preoccupations of medieval romance. The English and Italian texts that influenced Chaucer are themselves often responses to French literature, just as French literature and translations are frequently the vernacular channels through which classical culture and learning was conveyed and reworked for medieval audiences.

Cosmopolitan England

Chaucer's French background is both Anglo-Norman French and Continental French (French, like Middle English, was a language of dialects). During his lifetime the roles of both in relation to English society and literature were changing. Anglo-Norman was still widely used, especially in nunneries and the law, and for official documents (civic administration, parliamentary business, royal administration), as well, of course, as Latin. Anglo-Norman perhaps ceased to be a real spoken first language by the 1180s but continued to flourish as a language for administration and literature, producing a substantial proportion of the texts written in England up to the late fourteenth century: romances, chronicles, sermons, political satires, drama, learned and devotional works. Norman England was home to a major woman writer writing in French, in the mid-twelfth century: Marie de France, inventor of the Breton lay (the genre of Chaucer's 'Franklin's Tale'), and author, among other things, of two fabliau analogues to the 'Merchant's Tale'. Fourteenth-century authors still composed works in Anglo-Norman, notably Henry, duke of Lancaster's *Livre des seyntz medecines* (1354), the Chandos Herald's *Vie du Prince Noir* (c.1385), and Gower's *Miroir de l'Omme* (c.1374–9) and *Cinkante Ballades* (c.1399), but a sense that such composition increasingly inhabited a ceremonial or royal literary niche emerges from the fact that the first is by a duke, the second about a prince, and the last praises Henry IV. Chaucer's contemporaries still read and wrote Anglo-Norman, and multilingual English society facilitated easy shifting between languages, often within the same text. Such sociolinguistic fluidity also facilitated a gradual increase in writing in English during Chaucer's lifetime.

Parliament decreed in 1362 that lawsuits be conducted in English, though Anglo-Norman law-French remained common for centuries. Anglo-Norman was an acquired skill, learnt by upper-class English children. By the 1380s and 1390s English reading and writing was gaining ground, even among those classes. Ranulf Higden's 1363 preface to his *Polychronicon* famously complains that French (i.e. Anglo-Norman) is the language of instruction; his 1387 translator comments that schools have switched now to English, with the drawback that knowledge of French has declined. Chaucer's joke about the Prioress's ignorance of 'Frenssh of Parys' ('GP' 126) is typical of a long-standing slight embarrassment about the Anglo-Norman dialect in comparison with Continental varieties.

Major Latin authors were often read in French translations, in England as well as France (Valerius Maximus and Mathéolus, echoes of whose writings appear in Chaucer, only became widely known after translations appeared in France in the mid-fourteenth century). War with France doubtless discouraged the use of Anglo-Norman, though England's claim to French territories, Burgundian alliances, and relationships with northern Francophone regimes like Hainault meant there was not a simple, modern distinction between two nation-states. Moreover, Richard II pursued peace and was on good terms with Charles VI.

Books in French, in several dialects, composed in France and England, dominated the libraries of the fourteenth- and fifteenth-century laity, such as Thomas of Woodstock, the Black Prince, Humphrey, duke of Gloucester, Sir John Fastolf, and Edward IV. Some were lavishly decorated, often products of Continental workshops: luxurious and beautiful artworks as well as books for reading. Clerical and monastic libraries held primarily Latin texts, rarely French or English. Fourteenth-century letters of an official nature were generally Latin or Anglo-Norman French, the latter being usual for more personal letters, and business correspondence by merchants or for civic or estate administration. English letter-writing is still rare at the turn of the century. Letters sometimes start and end in French yet couch some of their message in English. Letters in French written by royalty survive, including some by Richard II while in Ireland. Two French narratives of his dramatic last year, 1399, were composed by, respectively, a Frenchman in his brother's household and a valet of the duke of Burgundy who accompanied Richard to Ireland and north Wales. The frequency with which English royalty married French-speaking wives; England's flourishing trade with the Low Countries, Burgundy, and France; the presence of foreign merchants in London, and of Francophone attendants, secretaries, diplomats, and sometimes high-born hostages, in court circles, all meant that Chaucer, born to a rich London merchant family, working as courtier, civil servant, and diplomat, moved throughout his career in a multilingual, cosmopolitan community and culture. Many visitors from across the Channel were important patrons or writers. Hostages taken during the Anglo-French wars included the French king Jean II, from 1356 to 1364, and Charles, duc de Berri, from 1360 to 1367, both patrons of Guillaume de Machaut. The Hainault poet, Jean de Le Mote, served Queen Philippa and her father, Guillaume de Hainault;

Jean Froissart was one of Philippa's secretaries, from 1361 to 1369; his *Paradis d'amour* (*c*.1361) is a source for the *Book of the Duchess*, and *Meliador* (*c*.1365) reflects his visit to Scotland around 1366. Oton de Grandson was a Savoyard knight in John of Gaunt's service for periods in the late 1370s and early 1390s. Chaucer's work, traditionally hailed as the first great liberation and flowering of English literature, benefited from an environment of growing lay literacy and of apparent enthusiasm for new English writing at Richard's court, but also from this multilingual, international environment, exposing him from youth to the latest fashions and experiments in French literature.

Royal princes seem to have moved between the French and English languages with ease. Froissart, who likes to compliment the great, mentions John of Gaunt's skill in reading French. Richard II's library contained French romances and poetry. Froissart presented some of his poems to Richard 'because he read and spoke French very well'; Philippe de Mézières addressed his *Epistre au roi Richart* to him. At the same time, however, Gower's English *Confessio amantis* was also composed in response to a request by Richard; Chaucer probably wrote the *Book of the Duchess* for Gaunt, and honours Richard's Queen Anne in the *Legend of Good Women*, as Clanvowe does in his *Cuckoo and the Nightingale*. Though Richard II clearly appreciated modern French art, French literature, and also the French monarchy's cultivation of grander styles of deference and dignity,[1] his court was at the same time a milieu that also fostered literature in English. Admiration for French literary achievements was not incompatible with cultivation of a new English poetry, much of it in courtly French genres.

Chaucer and contemporary French poetry

Older criticism saw Chaucer's career progressing from early imitation of French dream poetry—seen as a dead, conventional, and artificial model—to first an Italian period, which Kittredge called his 'emancipation' to more 'virile' writing, and finally a triumphantly English period of realism.[2] Recent criticism that has demonstrated the depth of Chaucer's engagement with Italy and Italian literature, notably in the work of Wallace and Havely, has had the indirect effect of leaving intact that older impression: that French influence was conventional and courtly, less adventurous and inspirational.

In fact, French influence is important throughout Chaucer's career. Furthermore, in contemporary French writing, especially the experimentation with lyric and *dit amoureux*, by Machaut, Froissart, Deschamps, and others, Chaucer found an avant-garde of exhilarating sophistication and innovation, and it was innovation precisely in areas that matched his own interests in dialogism, multiple discourses, and plural voices, encounters between different levels and spheres of experience. These French poets, above all Machaut, opened up new ways of exploring the self and consciousness, the relationship of passion to philosophy, and issues connected with the status of the artist and the contemporary poet's relationship to patrons and readers.

Such writers are not the only major French influences on Chaucer, but there is every reason to think that he saw himself, and was recognized by some of them, as one of their group, exploring what could be done with the *dit amoureux* and the ballade, forms that were being used with fluidity and technical virtuosity, pushing at the boundaries of how art could interrogate individual consciousness, authorship, and relationships between literature and life. Chaucer's dream poems are full of the phrasing and imagery of this French poetry.

Some specific influences are easily told. Firstly, like Eustache Deschamps, Chaucer employed the short lyric ballade for a range of subject matters beyond love: for political, personal, philosophical, moral, and humorous topics. A device Chaucer adopts from Machaut's *Jugement dou roy de Navarre* (1349) is to reverse the viewpoint of an earlier poem in a subsequent one. He thus presents his *Legend of Good Women* as obeying a command from the God of Love to reverse the alleged misogyny of *Troilus* and the *Romaunt of the Rose*. The *Canterbury Tales* experiments further with tales that reverse and 'quit' each other, and with audiences who veto and redirect the author's plans, as when Chaucer's pilgrims themselves, mid-work, halt certain tales or decide the next stage in the sequence. Machaut's and Chaucer's narrators, in *Navarre* and the *Legend*, are both told their previous poems are offences against women because they depict unfaithful women, and Machaut's allusions to the tragic fidelity of Dido, Ariadne, and Medea perhaps contributed to Chaucer's decision to depict faithful women in the *Legend*.

The French poets introduce themselves, but dramatized in various quasi-autobiographical personas, into their texts, often by name. The dreamer in a poem by Deschamps, for instance, is addressed as 'Eustache' by other characters and identified as the writer.[3] Chaucer's dreamers are greeted as 'Geffrey', or identified with his writings (e.g. *HF* 558, 729; *LGW* (G) 246–315, 405–20). This self-reference is part of a new assertiveness about vernacular secular literature, and a self-advertisement of the individual writer and his œuvre. This fourteenth-century movement (innovatory in an age when literature was often seen as celebrating, and owned by, its patron and when secular literature did not automatically command respect) is also discernible in Dante (1265–1321), but it is Chaucer's French contemporaries who play with recurrent self-reference and variations on the dramatized figure of the narrator, and seem to have inspired Chaucer in the dream poems, *Troilus*, and the *Canterbury Tales*. His dramatizations include a self-effacing narrator, who does not take himself particularly seriously; a narrator with a deferential relationship to others, producing situations where the author seems to be pushed around by his own characters; narrators who are observers and recorders rather than the primary actors in love-dramas; an ageing poet; a mere translator; or—a persona fitting the real-life position of Machaut, Chaucer, and others as secretaries and courtiers in the households of princes—one who writes at command. Chaucer uses these figures to create a stance for the author of detachment and lack of responsibility or control in relation to his text and its readers. This play with narrators has complex implications for the presentation of ideas in the poems, and for Chaucer's engagement with the socio-economics of fourteenth-century authorship. It takes us beyond the older critics' simpler notion of a realistically conceived fictionalized 'persona': Chaucer's dim-witted narrator, as constructed by Donaldson and Betherum in the 1950s.[4] In *Troilus*, for example, a narrator conceived as a detached translator with no experience of love forms part of a complex structure of simultaneous involvement with and detachment from the subject of love, which constitutes the real philosophical conundrum of Chaucer's poem.

Other writers in late fourteenth-century London and Westminster circles responded to the same French poets and fashions: examples are Usk's *Testament of Love* (*c.*1387), which uses the daisy image that Machaut and Froissart had employed, and Clanvowe's *Cuckoo and the Nightingale*, a St Valentine's Day vision (*c.*1385) like the *Parliament of Fowls*, and several of de Grandson's poems. In French and English courts, composing poetry was linked to other entertainments. There were tournaments on St Valentine's Day (Richard held one in 1385) besides poems in the day's honour. The poetry competitions called 'puys' apparently existed in England as well as France. Poets write of lords and ladies holding courts of love, declaring their judgements on matters of love, giving commands to poets, joining elegant, playful 'orders' like those of the Flower and the Leaf: groups of young courtiers who championed the respective merits of pleasure and self-control. Such motifs are certainly powerful in poetry and perhaps actually existed to some extent, at least in court social life.

Late fourteenth-century *dits amoureux* belong to a century-long process of development from the greatest of all love-visions, the *Roman de la Rose*. They became shorter. Dreams and gardens are not the only framing devices. *Dits* use many frames: narrators who fall asleep and dream, narrators who wake up and go on journeys, narrators who overhear, and narrators who enter into gardens, temples, islands, and other secluded and wondrous places. These may enclose allegories, debates, mythological figures, and parliaments; there are overheard laments, inset lyrics and fables, didactic speeches, and frequently authority figures or dream-guides. This was a capacious genre, permitting adventurous juxtapositions and contrasts of subject matter, mingling light and serious or amorous and philosophical themes. De Le Mote, Machaut, Froissart, and de Grandson use the *dit* as a showcase for inset tales, complaints, or lyrics. It is not surprising that Chaucer's *Legend of Good Women* combines a dream Prologue with a sequence of short tales, and the lyrico-narrative *dits* probably prompted the inclusion of lyrics in Chaucer's dream poems and *Troilus* and the complaint in the 'Squire's Tale' (499–629). Chaucer invented the use of an inset story near the start of a dream poem to raise issues for later exploration (his tales of Dido, Scipio, Ceyx and Alcione). Many *dits*, including Machaut's *Fonteinne amoureuse* and de Grandson's *Livre Messire Ode*, present an overheard voice, a lyric complaint, as a discrete element within a narrative with several disparate modes and themes. Similar counterpoint between lyric voice and narrative appears in Chaucer's *Anelida and Arcite*, the 'Complaint unto Pity', the *Book of the Duchess*, the 'Complaint of Mars', and the 'Squire's Tale', and is perhaps even a forerunner to that polyphony of voices and world-views that is central to the structures of *Troilus* and the *Canterbury Tales*.

Dream poems: creative responses, interpretative independence

The *Book of the Duchess* exemplifies the creative stimulation Chaucer found in working with several sources simultaneously. Its chief sources are the *Roman de la Rose*, Machaut's *Jugement dou roy de Behaingne* (1342?), *Jugement dou roy de Navarre*, *Remede de Fortune* (*c*.1341), and *Fonteinne amoureuse* (1361), Froissart's *Paradis d'amour* (*c*.1362), and perhaps his *Bleu chevalier* (*c*.1364).

We should not assume that using a source inevitably means that the source's meanings apply to Chaucer's own text. Thus, though the *Duchess*'s first twenty-four lines echo Froissart's *Paradis*, 1–12, Froissart explicitly attributes the melancholy described to love-sickness; Chaucer never does. And the interpretative uncertainty in which this places Chaucer's reader continues as an important structural element in his unfolding text. His Ceyx and Alcione episode uses Ovid's *Metamorphoses* book 9, Statius' *Thebaid*, Machaut's *Fonteinne amoureuse*, and possibly the *Ovide moralisé* (a sequence of Christian allegorizations of Ovid's *Metamorphoses* written around 1320). Chaucer, like Machaut, abbreviates the tale to focus on the bereaved wife, yet changes Machaut's husband's plea, 'remember me', to a plea that Alcione may recover from grief and accept his death. Like the anonymous *Songe vert* (1348?), Chaucer's poem may both lament the dead and delicately suggest remarriage. The *Duchess* was probably an elegy or memorial for Blanche of Lancaster but lacks any explicit consolation or religious message. What consolation a reader finds inheres in such details as this message from the dead spouse: interpretation depends on intense attention to the texture of Chaucer's writing. That means that substituting what his sources say for the usually more equivocal effects of what Chaucer's text says can imperil the kind of reading this poem requires.

At times critics have done just that. Some have argued for a Christian message in the *Duchess*, derived from Christian interpretations proffered by the *Ovide moralisé*.[5] Only in Chaucer's version does Ceyx ask Alcione to cease mourning (the *Ovide moralisé* requests black clothes and sorrow, Machaut's version remembrance). Chaucer also breaks off abruptly with Alcione's death, where several sources add a consolation: Ovid and Machaut have the metamorphosis of the couple into birds, the *Ovide moralisé* a promise of Christ's resurrection, interpreting Ceyx as the soul, Alcione as worldliness.

An otherwise extremely perceptive study of the poem by John Lawlor derived an interpretation (secular this time, not Christian) of Chaucer's poem from two sources: he argues first that Chaucer's narrator is a lover suffering from unfulfilled desire like Froissart's, and that this fact consequently plays a crucial role in the dialogue with the

Man in Black, and, secondly, that Chaucer offers John of Gaunt the message found in Machaut's *Behaingne*, that fulfilled love, even though cut short by death, is better than unfulfilled desire.[6] More recent criticism, however, treats sources less rigidly. Chaucer's poem seems to work on what is left uncertain or unspoken. The sources, for any readers familiar with them, may, at most, cause further ideas or answers to hover round the experience Chaucer's text gives us, but they do not substitute for it.

Each of Chaucer's dream poems takes elements from the tradition of *dits* and dream poetry and puts them in new juxtapositions that invite the reader's participation in the creation of meaning. The *House of Fame* uses the journey to another world, a dream, goddesses, debate, and a temple, but it is for Chaucer's readers to make sense of how its successive experiences and levels may relate to each other. His 'man of gret auctorite' (2158) reflects the traditional motif of the dream-guide, the inbuilt interpretation. But in this text—as we have it—he never arrives.

The *Parliament of Fowls* brings together material from Italian and Latin literature within frame devices of the walled garden and the assembly of birds, long established in French. Its complexities, however, go far beyond anything attempted by Chaucer's French or Italian contemporaries. It looks outwards, from the worlds of the *dits* and Boccaccio's garden and temple of Venus, towards politics and philosophy: the class conflicts of human society presented in the poem undermine Alain de Lille's vision of Nature as earthly harmony (from his *De planctu Naturae*), and the conflicts of passion are juxtaposed with Cicero's *Somnium Scipionis*, a vision of a cosmos where human desires seem very small. This same opposition between individual emotional intensity and cosmic impersonality is employed by Chaucer for the end of *Troilus*.

The *Legend of Good Women* reworks the motifs of the daisy, the Flower and the Leaf, and the dictatorial God of Love, to focus attention not on the dramas of masculine desire that dominate most French *dits*, complaints, and dream poems, from the *Roman de la Rose* on, but on perfect 'wifhod' (G 535), and on women who were martyrs to faithful love. Chaucer learned from Froissart to invent new, quasi-Greek, mythology: he reformulates Alcestis, Cybele, and Ariadne in his apotheosis of Alceste into a daisy and a star. Froissart invented a pseudo-Ovidian myth of Héro, whose tears at her lover's death were turned into daisies by the gods, in his seventeenth *Pastourelle* and one of his *dits* praising the daisy. Machaut's *Dit de la marguerite* (*c.*1364) and *Dit de la fleur de lis et de la marguerite* (1369) and Deschamps's *Lay de franchise* (1385) also use the daisy image. Chaucer's F Prologue takes this in a new, slightly mysterious direction by infusing his presentation with religious language. He calls the Flower and Leaf subjects on which his great predecessors have written songs (F 79), perhaps referring to now lost Flower and Leaf poetry or to Deschamps's allusions to the Flower and the Leaf.

While Ovid is the chief source for Chaucer's series of 'good women', his sympathetic handling of them and criticism of treacherous and ungrateful men probably reflects La Vieille's comments on Medea and Dido in the *Roman de la Rose* and the consequent defence of them in Le Fèvre's pro-feminine *Livre de Leësse* (*c.*1380; an answer to the notorious anti-feminist satire of Mathéolus). Critics until recently usually interpreted

Chaucer's heroines ironically, but there is no reason to take the *Legend*'s rebuttal of the standard misogynist attack on women's fidelity as anything but serious. The married love represented by Alceste and Chaucer's anti-misogynist God of Love, a moral judge completely unlike the God of Love in the *Roman de la Rose*, links, in fact, with a new anti-misogyny movement, praising marriage, found in de Mézières's writing and soon afterwards in Christine de Pizan's. She and later fifteenth-century feminists like Martin Le Franc redirected the tradition of courtly love *dits* to provide an elegant, glamorous vehicle for this more moral and respectful literary presentation of sexual desire and women. Chaucer's *Legend* stands at the beginning of this development.

Chaucer and French romance

French romance was the dominant influence on medieval European secular writing, imitated and translated in other European vernaculars. It was a central force in the cultural world of European aristocracy, reflecting and promoting that class's values and self-image. Chivalric romance forms the basis of much of its art, decoration, and life-style. Pageants and tournaments imitated romances, mythology, and allegory. Chaucer invokes these powerful associations in the bedchamber in the *Book of the Duchess*, illustrated with scenes from two deeply influential French romances, the *Roman de Troie* (c.1165) and *Roman de la Rose* (c.1237 and 1274). Like later references to Hector, Alexander, Roland, and Oliver, these allusions locate the encounter with the Man in Black within the vision of aristocratic ideals. A knight is the first human figure we see in the *Canterbury Tales*, conceived entirely in terms of those values ('honour', 'courteisie') and the warfare against infidels that romances, and the cultural ideology they served, portrayed as the highest secular masculine ideals. The crusaders' 1365 sack of Alexandria was, historically, strategically useless, with shameful massacre and looting. Chaucer's reference to it in the course of praising his perfect 'gentil' knight ('GP' 51) reflects the glamour of Machaut's chivalric romance *La Prise d'Alexandrie* (c.1369). Chaucer depicts Criseyde and her ladies listening to the *Roman de Thèbes* (*TC* 2. 100) and jokes about the popularity of Lancelot among women readers ('NPT' 3212–13). The social ideals of romance and echoes of particular romances appear throughout Chaucer's œuvre.

A centuries-long cultural tradition, especially one that presents a relatively unified world-view, like much medieval romance does (despite the rich variety contained within that genre), inevitably harbours internal conflicts and complexities. These emerge intriguingly in the 'Franklin's Tale'. Any reader familiar with the world of romances would accept that, in leaving Dorigen 'To seke in armes worshipe and hon-our' (811), Arveragus acts honourably. Modern readers might criticize him: almost certainly a misreading in terms of romance tradition and its usual assumptions, and the episode's role in the tale. The tension between that modern, critical approach (pro-wife) and the privileging of masculine military honour usual in romances (pro-glory) was not, however, always repressed in the history of romance: it surfaced in some early French romances, notably Chrétien de Troyes's *Yvain* (*c*.1177). Chaucer's tale, attempting radically to push back conventional views of male power in marriage and male ownership of woman's sexuality, comes up against several such problematic assumptions about masculine honour. Though the text interrogates conventional, gendered ideas about honour, it remains deeply imbued with masculinist rhetoric. The result, artistically, is some awkward moments in the text (749–52, 1457–86) and Arveragus' attempts to act generously and with 'trouthe', extending these principles to his wife's behaviour, clash with ideals of masculine honour as power. Unsurprisingly the provocative discussion of marriage and freedom that opens this tale echoes the *Roman de la Rose* (13959–66), a text whose diversity of views constantly challenges over-unified views of life.

Chaucer apparently resisted the temptation to compose his own large-scale romances on classic French romance subjects: Arthur, Lancelot, Tristan, the Grail, or Crusade cycle. His Arthurian mini-romance, the 'Wife of Bath's Tale', is related to English 'loathly lady' stories like *The Wedding of Sir Gawain and Dame Ragnell*. His 'Franklin's Tale' is his original reworking of the Breton lay, using it to raise questions: not only about freedom and generosity (1622) but about how a good God could create so dangerous a world (865–90). The 'Squire's Tale' is in the tradition of romances of Eastern origin and, though no close sources exist, several analogues are French, such as Adenet le Roi's *Cleomadès* and Girard d'Amiens's *Méliacin* (both based on the *Thousand and One Nights*). *Troilus and Criseyde* and the 'Knight's Tale' show Chaucer setting two of Boccaccio's classical narratives about passion against the challenge of Boethian philosophy. *Troilus* draws also on the *Roman de Troie*, one of the seminal French romances to idealize love and knightly warfare, yet conceives Pandarus partly in the very different spirit of uncourtly French fabliaux. Chaucer seems to use romances to set up provocative contrasts: between ideals of love and honour (and the romance genre which most embodied them) contrasted with the worlds presented by other types of literature, comic, philosophical, or cynical.

Perhaps he avoided subjects from mainstream romance traditions inherited from France because they all, in one way or another, entailed subscribing to some pre-ordained world-view. All of them, whether the baronial romance like *Guy of Warwick*, or Arthurian subjects or grail stories, incur implicit conscription to a cause: great families, royal ideology, transcendental religious absolutism. Chaucer's romances escape these restrictions, into classical, Celtic, and Eastern subjects. If Chaucer avoided the old-fashioned chivalric romance with its endless sub-plots, preferring to create shorter, more unified, romance-style tales and choosing instead the story collection for his greatest achievement, it was perhaps because a story collection within a frame-story offered a multi-stranded structure but one, unlike conventional romance, open to maximum variety, allowing clashes of styles, ideology, social classes, and genres.

Fabliaux

Of Chaucer's fabliau-style tales, the 'Reeve's Tale' has the closest French parallels, and comparisons with these are illuminating. Chaucer probably knew the thirteenth-century fabliau *Le Meunier et les ii clers*. He displays brilliantly all the skills that make a fabliau work: timing, pace, and suspense; low motives and high comic fantasy; malicious energies; slapstick and outrageous excess in the plot, all working up towards the exhilarating, justice-restoring, climax. Yet, without blurring these effects, he enriches them with new themes and satire. Kolve shows iconographic images of lust interwoven through the 'Reeve's Tale'.[7] Blood, in many senses, is a recurrent theme: Christ's blood, the parson's diversion of church funds for his illegitimate offspring (3983–6), the fisticuffs at the end, and the ambitions to elevate the peasant family bloodline to dizzy social heights through the daughter's marriage. The *Meunier* has the double entendres typical of fabliaux, including a cupboard-bed with its key, a penis-key analogy found in other fabliaux, including *Du Prestre ki abevete* (an analogue to Chaucer's 'Merchant's Tale', which itself uses it).

The *Meunier* has an unnamed 'city' and isolated mill; its unnamed characters only have attributes required by the plot: prettiness in the daughter, poverty in the students, a baby for the wife. Compared with its plot-centred stereotyping, typical of fabliaux, Chaucer gives localized and contemporary socio-economic verisimilitude, in his portraits of the family, their setting, attributes, the students' north-eastern accents, and so on. Animal imagery, common in fourteenth-century denigration of peasants, contributes to sharp social satire, which also targets corrupt clergy and a recent phenomenon on the late fourteenth-century economic scene: the rich peasant or tradesman (Chaucer's Reeve is himself one). Chaucer's denouement punishes Symkyn for upward mobility as much as dishonesty. The *Meunier*'s students are operating on their own, to improve their ailing finances. By connecting them to a college, defending its honour against the cheeky miller, Chaucer introduces another socio-economic force in contemporary England: colleges were the all-powerful financial power in Cambridge, a fact that made them targets of Cambridge's local form of the 1381 rising. There is class-warfare on several fronts in Chaucer's version. It also has an amusing injection of intellectual themes, like his other Oxbridge tale, the 'Miller's Tale': here Symkyn's well-worn joke against over-clever university styles of argument (4122–6); in the 'Miller's Tale' the themes of astrology, 'ymaginacioun', and God's 'pryvetee' (3163–6, 3611–13).

French tales are among the analogues to the Merchant's, Shipman's, Manciple's, and Summoner's Tales. The last elaborates its scatological bequest (resembling the fabliau *Le vescie a prestre*, 'The Priest's Bladder') and its stock fabliau types (worldly friar, canny peasant) with a dazzling mixture of theological and scientific discourse and with Chaucer's usual socially acute perspective on contemporary English interactions across the classes. Deschamps's misogynist *Miroir de mariage* influenced the debate on marriage in the 'Merchant's Tale'. French analogues to Chaucer's fabliaux do not lack art, wit, and satire, but the lines are sparer and less ambitious in contemporary socio-logical observation than Chaucer's extraordinarily richly textured comedies.

The Renart cycle and the 'Nun's Priest's Tale'

Sources for the 'Nun's Priest's Tale' include the twelfth-century *Roman de Renart* and Marie de France's Anglo-Norman *Fables*. As with fabliaux, Chaucer manages skilfully the characteristic pleasures of this genre (talking animals, roguish adventures, social satire, and a familiar, well-loved cast), while diversifying his own text with dream lore, science, philosophy, rhetorical grandeur, and classical allusions. As the adult-sized frame round the animals' world, he substitutes a poor widow of exemplary frugality (providing a deeper moral and political contrast with the overweening cock) for *Renart*'s comfortably-off peasant Constans de Noës, whose house overflows with food: poultry, salted meat, bacon, and corn. The *Renart* preface, comparing the story to Tristan and Paris's rape of Helen, and similar mock-heroic allusions, including Hecuba and Andromache, in another Renart text, *Renart le Contrefait*, probably inspired Chaucer's extravagantly mock-heroic style. *Renart*'s ironic repetition of the fox's duplicitous use of the friendly word 'cousin' perhaps prompted Chaucer's similar wordplay on cousinship and cozening in the 'Shipman's Tale' and on 'brother' in the 'Friar's Tale'. Chaucer's Fall of Chauntecleer, now detached from the longer Renart saga, becomes a comic continuation of his 'Monk's Tale' themes of Fortune and the Falls of Princes. Marie de France supplied the tale's moral about indiscreet talking; Chaucer, by adding his 'fruyt' and 'chaf' conclusion (3438–46) opens the tale up to optional further interpretations as an allegory of human sin and Adam's Fall, posing a dilemma about interpretation (religious or secular?) that makes this tale a microcosm of the similar puzzle represented by the whole of the *Canterbury Tales*.

French readings of Griselda and the 'Clerk's Tale'

The passages with which Chaucer ends the 'Clerk's Tale' display how many different potential interpretations its plot can generate. This is a virtuoso exhibition of disparate readings: three voiced by the Clerk (spiritual allegory, misogynist slur on modern wives, encouragement to termagants), another by the Merchant and the Host (a lesson for wives). Such bizarrely irreconcilable readings mirror the diverse reception of the Griselda story found in French texts, all or most undoubtedly familiar to Chaucer. Griselda was a popular topic in late fourteenth-century France.[8] Chaucer's main sources were the *Livre Griseldis* (*c*.1390?) and Philippe de Mézières's *Le Miroir des dames mariées* (1385–9), besides Petrarch's Latin (1374). The original plot itself was already highly provocative, containing oppression of women, apparent child-murder, and a barbaric, demonic folklore ancestry for the figure of Walter. It was also paradoxical since Griselda the victim is simultaneously heroic in her 'patience'. Petrarch insisted that the story does not teach women to imitate Griselda but must be read allegorically, with Walter representing God's testing of humans and Griselda the soul. The *Livre* repeats this reading, but de Mézières, the powerful defender of women and Christian marriage against misogyny, condemns Walter's cruelty while approving Griselda's (that is, the soul's) patience in tribulation. Chaucer similarly inserts condemnations of Walter (455–62, 619–23). Yet the tale appears in the *Menagier de Paris*'s book of instruction for a wife (*c*.1393) exactly as if its target audience were indeed wives, and endorses the message of wifely obedience (though saying that Walter's behaviour suits a socially unequal union with a shepherdess more than the author's with his own wife). Goodwin shows that at least one manuscript of the *Livre* alters it to present a conservative lesson of submission for wives.[9] The tale's potential for multiple and contradictory readings also includes feminist implications, in Griselda's heroic strength and her rebuttal of the medieval anti-feminist stereotyping of women as inconstant and rebellious, and some French manuscripts produced for women show the story being regarded as a philosophical and/or pro-women text, while other manuscript contexts foreground the religious, gender-neutral message.

Chaucer does not use French versions simply as cribs to help with a Latin source. Griselda demonstrates how Chaucer's cosmopolitan reading and use of multiple sources, like these varied French responses to Petrarch's original, can work together creatively with his own instinct towards dialogic narratives to produce exactly that type of writing that most characterizes his genius, seeming to inhabit simultaneously diverse worlds and sympathies and engender disparate interpretations.

The 'Man of Law's Tale' and Nicholas Trevet's *Chronicle*

Anglo-Norman literature was no minor cultural backwater. It had been ahead of Continental French in producing vernacular texts in the fields of history, science, philosophy, biblical translation, administration, and drama. Like Chaucer's work this testifies to the stimulation a multilingual culture can create.

Chaucer's most important Anglo-Norman inspiration is Nicholas Trevet's *Chronicle* (*c*.1334), source for the 'Man of Law's Tale'. Previous criticism of medieval literature generally undervalued pious works written for and by women; recent criticism recognizes the cultural significance and the qualities of medieval women's literature, including hagiography. Chaucer's hagiographical and quasi-hagiographical tales, like that of Custance, have enjoyed increasing analysis from these perspectives.

Acknowledgement of Trevet's own tale's merits has, however, lagged behind. Yet though Trevet is no Chaucer, he presents the tale interestingly, combining the modes of romance, history, and saint's life. Chaucer simplifies Trevet's typically romance-like plot, a concatenation of adventures and characters, filled with names and places, suiting its original context in a chronicle. Trevet's storytelling is vigorous: strong in concise but realistically conceived details. Trevet wrote for Marie, Edward I's daughter, a nun at Amesbury. His heroine is also a royal daughter and redoubtable woman of the Church, whose husband, like Edward I, wars against the Scots. She is resourceful, despite many vicissitudes, actively promotes the faith, is phenomenally learned, and knows many languages: a heroine any nun could admire and enjoy. Trevet shows an interest in language: an Anglo-Saxon character speaks English and God speaks Latin (his dark-age Britons unfortunately do not speak in Welsh), and Chaucer, perhaps stimulated by Trevet's interest in sixth-century languages, tells us that Custance speaks 'a maner Latyn corrupt' (519).

Trevet combines a sensational plot of implausible coincidences and marvels with everyday plausible details: his touches like the anger of the people attacking the anxious husband, Alla, as he rushes back from Scotland after getting dreadful news from home, and Alla's worried interrogation of the household on arriving home, are well imagined. Chaucer makes cuts. These make a more unified design and detach his Custance somewhat from this realistic, historically rooted, social environment, turning her into a universal figure of the human soul enduring adversity, and even more of a saint who, though buffeted round the physical world, marrying, and giving birth, is essentially separate from the world. She is an ethereal figure already dwelling mentally and spiritually with her heavenly father. Chaucer adds sententious and rhetorical appeals and judgements (perhaps reflecting the new context, a story told by a lawyer, one whose profession involves rhetoric). Trevet was an Oxford intellectual, renowned for works on astronomy, history, and philosophy; a strong link with Chaucer is his commentary on Boethius. Chaucer's learned elaborations within the tale may express homage to the wider œuvre of Trevet.

We can see some effects of Chaucer's changes in the episode of Hermengyld's murder. Trevet details Custance's discovery, in concretely imagined experiences from her point of view: waking up in a dark bedroom and realizing from moisture that her companion is soaked in blood, and raising the alarm, which brings in lights that reveal the slaughter. Trevet's constable stands up for Custance's innocence vigorously, despite the incriminating gory dagger planted on her pillow. As the murderer falsely testifies, God's hand slays him, declaring Custance's innocence. Trevet's is a drama of vigorous excitement and action. Chaucer removes Custance's agency. She does nothing; it is the constable who finds the body (603–5). Chaucer intensifies the sense of pathos and Custance's helpless, passive victimization, stressing that she had 'no champioun' (631). Similar shifts occur in Custance's second exiling. Her resourceful personality, realistic speeches, and reactions in the Anglo-Norman text are cut, with a corresponding intensification of the pathos of her plight and her lack of any aid save God and Mary's protection. Trevet's heroine, when a man tries to rape her, craftily says that her 2-year-old son is old enough to understand and remember what is going on, then persuades her assailant to walk to the front of the ship to look out for land; she creeps up behind him stealthily and tosses him into the sea. Chaucer's scene stresses impotence and pathos: 'this wrecched womman' reacts to threatened rape simply by crying 'pitously'. The baby wails too. It is the Virgin who miraculously causes the criminal to fall overboard (918–22).

Chaucer deepens a hagiographical colouring already present in Trevet's text. His tale also becomes more patriarchal, with Custance more dependent on autocratic men's whims, desires, and jurisdictions at every point. Her life's journey is directed initially by her royal father in Rome, the father to whom she is returned after her trials. Fortune and destiny ensure that she finds no resting place in the human world but her life's real director is the heavenly Father, who with Mary is more caring than any mortal turns out to be. Trevet depicted a strong woman, a servant of God and guarded by God, but situated in a concrete and historical social milieu, with capacity to act as well as suffer. Chaucer depicts a woman whose survival depends not on resourcefulness but on total submission to the divine power.

Chaucer's rhetorically heightened rendering also underlines the anti-Islamic element in the tale: the sultaness becomes a demonized monster:

> O Sowdanesse, roote of iniquitee!
> Virago, thou Semyrame the secounde!
> O serpent under femynynytee,
> Lik to the serpent depe in helle ybounde! (358–61)

He adds the theme of planetary influence (190–203, 295–315). The wider *Canterbury Tales* context also now affects the story's implications. Like the portrait of the Knight, it helps bring Christendom's relationship with Islam into the ambit of the *Tales*. As with Griselda and the Prioress's little 'clergeon', the tale becomes an exercise in literary pathos. The 'Man of Law's Prologue' links it with other tales of faithful but unhappy 'noble wyves' told by Chaucer (57–76). This Prologue also intriguingly introduces a complaint about poverty (99–121) whose sources are partly the deeply otherworldly *De miseria condicionis humanae* by Pope Innocent III and partly a very worldly condemnation of poverty from the *Roman de la Rose* (7921–8206).

Comparing Trevet's and Chaucer's versions illustrates the continuing influence of Anglo-Norman literature and illuminates some of the extraordinarily rich and varied elements contained within that strangely flamboyant and assertively written tale of extreme humility, the 'Man of Law's Tale'.

French influence on style and versification

The professional jargon through which Chaucer often characterizes people frequently contains French-derived terms: 'fee simple', 'chevyssaunce', 'poudre-marchaunt', 'magyk natureel', 'tables Tolletanes' (note the preservation of French noun–adjective order). French loan-words in English increased rapidly during the fourteenth century. Learned and elegant French words gave writers diverse and flexible vocabulary and stylistic confidence. Chaucer's achievement in creating in English writing that, in its own national terms, equalled the elegance of the French *dits* and lyrics led to praise of him in the fifteenth century for having enhanced the national language.

French loans often cluster in areas of fashion, warfare, administration, and law, areas marked by earlier Norman domination: Alison's '*ceynt . . . barred* al of silk', embroidered 'coler', smartly matching 'tapes' and 'voluper', all of a 'suyte', and that saucily pitched 'filet', making the rich tradesman's wife sharply stylish ('MT' 3235–43); the terms 'chivalrie', 'curteisie', 'noble armee', 'mortal batailles', 'sovereyn prys', 'bacheler', and 'chyvachie', characterizing the Knight and Squire; the legal register for the lawyer: 'justice', 'assise', 'patente', 'pleyn commissioun' ('GP' 45–67, 80–5, 314–15).

French loans' more regular patterns of final suffixes aided English rhyme, seen in the following passage of everyday diction:

> And after wol I telle of our *viage*
> And al the *remenaunt* of oure *pilgrimage*.
> But first I *pray* yow, of youre *curteisye*,
> That ye n'*arette* it nat my *vileynye*,
> Thogh that I *pleyn*ly speke in this *mateere*,
> To telle yow hir wordes and hir *cheere*,
>
> ('GP' 723–8)

and in the courtly ballade, 'Womanly Noblesse', with only seven English words (five ending -*nesse*) in thirty-two rhyme-words. Chaucer invented the iambic pentameter, perhaps partly influenced by French decasyllabics. He introduced into English literature the ballade, envoy, complaint, and rondel, experimenting like Machaut, Deschamps, and de Grandson with a variety of stanzaic patterns. His 'Complaint of Venus' reformulates three separate ballades by de Grandson to express a single story. While the poem compliments de Grandson's artistry and laments the English language's lack of rhyme (80–2), Chaucer still manages delicate verbal patterning (for example, in stanza four) and the demanding rhyme-scheme skilfully. He translates from one gender to another: de Grandson's expressions of masculine desire become a woman's lament. Chaucer's language alters to fit gendered perceptions of male–female difference: stanzas two and three, for example, strengthen the attributes and power of the, now masculine, beloved (such as his 'bounte, wysdom, governaunce').

Translations

Chaucer's major translations, the *Romaunt of the Rose*, *Boece*, and *Melibee*, helped develop the art of English translation, especially in the language's capacity, in lexis and syntax, to translate elegant philosophical and technical writing. Though Chaucer presumably translated all the *Roman de la Rose*, of the three extant fragments only the first is definitely thought to be his. *Boece* reflects his use of a multiple source: the Latin original (Boethius' *Consolation of Philosophy*), with Trevet's commentary and Jean de Meun's French translation.

Chaucer's 'ABC', however, illustrates his readiness, like many medieval translators, to reconceptualize a text. This prayer to the Virgin comes from the long French allegorical dream poem Guillaume de Deguilleville's *Pèlerinage de vie humaine* (c.1330). This was an 'anti-Rose', a tale of humanity's quest for Grace designed to counter the values of the *Roman de la Rose*. A feature of Chaucer's version is that he incorporates into his lyric several themes from its original larger setting, the *Pèlerinage* itself. Chaucer begins and ends his poem with the same line, creating the circular structure that was fashionable among English poets at the close of the fourteenth century.

'Melibee'

Nothing now seems less plausible than the older critical view that 'Melibee' is a ludicrously uninteresting piece, intended as a joke. Chaucer's 'own' tale presented to English readers a thought-provoking political debate about peace, vengeance, and violence. 'Melibee' translates Renaud de Louens's *Livre de Melibée et Prudence* (1337), a version of Albertanus de Brescia's *Liber de consolationis et consilii* (1246). Both texts had had a continuing history of being recontextualized to comment on changing political situations in different European contexts.[10]

What topical implications might Chaucer's version have? Among several historicist interpretations, Ferster links it to war with France and opposition to Richard II in the late 1380s.[11] But is it, as often assumed, really attacking Richard? After line 1199 Chaucer omits the biblical sentence 'Woe to the land that has a child as a lord and whose lord dines in the morning' (*Melibée*, 25. 2), perhaps to avoid offending Richard: he became king at the age of 10 and enemies criticized his self-indulgence. Chaucer omits a condemnation of those who use excessive force (12. 2) and there are other changes that possibly adapt *Melibée* for a Ricardian court audience.[12] Richard sought peace with France in the 1390s. Does Prudence's pacifism promote and complement royal policy?[13] Chaucer's 'own' tales, 'Melibee' and 'Sir Thopas', represent the two main traditionally acceptable roles for court poets: the 'adviser to princes' and the minstrel, the mere entertainer (parodied in 'Thopas', which also represents a chivalric warrior as ludicrous—another pacifist stratagem?).

Renaud's *Melibée* had a female dedicatee, a noblewoman at the court of Burgundy, and specifically declared its purpose to be that of instruction and benefit of princes and barons. It abbreviates some of the Latin Prudence's more dryly intellectual material, producing a more wifelike wise counsellor. Chaucer further omits a misogynist comment—voiced by the undisciplined hothead Melibée (*Melibée*, 3. 6). As a consequence,

Chaucer's Prudence forms part of a *Canterbury Tales* sequence of authoritative female speakers, challenging arguments voiced by males, including Cecilia in the 'Second Nun's Tale', the Wife of Bath, and the old woman in the 'Wife of Bath's Tale'.

Chaucer and the *Roman de la Rose*

The influence of the *Roman de la Rose* appears throughout Chaucer's work. Its phrases and themes become part of his own language; his use of proverbs and mythological allusions often echoes the *Roman*'s. Guillaume de Lorris began the poem around 1235; Jean de Meun's long continuation dates from around 1275. Guillaume's elegant allegory of a young man falling in love, presented as the entry into a walled 'garden of delight', representing courtly society as well as the pursuit of heterosexual desire, was the seminal influence on the great medieval tradition of amorous dream-literature. Its opening, depicting a narrator walking down a pretty path bordered with flowers, amid birdsong and perfect spring weather, arriving at a secluded paradisal place where love, beauty, joy, and lovers' sufferings are acted out, would reappear in many later poems including Chaucer's. Chaucer places an allusion to the *Roman* in the garden of coarse sensuality, loveless union, and adultery that forms the centre of the 'Merchant's Tale' (2031–3): the intertextual associations seem to contrast with January's senile lust and morally blinded mind. Yet the *Roman*'s own garden itself involves ambiguous echoes of the Fall in Eden, and its dreamer in becoming the thrall of the God of Love goes against Reason's counsel—and Reason in medieval thought is a voice of God.

The moral problematization discernible (for readers who choose to discern it) in Guillaume's plot and landscape gives way to an unequivocally challenging and satirical narrative in de Meun's continuation. Sensual and intellectual, obsessed with heterosexual desire yet notoriously misogynist (even to many medieval readers), cynical at times, pornographic at others, yet teaching Christian perspectives on Nature and Fortune, this continuation used Guillaume's theme of earthly sexual love to explore many serious, even academic, subjects, including contemporary theology and the nature of free will. A climate of debate, moral complexity, and questions about this world and its values animate it. Characters hold forth in long, provocative, often learned, speeches, with no indication which views (if any) are authorial or ironic. Given the interest in multiple discourses and voices that characterizes Chaucer's writing, it is easy to see why the *Roman* proved such a constant inspiration.

An example is the speech of La Vieille (the Old Woman): worldly-wise advice to both sexes, in the spirit of Ovid's witty, cynical *Art of Love*, on how to outwit each other and come out top in the quest for sex, money, and power. It is confusingly diverse in viewpoint: while it advises women on how to make the best of themselves, it presents to male readers a picture of women as dangerous, mercenary manipulators. Yet it also describes Phyllis, Dido, and Medea (the two latter often treated hostilely in earlier writings) as victims of exploitative, treacherous men, and this positive presentation influenced Le Fèvre, Machaut's *Navarre*, and Chaucer's *Legend of Good Women*. Apart from its internal inconsistencies, does the speech speak for the author? Does de Meun's cynicism contradict the apparent idealization of love by de Lorris or is the composite *Roman* somehow ultimately coherent? Like many aspects of the *Roman*, this speech, and that of the misogynistic Jealous Husband, provoked anger in the early fifteenth-century Debate of the Rose, where de Meun's defenders said readers should read cynical or anti-women passages like this as artistic ventriloquism, not blame them on the author.

La Vieille tells men, 'Never be generous; keep your heart in several places . . . sell it very dearly and always to the highest bidder', and tells women, 'A woman is the mistress of all markets' (13037–42, 13155). The 'Wife of Bath's Prologue' recalls such statements (414, 522–4). Even more provocatively Chaucer uses the speech in constructing his Prioress. La Vieille, an ex-prostitute, advises on beauty tricks to lure men, including dainty table manners (13385–456). Chaucer echoes this in the Prioress's portrait ('GP' 127–36): does he intend readers to see a shameless, man-hunting coquette beneath the habit of this sensitive woman of the Church, the head of a religious institution? Elsewhere, we have seen, Chaucer uses sources without directly adopting their original messages. Perhaps this is another case where associations from a source merely hover potentially, suggesting complexities in female celibacy (and also complexities in Chaucer's attitude towards women?). The concluding '*Amor vincit omnia*' (162) seems to encourage multivalent readings of the portrait as whole, within which incongruities can coexist.

The *Roman* is the main source for the 'Physician's Tale' and the 'Monk's Tale' stories of Nero and Croesus. De Meun gave Reason a long speech about Fortune, which includes the falls of Nero and Croesus, and the story of Virginia. Chaucer's Wife of Bath and Pardoner's self-revealing Prologues reflect the speeches of de Meun's 'Faux Semblant' ('false seeming'), which expose the rogue's modus operandi (10952–11976).

French literature inspired some of Chaucer's most sustained expressions of beauty, tragedy, satire, and humour. He is often most original and adventurous when drawing on sources, particularly multiple sources, and contrasting literary worlds, playing them off against each other. Deschamps's 'Ballade to Chaucer' (1385) praised him as 'Grant translateur', the 'great translator', who transplanted the *Rose* into England, the 'Aigles treshaulz' ('lofty eagle') of English literature, a Socrates in philosophy, Seneca in morality, and Ovid in poetry. Deschamps saw, early on, not only Chaucer's stature but the multifaceted nature of his genius. Chaucer criticism of the last thirty years, which has moved beyond earlier evaluations of Chaucer as pre-eminently a realist writer and replaced simple concepts of sources with a more complex recognition of intertextuality, has returned attention to the combination of gifts that Deschamps praised. Chaucer's reworkings of his sources and inspirations make the whole experience of translation, as he conducts it, a profound and creative one; he redirected the English vernacular and gave his poetic successors confidence, equalling what other European poets had begun to do for their vernaculars, though with characteristically understated representation of his own role in this. Translators from French and Latin after Chaucer often translate into Chaucer—into his vocabulary and style—as well as into English. As Deschamps observed, Chaucer's writing encompasses philosophical inquiry, moral debate, and a sympathy with sensual experience and emotional psychology that he shares with Ovid. He shows that a great poet joins a great tradition by being new. He can do this, as in the *Book of the Duchess*, by simultaneously producing a work that captures the essential spirit of his models, yet turning from their certainties into uncharted waters—here from certainties of consolation to his own poem's uneasy questioning. Or in rendering Virgil and Ovid's Dido into English in the *Legend of Good Women*, while creating new respect for her (partly in line with the *Roman de la Rose*). His highly original use in the *Legend* of Machaut's image of the daisy, resurrected each morning, acts, among other things, as a symbol, like that of new corn from old fields, of this complex understanding of poetry, in relationship to his predecessors, as both old and completely new.

FURTHER READING

Benson, Larry D., and Theodore M. Andersson (eds.), *The Literary Context of Chaucer's Fabliaux: Texts and Translations* (Indianapolis: Bobbs-Merrill, 1971). Introductions and translations for the fabliau background.

Brownlee, Kevin, *Poetic Identity in Guillaume de Machaut* (Madison: University of Wisconsin Press, 1984). Examines representation of consciousness, authorship, and patronage in Machaut's *dits*.

Calin, William, *The French Tradition and the Literature of Medieval England* (Toronto: University of Toronto Press, 1994). A readable introduction to French romances, hagiography, the poetry of Machaut and Froissart, and their relationship to English writing: Chaucer, Gower, and English romances.

Correale, Robert M., and Mary Hamel (eds.), *Sources and Analogues of the 'Canterbury Tales'*, i, Chaucer Studies (Woodbridge: Brewer, 2002). Invaluable: contains translations and introductions for the French background (volume ii will include Trevet's tale of Constance and French background to the 'Wife of Bath's Prologue').

Froissart, Jean, *Jean Froissart: An Anthology of Narrative and Lyric Poetry*, trans. Kristen M. Figg and R. Barton Palmer (London: Routledge, 2001). Facing-page texts and translations: includes 'Paradis d'amour', 'Dit de la Margheritte', 'Lay on the Death of the Queen of England' (interesting for comparison with the *Book of the Duchess*), and several lyrics. Quotes Froissart's Ballade 6, a source for 'Hyd Absalon' in Chaucer's *Legend of Good Women* (p. 32).

Muscatine, Charles, *Chaucer and the French Tradition: A Study in Style and Meaning* (Berkeley: University of California Press, 1957). Important study, especially on how the fabliau tradition contributes to Chaucer's characterization of Pandarus and the provocative tensions this introduces into *Troilus*.

Phillips, Helen, 'Chaucer's French Translations', *Nottingham Medieval Studies*, 37 (1993), 65–82. Argues Chaucer's handling of French sources is more sophisticated in style than traditionally assumed. Discusses *Romaunt of the Rose*, 'Complaint of Venus', 'Melibee', *Book of the Duchess*, 'An ABC'.

Phillips, Helen, and Nick Havely (eds.), *Chaucer's Dream Poetry* (London: Longman, 1997). Introduction and notes in sections 'Chaucer and Dream Poetry', the *Book of the Duchess*, and the *Legend of Good Women* include summaries and discussion of French backgrounds, including Flower and Leaf and daisy imagery (pp. 287, 302–3).

Wimsatt, James I., *Chaucer and his French Contemporaries: Natural Music in the Fourteenth Century* (Toronto: University of Toronto Press, 1991). Discusses de Le Mote (arguing for major early influence on Chaucer), Machaut, Froissart, Deschamps, and others, and their relationships to Chaucer.

Wimsatt, James I., *Chaucer and the French Love Poets: The Literary Background to the 'Book of the Duchess'* (Chapel Hill: University of North Carolina Press, 1968). History of courtly dream poems and *dits*, developing from the *Roman de la Rose*. Useful summaries of many of these poems in Chaucer's French literary heritage.

Windeatt, Barry, *Chaucer's Dream Poetry: Sources and Analogues* (Woodbridge: Boydell & Brewer, 1982). Invaluable translations and introductions for French sources.

NOTES

1. Nigel Saul, *Richard II*, Yale English Monarchs (New Haven: Yale University Press, 1997), 344–65.
2. George Lyman Kittredge, *Chaucer and his Poetry* (Cambridge, Mass.: Harvard University Press, 1970), 26–7, 72.
3. 'Lay amoureux', 296, in *Œuvres de Froissart*, ed. Kervyn de Lettenhove, 26 vols. (1867–77), ii. 202.
4. E. Talbot Donaldson, 'Chaucer the Pilgrim', *PMLA* 69 (1954), 928–36, repr. in Richard J. Schoeck and Jerome Taylor (eds.), *Chaucer Criticism*, i: *The 'Canterbury Tales'* (Notre Dame, Ind.: University of Notre Dame Press, 1961), 1–13; Dorothy Betherum, 'Chaucer's Point of View as Narrator in the Love Poems', *PMLA* 74 (1959), 511–20, repr. in Shoeck and Taylor (eds.), *Chaucer Criticism, ii: 'Troilus and Criseyde' and the Minor Poems*, 211–31.
5. e.g. James I. Wimsatt, 'The Sources of Chaucer's "Seys and Alcyone"', *Medium Aevum*, 36 (1967), 231–41.
6. John Lawlor, 'The Pattern of Consolation in the *Book of the Duchess*', *Speculum*, 31 (1956), 626–48, repr. in Shoeck and Taylor (eds.), *Chaucer Criticism*, ii. 232–60.
7. V. A. Kolve, *Chaucer and the Imagery of Narrative: The First Five Canterbury Tales* (London: Edward Arnold, 1984), 217–56.
8. See Amy W. Goodwin, 'The Griselda Story in France', in Robert M. Correale and Mary Hamel (eds.), *Sources and Analogues of the 'Canterbury Tales'*, i, Chaucer Studier (Cambridge: Brewer, 2002), 130–67.
9. Ibid. 135–6.
10. See William Askins, 'The Tale of Melibee', in Correale and Hamel (eds.), *Sources and Analogues*, 325–6.
11. Judith Ferster, 'Chaucer's "Tale of Melibee": Contradictions and Context', in Denise N. Baker (ed.), *Inscribing the Hundred Years' War in French and English Culture* (New Haven: Yale University Press, 2002), 73–89.
12. For examples, see Askins's notes in 'The Tale of Melibee'.
13. *Œuvres complètes d'Eustache Deschamps*, ed. le marquis de Queux de Saint-Hilaire and Gaston Raynaud, Société des Anciens Textes Français, 11 vols. (Paris: Champion, 1878–1904), ii. 138–9.

The Italian background

Nick Havely

Latin and Italian

> In hir langage mercy she bisoghte,
> The lyf out of hir body for to twynne,
> Hire to delivere of wo that she was inne.
>
> A maner Latyn corrupt was hir speche,
> But algates therby was she understonde.
>
> ('MLT' 516–20)

Geographical range makes Chaucer's 'Man of Law's Tale' one of the most European of his works. Its heroine, Custance, is from Rome. Driven by misfortune, tempest, and the grace of God from one end of the continent to another—from 'the See of Grece' (464, the Mediterranean) to 'oure occian' (505, the North Sea)—this Italian exile fetches up on the coast of Northumberland, where she is able to make her plight known to the English governor of the local castle through the use of 'corrupt Latin'. In this respect, the fictional Custance—inhabiting a notional Anglo-Saxon past—was somewhat luckier than a couple of actual Italian merchants found wandering in York during Chaucer's own time; they were thrown into prison for a while because it was said that nobody could 'understand their idiom'.[1]

In Chaucer's trilingual England, Latin coexisted with and was 'corrupted' by both French—now becoming 'increasingly a written language of record'—and English, which, in its various thriving dialects including Chaucer's east Midlands, was achieving status as a literary language.[2] The resulting mixed form of Latin, familiar in accounts and inventories, would have been accessible to the mercantile class into which Chaucer was born and would have been available to it as a basic kind of 'pidgin' when travelling in Continental Europe. For those of this class (like Chaucer) who had literary interests, it would also, together with French and more erudite Latin, have provided a portal to Italian.

The close linguistic and literary connections between Italian and Latin were obvious to English writers of the time. Around 1407, for instance, a Lollard advocate of translating the Bible into English looks towards continental Europe and notes that: 'it was translatid in-to Spaynesche tunge, Frenshe tunge and Almayne [German], and other londes also han the Bibel in ther moder [mother] tunge as Italie hath it in Latyn, for that is ther moder tonge'.[3] In a characteristically more devious way, Chaucer himself seems to have acknowledged the closeness of Italian to Latin at the beginning of book 2 of the *Troilus*. The *prohemium* (prologue) to this book begins (as we shall see) by rewriting the opening of Dante's *Purgatorio* (1–10); it goes on to present 'Chaucer' as historian and translator rather than original poet (11–21); and it concludes with an elaborate defence of what may seem 'straunge' in speech and manners (22–49). It is thus a piece of writing that shows concern with writing, language, and Italy. Not only does it begin by invoking Dante; it speaks of the route to Rome (36), and it also refers several times to Chaucer's 'auctour' (authoritative source, 18, 49), whom he elsewhere identifies in the poem as a certain Lollius (*TC* 1. 394, 5. 1653), but whom we know to have been Boccaccio, whose early vernacular romance the *Filostrato* is the English poem's main narrative source. What Chaucer means by 'Latin' in this context thus comes playfully close to Italian, when he asks his audience's indulgence for any shortcomings, since he is working as translator, and since

> of no sentement I this endite,
> But out of Latyn in my tonge it write.

> (*TC* 2. 13–14)

Chaucer would probably not have been able to substitute 'Italian' for 'Latin' in this line, although *italicus* and *italico* had been used in Italy to describe the language of Dante and Petrarch. Despite Dante's attempts early in the century (in *De vulgari eloquentia*, 'Of Eloquence in the Vernacular', *c.*1304) to identify the supreme form of the vernacular—and despite the prominence of his fellow Florentines Petrarch and Boccaccio—the Tuscan dialect that all three writers used had not yet become the unquestioned literary standard for Italy. Dante himself in the *Divine Comedy* used the adjective *latino* more frequently than *italico* to describe his land and its people; his own speech is recognized by souls in hell and purgatory not as *italiano* or *italico*, but as *tosco* ('Tuscan', *Inferno*, 23. 76; *Purgatorio*, 16. 137); and Boccaccio in his biography of Dante identified the language the poet used as 'our Florentine idiom'. *Italiano*, *italico*, and (in English) 'Italian' were in use at this time to identify the people of the peninsula, but it is not until the early sixteenth century that the word is regularly used in Italy to describe the language. And (so far as we know) the first reference in English to the writing of 'ytalyen' is a century later than Chaucer, in Caxton's preface to his edition of Malory (1485).

Lombards and Tuscans

Awareness of the diverse languages, regions, and peoples of Italy is nonetheless clearly evident among English writers of Chaucer's time. In France and England since at least the thirteenth century, terms like 'Tuscan' and 'Lombard' had been used to describe provinces of Italy and their inhabitants. These feature in book 5 of John Trevisa's translation of the encyclopedia *De proprietatibus rerum* (completed in 1397), where the country as a whole is said to 'bere[] the prys' ('stand supreme') among the lands of western Europe. *Mandeville's Travels* (*c.*1390–1400) mentions Tuscany along with the southern regions of Calabria, Campania, and Puglia; while Chaucer in the first few lines of the 'Clerk's Tale' (39–63) reproduces a quite precise description of the topography and boundaries of 'Lumbardye'. Chaucer, as we shall see, knew Lombardy well from his visit in 1378. 'Lumbarde' (as adjective and noun) had come to apply to Italians in general, including those merchants from Florence, Siena, and Bologna who had been active in the English wool trade since early in the thirteenth century; and it came to be recognized that 'Lombard' as a language might, alongside French or (corrupt) Latin, be a useful tool for the English when dealing with Italian traders.

Trade is one of the major activities that helped to shape English perceptions of Italy in the Middle Ages and to develop cultural contacts. Italians were playing a part in the English economy of the late fourteenth century, as they had been doing for a long time before. As early as 1221 Henry III was licensing groups of Italian merchants to participate in England's main export business—the wool trade—and, like later English monarchs (including Edward I and Edward III), he borrowed extensively from Italian financiers.[4] The sea route between England and Italy was in use by the late thirteenth century, with the Genoese exporting wool from London and Sandwich at that time. Venetian galleys began to visit northern Europe in 1314, and they are first reported to have arrived at Southampton, to a rather rough reception, in 1319. At the start of the Hundred Years War the majority of Italian merchants in England seem to have been from Florence and secondly Lucca; and—despite the hostility from some quarters in parliament, the use of forced loans by the Crown in 1337, and the royal default on loans that precipitated the collapse of the Bardi Company in 1346—at least sixty Florentine merchants continued to be active in England during the third quarter of the century. Over the second half of the fourteenth century the Genoese became the dominant Italian presence in England, using Southampton as their main port from 1383 on and exporting wool and importing essentials for the dyeing industry (such as alum and woad) along with luxury goods (fruit, spices, textiles). It is not surprising therefore that Chaucer's dealings as customs official and diplomat should have brought him into contact with Genoese merchants, two of whom—Giovanni di Mari and Iacopo Provano—accompanied him on his first journey to Italy in 1372–3.

Along with these particular Genoese, a number of individual Italian residents, especially those from the main communities in London and Southampton, came to play important parts in the English mercantile and cultural scene from Chaucer's time onwards. Moving within the circles frequented by Chaucer, there was, for instance, Gualtero dei Bardi, who was resident in London from about 1351–91 and King's Moneyer from 1361. Niccolò da Lucca, during the last quarter of the century, was successively the London representative for the Florentine firm of Alberti, then for the Guinigi company of Lucca, and again for the Alberti; and he combined this varied career with a role as valued agent on the Continent for John of Gaunt. In 1395 two members of the Alberti company performed a task of literary and political ambassadorship for Richard II, transporting a book of the miracles of Edward II to Rome and presenting it to the Pope.[5]

We do not know what specific books were brought back from Italy by this senior managerial class, nor precisely how they communicated with the likes of Chaucer and John of Gaunt. Tuscan merchants at this level, however, are known to have been among the early readers of, for example, Boccaccio's *Decameron*; and conversations between them and their foreign hosts and clients could have made use of a variety of languages—from English and French through 'corrupt Latin' to the 'Lumbard' that was reckoned to be of use to English traders in the Mediterranean.[6] The subsequent consolidation of the Italian communities, especially in London, was also likely to make cultural, as well as commercial, exchange easier. Groups, or 'nations', of Italian residents were subject to consular control in the early fifteenth century and by 1409 there was a Venetian vice-consul in London.[7]

It was not all plain sailing for Italian traders, however. Over the period, their conspicuous presence in several English cities also generated rivalry, resentment, and at times outright hostility. Already in the mid-thirteenth century the chronicler Matthew Paris was commenting on the size of houses bought up by Italian merchants in London.[8] The forced loans and defaults experienced by the Florentine financiers in the 1330s and 1340s have already been noted above; and towards the end of the century Gower in *Mirour de l'Omme* is expressing a commonly held attitude about 'Lombard foreigners' when he complains that 'in order to deceive, they put on an appearance of being our friends, yet beneath that they have set their hearts on plundering us of our silver and gold' (my translation). By the 1430s the *Libelle of Englyshe Polycye* is voicing a sturdy insular disdain for the luxury goods imported by the Florentines and Venetians, as 'nifles, trifles . . . thynges not enduryng', while also deploring the arrogance of these alien traders, who can 'ryde aboute' and buy up more Cotswold wool than 'we Englisshe may getyn in any wyse'.[9] Hostility of this sort was later to be expressed also in the alien subsidy acts of Henry VI's reign; through the fantasy of slaughtering Lombards in popular romance (*Beues of Hamtoun*); and in actual riots directed against Italian merchants at Southampton and London in the 1450s.[10]

Hostility towards aliens was recurrent over this period, especially in times of war or economic crisis; yet there is substantial evidence about the presence of Italian residents of various classes in the major cities of Chaucer's England. London, with its Lombard merchants' houses in Bread Street (looted by rioters in May 1456), was always the largest Italian community, followed by Southampton; but smaller numbers of Italians are found living in other towns, and they form a quarter of the Continental names recorded up to 1500 at the universities of Oxford and Cambridge.[11] Other kinds of transaction are reflected in references to Italian physicians and women servants, and the presence of Italian churchmen, from papal nuncios through learned friars to ordinary priests; while intellectual traffic and careerism in the fifteenth century was to bring several humanists from Italy to live and work in England. Meanwhile, we also need to consider the role of English travellers and other intermediaries in developing contacts with fourteenth-century Italy.

The English in Italy

English travellers in Chaucer's time could have reached Italy by a familiar and (for the time) not too lengthy route—through France and across the Alps—in about five weeks; and by the late fourteenth century there were a number of reasons for them to make the trip. Religious motives drew pilgrims to Rome, especially for the high spiritual value of the Jubilees in 1300, 1350, and 1390, which offered them remission of punishment for sins. For the more ambitious travellers to Jerusalem, like Margery Kempe and the Wife of Bath, Venice was the place to embark and get equipped for the sea voyage to the Holy Land. English scholars had been attracted to the major Italian universities (Salerno, Bologna, Padua) since the twelfth century, and small numbers of such students and lecturers (especially from the mendicant Orders) are on the records during the fourteenth and fifteenth.[12] Various kinds of business, too, drew other classes of English travellers: clerics visiting the papal court (in Avignon or Rome); military opportunists, like the mercenary John Hawkwood (d. 1394), whose equestrian portrait appears on the north aisle of Florence's cathedral and with whom Chaucer himself had dealings; and finally, diplomats on missions to Italian city-states, among whom on at least two occasions, in 1372–3 and again in 1378, was Chaucer.

Chaucer's own journeys were thus not literary or cultural excursions or study trips but official business. On the first of them his travels lasted about six months, from December 1372 until May 1373, and took him through Calais, down the Rhine, and across the St Bernard Pass. It was not a long journey by the standards of the time but it was not a comfortable one, since for most travellers there were risks of robbery, arrest, and (in winter) bad weather. One English traveller of the time, when crossing the Alps, had himself blindfolded and slung into an oxcart to overcome his fears; and another group is said to have strayed like sheep for several days in the Apennines. However, Chaucer made it, first to Genoa, where his mission was to arrange for the use of a seaport in England by Genoese merchants, and where he would have been yet more directly impressed by the evidence of the city's power in long-distance trade. By late February he had moved on to Florence, on secret business, probably to negotiate yet another loan for Edward III from the Italian banks.

In Florence in the spring of 1373 what might his first impressions of the city have been? In the first place English visitors would have been struck by the sheer scale of the place. Florence was then one of Europe's largest cities: even after the losses caused by the Black Death in the mid-century it still had around 60,000 inhabitants—considerably more than London, whose population at this time was nearer 40,000. During the period of its fastest expansion—from the 1280s to the 1330s, when the population may have reached the 100,000 mark—the city's third circle of walls had been built and must have been an imposing urban feature. Other new or reconstructed buildings of fourteenth-century Florence—the Palazzo della Signoria (the town hall), Giotto's 85-metre-high campanile (bell tower) beside the cathedral, and the vast Franciscan church of Santa Croce—would have conveyed an impression of civic power and prosperity.

The city was also one of major poets; and around this time Dante, Boccaccio, and Petrarch were being identified (by the city's chancellor, Coluccio Salutati) as the 'three crowns of Florence'. Dante had died in exile in Ravenna in 1321, some fifty years before; but in the year of Chaucer's visit Petrarch and Boccaccio were both still living and famous figures, although both of them were near the end of their careers. Petrarch in 1373 was living near Padua, as Chaucer's Clerk notes in the Prologue to his tale (26–38), and Boccaccio was still dividing his time between Florence and his native town of Certaldo. Chaucer never mentions Boccaccio by name in any of his works—even though works like the 'Knight's Tale' and *Troilus and Criseyde* are as much indebted to Boccaccio as the 'Clerk's Tale' is to Petrarch. But a visitor with literary interests and ambitions would have been aware of the author of the *Decameron* and *De casibus* as the grand old man on the Florentine literary scene; indeed plans were under way at this time for Boccaccio's last major project: his unfinished series of lectures on Dante's *Divine Comedy*. Chaucer could not have attended these lectures, since they began a few months after he had left Florence, but he could well have heard about the city's plans to put them on; and the idea of Boccaccio lecturing on Dante would have meant that during the time of Chaucer's visit to Florence links between the city's great authors were being recognized and cultivated.

Beneath this air of cultural, commercial, and political confidence, however, all was not well with Florence in the 1370s. Chaucer's second documented journey to Italy was from May to September 1378, to negotiate with Bernabò Visconti and the mercenary John Hawkwood on 'matters concerning the conduct of our war'.[13] By this time he would have become acutely aware of the contrasts between the declining 'associative polity' of Florence and the ascendant signorial despotism represented by Milan; hence images of Italian absolutism and the politics of Lombardy in the Clerk's and Monk's Tales ('ClT' 64–84; 'MoT' 2399–406) and in the Prologue to the *Legend of Good Women* (G 353–88) owe a good deal to Chaucer's encounter with the Visconti court in 1378 and to his awareness of Petrarch's earlier association with the 'tyrauntz of Lumbardye'.[14] The relationship between these missions to Florence and Milan and Chaucer's reinventing of Italian narratives was not, however, a straightforward matter of cause and effect. Unlike later more leisured English clerics or gentleman scholars, such as Abbot John Whethamstede in 1423 and John Tiptoft, earl of Worcester, in 1458–61, Chaucer did not go to Italy for lengthy periods to study and collect books. For him, a number of other diplomatic and cultural concerns framed his contacts with Italy. Among these was his continuing involvement with the politics and the literature of France.

French connections

French literary culture had, over the course of the fourteenth century, become pre-eminent in its own right and was also a significant intermediary for the transmission of Italian texts and influences. Since early in the century the papacy's residence in Avignon had drawn Italian financiers, merchants, craftsmen, and artists to the southern French city. With the expansion of its university and the Papal Library under the pontificate of John XXII (1316–34), the southern French city was also a growth point for learning in the pre-humanist period; and Petrarch, whose later childhood had been spent in Avignon, returned there in 1326–7 and again at intervals during 1337–53. Petrarch continued to maintain contact with and influence upon Avignonese culture long after he had settled in northern Italy and until near the time of his death (1374), thus contributing substantially to the 'history of Italian influence upon French culture which radiated from Avignon'; while his friend and contemporary Boccaccio visited the city on several occasions and several of his major Latin works—notably his encyclopedic *De casibus* ('Of the Fall of Famous Men') and the *Genealogie* ('Genealogies of the Pagan Gods')—are listed among the 2,000 or so manuscripts in the 1379 catalogue of the Papal Library.[15]

Petrarch's and Boccaccio's influence also extended to the intellectual culture of the French royal court during the 1360s and 1370s. Pierre Bersuire, the mythographer and translator of Livy, first encountered Petrarch when working on his moralization of Ovid at Avignon between 1330 and 1340; he met him again at Paris in 1360–1 when the poet was being received and lionized as ambassador to the court of John II; and it was at the court of John's successor Charles V ('the Wise') that among a number of major translation projects the first version of any of Petrarch's Latin works to appear in a modern vernacular was completed by Jean Daudin in 1376–7. Daudin's translation of Petrarch's moralistic encyclopedia *De remediis utriusque fortunae* ('Remedies for Both Kinds of Fortune') brings us close in both place and time to Chaucer. It is important to remember that Chaucer's contacts with France and Italy are interwoven during the late 1370s and that one well-documented visit to France (as a member of the mission to the Anglo-French peace negotiations at Montreuil-sur-Mer) took place between his two Italian journeys, during 1377. A pioneering new vernacular version of Petrarch could well have provided a talking point during breaks in those negotiations; and around this time Chaucer could also have made contact with another French friend of Petrarch, Philippe de Mézières. Philippe (1327–1405) was a dedicated promoter of reconciliation between the European powers in the interests of the crusade movement. He is known to have been in contact with Petrarch during 1369, and another potentially Chaucerian link is represented by his acquisition of Petrarch's Latin tale of Griselda (translated from Boccaccio's *Decameron*, Day 10), which he was to translate in his treatise on marriage and refer to in his political writing. This translation was imitated by the French version upon which Chaucer based his 'Clerk's Tale'.[16] Griselda's transformations, from Boccaccio's Italian to Petrarch's Latin and on to Philippe's French and Chaucer's English, reflect the busy interaction between the four languages in the later fourteenth century. They are a further reminder that, when thinking of the roles of Petrarch and Boccaccio in Chaucer's 'Italian background', we also have to bear in mind the 'middle ground' of France.

Authors and authority: Dante, Boccaccio, Petrarch

Chaucer's knowledge of the *Divine Comedy* and its author, however, probably did not owe much to his contacts with France. Dante's name recurs occasionally among French writers of the later fourteenth and fifteenth centuries; and the daughter of an Italian *émigré*, Christine de Pizan, pays tribute to him in several works around the turn of the century. But this is relatively slight recognition, compared with the critical industry that had grown up (in Latin and vernacular commentaries) around the *Comedy* in its native country; with the translations into Latin, Castilian, and Catalan that would appear early in the fifteenth century; and with the response to Dante in Chaucer's dream poems, *Troilus and Criseyde*, and the *Canterbury Tales*.

   In the fourteenth century, as now, Dante was regarded primarily as an authority on hell; and his text's own assertions about the authenticity of his vision reinforced this image. Hence, the very first known reference to Dante in English not surprisingly presents him as a source for the torments of the underworld. In book 1 of Chaucer's dream poem the *House of Fame* (written in the late 1370s or early 1380s) the narrator has been following the story of Virgil's *Aeneid* as depicted on the walls of a temple of Venus, and has reached the point in book 6 where the hero makes a journey through the world of the dead. At this point Dante is named as an *auctor* on hell, alongside Virgil and the late Roman poet Claudian:

> And also sawgh I how Sybile
> And Eneas, besyde an yle,
> To helle wente for to see
> His fader, Anchyses the free;
> How he ther fond Palinurus,
> And Dido, and eke Deiphebus;

And every turment eke in helle
Saugh he, which is longe to telle;
Which whoso willeth for to knowe,
He moste rede many a rowe
On Virgile or on Claudian,
Or Daunte, that hit telle kan. (439–50)

This looks like a routine reference, suggesting that Dante may be already known to readers, at least by repute, and placing him (as he placed himself) in the classical tradition, while implicitly noting the Italian poet's truth-telling claims, as one 'that hit telle kan'. This kind of authority is again acknowledged by Chaucer in the sinister comedy of the 'Friar's Tale', where a roving devil tells his prospective victim that he will soon become more of an expert on hell than Virgil was 'or Dant also' (1520); and very shortly after this, in the 'Summoner's Prologue', Chaucer satirically rivals Dante's imagining of ultimate evil by showing a friar being taken down to the depths of hell and shown where his colleagues nest, like bees, in Satan's 'ers' (1675–99). The latter scene derives from a long popular tradition of imagining hell as the ultimate grotesque debasement of human nature, and as such it parallels Dante's reimagining of such 'bestial signs' in his animalistic and militaristic devils (*Inferno*, cantos 21–2) and his thieves, who turn into serpents and back into thieves (24–5).

Chaucer also recognized the potential of the *Comedy* as a poem about love and the capacity of the soul for transfiguration as well as debasement. His highly ambiguous garden of love in the *Parliament of Fowls* presents outcrops of allusion to Dante's earthly paradise (*Purgatorio*, 28) alongside the more substantial strata laid down by his reading of Boccaccio's *Teseida*. Here a landscape that has been ominously, if ambiguously, introduced by a rewriting of Dante's inscription over the gate of hell (*PF* 123–47) comes to evoke not only its immediate source (Boccaccio's Garden of Venus in book 7 of the *Teseida*) but also the enclosed garden of the *Romance of the Rose*, and the earthly paradise on the summit of Mount Purgatory in which Dante the pilgrim meets Beatrice again. Even the most sceptical of those considering Chaucer's responses to Dante have had to allow that the most striking evocation of harmony in this scene—the accord between the wind in the leaves and the song of the birds (*PF* 201–3)—is closely modelled upon a feature of Dante's earthly paradise in *Purgatorio*, 28. 7–18.[17]

A yet more sophisticated and more extensive appropriation of Dante's invocatory language takes place at a climactic point in Chaucer's *Troilus* (3. 1261–7), when the speech through which Dante's St Bernard appeals to the Virgin Mary at the start of the final canto of the *Paradiso* (33. 13–21) is imitated in Troilus' invocation of the power of love when for the first time in bed with Criseyde:

Benigne Love, thow holy bond of thynges,
Whoso wol grace and list the nought honouren,
Lo, his desir wol fle withouten wynges;
For noldestow of bownte hem socouren

That serven best and most alwey labouren,
Yet were al lost, that dar I wel seyn, certes,
But if thi grace passed oure desertes.

In its second half, after 'bownte' (*bontate* in *Paradiso*, 33. 21), Troilus' invocation moves away from Dante and seems to lose some confidence in the process, particularly in the clumsy and breathless parenthesis that dominates line 1266. Yet in the first half of the stanza the resemblances between the two invocations are perceptible and powerful: the hopelessness of attaining grace without giving honour to its ultimate source; the imagining of that hopelessness through the metaphor (perhaps recalling the myth of Icarus) of attempting to fly without wings. Contextually, there is a parallel, too: just as Dante in *Paradiso* 33 is in the highest sphere of heaven, so Troilus has reached the uppermost point in the trajectory of his love affair. But what does Chaucer think he is doing with Dante here? Why is he putting in the mouth of a pagan—whose 'hevene' of the senses has been vividly and almost fetishistically depicted two stanzas before this (1247–53)—words that Dante's saint had addressed to the Virgin? An exalted and audacious allusion of this sort clearly requires the reader—as does Troilus' devotional discourse elsewhere in the poem—to ask what this lover's experience amounts to when viewed in the cosmic perspective that his own words open up.

By treating the language of Italian love-poetry in this way, Chaucer is following and surpassing the precedent of Boccaccio. In the *Filostrato* (*c*.1336–8) allusions to the *Comedy* (which had been completed not much more than fifteen years before) are frequent and specific; and in the first four parts of the poem they form a pattern that represents Boccaccio's Criseida as a reluctant and unstable Beatrice, his Pandaro as a disingenuous Virgil, and his Troiolo as a pilgrim of love who climbs from hell to paradise only to plunge down again into a hell of deprivation and despair. The *Filostrato*'s Troiolo is also inclined to quote from earlier Italian lyric, including Guinizelli, Cino da Pistoia, and Dante's *Vita nuova*. Yet Chaucer develops the Dantean dimension of the Trojan love-story more fully by drawing more than Boccaccio does upon the *Purgatorio* and *Paradiso*; and he also updates the lover's lyricism by drawing upon Petrarch.[18]

On the sole occasion when, in the *Troilus*, Chaucer turns to Petrarch's most well-known vernacular work, the *Canzoniere*, he does so in a very specific and innovative way. In the *Filostrato*, Boccaccio's hero Troiolo had shown a tendency to modulate into the sweet old style of earlier Italian poetry at moments of high stress or excitement (for example, in *Filostrato*, 1. 56, 3. 86, 4. 35, 5. 62–5). As early as book 1 of the *Troilus*, when his lover–hero is under similar pressure, Chaucer proceeds to outdo or update Boccaccio by giving his Troilus a more modern lyric voice—translating the fourteen lines of Petrarch's sonnet 88 into the three seven-line stanzas of the 'Canticus Troili' (1. 400–20).[19] This is the first English translation of a Petrarch sonnet before the sixteenth century, but, just as importantly, it forms part of Chaucer's process of developing his own lyric language in the *Troilus*. Elsewhere in his greatest complete poem, Chaucer also uses other authors (such as Boethius and Dante) to depart from, comment upon, and reinvent his source text (the *Filostrato*). We have seen how he uses the last canto of Dante's *Paradiso* for this purpose at the climax of the third book. Here, on the other hand, in the middle of book 1, he turns momentarily but significantly from 'Lollius' to 'the lauriat poete'.

Neither in the *Troilus* nor elsewhere does Chaucer speak of Boccaccio as his *auctour*, although he names Dante and Petrarch several times in other works (see below). This is a striking silence. Not much later (in the 1420s) Lydgate would be quite specific in naming the author and his place of origin as 'Bochas de certaldo', along with a major work ('the Genologye') and in assigning him status in the Italian pantheon of writers 'next Frraunceys Petrak' (*Siege of Thebes*, 3538, 3541, 3543). Various reasons have been advanced or suggested for Chaucer's refusal or inability to cite the author who was his most substantial source for two of his major works (the 'Knight's Tale' as well as the *Troilus*), as well as for a number of important passages elsewhere. By comparison with the daunting precedents of Dante and Petrarch, the early work of Boccaccio might have seemed less imposing for an ambitious later writer; and perhaps Chaucer might even have wished to avoid comparisons between what he was doing with the vernacular in *Troilus* and what Boccaccio had done in the *Filostrato*.[20] With this possible attitude in mind, we might see the enigmatic 'Lollius' whom Chaucer cites as his authority for the story of Troy and Troilus (*TC* 1. 394, 5. 1653; *HF* 1468) as, among other things, a playful allusion to the Middle English verb *lolle(n)* and hence to Boccaccio's early and sometimes awkward exercise of the vernacular tongue.[21]

Boccaccio's later and more ambitious vernacular poem, the epic twelve-book *Teseida delle nozze d'Emilia* ('The Theseid: The Marriage of Emilia', *c*.1339–41), must, on the other hand, have seemed a more magisterial performance, especially if Chaucer knew (or knew of) the author's own extensive commentary (*chiose*) to his work.[22] His treatment of this work in the 'Knight's Tale' is not confined simply to condensation of the narrative. His Knight gives a more sombre outlook to the colourful landscape of Boccaccio's epic; the gallant heroism of Boccaccio's main characters is scaled down; and once again other authors (notably Boethius) provide new perspectives on Chaucer's source text. Moreover, unlike the *Filostrato*, the *Teseida* provides him with material to quarry on a number of other occasions—for example, in the *Parliament of Fowls*, *Anelida and Arcite*, the 'Franklin's Tale', as well as the ending of the *Troilus* (5. 1807–34). (For more on the Teseida and the 'Knight's Tale', see Chapter 23.)

Boccaccio also seems to have cultivated a reputation as a Latin author, especially during the last quarter-century of his life. His monumental *De casibus virorum illustrium* ('Of the Fall of Famous Men') appeared in two versions (1355–60, 1373–4); his *De mulieribus claris* ('Of Famous Women') was written in 1361–75; and his encyclopedic project on pagan myth *De genealogia deorum* occupied him intermittently from the middle of the century until the 1370s, when copies begin to circulate. The influence of the *De casibus*, with its sequence of 'falls' from Adam to contemporary figures, is evident both in the plan and in the subtitle of Chaucer's 'Monk's Tale', which—with its account of the recent fall of Bernabò Visconti (2399–406) and its version of Dante's

Ugolino (2407–62)—is in several important ways an Italianate narrative.[23] Chaucer's version of the story of Cleopatra in his *Legend of Good Women* may have been influenced by both *De casibus* and *De mulieribus claris*; and he could also have recognized the latter as one important precedent (among others) for a programme of narratives about women. He may also have known something of the *De genealogia deorum*, in which the defence of poetry and of the author in books 14–15 would have been of considerable interest to writers of fiction, including Chaucer.

Poets and makers

Unlike Boccaccio in the *Genealogia*, or Petrarch (in his letters and the *Invectiva contra medicum* ('Invective against the Physician')), or Dante (in *De vulgari eloquentia*), Chaucer never wrote a theoretical or polemical treatise on poetry. Yet ideas about the art, craft, and status of fiction are implicit in his dream poems (especially the *House of Fame* and the Prologue to the *Legend of Good Women*), in the proems and the Epilogue to *Troilus and Criseyde*, and at various points in the framework of the *Canterbury Tales*. And while, for example, the French 'arts of rhetoric' and the traditions of Latin commentary on major texts and authors clearly formed part of the context for his concept of 'alle poesye' (*TC* 5. 1790), his sense of the Italian poets as powerful predecessors, especially Dante, also demonstrably helped to shape his poetic identity.

There are differing critical views about the degree of reverence or scepticism accorded to Dante as *auctour* by Chaucer, from the initial references in the *House of Fame* onwards. Yet his prominence as a precedent is evident from the fact that he and Petrarch are the only two vernacular writers to whom Chaucer gives the title of *poete*; for example, in the 'Wife of Bath's Tale' (1125–6) and the 'Clerk's Prologue' (31). This is a title that Chaucer never claims for himself, although it was conferred upon him by several of his French and English contemporaries and followers (such as Gower, Deschamps, and Lydgate). Instead, he describes himself less ambitiously as *makere*—for instance, at the end of *Troilus and Criseyde*, where he presents himself as the author of a 'litel . . . tragedye' rather than a more ambitious kind of 'comedye' (5. 1786–8). By the time he had completed the *Troilus*, Chaucer had made Dante a significant part of his poetic agenda by naming him or alluding transparently to the *Comedy* at a number of points of departure in his main works: at the end of book 1 and the beginnings of books 2 and 3 of the *House of Fame*; at the entry into the garden of love in the *Parliament of Fowls* (120–47); and perhaps most strikingly in the reworking of Dante's exordium to the *Purgatorio* (1.1–12) in the proem to book 2 of the *Troilus*:

> Owt of thise blake wawes for to saylle,
> O wynd, o wynd, the weder gynneth clere;
> For in this see the boot hath swych travaylle,
> Of my connyng, that unneth I it steere.

This see clepe I the tempestous matere
Of disespeir that Troilus was inne;
But now of hope the kalendes bygynne.

O lady myn, that called art Cleo,
Thow be my speed fro this forth, and my Muse. (1–9)

Tonally, this rewriting of the *Purgatorio* exordium is hesitant and tentative. Dante's image of his poetic craft—the *navicella del mio ingegno* ('the vessel of my [poetic] invention')—which so confidently hoists sail in the first two lines of the canto becomes here 'the boot . . . Of my connyng', which is literally split, between two lines. And Calliope, the Muse of epic poetry who is summoned to arise in all her power among the Italian poet's 'sacred Muses', is, in the *Troilus* proem, replaced by Clio, the Muse of history (or in some medieval traditions the Muse of beginnings). Nonetheless, this second *Troilus* prologue still signals a new beginning for the poem itself: a departure that is to take it in directions far different from those followed by its narrative source (the *Filostrato*). Chaucer may have been sceptical about the claims of fiction-writers to prophetic power and status—claims that continued to be made in his time. Yet one effect of his allusions to Dante's major poem here and elsewhere in his work is to stake a claim for English 'making' within the tradition of vernacular poetry to which the author of the *Divine Comedy* had earlier given such a powerful impetus. As all the examples so far cited from *Troilus and Criseyde* indicate, Chaucer, in the mid–1380s and in the midst of his main completed poetic project, is clearly dealing with the Italian poets in a confident as well as complex way. By this time, too, as is evident from his handling of the *Filostrato*, his knowledge of Italian was precise and confident: he draws upon the invocatory language of the *Comedy* here, as he draws upon other traditions and sources (Petrarchan lyric, Boethian philosophy, romance) to add resonance and perspective to his treatment of the Boccaccian text.

On the road and in the garden: the *Canterbury Tales* and the *Decameron*

Chaucer's dialogue with Italian authors continued in the *Canterbury Tales*. The first tale in the whole collection, the Knight's, extends the rewriting of Boccaccio's early vernacular narratives by condensing the twelve-book *Teseida* into not much more than 2,000 lines, while sharpening its metaphysical and existential questions; and another 'gentil', the Franklin, draws upon and develops a specific 'question of love' from book 4. 31 of Boccaccio's sprawling prose romance, the *Filocolo* (written 1336–8).[24] The authority of Italian writing and writers also continues to be at issue here. Dante is cited three times: as 'the wise poete of Florence' ('WBT' 1125); as authority on hell ('FT' 1520); and as 'grete poete of Ytaille' ('MoT' 2460)—and the invocatory language of St Bernard's prayer to the Virgin in *Paradiso* 33 is (by contrast with *Troilus*, 3. 1261–7) given an explicitly Christian context by the allusion in the 'Prioress's Prologue' (474–80) and the more extensive imitation in the 'Second Nun's Prologue' (36–56). Petrarch is acknowledged twice, as 'lauriat poete' in the 'Clerk's Prologue' (31) and (more briefly and less accurately) as the Monk's 'maister' and source for the story of Zenobia in his tale (2325) while the 'Clerk's Tale' itself can be seen as a kind of debate with the 'lauriat poete' and as a polemical restoration of Griselda to the vernacular, after Petrarch's 'abduction' of her from Day 10 story 10 (the last tale) of the *Decameron*.[25]

Narratives from Boccaccio's *Decameron* form the substrata of several of the *Canterbury Tales*, including the Clerk's. Boccaccio himself had rewritten Menedon's 'question of love' (*Filocolo* 4. 31) as another story (10. 5) of the last Day of his collection; and this 'revision' has been seen as comparable in some significant ways to Chaucer's reworking of the material from the *Filocolo* in the 'Franklin's Tale'.[26] And at least three of the comic tales in the *Canterbury Tales* have obvious analogues in Boccaccio's collection. The 'Reeve's Tale' (and possibly the Miller's too) has affinities not only with the tales of quitting and outwitting in French fabliau but also with specific stories in the *Decameron* (Day 9 story 6, Day 3 story 4); while the 'Merchant's Tale', it has been plausibly argued, may show the influence of several such sources (*Decameron* 2. 10 as well as 7. 9). Chaucer's most accomplished (and perhaps underrated) mercantile comedy the 'Shipman's Tale' also brilliantly recombines material and motifs from several sources including the first two stories of Boccaccio's Eighth Day.[27]

It is not only this evidence of parallels and complex reworking that reflects Chaucer's dealings with the *Decameron*. Although Boccaccio sought and achieved authoritative status for his Latin encyclopedic works, such as *De casibus* and the *Genealogia*, his 'hundred tales' had rapidly established themselves as a vernacular classic and are known to have circulated among the Italian mercantile class with whom Chaucer had dealings. A readership for the work in France around this time is also indicated by the fact that Laurent de Premierfait, the translator of *De casibus*, quickly followed that project with a version of the *Decameron* in 1414. Chaucer's response to the *Decameron* in the *Canterbury Tales* may not be so precisely demonstrable as is his use of the *Filostrato* or *Teseida*; but there are striking affinities in the narrative procedures of the two collections.[28] Again, as with *De casibus* and *De mulieribus claris*, Chaucer is very likely to have been aware of the narrative programme of the *Decameron* as an important vernacular project and precedent; and there may well have been an element of ambitious deliberation in adopting a framework which, instead of setting the stories in an idyllic garden with the plague-ridden city (Boccaccio's Florence) at a distance, puts them firmly on the road between two cities: fourteenth-century London and Canterbury. Recent discussion of the relationship between these two framed collections has focused not so much upon demonstrations of specific influence as upon shared themes and concerns, such as debate, voice, fiction, confession, anticlericalism, and modernity.

'Dante in English'? Six centuries of Chaucer's 'Italian background'

At first it seems to have been largely a question of status. Chaucer's establishment as poetic master for English writers of the fifteenth and sixteenth centuries led him to be enshrined in a temple of fame alongside Italian poets, especially Dante. Lydgate points in this direction in his famously obscure reference to Chaucer and Dante near the beginning of his own huge poetic project the *Fall of Princes* (itself based ultimately upon an Italian model, Boccaccio's *De casibus*):

> He [Chaucer] wrot also ful many day agone,
> Dante in Inglissh, himsilff so doth expresse,
> The pitous story off Ceix and Alcione,
> And the deth eek of Blaunche the Duchesse.

> (*Fall of Princes*, Prologue, 302–5)

'Dante in Inglissh' may refer in some way to Chaucer's *House of Fame*, which does indeed mention and allude to Dante, and which Lydgate certainly knew well. Yet, if the second line is read as a characteristically Lydgatean parenthesis, pointing forward to the third and fourth, the comparison invited could perhaps be between Dante as writer about love and Beatrice and Chaucer as celebrator of courtly love and loss in the yet earlier poem to which lines 304–5 explicitly refer: the *Book of the Duchess*. Either way, Lydgate is clearly promoting Chaucer's 'Inglissh' in relation to the Italian tradition, as his praise of the poet as one who sought to 'refourme' the language would suggest (275–8). In the next century, a number of English writers, such as John Horman (1519), John Leland (*c.*1540), and Sir Philip Sidney (*Apologie for Poetrie*, 1581), were concerned to develop this claim for nationalistic reasons. In his survey of 'illustrious British writers' (1548) John Bale (writing in Latin) presents Chaucer as a kind of Augustus figure who found English eloquence brick and left it marble, and he concludes that 'among his fellow English he was as Dante and Petrarch were among the Italians—still rightly thought of as the first restorer and celebrator of his country's language'.[29] Representation of Chaucer's 'earnest desire to enrich & beautifie our English tongue' as 'following the example of *Dantes* and *Petrarch*' recurs in the preface to Thomas Speght's edition of the poet's *Works* in 1598 and 1602; and in the preface to his *Fables* (1700), Dryden develops further the comparison between Chaucer and the three major Italians as writers who 'refin'd their Mother-Tongue'.[30]

Placing English Chaucer alongside the Italian pantheon was not always, however, a straightforward exercise in nationalistic celebration. In Dryden's time and later in the eighteenth century, comparing Chaucer with Dante—or with Petrarch, Boccaccio, and Ariosto for that matter—might also alert the neoclassically minded reader to these poets' shared 'Gothic' qualities: their lack of stylistic decorum at times and (as Joseph Warton complained in 1756) their 'very sudden transitions from the sublime to the ridiculous'.

Nonetheless, after 'Gothic' qualities had ceased to be a problem the issue of Englishness in relation to 'Italianizing' comes up on a number of occasions. Thus in the first year of Victoria's reign (1837) Chaucer is carefully defined in the *Edinburgh Review* as both 'Norman by descent' and 'the poet of the people', and as a writer who 'though borrowing largely from the early Italian poetry ... was at once a national poet'. What makes the 'poet of the people' or 'a national poet' also enters into more specific comparisons between Chaucer and the Italians. The *Edinburgh Review* article also contrasts Chaucer's 'Homeric' (dramatic) qualities with Boccaccio's 'Virgilian' features. Comparisons between Chaucer and Dante develop along similar lines later in the century. James Russell Lowell in 1870 characterizes Dante as 'the more universal poet' against Chaucer as 'the more truly national one'. Contrasts of this sort between the Italian and English 'fathers of poetry' subsequently became and remained common currency—with Swinburne in 1880 opposing the 'heavenly' in the *Comedy* to the 'earthly' in the *Canterbury Tales*—and even Mario Praz in his influential article of 1927 representing Chaucer as a 'bourgeois' who 'clings to the dear everyday world' and is 'little . . . affected by the sublimer sides of Dante's genius'.

As both Lowell's and Praz's articles also show, however, sweeping generalizations of this sort are often accompanied by some close attention to the basic nature of Chaucer's Italianizing. Lowell develops the traditional notion of the English poet as a linguistic Augustus when he argues that Chaucer 'found our language ... too apt to speak Saxonly in grouting monosyllables' and 'left it enriched with the measure of the Italian and Provençal poets'; and this seems to point the way for discussion of the Continental metrical models and their influence by academic critics such as W. P. Ker (1895) and George Saintsbury (1908).

Chaucer's appropriation of Italian sources had, long before this, been associated with his role as what Emerson (1845) called 'a huge borrower'. Already in the prologue to the *Fall of Princes* (283–7) Lydgate had drawn attention to the 'Lombard' origins of *Troilus and Criseyde*; and interest in Chaucer's use of such material is demonstrated not only by his editors but also by critics as diverse as Dryden (1700) and William Godwin (1803). By the 1870s the idea of an 'Italian period' in Chaucer's work (from his journey to Italy in 1372–3 through to the late 1380s) seems to have become established. This notion was given a seal of approval by the eminent Victorian editor and philologist F. J. Furnivall in his 1873 review of recent developments in Chaucer studies for *Macmillan's Magazine*; and in various forms it proved both durable and appealing. John Livingston Lowes—himself an assiduous investigator of Chaucer's Italian sources—came in 1930 to express some scepticism about the 'so-called Italian period, which was never Italian in the sense in which the earlier period had been French'; yet in the same article retains a sense of the seminal effect of the 1372–3 visit to Genoa and Florence: 'for Chaucer went to Italy, and learned to read Boccaccio and Dante, and all the while that knowledge of books and men on which we have dwelt was broadening and deepening'. The romantic (Wordsworthian or Goethean) appeal of Chaucer's crossing of the Alps early in 1373 has continued to strike a chord in later twentieth-century criticism.

J. A. W. Bennett imagines how the English poet might later on his journey have 'taste[d] the rapture of an Italian spring'; while Donald R. Howard's eloquent account of the Chaucerian party's descent into Lombardy might well be read to the accompaniment of Mendelssohn's Italian Symphony.[31]

By contrast to Lowes, Bennett, and Howard, David Wallace, near the turn of the millennium, prefers to imagine Chaucer on the docks at Genoa, confronting shiploads of slaves from the Levant.[32] This shift of emphasis—from interactions with books, high culture, springtime, and Italian sunshine to brute socio-economic circumstances—is striking. It reflects a concern to read Chaucer's Italian sources in the context of Italian history and politics, and as such represents an important recent development in the study of this particular 'background'. Other initiatives likely to extend the understanding of the interactions between England and Italy at this time may well include the work being done on the transmission of texts and influences through France and on the role of learned clerics during and before Chaucer's time.[33] The subsequent two-way traffic of clerics and humanists between England and Italy during the fifteenth century has been well documented.[34] Yet there is more still to be learned about the lives, interests, and activities of their fourteenth-century predecessors, English and Italian.

FURTHER READING

Boitani, Piero (ed.), *Chaucer and the Italian Trecento* (Cambridge: Cambridge University Press, 1983). A wide-ranging collection of essays, moving from historical and cultural contexts to Chaucer's dealings with particular Italian authors and texts. After twenty years this is still probably the most valuable general introduction.

Cooper, Helen, 'Sources and Analogues of Chaucer's *"Canterbury Tales"*: Reviewing the Work', *Studies in the Age of Chaucer*, 19 (1997), 183–210. An authoritative article, which asserts the primacy of the *Decameron* as model for the *Tales* on the basis of their 'convergence of interpretations as to what a story-collection might be', and reviews the parallels (see especially pp. 192–9).

Edwards, Robert R., *Chaucer and Boccaccio: Antiquity and Modernity* (Basingstoke: Palgrave, 2002). A concise recent study, arguing that 'Boccaccio's representations of antiquity and modernity furnish powerful models for Chaucer to extend, resist and reconceive'. It includes chapters on the 'Knight's Tale', *Troilus* and the *Legend of Good Women*, the 'cherles' tales', and the Clerk's and Franklin's Tales.

Hanly, Michael, 'Courtiers and Poets: An International Network of Literary Exchange in Late Fourteenth-Century Italy, France and England', *Viator*, 28 (1997), 305–32. Essential for the understanding of the intermediary role of French culture, this article provides a detailed account of those who transmitted knowledge of Italian writers via France in Chaucer's time.

Havely, Nicholas R. (ed. and trans.), *Chaucer's Boccaccio* (Cambridge: D. S. Brewer, 1980). Prose translations of the *Filostrato* and parts of the *Teseida* and *Filocolo*, with introduction, notes, and appendices.

Koff, Leonard Michael, and Brenda Deen Schildgen (eds.), *The 'Decameron' and the 'Canterbury Tales': New Essays on an Old Question* (Madison, Wis.: Fairleigh Dickinson University Press and

London: Associated University Presses, 2000). Discussions of reception, influence, and broader themes (locality, consolation, confession, anticlericalism) and five essays on specific tales.

Taylor, Karla, *Chaucer Reads the 'Divine Comedy'* (Stanford, Calif.: Stanford University Press, 1989). With reference to the *House of Fame* (chapter 1) and (primarily) *Troilus*, Taylor characterizes Chaucer's responses to Dante in terms of attitudes to narrative time, language, authority, and 'narrative authentication'.

Wallace, David, *Chaucer and the Early Writings of Boccaccio* (Cambridge: Brewer, 1985). A ground-breaking approach to Chaucer's transformation of Italian texts, insisting that any account of this 'must be preceded by some consideration of the literary and historical "formation" of the text that [he] is engaged with'. Chapter 6, 'The Making of *Troilus and Criseyde*', is a detailed and valuable account of Chaucer's dealings with the *Filostrato*.

Wallace, David, *Chaucerian Polity: Absolutist Lineages and Associational Forms in England and Italy* (Stanford, Calif.: Stanford University Press, 1997). An ambitious and extended essay in comparative historicism, with a particularly valuable account of Chaucer in Florence and Lombardy (pp. 9–64) and close attention to the Italian sources and contexts for the Knight's, Clerk's, and Monk's Tales.

Wetherbee, Winthrop P., *Chaucer and the Poets: An Essay on 'Troilus and Criseyde'* (Ithaca, NY: Cornell University Press, 1984). A wide-ranging and perceptive treatment of classical and vernacular intertextualities, with an especially illuminating chapter on Dante and the *Troilus* (chapter 5).

NOTES

1. Wendy Childs, 'Anglo-Italian Contacts in the Fourteenth Century', in Piero Boitani (ed.), *Chaucer and the Italian Trecento* (Cambridge: Cambridge University Press, 1983), 67.
2. William Rothwell, 'The Trilingual England of Geoffrey Chaucer', *Studies in the Age of Chaucer*, 16 (1994), esp. 46–54.
3. Curt Bühler, 'A Lollard Tract on Translating the Bible into English', *Medium Aevum*, 7 (1935), 173.
4. On the early role of Italians in the English wool trade, see Alwyn A. Ruddock, *Italian Merchants and Shipping in Southampton 1270–1600* (Southampton: University College, 1951), 16; and T. H. Lloyd, *The English Wool Trade in the Middle Ages* (Cambridge: Cambridge University Press, 1977), 138.
5. G. A. Holmes, 'Florentine Merchants in England, 1346–1436', *Economic History Review*, ser. 2, 13 (1960–1), 197.
6. Rothwell, 'Trilingual England', 53–4.
7. See Ruddock, *Italian Merchants*, 134–6.
8. Matthew Paris, *Chronica majora*, Rolls Series (1872–82), v. 246.
9. *The Libelle of Englyshe Polycye: A Poem on the Use of Sea-Power 1436*, ed. Sir George Warner (Oxford: Clarendon Press, 1926), lines 349–51, 456–9.
10. Ruddock, *Italian Merchants*, 162–8.
11. Childs, 'Anglo-Italian Contacts', 82.
12. G. B. Parks, *The English Traveller to Italy*, i: *The Middle Ages* (Rome: Edizioni di Storia e Letteratura, 1954), 136, 423.
13. Martin M. Crow and Clair C. Olson (eds.), *Chaucer Life-Records* (Oxford: Clarendon Press, 1966), 54.
14. David Wallace, *Chaucerian Polity: Absolutist Lineages and Associational Forms in England and Italy* (Stanford, Calif.: Stanford University Press, 1997), 13–54, 261–331.

15. Franco Simone, *The French Renaissance: Medieval Tradition and Italian Influence in Shaping the Renaissance in France*, trans. H. Gaston Hall (London: Macmillan, 1969), 43–50, 54–5, 64, 73.

16. Michael Hanly, 'Courtiers and Poets: An International Network of Literary Exchange in Late Fourteenth-Century Italy, France and England', *Viator*, 28 (1997), 309–10.

17. See e.g. Howard H. Schless, *Chaucer and Dante: A Revaluation* (Norman, Okla.: Pilgrim Books, 1984), 97.

18. On Chaucer's allusions to *Purgatorio*, see Nicholas R. Havely, 'Tearing or Breathing? Dante's Influence on *Filostrato* and *Troilus*', *Studies in the Age of Chaucer*, Proceedings, (1984), 55–9.

19. On the details of Chaucer's treatment of Petrarch here, see Ernest H. Wilkins, 'Cantus Troili', *English Literary History*, 16 (1949), 167–73.

20. For arguments along these lines, see David Wallace, *Chaucer and the Early Writings of Boccaccio* (Cambridge: Brewer, 1985), 152 and Karla Taylor, 'Chaucer's Uncommon Voice: Some Contexts for Influence', in Leonard Michael Koff and Brenda Deen Schildgen (eds.), *The 'Decameron' and the 'Canterbury Tales': New Essays on an Old Question* (Madison, Wis.: Fairleigh Dickinson University Press; London: Associated University Presses, 2000), 54–5 with n. 22, and 70 with n. 63.

21. Behind the name may lie the Middle English verb *lolle(n)*, which (according to the *Middle English Dictionary*) is related to a Middle Dutch verb meaning 'mutter, doze, sleep'. Meanings current in Chaucer's time were 'dangle' and 'limp', as well as the modern sense of 'lounge'.

22. On the question of Chaucer's knowledge of Boccaccio's 'self-commentary', see Nicholas R. Havely (ed. and trans.), *Chaucer's Boccaccio* (Cambridge: Brewer, 1980), 11.

23. On these features of the 'Monk's Tale', see Piero Boitani, 'The "Monk's Tale": Dante and Boccaccio', *Medium Aevum*, 45 (1976), 50–69.

24. On Chaucer's treatment of the *Teseida*, see Piero Boitani, *Chaucer and Boccaccio* (Oxford: Society for the Study of Medieval Languages and Literature, 1977). For the *Filocolo* as analogue to the 'Franklin's Tale', see Havely (ed. and trans.), *Chaucer's Boccaccio*, 154–61, and Robert R. Edwards, 'Source, Context, and Cultural Translation in the "Franklin's Tale" ', *Modern Philology*, 94 (1996–7), 141–62.

25. See Wallace, *Chaucerian Polity*, 261–98.

26. For discussion of this more complex kind of intertextuality, see Robert R. Edwards, *Chaucer and Boccaccio: Antiquity and Modernity* (Basingstoke: Palgrave, 2002), 154–72.

27. For a concise summary of views on the *Decameron* analogues for the 'Shipman's Tale', see N. S. Thompson, *Chaucer, Boccaccio and the Debate of Love: A Comparative Study* of the *'Decameron'* and the *'Canterbury Tales'* (Oxford: Clarendon Press, 1996), 214–20.

28. For discussion of these and other parallels, see Helen Cooper, 'Sources and Analogues of Chaucer's "Canterbury Tales": Reviewing the Work', *Studies in the Age of Chaucer*, 19 (1997), 183–210.

29. Bale, *Illustrium maioris Britanniae scriptorum*, fo. 198ʳ.

30. Most of the examples cited here and later in this section can be found, under the dates mentioned, in D. S. Brewer (ed.), *Chaucer: The Critical Heritage*, 2 vols. (London: Routledge & Kegan Paul, 1978).

31. J. A. W. Bennett, 'Chaucer, Dante and Boccaccio', in Boitani (ed.), *Chaucer and the Italian Trecento*, 90; Donald R. Howard, *Chaucer and the Medieval World* (London: Weidenfeld & Nicolson, 1987), 175–6.

32. *Chaucerian Polity*, 21–2.

33. See Hanly, 'Courtiers and Poets', esp. 331–2.

34. e.g. Roberto Weiss, *Humanism in England during the Fifteenth Century*, 3rd edn. (Oxford: Blackwell, 1967), and more recently Suzanne Saygin, *Humphrey, Duke of Gloucester (1390–1447) and the Italian Humanists* (Leiden: Brill, 2002).

19 | The Bible

Valerie Edden

The 'Miller's Tale' is a comic tale of bawdy, in which a young Oxford student proves his superiority to his ageing, artisan landlord, John, by bedding his attractive young wife. It provokes laughter not only because it breaks taboos with its indecent puns and frank reference to bodily functions but also because of the ludicrous plot which Nicholas employs to win Alison in her husband's house and in his very presence and also because this love-triangle is complicated by having a second would-be lover, Absolon. It comes, therefore, as a surprise that a tale so rooted in profanity, so obviously designed to provide 'solaas' rather then 'sentence' (see 'GP' 798), depends for its effect upon the biblical texts to which it alludes.

Nicholas's plot hinges on John's ignorance of the details of the story of Noah. He tells him that on the Monday following there will be a second flood of twice the scale of Noah's flood and persuades him to outdo Noah's response by building three individual vessels to save himself, his wife, and his lodger ('MT' 3516–21, 3547–50). What John has forgotten is that the biblical narrative ends with God establishing the rainbow as a sign of his promise that never again will the whole world be destroyed by flood (Genesis 9: 13–15).

Similarly the name of Nicholas's rival seducer, Absolon, and his golden curls raise expectations in a reader who knows the story of his biblical namesake. Absolon (the name is 'Absalom' in English Bibles), son of David, was a byword for masculine beauty with his flowing hair and his handsome appearance. He was also a villain who got his well-deserved come-uppance when, in an attempted coup to oust his father, he met his death when he was caught by his hair in an oak tree and lost his footing on his mule (2 Samuel 14–18).

There are less obvious allusions. There is something of a jest to be found when Absolon borrows a hot ploughshare from the blacksmith Gerveys, using it as a weapon of revenge (3775 ff.), thus turning upside down the prophecy of Isaiah that swords shall be turned into ploughshares (Isaiah 2: 4; compare Micah 4: 3): a topsy-turvy allusion for a topsy-turvy moral world.

When Nicholas practises singing in his room, he sings a well-known song to the Virgin Mary, 'Angelus ad virginem' (3216), commemorating the Annunciation, the visit of the Angel Gabriel to tell Mary she was to bear the son of God (Luke 2). Some critics see in this an invitation to read the tale as a parody of the Annunciation, with

Nicholas as Gabriel, Alison as Mary, and John as Joseph. Even those sceptical of such a parody would acknowledge the comic effect evoked by the comparison.

There is a different type of 'biblical' allusion when John swears 'by hym that harwed helle!' (3512). This refers to the story in which Jesus descends into hell between his death and resurrection to defeat the powers of evil and release the souls of the righteous of the pre-Christian era. It is not strictly biblical at all. It is related in the Gospel of Nicodemus, a fourth-century text long since dismissed as spurious by the Church but which held the popular imagination for centuries. It is important for modern readers of medieval texts to familiarize themselves with such apocryphal texts and to acknowledge the extent of their influence.

In this present age a good knowledge of the Bible is the prerogative of a devout and/or learned minority. This was not the case in Chaucer's time. The Bible was familiar to literate and illiterate alike. Formal education began and often ended with the (Latin) Bible. Young boys learnt their letters by reading the Psalms, and university students were required to debate fine points of biblical scholarship in order to graduate. Those who could not read also had access to the Bible. Illustrations of biblical texts abounded, not only in books but also as murals in churches, on church furniture, and as sculptures. Such illustrations do not simply replicate biblical texts; inevitably they interpret them. Noah was commonly interpreted as a 'figure' of Christ and his ark as a figure of the Church, and so the latter was commonly presented as a ship. Such 'figural' interpretations will be discussed below. In the 'Miller's Tale' the story of Noah is treated literally, without regard to its figural significance.

Key episodes from the Bible were made familiar by the cycle of plays performed annually by the craft guilds in many towns, hence 'mystery' plays since a man's 'mister' was his trade. The Miller himself is said to cry out 'in Pilates voys' ('MP' 3124), shouting loudly as Pilate was required to do. We are told that Absolon took part in such dramas, playing the blustering Herod (3384). Inevitably these plays embellished the biblical narratives they dramatized, adding not just characterization and local colour, but material passed down through oral tradition. The power of such tradition even today may be well illustrated in the practice of school nativity plays, whereby three kings called Caspar, Melchior, and Balthazar visit the baby Jesus; one king is black, one brown, one white, thus representing the peoples of the world. Such details are not to be found in the biblical account of the visit of three astrologers from the East, though they may be traced back to a time before Chaucer.

Those among Chaucer's audience who knew the mystery plays would find the 'Miller's Tale' enriched by a web of references linking John the carpenter to both Noah and Joseph, the husband of Mary. Nicholas, we remember, has persuaded John to build vessels to survive the coming deluge, 'thanne shul we be lordes al oure lyf | Of al the world, as Noe and his wyf' (3581–2). He reminds him too of the difficulties experienced by Noah in getting his wife into the ship. Noah's trouble with his wife, like the figures of Caspar, Melchior, and Balthazar, does not figure in the Bible. It is through the drama that the legend of Mrs Noah as a shrewish harridan, prompted by the Devil, was transmitted. The obduracy of the commonsensical Mrs Noah in the face of her husband's crazy shipbuilding scheme was a splendid opportunity for comedy. John reminds us of another troubled husband, for the old man is a carpenter like Joseph. The mystery plays, drawing on a tradition that made Joseph an old man, portrayed him, like Noah, as a man whose wife caused him trouble. 'Joseph's trouble about Mary' was a common theme in drama and song and gave another opportunity for comedy as he became the butt of jokes about his pregnant young wife-to-be and her story about the virginal conception of her baby. It is worth commenting, too, that while the implied parallels drawn between John, Noah, and Joseph help to make him a foolish and gullible old man, they also draw attention to the thoughtless cruelty of youthful comedy against old men, given that Noah and Joseph were both innocent and righteous.

This discussion of the 'Miller's Tale' has served to show the pervasive influence of biblical allusion even in a comic fabliau and to show particularly the need to look beyond the biblical text to the wealth of tradition, learned and popular, that shaped the way such material was understood in the late Middle Ages.

The composition of the Bible

But what was the Bible and to what extent does the volume we now possess resemble the Bible Chaucer might have read? As the sacred book of the Christian faith, it is accepted by Christians as a record of God's revelation of himself to humanity. It is not one book but many, a collection of sacred writings. The Christian Church grew out of Judaism, and the most substantial section of the Bible, the Old Testament, is taken over from the Hebrew Scriptures. Initially the Church used a version of them translated into Greek (known as the Septuagint), a version abandoned by the Jewish authorities early in the Christian era. The Hebrew Scriptures comprise the Law (the Torah) and the Prophets. The Law is contained in the five books known as the Pentateuch, which contains a narrative account of the Creation and the early history of God's 'Chosen People' as well as the legal code. The writings of the prophets do not prophesy in our modern sense of 'foretell', but proclaim the will of God to his people. To these were added the 'Writings', which included books of history, the Psalms (the hymns used liturgically in the Second Temple, the central sanctuary of the Jewish religion from the sixth to the first centuries BC), and a number of books of wisdom (proverbs).

The early Church gathered together a collection of writings of its own to supplement the Old Testament. Letters written by Paul (in the middle of the first century) are the earliest to have been written. They also collected four Gospels, narrative accounts of the life of Jesus, incorporating material which had circulated orally, including the 'sayings of Jesus' and a narrative of the life of the first Christians (the Acts of the Apostles). By the late fourth century the Christian Scriptures, known collectively as the New Testament, were generally accepted as including these texts together with other letters and the Revelation of John, a series of visions about the kingdom of God, written in the form of an apocalypse, a prophecy whose meaning is veiled and mysterious.

About the year 382, under Pope Damasus, a decision was made about which texts of both the Hebrew Scriptures and the Christian writings should be accepted as authoritative (that is the 'canon' of the Scriptures) and the Bible as we know it was born. This did not stop the circulation of apocryphal Hebrew texts, which had been rejected by the Jewish authorities around AD 100, or of Christian writings of dubious authenticity, such as the Gospel of Nicodemus and other 'gospels' that related stories such as the infancy of Jesus and the birth of the Virgin Mary. At about the same time Damasus entrusted to Jerome the task of preparing a Latin Bible, working from Hebrew texts rather than the Septuagint for the Old Testament. Jerome's translation, the Vulgate, has remained the authoritative version of the Catholic Church.

The interpretation of the Bible

The Greek word βιβλια is plural (i.e. books), as is its Latin derivative *biblia*. However, by the twelfth century it had become a singular noun. The change is a significant one and goes hand in hand with a new tendency for the various biblical texts to be gathered together rather than circulate separately. Thus understood, the Bible becomes a single narrative telling the story of salvation, beginning with Adam's fall from grace. The climax is the death of Jesus, the Messiah, which saved humanity from the consequences of its own fallen, sinful state. The Hebrew Scriptures are appropriated as Christian writings, deriving their true meaning (which had been hidden from their original writers and readers) in relation to the gospel story. As history they record the preparation of the Chosen People, Israel, for the coming of Jesus.

This way of reading the Scriptures was reinforced by the circumstances in which they were most commonly read, not in formal study but during worship. From the fourth century onwards selections were chosen to be read at each service during the day and gathered together in a lectionary, a table of readings for the whole year. So, for example, the Old Testament reading for Good Friday was Exodus 12, the account of the Passover, in which the Israelites were able to escape from slavery in Egypt by sacrificing a lamb and marking their doorposts with its blood. By placing this passage alongside the account of the Crucifixion in John's Gospel, the two events are made parallel; Christ is understood as the new sacrificial lamb.

Matthew's Gospel reports Jesus as speaking of his impending death and resurrection in terms of Jonah's three days and three nights in the belly of the whale. Jewish scholars were allegorizing the Hebrew Scriptures by the beginning of the Christian era, and the Christian Church extended the practice into 'typological' reading, that is, reading people and events in the Old Testament as foreshadowing people and events in the New. Thus the Crucifixion is prefigured by Abraham's sacrifice of Isaac (Genesis 22) and Moses' lifting up the serpent in the desert (Numbers 21: 9); Melchizedek, the priest who offered Abraham bread and wine (Genesis 14: 18) is seen as prefiguring Jesus' blessing bread and wine at the Last Supper and so instituting the sacrament of the Eucharist; Leah and Rachel, the two wives of Jacob (Genesis 29), are interpreted not so much as real women but as aspects of Jacob's life and character. Over the centuries biblical scholars developed elaborately sophisticated 'spiritual' readings, often uncovering many layers of allegorical meanings. While such elaborate readings may have been known only to those with a university education, the practice of reading 'spiritually' was popularized by pictorial representations of Bible stories, in which gospel scenes are presented together with their Old Testament 'types', as mentioned earlier. In Figure II.1 Christ is shown carrying the Cross to Golgotha (John 19: 16–17). Placed alongside are Old Testament foreshadowings of this event: Isaac bearing wood for Abraham's sacrifice (Genesis 22: 3), the widow gathering wood in Zarephath (1 Kings 17: 10), and Old Testament prophecies (Isaiah 53: 7; Jeremiah 11: 19) of the lamb led to the slaughter.

Chaucer's alphabetical poem, 'An ABC', speaks of Moses' burning bush (Exodus 3) as a 'signe of [Mary's] unwemmed maidenhede' (91), since the bush which burnt with fire but was not consumed was understood as symbolizing her virginal conception of Christ. Similarly, Abraham's sacrifice of Isaac is understood to prefigure the sacrificial death of Christ on the cross ('An ABC', 169). When, in the 'Merchant's Tale', the aged January sings a love-song to his young bride and quotes from the Song of Songs (2138–48), eliciting from the narrator a comment about his 'olde lewed wordes' (2149), there is a double irony at work. The word 'lewed' here is no doubt intended by the Merchant in its main sense of 'lascivious', though for the medieval reader it will inevitably also mean 'lay', that is non-clerical. January is deceived in thinking that May may be appropriately compared with the idealized bride in the biblical text; the Merchant is mistaken in thinking the words were usually read in this literal way to commend a young woman's physical beauty. However, the beautifully erotic 'Song' found its way into the canon of Scripture; it was read 'spiritually' from a very early date to signify the love of Christ for the Church and, after the twelfth century, for the Virgin Mary. Moreover, the image of virginity which January borrows (the enclosed garden, Song of Songs 4: 12) is at once a standard medieval figure of Mary's virginity and also under-lines the tale's plot, in which January builds a walled garden in which to make love but also to guarantee his wife's chastity. This garden image sets off a chain of other allu-sions, to the paradisal garden of Eden (always walled in medieval illustrations) which was yet the scene of the Fall, and to the garden which is the scene of love in the *Romance of the Rose*.

The practice of reading through the surface meaning of a text to find the kernel of truth hidden within it resulted in a complex and sophisticated theory of authorship and the assumption that texts, secular as well as sacred, could be read on a number of different levels. To take a Chaucerian example, one might consider the Clerk's tale of

Fig. II.1 Christ carrying the cross, with typological scenes from the Old Testament. Illustration from the Eton Roundels, mid-thirteenth century (Eton College, MS 177).

patient Griselda, which is derived from Petrarch's version of the story, in which Griselda's obedience to her husband exemplifies humility and obedience to God's will. When, at the close of the tale, the Clerk claims that this is also his meaning, it is not only modern readers who question his judgement, doubting among other things the possibility that Walter, the husband, can be equated with God. The Host and the Merchant make it clear that they have understood the tale quite differently, as a story about an ideal marriage. There has been a major debate about the extent to which Chaucer's poetry is to be read with the aim of discerning such 'spiritual' truth. This will be discussed below (see 'Chaucer's "biblical poetics"').

Biblical translation and the 'plain text': the Wycliffite controversy

The issue of translation was a live one in Chaucer's time. The Psalms had been translated into English many times from the Anglo-Saxon period onwards and there were paraphrases of other books. Recent scholarship has revealed the full extent to which vernacular biblical paraphrase and versification were available by Chaucer's time.[1] However, biblical translation became a matter of considerable controversy when, inspired (and possibly encouraged) by John Wyclif, the first complete English prose translation of the Bible was prepared. Official condemnation of this translation came in 1409 on the grounds that it was dangerous to put sacred writings into the hands of ignorant men who might misinterpret them.

The issue was more complex than this accusation allows. The Wycliffite translation was condemned not only because it was in the vernacular but also because it presented the text without the commentary which traditionally accompanied it. It was usual for the biblical text to be surrounded, at times almost submerged, by commentary drawn from the fathers of the Church, written in all four margins and sometimes between the lines as well. Such commentary is known as 'gloss' and there were a number of standard glosses, the *Glossa ordinaria*, Peter Lombard's *Magna glosatura*, and Nicholas of Lyra's commentary. Such practices are not totally unfamiliar to modern readers; one thinks of modern scholarly editions, with their bulky apparatus and learned commentary, as, for example, Barry Windeatt's edition of *Troilus and Criseyde*.[2] Wyclif and his followers (the Lollards) believed in the right of all individuals to read the Scriptures and interpret them, since their plain meaning was felt to be apparent even to the simple and ill educated. They thus challenged the clerical monopoly on the Bible. Chaucer was well aware of the nature of these disagreements about who might read and who might interpret the Bible.

Scholars disagree about the impact of Wycliffite ideas. There are those who see Lollardy as preparing the ground for the Reformation, promoting a Bible-centred faith in many ways similar to Protestantism.[3] Others emphasize the strong survival of 'traditional' Catholic parish life well into the sixteenth century,[4] though this seems truer in rural parishes than in the towns.

There were a number of key Wycliffite positions (not all of them found in the writings of Wyclif himself):

1   That the plain text of the Bible is to be read, stripped of its gloss.

2   The unity of sacred Scripture: *tota scriptura est unum dei verbum*, 'the whole of Scripture is the single Word of God'.

3   That sacred Scripture is to be read as a whole, that is, not in fragments or disconnected extracts.

4   That a proper understanding of the Bible depends upon the virtue of the interpreter.

5   The literal meaning is privileged. Note that 'literal' does not have its modern sense, but signifies the meaning intended by the author (God in the case of the Bible) and includes an acceptance of 'spiritual' readings, which would nowadays be considered figurative, such as allegorical, tropological (conveying moral truth), or anagogical (concerning the next life).

6   That the Bible be made available in the vernacular to be read by the laity.

7   That the Bible be considered the only authority for the Christian (as distinct from the teachings of the Church).

8   That every man may interpret the Bible for himself (provided he has a 'moral disposition' (see point 4 above)).

Neither side in the Wycliffite controversy approximates what might be called a modern scholarly approach to reading the Bible, as a text showing the developing understanding of the nature of God over time, especially in the Old Testament, and in which individual books may be illumined by knowledge of the circumstances in which they were written. Such a historical perspective was first expressed in England by John Colet at the close of the fifteenth century. Fourteenth-century readers had different preoccupations. Their concerns included establishing who had the right to interpret the sacred text and how truth might be discerned among conflicting readings. Such issues of truth and textual authority are raised repeatedly in Chaucer's poetry. (For more on Chaucer and Wyclif, see Chapters 5, 7, and 16.)

Chaucer's use of biblical allusions

It is not easy to quantify the extent of Chaucer's scriptural references and allusions. It is not just that allusions may be (and frequently are) disputed, but that a passage that does not refer explicitly to any biblical text may refer to the gist of a text or may well reflect a debate about the interpretation of Scripture. Many references to Adam, Christ, and the Virgin Mary refer generally to their role in the Christian story rather than to any specific biblical text. Besserman's index lists almost all the instances claimed to be biblical allusions in Chaucer and so leaves the reader free to choose or discard examples as s/he thinks fit.[5]

The most straightforward biblical allusions work by drawing a comparison and thus enriching the text, as, for example, when the fair Lady White in the *Book of the Duchess* is compared to Esther in her 'debonairte' (graciousness, meekness, 986), or in the ballade 'Truth', where Chaucer weaves the poem round the biblical text 'And trouthe thee shal delivere, it is no drede' (John 8: 32). At times the Bible is cited as a proof-text, as an authoritative source of wisdom and truth, making particular use of the wisdom books (Proverbs, Ecclesiastes, and the apocryphal Wisdom of Solomon and Ecclesiasticus). So, the Parson, declining to tell a fable, gives as his authority Paul's words to Timothy: 'They will stop their ears to truth and turn to fables' ('ParsP' 31–4; 2 Timothy 4: 4; see also 1 Timothy 1: 4, 4: 7). So too Pandarus, persuading his niece Criseyde not to reject Troilus' advances, adduces, 'The wise seith, "Wo hym that is allone, | For, and he falle, he hath non helpe to ryse"' (*TC* 1. 694–5), quoting Ecclesiastes 4: 10, though the original refers clearly to friends and not sexual partners.

More typically Chaucer uses the biblical text in an indirect way: either ironically or in some other way that allows us to reflect on the *dissimilarity* between the context of the biblical text and the situation or character in Chaucer's text. We have already discussed the irony in January's quoting from the Song of Songs in the 'Merchant's Tale'. The problem with irony is that it depends on the reader's being able to assume that the author cannot have meant us to take his statement straight. Chaucer is an author whose precise beliefs and assumptions are notoriously difficult to pin down, quite apart from his habit of putting utterances in the mouths of fictional and therefore unreliable characters. Now and then one may be confident that irony is totally absent (despite the pleas of critics), for example in the biblical quotations in the 'Parson's Tale'. When the sorrowing mother in the 'Prioress's Tale' is compared to 'this newe Rachel' (627), it is most likely that both the Prioress and her creator speak without irony, inviting us to consider Rachel as the paradigm of maternal grief, rather than reflecting on the incongruity of an Old Testament allusion in a text marked by antisemitism or on its inappropriateness to the situation of this particular mother.[6]

In the 'Merchant's Tale' January reflects on all the reasons why in old age he should take a young wife. Much of his reasoning is self-deceiving or illogical. His claim that sexual sin is not possible between a man and his wife is supported by the analogy 'Ne hurte hymselven with his owene knyf' (1840), which is obviously nonsense, since the latter event is quite possible. So when he cites a list of good women from the Bible and advises men to follow the wise counsel of their wives, critics have been quick to find irony and to point to ways in which these good and faithful wives were also deceivers. Rebekah encouraged her son Jacob to deceive his father, Isaac, and take the inheritance intended for his elder brother Esau (Genesis 27). Judith brought about the death of Holofernes through her cunning (apocryphal book of Judith). Esther used her position as queen to destroy Haman, the king's chief officer, because of his hostility to the Jews (Esther 3–8). Abigail used deceit to save her wicked husband, Nabal, but married David after Nabal's death (1 Samuel 25). While these women hardly seem model wives, it is far from certain that they are being cited here as negative *exempla*. The list is derived from Albertano of Brescia's *Liber consolationis et consilii*, which is the source of Chaucer's 'Tale of Melibee'. In this tale these women are cited unambiguously to prove that women may be 'ful discret and wis in conseillynge' (1097). All four women are presented as heroines in the Old Testament. The son whom Rebekah favoured was Jacob (Israel), father of the twelve tribes of Israel. Judith and Esther both saved Israel from her enemies. Abigail's main role is to save King David from wrongful bloodshed. If there is irony in January's citing these four women, it is not because he is mistaken in thinking that they are good. Chaucer's touch, as ever, is lighter than this. It is only in hindsight, after January chooses May and the story unfolds, that we realize he has ignored his own advice, choosing a woman he (falsely) believes to be totally compliant and submissive to his will, rather than one like the four biblical wives, whose clever schemes and politically prudent actions make them assets indeed. The references to these women, with their courage and variety of virtues, cause us to reflect that January, in contrast, has only one standard of wifely virtue, a sexual one.

When, in the 'Physician's Tale', Virginia reminds her father that even Jephtha allowed his daughter 'grace . . . | to compleyne, er he hir slow' (240–1), we may notice both similarities and dissimilarities between her predicament (her father intends to kill her rather than allow her honour to be sullied by submitting to the lust of the judge Apius) and that of Jephtha's daughter, whose sacrifice is required because of a vow to the Almighty (Judges 11: 1–40). Referring to medieval biblical commentaries does not help us know how to respond to the allusion, since Jephtha's sacrifice is condemned by some commentators and compared by others to Abraham's sacrifice of Isaac, widely believed to prefigure the sacrifice of Jesus on the Cross. No doubt the more learned among Chaucer's audience also recalled the story of Iphigenia, whose father, Agamemnon, was obliged to sacrifice her. One may at least comment on the effect of the mingling of classical and biblical references and note that Virginia's invocation of the distinctively Christian idea of 'grace' is unsettling in its pagan context, though critics disagree about the impact of this juxtaposition of different cultural values. Those poems of Chaucer set in the pagan past, that is *Troilus and Criseyde* and the Knight's and Franklin's Tales, are generally remarkable for the absence of biblical and Christian references.

Most frequently we are left with the possibility that some irony may be present but that any heavy irony would be reductive, and would close down a text left suggestively and playfully open. There are many examples of allusions that raise more questions than they answer. The 'Nun's Priest's Tale' retells the fable of the cock Chauntecleer in a way that enables him to allude jestingly to a number of issues that exercised the minds of fourteenth-century scholars, such as predestination and free will, the nature of dreams and the use and abuse of language, not to mention the use and abuse of biblical interpretation. The tale contains a number of allusions to the biblical account of the Creation and Fall. The tale's setting in May is in fact calculated with reference to the month of March, 'whan God first maked man' (3188). When Chauntecleer woos Pertelote, commending her beauty, he quotes, '*In principio, | Mulier est hominis confusio*' ('In the beginning, woman is man's downfall'), mistranslating the Latin maxim as 'Womman is mannes joye and al his blis' (3163–6). Chauntecleer no doubt thinks the joke is against his wife, who in her role as a mock-romantic heroine will have no Latin. 'In principio', the opening words of both Genesis and John's Gospel, were widely believed to have magical power and are used here simply to assert that what follows is true. As the maxim suggests, in the Middle Ages Genesis 3 was invariably understood to suggest that blame for the Fall was to be laid upon Eve and that Adam allowed her to lead him astray because of his uxoriousness. What Chauntecleer fails to realize is that his mistranslation is also true, in that he too will suffer the consequences of his uxoriousness, prompted by the 'joye' he takes in his wife. He may know his Bible but is comically incapable of applying it to his own circumstances, just as he fails to act on his knowledge of biblical and classical dreams.

Later, when the narrator reflects on the meaning of his fable, he refers once more to Genesis 3:

> Wommennes conseils been ful ofte colde;
> Wommannes conseil broghte us first to wo
> And made Adam fro Paradys to go,
> Ther as he was ful myrie and wel at ese. (3256–9)

He then swiftly withdraws his chauvinist generalization, disingenuously claiming, 'Thise been the cokkes wordes, and nat myne' (3265). The passage is comic, not least because of its slipperiness. The reader responds first by accepting the element of truth in the accusation: Chauntecleer was mistaken to listen to Pertelote when she dismissed his prophetic dream as an insignificant nightmare. However, a moment's reflection leads us to acknowledge that Chauntecleer's fall had other causes, since it was lust that drove him down to the floor from the safety of his perch and his vanity led him to be beguiled by the fox's flattery. At this point we may reconsider and resist the parallel between this barnyard scene and the fall of Adam and Eve. Chauntecleer makes a poor Adam, given his vanity, pomposity, and his love of his own voice. Nor is Pertelote a temptress, save in the sense (advanced at times by medieval preachers) that feminine beauty was in itself a temptation.

It is here that critics diverge. Some take the parallel between the fable and Genesis as the key to understanding the tale, seeing the beam upon which Chauntecleer perches as the forbidden tree and the barnyard as Eden. They thus take entirely seriously the narrator's injunction to 'Taketh the fruyt, and lat the chaf be stille' (3443, Augustine's rewording of 2 Corinthians 3: 6). Others refuse to see a single meaning or moral in a tale in which, however much we learn about fallen mankind, laughter predominates, whether the last laugh is on the Nun's Priest, who bears such an uncanny resemblance to his cockerel protagonist in his love of rhetorical display and his male vanity, or on us all in that we are all implicated in the satire by our common humanity.

The story of Adam and Eve is told and retold in the *Canterbury Tales*, for example in the 'Tale of Melibee' and by the Monk and the Pardoner. The Parson also uses it in a completely orthodox way to account for the innate human inclination to sin and for the waywardness of the flesh in particular ('ParsT' 323–30). As Alfred David points out, each retelling offers a different view of the human condition and human sexuality.[7] Thus in the 'Merchant's Tale', May's betrayal of a husband who believed a young wife could give him paradise on earth takes place in a garden and involves a tree and a distinctly human serpent, her lover Damyan. The tale presents a bleak and brutish picture of human relationships and seems to endorse an idea of human sexuality as a particular symptom of the fall from grace.

The presence of explicit biblical allusion is largely uncontroversial, though critics may disagree over the significance of a particular instance. There is inevitably disagreement about implicit allusion, where one reader finds a biblical parallel that is used to unlock the text and others deny its presence at all. One instance is the invitation to consider the diet of a number of the Canterbury pilgrims (the Prioress's roast meat, the Monk's fat swan, the Franklin's house, in which it snowed with meat and drink) in the light of the text 'Man shall not live by bread alone' (Matthew 4: 4), a text not explicitly mentioned here or elsewhere in the *Canterbury Tales*. This implied biblical allusion has been taken to condemn the carnality of those whose food consumption is mentioned.[8]

Chaucer and the 'glosing' debate

As well as explicit or implicit allusion, a third use of the Bible may be distinguished in Chaucer, where the allusion is to the debate about biblical interpretation, raising questions about who has the right to act as interpreter and broader questions about the relationship between textual authority and truth. We have already mentioned the debate about the glossing of the Scriptures. The word 'gloss' had acquired largely negative connotations by the late fourteenth century, suggesting an interpretation which is specious or over-elaborate or too clever by half. Its use in Chaucer's works is generally pejorative. The Squire, describing the gifts given to Cambyuskan, exclaims, 'This is a verray sooth, withouten glose' ('SqT' 166). The Manciple, who goes on to tell a slippery tale which makes a point about the dangers of telling the plain truth, promises the Cook, 'Of me, certeyn, thou shalt nat been yglosed' ('ManP' 34), where 'yglosed' seems to suggest both deceit and flattery. When the Monk speaks of Fortune 'glos[ing]' ('MoT' 2140), the meaning is unequivocally 'deceive'.

While glossing had been a clerical activity for centuries, it had become an issue of particular debate in Chaucer's time. It was an issue raised repeatedly in satire against the friars, which took them to task for failing to live up to the ideals of their founders, particularly Francis of Assisi and his espousing of Lady Poverty. Among the criticisms levelled against the friars, who by Chaucer's time were more often than not better educated than local parish clergy, was that they glossed the Scriptures to their own advantage, to flatter rich patrons and to deceive others:

> I fond there freres, alle the foure orders,
> Prechynge the peple for profit of the wombe:
> Glosed the gospel as hem good liked.
>
> (*Piers Plowman*, prologue, 58–60)

The 'Summoner's Tale' is a story about a friar with these very skills, who boasts to the humble Thomas, lying on his sickbed, of his ability to elucidate difficult passages:

> And therfore wol I teche yow al the glose.
> Glosynge is a glorious thyng, certeyn,
> For lettre sleeth, so as we clerkes seyn. (1792–4)

His own 'glosynge' perfectly illustrates the charges made by those who, like the Summoner, opposed the friars, for it is a model of dissimulation and self-interest. First he cites Jerome's understanding of the implications of Genesis 3, that gluttony contributed to the Fall. Then he preaches a sermon about the merits of fasting and abstinence on a visit to a house where he habitually cadges his dinner. He goes on to claim that a gloss on the beatitude 'Blessed are the poor in spirit' (Matthew 5: 3) explains that the poor in spirit are friars and that the prayers of friars are therefore particularly effective. Thomas rightly judges this to be an attempt at begging from him ('ST' 1918–53).

There is a second more specific context to these references to 'glosing'—the debate about the interpretation of the Scriptures, prompted by the ideas of Wyclif and his followers discussed above. Chaucer, whose work suggests no clear relation to the various political factions of his time, is equally non-committal about contemporary religious controversies. Nonetheless, there was support for Wyclif and his views at court and among Chaucer's particular circle. Lollard (Wycliffite) views were a matter of public debate by the 1390s and Chaucer was well informed about the issues at stake.

The relation of truth to text and the whole issue of textual authority in secular texts had been explored in some depth in Chaucer's pre-*Tales* poems, particularly the *House of Fame* and the *Legend of Good Women*. These same issues in relation to sacred texts are debated in the *Canterbury Tales*, notably by the Wife of Bath. Her tale with its lengthy Prologue takes issue with clerical orthodoxy on a variety of issues, including the role and worth of women, the respective merits of marriage, widowhood, and virginity, and sexual relations. She challenges clerical misogyny and the anti-feminist stance of many clerical writings. She points out the male monopoly on glossing the Scriptures and boldly asserts that she too can understand the Bible. She is well aware that those who interpret the Scriptures make choices between readings and that, since biblical teaching was believed to have authority, their role gives them power and influence over people's lives. She comments too that anti-feminist clerics tend to ignore all the good women in the Bible. The Friar understands her position well, rebuking her:

> Ye han heer touched, also moot I thee,
> In scole-matere greet difficultee.
> Ye han seyd muche thyng right wel, I seye;
> But, dame, heere as we ryde by the weye,
> Us nedeth nat to speken but of game,
> And lete auctoritees, on Goddes name,
> To prechyng and to scoles of clergye.

('FP' 1271–7)

Despite her initial claim to value experience more than 'authority' ('WBP' 1–2, that is, the authority of the Church and its scholars), she conducts her own debate in the manner of an academic theological dispute, analysing a number of biblical passages and choosing between different interpretations and offering her own. Five times married herself, in her Prologue she defends serial monogamy by adducing scriptural texts that condone marrying more than once. She cites the views of Jerome, who had based his argument that people should marry once only on the fact that the Gospels record Jesus attending a wedding on one occasion only, at the marriage feast of Cana (John 2). Against this she balances the biblical injunction to 'go forth and multiply' (though she herself is apparently childless, as a number of critics have pointed out) and a number of examples of polygamy in the Old Testament, and she comments on the difficulty of drawing conclusions on the matter from Jesus' meeting with the Samaritan woman at the well (John 4). Later she argues that Jesus' command to be perfect (Matthew 19: 21) is addressed to a particular young man and cannot therefore be held to be binding on everyone.

The Friar's reference to 'game' may serve to remind us of the extent of game here, where pro- and anti-feminist arguments are played off one against the other, but in terms wholly defined by the anti-feminist literature which the Wife is attacking. Sympathy for her championing the right of women to read and interpret for themselves should be balanced against the realization that Alison's biblical exegesis is at times both outrageous and either wilfully partial or plain ignorant. On occasion, she suppresses parts of a text or quotes one out of context. Much of her Prologue comprises a sustained response to Jerome's *Adversus Jovinianum*, an authoritative anti-matrimonial and anti-feminist text in the Middle Ages.[9] To refute Jerome, she gives her own view of two key passages in the Pauline epistles in which marriage is discussed. From 1 Corinthians 7 she quotes Paul's statement that men should yield their wives the 'marriage debt', interpreted by the Church to mean that sexual relations are due to each partner in marriage. She ignores both the immediate context (the statement that husbands and wives indeed have a mutual obligation in this respect) and the argument of the whole chapter, which rather grudgingly concedes the need for marriage but commends chastity for the unmarried and widows and even mutually agreed abstinence within marriage. Moreover, medieval canon law excused the conjugal debt to elderly and infirm husbands, such as the Wife's first three husbands. The term 'debt' also leads her into an equation of sex and money ('WBP' 153–5), which is certainly not biblical though it may well reflect a commonly held medieval view that women were little more than chattels, which she is comically turning to her own advantage. She goes on to quote Ephesians 5, where Paul advises husbands to love their wives, once again ignoring the verse following, in which he tells wives to reverence their husbands (the Latin of the Vulgate uses *timere*, 'to fear'), and the wider context, in which wives are explicitly told to 'submit to [their] husbands as though to the Lord' (Ephesians 5: 22). It is at this point that the Pardoner can no longer restrain himself and interrupts her in full flow.

It will be clear that some of the issues raised by the Wife are points raised by the Lollards. It is also true that she epitomizes the social background in which Lollardy flourished and uses Lollard sect vocabulary, as Blamires points out.[10] It is equally clear that she totally disregards much other Lollard teaching, both about the Bible and, crucially, the outright condemnation of pilgrimages. She may claim her right to interpret Holy Writ for herself but she blatantly disregards the 'whole book', selecting her texts carefully for her own purposes, and is hardly concerned with her own 'moral disposition'.

The Wife's abuse of scriptural authority raises questions about how the Scriptures may be interpreted and by whom. It also raises more general issues about the use of authoritative texts and about how they may be said to embody truth, matters considered elsewhere in the *Tales* (for further discussion of the Wife of Bath, see particularly Chapter 21). An extreme response to such questions is that of the Parson, who cites scriptural authority to justify his refusal to follow the other pilgrims in telling a (fictional) story ('ParsP' 31–4).

Chaucer's 'biblical poetics'

An area of major and ongoing critical controversy since the 1960s has been the claim that Chaucer's poetry is imbued with what Besserman has called 'biblical poetics'. The interpretative practices employed for reading biblical texts are held to have become so much a habit of mind in the Middle Ages that they profoundly influenced the practice of secular writers, and can thus provide a sound methodology for reading medieval secular writings. The seminal work here is D. W. Robertson, Jr.'s *A Preface to Chaucer* (1962). The articles in which Robertson first outlined his position were written in the late 1950s, while *A Preface* was published only a little later than Muscatine's *Chaucer and the French Tradition* (1957). Both writers reacted against the view then generally held that Chaucer was to be admired principally for his realism and for his understanding of human psychology, and rather claimed a historicist agenda: Muscatine speaks of Chaucer as 'supremely an artist of his own age' and Robertson notes 'Chaucer's literary art is . . . distinctly a product of its time'.[11] Muscatine, with his 'Gothic' Chaucer, uses a liberal historiography and is greatly influenced by New Criticism, whereas Robertson claims to use an objectively accurate account of the world-view of the fourteenth century to interpret his Christian Chaucer, a critical approach as conservative as Muscatine's is liberal and humanist.[12]

It is helpful to follow the steps in Robertson's argument. Firstly, he discusses medieval biblical exegesis, the practice of reading through the literal level of the text to find the spiritual truth beneath it, the kernel within the husk, the fruit within the chaff. Drawing particularly on Augustine's *De doctrina Christiana*, he goes on to describe how the early fathers of the Church extended this 'spiritual' reading to justify their continued enjoyment of classical, pagan literature. Augustine offers an analogy with the Israelites' taking gold out of Egypt (Exodus 3 and 11), and Jerome cites the instructions to the Israelites on how to purify a Gentile woman before marrying her (Deuteronomy 21). One way of 'purifying' pagan literature was to read it as allegory, and there are several late medieval Christian allegorical readings of pagan writers, such as Pierre Bersuire's *Reductorium morale* and the French *Ovide moralisé*. So, for example, Bersuire suggests that the pagan god Mars may be interpreted as the princes and tyrants of this world or alternatively as the sin of discord, and that Diana may be interpreted as the Virgin Mary.[13] No one now would dispute the importance of allegorization and other non-literal ways of reading in the Middle Ages, though subsequent research, such as that of Minnis and Scott, has modified our understanding of medieval literary criticism, revealing the variety of critical practice available.

Robertson's argument becomes more contentious when he goes on to claim that this allegorical way of reading generally determined the way in which secular writers created new works: writing is seen as a process of encoding sacred truth and reading as a process of decoding the sacred message hidden beneath the 'veil' of the literal level. The approach is succinctly described by Huppé, Robertson's one-time colleague: '[We assume] that Chaucer would have wished to convey a fairly specific kind of doctrinal truth because he wrote in a literary tradition older to be sure than St. Augustine but certainly stemming in the Middle Ages from his vast authority.'[14] The opposition between *caritas*, divine love, and *cupiditas*, carnal and worldly love, which Augustine develops in his writing, is taken by Robertson to be Chaucer's 'o sentence' ('one meaning'). The commendation of divine love, embodied in the final stanzas of *Troilus and Criseyde* (5. 1835 ff.), is pursued by Robertson throughout all of Chaucer's poems and held to be the principal message of the Bible and Boethius' *Consolation of Philosophy* and many other medieval texts.

Two examples will illustrate the application of this to the *Canterbury Tales*. Robertson reflects on the references to music in the 'Miller's Tale'. The miller's bagpipe, with its resemblance to male genitalia, represents the 'old dance' of lust and cupidity to be contrasted with the new song of grace. So, since Nicholas woos Alison, kisses her, and 'maketh melodie' (3306), and their love-making is described elsewhere as 'revel' and 'melodye' (3652), Robertson claims that we are to understand the tale as an exemplification of lust and its consequences.[15] Huppé reads the whole *Canterbury Tales* for its 'moral design': 'It must be read with a full savoring of its sense, but with the expectation that the sense is designed richly to embody a sentence, an underlying meaning in accord with Christian truth.'[16] The Host may mistakenly want entertainment as well as moral improvement from the tales, but the actual pilgrimage to Canterbury is a metaphor for the spiritual journey to the heavenly Jerusalem and each pilgrim is seen to embody either *caritas* or *cupiditas*.

'Robertsonianism', or more commonly 'patristic exegesis', was from its inception a dominant critical movement, particularly in the United States. Lee Patterson, in his account of the hidden contemporary assumptions and agenda that underlie contemporary scholarly work on the Middle Ages, considers that Robertsonianism and its heirs are deeply implicated in the whole institution of academic medieval studies, committed to a professionalism in which certain specific skills and knowledge are a prerequisite for the right to interpret medieval literature.[17] The influence of Robertson may be seen in a number of more recent critics, including Besserman, Fleming, Jeffrey, Kaske, Olson, and Chauncey Wood, though Robertson's original practice has been modified somewhat. Besserman acknowledges the validity of many of the charges brought against exegetical criticism,[18] but his *Biblical Poetics* is thoroughly Robertsonian even if it engages with recent critical positions.

There has, however, been vigorous opposition to such exegesis from the first reviews of Robertson onwards. It has been argued that Chaucer's reading of the Bible is typically literal, even if he is aware of allegorical readings. The main accusation against Robertson, however, is that, since all serious medieval literature is held to illustrate the same theme, the supremacy of *caritas*, meaning becomes universal and unproblematic. The rejection of carnal love in favour of the love of God is the same spiritual truth whether the love is Troilus' youthful idealism or Palamon and Arcite's devotion to Emelye or Nicholas's uncomplicated pursuit of sexual pleasure. In which case, it is argued, how is it that Chaucer needed to revoke all his 'translacions and enditynges . . . that sownen into synne' at the end of the *Canterbury Tales* ('CR' 1085–6)? Robertsonian exegesis is thus condemned as totalizing and reductive. A related criticism is that the assumption that all medieval writers had a similar message and responded in the same way to tradition allows no possibility of individuality or self-expression.

Another fundamental challenge comes from critics whose view of late medieval Christianity and intellectual life differs from Robertson's, including those who do not directly address Robertson's work. He presents a view of the Christian Church in the Middle Ages as speaking with a single voice over many centuries, proclaiming a stable orthodoxy that is biblically based and largely Augustinian in theological outlook. In recent decades Church historians have presented the late medieval Church as much more diverse, conducting biblically centred teaching alongside the whole round of parish life with its traditions, its devotion to the saints, and its sacraments as a means to salvation and as a moral guide, together with various strands of popular religion and some influence from heretical movements. Recent studies of parish life and of popular religion have clearly shown the diversity of late medieval Christian belief and practice.[19] The 'Middle Ages' of which the exegetes write is (it may be argued) a fiction, in which the sea of faith was not only at the full but accepted in a stable form by the whole community of believers. On the contrary, medieval Christianity had many competing voices, responding to particular intellectual debates and particular circumstances in various ways. (On exegetical criticism, see also Chapter 9.)

Similarly, there were varied ways of establishing Christian truths and of interpreting the Bible. In late fourteenth-century England contentious issues included others beyond those raised by Wyclif and his followers. The material surveyed by Morey in *Book and Verse* shows the extent to which biblical paraphrases and versions varied in originality and sophistication and also the variety of uses to which biblical material was put, including the recreational, the delight afforded by a good story. It has been proposed that other views of textual interpretation and tradition were available to Chaucer in addition to those of Augustine. Alastair Minnis argued that Chaucer was influenced by a later medieval learned tradition of textual commentary and that he may well have considered 'All that is written is written for our doctrine' (Romans 15: 4) not as commending allegorical and typological readings but rather as justifying the juxtaposition of unlikely sacred and pagan material.[20] Sheila Delany argued that Chaucer's poetry reflects the intellectual tradition of sceptical fideism, which attempted to hold together conflicting and contradictory truths.[21] Lisa Kiser moved beyond Delany's position to see Chaucer's texts, far from embodying a stable and Christian orthodoxy, as exploring the difficult relationships between written texts and historical or experiential reality: 'The only truth that emerges from Chaucer's work, then, is that truth is impossible to ascertain.'[22]

FURTHER READING

Besserman, Lawrence, *Chaucer and the Bible: A Critical Review of Research, Indexes, and Bibliography* (New York: Garland, 1988). This book provides a comprehensive index of Chaucer's biblical allusions and citations.

Besserman, Lawrence, *Chaucer's Biblical Poetics* (Norman: University of Oklahoma Press, 1998). Besserman argues that medieval Augustinian biblical hermeneutics formed the basis of Chaucer's 'biblical poetics', determining his practice as a poet together with his understanding of the relationship between truth and written texts.

Huppé, Bernard F., *A Reading of the 'Canterbury Tales'* (New York: State University of New York, 1964). Presents the thesis that the overall design of the *Tales* is to convey Christian doctrine in a literary tradition deriving from Augustine.

Jeffrey, David Lyle (ed.), *Chaucer and Scriptural Tradition* (Ottawa: University of Ottawa Press, 1984). This is a collection of essays examining Chaucer's use of biblical material. It is largely 'Robertsonian' in approach.

Kiser, Lisa, *Truth and Textuality in Chaucer's Poetry* (Hanover: University Press of New England, 1991). This book challenges much previous work on Chaucer's attitudes to textual tradition and interpretation.

Morey, James H., *Book and Verse: A Guide to Middle English Biblical Literature* (Urbana: University of Illinois Press, 2000). This is an annotated bibliography of Middle English biblical literature. It provides an insight into the variety of use made of the Bible and thus a context for understanding Chaucer's use of biblical material.

Robertson, D. W., Jr., *A Preface to Chaucer: Studies in Medieval Perspectives* (Princeton: Princeton University Press, 1962). This is the book that first promoted the view that medieval biblical exegesis was a major influence on Chaucer.

NOTES

1. James H. Morey, *Book and Verse: A Guide to Middle English Biblical Literature* (Urbana: University of Illinois Press, 2000).

2. *Troilus and Criseyde: A New Edition of 'The Book of Troilus'*, ed. B. A. Windeatt (Harlow: Longman, 1984).

3. Anne Hudson, *The Premature Reformation: Wycliffite Texts and Lollard History* (Oxford: Clarendon Press, 1988).

4. Eamon Duffy, *The Stripping of the Altars: Traditional Religion in England c.1400–c.1580* (New Haven: Yale University Press, 1992), and his *The Voices of Morebath: Reformation and Rebellion in an English Village* (New Haven: Yale University Press, 2001).

5. Lawrence Besserman, *Chaucer and the Bible: A Critical Review of Research, Indexes, and Bibliography* (New York: Garland, 1988).

6. As claimed by Edmund Reiss, 'Biblical Parody: Chaucer's "Distortions" of Scripture', in David Lyle Jeffrey (ed.), *Chaucer and Scriptural Tradition* (Ottawa: University of Ottawa Press, 1984), 54.

7. Alfred David, 'Chaucer's Adams', in Thomas Hahn and Alan Lupack (eds.), *Retelling Tales: Essays in Honor of Russell Peck* (Cambridge: Brewer, 1997), 61–72.

8. Chauncey Wood, 'Artistic Intention and Chaucer's Uses of Scriptural Allusion', in Jeffrey (ed.), *Chaucer and Scriptural Tradition*, 44–6.

9. Robert P. Miller (ed.), *Chaucer: Sources and Backgrounds* (New York: Oxford University Press, 1977), 417–33.

10. Alcuin Blamires, 'The Wife of Bath and Lollardy', *Medium Aevum*, 58 (1989), 224–41.

11. Charles Muscatine, *Chaucer and the French Tradition: A Study in Style and Meaning* (Berkeley: University of California Press, 1957), 247; D. W. Robertson, Jr., *A Preface to Chaucer: Studies in Medieval Perspectives* (Princeton: Princeton University Press, 1962), 241.

12. For a fuller account of this period of Chaucer criticism, see Lee Patterson, *Negotiating the Past: The Historical Understanding of Medieval Literature* (Madison: University of Wisconsin Press, 1987), 22–34. See also Chapter 20 of this Guide.

13. A. J. Minnis and A. B. Scott (eds.), *Medieval Literary Theory and Criticism c.1100–c.1375: The Commentary Tradition*, 2nd edn. (Oxford: Clarendon Press, 1991), 369–71.

14. Bernard F. Huppé, *A Reading of the 'Canterbury Tales'* (New York: State University of New York, 1964), 5.

15. *A Preface*, 133.

16. *A Reading*, 9.

17. *Negotiating the Past*, 37–9.

18. *Chaucer and the Bible*, 24–7.

19. On parish life, see Duffy, *Voices of Morebath*, and R. N. Swanson, *Faith, Religion and Observance before the Reformation* (Manchester: Manchester University Press, 1993). On popular religion, see

Aron Gurevich, *Medieval Popular Culture: Problems of Belief and Perception*, trans. János M. Bak and Paula A. Hollingsworth (Cambridge: Cambridge University Press, 1988), and Gábor Klaniczay, *The Uses of Supernatural Power: The Transformation of Popular Religion in Medieval and Early Modern Europe*, trans. Susan Singerman (Cambridge: Polity Press in association with Blackwell, 1990). The first two books deal with England, the second two more generally with Europe.

20. A. J. Minnis, *Medieval Theory of Authorship: Scholastic Literary Attitudes in the Later Middle Ages* (London: Scolar Press, 1984), 167, 205–9.

21. Sheila Delany, *Chaucer's 'House of Fame': The Poetics of Skeptical Fideism* (Chicago: University of Chicago Press, 1972).

22. Lisa Kiser, *Truth and Textuality in Chaucer's Poetry* (Hanover: University Press of New England, 1991), 147.

Part III

Readings

20 | Modern Chaucer criticism

Elizabeth Robertson

Modern academic criticism of Chaucer spans many decades and historical moments, but can be characterized by a shift away from the palaeographical, philological, and historical biases of nineteenth-century scholarship towards more general literary appreciation. Such criticism could not have emerged without the presence of the relatively stable text produced by earlier scholars—and, of course, crucial works of textual scholarship continued to be produced. In general post-Victorian Chaucer criticism was guided by Matthew Arnold's influential view of literature as morally salvific, but although Arnold praised Chaucer's humanity and his poetic skill, Chaucer for him lacked 'high seriousness', that is, the tragic moral vision of the great English poets such as Shakespeare.[1] To later Chaucerians, however, Chaucer's humanity and insight into character absolved him of Arnold's charge. Many modern Chaucerians valued Chaucer first and foremost as a storyteller, a 'naive', unself-conscious narrative poet at one with the natural world. To these critics Chaucer, using an accessible quotidian language, portrayed the beauty of an unspoiled England, unmarked by contradiction or conflict.

The earlier twentieth-century critic of Chaucer, with few exceptions, was an urbane secular humanist and found Chaucer to be the same, with his fine delineation of human character and the human comedy. Chaucer's portraits are psychologically astute, even though untouched by the revolution in psychoanalysis occurring at the same time. As the century progresses, the vision of Chaucer as a 'congenial soul', as Stephanie Trigg puts it, a man among men just like 'us', marks Chaucer as a bulwark against the erosion of humanity experienced because of the world wars.[2] Although the historical 'moment' of many critics of the period is never addressed directly, the almost exclusive focus on poetry as it illuminates character reveals the press of a history seeking to restore rational humanism to a world gone awry. The history embraced by these critics is one of 'presentism'; that is, as Richard Halpern argues in his book *Shakespeare among the Moderns*, earlier twentieth-century critics can be characterized by what he calls their use of 'historical allegory', a concept emerging from T. S. Eliot, who argued that such a historical sense 'involves a perception, not only of the pastness of the past, but of its presence . . . [it is] a sense of the timeless as well as of the temporal and of the timeless and of the temporal together'.[3] Even those critics who claimed the importance of historical understanding for an appreciation of Chaucer, such as D. W. Robertson (see below), share such presentism.

The modern criticism discussed in this chapter occurs in two waves: the first includes predominantly American post-Victorian humanist critics; the second comprises the work of post-Second World War English and American New Critics. The earlier group of critics, almost exclusively male, wrote 'monumental' criticism, eloquent and passionate illuminations and appreciations, though arguably there was a curious evasion of Chaucer's poetry itself. Although admired for his skill in evoking the world of the everyday, Chaucer's poetic technique received little attention until later in the century with the work of the New Critics. Instead, the earlier critics focused on his movement away from the medieval rhetorical traditions that he both learned from, and learned how to avoid, towards a realism of the everyday that is assumed rather than defined. They chart Chaucer's artistic development as a movement towards such realism. However, the claims made for Chaucer's realism are strangely contradicted by the refusal to wed a knowledge of historical actuality and locality to the text. Even critics who study Chaucer's engagement with the rhetorical tropes of his day, or his use of historical material, or even his philological skills, do so in the service of delineating his artistic development as a realist. For many of these critics, Chaucer's poetry is a transparent window onto fourteenth-century life—but the life that he captures is ultimately transhistorical. History is used to buttress pre-existing realist notions about Chaucerian character and community; anything that does not fit those notions is left out. The information gleaned from the study of Chaucer's use of rhetoric, his sources, or the events of his own time, is all refracted through the presentism of the critic, serving to illuminate Chaucer's affinity with transhistorical humanist values. And although such presentism is now acknowledged in some senses to be inevitable, the difference of emphasis between the modern understanding of the Chaucerian past and the postmodern relates to the former's obscuring of its habit of imposing its own values and morals on the past.

Earlier modern critics of Chaucer also share an assumption of Chaucer's historical disinterestedness as a poet. Although keenly involved in fourteenth-century court life, Chaucer is quintessentially a poet, as Thomas Lounsbury says, 'for all time and not of the time'.[4] Just as it typically avoids the details of the poetry itself, such criticism persistently avoids medieval social, political, and ecclesiastical contexts, which are engaged only in the most general terms. Most earlier critics agree that Chaucer's religion was secondary to his humanism; as Linda Georgianna has demonstrated, modern Chaucer was a 'liberal apostle of humanism', a thinking Christian who 'was rational and discreet rather than emotional, sensual and popular'.[5] Chaucer, even to those critics who acknowledged his Catholicism, was a man of morality, rather than of faith.

Post-Victorian American criticism

The American critic considered responsible for bringing Chaucer into the university curriculum in the United States was Thomas Raynesford Lounsbury (1838–1915), a professor at Yale for thirty-six years, who brought together and carefully analysed previous Chaucer scholarship in his three-volume collection *Studies in Chaucer* (1891). This encyclopedic work consists of eight chapters covering such topics as the Chaucer biography and legend, texts and canon, Chaucer's learning, his place in the development of the English language, and the nature of his religion. Lounsbury concludes with a study of Chaucerian reception, and an appreciation of Chaucer as a literary artist.

Lounsbury gathers and evaluates most of the Chaucerian scholarship to date and much subsequent criticism generally embraced his measured conclusions. His analysis is pervaded by his strong sense of who Chaucer is—a learned man, but not a scholar; a skilful and innovative versifier; a humorous teller of stories which, though sometimes bawdy, are never immoral; a diplomat whose views on religion and politics will never be known, but whose humanity and common sense suggest his disapproval of war and cruelty; and a sceptic, if not an agnostic. Although he claims to base his views on Chaucer's poetry, Lounsbury evades discussions of the poems themselves except in the most general terms. The *Canterbury Tales* functions for him as examples of Chaucer's skill at capturing what are assumed to be universal human emotions ranging from the fear of old age on the Wife of Bath's part to the admirable endurance Griselda displays in the face of irrational torture. Despite Lounsbury's acknowledgement of Chaucer as a self-conscious literary craftsman, the poetry reveals, in his view, sensitivity and humanity, rather than poetic and artistic mastery. Lounsbury defends Chaucer against the charge of immorality by arguing that the scope of his vision has a notable breadth, such that 'all views of human nature are acceptable' (*Studies*, iii. 348). Furthermore, he challenges Arnold's assessment of Chaucer by asserting the poet's 'consciousness of the burden of sorrow that rests upon human life' (iii. 362). His comic joyfulness is permeated by the recognition of the instability and transitoriness of all earthly joy.

Like many modern critics, Lounsbury assumes Chaucer to be an agnostic. His firm conviction of Chaucer's religious scepticism has been attacked by Georgianna in an influential essay, 'The Protestant Chaucer', in which she demonstrates Lounsbury's dismissal of those elements of Catholicism particularly distasteful to Protestant readers: miracles, mysteries, and a non-rational commitment to faith. To Lounsbury, the 'Second Nun's Tale' is the weakest of the tales, and the 'Prioress's Tale' the most effective because of its 'tenderness'; such things as its problematic antisemitism and violence are not of consequence in Lounsbury's response (ii. 49). Lounsbury characterizes the religious aspects of the tales, in Georgianna's summary, as 'audacious, extravagant, unnatural, ludicrous, grotesque, and absurd' ('Protestant Chaucer', 60). Indeed, this religious agnosticism reveals precisely Chaucer's modern temperament, enabling Lounsbury to conclude that Chaucer could not have been a Lollard because 'his business was the portrayal of men as they are, and not the effort to make them what they ought to be, or what he thought they ought to be. So far as Chaucer had any conscious aim at all, it was to mirror the life of his day, and not to reform its morals' (*Studies*, ii. 472). Lounsbury's assumption of a universal condition of humanity here is typical of earlier modern criticism.

Lounsbury's assessment of Chaucer's general character and temperament as a writer continued to shape academic criticism despite his followers' interest in topics such as Chaucer's sources, historical backgrounds, and use of rhetorical tropes. John Mathews Manly (1865–1940), professor of English at the University of Chicago from 1889 to 1933, offered two different perspectives on Chaucer's work, one a study of his use of rhetoric, the other a meticulous study of the historical backgrounds of Chaucer's Canterbury pilgrims. Despite their engagement with historical contexts, both emphases in different ways ultimately refine Lounsbury's sense of Chaucer's development as an astute observer of a transhistorical everyday life and manners.

Perhaps most influential was Manly's 1926 British Academy lecture 'Chaucer and the Rhetoricians'. Manly discusses the principal rhetorical tropes known to Chaucer and shows his use of such figures as description, digression, apostrophe, prosopopoeia, circumlocution, and occupatio. In this he assumes that extensive use of rhetorical tropes is a sign of Chaucer's poetic immaturity; as he matures, such inherited devices drop away and the poetry becomes a transparent conduit to the world and the life of character. Thus we have Chaucer's 'growing recognition that for him at least the right way to amplify a story was not to expand it by rhetorical devices, but to conceive it in terms of the life which he had observed so closely'.[6] Manly accounts for the fact that some of Chaucer's latest works foreground rhetorical tropes as an aspect of the pilgrim–teller, that is, as part of the dramatic realism of the *Canterbury Tales*. Within this framework it is not surprising that the tales most closely associated with their tellers are especially valued by Manly because Chaucer's 'advanced method is displayed in them', that is the advanced method of realism.[7]

Manly's longer study, *Some New Light on Chaucer*, also published in 1926, similarly values Chaucer for his realism, but here, employing what might be called an old historicist technique, he takes a different tack to instance that realism. Using historical materials painstakingly uncovered by him in collaboration with Edith Rickert, he identifies numerous historical figures who occupied the various estates described by Chaucer in the 'General Prologue'. He then ponders the details found in Chaucer's portraits in order to determine which of these historical figures was most likely to have acted as the model for the characters of the 'Prologue'. Manly emphasizes the 'realistic' nature of the portraits above all, a position challenged thoroughly by Jill Mann in her later work, in which she demonstrates Chaucer's uses and development of the conventions of estates satire.[8] As a lively account of personages familiar to Chaucer, Manly's study is interesting background for an appreciation of Chaucer's London. The actual identifications of the pilgrims with such personages are unconvincing, in part because of Manly's refusal to consider the rhetorical elements of the portraits and in part because the identifications are guided by firm prior convictions about the character of each pilgrim.

In 1914 George Lyman Kittredge delivered six lectures on Chaucer at Johns Hopkins University that, as the culmination of his views on Chaucer developed over a prestigious career at Harvard, established the American understanding of Chaucer for generations to come. Indeed, the focus of Chaucer criticism has arguably only recently expanded beyond the topics of these lectures: Chaucer's biography, the *Book of the Duchess*, the *House of Fame*, *Troilus and Criseyde*, and the *Canterbury Tales*—more or less the syllabus for Chaucer courses in America to date. Chaucer's short poems, his *Treatise on the Astrolabe*, the *Legend of Good Women*, and his translations are ignored, along with larger questions of history, politics, gender, and religion.

Like many later Chaucerians, Kittredge was described by his student B. J. Whiting as a man much like Chaucer himself was supposed to be: playful, learned but not oppressively so, a convivial man who enjoyed cigars, scatological jokes, the history of words; an orthodox Congregationalist and conservative in politics, though in favour of women's suffrage. In the tradition of Lounsbury, Kittredge begins his lectures with the sketch of a Chaucer who is praised above all for his understanding of 'changeless human nature', for 'he knew life and loved it, and his speciality was mankind as it was, and is'.[9] Although well trained in rhetoric, Chaucer wears his learning lightly and is no scholar. Historical difference is swept away, for the problems of the modern era—labour disputes, war, 'the Eastern question', imperialism, financial disputes, and religious controversy—are also precisely the problems of Chaucer's own age. Chaucer himself is viewed as the first modern: 'Chaucer was born in a time of great religious and political and literary activity, not so much at the end of the middle ages as at the beginning of the modern world' (p. 5). Kittredge was sceptical about what had become the standard categorization of Chaucer's work into three distinct periods—the French, the Italian, and the English—but he still regarded the culmination of Chaucer's powers as occurring when he turned to 'English life and English character' (p. 27). Here Kittredge reveals like many modern Chaucerians, American and English alike, a nostalgia for an idealized England of the past. Unlike some of his sceptical peers, Kittredge values religion and asserts that Chaucer took his religion seriously, but what that religion was and how it might have infused his writing is not in Kittredge's view a suitable subject for criticism; religion is valued for its morality, but is considered something private, not to be publicly scrutinized. Politics is similarly not significant to his understanding of Chaucer except in his reference to Chaucer's general affable diplomacy.

Kittredge acknowledges Chaucer's poetic innovations such as his use of rhyme royal and the heroic couplet, and he admires his stylistic economy, but far more important is Chaucer's dramatic power: 'next to Shakspere [*sic*], Chaucer is the greatest delineator of character in our literature' (p. 29). It is in fact through Shakespeare that Kittredge understands Chaucer, comparing the *Canterbury Tales*, the height of his study of character, to a five-act play enlivened by a variety of characters whose tales exist not as various forms and styles of poetry, but rather as responses by one teller to another. The works that precede the *Tales* are primarily character sketches leading to the fuller realizations of the *Tales* themselves. The *Book of the Duchess*, for example, is a psychologically astute and sensitive mourning poem, and *Troilus and Criseyde* 'an elaborate psychological novel' and Chaucer's 'most sustained early effort at the delineation of character' (p. 112).

Kittredge's most lasting influence on Chaucer criticism was his formulation of this dramatic theory of the *Canterbury Tales*, that is, a way of reading the work that sees each tale primarily as a reflection of its teller. He finds Chaucer's modernity precisely in such drama; for example, in the delicacy of the Knight's interruption of the long-winded peroration of the Monk ('NPP' 2767–79). Chaucer's human comedy reaches its climax in one 'act', famously described by Kittredge as 'the marriage group', that is, the 'Wife of Bath's Tale', the 'Clerk's Tale', the 'Merchant's Tale', and the 'Franklin's Tale'—each a response to the other. Troubling aspects of the tales—the brutality of the marriage night in the 'Merchant's Tale', the rape in the 'Wife of Bath's Tale', the torture of Griselda in the 'Clerk's Tale', and the contemplated suicide of Dorigen in the 'Franklin's Tale', as well as the stylistic differences between them—are completely overlooked in Kittredge's unruffled survey of a dramatic struggle of the tellers as they explore dominion, obedience, mutuality, and love.

So fond is Kittredge of the pilgrims that he turns to the anonymous fifteenth-century *Tale of Beryn* and its associated interlude describing the pilgrims' arrival at Canterbury to reinforce his delineation of the fullness of their personalities. He imagines the parallel of a 'smoking-room of a small steamship with only three or four dozen passengers' who 'empty their hearts to one another with an indiscretion that may shock them' (p. 158). Kittredge's Chaucer is indeed as Trigg puts it a 'congenial soul', one who, like his characters, would be at ease in the men's clubs Kittredge himself frequented. He closes his book with a typically modern commendation not of Chaucer's poetry, but of Chaucer the man: 'Geoffrey Chaucer, poet, idealist, burgher of London, Commissioner of Dykes and Ditches, who loved his fellow-men both good and bad, and found no answer to the puzzle of life but in truth and courage and beauty and belief in God' (p. 213).

John Livingston Lowes dedicates to Kittredge his 1932 Swarthmore lectures, later published as *Geoffrey Chaucer and the Development of his Genius*. Lowes's task was twofold: to enhance our understanding of Chaucer by providing us with backgrounds that we have lost, and to provide a general appreciation of Chaucer. Although he describes Chaucer as producing 'timeless creations upon a time-determined stage', the historically determined aspects of his work presented in the first half of Lowes's book have little to do with the appreciation of Chaucer's poetry in the second half.[10] Lowes fills in for us a cultural backdrop of medieval ideas, such as the history of the names of the days of the week, the fourteenth-century's understanding of the planetary hours, the signs of the zodiac, the *mappa mundi*, the humours, and early science (such as the lore of magnets), but the subsequent appreciation of Chaucer's poetry is much in keeping with the general tenor of criticism of the day. Having compared Chaucer to his French and Italian sources, Lowes concludes with praise of the *Canterbury Tales*, in which he finds the 'General Prologue' to be the essence of Chaucer's modernity. His book thus embodies two common early twentieth-century approaches: on the one hand a search for extra-textual historical evidence to support Chaucer's realism, and on the other a general appreciation of the dramatic qualities of Chaucer's poetry.

Post-Victorian English criticism

Post-Victorian Chaucer criticism in England was primarily devoted to the editing of Chaucer's works. While the two greatest English medievalists of the period, J. R. R. Tolkien and C. S. Lewis, have relatively little to say about Chaucer, their eminence as the two chairs of medieval studies in Oxford and Cambridge respectively makes note-worthy their contributions to Chaucer studies in the modern tradition. Tolkien delivered one major lecture on Chaucer (given in Oxford in 1926 to the Philological Society), later published as 'Chaucer as a Philologist'. Here he sets out to prove that Chaucer was unusually attentive to dialect, particularly the northern dialects found in the speech of the two students of the 'Reeve's Tale'. He was dialectologist enough indeed to Tolkien to have easily passed an Oxford exam in linguistics.[11]

C. S. Lewis focuses his critical attention less on philological matters and more on the history of ideas: in his later *The Discarded Image* (1964), the medieval idea of the cosmos; in his earlier *The Allegory of Love* (1936), the idea of 'courtly love'.[12] In the earlier work, perhaps best known for bringing Spenser into critical fashion, Lewis defines the medieval understanding of courtly love, tracing the history of allegorical love poems from the eleventh-century love lyrics of the Provençal troubadours to the sixteenth-century English allegory, Spenser's *Faerie Queene*. Focusing only on Chaucer's love poems, Lewis considers a selection of his shorter pieces, including several complaints. He analyses the *Book of the Duchess* more extensively, praising it for its sensitive portrait of loss and love, and defends the *Parliament of Fowls* from those critics who had either dismissed it as merely occasional or predominantly a satire of the lower classes, proclaiming it a 'supremely happy and radiant work'.[13] Typical of early modern critics is Lewis's nostalgia for a delicate, 'pre-industrial' poetry: 'it is only natural that we, who live in an industrial age, should find difficul-ties in reading poetry that was written for a scholastic and aristocratic age. We must proceed with caution, lest our thick rough fingers tear the delicate threads that we are trying to disentangle' (p. 174). Lewis is concerned to preserve the unself-conscious Chaucer that modernity might threaten. He suggests in this regard that too much attention has been given to Chaucer's 'mocking' tone and not enough to recognizing Chaucer as 'a great model of poetical style' (pp. 163–4). Like other modern critics, Lewis is attentive to Chaucer's universality, which he describes in terms of his psychological astuteness and sensitivity to feeling. Citing Dryden's comment that Chaucer was 'a perpetual fountain of good sense', he contrasts the medieval Chaucer with later poets: 'a profound and cheerful sobriety is the foundation alike of Chaucer's humour and his pathos. There is nothing of the renaissance frivolity in him' (p. 176).[14]

Chaucer's finest treatment of courtly love for Lewis is found in *Troilus and Criseyde*. He argues for its close relationship with the *Romance of the Rose* and the works of Boccaccio. In some senses, this careful study of Chaucer's transformation of his sources marks the beginning of much twentieth-century interest in source study, a dominant strand of later Chaucer criticism. Although not allegorical, *Troilus and Criseyde*, according to Lewis, grew nonetheless out of his deep acquaintance with the *Rose*. After demonstrating how Chaucer transforms scenes from the *Rose* into specific moments in the *Troilus*, Lewis eschews the poem's satire, humour, conflict, and contradiction, in offering generous readings of the poem's three main characters as psychologically realistic: Troilus the most devout of lovers, Pandarus the most sincere of friends, and Criseyde struggling with her wholly understandable fear. 'A great poem in praise of love', Lewis concludes, adding that despite its frank portrait of sexual love, *Troilus and Criseyde* avoids the pornography of Ovid because of its concreteness: 'with Chaucer we are rooted in the purifying complexities of the real world' (p. 196).

This last statement captures some of the typical dialectics of modern criticism that pulls on the one hand towards 'realism', and on the other to the universal. Earlier critics celebrate the transparent realism of Chaucer's poetry, a realism that reveals universal humanist values; to Lewis, the reader finds a purifying complexity that leads to elevated feeling. Lewis hovers on the edge of sexuality, but refuses to look over that edge. The eroticization of criticism, an intense concern not with the emotions of sexuality but with the nature of desire and sexual identity, becomes the territory of the postmodern critic.

Post-Second World War critics

The modern Chaucer established by these early humanists reaches its fullest expression in the post-war American New Critical writings of E. Talbot Donaldson and Charles Muscatine. These critics, in keeping with New Criticism generally, shift the focus away from a general appreciation of Chaucer's realism towards a close attention to form and style, although in keeping with earlier criticism, that style is ultimately viewed as enhancing the representation of character. Infused with secular liberal humanism, New Criticism celebrates the autonomy of the individual, and is particularly interested in literary paradox, irony, and complexity. The latter two elements are especially valued in New Critical studies of Chaucer.

Charles Muscatine's *Chaucer and the French Tradition* (1957) is typical of this focus. According to the introduction, the work

seeks to determine Chaucer's 'meaning' as a complex whole; by giving form and style their due attention as essential, inseparable concomitants of meaning, it will try to balance the traditional preoccupation with 'content' alone. It sees realism as a technique and a convention, not as an end in itself, and it sees convention as a potentially powerful tool, not as something to be avoided or rebelled against . . . Rhetoric, too, it takes to be an instrument and not a vice. Liberated in great measure by post-Victorian scholarship itself, it does not confine its attention to narrowly textual sources in tracing and using the literary history behind Chaucer, but attempts broadly to explore his stylistic heritage.[15]

In some ways, Muscatine's readings emerge naturally from Lewis's illuminating analysis of stylistic innovation in *Troilus and Criseyde*, a study Muscatine greatly admires.

Muscatine divides Chaucer's work into two kinds: that characterized by a formal or elevated style—one that makes use of rhetoric and convention—and that characterized by realism. His categories preclude consideration of the religious tales, which he ignores, instead offering paradigmatic readings of the courtly, formal, rhetorical, and ornamental style of such tales as the 'Knight's Tale' on the one hand, and the 'realistic' bourgeois style of the fabliaux, which he equates with the tastes of an emergent middle class full of 'naive realism . . . commerce . . . and common sense' (pp. 58–9). According to Muscatine, Chaucer absorbs and transforms these two styles through his acquaintance with French poetry, most importantly his profound knowledge of the two styles as manifest in the contrasting work of Guillaume de Lorris and Jean de Meun in the *Romance of the Rose*. He analyses the *Canterbury Tales* as examples of the elevated style, the bourgeois style, and the mixed style. Like Gothic art, the *Canterbury Tales* gains meaning through juxtaposition and coordination, reflecting 'the tension between phenomenal and ideal, mundane and divine, that informs the art and thought of the period' (p. 168). The variety of pilgrims thus becomes of interest less because of 'realistic' presentation than because of the range of attitudes they represent.

As he develops, however, Chaucer hones these styles in order better to express transhistorical human values. In the end, therefore, character still dominates Muscatine's analysis as it does the work of his teacher Donaldson, and as it does in earlier modern criticism. Muscatine picks up on Manly's concern with describing Chaucer's stylistic methods, but where Manly saw his use of rhetoric as a sign of immaturity, Muscatine argues that Chaucer uses rhetoric in order to enhance the mimetic qualities of his characterizations. The mixed style 'expresses the great capaciousness of Chaucer's humane vision' (p. 243). At the centre of Muscatine's work, as Lee Patterson points out, is the New Critical emphasis on both complexity for its own sake and as a celebration of the autonomy of the self: 'since objectivity is possible only to a dehistoricized and socially unconditioned subject, Chaucerian mimesis stands as the poetic equivalent of the liberal assertion of the freedom of the individual from a determining historical context'.[16] Where earlier critics saw Chaucer moving towards an anti-rhetorical simplicity of expression, Muscatine argues for his complexity, yet a complexity leading to an aesthetically unified project, one located in the centrality and autonomy of the conscious self.

Although E. Talbot Donaldson was Muscatine's teacher, he did not publish his work on Chaucer until after the latter's appeared: first his edition of Chaucer's poetry, followed by critical studies of Chaucer and related medieval topics in *Speaking of Chaucer* (1970). This work established a school of thought about Chaucer that has flourished to this day. In the latter book Donaldson expresses clearly and emphatically his disagreement with another concurrent influential school of criticism in the United States known as exegetical criticism, criticism that privileged the medieval literary text's engagement with theological writing promulgated by D. W. Robertson. As a New Critic, Donaldson focuses on Chaucer's style, but these interests primarily centre on the complexities produced by Chaucer's unexpected shifts in tone. Such an analysis is in the service of illuminating liberal humanist values, especially from a masculine perspective. Often witty, and above all accessible, Donaldson's analyses at times include appeals to assumed shared masculine understandings of the world where adultery is 'exciting' and where the reader cannot fail to share the narrator's love for Criseyde, assumptions targeted in Carolyn Dinshaw's later feminist critique of Donaldson.[17] Donaldson shifts the focus away from the pilgrim narrators and towards hitherto unobserved 'characters': Chaucer the pilgrim and the narrator of the *Troilus*, figures whose presences introduce levels of irony into the poems. Several of his discussions make liberal use of a Chaucer concordance, showing us the complex effects produced by the use of terms such as 'hende', 'coy', 'softe', or 'sin'. The diction of the 'Merchant's Tale', for example, affronts 'our aesthetic sense, bringing our emotions into play in such a way as to confuse our moral judgment' (p. 35). Often he praises Chaucer for his 'ability to describe things simultaneously from several distinct points of view while seeming to see them from only one point of view, and thus to show in all honesty the complexity of things while preserving the appearance of the stylistic simplicity which we feel to be so honest and trustworthy'(p. 47). Like Muscatine, Donaldson therefore values Chaucer's complexity—a complexity like that of the modern liberal world. He warns that Kittredge's emphasis on *Troilus* as a brilliant psychological novel and as a study in character neglects the difficulties created by the multiple points of view and further complicated by the filter of the narrator. Yet he concludes by at the same time praising Chaucer's characterization: Criseyde, for example, is his 'supreme achievement in the creation of human character' (p. 67). In keeping with New Criticism more generally, the ends of complexity are contained within a vision of aesthetic autonomy impervious to historical and political contexts, and one that is congruent with a claim for the transhistorical status of the text's protagonists.

Often Donaldson's judgements are based on 'common sense' or on values that he 'shares' with his fellow readers—assumed to be male. He thus explains his choice to discuss Chaucer's representations of four female characters: 'I choose women because they are, obviously, the most complex topic that a man can try to deal with, a subject that no honest poet can hope to treat simply' (p. 47). Emelye in the 'Knight's Tale' is like spring itself; in the 'Merchant's Tale' there is something 'impenetrable about May's loveliness'; in *Troilus and Criseyde*, Criseyde is enchanting; and the Prioress of the 'Prioress's Prologue and Tale' is a romance heroine out of place (p. 52).

The New Critical humanism exemplified by Donaldson flourished alongside the Robertson school of exegetical criticism. Since this is treated elsewhere at length in this volume (see Chapters 9 and 19), a few remarks will suffice here. Robertson's most significant contribution was his departure from the overriding modern assumption that Chaucer was 'like us', stressing instead the difference of the Middle Ages, a difference to be recovered only through the lens of historical understanding. Robertson's understanding of the 'medieval mind' insisted that patristic thought then permeated all poetry for all audiences in the same way. In critiquing exegetics, Donaldson admits the value of knowledge of patristic thought for an understanding of medieval poetry, but disputes the proposition of Robertsonian critics that 'all serious poetry written by Christians during the Middle Ages promotes the doctrine of charity by using the same allegorical structure that the Fathers found in the Bible' (*Speaking of Chaucer*, 134). Donaldson especially objects to the universalizing mandate of exegetics, arguing that such critics 'have been kidnapped by their preconceptions' (p. 141). He demonstrates the distortions produced by these preconceptions in his readings of *Piers Plowman* and the *Canterbury Tales*, especially the 'Nun's Priest's Tale', where he concludes that, contrary to exegetical readings describing the tale as a parable of the Fall, the meaning lies less in the moral that can be gleaned from it than in the 'chaff', that is, the variety of philosophical, moral, and poetic questions the poem embraces. Despite their differences, these two critics, as Dinshaw has observed, share common patriarchal assumptions; to her, theirs is a sibling quarrel (*Chaucer's Sexual Poetics*, 28).

Later twentieth-century trends

In the remainder of this chapter there is only space to remark on a few of the arguments stemming from the traditions we have been following thus far that characterize Chaucer criticism of the later decades of the twentieth century. In the 1960s and 1970s the work of several British critics continued to be informed by New Critical perspectives. Shifting the critical gaze from the pilgrims to Chaucer's narrators and from the *Tales* to the dream visions, A. C. Spearing's *Medieval Dream-Poetry* of 1976[18] is the first book to explore the subtlety of Chaucer's self-reflexive use of the dream vision form, especially in his use of the tradition of the dream narrator. Together with Elizabeth Salter, Spearing began a reassessment of Chaucer's particular skills and techniques as a religious poet. His essay 'Chaucer's "Clerk's Tale" as a Medieval Poem' in his *Criticism and Medieval Poetry* of 1972,[19] along with Salter's discussion of the 'Clerk's Tale' in her elegant *Chaucer: the 'Knight's Tale' and the 'Clerk's Tale'* (1962),[20] attributes some of the puzzling difficulties of tone in the 'Clerk's Tale' to Chaucer's interest in integrating religious ideals with everyday life, a topic of increasing critical interest in recent years.

Other critics challenged the predominance of Kittredge's dramatic reading of Chaucer. Thus Derek Pearsall in his *The Canterbury Tales* of 1985[21] summarizes and judiciously assesses previous criticism on each tale, stressing the need to view the tales as individual poems rather than as 'performances' by their tellers. He argues that the tales are best understood within the categories of the genres they embrace, such as prologues, romances, comic tales, and religious tales. Muscatine's student C. David Benson takes issue with Kittredge's dramatic theory in his *Chaucer's Drama of Style*

(1986),[22] arguing like Pearsall that rather than viewing the tales as dramatic expressions of their tellers, one should study them as stylistic discourses in and of themselves. Another assault on the age-old assumptions about the 'realistic' nature of Chaucer's characters comes from Jill Mann in her 1973 *Chaucer and Medieval Estates Satire*, where she counters Manly's response to the pilgrims by demonstrating with great skill and thoroughness Chaucer's use and transformations of the conventions of medieval estates satire.

Another strand of criticism that challenges reductive Robertsonian notions of history results in works like John Burrow's *Ricardian Poetry* of 1971,[23] which explores Chaucer's relationships to other major fourteenth-century English poets, Langland, Gower, and the *Pearl*-poet, arguing that all share features indicating their position as poets writing in the historical period of Richard II. David Aers was for a long time one of the few critical voices in the post-war era calling for a reconsideration of Chaucer within specifically historical contexts. In his 1980 book *Chaucer, Langland and the Creative Imagination*[24] he demonstrated Chaucer's active engagement with social, theological, and ecclesiastical issues, arguing that Chaucer affirms his culture while espousing its contradictions and tensions. Aers called for a re-evaluation of Chaucer in relationship to Langland and for the necessity of the historical contextualization of Chaucer's work which he subsequently enacted in numerous essays and collections. In 1987 Lee Patterson's re-evaluation of Robertsonian historicism led to a call for a new theoretically informed historicism, which he then practised in his 1991 book *Chaucer and the Subject of History*.[25]

In the last decades of the century Chaucer's representation of women began to garner critical attention. In 1991 Mann followed her study of estates satire with one of the first extended treatments of women in Chaucer's work (*Geoffrey Chaucer*[26]), in tandem with Carolyn Dinshaw's crucial *Chaucer's Sexual Poetics* (1989). A few years later Elaine Tuttle Hansen published her *Chaucer and the Fictions of Gender* (1992).[27]

As we move towards the end of the twentieth century, we find tension, contradiction, and indeterminacy of meaning as well as further aspects of gender and sexuality beginning to fascinate Chaucer critics. All such studies are properly in the realm of postmodern criticism, and Chaucer the naive, bawdy, witty realist, a simple man among men, can no longer be said to exist academically. And yet, although many of the universalizing tendencies of earlier criticism have been abandoned, and we have now turned to those concerns such criticism seemed wilfully to shut out—the concerns of social class, the effects of war and race, gender and sexuality issues, the presence of the unconscious—nonetheless we still value Chaucer both for the sweep of his comic vision and for his humanity, and we should continue to recognize the degree to which our own new presentisms shape our critical preoccupations. The following chapters of this part of the Guide will trace our present approaches to Chaucer.

FURTHER READING

Brewer, Derek (ed.), *Chaucer: The Critical Heritage, ii: 1837–1933* (London: Routledge & Kegan Paul, 1978). An invaluable collection of selections of late nineteenth- and early twentieth-century academic and literary responses to Chaucer.

Dinshaw, Carolyn, 'Reading Like a Man: The Critics, the Narrator, Troilus, and Pandarus', in her *Chaucer's Sexual Poetics* (Madison: University of Wisconsin Press, 1989), 28–64. This chapter of Dinshaw's feminist discussion of Chaucer demonstrates the similarities between E. Talbot Donaldson and D. W. Robertson, especially in their interpretations of female characters.

Ellis, Steve, *Chaucer at Large: The Poet in the Modern Imagination* (Minneapolis: University of Minnesota Press, 2000). Explores the modern non-academic response to Chaucer and considers its relation to academic criticism.

Georgianna, Linda, 'The Protestant Chaucer', in C. David Benson and Elizabeth Robertson (eds.), *Chaucer's Religious Tales* (Cambridge: Boydell & Brewer, 1990), 55–70. Discusses the ways in which Protestant biases of modern critics shape their understanding of Chaucer's poems.

Guillory, John, *Cultural Capital: The Problem of Literary Canon Formation* (Chicago: University of Chicago Press, 1993). This book provides a theoretically provocative context for considering the ways in which economics and institutions shape the formation of literary canons.

Halpern, Richard, *Shakespeare among the Moderns* (Ithaca, NY: Cornell University Press, 1997). Studies Shakespeare's reception among the moderns, showing how many aspects of postmodernism have their roots in modernist criticism.

Patterson, Lee, *Negotiating the Past: The Historical Understanding of Medieval Literature* (Madison: University of Wisconsin Press, 1987). Begins with a summary of post-Victorian and modern non-academic and academic criticism of Chaucer and offers a re-evaluation of Robertson's historicism as a guide for new historicist understandings of Chaucer.

Trigg, Stephanie, *Congenial Souls: Reading Chaucer from Medieval to Postmodern* (Minneapolis: University of Minnesota Press, 2002). This comprehensive study surveys scholarship and criticism of Chaucer from Chaucer's lifetime to the present.

NOTES

1. Matthew Arnold, Introduction to Thomas Humphry Ward (ed.), *The English Poets* (1880), pp. xxxi–xxxvi.
2. Stephanie Trigg, *Congenial Souls: Reading Chaucer from Medieval to Postmodern* (Minneapolis: University of Minnesota Press, 2002).
3. T. S. Eliot quoted and discussed in Richard Halpern, *Shakespeare among the Moderns* (Ithaca, NY: Cornell University Press, 1999), 3.
4. Thomas R. Lounsbury, *Studies in Chaucer*, 3 vols. (New York: Russell & Russell, 1962), iii. 366.
5. Linda Georgianna, 'The Protestant Chaucer', in C. David Benson and Elizabeth Robertson (eds.), *Chaucer's Religious Tales* (Cambridge: Boydell & Brewer, 1990), 60, 63.
6. Quoted in Derek Brewer (ed.), *Chaucer: The Critical Heritage, ii: 1837–1933* (London: Routledge & Kegan Paul, 1978), 399.
7. Manly, 'Chaucer and the Rhetoricians', in Brewer (ed.), *Chaucer: The Critical Heritage*, ii. 402.
8. See Jill Mann, *Chaucer and Medieval Estates Satire* (Cambridge: Cambridge University Press, 1973).
9. George Lyman Kittredge, *Chaucer and his Poetry* (Cambridge, Mass.: Harvard University Press, 1915), 1, 2.
10. John Livingston Lowes, *Geoffrey Chaucer and the Development of his Genius* (Boston: Houghton Mifflin, 1934), 6.

11. J. R. R. Tolkien, 'Chaucer as a Philologist: The "Reeve's Tale" ', *Transactions of the Philological Society* (1934), 1–70.

12. C. S. Lewis, *The Discarded Image: An Introduction to Medieval and Renaissance Literature* (Cambridge: Cambridge University Press, 1964); *The Allegory of Love* (Oxford: Oxford University Press, 1936).

13. *The Allegory of Love*, 173–4.

14. For Dryden's comment, see John Dryden, Preface to *Fables Ancient and Modern* (1700), in *The Poems of John Dryden*, ed. James Kinsley, 4 vols. (Oxford: Clarendon Press, 1958), iv. 1452.

15. Charles Muscatine, *Chaucer and the French Tradition: A Study in Style and Meaning* (Berkeley: University of California Press, 1957), 1.

16. Lee Patterson, *Negotiating the Past: The Historical Understanding of Medieval Literature* (Madison: University of Wisconsin Press, 1987), 25.

17. Carolyn Dinshaw, 'Reading Like a Man: The Critics, the Narrator, Troilus, and Pandarus', in her *Chaucer's Sexual Poetics* (Madison: University of Wisconsin Press, 1989), 28–64. For Donaldson on Criseyde, see *Speaking of Chaucer* (London: Athlone Press, 1970), 65–83.

18. (Cambridge: Cambridge University Press).

19. 2nd edn. (London: Edward Arnold, 1972), 76–106.

20. (London: Edward Arnold, 1962), 37–65.

21. (Repr. London: Routledge, 1995).

22. *Chaucer's Drama of Style: Poetic Variety and Contrast in the 'Canterbury Tales'* (Chapel Hill: University of North Carolina Press, 1986).

23. J. A. Burrow, *Ricardian Poetry: Chaucer, Gower, Langland, and the 'Gawain' Poet* (London: Routledge & Kegan Paul, 1971).

24. (London: Routledge & Kegan Paul, 1980).

25. (Madison: University of Wisconsin Press, 1991).

26. Harvester Feminist Readings (Hemel Hempstead: Harvester Wheatsheaf, 1991).

27. (Berkeley: University of California Press, 1992).

21 | Feminisms

Gail Ashton

To read a text from a feminist standpoint in the early years of the twenty-first century can be an uncomfortable experience. Too often we shy away from identifying ourselves or our readings as feminist, dismissing this as an over-theorized, even outdated, activity. Alternatively, we take for granted our understanding of the nature of a feminist enterprise with its focus on the dynamics of gender, sexuality, and power without considering the problematic beginnings of the category of feminism itself.

A feminist literary practice has its own history. Grounded in the political conscious-ness of the 1960s and a drive to uncover hundreds of years of oppression and potential resistance to it, its early years were marked by a woman-centred approach. Its aims were radical: to question traditional patriarchal or male-dominated notions of order and authority and to attempt to redress the balance by uncovering the marginalized voices of women—as figures in literary texts and as 'lost' women authors. A feminist reading concerned itself with the representations of women in literature: as both victimized and resisting figures, as entities ignored or misread from a patriarchal per-spective that alternately erased or denigrated them, or else sympathized with them as fragile objects in need of chivalrous protection. Its focus too was on the question of the specificity of women's writing, on how it might (or might not) be distinct from that of men's. In a parallel move, French feminism (a conceptual rather than a national term) shifted attention away from the gender of an author and representations of the female to an examination of the style of a text, to reading and writing as gendered activities unconnected to biological sex.

These were ground-breaking enterprises rooted in the theoretical fields of deconstruction—with its concern for language—and psychoanalysis, with its emphasis on the unconscious. These areas were most notably brought together and developed by Jacques Lacan to suggest that the unconscious might be at work in a text to produce effects originating in the displacement or repression of fear and desire. A feminist reading often seeks out these silences or gaps in a text—its unconscious—and fully accepts that we can read against the grain of authorial intention.

Psychoanalysis assumes that the biological difference between men and women affects their experiences and perceptions of the world. This gender difference or 'binary'—male–female—is also offered as a hierarchical tradition, where the female is presented as a negative imprint of the male and so merely affirms *his* identity. In this way, the feminine can only be represented in masculine terms. Lacan suggested that in the same model, woman was 'other' to the male and signified only as absence or lack (without male attributes). Thus she cannot be represented at all in the masculine world, an idea particularly elaborated by French feminist theorists. Here, the possibility that women's experience might be different from men's gives rise to questions about how that experience might be expressed as well as how to define gendered identity. 'Feminine' and 'masculine'—and corresponding notions—become problematic terminologies embedded both in the structures of language and in cultural or social constructions of such identities.

The suggestion that gender is not based on biological sex but is, instead, a social construction has undoubtedly impacted upon contemporary feminism.[1] If gender is made or learned, then gender identity is unstable. Equally its relationship to sexuality is a troubled one. Increasingly, a feminist reading must take account of these—and other—notions. Early feminist inquiry assumed that its object, woman, was fixed, a category conflating all differences—of class, sexuality, gender orientation, ethnicity—and thus leaving no room for ambiguity. Increasingly this simplistic equation is under threat. French feminist thought argues that 'woman' cannot be represented. Other theorists suggest that even anatomical sex, just like gender, is not an easy or natural category.[2] Instead the body is a concrete and social phenomenon with its own shifting contexts and histories.

Feminisms is not, then, a 'woman' question or even singular, as either a term or an enterprise. Instead it is dynamic and composed of differences. It now emerges in other theoretical fields such as masculinities, gender studies, and queer theory. Closely allied to psychoanalytical theory, feminist readings have traditionally assumed a heterosexual model, thus ignoring other sexualities and tending to adopt an adversarial approach to men. The French feminist Luce Irigaray[3] has consistently argued that a patriarchal set-up is as damaging to men as it is to women, an area of inquiry, in part, redressed by readings exploring constructions of masculinities, while the introduction of lesbian and gay studies approaches some of these problems from a different angle.

This blurring of conceptual boundaries finds expression too in gender studies, an increasingly 'natural' home for feminisms. Here the focus is on the cultural constructions and problematic status of *apparently* natural categories such as gender, sex, masculinity, and femininity, a rereading that troubles these areas to examine how these categories are composed and represented. Queer theory goes even further to problematize and refuse all labels and identities, stir up differences and destroy binaries—male–female, masculine–feminine, heterosexual–homosexual—by searching for explicit *or* implicit homosexual touches or connections in literature.

Chaucer and feminist readings

A present-day feminist reading is, therefore, entirely different from one of even ten years ago, a development reflected in academic studies of Chaucer. Even in the 1970s dominant modes of reading Chaucer were highly conservative, frequently emphasizing exegetical readings (the search for moral allegory and spiritual 'Christian' truth hidden in all narratives). Chaucer is unusual for a medieval writer in that women are sometimes the centre of his stories, but this does not necessarily make him a proto-feminist. Even so, early feminist readings of Chaucer saw in his texts traditional oppositions—women represented as either the Virgin Mary or Eve—and so tended to label Chaucer as a patriarchal product of the system within which he writes.

Especially productive of a range of feminist interpretations is the Wife of Bath. Critics differ widely in their views. Some view her as a realistic figure expressive of the role of women in medieval society, others as a comic female grotesque affirming traditional misogynistic views of 'woman'. Elsewhere she is read as subversive, or alternatively as a victim unable to escape indoctrination by patristic teaching.

The first full-length feminist work on Chaucer appeared as late as 1989 in the shape of Carolyn Dinshaw's ground-breaking *Chaucer's Sexual Poetics*. Dinshaw argues that the Wife 'makes audible precisely what patriarchal discourse would keep silent'.[4] This she does through mimesis, a process that is a deliberate enactment of the stereotypical woman of misogynistic texts—lecherous, deceitful, extravagant, and noisy—in order to make overt the limitations of such extreme and oppressive portraits. More generally, Dinshaw presents Chaucer as an author who celebrates the feminine through his investigation of reading and writing practices. She suggests the Wife of Bath makes us attentive to the possibility of a 'feminist' re-visioning by encouraging us to rethink the gendered ways in which we, and medieval audiences, might read, in offering her own literal body as an erotic and playful text.

Other critics equally recognize the *potential* for subversion in the Wife of Bath, if not in Chaucer, but remain more sceptical of its actuality. Like Dinshaw, Catherine Cox suggests Alison writes *herself* through the metaphors of her own body. In a potentially disruptive manoeuvre, she takes pleasure in sex and in excessive talking. But though her tongue becomes an erotic strategy, it only *promises* to destabilize the masculine. Cox sees the Wife as an ambivalent figure, produced by, and reiterating, masculine, especially clerical, discourse, however much she might twist this for her own ends. The end product is 'anti-anti-feminist', a repudiation of anti-feminism that illustrates and supports its attack by taking the conventions of the very discourse it seeks to critique to offer only an idiosyncratic and personal response rather than something new. Thus it seems to validate the assumptions it sets out to dismantle.[5]

Similarly, for Susan Crane women—and some men—in Chaucer's texts use the language and paradigms of femininity to reaffirm conventional portraits at exactly the same time as they 'press against their positioning' within that framework partially to rework it.[6] She too believes that the Wife impersonates masculine discourse in a gesture towards an insubordination that cannot finally be sustained. Crane admires Alison's unbridled feminine and carnivalesque performance but thinks it remains only a 'seized power' that writes out all possibility 'of feminine authority'.[7]

Elaine Tuttle Hansen's seminal text *Chaucer and the Fictions of Gender* was an early and pessimistic intervention in feminist approaches to Chaucer that, interestingly, apparently forecloses feminist readings at the same time as opening up the field for later developments in masculinist and gender studies. She claims Chaucer replicates rather than transcends the concerns of his own culture and offers a focus, not on women, but on men troubled by insecure and conflicting representations of masculinity. For Hansen, the Wife of Bath remains 'a dramatic and important instance of woman's silence and suppression in history and language' that endorses the anti-feminism the Wife rails against and that reaffirms traditional binaries.[8] More generally, she hears in Chaucer's work not a genuinely female voice but 'something of a monotone making known both feminine absence and masculine anxiety'.[9]

Hansen's insistence on Chaucer's concern with the instability of gender anticipates more recent work. Most notably, Dinshaw's later investigations are markedly less radical and take her into 'queer theory', where potential transgressions, however unsettling, always seem to be recontained.[10] Equally Karma Lochrie's innovative work on how secrecy operates to both disguise and produce an ideology of gender uncovers an anxiety that is ultimately always stabilized.[11]

Twenty years ago a feminist reading was fresh and provocative. However much contemporary feminist investigations disturb, they have become ironically respectable as evidenced by their inclusion in a mainstream post-16 education system. Today's feminism must accommodate diverse approaches and schools of thought. Its plurality as a field is its strength, an openness that has ensured its development and perhaps resisted an inevitable drift towards conservatism. A feminist reading now is often highly theorized, one perhaps best described as gendered reading, and much in evidence in academic journals like *Exemplaria* and *Medieval Feminist Forum*; formerly *Medieval Feminist Newsletter*, the latter's new name is designed to reflect its more nuanced intervention in the field. Feminism is now concerned less with 'female' and more with 'feminine' as a subject position dissociated from biological sex and open to interpretation. It problematizes and searches for tensions and ambiguities rather than seeking answers.

Increasingly, too, it is interested in intersections, not least between theory and history. It accepts that a figure like the Wife of Bath is produced by and within a range of medieval discourses—including those related to the body and gender—specific to her cultural and historical context. At the same time, it actively questions the ways in which these discourses seek to fix themselves and conceal their incoherence. Above all, feminism(s) is not a historical movement now complete, as some believe—though we can track its trajectory through time—but a concept or mode of thinking that brings together both contemporary and historical ideas, an acute awareness of both our own and other practices.

Much remains to be done, at least in medieval studies where, so far, ethnicity, class, and colonization are only beginning to receive critical attention (see, for example, Chapter 26). I foresee a feminist agenda venturing further into postcolonial study and deeper into a practice that takes account of the discontinuous nature of history, and accepts both its specificity *and* its blurring.

The Wife as oral construction

Of all Chaucer's Canterbury pilgrims the Wife of Bath seems the most obviously a feminist prototype. We hear a strong female voice speaking at length in both her tale and her Prologue, a story in itself that recounts the life of a medieval woman, one who seemingly condemns clerical and anti-feminist tracts seeking to define and contain *all* women. Her Prologue is, then, a vigorous two-fingered reply to teachings that enjoin meekness, obedience, and restraint in speech, dress, physical and sexual behaviour.

But the nature of the Wife's voice is far more problematic than first appears. It comes to us filtered through layers of fiction—through Chaucer the pilgrim, the dramatic frame of the *Tales* and its (partial) readings, and through the ever-receding writer, Chaucer himself. Moreover, 'she' is, in part, a literary device common to both classical and modern texts, a personification of vice: here the troublesome and sexually voracious virago browbeating her husbands. We see this type elsewhere in medieval literature, most notably in the *Romance of the Rose*, where the figure of La Vieille, the old hag, boastfully reveals her secret tricks of the trade for dominating men. The Wife of Bath is a composite figure, a literary type that at the same time as offering what is, to a twenty-first-century audience, an energetic and attractive assertion of equality, also conforms to medieval anti-feminist stereotypes.

The Wife *seems* to offer a personal and directly related history of the abuse and suppression of women. Right from the start of her Prologue she asserts her lived experience over the authority of the written word. We witness the careful construction of an 'I', a first-person testimony complete with her own views and reported speech. Notice the prevalence of personal pronouns in the opening thirty lines or so and the opinionated nature of the monologue—'wel I woot' ('WBP' 27, 30), 'I wel understonde' (29), 'herde I nevere tellen in myn age' (24)—that refuses the monolithic authority vested in Jankyn's many books, all bound in 'o volume' (681), to declare finally 'I wolde nat of hym corrected be' (661).

This personal and confessional quality is enhanced by the oral nature of her narrative. She repeats herself and often loses the thread of her thoughts (586, 711–12). She continually hints at, yet delays, the crux of the story: Jankyn's beating of her for a book (586, 667–9, 711–12). She appears endearingly human with her poignant cry, 'Allas, allas! That evere love was synne!' (614), her comments on age (474–8), and the recollection of her lively youth (469–73). But the Wife is not the fully rounded, psychologically 'real' 'Talking Head' we imagine her to be. There is no careful revelation of character, or even consistent dramatization. Instead, Chaucer clearly exposes those oral features of her narrative to undercut what seems to be a full, personal recollection of events and remind us of the ways in which she is constructed, not as character but as a text.

There is an ambiguity at the heart of the Wife's apparently personal confession, one revealed not only through her own experiences but through a mimicry of the masculine discourse that produces her. She offers intimacy, not least through the technique of asking direct questions. But this remains a formal rhetorical trick in the style of male clerical sermonizing. In this question-and-answer debate mode the Wife sets up a series of interrogations that engage with the tradition of patristic writing and allow her both to mimic *and* to undermine its authority. Equally, she presents us with another technique from masculine discourse in the sequence marked by the repeated 'thou seyst' or its equivalent (257–450); you say we do this, she says, and so we do that. Here, as she describes women's 'unacceptable' behaviour, Alison shows how she conforms to the exact picture of anti-feminism she is attempting to negate. So, the Wife both denies *and* exemplifies a construction of the feminine based on patristic and theological commentaries, authored by the likes of Theophrastus, St Jerome, and Walter Map—those same written, anti-feminist tracts that Jankyn cites.

This simultaneous interchange is seen too in Chaucer's emphasis on the orality of the Wife's Prologue. On the one hand this is an attempt to take us away from the authority of written texts and produce, instead, a different kind of text. The direct opening of the Prologue and its insistent declaratives clearly flag it up as a story to be heard. Throughout, emphasis is on speech and, also, hearing, a correspondence that draws attention to the possibility of dialogue *between* discourses rather than a simple refutation of clerical anti-feminism. Observe the repetition of 'seye' or 'sayde' and the conversational tags and fillers—'eek', 'lo'—that punctuate her performance, as well as references to 'herkneth' or to listening (234, 224, 14, 828). It seems to be a spontaneous outpouring, a possibility of exchanging views. Certainly, in the everyday speech act this resembles we anticipate a conversation.

Yet, this remains a scripted, and so fixed, performance, in which 'herkneth' is a command to pay attention and the other oral markers are formal components of the clerical sermonizing in which it is rooted. Here too the partially deaf Wife refuses to listen; she speaks *for* her dead husbands, and at length. The oral and informal nature of the Wife's personal testimony, her colloquialisms, oaths, and coy euphemisms (contradicting her sexual frankness elsewhere), work, then, *in tandem* with the more formal features of traditional masculine discourse. An authoritative and textual tradition of anti-feminism *plus* a lived experience signalled through the marks on and practices of the Wife's actual physical body—a different text—continually play themselves out in the Prologue. Alison's testimony is composed of sound and body, is oral and, hence, 'feminine', as we shall see. Yet it exists, too, as a literary document and one, moreover, authored by a man.

The figure of the Wife is produced by and within those same texts that construct her as an anti-feminist stereotype, yet brings into play all that they try to condemn and silence: female pleasure in bodies, in sex, or joy in physical activities like singing, walking out, or chatting. In this way, she resists *written* claims to containment and definition, but can only do so by offering a monologue, an *oral* version of Jankyn's texts bound in one volume with which her struggle begins.

Departures

What is the gender of this textual construction, this narrative sequence we call the Wife of Bath? Gender—like a body—is fabricated and repeatedly performed. It is not a biological given. Hence, the Wife is not feminine—or even a feminist—simply because we know she is female. The formal debate style at the heart of her Prologue is associated with the masculine, for it seeks to own and control its audience. At the same time, the oral features and confessional, intimate tone of Alison's dramatization mark it as feminine. It is offered as gossip,[12] a marginal and secret speech enjoyed and exchanged by women, and, hence, stigmatized, lacking in authority—certainly not to be taken seriously as a 'feminist' reply.

Yet even this is ambiguous. Written transmission of words carries authority for it fixes discourse, often offering a single answer or world-view. This is a system traditionally categorized as masculine. In contrast, oral stories are dramatic, ripe for adaptation and reinvention. They implicitly invite audience participation or informal response and thus are productive of dialogue, a discourse that is multiple and rebelliously feminine. If the Prologue is non-authoritative gossip passed between women, then we would expect the Wife's audience to be female. Yet she makes only one direct address to women (225), and that in the midst of her formal, masculine question-and-answer debate. Elsewhere, it is apparent she speaks to men with her 'lordynges' (4, 112, 379) or 'Now, sire' (193).

The Prologue does, then, contain traces of the masculine, but this is quickly turned around to produce something that mingles discourses and styles, both replicates *and* refutes anti-feminist authority to present a construction that actually foregrounds all that is repressed and denigrated as feminine. It verbally uncovers the female body, confesses its life history and its secrets, to make it a public spectacle, both a visual and an audible body where the feminine is seen *and* heard.

Despite her intensely corporeal presence, the Wife of Bath ultimately evades our view. Hers is a body constructed through fragmented parts and the materiality of sound, both of which ally her with the feminine, with all that is unrepresentable within patriarchal discourse. That body is revealed piecemeal. Like a striptease, the Prologue delays and suspends its story to arrest our concentration on isolated fragments and to circle around what lies at its heart—the reiteration of how the Wife was beaten for a book. We catch only glimpses of a more subversive performance that never quite coheres. Yet in this textual embodiment of her as a speaking voice we might, too, discover a feminist re-visioning of the Wife's stories.

Alison's discursive performance focuses on her as disruptive noise, on the physical act of making sound that lies beneath what she verbally declares. It is this sound, with its multiplicity that evades definition, that, according to Sturges, might be termed the 'repressed feminine'.[13] It is set up in opposition to the singularity of meaning in masculine authoritative written texts (remember Jankyn's 'o volume'). Lacanian psychoanalytical theory describes how we come to language by accepting the Law of the father and so, regardless of our sex, aligning ourselves with the masculine symbolic world, with its connotations of rationality, regulation, and order. Thus we begin to name, and hence appropriate, objects and ideas, to give and accept identities.

In order to do this, we must repress all that Lacan depicts as feminine. We push aside a pre-symbolic mother-and-child unity, a world centred on the body and sensual pleasure, on sound rather than 'language': babble, rhythm, song, tears, laughter. This is sound we cannot fully name or describe. We cannot write or script it. Constantly suppressed but never fully dismissed, it continually threatens to erupt and so is troubling and anti-authoritarian, as much a part of our social world as is its principal defining discourse.

This, then, is my interpretative framework. I read the Wife as a textual body upon which are inscribed competing discourses, the masculine and the feminine (not male and female). I see her Prologue as a story not about 'maistrie' but about dialogue, an endless and unresolved exchange of alternatives whereby the repressed feminine, integral to the masculine frame of reference that seeks to exclude it, makes known its presence.

Alison: noise and sound

What psychoanalysts call pre-symbolic and Sturges terms non-scriptible (as opposed to scriptible, the written text),[14] medieval linguistic theorists called 'acoustic': material sound, of the body and its senses, something irrational rather than 'intelligible' which might be represented in letters. Medieval patristic writing condemned the acoustic as 'pure voice' or 'struck air',[15] a distraction from the Word of God and allied to oral speech. In turn, this was connected to gluttony and sexual incontinence, a conflation that finds expression in the Prologue, as we shall see. This is the feminine repressed in both women *and* men in order for us to function coherently within the social order.

The Wife's performance is not simply oral but is firmly associated with sound. Laughter is an important element in her (self-)construction. The 'General Prologue' reveals that her manner is to laugh and 'carpe' (474). Later, claiming 'myn entente nys but for to pleye' ('WBP' 192), she laughs when she recalls how she made her husbands 'work' all night in bed (202). She is implicitly chuckling too when she remembers the 'jolitee' of her youth, telling how this 'tikleth me aboute myn herte roote' (471). We imagine her laughing as she reveals how she pretends to lament—more sound—at husband number four's funeral, all the time peeping between her fingers to ogle Jankyn's legs (587–99).

What is emphasized is something not to be articulated or scripted, a sound indicative of an abandoned but repressed joy in a sensual body. Alison tells us she was young and wanton, 'joly as a pye' (456), a bird famed for its noise. We laugh when she describes how she uses sound to wear down her old husbands; notice the onomatopoeic vocabulary as she constantly 'pleynes' (complains) with 'continueel murmur or grucchyng' (406), or relates how she can 'byte and whyne' (386).

Equally, rhythm and song exert continual pressure on scriptible language. Ironically, her hard-pressed husbands struggling to perform sexually for her *songen* "Weilawey!"' (216, my italics). Alison herself sings like a nightingale when drunk (458–9)—which is often—and remarks that men like women for many reasons, some because they can sing or dance (259). Here, singing is tied to sexual allure, just as greediness and promiscuity are frequently linked in medieval writings.

The repressed feminine is, thus, expressed through a range of sounds that cannot properly be written down. Inextricably connected to gluttony and sexual licence (or 'appetit', 417), its predominant quality is purely oral. This is the medium through which the Wife is constructed. Deep within the repressed feminine too is that tendency towards disruption witnessed in the wider context of the *Tales*. The most extensive elaboration of this occurs at the end of the 'Clerk's Tale'. The Clerk recounts the story of silent and patient Griselda, the Wife's antithesis. As he concludes, a new discourse bursts into the dramatic frame ('ClT' 1176–1212) claiming to speak on behalf of the Wife of Bath and 'al hire secte' (1170–1). This disruption—in the form of a song—destroys the contained and scriptible narrative presented by a male cleric, the clerk. It is an oral, and hence feminine, response, not the taken-in-turn reply of a formal question-and-answer debate, but an explosion into the Clerk's *exemplum* of that good wife Griselda.

The envoy to the 'Clerk's Tale' calls on the audience to 'Herkneth my song that seith in this manere' (1176). This reply matches the Wife's Prologue with its emphasis on the feminine, the oral features of 'herkneth' and 'seith' and song that urge all women to reject the authority of exemplary women. Follow Echo, it demands, who—rather like Alison in the multiple discourse of her Prologue—*always* replies, and indeed contradicts ('ClT' 1189–90). It calls on women to 'clappeth as a mille' (1200) and to use their 'crabbed eloquence' (1203) to make men 'wepe, and wrynge, and waille!' (1212). Don't let humility nail your tongue, says the envoy, or allow clerks to write of you stories like the one of Griselda (1184–7). What is striking in this exchange is the sheer force and noise expressed by the repressed feminine that the Wife embodies. Here is a material, corporeal performance that asserts non-scriptible sound over masculine scriptible and clerical stories. It is not the Wife's words that are crucial but her voluble and bodily presence in the text(s) that constructs her.

The repressed feminine

If the repressed feminine identifies itself through a performance composed of sound, so too its presence is marked by the physical. Any body is both a discursive (produced by a range of 'texts' including non-verbal and iconographic ones) and a social construct, one that we seek to contain by making it legible. Thus we inscribe it, make it scriptible. Our contemporary world does this by assigning codes of gender and sexuality, by bringing a body under surveillance through, for example ID, DNA, or fingerprinting.

In the Prologue the Wife seems to bring her own body into play. As we have seen, she offers us its history and tells of its bodily and sexual crimes. Alison is of the flesh, associated with excess of the body and with noise. Hers is, then, an unruly material body, feminine according to anti-feminist thought and, hence, subordinate to the medieval masculine with its 'higher' order of mind, rationality, and spirit. Hers is the repressed feminine at the heart of us all, undisciplined and non-scriptible sound and body, at once denigrated *and* powerfully subversive.

Alison's insistent association with bodily activity is not simply sexual, though her liking for wandering by the way ('GP' 467) has a double meaning. She goes on pilgrimages and attends festivals, plays, and processions. When her husband is absent, she is off out into the fields in search of Jankyn ('WBP' 548–52). Her list of anti-feminist proscriptions includes walking and playing in friends' houses (243–5). Alison demands freedom, for women to be 'at oure large' (322). This delight in activity is replicated in her tale with its centuries-earlier setting when fairies roamed the land and the elf queen and her attendants might be seen dancing on the green ('WBT' 857–64), or when ladies dance and magically disappear as the knight errant approaches (991–6). To be open, not closed in, the feminine asserted or at least acknowledged, not repressed: this is the desire that drives her text, yet one without easy resolution.

For gendered identity is persistently troubled not just by the repressed feminine in terms of sound or physicality, as seen earlier, but also by the same feminine's insistent alliance with a body in pieces. Medieval thought classified a 'proper' (masculine) body as one that was whole or sealed, without dangerous apertures where sin might enter. In contrast, an 'improper' body was fragmented and regarded as feminine, an association analogous to a fear of the female body and, in particular, its vaginal orifice. This feminine body is threatening; it has gaps—from which leak sound and fluid; it is grotesque, distorted in pregnancy, for example, and so exceeding its own bounds. Presented to us in pieces, Alison's is a feminine body. We view her not as a whole but as a series of parts witnessed through a description of bodily markings: dress, birthmarks, and 'queynte'. In this way, then, the Wife, allied with the monstrous, is an unsettling figure.

Alison as monster

When Jeffrey Cohen identifies the figure of the monster, he marks it as both masculine—huge, strong, and aggressive—*and* feminine, allied to corporeality and to excess.[16] The monster, too, is indelibly marked by fragmentation. It dismembers its enemies and is killed only by beheading. Both compelling *and* threatening, its presence must be suppressed in a move reminiscent of the repression of the feminine. The monster's is a carnal body, obscene and grossly feminine in its emphasis on consumption and (carnal) appetite. We fear its huge mouth might open up and eat us. This terrifying aperture marks it as an example of the improper body discussed earlier. The Wife's seemingly conventional depiction as an anti-feminist caricature ignores the ambiguous complexity of her figuration. Her description is almost exclusively corporeal, an intensely bodily yet fragmented depiction that allies her with a 'monstrous' femininity. Focus is on her teeth ('GP' 468), her face (458), hips (472), and her legs and feet clad in scarlet stockings and supple new shoes (456–7).

Equally, just as her oral performance intermingles masculine and feminine styles, so too her gendered presence remains monstrously uncertain. She is, at first sight, 'typically' feminine, loving fine clothes and ostentatious display; think of her hat with its lavish head coverings ('GP' 453–5). Her skin is 'fair' in the mannered idealism of the courtly lady, her star sign Venus, the goddess of love. Yet her constellation is a dual one for she is born with Mars, god of warfare and aggression, in the ascendant ('WBP' 613). Her complexion is equally fair *and* florid ('GP' 458), its scarlet tones mirroring the bloody aggression of Mars (generally, rosy and vibrant hues were reserved for male figures in classical and medieval art). Attention is called to the spurs she wears (473).

But it is her hat that, like the monster, allows this figure to slip between masculine and feminine positions, to keep the body in play and so multiply possibility and resist definition. Alison's enormous headgear with its weighty coverings provokes comment from Chaucer the pilgrim ('GP' 453–5) and renders her monstrously excessive. This feminine corporeality is echoed in the large size of her overskirt and hips, both of which draw attention to the genital region. If we look closely, we see that the lower portion of her description—her hips, skirt, legs, feet—focuses upon the bodily strata traditionally associated with the feminine. Yet her exceptionally large hat relates her to the masculine. To highlight the head invokes associations with the rational and abstract, as opposed to feminine unruly corporeal substance. The hat is compared to a 'bokeler or a targe' (471), a shield or a target, again stressing the masculine with its warrior-like intimations. More disconcerting is the fact that both of these implements were employed as metaphors in some medieval poetry for the *mons veneris*, or, as the Wife terms it, the 'chambre of Venus' ('WBP' 618).[17] This threatening bodily aperture suddenly focuses her portrait in a new way.

The Wife, *seemingly* huge in size, profoundly corporeal, is at once masculine *and* feminine. We have already seen how her mouth is ever open, emanating sound.

Medieval etymology persistently links the mouth and the vagina in fabliau stories.[18] In medieval iconography the vagina is frequently represented as the *vagina dentata*, a horrific mouth that opens and closes, and has teeth. In the 'improper' body that is Alison, neither mouth nor vagina are ever closed.

Alison: a talking 'queynte'

Like the monster in which she is rooted, the Wife's 'appetit', here for sex ('WBP' 417, 623), knows no bounds. She is a self-confessed 'lusty oon' (605), her 'coltes tooth' (602) and gap teeth ('GP' 468) disturbing reminders of that all-consuming *vagina dentata* image. Her sexuality is continually expressed in images of consumption; even her fake pleasure in the beds of her old husbands is imaged as 'in bacon hadde I nevere delit' ('WBP' 416–18). Her gluttonous drinking (459–63) leads to the proverb 'A likerous mouth moste han a likerous tayl' (466), the pun on 'tail' again collapsing the distinction between the carnal excesses of mouth and vagina.

Alison's obsessive referencing of her genitalia insistently demands our attention and helps to construct her as a 'talking queynte'. She claims to have 'the beste *quoniam* myghte be' (608) and says she cannot withdraw 'My chambre of Venus from a good felawe' (618). Her husbands will have her 'queynte right ynogh at eve' (332) for she keeps her '*bele chose*' only for them (447, 510). Here the Wife is constructed in classic anti-feminist terms through her corporeal and carnal nature in a manner that irremediably retains her within a masculine frame of reference as a terrifying figure. She is reduced to body; worse, to her consuming genitalia.

Yet at the same time her insistence on the physical and its pleasures, on fragmented body parts, on appetite, on the fluidity of gender that marks the monstrous offers a compelling example of the way the repressed feminine is brought into play, erupts into the open and *sings*. The same masculine authoritative discourse that scripts her is burst asunder and the feminine asserted; not as something better or even equal, but simply as different, as productive rather than reductive of meaning.

Asserting the feminine

The Wife's contempt for the anti-feminist tracts that attempt to erase her non-scriptible body is imaged in highly physical terms. She describes the cleric in his dotage, writing of women's failure to keep their marriage vows when *he* is unable to perform 'Of Venus werkes worth his olde sho' ('WBP' 707–10). Here masculine authority is depicted as decrepit and static in contrast to the energy and movement enjoyed, as we have seen, by the repressed feminine.

It is interesting to note too what women apparently do to men in Alison's personal reading of Jankyn's books. Sampson loses his hair and both his eyes, thanks to Delilah.

Hercules is set on fire. Xantippa 'caste pisse' on Socrates' head (729). Lyria and Lucia both poison their husbands. Other women drive nails into the brains of their men as they sleep or slay men in their beds after which 'hir lecchour dighte hire al the nyght' while the corpse lies upright on the floor (765–8).

We recognize in all this misogynistic fears of physical violence and fragmentation embodied in irrational and monstrous women. Yet this is an attempt to script actively and *physically* the non-scriptible feminine upon a masculine body in an inverse of the usual scenario. It is this emphasis on the body and its crimes that blurs the distinction between masculine and feminine. The male body is feminized: rendered passive, penetrated (nails in the brain), and marked while the feminine performs, often sexually. It is reduced to its parts—heart, head, eyes, brain—those segments traditionally associated with masculine intellect and rationality, with sight and cognition or ways of knowing and appropriating the world, all here under attack. Physical activity, pleasure, *pieces* of body are asserted over unsuspecting, paralysed wholeness.

This reaches its height in the final and literal battle of the Wife's narrative. Alison literally fragments the authority of the scriptible by tearing three pages from Jankyn's book of wicked wives ('WBP' 788–810). He strikes her, the blow to her ear leaving her partially deaf (794–6); though masculine discourse is not finally refuted (she is not completely without hearing after all), now she need no longer fully listen to the authority of the written as Jankyn reads it to her.

The Wife does win. While he afterwards destroys his book, she governs his *tongue* and his *hand* (815). Sound and body are conflated in an assertion of the repressed feminine that echoes the close of the envoy's song that concludes the 'Clerk's Tale' discussed earlier. There, women are urged to make so much noise that the sound might pierce the breast and 'aventaille' (neck-guard) of their husbands ('ClT' 1204). This is the lesson the envoy—offered on behalf of that textual construct the Wife of Bath and all her sect—teaches: to turn the unrepresentable (sound) into a version of script marked on the bodies of the men who resist and are even armoured against it, leaving not a clear scriptible presence but perhaps the best the Wife can hope for, a trace.

Like the monster, too, the Wife always exceeds. She spills over, breaking the confines of her own story to 'appear' elsewhere in the *Tales*, and even beyond. The title of Evans and Johnson's critical work *Feminist Readings in Middle English Literature: The Wife of Bath and All her Sect* (1994) points up a debate that turns on the multiplicity of feminist readings produced by a figure like the Wife and by a feminist enterprise in general. Associated with feminine excess—of words, body, sound, all that the masculine seeks to subordinate—the Wife is not 'proof' of masculine anti-feminist notions but a proliferation of possibilities.

Insistently feminine yet constructed through the masculine, it is the Wife's monstrous textual body rather than the words of a 'real' character that speaks itself: through its body parts and through the sound it makes. Perhaps this assertion of the feminine is conservative in scope, its attempt to represent the unrepresentable— 'woman'—driving her back into nonsensical babble. But to read *through* rather than *with* the Wife (in other words, to read her as textual and not as a 'lifelike' character) makes us aware of how the repressed feminine exists *within* and not independently of the dominant masculine. What we deny or repress indelibly marks us. Like the monster, then, the Wife—or rather her shifting and excessive figuration—always returns to haunt us.

FURTHER READING

Cox, Catherine, *Gender and Language in Chaucer* (Gainesville: University of Florida Press, 1997). This is a challenging but interesting book that offers both a highly theoretical and a close reading of Chaucer's texts. For her comments on the Wife of Bath, see especially pp. 18–38.

Crane, Susan, *Gender and Romance in Chaucer's 'Canterbury Tales'* (Princeton: Princeton University Press, 1994). Crane's concern is with the problematics of the romance genre that typically has as its paradigm male domination over a passive, female love object. Crane rereads the genre to offer a cautious endorsement of Chaucer as a proto-feminist writer.

Dinshaw, Carolyn, *Chaucer's Sexual Poetics* (Madison: University of Wisconsin Press, 1989). In its time this was a ground-breaking work that celebrates Chaucer as a feminist author and the Wife in particular as a radical figure. See especially pp. 113–31.

Evans, Ruth, and Lesley Johnson (eds.), *Feminist Readings in Middle English Literature: The Wife of Bath and All her Sect* (London: Routledge, 1994). This is an exceptionally useful if dated beginning to any general reading of feminist approaches to Chaucer. The introduction remains valuable and the volume contains material on the Wife.

Hansen, Elaine Tuttle, *Chaucer and the Fictions of Gender* (Berkeley: University of California Press, 1992). This remains a seminal and influential text, not least for its prefiguring of a more complex and less exclusive visioning of feminism. Hansen questions the notion of Chaucer as a feminist writer by arguing that his work seeks to reinforce male positions even when it seems most concerned with women. It is a particularly rewarding read in conjunction with Dinshaw. Read pp. 26–57 on the Wife.

Lochrie, Karma, *Covert Operations: The Medieval Uses of Secrecy* (Philadelphia: University of Pennsylvania Press, 1999). This is an exceptionally stimulating text that perfectly exemplifies the ways in which feminist readings have moved into more complex theoretical fields. Lochrie offers an intelligent and perceptive analysis of both medieval and contemporary ideas about gender. See pp. 55–80 for her comments on the Wife of Bath.

NOTES

1. The best-known name in this field is undoubtedly Judith Butler. See *Gender Trouble: Feminism and the Subversion of Identity* (New York: Routledge, 1990) or *Bodies that Matter: On the Discursive Limits of Sex* (New York: Routledge, 1993).

2. See Toril Moi, *What is a Woman? and Other Essays* (Oxford: Oxford University Press, 1999) for a critique of contemporary gender theory and a persuasive intervention of her own.

3. Luce Irigaray, *This Sex which is Not One*, trans. Catherine Porter with Carolyn Burke (Ithaca, NY: Cornell University Press, 1985) or *Je, tu, nous: Toward a Culture of Difference*, trans. Alison Martin (New York: Routledge, 1993).

4. Carolyn Dinshaw, *Chaucer's Sexual Poetics* (Madison: University of Wisconsin Press, 1989), 115.

5. Catherine Cox, *Gender and Language in Chaucer* (Gainesville: University of Florida Press, 1997), 37.

6. Susan Crane, *Gender and Romance in Chaucer's 'Canterbury Tales'* (Princeton: Princeton University Press, 1994), 55.

7. Ibid. 130–1.

8. Elaine Tuttle Hansen, *Chaucer and the Fictions of Gender* (Berkeley: University of California Press, 1992), 27, 37.

9. Ibid. 12.

10. See Dinshaw, 'Chaucer's Queer Touches/A Queer Touches Chaucer', *Exemplaria*, 7 (1995), 79–92, and *Getting Medieval: Sexualities and Communities, Pre- and Postmodern* (Durham, NC: Duke University Press, 1999).

11. Karma Lochrie, *Covert Operations: The Medieval Uses of Secrecy* (Philadelphia: University of Pennsylvania Press, 1999).

12. Lochrie suggests that the Wife 'translates' anti-feminist discourse into gossip thereby authorizing her own feminine speech. But since gossip is itself a secret, and hence deviant, discourse, though it raises questions it can never finally repudiate dominant modes. See ibid. 56–8.

13. Robert Sturges, *Chaucer's Pardoner and Gender Theory: Bodies of Discourse* (New York: Macmillan, 2000); see esp. pp. 1–4, 81–91.

14. Ibid. 81–106.

15. Ibid. 85–6.

16. Jeffrey Jerome Cohen, *Of Giants: Sex, Monsters and the Middle Ages* (Minneapolis: University of Minnesota Press, 1999).

17. For the tracking of this web of references concerning the Wife's hat, I am indebted to Leonie Kenyon's BA dissertation, May 2003, University of Manchester.

18. See E. Jane Burns, *Bodytalk: When Women Speak in Old French Literature* (Philadelphia: University of Pennsylvania Press, 1993).

22 | The carnivalesque

Marion Turner

A conspicuous feature of late medieval culture is festivity and carnival. Parodies of the mass, subversive gargoyles and misericords (carvings on tip-up seats) in churches, the boy bishop ceremony, and the festive election of temporary 'Lords of Misrule', are some of the cultural forms that exemplify the idea of the carnivalesque.[1] In modern critical discussions about Chaucer's time—the late fourteenth century—carnival is invoked to describe social practices and cultural events from the ritual behaviour of the rebels during the Peasants' Revolt to the festive procession of Chaucer's pilgrims behind the bagpipe-playing Miller ('GP' 565–6). Indeed, in recent years the most popular aspects of Chaucer's texts outside academic circles have been those that might be termed 'carnivalesque': those parts of the *Canterbury Tales* that emphasize the lower bodily stratum and that celebrate the dethroning of the father figure (for example, the 'Miller's Tale', the 'Merchant's Tale', the 'Wife of Bath's Prologue and Tale') are undoubtedly the most well-known of Chaucer's writings.

Bakhtin and his readers

Mikhail Bakhtin (1895–1975) was the most famous and influential expositor of the concept of carnival. His best-known work, *Rabelais and his World* (written in the Soviet Union in the 1930s and submitted as a Ph.D. thesis in 1940), deals at length with ideas about folk culture and festive practice. According to Bakhtin, in the Middle Ages 'a boundless world of humorous forms and manifestations opposed the official and serious tone of medieval ecclesiastical and feudal culture'.[2] Carnival was the indestructible life of the people, a celebration of freedom, an assertion of change and renewal, a revelling in the body, a festival of laughter, a challenge to hierarchy and order, a proliferation of discourses, in which boundaries were exploded and variety was celebrated. Bakhtin declares that carnival is 'the people's second life, organised on the basis of laughter' and that it is the 'feast of time, the feast of becoming, change, and renewal'.[3] Mimicking 'serious' rituals and figures, turning the world upside down or inside out, is an important manifestation of carnival, visible in many medieval customs and in much medieval art and architecture. The lowering of what was high and the collapsing of hierarchy is a vital feature of grotesque realism, an integral part of the carnivalesque. Bakhtin writes:

In grotesque realism, therefore, the bodily element is deeply positive . . . The material bodily principle is contained not in the biological individual but in the people, a people who are continually growing and renewed. This is why all that is bodily becomes grandiose, exaggerated, immeasurable . . . The leading themes of these elements of bodily life are fertility, growth, and a brimming-over abundance . . . The essential principle of grotesque realism is degradation, that is, the lowering of all that is high, spiritual, ideal, abstract; it is a transfer to the material level, to the sphere of earth and body in their indissoluble unity.[4]

Grotesque realism, then, is an exuberant celebration of primal, earthy materiality, an encomium to the idea of 'the people'.

It is also an inversion of acceptable, official forms—and an attack on socialist realism, an important concept in 1930s Soviet culture. A crucial aspect of the carnivalesque is the emphasis on stylistic variety, and generic instability and openness. Bakhtin is interested in the influences of genres such as Menippean satire (characterized by its mockery of 'serious' forms) and Socratic dialogue (characterized by an emphasis on interlocution and dialogic ways of thinking). He is concerned with texts that are 'carnivalesque': multi-voiced, generically mixed, parodic. In *Problems of Dostoyevsky's Poetics* he argues that Dostoyevsky's works are not monologic texts, dominated by an author's voice; rather they allow many separate and unmerged voices to speak. Bakhtin suggests that voices within texts can gain their own independence and power and he stresses the importance of presenting diverse, multiple perspectives and ideas, as opposed to trying to find a univocal truth. Such voices are themselves double, encapsulating a dialogue between character/narrator and author.[5]

Bakhtin is interested in the social contexts of utterances, arguing that the environment of any utterance constructs its meanings. He uses the term 'heteroglossia' to describe the forces enabling those meanings. The fact of heteroglossia creates a dialogic world in which everything interacts and meanings exist in a state of flux and debate. Carnivalesque heteroglossia is playful and parodic, multifaceted and marginal, indeterminate and insurgent. It challenges official languages, which seek to impose order and to fix meanings.

Bakhtin is passionate in his characterization of carnival forms as genuinely anarchic and powerful, as social practices that create and celebrate change. Anatoly Lunacharsky, the Commissar of Enlightenment in the Soviet Union, held a view directly opposed to Bakhtin's: he argued that carnival functioned as a 'safety valve' for emotions and desires that might otherwise have been channelled into revolutionary activity. Indeed, at the heart of much debate about 'the carnivalesque' is the extent to which it can truly be seen as subversive. On the one hand, carnival mocks and attacks high culture and hierarchy, but on the other, it does so in a contained and sanctioned manner, and is thus often seen as a form that actually serves to protect and to maintain hierarchies. As a controlled form of protest, it allows the people to express their discontents through parodies and festivities for a short and predetermined period of time, but does not ultimately threaten the upper echelons of society. According to 'safety valve' theories, carnival allows the release of pent-up tensions, which enables society to continue unchanged. Since Bakhtin's work became widely known in the West, many critics (including theorists such as Terry Eagleton and Michael Camille) have emphasized the controlled and permitted aspects of carnival, seeing it as a device for letting off steam within a constraining social order. In their important book *The Politics and Poetics of Transgression*, Peter Stallybrass and Allon White provided an influential reading of Bakhtin. Pointing out that carnivalesque activities often violently abuse and scapegoat the weakest elements of society, *not* the strongest, they suggested that carnival can be complicit with the status quo.[6] However, they also discussed the fluid nature of the carnivalesque, arguing that although carnival may usually have no dramatic trans-formative effects, in certain conditions it can provide a site for genuine transgression and opposition. Carnival can be viewed as a dynamic entity that functions differently in diverse circumstances rather than as a stable cultural idea; in other words, it can be appropriated and manipulated in a variety of ways.

The carnivalesque in medieval culture

A relatively straightforward example of a carnivalesque ceremony is the custom of the boy bishop. The tradition was popular all over England from the thirteenth century to the sixteenth, in monastic houses, in urban and provincial churches, and in educa-tional establishments such as Eton, Winchester, and Westminster schools, King's College, Cambridge, and All Souls, New, and Magdalen colleges in Oxford. The boy bishop was usually elected on St Nicholas's Day (6 December), and the principal occa-sion for his rule was the Feast of the Holy Innocents (28 December). The festivities started during the Magnificat, at the verse 'Deposuit potentes de sede' ('He hath put down the mighty from their seat'). These words were greeted by laughter throughout the chapel, bells were jangled, and the boy bishop replaced the bishop, dean, or abbot, while the other boys changed places with other clerics. The boy then acted as a priest, sometimes even preaching and soliciting alms, burlesquing the usual religious prac-tices of the house. Festive inversion and mockery are manifest in this tradition, as is the fact that such rebellion was sanctioned and permitted—although that is not to say that it could not transgress its imposed limits.

Similarly, the misericords that decorated medieval churches often displayed scenes that subverted hierarchy, challenged the 'father', and elevated the low and the bodily—but did so under the auspices of the Church. One common subject was domestic violence, with women winning out. A misericord from Westminster Abbey, for example, depicts a woman beating the naked buttocks of a man, who is holding a winding frame and wool (see Figure III.1).[7] Such scenes of the battle of the sexes convey an idea of hierarchies inverted and challenged. They are also very similar to Harry

Fig. III.1 Battle and inversion of the sexes. Misericord, early sixteenth century (Westminster Abbey).

Bailly's account of his own marriage. Harry claims to be dominated by an aggressive, emasculating wife, Goodelief, 'byg in armes' ('MoP' 1921), who taunts him, saying

> I wol have thy knyf,
> And thou shalt have my distaf and go spynne!
>
> ('MoP' 1906–7)

The potential subversion of this image is contained within the discourse of the 'authoritative' male voice.

A more complex example of the function of carnival can be seen in the Peasants' Revolt of 1381. A feast day, Corpus Christi, was appropriated for rebellion, and that rebellion was acted out with the trappings of carnival. Chroniclers describe the rebels treating executions as a game, crying 'A revelle! A revelle!' as they burnt Lambeth Palace,[8] inverting hierarchy by making knights act as servants to the rebels, and generally blurring the distinction between rebels and revels. In this case, the traditions of carnival seem to have been exploited and manipulated to produce symbolic acts that were oppositional and rebellious.[9] The revolt provides a fascinating negotiation between festivities and anarchy, yoking together protests against the Church and state with acts of play and symbolic gestures. Narratives of the revolt suggest that contemporary chroniclers and churchmen were very much awake to the potential dangers of carnival behaviour. These chronicle accounts suggest that just as revelry might become rebellious, so rebellion could metamorphose into revels.

The playful forms adopted by Wat Tyler (one of the leaders of the Peasants' Revolt) as he drank, played with his knife, and spoke with familiarity to the king serve a very different function in their chronicle setting from the festive inversion of the boy bishop ceremony. Comparing such diverse manifestations of the carnivalesque in medieval culture affirms its shifting, circumstantial nature, its availability for use in different situations and for various purposes. Moreover, the meaning of play to Wat Tyler, for example, would have been very different from its meaning for the king, or from its meaning for the chroniclers. The carnivalesque cannot be limited to a particular function; it is fundamentally open and incomplete in nature.

Late medieval pilgrimage is an important subject of study for anyone interested in Chaucer's manipulation of carnival forms. Pilgrimage was falling into disrepute at this time, and was frequently viewed as an excuse for a holiday, for sexual promiscuity, for singing and tale-telling, and generally for enjoying the journey, rather than focusing on the journey's goal. Criticism of the carnival aspects of pilgrimage was characteristic of Lollard (heretical) dissent. William Thorpe, suspected of heresy, and examined before the archbishop of Canterbury in 1407, afterwards penned his own account of his defence. It included a polemical attack on the practice of pilgrimage at this time:

Also, sire, I knowe wel that whanne dyverse men and wymmen wolen goen thus aftir her owne willis and fyndingis out on pilgrimageyngis, thei wolen ordeyne biforehonde to have with hem bothe men and wymmen that kunnen wel synge rowtinge songis, and also summe of these pilgrimes wolen have with hem baggepipis so that in eche toun that thei comen thorugh, what with noyse of her syngynge, and with the soun of her pipinge, and with the gingelynge of her Cantirbirie bellis, and with the berkynge out of dogges aftir hem, these maken more noyse than if the king came there awey with this clarioneris and manye other mynystrals. And if these men and wymmen ben a monethe oute in her pilgrymage, manye of hem an half yeere aftir schulen be greete jangelers, tale tellers, and lyeris.[10]

Thorpe describes a scene of carnival: a cacophony of noise, of divergent voices, of music and chaotic festivity. The pilgrimage is described as something that subverts a spiritual ideal, representing what happens when men and women follow 'her owne willis'. It is also depicted as socially and politically subversive. Thorpe explicitly compares the behaviour of the pilgrims to the behaviour of the king and his followers, contrasting the bagpipes and bells with the clarions; the 'rowtinge songis' with the king's minstrels. The carnival aspects of pilgrimage challenge both the ultimate father, God—Thorpe declares that the pilgrims 'dispisen God' (p. 35)—and the father figure of the king, sweeping these figures of authority aside and celebrating the life of the people. In Thorpe's description, pilgrims also celebrate the body, 'spendynge these goodis upon vicious hostelries and upon tapsters, whiche ben ofte unclene wymmen of her bodies' (p. 36). He explicitly states that they have gone on pilgrimage 'more for the helthe of her bodies than for the helthe of her soulis' and that they privilege 'worldli or fleischli frendschip' over the 'frendschip of God' (p. 35). Even the musical instruments, the bagpipes, are testicular and bodily. Thorpe conjures up an image of a carnival procession, wending its way through England, spreading dangerous noise and exuberant enjoyment. The overt declarations that the pilgrims' behaviour is not 'thankful to God', and the implication that it may act against the king's authority, construct pilgrimage as a carnivalesque site of potential anarchy.

Thorpe's description of the pilgrimage is also reminiscent of charivari, known as 'rough music', a ritual enacted to protest against irregular marriages and to shame the participants. It usually took the form of a rowdy procession characterized by shouting, banging, and discordant noise. Charivari implicitly challenged the Church's jurisdiction over marital matters but it was also inherently conservative, in its scapegoating of women, adulterers, and other weak or marginalized members of society. The noisy pilgrimage that Thorpe describes likewise rebels against the Church's idea of pilgrimage, but was perhaps not seen as threatening the status quo. It is a dissident speaker (Thorpe), rather than the Church itself, who attacks the carnival rout: like charivari, such holiday noise might have been viewed not as genuinely subversive, but rather as a contained and temporary outlet for unruly spirits.

Chaucerian carnival

The carnivalesque aspects of Chaucer's *Canterbury Tales* have been discussed by various critics in recent decades; indeed, its festive aspects are conspicuous. The *Tales* depicts a group ruled by a temporary lord (Harry Bailly), in the mode of a festive (albeit fairly conservative) Lord of Misrule, who wants to encourage drinking, amusement, and play, but also wants to uphold the privileges of the Knight and the Monk. The group itself assaults hierarchy by refusing to allow the tales to be told according to social order and at least tacitly supporting the Miller's interruption. The pilgrims set off in fertile springtime; their journey is enlivened by taverns, noise, and tale-telling; many of the tales are fabliaux which celebrate the body and the world turned upside down; and the text is informed by polyvocality, by a hullabaloo of diverse voices and discourses. This section will investigate the use made of the idea of the carnivalesque by three Chaucer critics.

In *Chaucerian Play: Comedy and Control in the 'Canterbury Tales'*, Laura Kendrick argues that the carnival aspects of the *Canterbury Tales* function as sanctioned subversion. She characterizes Harry Bailly as a Lord of Misrule who is rebelling against restrictions, and whose order is 'a rejuvenating antithesis'.[11] Kendrick suggests that 'Chaucer builds the authority to be dethroned into the text of his *Canterbury Tales*' (p. 100) describing, for example, the Miller's challenge to the 'repressive authority of the "Knight's Tale"' (p. 121) and the dethroning of the father in the fabliaux told by the Miller, Reeve, Shipman, and Merchant (p. 116). In her emphasis on the reviving aspects of this pilgrimage, on its springtime setting and its playful character, Kendrick depicts Chaucer's pilgrimage as a Bakhtinian seasonal festival of plenty, a joyous celebration of life and fertility. She stresses the idea that this pilgrimage takes place in the 'safe bounds of festive time' and that it is 'sanctioned' (p. 128). According to Kendrick, Chaucer had a 'therapeutic, equilibrating intention' (p. 126) hoping to 'promote social stability' (p. 129). He accomplishes this promotion through the medium of the 'Parson's Tale', which 're-establishes proper order and authority' (p. 129). Kendrick is firmly of the opinion that the carnival functions as a safety valve.

Paul Strohm's *Social Chaucer* is concerned with the concept of polyvocality, with Chaucer's texts as 'places crowded with many voices representing many centers of social authority'.[12] Strohm argues that Chaucer's concern with generic diversity and instability, with polyvocality and stylistic variety, itself represents a dynamic approach to the social. Characterizing the *Canterbury Tales* as polyphonic, Strohm notes: 'The polyphonic work is, as Bakhtin has reminded us, "dialogic through and through" and is grounded not simply in a perverse human nature that refuses to recognize transcendent truth but in an experience of a society constituted by various groups, each with its own version of reality' (p. 171). The work celebrates difference but, in Strohm's argument, it is not anarchic, or ultimately conflictual. Rather, the text is 'conciliatory' (p. 172). In his reading of Chaucer, the text is almost endlessly accommodating to diversity: it imagines 'heterogeneity as a normal condition of civic life' (p. 182). This is a very different reading of the *Canterbury Tales* to Kendrick's interpretation of the text as conservative and hierarchical. Strohm discusses the monovocality of the Parson's treatise, and the Parson's aspiration to have the final and definitive word, but argues that the text resists such closure, and that the Parson's views must 'take their chances, among a multitude of contending conceptions' (p. 181). According to his reading of the *Tales*, the text is socially imaginative and potentially transformative. It presents, above all, a vision of social possibility, and refuses to inscribe carnival within a finally stable hierarchy.

Polyphony is also a central concern in John Ganim's *Chaucerian Theatricality*. Ganim emphasizes the centrality of quotation, dialogue, parody, and multiple voices in the *Tales*, and is particularly concerned with Bakhtin's theories of performance and language. He locates Bakhtinian concepts of carnival within and alongside other performative aspects of medieval culture, contrasting the imagery of civic processions with the imagery of carnival, and discussing the importance of both models in the first fragment of the *Tales*. Ganim suggests that the 'General Prologue' alludes to the city procession, but that the tales then degenerate/regenerate according to the modes of carnival.[13] *Chaucerian Theatricality* argues that the *Canterbury Tales* depicts marketplace theatricality, yoking carnival to other performance types, including the tournament and the mystery plays (p. 35). Ganim explores the deployment of the carnivalesque in the obviously subversive, festive tales, such as the Miller's, but he also looks in detail at the carnivalesque aspects of the ostensibly 'serious' tales such as the Clerk's. Ultimately, Ganim argues that Chaucer sometimes foregrounds, sometimes obscures, the power of the 'noise of the people', contending that Chaucer had an 'ambivalent and problematic relation to the power of popular discourse' (p. 120).

The *Parliament of Fowls*

This section will explore how ideas of the carnivalesque might inflect a reading of the *Parliament of Fowls*. The *Parliament of Fowls* is the *Canterbury Tales* writ small. Like the *Tales*, it is a profoundly polyphonic work, taking as a principal theme the idea of discursive variety. Both the *Parliament of Fowls* and the *Canterbury Tales* imitate—and mock—a late medieval institution (parliament, pilgrimage) and both texts set up hierarchies only to subvert them. Unlike the approaches of the critics discussed above, my reading will ultimately emphasize the conflictual dynamic of social forms in Chaucer's texts.

When the birds assemble, Nature 'Bad every foul to take his owne place' and she seats them according to their social standing, with the 'foules of ravyne' being 'hyest set' and 'foul that lyveth by sed sat on the grene' (*PF* 320–8). Nature is eager to enforce a sense of hierarchy, privileging the tercel eagle whose 'royal' nature she is careful to mention and who, she points out to the other birds, is 'above yow in degre' (393–4). She tells the birds that this most noble bird gets to choose first, and emphasizes that after him the others may choose 'by ordre' (400). The discourse of the royal tercel (416–41) is markedly courtly (like the discourse of the 'Knight's Tale'). He makes use of many of the classic tropes of courtly love: asserting that he will die without his love, begging for pity and mercy, emphasizing that his love is greater than anyone else's, speaking in hyperbolic terms about his feelings, using images of binding, and stressing the idea that his love is a kind of service. His courtliness is also revealed in the compliments that he pays to his lady, and in his deferral to her opinion: the first-person pronoun is delayed until the second line of his speech (417), and he makes it clear that he does not want to coerce her. The stress that he lays on his 'trouthe' (426) is characteristic of courtly lovers. His syntax is decidedly non-colloquial and formal: his first sentence lasts eight lines, and all of his sentences end with the end of the verse-line; his discourse is adapted to the formal verse structure.

Two other noble birds then assert their own undying love for the formel, and the three talk of their love all day. At this point, the people, represented by the other birds, can take it no more. Their voices burst into the text, and arrest the hierarchical proceedings:

> The noyse of foules for to ben delyvered
> So loude rong, 'Have don, and lat us wende!'
> That wel wende I the wode hadde al to-shyvered.
> 'Com of!' they criede, 'allas, ye wol us shende!
> Whan shal youre cursede pletynge have an ende?
> How sholde a juge eyther parti leve
> For ye or nay withouten any preve?'
>
> The goos, the cokkow, and the doke also
> So cryede, 'Kek kek! kokkow! quek quek!' hye,
> That thorugh myne eres the noyse wente tho.
> The goos seyde, 'Al this nys not worth a flye!
> But I can shape herof a remedie,
> And I wol seye my verdit fayre and swythe
> For water-foul, whose be wroth or blythe!' (491–504)

These stanzas are entirely different in tone from what has come before (and might remind readers of the Miller's interruption of the Knight in the *Tales*). 'Noyse' is twice repeated, as is 'cried'; the racket is so great that it seems that the wood might break apart; it rings out through the narrator's ears. The alliterating avian noises—'Kek kek! kokkow! quek quek!'—underline the bestiality of the speakers. The diction and syntax also reveal the informality and rudeness of these birds. Colloquial phrases such as 'cursede pletynge', the goose's proverbial 'Al this nys not worth a flye!', the abrupt imperatives 'Have don', 'Com of', and the short sentences that break up the flow of the verse, mark the 'low' character of these speakers and their form of speech. They represent the exuberant lower orders, rebelling against authority and attacking hierarchies; they refuse to submit to Nature's ordering of events, and insist upon their right to be heard. One of the most dazzling aspects of these stanzas is the mockery of legal discourses, reminiscent of Bakhtin's description of carnivalesque language parodying formal discourses. The lower birds use the formal discourse of judgement and law courts for their own ends, and to judge their social superiors. They point out that there is no 'preve' about who loves the formel best, they construct themselves as 'juge' of the situation, and the goose refers to a 'verdit'. The fact that these churlish birds assert their rights to sit in judgement on royalty completes the inversion of socio-political norms (while also aping the actual role of parliament, which did curb the king). Furthermore, the purport of what they say is far from meaningless 'noyse': it is hard to fault their common-sense assertion that it is impossible to know who loves the formel the best, or the assumption underlying their critique—that courtly love has little to do with actual mating.

Above all, this chaotic intrusion of multiple, competing voices highlights the polyphonic nature of the text. The speech of the highest-class birds is not allowed to be authoritative and the other birds do not have to speak according to the desire of the royal tercel. Instead, they create a space for expressing divergent opinions and insist that those opinions must be heard. The *Parliament* continues to stage a genuine debate, in which birds of different social levels are all allowed to give their views and judgements. While 'auctorite' was usually conferred by age, status, and fame, the lowly cuckoo calmly asserts,

> I wol of myn owene autorite,
> For comune spede, take on the charge now. (506–7)

The idea of finding authority in oneself, without need of external validation, is radical indeed. One of the central ideas in texts such as the *Parliament*, the *Canterbury Tales*, and the *House of Fame* is the importance of allowing diverse characters to speak and to express their views. Chaucer's texts are profoundly dialogic.

The vitality of the discourse of the lower-level birds continues to dominate the debate. The attitude expressed by these birds calls to mind Bakhtin's description of grotesque realism, earlier cited. He comments that the essence of this carnival form is 'the lowering of all that is high, spiritual, ideal, abstract . . . a transfer to the material level'. In the same way, the churlish birds attack the idea of courtly love, emphasizing instead the importance of immediate physical satisfaction, and ridiculing the abstract, idealizing tendencies of the courtly lovers' speeches. The common sense of the goose's advice 'But she wol love hym, lat hym love another!' (567) or of the duck's incredulous 'That men shulde loven alwey causeles! | Who can a resoun fynde or wit in that?' (590–1) contrasts markedly with the idealized, unworldly words of the courtly lovers who exclaim, 'God forbede a lovere shulde chaunge!' (582). These higher-class birds are dismissive of the discourse of the plebeian birds precisely because it is associated with physical needs. They stress the physicality of their 'inferiors' in their insults: the gentil tercelet associates their speech with the 'donghil' (597) and the merlin twice disparages the cuckoo by terming him a 'glotoun' (610, 613). The churlish birds are thus connected not only with sex, but also with excretion and overeating; their bodies are depicted as grotesquely functional.

The body is, as we have seen, central to the carnivalesque and its grotesque realism. The complaints that the goose and the duck make against the noble birds are grounded in their incomprehension of the idea of courtly love, with its emphasis on suffering and deferral, rather than immediate, easy pleasure. Mating is the whole purpose of the parliament, and the birds interrupt the eagle's formal debate because of an impatient desire to get on with the business of pairing off. The goose's insistence that if your chosen one will not love you, you should choose another mate, privileges bodily imperatives over spiritual or cerebral love. The image of these birds at the end of the poem, when they are full of 'blisse and joye' as they fold their partners in embraces and wind their necks together (669–71), is an exuberant celebration of the body, and fertility. The song that the birds then sing, with its refrain 'Now welcome, somer, with thy sonne softe' (680), stresses ideas of cyclical renewal and change that underline the importance of bodily, physical regeneration. This song, however, is a French roundel, originating in the country of courtly love, and in a form that emphasizes stasis by repeatedly returning to the same idea. It thus also represents the fate of the higher members of the social hierarchy in this poem: the competing eagles who do not find a mate, who do not procreate and regenerate, who—in contrast to the vibrant, vital 'people'—remain in a world in which satisfaction is deferred. The bleak conclusion for these birds throws into greater relief the success of the joyous churls, who can celebrate life and renewal with their mates. The stasis of the roundel reminds us, however, that social change has not been effected.

In my analysis of the *Parliament of Fowls* I have imagined the different birds in the poem in oppositional terms, representing the establishment, hierarchical forms, and order (the eagles *et al.*), versus the people, subversion, and carnivalesque freedom (the goose, the duck, *et al.*). It is also possible, however, to interpret the poem as a carnival within a carnival, locating the centre of stability outside the action of the poem itself. According to this reading, the behaviour of the aristocratic birds can itself be interpreted as carnivalesque. Chaucer's poem leads us into the world of the dream vision, a temporary other world of imaginative freedom reminiscent of carnival. The poem burlesques the central political institution of parliament, by imagining a parliament of birds, convened not for political purposes but for discussing personal matters of love, and by repeatedly using legal language to discuss love and mating.

The higher-class participants are aficionados of the code of courtly love. This cultural idea is itself playful in its essence. Describing the formal, courtly speeches of the three eagles, the narrator emphasizes the need for 'leyser' (487) to appreciate them. Courtly love is opposed to seriousness and work; it is for those who have endless time for leisured speech, and takes place in a temporary, artificial arena. The tropes of courtly love construct a 'world upside down', inverting the gender hierarchies that structure patriarchal society. The conventions of the courtly love genre, like many carnivalesque practices, place women on top: the lady is the powerful ruler who commands the abject, powerless male lover. In the royal tercel's speech to his lady, he terms her 'sovereyne' (422), treating her as his social superior, and as a god who can dispense mercy and grace (421). Such language is potentially subversive, challenging both the political and the ecclesiastical norms, by setting up a woman as king and god (the 'Merchant's Tale' provides an example of the blasphemous possibilities within courtly love, when January misuses the Song of Songs in the service of his own lust, 'MerT' 2138–48). At the end of the *Parliament*, however, the real world of male-dominated hierarchy reasserts itself, and we are reminded that courtly love is mere temporary play. Nature makes it clear that the lady (like Emelye in the 'Knight's Tale') cannot choose chastity, but must, after a year, submit to the laws of patriarchy and the forms of hierarchically ordered society by selecting her mate from among those who have chosen her. The formel acknowledges her subjection, commenting that she, like 'everich other creature', is 'evere under [Nature's] yerde' (640–1). In this context, carnival is put firmly in its place, as a brief reversal that should not threaten the status quo. This narrative dynamic is at odds with the lower-class birds' successful insertion of their voices and bodies into the discursive world of the text, which might suggest a more positive interpretation of the function of carnivalesque forms.

My own reading of the *Parliament* interprets the text as socially pessimistic. The roundel sung by the birds, coupled with the conventional awakening of the dreamer, which returns us to his position at the start of the poem, decisively closes the poem on a note not of change but of stasis. As the roundel is sung to Nature, this ending associates that figure herself with 'unnatural' sterility. No birds have changed their opinions during the lively debate, and speech has not had the power to persuade, to alter perspectives, or to effect change. The creatures do not exist, however, in a controlled hierarchy; rather the birds' ability to assert themselves, and their overt antagonism towards each other, suggest that the society depicted is riven with faction, discord, and fragmentation. These birds represent neither powerful, community-based popular culture, as Bakhtin might have it, nor the controlled, puppet-like lower classes that some of his critics imagine. Society is portrayed as an essentially conflicted locus, torn apart by self-interest and aggressive instincts that cannot be tamed or altered. Although the eagles agree to submit to authority, and to defer the female's decision for a year, this does not represent a taming of instinct, as they are driven not by sexual desire but by the sterile aesthetic of courtly love, which privileges deferral and elaborate longing over consummation. Moreover, the sexual desire which drives some of the other birds is not presented as something joyful in this poem, and the body is not a positive emblem: the temple of Venus is decorated with images of unhappy lovers (285–94), many of whom were famous for their incest, betrayals, or miserable fates. Chaucer even altered his source to replace Cupid's associates Comeliness and Affability with Lust and Pleasaunce (218–19). Nature, of course, is not Venus, but this early description of the unpalatable characteristics of sexual desire undermines Nature's rule over love, suggesting that Nature itself may be aberrant and destructive. The depiction of mating and love in the poem is dark and pessimistic.

Finally, modern readers should not forget that all of the discourses in the poem appealed to the higher echelons of society, the only people who would have had access to poetry and to manuscript culture. Fabliau, represented by the 'churlish' birds, like romance, represented by the 'gentil' birds, was a genre read and understood by the more privileged elements of society, and 'the people' had little chance of participating in a textual world. It is practically impossible to find strands of literary culture that were genuinely 'low' in this period.

Reading Bakhtin and Chaucer in the twenty-first century

We are all products of our historical moment, and reading Bakhtin in a capitalist country in the twenty-first century is a very different experience from reading Bakhtin in the mid-twentieth century in the Soviet Union. Many aspects of Bakhtin's thought speak directly to his own time, and his work has sometimes been interpreted as a veiled critique of Stalinist society. Certainly, his idea of the common man and of popular culture is constructed against Gorky's idealization of the common man as Soviet hero, and Bakhtin's promotion of 'grotesque realism' functions in opposition to the state-promoted genre of 'socialist realism'. The historical specificity of texts does not, however, preclude their being of use in other periods; indeed one of the joys of literary study is the way in which the discipline continually renews itself as differently situated generations read texts in new ways, and find different meanings and signification in their subjects of study. Writing after the collapse of the Berlin Wall, looking back on a century in which social experiments repeatedly resorted to genocide or the culture of the gulag and ultimately collapsed, brought up in a generation whose social disaffection and atomization is a cause célèbre, I find it hard to sympathize either with Bakhtin's utopian vision of social community or with the concept of an all-controlling state. Unlike the majority of those who have written on Chaucer in the past, I cannot find a positive image of the social anywhere in Chaucer's texts. It is only in recent years that the possibility that Chaucer was not a social idealist (whether innovative or conservative) has been entertained.

Furthermore, our perception of the function and power of carnival is necessarily affected by its enactment in our own time. The development of May Day provides an example of the changing manifestations of carnival. In Chaucer's time May was constantly associated with pairing up, courtly love, and dancing (*PF* 130). Guillaume de Lorris and Jean de Meun's *Romance of the Rose*, the 'Knight's Tale', the 'Franklin's Tale', John Gower's *Confessio amantis*, and John Clanvowe's *Boke of Cupide* are just some of the poems that associate May and love. The *Floure and the Leafe* emphasizes that the courtly game of choosing the flower or the leaf (important in the F version of Chaucer's Prologue to the *Legend of Good Women*) was associated with May Day in particular, a festival connected with pagan fertility rites and the play of love (indeed, some critics have connected the *Parliament of Fowls* itself with May traditions, as it is unclear whether or not St Valentine's Day was celebrated in February at this time). In the nineteenth century, 1 May was co-opted for trade unions and workers' rights. It was reconfigured as International Workers' Day, a day for celebrating workers' solidarity and staging protests for shorter working days. In the Soviet Union—Bakhtin's eulogies on free carnivalesque activities notwithstanding—the pre-eminent festival was the state-endorsed May Day, and the May Day parades, highly ordered and choreographed by the authorities, remain among the most enduring images of Stalin's regime. Ten years ago I might have written that May Day had run its course, and was relegated to the status of a minor festival. However, in the last few years it has been reclaimed, and is now the staging ground for demonstrations by anti-capitalist and anti-globalization protest groups. This re-emergence of May carnival might encourage a number of conclusions: one could dwell on the enduring importance of carnival, or on its continued impotence, as anti-capitalism demonstrations have done nothing tangible to check the advance of multinationals, exclusive trade agreements, and global branding. Yet it is difficult to judge the efficacy of carnival and protest without historical perspective, and the fact that we cannot know the long-term effects of such actions is a valuable lesson for readers of the past. The Peasants' Revolt, or the York mystery plays, look different with hindsight: cultural and political forms and events have diverse meanings at different times.

The examples of carnival that have been most striking in the last few months—I am writing in the summer of 2003—have served to suggest that it has little or no power to effect change. Who can forget, for example, the Iraqi dethronement of Baghdad's giant statue of Saddam Hussein in April, which was enabled by an American tank, and was immediately claimed for the authoritative superpower by a marine's enthusiastic draping of an American flag over the statue's head? It is hard to imagine a starker reminder of the control exerted over the actions of 'the people', who seemed merely to act out the desires of the new father figure, although their *intentions* probably had nothing to do with supporting American colonial ambitions. Moreover, the crowd at the statue were not necessarily representative of Iraqi society as a whole, which proved to be deeply divided in its attitudes and to be made up of groups with very different interests. It is difficult to fit such a moment of 'carnival' into any one theoretical model.

It is also crucial to note that carnival's symbolic efficacy may be more important than its immediate effect. Annual carnivals with a political message such as gay pride marches may not effect tangible change, but their symbolic social importance plays a vital social role. Such celebrations also mark the way in which carnival can now be enacted and used by relatively marginalized social groups (who in the past were often the target of abuse in 'carnival' activities such as charivari). This modern appropriation of carnival forms from a generic mass of people for the use of minorities changes the cultural possibilities of carnival. This multiplication of carnival possibilities highlights something that has always been important in carnival and rebellion, and that we can detect in events such as the Peasants' Revolt or Chaucer's pilgrimage: participants in carnival are individuals who use the carnivalesque for varied motives. Carnival reveals the tensions and differences within society, and reminds participants and spectators of the impossibility of social wholeness or unity by creating a locus in which varying points of view can be imagined. It provides a site for multiple voices to speak and for that heteroglossia so valued by Chaucer to be revealed—without suggesting that true change or transformation can be effected.

FURTHER READING

Bakhtin, Mikhail, *Problems of Dostoyevsky's Poetics*, ed. and trans. Caryl Emerson, introd. Wayne C. Booth (Manchester: Manchester University Press, 1984). Particularly useful for understanding Bakhtin's ideas about genre, language, and polyphony, and contains substantial sections on carnival.

Bakhtin, Mikhail, *Rabelais and his World*, trans. Hélène Iswolsky (Bloomington: Indiana University Press, 1984). Bakhtin's seminal text on carnival uses Rabelais's sixteenth-century work *Gargantua and Pantagruel* as a lens for exploring the carnivalesque. This book provided a starting point for much discussion of the carnivalesque in the twentieth century.

Camille, Michael, *Image on the Edge: The Margins of Medieval Art* (London: Reaktion, 1992). Packed with illustrations, *Image on the Edge* discusses marginalia, and the subversive, world-upside-down aspects of much medieval art.

Davis, Natalie Zemon, 'Women on Top: Symbolic Sexual Inversion and Political Disorder in Early Modern Europe', in Barbara A. Babcock (ed.), *The Reversible World: Symbolic Inversion in Art and Society* (Ithaca, NY: Cornell University Press, 1978), 147–90. Good general discussion of gender inversion in early modern festivals, art, and literature.

Ganim, John M., *Chaucerian Theatricality* (Princeton: Princeton University Press, 1990). One of the best deployments of Bakhtinian ideas by a Chaucer critic. Uses Bakhtin selectively and critically.

Kendrick, Laura, *Chaucerian Play: Comedy and Control in the 'Canterbury Tales'* (Berkeley: University of California Press, 1988). Interprets the *Canterbury Tales* as a carnival text, which finally emphasizes the power of the establishment and the temporary release of carnival.

Minnis, Alastair, *Oxford Guides to Chaucer: The Shorter Poems* (Oxford: Clarendon Press, 1995). The best introduction to Chaucer's shorter poems, this is the ideal place to start to find out more about the *Parliament of Fowls*.

Stallybrass, Peter, and Allon White, *The Politics and Poetics of Transgression* (London: Methuen, 1986). Deals with post-medieval texts, but provides an important reading of Bakhtin useful for students interested in any period.

Strohm, Paul, *Hochon's Arrow: The Social Imagination of Fourteenth-Century Texts* (Princeton: Princeton University Press, 1992). Examines texts by Chaucer and his contemporaries, and uses Bakhtinian ideas, particularly in analysing accounts of the Peasants' Revolt. Strohm's idea of the 'textual environment' is influenced by the Bakhtinian concept of heteroglossia.

Strohm, Paul, *Social Chaucer* (Cambridge, Mass.: Harvard University Press, 1989). One of the most significant recent works of Chaucer criticism, this influential book deploys Bakhtinian theories, especially ideas of polyphony and heteroglossia, to talk about Chaucer's poetry.

NOTES

1. See Miri Rubin, *Corpus Christi: The Eucharist in Late Medieval Culture* (Cambridge: Cambridge University Press, 1991), 345–6; Michael Camille, *Image on the Edge: The Margins of Medieval Art* (London: Reaktion, 1992); Walter Clifford Mellor, *The Boy Bishop and Other Essays on Forgotten Customs and Beliefs of the Past* (London: G. Bell, 1923); Sandra Billington, *Mock Kings in Medieval Society and Renaissance Drama* (Oxford: Clarendon Press, 1991), esp. 30–54.

2. Mikhail Bakhtin, *Rabelais and his World*, trans. Hélène Iswolsky (Bloomington: Indiana University Press, 1984), 4.

3. Ibid. 8–10.

4. Ibid. 19–20.

5. Mikhail Bakhtin, *Discourse in the Novel*, in his *The Dialogic Imagination*, ed. Michael Holquist, trans. Caryl Emerson and Michael Holquist (Austin: University of Texas Press, 1981), 324–5. For heteroglossia, see pp. 263, 428.

6. Peter Stallybrass and Allon White, *The Politics and Poetics of Transgression* (London: Methuen, 1986), 19.

7. See Marshall Laird, *English Misericords* (London: John Murray, 1986), 26, and G. L. Remnant, *A Catalogue of Misericords in Great Britain* (Oxford: Clarendon Press, 1969), 98.

8. *The Westminster Chronicle: 1381–1394*, ed. L. C. Hector and Barbara F. Harvey (Oxford: Clarendon Press, 1982), 2.

9. Paul Strohm, *Hochon's Arrow: The Social Imagination of Fourteenth-Century Texts* (Princeton: Princeton University Press, 1992), 49.

10. Thorpe's text is printed in Matthew Boyd Goldie, *Middle English Literature: A Historical Sourcebook* (Oxford: Blackwell, 2003), 33–7.

11. Laura Kendrick, *Chaucerian Play: Comedy and Control in the 'Canterbury Tales'* (Berkeley: University of California Press, 1988), 111.

12. Paul Strohm, *Social Chaucer* (Cambridge, Mass.: Harvard University Press, 1989), p. xiii.

13. John M. Ganim, *Chaucerian Theatricality* (Princeton: Princeton University Press, 1990), 34.

23 | Postmodernism

Barry Windeatt

And I come after, glenyng here and there.

(LGW (F) 75)

Cultural belatedness: Chaucer's postmodernity

Postmodernism, as its name implies, defines itself by its cultural 'belatedness'. Of its essence, postmodernism is subsequent to prior developments and innovations, just as Chaucer's own cultural moment also enables him to seize the poetic opportunities of both belatedness and innovation. As a poet in the England of his time, Chaucer could think of himself as succeeding to a sophisticated modernity: the world of Latin learning, and of French and Anglo-French courtly culture. Yet circumstances allowed Chaucer to articulate an established culture in a new voice and from new perspectives: to write with all the accumulated assurance of mature tradition in a vernacular language, English, that was newly being used again for higher purposes. This is Chaucer's own postmodernity, as also is his medieval author's tendency to turn to 'olde bokes' for his subject matter and openly to represent himself as so doing, even where he is not. To these forms of belatedness our postmodern condition may offer an informing correlative in reading his works. Chaucer was unique in his cultural moment and has been unique in his posterity, the subject of a continuous tradition of commentary over six centuries of subsequent English literature. To review those centuries of reception of Chaucer, and to observe how succeeding ages marvel complacently that Chaucer has achieved so much of what each age prefers, is to be reminded of just how much the postmodern present will colour the way Chaucer is read now. If this helps guard against the condescension of claiming Chaucer as some harbinger of postmodernism, it can also question the focus of current readings of Chaucer, not so much to set postmodernism aside as to explore how far it may inform understanding of Chaucer's accomplishments.

A postmodern perspective on Chaucer may be all or anything that a theoretically informed contemporary view might draw upon, for postmodernism understands itself to subsume and supersede any preceding theories and '-isms'. This may explain why there is a rather small corpus of professedly postmodern criticism of Chaucer, although postmodern ideas and practice have had a wide if diffused impact on Chaucer criticism and underlie many feminist and poststructuralist readings of his work.[1] Even so, does the very periodicity of postmodernism limit its application to Chaucer? What could be the relevance to Chaucer of postmodernism's preoccupation with its own succession to modernism, or its implication in the uniquely modern mass media of this post-industrial age? In practice, postmodernism's reconceptualization of the boundaries of art and culture in the present have lent modern readers new modes of reading and idioms for critical discourse that can defamiliarize not only what is characteristic about Chaucer's fourteenth-century work, but also those nineteenth- and twentieth-century constructions of the Middle Ages in their own image, through which Chaucer has so often been read.[2]

Chaucer and the themes of postmodernism

Postmodernism dismisses as superseded any totalizing and legitimizing cultural meta-narratives and myths (the *grand récits* of Jean-François Lyotard, influential theorist of the postmodern). It might seem therefore that nothing could have less application to medieval Christendom than postmodernism.[3] This is to adopt a certain view of the Middle Ages—that view itself a defining myth of the post-medieval world—that of all periods the medieval is most circumscribed by its all-explaining meta-narrative of Christian faith and dogma. Yet, seen in a postmodern light, who could be more evasive than Chaucer towards the *grands récits* of his culture? Taken as a whole, his work is not exactly in the service of reaffirming Christian orthodoxy. Although Chaucer could hardly ignore material from clerical culture, he does not write as if from within that culture and shows no significant engagement with the allegorical mode so pervasive in medieval writing. Such disengagement will seem less surprising to today's readers, conditioned by postmodernism to regard as superseded the hermeneutic binary models of depth-as-against-surface, hidden-as-against-revealed, latent versus explicit (in which one term is posited as dominant and hence in the position of meta-narrative). Written within a more postmodern awareness, some recent criticism resists the anachronistic twentieth-century determination to discover ironies everywhere in Chaucer's poetry. Irony has been invoked too often to resolve every instance of unevenness and disjunction which, although disconcerting to modern readers, is more likely to reflect a late Gothic style of busy ornamentation and an exultancy in surfaces and patterning. For some readers of Chaucer in the postmodern present, there will also be illuminating parallels between postmodern scepticism about the possibility of anything eternal or immutable and Chaucer's marked imaginative engagement with change as both theme and form. Throughout the twentieth century his storyteller's fascination with causation and free will tempted critics to claim him to be a sceptic at heart (this being modern, and hence good). Not that Chaucer's avoidance of the medieval *grands récits* is confined to the religious, for he is strikingly unengaged with the great Arthurian narrative cycles and, more generally, his comic sense keeps him coolly detached from the whole romance project both in subject and in form.

For today's reader, Chaucer's oblique approach to the serious will seem more postmodern than modernist. The very plausibility of seriousness itself has been eroded by the intrinsic playfulness of postmodernism, for the postmodern cannot keep a straight face and is essentially insubordinate and parodic. Modernism's solemn and pessimistic sense of tragic individualism has modified into postmodernism's wry resignation to disempowerment in a globalized, consumerist environment of modern media and communications. That lack of 'high seriousness' in Chaucer regretted by the Victorian critic Matthew Arnold can now be seen not so much as some feckless failure in Chaucer's proper moral development as a poet, than as designedly his way of observing a world.[4] It is a world where individuals are powerless and passive within experience that is more pitiable and plangent than tragic, or even as blankly amoral as the brutally unillusioned 'comic' tales. Without a postmodern perspective, past assessments of Chaucer's seriousness have been disconcerted unnecessarily by tonal juxtapositions. Flippancy may seem to follow fast on the heels of lofty rhetoric and 'punctures' it (but by which period's sense of literary decorum?). What may seem a comically excessive high style (but how is 'excess' to be judged?) sits quirkily in an apparently inappropriate context. Little of such juxtaposition is so distant from the postmodern present. Deriving from its sense of the disappearance of the unified subject or individual character comes postmodernism's view that unique and personal styles are no longer available or inventable. Instead, there can be only a cannibalization and medley of past styles, in what is quintessentially pastiche and the eclectic, destabilizing all boundaries and distinctions between high and mass culture. Such a postmodern aesthetic, defined by the delimitations of coming after prior cultural developments, offers parallels and contrasts with what Chaucer makes stylistically of his own position. Endlessly puzzling challenges to interpretation are prompted by Chaucer's eclectic enlistments of stylistic varieties within his poems, which juxtapose learned allusion or neologism with echoes from the pulp fiction of the medieval popular romances.

Postmodernism views the world as entirely textualized, and Chaucer's familiar self-fiction of the author within his works as a definingly bookish figure comes into sharper focus from such a postmodern perspective. The Prologue to the *Legend of Good Women* opens by insisting how much of any individual's world is textualized (F 4–28), for in so far as no one can test everything against 'experience', our awareness is informed and defined by a culture of texts (F 27–8), and there is nothing that cannot but be textual, as the 'Wife of Bath's Prologue' suggests. With its emphasis on textualization, postmodernism claims that there can be no representation of reality, no mimesis, because there is no extra-fictional reality outside of texts to be represented. To compare Chaucer's methods with such an approach can remind his (post)modern readers how much his work reinterprets earlier texts, and how little of his creative ambition would have been engaged by anything akin to the endeavours of novelists or dramatists in a realist tradition to create 'lifelike' characters in 'realistic' situations.[5] From postmodernism's textualized perspective, traditional possibilities for representation of unified and developing 'character' and 'plot' are dissolved into an acceptance that such can be no more than questions of perception. Nor, in a characterless and plotless postmodern universe, is history available to bring the past's perspective to bear on the present, since for postmodernism there can be no historical reality, only a sense of historiography, of how 'pasts' are constructed by their interpreters.[6] Such is a useful correlative to Chaucer's own alertness to historical difference as imaginative parallel rather than as alternative actuality.

Chaucer and postmodernist forms

Postmodernist readings of form and style reflect postmodernism's own anti-interpretation of the human condition as resistant to interpretation. There is an open-ness to multiple perspectives, 'pluriformity', and relativism. This in turn has been echoed in many later twentieth-century readings of a Chaucer construed as ambivalent and equivocal, typically working through the multiple voices accorded by framed tales and unreliable narrators. Postmodernism contests notions of 'totality', 'unity', and the unitary in texts. This has emboldened Chaucer criticism—sometimes through parallels with the medieval visual arts—to revise earlier, essentially post-Romantic judgements of what integrates Chaucer's poems and how effectively.[7] From a postmodernist view of the subject as essentially fragmented (rather than alienated, as in modernism) comes interrogation of notions of completeness, which has been very pertinent in the post-modern reception of Chaucer. The list of Chaucer's uncompleted works might include: *Anelida and Arcite*; the *Legend of Good Women* as a series, and the last legend of Hypermnestra as a unit within that series; an anticipated later part of the *Treatise on the Astrolabe* was not executed; only the first fragment of the *Romaunt of the Rose* is con-vincingly attributed to Chaucer; the *Canterbury Tales* was left as some ten 'Fragments', interlinked within themselves but unassembled with each other as a larger sequential whole, while some tales (of the Cook and the Squire) are apparently uncompleted. To reconsider what constitutes a fragment or the fragmentary, as against a 'whole', can be to reclaim a significant aspect of Chaucer's œuvre, for the brief narrative and the fragment are the norm of what he worked with, and left. If it is the *Book of the Duchess*, *Parliament of Fowls*, *Troilus and Criseyde*, the *Boece* translation, and most of the extant *Canterbury Tales* and its link passages that Chaucer brought to completion, it is the brief span of many of these works that is notable, with the obvious exceptions of *Troilus*, *Boece*, and the 'Knight's Tale' (although the latter is much abbreviated from Boccaccio).

Chaucer is a poet of beginnings (of prologues, introductions, and story openings) more than of endings; he is a narrative poet who finds it easier to start than to con-clude, perhaps because his additions to his sources generate more questions than he can contrive to find answers for. Authority figures—like Duke Theseus in the 'Knight's Tale' or Dame Nature in the *Parliament of Fowls*—attempt qualified or postponed resolutions. *Anelida* and the 'Squire's Tale' move from epic or romance narrative into female complaint, for which there seems little available consolation or an obvious point to stop. Yet although Chaucer has left many ostensibly incomplete works, whether some actually are uncompleted remains a puzzle for interpretation, so that the very concepts of completion and completeness become problematic. If there is room for tales interrupted and truncated because unendurably bad or monotonous ('Sir Thopas', the 'Monk's Tale'), there is also room for uncertainty as to whether the Franklin's words to the Squire were to constitute an interruption of the Squire's incomplete tale. If the fragmentary 'Cook's Tale' stops dead at such a provocative line (4422), Chaucer perhaps planned to have it interrupted: a tale that could only go as far as a censored fragment. A very much larger fragment (if indeed it is one), the *House of Fame* is usually labelled 'unfinished' in modern editions, because it breaks off just as an unnamed 'man of gret auctorite' is arriving on the scene, although Chaucer perhaps preferred his poem to foreshadow tantalizingly the man's contribution, but to fade out before specifying it. Although Chaucer models aspects of his dream poems on the courtly disputations in the poems of his older French contemporary Guillaume de Machaut, he shows less interest in imitating the arbitrations by grand personages that provide the conclusions to these French poems, just as in his borrowings from Boethius it is the questions and paradoxes, not the answers, that fuel Chaucer's inventiveness.

Postmodernism's scepticism about the possibility of closure has found an echo, to modern perceptions, in the difficulties both formal and thematic that Chaucer experienced in bringing to a close not only his apparently fragmentary works but also those poems that have a conclusion. Pandarus repeats a very old commonplace in declaring 'th'ende is every tales strengthe' (*TC* 2. 260), but the very strength of Chaucer's realization of his narratives often makes the ending not so much a weakness as a challenge. Postmodern readers are well placed to see that Chaucer's endings are symptomatic of how much more engaged he is by series and sequences than by decisive or rounded conclusions. If the dream poems appear to stop rather than conclude, this only underlines their internal momentum as a series of dreamscape interiors, outdoor scenes, and tableaux, through which the dreaming 'I/eye' of the narrative persona moves successively. In these poems a liking for lists is one pointer to a larger structuring disposition to the series as an organizing principle of the works as a whole. To the postmodern reader, the dream poems can parallel some of the technique and effect of montage in film, accumulating meaning through the visualizing medium of scenes and images coordinated by juxtaposition, cutting, and transition. Montage can also offer a meaningful correlative for the seemingly disconcerting series that is the *Legend of Good Women*, in which murderesses of their children like Medea and Philomela are set alongside Lucretia, and Cleopatra is lined up with Dido, or even the hapless girl Thisbe, in a compendium or legendary of 'good' women. The strange omissions and skewings of focus, the quirkily 'inappropriate' flashes of flippancy, and the intrusive cutting effected by an ostentatious concern to abbreviate, have often been interpreted as tokens of Chaucer's weariness with the whole project of a series. Yet, for the postmodern reader, the provocative selection of material and the challenging disjunction within the series make it one of Chaucer's most experimental fragments, not least in the reshuffling of sequences that marks his revision between the Prologue's two surviving versions. The Prologue's convenient fiction that this project's theme has been imposed on its writer as a punishment makes a joke of its own belated moment in a sequence of what has already been written, by Chaucer and others. It is an enabling ruse that in practice allows Chaucer wide thematic and formal latitude under the pretence of dutifully conforming with a difficult subject not of his choosing.

From a postmodern perspective, what was once viewed as on the margins, hence marginal, can be turned inside out and become 'ex-centric', less to displace what is 'central' (for where is the centre now?) than to explode any such priorities and categorization. The *Legend* challenges readers to rethink what constitutes the centre in these narratives. More widely in his work, Chaucer's choice of focus unsettles what was previously central to the story. In his realization of the inward life of Criseyde, Chaucer radically revises what was previously central or marginal to every aspect of that narrative, all the while casting himself as merely the slavishly close translator of a source and in no sense an original creative artist. Such a self-consciousness in his poems about the compositional process, whereby the scaffolding remains part of the constructed edifice, lends Chaucer's poems a reflexiveness redolent of the postmodern emphasis on performativity. Chaucer's self-fictionalization evidently proved its worth to him as a stratagem: he keeps on recycling aspects of it from the early *Book of the Duchess* to his last self-characterization in the frame to the *Canterbury Tales*. Throughout, the author casts himself as a humble dullard and ineffectual poet, marginalized within his own creation by the stronger characters with whom he has peopled his imaginative world. As a self-projection, this resembles some wry postmodern revision of that still-influential post-Romantic form: the 'biography of the great artist'. Here, however, the expected profile of progress and development has become something more fragmented and discontinuous. At once endearingly self-effacing yet artfully enabling, Chaucer's self-fictionalization strikes a particular chord with readers acclimatized to postmodern assumptions that artistic originality or individual genius are no longer possible, and have given way to an art that can only recombine past elements in an age of multiple mechanical reproduction. Yet, in practice, there are illuminating parallels between the ways that Chaucer and postmodern artists get on with being original and individual, by means of artistic interventions that can indeed make something new by recombining past elements.[8] Not least, Chaucer achieves this through his adaptive combinations of borrowed, rewritten, and invented materials, of which the Merchant's, Nun's Priest's, and Pardoner's Tales are among his boldest conjoinings.

For postmodern readers, it is the self-reflexiveness of Chaucer's writing that has made his work seem to anticipate modern theoretical concerns. Recent reception of Chaucer's dream poems, including the *Legend* Prologue, has emphasized their metafictional identity. As fiction about fiction, the dream poems may be read as the poet in search of a subject. Such poems fictionalize the play of intertextuality, where the dreaming poet—removed from normal waking consciousness—finds inspiration through imaginative interaction with his reading of other literature, and so composes the new poem that the reader now reads. Interpreted in this vein, the dream poems have contributed to a greater emphasis on Chaucer's self-reflexiveness, and to comparisons with postmodernism's collapsing of traditional distinctions between critic and artist, theory and practice.[9] The contemporary emergence of the artist–theorist, or theorist–artist, provides a postmodern correlative through which to explore the inventiveness of Chaucer's reflexive and experimental modes. Moreover, this postmodern erasure of earlier boundaries between artist and critic has eroded the critics' traditional authority over the text, disempowering their claim to unlock texts with the keys provided by particular critical schools and agendas. Hence the hostility shown by historically minded critics to postmodernism's ahistorical stance and the supposed depthlessness of pastiche. Hence the righteous indignation of politically minded critics at what is represented as postmodernism's kitsch trivializing, its ethical blankness and unconcern for social dimensions. For the reading of Chaucer, however, such a postmodern revision of critical authority is peculiarly in keeping with his poems' resistance to any monolithic interpretation, through their signals that an openness to any number of critical possibilities is inseparably part of the poem.

Magic, or realism, or magical realism?

At the beginning of the Squire's uncompleted tale, a mysterious stranger presents to the court of Tartary four magical objects: a steed of brass to transport its rider at will to any destination; a magic mirror and sword (of which more later); and a ring that gives its owner the power to understand the utterance of the birds (110–67). This is the stuff of romance, but for the postmodern reader a correlative suggests itself between many of Chaucer's narratives and the techniques of modern magic realism, where essentially naturalistic fictions may embrace fantastic, non-naturalistic elements. Canacee, the heroine of the 'Squire's Tale', uses the ring and overhears a female falcon's lament, but what is striking elsewhere in Chaucer's poems (*House of Fame, Parliament of Fowls*, 'Nun's Priest's Tale', 'Manciple's Tale') is that no magic device is needed for the narrator to understand the language of birds. Indeed, one of Chaucer's short poems, the 'Complaint of Mars', is declaimed to the poet by a bird (the reason is never given), and although the steed of brass can carry its rider 'to fleen as hye in the air | As dooth an egle' ('SqT' 122–3), the poet figure of the *House of Fame* needs only to enter the magic realism of his dream-life to have the same experience. The 'Squire's Tale' may not progress much past the beginning of a romance because it is the interaction of naturalism with fantasy that is more characteristic of Chaucer's imagination than a romance with magic props and contraptions.

The postmodern reader of magic realism has an advantage in approaching Chaucer's retelling, in the 'Man of Law's Tale', of the traditional tale of the twice-unwelcome daughter-in-law, expelled from their lives by not one but two murderous mothers-in-law, who have their son's alien wife cast adrift on the high seas. Chaucer derives his poem from an episode in Nicholas Trevet's chronicle history of England, written in Anglo-French prose. Here Chaucer found the story of a quasi-allegorical heroine, the Roman emperor's daughter Constance, whose conduct allows her to represent an embodiment of constancy in an age of miracles during the early history of Britain. By making a free-standing narrative from an episode within his source, and by making it a tale told by a lawyer, Chaucer at once poses questions about the generic identity of his material, which must establish itself to readers on its own terms. Although Chaucer maintains the storyline of his source, approximately half of his tale is given over to commentary on the narrative events, partly influenced by Chaucer's work on his now lost translation of Pope Innocent III's *De miseria condicionis humane* ('On the Wretchedness of the Human Condition'). Such an added commentary—in the form of apostrophes, prayers, and rhetorical questions interpolated into the narrative—recurrently confronts readers with what cannot be explained in a legendary story. Thus, Trevet's chronicle notes carefully (if implausibly) that at her two castings adrift Constance's boat was provisioned in advance for voyages of three and five years, which prove to be the precise duration of her wanderings. By contrast, the 'Man of Law's Tale' marks these junctures with an ostentatious flurry of rhetorical questions that equates Custance's survival with that of Daniel in the lions' den, Jonah in the whale, and St Mary of Egypt, who lived as a hermit in the desert (470–501). How Custance is sustained at sea is aligned with Christ's miracle in feeding the five thousand (502–3), and to question how she evades a rapist during her second sea journey is likened to questioning how David overcame Goliath, or how Judith slew Holofernes (932–45), both Old Testament examples of virtue triumphant over force. The effect of combining narrative with commentary upon it is to insist over and again that what is miraculous must be accepted as such and cannot be explained (470). Custance cannot evade a trumped-up murder charge unless Christ openly performs a miracle (636); before her second casting adrift she puts her faith in Christ to save her but accepts that it is beyond any human understanding ('He kan me kepe from harm . . . | . . . althogh I se noght how', 829–30). Yet if good triumphs beyond understanding, so does evil: rather than accounting for the singular wickedness of the two mothers-in-law the commentary's apostrophes fall back on misogynistic archetypes and find the women's malice beyond expression ('I ne have noon Englissh digne | Unto thy malice', 778–9). More largely, although our fates may be written in the stars, neither the Sultan's fate nor Custance's are avoided, because human intelligence is too slow or too negligent to decode 'thilke large book' of the heavens (190, 315), and so explanation and understanding remain unavailable.

Yet while Chaucer retells what could be a saint's life in a voice that prominently insists on the story's miraculous nature, he also includes an imaginative identification with the sufferings of his heroine. In a tale where event and motive are the stuff of legend, Chaucer has portrayed a sentient heroine whose faith and duty can include some tender expression of feeling—as in her prayerful 'exit aria' (826–61)—as well as a keen sense, actually misplaced, of her husband's cruelty as it appears to her. The overall effect is intriguingly strained, as if Chaucer has set out to make a strange tale stranger. Why should the Roman emperor send his only child and heir away to be married to an unknown Muslim? In some versions of this tale the daughter accepts marriage in order to escape her widowed father's incestuous interest in her. Chaucer elides this, yet the 'Man of Law's Introduction' protests (too much?) that incest is never a theme of Chaucer's (77–89), before his tale of two husbandless mothers who wish their son's wife dead. Why does Chaucer's Custance not reveal her imperial rank and identity in Northumberland (where her mother-in-law resents her son's marriage to this refugee woman of unknown lineage)? Why does she not identify herself when returned to Rome and living unrecognized for years in the house of her own aunt? Why does Chaucer reverse the incest theme by his rewriting of the end of the tale, so that its emotional climax is not so much the heroine's reunion with her husband as the pathetic scene in which Custance falls at her father's feet begging him not to send her away again among heathens? In the Man of Law's telling, the tale becomes a bleak parable of the soul's solitariness, alone with God in this world, as reflected in Custance's hermetic self-containment. True to God and herself, Custance passes on life's voyage through a world variously exclaimed upon as beyond understanding and full of the miseries of the human condition, such as drunkenness and poverty. Not that our own appraisal of the tale-teller's prominent commentary on the tale—including distaste for poverty, his clumsy remarks on married women's obligations to their husbands, his snobberies (99–130, 708–14, 1086–92)—can be other than part of the whole. In a small but telling touch, the allegorical figure of Constance in the source is renamed Custance in Chaucer's version, for her conduct is evidently not now confined to interpretation in allegorical terms.

Chaucer seems incapable of presenting an unbelievable character, not because he is always a naturalistic writer but because what appears most naturalistic in his writing is its unerring truth to identifiably human feeling, instinct, and observation. This is often despite his borrowed stories' fantastic situations and legendary settings, or perhaps because of them. That Custance lives in an age of miracles allows for her to survive ordeals extreme and horrifying beyond any limitations of the merely realistic. Yet at the centre of this narrative is no steely saint but a sentient, suffering woman, and the interface between the miraculous and the human prompts a highly self-reflexive narrative. In Chaucer's practice here and elsewhere there is much to prompt the postmodern reader to comparisons with magic realism, for in the sense that so many of his tales represent varieties of nightmare for those within them, Chaucer is everywhere a dream poet and not simply in his four 'dream poems'. The *Canterbury Tales* includes nightmarish narratives of how an obsessive husband (in the 'Clerk's Tale') tests his wife's obedience to him by apparently having their children serially murdered; how a happily married husband (in the 'Franklin's Tale') sends his wife to another man who is obsessed with her, rather than have her break a rash promise to that man; or how a father feels entitled to behead his young daughter rather than let a crooked judge kidnap and rape her (in the 'Physician's Tale'). The *Canterbury Tales* makes room for the licensed magic of fable (talking chickens, fox, and crow in the 'Nun's Priest's Tale' and 'Manciple's Tale'). There is also the sacred magic of saints' lives and miracles (a child murder-victim's corpse carries on singing lustily until it is discovered in the 'Prioress's Tale'). As a rule, in medieval fables and saints' lives, magic remains in its customary generic compartments. Chaucer's boldness lies in juxtaposing magic and fantasy with his own version of realism through truth to human feeling, in ways that explore more than they resolve some of the most disturbing tensions in human life: a wrinkly old lady, who has outsmarted a callow toyboy into a shotgun wedding, can turn herself into a young woman again (in the 'Wife of Bath's Tale'); Pluto, god of the underworld, enables a blind old man to see his young wife's flagrant adultery (in the 'Merchant's Tale'), but Pluto's wife, Proserpina, whom he originally abducted, gives the guilty young wife the wit to persuade her husband not to believe his own eyes; two former friends (in the 'Knight's Tale') spend untold years in a rivalry to the death over a girl who is entirely unaware of them, since neither ever gets an opportunity to declare himself to her.

Post-romance

His spirit chaunged hous and wente ther,
As I cam nevere, I kan nat tellen wher.
Therfore I stynte; I nam no divinistre;
Of soules fynde I nat in this registre,
Ne me ne list thilke opinions to telle
Of hem, though that they writen wher they dwelle.

('KT' 2809–14)

The magic sword in the 'Squire's Tale'—that can pierce any armour and inflicts a wound that may only be healed by a touch of the same blade—is an emblem of romance's marvellous power of second chances: to follow hurt with healing, to reverse and redress all that has gone amiss. In the 'Knight's Tale'—where a wound does not heal and magical redress is unavailable—Chaucer makes romance venture beyond itself, into unfamiliar terrain. Chaucer derives his tale from Boccaccio's Italian narrative poem *Il Teseida delle nozze d'Emilia* ('The Story of Theseus concerning the Nuptials of Emilia'). This, as its title suggests, attempts to meld a romance-type narrative of love with the epic career of Theseus, against the background of ancient Thebes and its woes. Tensions between romance and epic history in Boccaccio's uneasy generic hybrid have prompted Chaucer, through a critique of the idealization of romance and its stylization, to arrive at a stage of post-romance in both form and theme.[10]

Now that postmodernism has blurred and destabilized generic boundaries and definitions, today's readers are well placed to appreciate that Chaucer makes the problem of how to read a text into part of the process of reading it. Chaucer's mode of postmodernity in the 'Knight's Tale' is to reconfigure his source into an almost diagrammatic pattern of contrasting extremes. In the *Teseida* two Theban prisoners of war, Palemone and Arcita, kept by the Athenian ruler Teseo under a permanent house arrest befitting their rank, fall in love with Emilia when they glimpse her in a garden; by enquiries they discover her identity. For her part, Emilia is not unaware of their feelings for her. In the 'Knight's Tale' Palamon and Arcite are pent up in a thick-walled prison tower, juxtaposed with the delightful garden where Emelye gathers May flowers. When first Palamon and then Arcite catch sight of Emelye through the iron-barred window of their prison, it is only Palamon who wonders whether Emelye is a goddess or woman, and the 'Knight's Tale' never mentions how they discover her identity. Boccaccio's Palemone and Arcita are equally unsure whether Emilia is a goddess and for some while behave like comrades in a shared affliction. Once smitten with love, Chaucer's Palamon and Arcite quarrel immediately: all former bonds of sworn brotherhood are dissolved into competitive enmity, and Arcite derides Palamon for his idealizing ('KT' 1158–9). In the *Teseida* it is only at their encounter in the grove, after each lover unsuccessfully asks the other to give up his claim to Emilia, that Boccaccio's Palemone and Arcita finally quarrel and start fighting. By contrast, the meeting in the grove of Chaucer's two knights is their chosen opportunity to pursue with weapons the verbal duel that has sundered them from the instant they both fell in love. What Theseus will later call 'this foule prisoun of this lyf' (3061) is symbolized in the circumstances of the heroes, whose whole capacity to see the world is shaped by one heavily barred window. The unknowable identity of the girl who is the object of their passion, and her obliviousness (in Chaucer's version) of their love for her, are emblems of the uncertain relation between knowledge and desire as this constructs itself for an unknown, scarcely glimpsed image of idealized woman. This desire is all one way: Emelye's possible desire for them, or lack of it, is never part of the desire for her of Palamon and Arcite. Desire is uninformed, and brings less self-knowledge than selfishness, that will renege on all other obligations.

The nightmarish twist to romance in the 'Knight's Tale' is that the lover's self has a twin, a shadow and hence a rival—but there is only one lady. The conventional romance ending of winning the lady in marriage can only be attained, unconventionally, if this rivalrous shadow self is killed off. Through this twinned hero can be presented schematically something of the divided knightly self and its exclusive drives: erotic and idealizing, combative and competitive. Whether or not Palamon and Arcite differ as personalities is irrelevant in the world-view of a tale where individual human character can hardly make much difference. Not that Chaucer's Palamon and Arcite present mirror images of each other: their association with Venus and Mars, and with more passive and active dispositions respectively, is differentiated at the emblematic level on which the 'Knight's Tale' works. Chaucer's synchronizing of the rivals' quarrel with the instant they see Emelye brings their divided self into much sharper focus, for from that point the rival lovers are obsessed with excluding the other (1227–39, 1281–94). Their eventual duel is no romance-like joust between relatives or comrades who fail to recognize each other, but a willed fight to the death (1643–4). When Teseo discovers the rivals duelling in the *Teseida*, Arcita first wins an amnesty for both lovers and then leaves Palemone to identify himself (5. 83–90), but Chaucer alters this entirely (1714–41). His Palamon not only identifies himself but vindictively denounces Arcite; resigned to his own execution, Palamon's concern is that Arcite be killed too (presumably so as not to enjoy Emelye), and he seems resentful of Arcite's reinvention of himself in another identity, disguised as Philostrate.

If this incident has a nasty edge, it is because the 'Knight's Tale' does not unfold in that conventionally benign universe where the progress of romance educates and eventually rewards the well-meaning hero's aspirations. Here the lovers' frustrations move them to philosophical disquisitions—framed and expressed through recollections of Boethius—on an unjust world. This is also a romance world that is disconcertingly more crowded than usual. The twin heroes are not alone, pursuing their romance, to quest their way to their own salvation. The impasse which is their story must be resolved by an older man, and the comparison with Theseus diminishes Palamon and Arcite into subjects rather than agents. In their attempt to resolve their quarrel between themselves, unwitnessed and in isolation, they offend in going outside the rules of knightly society (1711–12). The resolution of their disagreement must be brought within society, witnessed and socialized, perhaps not least because it evidently cannot be resolved to the satisfaction of all parties. The lovers' personal and private rivalry becomes a political problem of governance for Theseus in his public exercise of authority and dispensation of justice. Although Boccaccio's *Teseida* devotes many more lines to the figure of Teseo, the effect of Chaucer's radical condensation is to create a more dynamic role for his Theseus, who is all the more interesting for having passions almost strong enough to master him, but which he succeeds in mastering with reserves of reason, as also with his sense of the ridiculous. His impulse of compassion for the suppliant Theban widows, and his instant resolve to right their wrongs by punishing Creon's sacrilege (952–1000), are paralleled by his later moderation of his indignant wrath when his queen and other ladies beg him to spare Palamon and Arcite (1760–81). His wry sense of the absurdity of the rival lovers' predicament ('She woot namoore of al this hoote fare, | By God, than woot a cokkow or an hare!', 1809–10) bluntly expresses many a reader's private sentiments, and thereby strengthens the tale by acknowledging the very incoherence of desire that is part of its subject.

Theseus' attempt at resolving the unresolvable conflict between Palamon and Arcite is literally a constructive one: to create a purpose-built arena in which the inevitable outcome of a winner and a loser is to be ceremonialized into the carefully choreographed equipoise of equal opportunities. Since the third of the tale's four parts is largely devoted to an account of the lists, the creation and decoration of this emblematic construction forms a key part of the thematic scheme of the tale. Before their combat, Boccaccio's Arcita and Palemone pray to their respective patron deities, Mars and Venus, and their personified prayers are imagined as travelling to deliver their petitions to the temple homes of Mars in the Thracian fields and of Venus on Mount Cithaeron. In the *Teseida* it is these divine residences that are described, while the setting for the combat is not specially constructed or described. The effect of Chaucer's recombining of these elements in the 'Knight's Tale' is that the lists—with integral temples to the three patron deities of the protagonists whose lives will be determined in those lists—are turned from being, as in Boccaccio, a direct expression of the gods' natures and attributes into a work of art (the painters' accomplishment is stressed, 2049, 2087–8) emblematic of the human endeavour to discover meaning and order, and to interpret. In the *Teseida* prayers establish direct contact with the gods, whereas in the 'Knight's Tale' prayers receive only ambiguous signs needing interpretation. For all the creative flurry of building and painting in the 'Knight's Tale', the temples in Chaucer's story have been revised into an emblem not of the links (as in the *Teseida*) but of the disjunction and distance between gods and mortals, and of how mortals are left to interpret as they can the forces that determine human life. Where Chaucer found a binary structure in the *Teseida*, he has introduced triangulation, and thereby a shift in thematic dimensions. Where Boccaccio had the two male lovers pray to Venus and Mars, Chaucer adds thirdly a temple of Diana and interpolates Emelye's unsuccessful prayer to Diana between the prayers of Palamon to Venus and of Arcite to Mars. By adding the goddess and her temple Chaucer gives voice to Emelye, the unconsulted object of desire, if only to underline how this woman's preferred choice to stand aside from sexual experience is to be overridden. Boccaccio's Venus and Mars disagree over the incompatible prayers of the two lovers for love and for victory, but they resolve their quarrel when Mars concedes gallantly to Venus. Instead, Chaucer introduces Saturn as an arbitrating third force: it is now Saturn, not Venus, who arranges the 'furie infernal' (2684) and whose resolution of the conflict derives from attributes that range from meaningless anarchy to the calculations of realpolitik.

Chaucer's revision of the romance theme in the 'Knight's Tale' remakes the implication of his material in a coolly anti-illusionist spirit as a post-romance. The soul of Boccaccio's Arcita had soared up into the heavens after his death, but Chaucer reserves that exaltation for the soul of his Troilus in *Troilus and Criseyde*. Instead, the 'Knight's Tale' focuses clinically on Arcite's death as a physical process and declines to discuss the afterlife of his or any other souls. Chaucer's specification that his three protagonists pray to their patron gods at the correct planetary hours ruled by those gods (2209–12, 2271–2, 2367–8) makes clear that in this narrative the 'gods' are less the deities of pagan mythology than their namesakes in the planetary forces that were believed to shape character and conduct. In this sense the 'Knight's Tale' remains focused not on souls or divinities but on this-worldly experience, in which the planetary gods—far from being nobler supernatural forces—reflect back aspects, conjunctions, and confrontations of human attributes. Into this bleakly humanist vision

Chaucer introduces his Theseus' speech discerning order and consolation in experience (2987–3074), something unattempted at this point in Chaucer's source. Driven by older critical imperatives, which always hoped to see literary texts making sense of their world and of ours, twentieth-century criticism generally found Theseus' final oration a noble failure, or ironically inadequate, or both. In effect, the speech is a paradigm of logocentric thinking that is deconstructed by the tale itself. For postmodern readers, it is open to interpret the limited consolations and resignations of Theseus' speech as only appropriate to his pragmatic project, which is no more than to 'maken vertu of necessitee' (3042) in a post-romance world.

Postscript

Of the empowering gifts presented at the opening of the 'Squire's Tale', the magic mirror gives the power to foresee the future. To the question 'What will be the future developments in postmodern criticism of Chaucer?' postmodernism might reply that any foreseeable developments cannot but be postmodernist to some degree. Postmodernism parodies the notion of progress as a superseded myth, and its sense of coming very near the end of foreseeable cultural development is its own contemplation of mortality, or art of dying, in a post-religious age. If postmodernism can subvert the moralizing tendency to religiose interpretation in twentieth-century Chaucer criticism, something will have been gained. A postmodern approach could usefully deconstruct what may be called the fallacy of a homogeneous past, whereby modern criticism implicitly or explicitly constructs a medieval mindset more coherently unified, less troubled and divided, than a contemporary one. That mirror of enchantment in the 'Squire's Tale' gives the power not only to foresee future changes in fortune but also to look into characters' inner lives, distinguishing friend from foe and unmasking the 'subtiltee' of faithless lovers (132–41). As such, this gift of a magic mirror, left unused in the Squire's romance, can be an emblem of the privileged foresight and insight that is fiction's gift to its readers in most of Chaucer's poems. The present of a mirror implies that viewers may see something in themselves of future changes to come, and our postmodernist present's acute self-awareness of its cultural moment has the power to shape a more informed understanding of Chaucer's thematic and stylistic variousness in his own cultural moment, at once belated and experimental.

FURTHER READING

Bertens, Hans, *The Idea of the Postmodern: A History* (London: Routledge, 1994). A crisp overview of developing ideas about the postmodern.

Connor, Steven, *Postmodernist Culture: An Introduction to Theories of the Contemporary*, 2nd edn. (Oxford: Blackwell, 1997). Includes chapters on postmodernism and architecture, law, literature, performance, television and film, popular culture, and cultural politics.

Docherty, Thomas (ed.), *Postmodernism: A Reader* (Hemel Hempstead: Harvester Wheatsheaf, 1993). Useful selections from a range of postmodernist theory, including extracts from Fredric Jameson's classic study *Postmodernism, or, The Cultural Logic of Late Capitalism* (1991), and from essays by such students of postmodernism as Jean Baudrillard, Jürgen Habermas, and J.-F. Lyotard.

Ellis, Steve (ed.), *Chaucer: The 'Canterbury Tales'*, Longman Critical Readers (Harlow: Longman, 1998). Reprints a selection of recent, theoretically informed Chaucer criticism, with a helpful introduction.

Ferster, Judith, *Chaucer on Interpretation* (Cambridge: Cambridge University Press, 1985). An attempt to analyse Chaucer's treatment of personal identity, political power, and literary meaning in the context of modern hermeneutic theory, chiefly that of H.-G. Gadamer.

Hutcheon, Linda, *A Poetics of Postmodernism: History, Theory, Fiction* (London: Routledge, 1988), and *The Politics of Postmodernism*, 2nd edn. (London: Routledge, 2002). Two lucid and original introductions to postmodernism, its self-reflexive and parodic nature, in a range of art forms including architecture and photography as well as literature.

Jordan, Robert M., *Chaucer's Poetics and the Modern Reader* (Berkeley: University of California Press, 1987). A pioneering endeavour to re-evaluate Chaucer's rhetorical practice from a postmodern perspective.

Leicester, H. Marshall, Jr., *The Disenchanted Self: Representing the Subject in the 'Canterbury Tales'* (Berkeley: University of California Press, 1990). An important application to Chaucer of a poststructuralist approach.

Lyotard, Jean-François, *La Condition postmoderne* (1979); trans. Geoff Bennington and Brian Massumi as *The Postmodern Condition: A Report on Knowledge*, foreword Fredric Jameson (Manchester: Manchester University Press, 1984). Classic study by a primary theorist of postmodernism, focusing especially on the role of technology and the control of information in the postmodern world.

NOTES

1. Some recent studies include M. Keith Booker, 'Postmodernism in Medieval England: Chaucer, Pynchon, Joyce, and the Poetics of Fission', *Exemplaria*, 2 (1990), 563–94; Andrew Taylor, 'Chaucer our Derridean Contemporary?', *Exemplaria*, 5 (1993), 471–86. See also Thomas Hahn, 'The Premodern Text and the Postmodern Reader', *Exemplaria*, 2 (1990), 1–21.
2. See Stephanie Trigg, *Congenial Souls: Reading Chaucer from Medieval to Postmodern* (Minneapolis: University of Minnesota Press, 2002).
3. But see Kevin J. Vanhoozer (ed.), *The Cambridge Companion to Postmodern Theology* (Cambridge: Cambridge University Press, 2003), and Graham Ward (ed.), *The Postmodern God: A Theological Reader* (Oxford: Blackwell, 1997); also Edith Wyschogrod, *Saints and Postmodernism: Revisioning Moral Philosophy* (Chicago: University of Chicago Press, 1990), and especially Catherine Pickstock, *After Writing: On the Liturgical Consummation of Philosophy* (Oxford: Blackwell, 1997).
4. Matthew Arnold, Introduction to Thomas Humphry Ward (ed.), *English Poets* (1880), pp. xxxi–xxxvi.
5. See Brian McHale, *Postmodernist Fiction* (London: Methuen, 1987).
6. See Paul Strohm, *Theory and the Premodern Text* (Minneapolis: University of Minnesota Press, 2000), ch. 10: 'Postmodernism and History', and Lee Patterson, 'On the Margin: Postmodernism, Ironic History, and Medieval Studies', *Speculum*, 65 (1990), 87–108. See also Elizabeth Deeds Ermarth, *Sequel to History: Postmodernism and the Crisis of Representational Time* (Princeton: Princeton University Press, 1992).

7. See Phyllis Portnoy, 'Beyond the Gothic Cathedral: Post-Modern Reflections in the *Canterbury Tales*', *Chaucer Review*, 28 (1994), 279–92.

8. See Patricia Waugh, *Practising Postmodernism / Reading Modernism* (London: Edward Arnold, 1992).

9. See Valerie Allen and Ares Axiotis (eds.), *Chaucer*, New Casebooks (Basingstoke: Macmillan, 1997): 'But Chaucer's mongrel poetry enacts what postmodernism was later to call *écriture*—that is, a writing which is not "literary" in the traditional sense but *textual*, a transgressive writing which collapses the genre distinction between literary and critical writing . . . premodern Chaucer, more than later poets who submissively complied with the Enlightenment aesthetic of rules, can be said to be a forerunner of postmodernism' ('Postmodern Chaucer', 12–13).

10. On romance and postmodernism in later fiction, see Diane Elam, *Romancing the Postmodern* (London: Routledge, 1992).

24 | New historicism

Sylvia Federico

'New historicism' is a phrase most closely associated with Stephen Greenblatt's approach to Renaissance literature and culture. Greenblatt, along with Louis Montrose and Jonathan Goldberg and others, practised a form of historical inquiry that reads cultural phenomena (such as public executions, riots, and royal processions) as texts. In this, the new historicists, like Marxists, expanded the scope of literary studies to include historical realities. But the new historicism pointedly differed from Marxism in terms of how the political function of those historical realities was perceived and interpreted. Where Marxist criticism focused on identifying the forms of economic production that established and maintained cultural hegemony, and sought out pockets of resistance to that hegemony, new historicist criticism looked instead to elaborate the symbolic significance of events. New historicism did not advocate; it merely described. Many of these interpretations were dazzling; but, as Lee Patterson's important review of the situation points out, new historicism was open to the charge of neglecting the continuing struggles of real history in favour of ostensibly apolitical cultural narratives.[1]

While the new historicism as practised by Chaucerians partakes of these distinguishing features and problems, it is distinct in several ways owing to the different shape of the development of the field of Chaucer studies. It is so different, in fact, that the phrase 'new historicism' really ought not to be applied to the sort of historicist research Chaucerians do these days. For most of the twentieth century, Chaucerian historical criticism was deeply conservative—both in method and in politics. Unlike the field of Renaissance studies, Chaucer studies in general did not warm to Marxist analyses and their renewed emphasis on history. Instead, the anti-historical New Criticism flourished uneasily alongside exegetical criticism, which was a type of religious analysis that could be considered historicist only in a very narrow sense.[2] The 'new historicism' in Chaucer studies thus refers not to the Greenblattian school, which came out of the Marxist and cultural materialist trends of the 1970s, but is instead a form of cultural analysis that looks back to the turn of the twentieth century for its critical heritage.

Traditional Chaucerian historicism emphasized the importance of specific late fourteenth-century people, places, and events that may have had an influence on Chaucer or on his writing. Detailed archival studies on topics such as his various jobs and political appointments, his international travels, court affiliations and business affairs, and his whereabouts during notable crises like the 1381 Peasants' Revolt or Richard II's parliamentary controversies sought to illuminate better the meanings of the poems. Particular attention was paid to Chaucer's possible connections at court, and to his literary and political sponsors. The value of this 'old' historicism is not just that it brought to light much information about Chaucer's life and about the late fourteenth-century contexts for his work, or that it established many credible hypotheses for the chronology of the poems; more broadly, it underscored the importance of contextual reading for an understanding of medieval texts and cultures. The new Chaucerian historicism accepts many of these foundational premises, but its reading of history is influenced by theoretical perspectives that call into question the nature of 'reading', on the one hand, and of 'history', on the other.

New Chaucerian historicism owes much of its interpretative power to its insistence on locating the textual in all things. Rather than privileging the notion of an external truth, against which the subjective literary text can be measured, this new historicism inherits from deconstruction a distrust of the boundary between the nature of reality and the nature of textuality. Quite simply put, history is generally thought of as having to do with tangible reality—with events, with things that actually happened—whereas literature is typically thought to reside in the sphere of the figurative, the symbolic, the imaginary. New historicism treats history as a text: the reality referred to by historical documents is not an external truth but is rather a textual phenomenon, created in and by the text that claims merely to record it. As Patterson puts it, 'the symbolic constitutes the real'.[3]

When we apply this notion of textuality to archival documents, we come up against the central tension of new historical critical practice: how do we try to come to terms with facts, or lived historical truth, within a post-deconstructive framework that interrogates the epistemological foundation of the very idea of facts? That is, we all know that events do happen, and that historical realities such as poverty, rebellion, and rape occur in real time and affect real people. But we also know that the documents that record such historical events are not simply pure reflections of what happened; they are, like any text, subject to a number of motives and distortions. To a certain extent, it is possible to suggest that we will never know what happened in the past; all we have are the textual traces that claim to represent events. This does not mean, however, that therefore what really happened does not matter—or that we should stop trying to find out. But it does mean that we must be mindful of the distortions of the archival text: just as we would never assume that the meaning of a line of poetry is transparent or uncomplicated by levels of significance, so also must we be wary of trusting a historical document to accurately or simply tell the truth that it claims to tell. What we try to do instead is to locate the truth (or truths) the text is telling.

The documentary text thus stands not as an answer to our questions about history, and therefore as a solution to the mysteries of the literary text, but rather as a provocateur of new questions: what kinds of social and political systems govern (and fail to govern) the production, distribution, and interpretation of the text, and what sorts of effects might these systems have on our ability to know the past? In addressing these questions, we move back and forth between the impulse to recover the real, on the one hand, and the impulse to resist the (illusion of the) real, on the other. As a final note, we should also point out that the new Chaucerian historicism understands history to include groups typically abstracted or overlooked in the chronicles of aristocratic heritage and warfare that constitute much traditional historiography. These groups might include women, the middle class, and the poor, members of religious, political, and ethnic minorities, and the diseased or disabled. In the discussion that follows, a focus on the topic of rape in and around Chaucer's poetry will show how the theoretical points I have outlined might work in practice.

Chaucer at Chancery

In the archives at the Public Record Office in London lurks a text that has distressed and excited Chaucerians for years. Known as the Cecily Chaumpaigne release, the document enrolled in Chancery is more notorious for what it does not say than for what it does. It is so notorious, in fact, that it carries the double status of being more or less universally acknowledged and yet also more or less universally dismissed by readers of Chaucer—it is the kind of text every Chaucerian knows about but few want to discuss. The record is traumatic in two important senses: firstly, in that it refers, however obliquely, to an instance of sexual violence, an occasion on which a woman named Cecily Chaumpaigne presumably was hurt, and secondly, in so far as it seems to implicate our father of English letters, Geoffrey Chaucer, as a rapist. As we shall see, the legal-textual machinery of Chancery tidied up the first trauma, while the critical-textual machinery of Chaucerians has tidied up the latter.

The Cecily Chaumpaigne release is not a rape charge; it is more precisely a *release* from the charge of rape. The text, as inscribed on 4 May 1380, releases 'Galfrido Chaucer armigero' (Geoffrey Chaucer, esquire) from 'all manner of actions such as they related to my rape or any other thing or cause' ('omnimodas acciones tam de raptu meo tam [sic] de aliqua alia re vel causa').[4] Given this archival clue, an 'old historicist' might try to investigate further to determine what really happened: did Chaucer rape Cecily Chaumpaigne or not? Who exactly was Chaumpaigne, and what was her relationship to Chaucer? But in addition to the usual difficulties of such research, these questions have been rendered more or less unanswerable by the notorious confusion over the meaning of the term *raptus* (from the verb *rapere*). Medieval law lumped rape and abduction together under the same name, making any distinction between the two largely impossible when the term *raptus* was used without context. Most studies of the Chaumpaigne release conclude, often with palpable relief and sometimes despite their own findings, that we cannot tell with any certainty just what happened.[5] And yet this text continues to be especially charged: it is, after all, a rape we are talking about (or not talking about). And while obviously the release does not claim that Chaucer raped Chaumpaigne, in another sense of course that is exactly what it is saying.

In our attempt to understand, or at least partly unravel, this text, Christopher Cannon helped enormously when he discovered a memorandum, enrolled three days after the original release, regarding the same case. In this memorandum the original phrase *de raptu meo* has been replaced with a generic phrase that could cover practically any crime; instead of 'my rape', here Cecilia releases Chaucer from 'all manner of actions both concerning felonies, trespasses, accounts, debts, and any other actions whatsoever'.[6] As Cannon notes, the replacement of *de raptu meo* (a 'singular and unusual phrase') with a standard and general phrase in the memorandum is 'too complex a substitution, too long and too flawless in its concealment, to be a probable accident'.[7] Cannon speculates that Chaucer, using his influence and with the help of his friends, had the memorandum enrolled specifically because the charge of *raptus*, and even a release from the charge of *raptus*, was enormously stigmatizing. Such an action would not constitute subterfuge or tampering exactly, because the legal function of both documents is the same. Cannon's point is that the word *raptus* was itself inflammatory: it was, he argues, 'so bold that three days later, whether by coercion, persuasion, or some more complicated manipulation in the court of the king, this strong word—this mention of rape—had to be quietly, but emphatically, retracted'.[8]

Cannon takes the issue one step farther by linking his linguistic analysis of the word *raptus* to a political analysis of Chaucerians. In pointing out the motivated reticence of the critics in regard to the release, he notes that their rhetorical strategies are similar to those found in the revised memorandum:

Modern scholars have shrunk from even mentioning *raptus* or rape . . . they have repeatedly tried to protect Chaucer's reputation from any association with . . . rape by simply avoiding that wrong's mention. Like the writer of the memorandum, these writers have preferred to introduce or discuss the Chaumpaigne release under cover of a wide range of neutral phrases.[9]

The critics have been just as disturbed as Chaucer's contemporaries by the mention of rape, and like them they have tried to make it go away.

When we focus on the questions that we (happily know we) cannot answer—did *raptus* mean rape or 'mere' abduction? did it or did it not happen? who was Cecily Chaumpaigne in relation to Chaucer?—we lose sight of the many significances of the problem, not least of which are the ethical considerations that arise from knowing that Chaucer may have raped someone. Even if we cannot know with certainty that Chaucer did or did not rape Cecily Chaumpaigne, we can—and should—ask what rape meant for Chaucer, his contemporaries, and his readership. For these questions we look to texts: Chaucer's poetry, that of his friend and fellow poet John Gower, the writings of cultural commentators such as the chronicler Thomas Walsingham, as well as legal and political documents from the period.

Representations of rape

Rape figures as a topic in a number of Chaucer's poems, most obviously and unambiguously in the 'Wife of Bath's Tale', where the language describing sexual viola-tion is clear. There is no ambiguity as to whether this is rape or abduction. The 'lusty bacheler' (883) is described as forcing the maiden to have sex against her will: 'maugree hir heed, | By verray force, he rafte hire maydenhed' (887–8). The rest of the tale concerns the legal and ethical issues arising as a result of rape; it confronts the problem of what constitutes appropriate punishment for the crime of rape, and more generally what society ought to do with a rapist. While in the Arthurian society of the tale the sentence for rape is death, for 'swich was the statut tho' (893), the queen's fought-for exception to the rule suggests that Chaucer is investigating what rape means, culturally and socially, rather than viewing it simply as a juridical issue. Indeed, when the queen sets the knight on his quest to discover what it is that women really want, one could argue that a re-education of sorts has been decreed. If the knight is to truly satisfy the quest, he must learn compassion for women—to consider their subjectivity—and this, presumably, would prevent him from reoffending. Compared to the penalty provided by the law, obviously this sentence is light.

In the courtroom drama scene that occurs once he returns from his quest, the knight demonstrates a certain schoolboyish quality in his clever response. Do with me what you will, he says, and resignedly pronounces that

> Wommen desiren to have sovereynetee
> As wel over hir housbond as hir love,
> And for to been in maistrie hym above. (1038–40)

In the contexts of the 'Wife of Bath's Prologue' and the barbed references to the Wife by the 'schoolboy' of the pilgrimage, the Clerk ('CIT' 1163–75), this answer reads not so much like the revelation of women's consciousness that was meant to teach a rapist a moral lesson, but rather like a patronizing wink between men who have been caught denying women their sovereignty.

What follows, however, is a reversal of this power structure and perhaps a questioning of the social structure of gender relations as well. The old hag testifies as to her relation-ship with the knight and what they had agreed upon; before she gave him what he wanted, she received from him a promise to give her whatever she might ask for in the future: 'he plighte me his trouthe there' (1051). In now demanding marriage at court, particularly in a courtroom assembled to decide justice following a rape, the hag is mimicking a very common form of discourse in the later Middle Ages. Before Richard II enacted a statute that discouraged it, it was fairly routine practice for rape cases to be resolved by marriage.[10] Shockingly (to our modern sensibilities), if a rape victim married her assailant, the sex was said to be retroactively legal because the consent was granted after the fact. Such cases often involved the woman's family demanding marriage from the man who hurt (and ruined) their daughter, but in many cases—and the reason why the statute was enacted to stop the practice—the rape was committed with the goal of marriage in mind. Men who wanted to marry well, but for whatever reason were barred from pressing their suit in the customary way, would sometimes rape their intended with an eye towards then being 'forced' to marry her as a punishment. Sometimes a woman consented to the rape if she found marriage to the man desirable: it was common for lovers whose parents objected to the match to stage a rape so that they could marry. Such arrangements of consensual rape (if we can even fathom such a thing), or 'heiress rape' as it is called by some modern historians, underscore the point that the legal and cultural definitions of rape in the later Middle Ages were by no means clear. Indeed, they were so problematic that Richard II was moved to clarify the law in 1382.

During a parliamentary session that also dealt with the crimes of the rebels of 1381, Richard II enacted a statute to deal with the apparently widespread phenomenon of consensual rape. The 1382 statute did not emphasize justice for the woman involved; rather, it tried to limit the economic damage done to her family. The statute notes that as the 'offenders and ravishers of ladies, and the daughters of noblemen, and other women . . . [are] in these days offending more violently, and much more than they were wont', it is ordained that even when a woman consents after the fact and marries her attacker, the couple may not inherit. The statute makes 'heiress rape' even less attractive by enabling the woman's husband or father to sue the attacker even if she has consented after the fact. Furthermore, the statute forbids a resolution of the matter through a trial by battle, a popular alternative to the law for aristocrats: 'the defendant in this case shall not be received to wage Battel, but [it is ordained] that the Truth of the Matter be thereof tried by Inquisition of the Country'.[11] I shall return to this statute, and the famous case that prompted it, shortly. It is important to note, however, that in its focus on providing a financial disincentive for 'heiress rape', the law removed marriage as a legitimate means of redress for women who had been raped in the true sense of the term—that is, against their will and without their consent. And despite the rampant confusion over what *raptus* really meant in the late fourteenth century, Richard's statute in no way clarifies that issue; its focus is single-mindedly on the matter of inheritance.

Chaucer's 'Wife of Bath's Tale', which is usually dated in the early to mid-1390s, engages the issue of rape and the law in ways that might ask us to consider the victim. But while the hag's testimony in court mimics the discourse of a rape case, she is of course not the rape victim. And the real victim, the silent 'mayde', disappears from the tale straight after the rape. Rather than emphasizing the plight of the woman forced to have sex against her will, Chaucer focuses instead on the plight of the man who forced her. In being forced into marriage, the rapist–knight of the 'Wife of Bath's Tale' paradoxically inhabits the position of the victim. His fear and loathing of his bride on their wedding night, and his resignation to the ugly truth of what he must do, indicate that he has been deprived of agency in sexual congress: in this sense, he is assigned the role of a rape victim. And yet, of course, he is not a rape victim—to suggest as much is to diminish the seriousness of the crime against the 'mayde', who is so unambiguously raped at the beginning of the tale. But while she is certainly victimized, he both is and is not. The fact that he lives at all is in itself problematic; the fact that he continues to live as a misogynist is worse. It is even possible to suggest that, to certain audiences, his current punishment—having to have sex with an old, ugly woman—is darkly funny in so far as the depiction is a playful rendition of non-consensual sex, a sort of joke about rape. Depending on how the situation is looked at, and by whom, the knight's predicament on his wedding night is a shame, a farce, or a crime.

As readers, we have entered a grey area, where rape is and is not punished, and sexual victimization is both serious and comic. How do we (and how does Chaucer) get out of this thicket? Magic, of course, helps: when the hag transforms herself into a beautiful young woman, all of this complication can be made to go away. But even before this easy ending, the tale provides us with a solution—if not to the problem of rape then at least as an interpretative key to the questions it raises. The knight's failure to learn his lesson has been until this point in the tale demonstrated in his attitude towards the old hag's appearance; because she is physically unattractive to him, he cannot see her as a person. He views women purely as sexual objects. It is only once she has instructed him in the concept of *gentilesse* that he can accept her authority, and thus her 'personhood', suggesting that it is this lecture which finally accomplishes his reform. The tone of the tale shifts here as well, from bantering entertainment to high-toned moralizing.

The hag tells the knight that 'he is gentil that dooth gentil dedis' (1170), and 'He nys nat gentil, be he duc or erl, | For vileyns synful dedes make a cherl' (1157–8). This speech on *gentilesse* is original to Chaucer's version of the story, as is the rape of the 'mayde'; none of the analogues includes the sexual violence at the tale's beginning or the emphasis on social class at its end. The combination of these two original details is particularly relevant to our discussion of the cultural value of rape in the late fourteenth century: we have seen how Richard II's statute of rapes is more concerned with class—specifically with economic and social protection from undesirables—than it is with the punishment of sexual violations. Rape, we could suggest in a preliminary way, is not about rape in the later fourteenth century; it is about money and class.

In the 'Physician's Tale' we encounter again a situation in which a rape (in this case a plotted rape that does not occur) is situated in an unusual legal context; and once again, as in the 'Wife of Bath's Tale', here also the topic of rape is bound together with the topic of social class. Of Virginia, a knight's daughter, it is said that

> No countrefeted termes hadde she
> To seme wys, but after hir degree
> She spak. (51–3)

She is pure on a number of levels: blood, morals, and words. Simply put, she is truth. And her status as such is exemplary:

For in hir lyvyng maydens myghten rede,
As in a book, every good word or dede
That longeth to a mayden vertuous,
She was so prudent and so bountevous.
For which the fame out sprong on every syde,
Bothe of hir beautee and hir bountee wyde. (107–12)

Apius, Virginia's evil admirer, hears about this notable beauty and goodness and is consequently provoked to corrupt her. He is a 'justice', 'juge', and 'governour . . . of that regioun' (121–3). Where Virginia is truth, he is law. The law, in other words, corrupts the truth—or tries to corrupt it, as happens in this instance. More specifically, the law tries to get away with rape. Going over his options as to how to achieve the gratification of his desire, Apius ponders how legally to get away with it:

Anon the feend into his herte ran,
And taughte hym sodeynly that he by slyghte
The mayden to his purpos wynne myghte.
For certes, by no force ne by no meede,
Hym thoughte, he was nat able for to speede;
For she was strong of freendes. (130–5)

It is still rape, as he knows and as Chaucer knows, but it will not be able to be prosecuted as rape in court. Apius conscripts Claudius, a 'cherl' (140), and tells him his plan 'in secree wise' (143). The secrecy is emphasized when Apius further threatens Claudius with death if he tells anyone about the plot: 'He sholde telle it to no creature, | And if he dide, he sholde lese his heed' (144–5). In so far as a rape is planned that will not technically (legally) be a rape, the tale explores the gulf between victimization and punishment. But in its emphasis on the alliance between the law and a 'cherl', the tale explores the violence that occurs when 'this false juge' (154) *is* a churl.

Claudius launches a false accusation in Apius' court, and asks for justice in the language of a bill of complaint. He claims that Virginia is actually his servant, who was stolen from him some years earlier. In telling the story of the girl's abduction, which legally would be termed *raptus*, Claudius furthermore revises Virginia's social status when he claims

How that a knyght . . .
Agayns the lawe, agayn al equitee,
Holdeth, expres agayn the wyl of me,
My servant, which that is my thral by right,
Which fro myn hous was stole upon a nyght,
Whil that she was ful yong. (180–5)

In calling a knight's daughter a 'thral', Claudius underscores the issue of social class in a way that competes for significance with the planned rape itself. The problem of confusing (or wilfully disregarding) norms of social class is further highlighted when Apius refuses to allow Virginius an aristocratic defence, by battle or by witness testimony, and brings the matter quickly to its base end: 'The cherl shal have his thral' (202). Following this perversion of the law, Virginia is then perversely murdered by her father to spare her, and him, not just the shame of rape but the shame of being thought a 'thral'.

Justice is arguably restored in the end when, suddenly, 'a thousand peple in thraste' (260) to save Virginius from being executed for killing his daughter. They suspected, 'By manere of the cherles chalangyng, | That it was by the assent of Apius' (264–5). The people are familiar not only with the language of legal challenges, but also with its tendency towards corruptibility—and perhaps with the courtroom as a site given to the corruption of truth.

So what happens to corrupters of truth, to men who plot to rape women, to men who disregard the distinction between 'gentils' and 'cherls'? Apius kills himself in prison, and Claudius 'Was demed for to hange upon a tree' (271). It is a churl's death for a churl's deeds—he is not, after all, to be granted the aristocrat's quick death of beheading threatened by Apius (as also threatened to the knight in the 'Wife of Bath's Tale'). But while Claudius is ultimately spared the mandated punishment for his part in the 'conspiracie' (149) when Virginius intervenes and gets the sentence commuted to exile, we learn that 'The remenant were anhanged, moore and lesse, | That were consentant of this cursednesse' (275–6). The existence of this unnumbered 'remenant' comes as some surprise, as it contradicts what we had been given to understand before: that Apius and Claudius were alone in their plot, 'in secree wise'. This 'remenant', moreover, is of a socially mixed composition; but whether they were 'moore or lesse'—that is, whether they were high or low—they were all hanged as churls. The tale at this point is very far from its concern with the plight of Virginia, the victim, and much more concerned with the relationships between the men who victimized her. What are we meant to take away from this story of crime and multiple, often inappropriate, punishments? What kind of justice has been served?

Rape and revolt

The framing narrative of the *Canterbury Tales* is often helpful for gauging the pilgrims' responses to an ambiguous text. In the case of the 'Physician's Tale', both the Physician himself and the Host, Harry Bailly, offer commentary. The Physician's moral emphasizes the socially equalizing nature of the fear of death. Everyone, 'be he lewed man, or ellis lered' (283), who dies unabsolved is going to be punished in the afterlife for his sins. The Host also emphasizes how the churl and the justice are both 'fals' (288), but he reserves most of his condemnation for another group of villains:

> 'Harrow!' quod he, 'by nayles and by blood!
> This was a fals cherl and a fals justise.
> As shameful deeth as herte may devyse
> Come to thise juges and hire advocatz!
> Algate this sely mayde is slayn, allas! . . .'

> ('ParI' 287–91)

While Harry does manage to spare an afterthought for the innocent Virginia, for him the tale is about the evil of the false justice, meaning not only Apius in particular but more generally the sort of manipulation of the law practised by an unnumbered and yet specific ('thise') group of 'juges and hire advocatz'.

The Host expresses a general hatred for the corrupt judiciary system, which he sees as typified by Apius' specific example. In this expression of hostility towards judges and lawyers, and the wish for them to die a grisly, violent death, we bump up once again against the spectre of the 1381 Peasants' Revolt, much of whose violence was aimed at lawyers. The rebels in 1381 focused their action on several groups, but members of the legal profession were especially targeted because they were seen as supporting the 'untrewe' (unfair) policies of landowners. In actual practice, lawyers were killed indiscriminately, whether they were honest or not. As the contemporary chronicler Thomas Walsingham writes, the rebels executed 'all the lawyers in the land whom they could capture—not only apprentices but also old justices and all the kingdom's jurors, without respect for piety; for the rebels declared that the land could not be fully free until the lawyers had been killed'.[12] When Harry Bailly conjures the image of numbers of slaughtered lawyers, and the tale itself concludes with the image of countless criminals being hanged for their part in a conspiracy, the Revolt asserts itself as a symbolic presence in the story of Virginia.

The 'Physician's Tale' is usually dated before or at the beginning of the period during which Chaucer wrote the *Canterbury Tales*, and some readers have suggested that the tale initially may have been written for, or at least under the influence of, the *Legend of Good Women*. The noted critic and editor J. S. P. Tatlock suggested the tale may also have been related to the consensual rape (what he termed the 'elopement') of John of Gaunt's daughter, Elizabeth, in 1386, and that the tale was written when the couple returned to England, in 1388.[13] I think that there is some possibility in both hypotheses, but there is yet another specific case that may help us better understand the dynamics of rape and class found in the 'Physician's Tale'. This is the case that prompted Richard II to enact his statute of rapes.

In the summer of 1382 Sir Thomas West petitioned John of Gaunt for help in avenging the rape of his daughter, which he described in the following terms: a new but trusted family friend named Nicholas Clifton lured Thomas's wife, Alice, and daughter Eleanor to the woods, with the intention of raping Eleanor. His men 'made assault on the said Alice and Eleanor and their meinie with drawn swords, bows and arrows drawn back to the ear, and ravished the said Eleanor with most evil affray to the said Alice and her company, who thought that the great and treacherous insurrection had been renewed'.[14] Petitioned by West, Gaunt presumably pressed this suit with the king, who then enacted the statute in the 1382 parliament. In a second petition West tried to have the statute made retroactive, but he failed in this endeavour. Eleanor, described as 'ravished and deflowered' in the second petition, subsequently married Clifton.[15]

An armed attack on women, and the rape of a young woman, reminds the victims of 'the great and treacherous insurrection', the 1381 Peasants' Revolt—that other social problem dealt with along with 'heiress rape' in the 1382 parliament. Perhaps it is merely a coincidence, or an accident of history, that rape and the Revolt were both treated in the same session of parliament. There is nothing that obviously links the two, and the proceedings do not state or even imply a connection between these matters of parliamentary business. But in fact, rape appears in several famous descriptions of the 1381 rising. For instance, in his account of the rebels' invasion of London, Gower writes that the city was as 'powerless as a widow' and 'defenceless as the savage throngs approached and entered her by violence [adeunt urbem turbe violenter agrestes, | Et . . . ingrediuntur eam]. The madness plunged [ruit] into any- and every-thing forbidden.'[16] Similarly, describing the rebels' entrance into the king's private apartments in the Tower on 13 June, Walsingham writes that 'the most vile of rustics poked their nasty sticks into places they did not belong, rolled around on the bed, and propositioned the king's mother with kisses'.[17] In using this kind of charged imagery, the poet and the chronicler assert a connection between rape and rebellion that echoes the 'accidental' proximity we saw in the parliamentary proceedings.

The language used by these contemporary commentators clearly is meant to underscore the heinousness of the 1381 rising by likening it to sexual violation. The body politic, gendered feminine, was corrupted by monstrous churls. We do not have to look far to discern the logic of this metaphor: both in the case of rape as it was understood and adjudicated in the 1380s and in the case of the Revolt, the significance of the violation has to do with social class—it is about the lower classes getting into a place (in society) where they do not belong. Rape, in other words, was so already *about* class that it was the perfect metaphor to use for the revolt.

The invisibility of rape

But even though it seems to call attention to rape, the use of metaphor here threatens to disguise the reality of the crime—as much as the law disguised it. The legal attention to rape, as we have seen, made invisible what it claimed to address: the violence done to the woman was lost in the focus on inheritance, as it had been in the grotesque concept of consent granted after the fact. Figurative representations of rape likewise occlude the reality of women's lived experience: metaphor helps medieval authors to contain the issue of violence rhetorically, and permits later commentators in turn to forget or even dismiss the possibility of crimes against women in the Middle Ages. For instance, despite (or perhaps because of) the metaphorical rapes that appear in descriptions of the rising of 1381, until quite recently most historians were oblivious to the fact that 'real' women were even involved in the rebellion. As it happens, women participated in the Revolt in a number of ways, both as instigators and as victims of violence.

The rising of 1381 is usually remembered for its dramatic moments: the rebels' storming of the Tower, their tense meetings with the king, their wholesale slaughter of lawyers and Flemings in the street. But the overwhelming majority of legal documents related to the rebellion are cases of civil trespass in which a group of rebels entered someone's house, stole or destroyed documents, and threatened or hurt whoever they found at home at the time. Many of the victims were women who were harassed, humiliated, beaten, and robbed by bands of marauding rebels roving from house to house.[18] In this context of violent lawlessness enacted largely within domestic space, it is easy to imagine that rape may have been common. Indeed, it is hard to imagine that it did not happen. But the historical record is reticent on this topic: there are but a handful of cases that specify the charge of rape in unambiguous terms. Most of the cases in which the context suggests that rape may have been involved use the legal phrase *rapuit et abduxit*, which, because of the ambiguity belonging to the term *rapere*, leaves open the technical possibility that the women in question were only carried off.

As with the case of Cecily Chaumpaigne, the best evidence we have that rape occurred during the rising of 1381 is not really evidence at all. At the urging of his new queen, Anne of Bohemia, Richard II offered a general amnesty to all rebels—with a few notable exceptions. The amnesty excludes traitors, murderers, *and rapists*: 'proditoribus murdris et *raptibus mulierum* exceptis' (my italics).[19] Of course this does not prove that rape occurred (though treason and murder did), but the wording of the amnesty certainly suggests that rapists were prevalent enough to warrant special mention as an exclusion. But though the circumstances vary enormously, we seem to keep coming to the same frustrating conclusions: despite all indications, despite what all common reasoning would suggest, and despite our ethical sensibilities, rape cannot be proven and consequently rape will not be punished.

Rape and punishment

The pardon for the rebels was urged by Anne of Bohemia, who also pardoned the very well-connected Nicholas Clifton for his rape of Eleanor West.[20] Anne also pardoned Chaucer, not for his rape of Cecily Chaumpaigne, but, in her figuration as Queen Alceste in the Prologue to the *Legend of Good Women*, for other crimes against women. The crimes here are textual rather than sexual, though—as we saw before in Virginia's booklike purity in the 'Physician's Tale'—this is not an especially firm distinction. The God of Love accuses the narrator of having

> translated the Romauns of the Rose,
> That is an heresye ageyns my lawe,
> And makest wise folk fro me withdrawe.
>
> (*LGW* (G) 255–7)

He further demands whether the narrator had not also written *Troilus and Criseyde*:

> Hast thow nat mad in Englysh ek the bok
> How that Crisseyde Troylus forsok,
> In shewynge how that wemen han don mis?
>
> (264–6)

Clearly the narrator here is an author, and is more specifically the author of Chaucer's poems; it is, in other words, a very self-conscious version of Chaucer himself. And the poet is in this instance imagining himself, however comically, as a criminal called to answer a charge of mistreating women. It is not rape, of course: the God of Love makes clear that he is offended by poems. Indeed, part of the humour of Chaucer's familiar self-deprecatory presentation is that he is not actually violating women, just writing about them. He is no lover, no seducer, no rapist—but rather merely a man of books. Once again, we find ourselves confronted with Chaucer's sexual wit: this is not a rape case, just a bit of fun that sounds like a rape case.

Despite the queen's intercession, 'Chaucer' is deemed guilty of writing evil things about women and is subsequently sentenced to write good things about them. The anti-feminist thrust of this point sets the tone for the Prologue. As with the 'Wife of Bath's Tale', we have a courtroom drama that pastiches a rape trial—and here, too, the offender's punishment is a joke. It is a joke in the sense that it is too lenient: the queen notes that his 'penaunce is but lyte' (485) and the god says the narrator 'deserved sorer for to smerte' (490). But it is a joke also in the sense that it is comic. The whole Prologue can be read as a misogynist joke, in so far as it is a sarcastic gibe at the notion of true women—and the legends that follow often seem like a bored response to the narrator's sentence, like writing one hundred times on a blackboard, I will not rape women.

To suggest that Chaucer may have been commenting upon the Chaumpaigne proceedings does not necessarily implicate him in the rape; in fact, we could just as easily see him as unfairly accused. Indeed, in this scenario, *his* good name is ruined by the accusation; he has been violated. As Alceste reminds us, 'This man to yow may wrongly ben acused, | There as by ryght hym oughte ben excusid' (338–9). In continuing to suspect him of rape—when he went to all the trouble of erasing the blemish—we continue to victimize him through our misinterpretation. As Carolyn Dinshaw has observed, Chaucer was especially sensitive to his texts being misread, and figured the dynamics of misinterpretation in sexual terms. In the comic short poem 'Chaucers Wordes unto Adam, his Owne Scriveyn', Chaucer castigates his error-prone scribe, accusing him of negligence and 'rape'. While 'rape' is primarily glossed here as haste, Dinshaw's discussion shows how Adam's miswriting of Chaucer's text puts the author in the position of 'the victim of scribal rape; his text, his work, his intent are violated by the pen of the scribe'.[21] For Chaucer, in this instance, a misunderstanding is a rape; it is, as much as the corruption of Virginia in the 'Physician's Tale', a violation of truth. And whether he raped her or not, the Chaumpaigne proceedings were known to a group of Chaucer's well-placed contemporaries.

Rape and social position

We have come no closer to determining what really happened between Chaucer and Cecily Chaumpaigne. But we have come closer to understanding what and how rape signified in the late fourteenth century. Whereas, according to one critic, in Chaucer's writing 'rape remains a constant touchstone for determining justice between the sexes',[22] I would argue instead that, for Chaucer and his contemporaries, rape is a constant touchstone for determining justice between the classes. The rebels in 1381 were understood as using rape as a means of social warfare, but this is not as shocking as it initially sounds; for, as we have seen, up until Richard's 1382 statute, rape was deployed as a tactic for upward social mobility by the second sons of the aristocracy. The cultural value of rape in the late fourteenth century was such that the rebels' violence was but an imitation of an apparently acceptably violent practice among the upper classes.

We have seen how men in high places, such as Sir Thomas West, could affect the law as it related to rape. A good king, as Alceste notes, should hear his people's 'excusacy-ouns, | And here compleyntes and petyciouns' (*LGW* (G) 362–3)—and West's petition was duly heard. But even those on the wrong side of the law could nevertheless trans-late their violent behaviour into a social benefit. Nicholas Clifton, after being par-doned by Anne for his rape of Eleanor, attached himself to the king's half-brother John Holland (the man who raped Gaunt's daughter in 1386) and was then knighted two years later.[23] Geoffrey Chaucer esquire was no Thomas West, no Nicholas Clifton—but with the help of his friends as witnesses, all of them prominent men in the court of Richard II (including Sir William Beauchamp, chamberlain of the king's household; Sir John Philipot, Member of Parliament and mayor of London; Sir William Neville and Sir John Clanvowe, knights of the king's chamber; and Richard Morel, a member of the powerful Grocers' guild), Chaucer was released. Manipulating the law, or at least massaging the documents, was something a well-connected man could do. And rape, whether or not it happened, was something a polite man could joke about—even if he was not of the status himself to be directly pardoned.

As Dinshaw observes, the Chaumpaigne release 'reminds us that there are not only *figurative* rapes . . . and there are not only *fictional* rapes . . . but there are *real* rapes as well'.[24] These signposts flagged by Dinshaw constitute precisely the intersection at which the new Chaucerian historicism finds itself today. Instead of using the real to gloss the figurative and fictional (and thus privileging historiography's claim to truth-fulness), our current practice attempts to read the figurative, the fictional, and the real simultaneously—and to explore the mutually dependent and mutually constructing nature of these terms. No longer trapped by the simple (and illusory) binary distinction between true experience and its false textual appearance, Chaucerian historicist prac-tice will in coming years continue to look beyond traditional definitions of disciplinary boundaries. Psychoanalysis and geography may both be very useful for helping us understand the interconnectedness of the real, the remembered, and the represented.

FURTHER READING

Colebrook, Claire, *New Literary Histories: New Historicism and Contemporary Criticism* (Manchester: Manchester University Press, 1997). Very clear and basic guide to how (several versions of) new historicism fit into the larger context of contemporary literary studies.

Gallagher, Catherine, 'Marxism and the New Historicism', in H. Aram Veeser (ed.), *The New Historicism* (New York: Routledge, 1989), 37–48. Excellent discussion of how new historicism is indebted to Marxism but also how it has moved away from (some would say dodged) the political issues most closely associated with Marxist studies.

Goldberg, Jonathan, 'The Politics of Renaissance Literature: A Review Essay', *English Literary History*, 49 (1982), 514–42. A discussion of how different forms of literary analysis are informed by political concerns, this essay constitutes one of the seminal statements of early new historicist thought.

Greenblatt, Stephen, *The Power of Forms in the English Renaissance* (Norman, Okla.: Pilgrim Books, 1982). Greenblatt's first major statement on the intersection of history and literature. Although somewhat dated by now, the book is important to the history of the field.

Montrose, Louis, 'New Historicisms', in Stephen Greenblatt and Giles Gunn (eds.), *Redrawing the Boundaries: The Transformation of English and American Literary Studies* (New York: Modern Language Association of America, 1992), 393–418. A lucid examination by one of new historicism's earliest practitioners, some ten years after its arrival, of how this critical practice has changed the face of literary studies.

Patterson, Lee, *Chaucer and the Subject of History* (Madison: University of Wisconsin Press, 1991). One of the earliest major statements on the role of history in the field of Chaucer studies. Contains an excellent overview of how Chaucerian criticism has kept pace (or not) with critical trends in other literary periods.

Scala, Elizabeth, 'Historicists and their Discontents: Reading Psychoanalytically in Medieval Studies', *Texas Studies in Literature and Language*, 44 (2002), 108–131. Important new work on the relationship (or lack of relationship) between psychoanalysis and new historicism in medieval literary studies.

Strohm, Paul, 'Chaucer's Lollard Joke: History and the Textual Unconscious', *Studies in the Age of Chaucer*, 17 (1995), 23–42. Ground-breaking work on how psychoanalytical insights can inform literary texts, by an early proponent of historical studies in Chaucer.

Summit, Jennifer, 'Topography as Historiography: Petrarch, Chaucer, and the Making of Medieval Rome', *Journal of Medieval and Early Modern Studies*, 30 (2000), 211–46. Very exciting new work emphasizing how the description of physical landscape is itself a form of history-writing.

Wallace, David, *Chaucerian Polity: Absolutist Lineages and Associational Forms in England and Italy* (Stanford, Calif.: Stanford University Press, 1997). Exceptional study on the international historical contexts of Chaucer's work.

NOTES

1. See Lee Patterson, *Negotiating the Past: The Historical Understanding of Medieval Literature* (Madison: University of Wisconsin Press, 1987), for an excellent discussion of the history of historicism in Chaucer studies.
2. See ibid. 3–39 and Ch. 20 of this Guide.
3. Ibid. 61.
4. Martin M. Crow and Claire C. Olson (eds.), *Chaucer Life-Records* (Oxford: Clarendon Press, 1966), 343.

5. Christopher Cannon, '*Raptus* in the Chaumpaigne Release and a Newly Discovered Document concerning the Life of Geoffrey Chaucer', *Speculum*, 68 (1993), 74–94, discusses the ambiguity of the legal terminology and notes the 'obsession' in Chaucer criticism over whether *raptus* means abduction or rape (p. 88).

6. Public Record Office, London, KB 27/477 m. 58d; cited and translated in Cannon, '*Raptus*', 89.

7. '*Raptus*', 92.

8. Ibid. 94.

9. Ibid. 92.

10. See J. B. Post, 'Ravishment of Women and the Statutes of Westminster', in J. H. Baker (ed.), *Legal Records and the Historian* (London: Royal Historical Society, 1978), 150–64.

11. 6 Richard II, Statute 1, c. 6, printed in *Statutes of the Realm* (1816; repr. 1963), ii. 27.

12. Thomas Walsingham, *Historia Anglicana*, ed. Henry Thomas Riley, 2 vols. (1863), i. 453–5; trans. R. B. Dobson, *The Peasants' Revolt of 1381* (London: Macmillan, 1970), 133.

13. J. S. P. Tatlock, *Development and Chronology of Chaucer's Works* (London, 1907; repr. 1963), 152–5.

14. J. B. Post, 'Sir Thomas West and the Statute of Rapes, 1382', *Bulletin of the Institute of Historical Research*, 53 (1980), 25–6.

15. Ibid. 27.

16. John Gower, *Vox Clamantis*, in *The Major Latin Works of John Gower*, trans. Eric W. Stockton (Seattle: University of Washington Press, 1962), 69–70.

17. *Historia Anglicana*, i. 459; my translation.

18. See Sylvia Federico, 'The Imaginary Society: Women in 1381', *Journal of British Studies*, 40 (2001), 159–83.

19. Public Record Office, C 67/29.

20. Nicholas Clifton was pardoned for the rape of Eleanor West 'at the supplication of Queen Anne' (*Calendar of the Patent Rolls, 1381–1385* (1891–1916), 236).

21. Carolyn Dinshaw, *Chaucer's Sexual Poetics* (Madison: University of Wisconsin Press, 1989), 10.

22. Jill Mann, *Geoffrey Chaucer* (Hemel Hempstead: Harvester Wheatsheaf, 1991), 45; cited by Christopher Cannon, 'Chaucer and Rape: Uncertainty's Certainties', *Studies in the Age of Chaucer*, 22 (2000), 68.

23. See Post, 'Sir Thomas West', 29.

24. *Chaucer's Sexual Poetics*, 11.

Queer theory

Glenn Burger

Sexuality and Chaucer studies

Talking about sexuality and Chaucer often seems to lead inevitably to the dominance and centrality of *hetero*-sexuality (understood both as male–female sexual relations and, more broadly, as that modern sex–gender system in which proper male–female relations represent and reproduce dominant social relations). What little we know about Chaucer's life reveals a successful civil servant and married man, whose only recorded sexual involvement is the rape of Cecily Chaumpaigne (see Chapters 1 and 24).[1] Chaucer's early literary production focused almost entirely on romantic love and sexual relations between courtly men and women. And in his last great work, the *Canterbury Tales*, the body in all its sexed and gendered stylizations—first in the portraits of the 'General Prologue' and then more generally in the dramatic fiction of the crucial relationship of tale-tellers to tales—emerges as foundational for our critical judgement and understanding. Such attention to embodiment in the work of representation seems 'naturally' to produce a compulsory heterosexuality as central to the project of the *Tales*. Marriage relations, and the social structures that depend upon them, provide the subject matter of a majority of the tales, and a debate about marriage provides their literal centre in the ordering of the tales in the Ellesmere manuscript (that is, the tales told by the Clerk, Merchant, and Franklin in reply to the Wife of Bath's argument for female sovereignty in marriage). And social dissidence is most often represented as sexual dissidence, both within the action of the tales and within the fictionalized social relations of the Canterbury pilgrimage. Two of the troubling characters within the Canterbury project, for example, the Wife of Bath and the Pardoner, are problematic at least in part because they so clearly get 'proper' sexuality wrong. Less obviously, we might also see a certain heteronormativity at work in the *Tales'* attempts to inscribe the 'real' Chaucer (that magisterial, ironic artist figure looming large behind the fictions and a worthy foundation for a modern English literary tradition) by disavowing so clearly his fictionally embodied other, that feminized, 'elvyssh' pilgrim Chaucer comically misfiring with the 'Tale of Sir Thopas' (see the Host's description of the pilgrim Chaucer in the tale's Prologue, 691–711).

But how natural or inevitable is such a heterosexual Chaucer? How medieval or modern? What kind of queer torsions have been necessary to produce such presumptively heterosexual and modern readings of the author, his works, and his place in history? One obvious place to turn in taking up these questions has been Chaucer's treatment of that most vilified and marginalized of Canterbury pilgrims, the Pardoner. Beginning in 1915 with George Lyman Kittredge's influential character-ization of the Pardoner as 'the most abandoned character' among the Canterbury pilgrims, critics have been preoccupied with proving the absoluteness of the Pardoner's moral depravity and the anomalous position it puts him in in relation to the rest of the pilgrims.[2] One recurring piece of evidence, based on the narrator's description in the 'General Prologue' (especially the comment 'I trowe he were a geldyng or a mare', 691), has been the troubling unnaturalness of the Pardoner's body and physical presence. Consequently, the Pardoner has often seemed the 'natural' place for critics to turn in deciding how sexuality matters in Chaucer. Because of the Pardoner's representation as physically deficient, in various ways not a 'real' man, it is not surprising that many modern readers would see him as in a position analogous to, or as a precursor of, or as even really and truly, a gay man.[3] However, other critics have maintained the Pardoner's heterosexuality, citing his claims to frequent sexual activity with women ('ParP' 453) and medieval medical attributions of effeminacy to an over-abundance of heterosexual activity.[4] What is interesting about this critical debate is its underlying assumption that we can discover who a person truly *is* by uncovering their essential biological nature—an assumption intrinsic to those medical and juridical discourses producing modern sexuality described by Michel Foucault in *The History of Sexuality*.[5] As a result, such attempts to settle the worth of the Pardoner in terms of his sexual identity can all too easily end up reproducing modern sexuality as we know it—and especially the foundational status of the homo–hetero binary—as if it were the only possibility for medieval and modern reader alike.

How, then, to resist the oppressive power of dominant modern (hetero)sexuality on our readings of the past and our attempts to intervene within present critical debates? Anti-homophobic readings of the Pardoner over the past decade have been less con-cerned with proving who the Pardoner really is and more with exploring how such identifications with or against the Pardoner both arise out of but also can resist the structures of medieval and modern sexual politics. Steven F. Kruger, for example, has provocatively explored the paradoxical power inherent in claiming the Pardoner as a kind of gay 'ancestor' and thus 'writing the *Canterbury Tales* into a history of gay subversion and resistance'.[6] Using the example of Allen Barnett's short story 'Philostorgy, Now Obscure'—where Preston, the main character recently diagnosed with AIDS, finds himself newly identifying with the Pardoner's 'camp sensibility' and claiming him as 'the first angry homosexual'[7] in order to evoke a gay history more responsive to the anger of the current post-AIDS moment—Kruger considers the com-plex processes of historicization that might be put in play by such an 'anachronistic' desire. In discussing the question of whether or not the Pardoner might be homo-sexual, indeed whether or not one can even use such a term born out of modern medical and juridical discourses, Kruger focuses not on proving 'the Pardoner's (indeed unprovable) homosexuality' but rather on Chaucer's wanting us to see, 'as part of the Pardoner's "sexual queerness", the possibility of homosexuality'.[8] So too, Kruger's engagement as gay medievalist with the alterity of the Middle Ages leads neither to simple reclamation of a gay ancestor nor to a sanitization of the medieval moment:

> To embrace the Pardoner, to claim the Pardoner as somehow our own, is not just to embrace a gay ancestor—if that is what he is—but also to take to ourselves a self-proclaimed hypocrite and cheat, and, worse yet, to make ourselves (as we identify with the Pardoner) the target of the strong, and violent, hatred of the tale's conclusion (the Host's verbal, but almost physical attack on the Pardoner). The Pardoner may be intended by Chaucer to be the medieval equivalent of a gay man, but if so he is a character written out of homophobia.[9]

Thus, even while acknowledging that Chaucer 'admits in the standoff between Pardoner and Host the possibility that an angry homosexual voice might present real challenges to dominant heterosexual paradigms',[10] Kruger is careful to situate such empowerment within the context of a certain medieval homophobia structuring the tale's linking of sexuality and sin. Only by means of such a careful historicization can a modern claiming of the Pardoner reveal 'the artificiality, the unnatural and violent constructedness of heterosexual paradigms'.[11]

I have also argued elsewhere for the need to resist the turn to the supposed know-ability of the Pardoner's body and the stabilizing identity politics it has so often supported.[12] Instead, we should attend to that perverse dynamic—made especially visible in the moment when the Host is urged to kiss the Pardoner—that continues intimately to link the Pardoner and 'gentil' pilgrims even while such proper Christian subjects attempt his disavowal. The different kinds of kisses imagined by the Host and the Knight, and especially the conceptual dissonances they embody, draw attention to themselves as socially constructed performances; and in presenting the pilgrimage body as spectacle, the kiss exposes the limitations of identities put into the discursive marketplace by the linguistic economy of this society. Therefore, while the prevailing discourse of power in the 'Pardoner's Tale' seeks everywhere to establish the Pardoner as (an)other self, culture's opposite, the 'dangerousness' of the Pardoner is not that he represents another essentialist self (homosexual rather than heterosexual or eunuch rather than potent male) or that he is some symbolic black hole of absolute non-meaning. What is transgressive about the Pardoner, what provokes the violent responses of his audience, is precisely the way that he is *not* other, most obviously the way that the cupidity his audience attempts to fix in him alone actually fuels the discursive economy of relics and commerce in the dominant culture.

In a somewhat different vein, Carolyn Dinshaw's recent provocative discussion of the 'touch of the queer' has sought to underscore the foundational status of a hetero-sexual Chaucerian body for an Anglo-American literary and social tradition, along with the deconstructive work that a modern queer touching the dissident energy of the Wife and Pardoner might accomplish. Dinshaw frames her analysis of the Pardoner with the historical example of a late fourteenth-century English cross-dresser, John/Eleanor Rykener, and the polemics of Wyclif and his Lollard followers in order to suggest 'that the fierce silencing of the Pardoner on the pilgrimage marks a larger cultural response to the intertwined phenomena of sexual indeterminacy and intimations of heresy'.[13] Thus she claims that the Pardoner's 'illegibility' (to the narrator in the 'General Prologue', to the other pilgrims, and to a succession of later critics) becomes clearer in light of the 'nexus of normative sexuality and religion' laid out in the opening lines of the 'General Prologue'. The lines' 'intense masculinization of spring fecundity' and their focus on a penetrative act that fosters generation as the inaugural moment of the *Canterbury Tales*—'Whan that Aprill with *his* shoures soote | The droghte of March hath *perced* to the roote', (1–2, my italics)—as well as their universalizing voicelessness and magisterial diction, have thus worked to construct a foundational author figure himself revered for his generative powers as the father of English poesy, thereby contributing 'to the scholarly establishment of a tradition of English literature consonant with larger heterosexualized literary structures: literary production itself has been construed as a heterosexual act'.[14] But if the 'General Prologue' 'sets up a norm whose function is to configure the intelligible and unintelligible', the queer vibrations animated by the activities of the Wife and Pardoner and felt through the touch of the modern queer critic can also make visible 'the workings of that norm, show the unnaturalness in the bosom of the "natural", reveal the perversion at the heart of the orthodox'.[15]

While much of queer Chaucer criticism has remained focused on 'recognizably' sexually deviant characters like the Pardoner (or more recently, the Summoner), attention has also broadened to queer the actions of sexuality more widely—whether to rethink the perverse dimensions of the focus on marriage in the *Canterbury Tales*, male bonding and chivalric masculinity in *Troilus and Criseyde*, gender and genre in the Chaucerian fabliau, or the queer inter-implications of sexuality, race, and religion. It is this kind of broader reorientation that I undertake later in this chapter by reading the 'Shipman's Tale' in light of its queer conflation of the new money economy, female sexuality, and the lay bourgeois married household. Before that, though, it is worth taking up in greater detail what 'queer' and queer theory are attempting to conceptualize and reconfigure in terms of modern sexuality and its legacy, and why queer theory might therefore provide a useful intervention at this moment in the history of sexuality.

Queer matters

Why choose to use a term like 'queer', one with such a negative history, instead of more positive categories like gay or lesbian? Is it significant that 'queer' functions as much as a verb or adjective as it does as a noun? Does this shift from an emphasis on proper naming to process and impure identification matter? No doubt, in asking such questions queer activists, and queer theorists in particular, may appear at times to be splitting hairs or obsessively concerned with names and terms. But as any member of a minority or marginalized group will attest, names can carry more than symbolic power; language and the processes of representation have political consequences. I want, therefore, to begin this discussion of queer theory and Chaucer by considering first the contested and politically resistant power of queer as an analytic term, hoping thereby to show how queer theory can open up new possibilities in the present moment and provide a different lens on that present's dynamic relationship with the past.

At first glance, 'queer' would appear to be the term least likely to be adopted by those resisting the oppressive and prescriptive power of modern regimes of sexuality. 'Queer' as an epithet for homosexual man or woman has long been a staple weapon in the arsenal of homophobic discourse, identifying, disavowing, and marginalizing those failing to conform to whatever has been defined as 'normal' in the heterosexual practices of the day. Not surprisingly, then, the first generation of more successfully mainstream gay activism in the 1970s and 1980s chose 'gay' as a new, affirming term of self-identification precisely to replace such abusive and pathologizing terms as 'queer'. Why, then, has 'queer' become an increasingly popular form of expression for large sections of the gay–lesbian–bi–transgendered communities in the 1990s and the early twenty-first century? In large part the deployment of 'queer' marks a growing aware-ness of the limitations and blindnesses of the kind of identity politics that motored so many of the liberation movements of the 1970s and 1980s, including much useful and productive gay–lesbian activism.

For some—lesbians of colour, the transgendered, non-Western, non-heterosexual groups, and so forth—the successes of gay liberation have often seemed dis-proportionately to benefit middle-class, white gay men and lesbians. So too, the very proliferation of ever more specific and fragmenting identity categories—gay man, les-bian, bisexual, transgendered—indicates the narrowing and potentially minoritizing effects of an identity politics that demands that I *be* one thing only. Does one have to give up being black or Asian or Hispanic or become Western and middle-class to be gay? Is there room in an increasingly mainstream gay community for less socially acceptable forms of erotic desire and sexual practice (such as the sadomasochistic) or of sexual identity (such as the transgendered)? Can gay liberation, with its current emphasis on stabilizing and safeguarding various minority identities, fundamentally change things as they are? Don't the foundational structures of modern identity-making itself need to be challenged and taken apart? That is, while a politics organized around the validity and worth of gay or lesbian identities has clearly brought signifi-cant gains for at least some formerly marginalized and dispossessed groups, has it really expanded options beyond the homo–hetero binary delineating modern sexual-ity or challenged the 'natural' dominance and centrality of heterosexuality in that binary?

The turn to 'queer', then, registers the desire for a more mobile, less stable, set of identifications than those provided by the categories of an often essentializing identity politics (where 'gay–lesbian' replaces the previously normative terms of the homo–hetero equation). The use of 'queer' as adjective and verb as much as noun, as well as the variety and shifting nature of the subject positions and sexual practices it represents, foregrounds the provisionality, even undecidability, of such identifications. If 'queer' signals a desire for more fluid, dynamic subject positions than those made possible by the binaristic thinking of homo–hetero, gay–straight, lesbian–gay man, and so on, the politics arising out of it might better envisage new forms of coalition-building and new room to manoeuvre within established sex–gender systems.

Queering identity/historicizing modernity

Beginning in the late 1980s and early 1990s a growing number of cultural critics and theorists began to engage with this turn to 'queer' in sexual activism and popular culture, in search of a more thoroughgoing and multivalent challenge to modern discourses of sexuality and identity than that offered by the focus on identity that dominated so much of current feminist and sexuality studies. The academic discussion that developed, loosely grouped under the rubric 'queer theory', crosses a variety of disciplinary boundaries, historical periods, and critical–theoretical approaches. Certainly there is no one monolithic thing that is queer theory. But we can isolate three areas of investigation—the body and identity, the relationships of pleasure, power, and politics, and the historicization of modernity—where queer theory has made provocative and powerful interventions.

Judith Butler, for example, in her books *Gender Trouble* and *Bodies that Matter*,[16] has interrogated the naturalness of the 'sex is to nature as gender is to culture' equation, and with it the foundational status of a pre-existent known biological body for the modern sex–gender–sexuality system, by theorizing the performativity of both sex and gender. As Butler puts it,

performativity describes this relation of being implicated in that which one opposes, this turning of power against itself to produce alternative modalities of power, to establish a kind of political contestation that is not a 'pure' opposition, a 'transcendence' of contemporary relations of power [as some uses of gay or facile notions of performativity as simple performance might suggest], but a difficult labor of forging a future from resources inevitably impure.[17]

In stressing performativity in this way, Butler does mean that either sex or gender is simply a role we choose to try on or take off. But neither is the material body we think we can 'know' and take for granted somehow able to be talked about, imagined, lived as if it were outside the effects of culture and language. Instead, our sexed and gendered bodies are the tangible effects of the 'congealing' of a set of legal, medical, philosophical, cultural statements repeated again and again over time and throughout a variety of discursive terrains in such a way as to stylize the body in profoundly structural ways. Thus, the body that we think of as natural, as a given, is instead a discursively created social phenomenon that has its own particular history and madeness. Take the performative utterance 'It's a boy/It's a girl'. Performative in that in making it we trust we make it fact, it is an utterance sometimes literally spoken thus by doctor or parent at birth but repeated again and again in the clothes we are given as children and later 'choose', the career choices we make, the force of laws enacted upon us, and so on. Moreover, the binaristic force of its boy–girl structure has always already shaped and stylized the supposedly natural, pre-existent material body it envisages, sometimes by literally ignoring or disallowing the evidence of the eyes or the evidence of the psyche (as in the case of transgendered individuals).

Butler's queer performativity, by deconstructing the naturalized body of modern regimes of sex–gender–sexuality, is one example of how the insights of queer theory work to undo the dominance of compulsory heterosexuality within modern regimes of sex–gender–sexuality in very different ways from the politics of gay liberation. Such a performative model of sexuality, for example, might suggest that certain aspects of gay–lesbian identity politics, while immensely useful in winning rights for many previously disavowed citizens, to the extent that they are based on notions of a stable identity presupposing biological or psychological 'facts' about the body still in crucial ways reproduce some of the basic foundational structures of modern sexuality. If so, a politics worked through in terms of stable identities could unwittingly perpetuate a system in which heterosexuality presents itself as natural, unquestionably central, normative, and dominant (one in which gay men and lesbians, and certainly those 'deviants' still outside the pale, remain at best tolerated minorities). Rather than fantasize a new, improved 'gay' subject outside heterosexuality, but still maintaining the status of heterosexuality largely untouched, queer theory would focus more on exploring ways of resisting modern regimes of sexuality and identity *from within* the various cultural scripts that shape us as modern sexed–gendered subjects.

Queer theory's emphasis on the *processes* by which power circulates through modern systems of sex–gender–sexuality, as well as on the queer torsions such circulation produces, accounts for its intimate relationship with sexuality studies and many points of overlap with gay–lesbian politics. But it also marks a significant reorientation *away* from a delimited focus on the history of homosexuality or a politics of simple mainstreaming of previously marginalized groups such as gays and lesbians. Queer theory's privileging of erotic over identitarian politics has tended to turn it away from the delineation of the specificities of same-sex desire towards the articulation of a personal, political, and cultural praxis that remains as open as possible to the fullness of identifications that desire can excite.

Queer theory remains intent on exploring the crucial and disruptive role that perverse pleasure plays in the relationships between desire and power (both dominant and marginalized). Hence, queer theory emphasizes the processes by which queer subjects become integral to a dominant heterosexuality's construction of the natural and unnatural, centre and margin, inside and outside. Conceptual models such as Eve Kosofsky Sedgwick's epistemology of the closet, Judith Butler's queer performativity and transgressive reinscription, Jonathan Dollimore's perverse dynamic, Lee Edelman's homographesis, or Judith Halberstam's female masculinity, as well as attention to the queer crossings of conceptual divides that can take place through the pursuits of drag queens–kings or transgendered individuals, have all become important means by which queer theory has worked to make visible both the structuration of dominant power within and through the modern sex–gender system *and* the processes of queer resistance.[18]

Although queer theory has often been accused of an ahistoricist presentism, it does, I think, offer a way to think the history of sexuality differently, much as postcolonial theory attempts to think 'beyond' nationalist and racial historicizing in useful ways. Queer theory seeks to historicize modern regimes of sex, gender, and sexuality, recognizing them as neither natural nor a progressivist supersession of previous epistemological frameworks. Perhaps its most important insight has been the exposure of modern heterosexuality (and the entire sex–gender regime that supports it) as a creation of modern economic, legal, and medical discourses—something *un*natural, with its own history. Thus, the work of historicization is not simply to chart the triumphant march of modernity and progress as inevitable and natural. Rather, the work of historicization, in challenging the naturalness of things as they are, exposes not only the blindnesses and wilful ignorances of the present, but also that which has been left behind. A queer history of sexuality, then, might expose the constructedness of modern heterosexuality, thereby reading the past not through the lens of a presumptive modern heterosexuality (where the past must either reproduce heterosexuality as we know it or function as the primitive backdrop to the march towards modern fulfilment). Queer theory thus provides one important way to open up conceptual space for different modes of desire and sex–gender systems within the present *and* for a recognition of the difference of the premodern outside the workings of modern (hetero)sexuality.

Late medieval proto-capitalism and category confusion in the 'Shipman's Tale'

In the remainder of this chapter I want to consider the perverse intersections of the new money economy, female sexuality, and the bourgeois married household that dominate the plot of Chaucer's 'Shipman's Tale'. I focus on the tale's attempts to understand individual desire and the social relations arising out of it in terms of exchanges in the marketplace. And I argue that such a queer project manifests not only the new signifying power attained by a late medieval sex–gender system increasingly organized around bourgeois conjugality, but also the growing authority of the logic of the marketplace as a reliable model for productive social relations. At the same time, such an emphasis on the new calls into question the traditional foundations for medieval assessments of moral worth and the natural order. Queering the tale this way will, I hope, move us far beyond a simple preoccupation with sexuality and take us into wide-ranging and fundamental issues relating to social structures, historical change, and ultimately to questions of reading and literary structure itself.

Commercial exchange is everywhere in the 'Shipman's Tale'. A wealthy merchant makes 1,000 franks from his commercial transaction; a monk profits sexually by borrowing 100 franks from the same merchant and lending it to the merchant's wife in return for a night in bed with her; the wife gains the 100 franks she needs to pay for clothing she has bought—first by trading her body for the monk's borrowed money, and then by claiming to her husband that she thought the monk had given her the money in return for the merchant's past hospitality; the merchant 'forgives' his wife's debt in recognition of the sexual and other satisfactions she provides him as his wife. Moreover, the logic of exchange not only motivates character and action in the tale, it defines the very structures of language itself. A number of crucial puns brings together normally different and separate conceptual fields in ways that exploit and make explicit the queer contiguities occurring in the tale's plot. The monk, claiming the merchant 'as for cosynage' (36) and counted a 'cosyn' (69) by the merchant because of a shared village background, cheats (or 'cozens') his sworn brother when he buys the wife's sexual favours with the merchant's own money.[19] Later the monk assures the merchant that he has repaid his loan to the merchant's wife, who knows it for sure 'by certeyn tokenes' (359) that he could tell about (that is, by the imprint of their sexual exchanges on her body rather than the expected exchange of coins). And most notably, the representation of conjugality (and the bourgeois household founded upon it) as a kind of marketplace perversely conflates a money economy with wifely constancy and sexual satisfaction in the 'tail'–'tally' pun that runs throughout the plot but that is made comically explicit in the final bedroom conversation between wife and husband: 'I am youre wyf; score it upon my taille, | And I shal paye as soone as ever I may' (416–17).

Such exchanges in the tale work to bring together the incommensurable—things, characters, concepts, semantic fields that would, more properly, elsewhere be kept apart. Thus, the same merchant who at the beginning of the tale lectures his wife about how 'litel kanstow devyne | The curious bisynesse that we [merchants] have' (224–5), urging her to carry out her housewifely duties faithfully in his absence, ends up lectured by his wife about just how market forces govern the business of their conjugal relations and matters of the household. The tale's emphasis on market forces also calls into question the foundations upon which 'normal' relations of moral worth and natural order are judged, suggesting that no recourse is available to some stable, secure point of origin, ethical or otherwise. The merchant's claim to kinship or 'cosynage' with the monk, based on their common village origins (with all its promise of connection between present personally chosen associations and a stable, originary feudal order), is summarily exchanged by the monk for possible sexual satisfaction with the merchant's wife:

> 'Nay,' quod this monk, 'by God and Seint Martyn,
> He is na moore cosyn unto me
> Than is this leef that hangeth on the tree!
> I clepe hym so, by Seint Denys of Fraunce,
> To have the moore cause of aqueyntaunce
> Of yow, which I have loved specially
> Aboven all wommen, sikerly.
> This swere I yow on my professioun . . .' (148–55)

Similarly, the monk profits from his 'professioun' of holy orders and kinship here not because it makes evident some transcendent moral ideal, social structure, or religious identity, but because it provides a convincing cover for sexual negotiation and a useful rhetorical flourish in his wooing of the wife.

While there is nothing remotely homo about the sexual perversity of the tale, there is much that is queer in terms of medieval thinking about sex, gender, and sexuality. The supposedly celibate monk who desires the merchant's wife and effectively buys her sexual favours with a loan she desperately needs, the wife who 'sells' her body thus to improve her social and marital position, the merchant who puts monetary profit ahead of his duties as head of the household, all provide reverse images of a medieval sex–gender system very different from modern heterosexuality. In such a system, which the antics of the 'Shipman's Tale' comically invert, the inherent worth and superiority of celibacy is institutionalized in a social hierarchy that privileges celibate cleric over married husband, virgin over wife. Sexual activity and erotic desire must be rigorously controlled and harnessed in service to the common good or they will undermine the valuable work of reason and the will and thus undo the boundaries of the individual and the social order itself. Because sexual activity can only be justified to the extent it works to reproduce the race, it must be expressed within the sanctioned channels of proper marital sex in the missionary position, and only at times when procreation could occur. Anything else for medieval theologians constitutes a sodomitical perversity on par with same-sex activity (for further discussion of this, see Chapter 12).

The disturbances to traditional order wrought by the sexual activity taking place in the 'Shipman's Tale' are paralleled by the apparently reductive equation of monetary profit, sexual commerce, and successful marital relations made by the merchant's wife. The wife's exchange of sex for money, by mimicking merchant pursuit of profit (traditionally justified as for the common good), thereby threatens to undo the traditional 'natural' superiority of husbands within the married state. Similarly, the monk's devaluation of a traditional kinship tie that the merchant claims with him and his willingness to exchange such cousinship for the fleeting satisfaction of a night with the merchant's wife also constitute a perverse undoing of traditional village social relationships arising out of medieval feudalism. These exchanges on the part of wife and monk thus threaten the supposedly essential truth and value of traditional medieval identities, but they also run the risk of tainting newer identities and practices struggling to gain stability and dominant positions within late medieval society—those of the merchant and bourgeois–gentry household. Social arrangements are changing rapidly in the late fourteenth century as a new class of individuals, representing economically and politically powerful landowning and mercantile interests but not part of the traditional aristocratic or clerical ruling classes, comes to the fore. And this new merchant–gentry class is seeking ways of representing themselves and their interests within an older medieval social and cosmic order. As we will see, both marriage and the money economy provide important locations to negotiate such processes of identity formation and self-authorization.

Money, exchange, and equality

Joel Kaye has argued that the ubiquity and necessity of the newly emerging money economy in the late Middle Ages produced two different responses from theorists in the period.[20] The first, what he calls an arithmetic model, tried to reconcile the pursuit of profit with older, natural law definitions of economic equality. Merchant profit escaped the charge of usury, of making something out of nothing, only when a commercial exchange involved a reasonable risk for the merchant *or* when the 'work' of the merchant bringing one good prevalent in another land to a country where it was scarce added to common profit. In this way, one could decide the real value of an exchange, arithmetically, by gauging the extent to which it matched or fell away from the 'natural equality' that ruled all things in God's universe. It seems to me that many modern critical approaches to the 'Shipman's Tale' reproduce such an approach to the tale's exchanges in seeking to work out a 'plus' or 'minus' figure for the merchant's morality—either by invoking medieval models of natural law in order to decide the moral worth of the tale and the merchant or by invoking the historical situation of merchants in order to decide how representative the tale's treatment of the merchant class and its emergent social power might be. Such criticism has ranged from condemnations of the merchant as corrupted by his occupation and its focus on material rather than spiritual profit, to endorsements of his class's ingenuity, hard work, and competitiveness, to more nuanced historicizations of the tale's representation of the complexity and contradiction inherent in the merchant's social situation and the money economy he inhabits.

It is the second, newer medieval theoretical response to an emergent monetized economy—what Kaye calls a geometric model of exchange—that seems more relevant, however, in addressing the specificities of exchange in the 'Shipman's Tale'. The older arithmetic model imagined the necessity of an intervening judge to decide the natural relationship between two different points of exchange. In the newer geometric model, the idea of money as an impersonal instrument within economic exchange replaces the necessity for the personal activity of the judge in the older arithmetic model, and the logic of the marketplace replaces the morality of the stable natural order. Money offers exactly the kind of flexible, relational medium needed to equate the unequatable, and thereby to negotiate the problem of value incommensurability within the dynamic processes of the marketplace of the fourteenth century. For as Kaye notes,

in the marketplace, not only were doctors brought into relation with farmers . . . but armies were bought, labor and land commoditized, subjective services (including indulgences) commuted into cash, social position and duty increasingly graded by numbered income, and personal qualities measured by and translated into a numbered money price.[21]

Money is thus seen to function as a geometric line linking incommensurable goods and services (and agents and desires), and value derives from a set of fluid and contingent marketplace estimates.

In this geometric model, money acts as an instrument of relation by measuring and giving a numerical value to such an accidental continuous quality as need (from which all exchange results). Need thus functions as the necessary common quality or 'third term' in the measurement and relation of commodities in the marketplace, and money as the continuum recognized to measure need. Market exchange, then, could be seen as a system governed by its own logic and possessing its own equilibrium (its own 'nature' as it were) despite the inequality and incommensurability of individual points of exchange within this system.

Such a model for the market suggests an alternative to the moralizing language of blame that so easily provides a ready-made model for deciding the worth of the 'Shipman's Tale' or its characters. I give as an example Lee Patterson's insistence, like the merchant at the beginning of the tale, on the natural incommensurability of household and marketplace:

That the profit these transactions generate is unfounded continues to pose the central question . . . The marriage between merchant and wife, the kinship between monk and merchant, and the friendship between wife and monk are natural relations that are degraded—commodified—when they enter into the exchange system. Profit is what accrues from the reduction of the matrimonial bond, and of the ties of kinship and friendship, to business relationships. The argument of the *Tale*, in short, is that profit derives from the commodification of the natural order.[22]

Yet it is precisely the tallying wife whom the merchant acknowledges as valuable at the end of the tale, and in doing so, he in some measure accepts the business of the household (and with it wifely activity) as business, different from but still on a continuum of geometric measurement with his 'normal' business. In turn, the exchanges between wife and merchant link the work of identity formation within the household (organized in and through economies of gender, sexuality, and desire) with that of the outside world. And they do so in a way that privileges the value of the private, enclosed, 'unnatural' system of household and fabliau story in honing crucial skills of individual estimation and measurement. Far from degradation and empty commodification (as Patterson suggests), the tale's conflation of the wife's body–sexual favours– tail and money–commercial exchange–tallying reclaims the perverse from a solely negative meaning to indicate productive procedures. In doing so, the tale's queer sexual politics profitably mobilizes the room for manoeuvre present in new, developing models of lay conjugality and ties them to the logic of the marketplace in order to promulgate new conceptual frameworks and modes of social organization.

Medieval conjugality and late medieval bourgeois identity formation

I have argued elsewhere that an emphasis on the representational power of conjugality by bourgeois lay groups within late medieval society increasingly came to provide an important way for them to identify their bourgeois–gentry identity and made the married estate in the period an unstable 'middle' category within traditional medieval modes of social organization.[23] That is, conjugality becomes an important category with which to think through the complex and contradictory desire of a newly emerging late medieval–early modern 'middle' class.

The new emphasis in canon law and theology on individual consent as the basis for marriage proceeded out of its revaluation as a sacrament by canon lawyers such as Peter Lombard and others in the twelfth century. This sacramental function for marriage in turn encouraged a much greater emphasis on the value of the personal relations it established between a man and woman. This is seen, first of all, in the way that an appreciation of the intrinsic goodness of the married state led to the articulation of a so-called 'conjugal debt' in canon law, stipulating that each spouse owed the other right of access to proper marital coitus (for more on this, see Chapter 12). The right of spouses to their marital due could therefore be abrogated only by mutual consent. But canon law also calls for the desirability of growth in marital or conjugal affection, making marital affection not only a requirement for the establishment of marriage but also a required part of married life that endured during the entire marriage. Such marital affection (in an age of arranged or business marriages) was often articulated in what might seem to us as very material terms—a sexual partner; a place in society; nourishment, shelter, and clothing suitable to one's rank; and so forth. There is, though, some evidence of the capacity for this understanding of marriage as sacrament to articulate a kind of conjugal love that goes beyond either the external aspects of marital affection or the contractual obligations of equal sexual rights: conjugality as a kind of love between partners and equals that had heretofore been imaginable only between male friends.

Lay conjugality and the individual bourgeois household it constructed thus came to function in the later Middle Ages as sites governed by their own logic and possessing their own equilibrium despite the inequality and incommensurability of individual agents within the system. Previous dynastic models of marriage exchange might have provided a kind of arithmetical exchange that would have established the comparable nobility and worth of each participant and their difference from inferiors. What I am suggesting here is that the new interest in lay conjugality reconfigures the married estate, previously often defined as 'inferior' to celibacy, in a way that allows it to structure an empowering identity for individuals and groups not previously given representational force. Moreover, this evolving conjugality often facilitates new forms of exchange within marriage by commodifying the feminine and the wifely role in newly profitable ways so that it can function, like money for the market economy, as the instrument of relation for the emerging household economy. Deportment books directed at marriageable daughters or young wives, such as the *Ménagier de Paris*, or the immensely popular stories of patient Griselda's forbearance and the wise Prudence's advice to her husband, Melibee, write on the bodies of these good women a bourgeois–gentry identity for the feminine, and via that foundation, a new, potentially dominant form of masculinity for their male authors and readers. Marriage, then, by the later Middle Ages has become something 'good to think with' for an emergent class within dominant culture. And in this restructuring of lay gender relations within conjugality, the feminine is accorded some measure of use value and a certain limited degree of autonomy, even as such redefined marital relations continue to try to keep the feminine under the masculine control of a properly husbanded bourgeois household.

The extent to which the comic action of the 'Shipman's Tale' promises to 'handle' the perverse threats posed by the new conjugality and commerce to an older social order allows it to represent a successful rebalancing of old and new within the merchant household as 'natural' and hegemonic. But the 'Shipman's Tale' also represents what is destabilizing and transgressive about these new market and conjugal exchanges in its refusal to fix their value in arithmetical fashion, to render them either wholly proper or improper. Instead, the sexual and commercial exchanges taking place in the tale can be seen as governed by their own logic and possessing their own equilibrium despite the inequality and incommensurability of their agents within the tale. And the tale's complex interweaving of conjugality and commerce, both disavowing the potential perversity of the wife's sexual commerce *and* privileging aspects of lay sexuality and authorizing bourgeois–gentry subjectivity in the thriftiness of the husband, can make possible a place for certain aspects of the new conjugality and commerce within an older medieval representational system, although not without much anxiety and contestation.

The tale's exploration of the logic of the marketplace in negotiating and under- standing the value of social as well as economic relations suggests, too, the possibility of a larger reorientation of readerly desire and the hermeneutic structures such desire estab- lishes. In Fragment VII of the *Tales*, fabliau ('Shipman's Tale') is exchanged for anti- semitic miracle story ('Prioress's Tale'), for tragedy ('Monk's Tale'), for truncated mock romance ('Tale of Sir Thopas'), and didactic moralization ('Tale of Melibee'), and for beast fable ('Nun's Priest's Tale'). This succession of apparently incommensurable points of exchange, often without even the rudimentary structuring relationships of dramatic suitability of tale-teller and tale or the social contest established elsewhere in the fictional frame of the *Tales*, produces a disorienting generic variability and troubling lack of 'natural' or 'literary' connection if viewed through traditional hermeneutic lenses. By representing and valuing a more contingent and fluid model of reading and understanding, a geometric rather than arithmetic one, the 'Shipman's Tale' sketches in particularly bold strokes a different way of approaching the apparently incommensurable exchanges that structure Fragment VII (and indeed, the fragmented, contingent relationships within the *Canterbury Tales* as a whole).

FURTHER READING

Bowers, John, 'Queering the Summoner: Same-Sex Union in Chaucer's *Canterbury Tales*', in R. F. Yeager and Charlotte C. Morse (eds.), *Speaking Images: Essays in Honor of V. A. Kolve* (Asheville, NC: Pegasus Press, 2001). Explores how, in the relationship between the Pardoner and Summoner, Chaucer dramatizes the deviant paradigm of a union between two men based upon the contractual bond of adoptive brotherhood.

Burger, Glenn, *Chaucer's Queer Nation* (Minneapolis: University of Minnesota Press, 2003). Shows a Chaucer uneasily situated between the medieval and the modern, representing in the *Canterbury Tales* new forms of sexual and communal identity but also enacting the anxieties provoked by such departures from the past.

Burger, Glenn, and Steven F. Kruger (eds.), *Queering the Middle Ages* (Minneapolis: University of Minnesota Press, 2001). The essays in this volume, including several on Chaucerian material, present work that queers stabilized conceptions of the Middle Ages, allowing us to see the period and its systems of sexuality in radically different, off-centre, and revealing ways.

Dinshaw, Carolyn, *Getting Medieval: Sexualities and Communities, Pre- and Postmodern* (Durham, NC: Duke University Press, 1999). Especially interesting for its careful and nuanced theorization of the interrelationships of sexuality and community, as well as of the processes of historicization for the postmodern reader.

Jagose, Annamarie, *Queer Theory: An Introduction* (New York: New York University Press, 1996). Provides a clear and concise explanation of queer theory, tracing its history and surveying the contributions of major queer theorists.

Kruger, Steven F., 'Claiming the Pardoner: Toward a Gay Reading of Chaucer's "Pardoner's Tale"', *Exemplaria*, 6/1 (Spring 1994), 115–40. One of the first articles to bring the insights of queer theory to Chaucer studies, providing a compelling argument for a gay reading of the Pardoner from within modern sexuality that honestly seeks to come to terms with the anachronism and political engagement that such reading necessarily involves.

Lochrie, Karma, *Covert Operations: The Medieval Uses of Secrecy* (Philadelphia: University of Pennsylvania Press, 1999). Providing readings of the Parson's and Miller's Tales and other late medieval English texts, this is particularly interesting for its theoretical and historical discussion of the importance of medieval heterosexual sodomy and the crucial difference of medieval sexuality from modern heterosexuality.

Zeikowitz, Richard, *Homoeroticism and Chivalry: Discourses of Male Same-Sex Desire in the Fourteenth Century* (New York: Palgrave, 2003). Explores the discourses of male same-sex desire in various fourteenth-century chivalric texts, including Chaucer's *Troilus and Criseyde*.

NOTES

1. See Christopher Cannon, '*Raptus* in the Chaumpaigne Release and a Newly Discovered Document concerning the Life of Geoffrey Chaucer', *Speculum*, 68 (1993), 79–94; and Christopher Cannon, 'Chaucer and Rape: Uncertainty's Certainties', in Elizabeth Robertson and Christine M. Rose (eds.), *Representing Rape in Medieval and Early Modern Literature* (New York: Palgrave, 2001), 225–79.

2. George Lyman Kittredge, *Chaucer and his Poetry* (Cambridge, Mass.: Harvard University Press, 1915), 211.

3. See e.g. Monica McAlpine, 'The Pardoner's Homosexuality and How it Matters', *PMLA* 95 (1980), 8–22.

4. See e.g. Richard Firth Green, 'The Sexual Normalcy of Chaucer's Pardoner', *Medievalia*, 8 (1985), 351–7.

5. Trans. Robert Hurley, 3 vols. (New York: Pantheon Books, 1978–86).

6. 'Claiming the Pardoner: Toward a Gay Reading of Chaucer's "Pardoner's Tale" ', *Exemplaria*, 6/1 (Spring 1994), 119.

7. Ibid. 117.

8. Ibid. 125.

9. Ibid. 121

10. Ibid. 137.

11. Ibid. 138.

12. Glenn Burger, *Chaucer's Queer Nation* (Minneapolis: University of Minnesota Press, 2003), 140–59.

13. *Getting Medieval: Sexualities and Communities, Pre- and Postmodern* (Durham, NC: Duke University Press, 1999), 116.

14. Ibid. 121.

15. Ibid. 126.

16. *Gender Trouble: Feminism and the Subversion of Identity* (New York: Routledge, 1990); *Bodies that Matter: On the Discursive Limits of Sex* (New York: Routledge, 1993).

17. *Bodies that Matter*, 241.

18. Eve Kosofsky Sedgwick, *Epistemology of the Closet* (Berkeley and Los Angeles: University of California Press, 1990); Butler, *Bodies that Matter*; Jonathan Dollimore, *Sexual Dissidence: Augustine to Wilde, Freud to Foucault* (Oxford: Clarendon Press, 1991); Lee Edelman, *Homographesis: Essays in Gay Literary and Cultural Theory* (New York: Routledge, 1994); Judith Halberstam, *Female Masculinity* (Durham, NC: Duke University Press, 1998).

19. See Gerhard Joseph, 'Chaucer's Coinage: Foreign Exchange and the Puns of the "Shipman's Tale"', *Chaucer Review*, 17 (1983), 351–2, for a discussion of why such a pun might be read into the tale.

20. Joel Kaye, *Economy and Nature in the Fourteenth Century: Money, Market Exchange, and the Emergence of Scientific Thought* (Cambridge: Cambridge University Press, 1998).

21. Ibid. 218–19.

22. Lee Patterson, *Chaucer and the Subject of History* (Madison: University of Wisconsin Press, 1991), 356.

23. *Chaucer's Queer Nation*, 37–77.

26 | Postcolonialism

Jeffrey J. Cohen

Postcolonial criticism explores those contact zones where multiple cultures clash, compete, coexist. Its analyses are, in the words of one highly regarded practitioner, predicated upon the critical examination of 'the unequal and uneven forces of cultural representation involved in the contest for political and social authority'.[1] Postcolonial critique emphasizes the heterogeneity of cultures, their commingling of differences in history, language, creed, custom, desire. Without a great deal of violence such differences cannot be assimilated into a uniform whole. Postcolonial critique aims to restore to the world its multiplicity, its pluralism, often by exploring minority histories that have been obscured. Although medievalists have only recently begun to cite postcolonial criticism explicitly in their work, its concerns have long been evident in their research.

Postcolonial practice

The postcolonial criticism most widely influential in the academy derives mainly from the study of English imperialism, from Europe's enduring fantasies of the East (christened 'orientalism' by Edward Said, see below), and from the decolonization of former French possessions. South Asia has received the most attention in the United States and England. Yet the intellectual genealogy of postcolonial critique spans the inhabited continents, and addresses a vast array of cultures and histories, from the Caribbean and Latin America to Africa, Canada, Australia, and the United States. Postcolonial critique is connected to ethnic, race, and area studies, as well as to feminism, disability studies, and cultural materialism, not least because all these schools demonstrate an abiding concern with the excluded and disempowered. Postcolonial criticism evinces a deep sense of social justice. The world is assumed to be utterly messy and protean, a state of impure being described variously as creolization, doubleness, mesitizaje, métissage, or hybridity. Attempts to sort and organize this turbulence more often than not reveal a desire to contain, degrade, and colonize whatever is perceived as foreign and threatening. Distrustful of official accounts of history, postcolonial criticism turns to the past in order to discover the contingencies that have formed the present.

Canonical Chaucer

Postcolonial critics cast a suspicious eye upon the claim that some few texts should be revered simply because they are part of a self-evident register of Great Works, and are interested in who gets left out from such lists. Some foundational scholarship in postcolonial theory ties education intimately to the aims of empire, especially when native or minority knowledges are denigrated so that the English language and Christian religion can be promulgated as universals. What world-view is being instilled as part of the educational process? Does imbuing an awe for Anglophone culture imply an inherent superiority? When a fourteenth-century poet like Chaucer is widely studied while contemporary authors writing in Scotland, Ireland, and Wales (or writing within England in, say, Hebrew) are not, are imperialistic objectives being silently reaffirmed?

That pedagogical traditions do change—and change radically—is obvious from a glance at Chaucer's education. He did not grow up reading classic English literature, for the simple reason that there wasn't any. For the educated class to which he belonged literacy meant Latinity, since Latin was the international language for keeping records, composing official documents, and recording history, and was the language of the authoritative literary classics. To go to school was to be disciplined into a discourse shared by a powerful masculine elite, bestowing prestige and cultural capital upon those in its possession. At court Chaucer would have spoken the Anglo-Norman dialect of French, an enduring inheritance from William's conquest of the realm. A colonizer's language, French had by Chaucer's day become a marker of social class rather than of ethnic difference. Chaucer probably wrote his first poetry in this elite tongue, but that did not render his relation to French and France any less ambivalent. He knew all too well the ebbs and flows of violence between England and its continental neighbour, not least because in 1359 he was captured while part of an invasion force. Chaucer never mentions the French presence in English history. The 'Man of Law's Tale' is set in the Anglo-Saxon past of the land; even though its narrator knows all the legal judgments from 'the tyme of kyng William' ('GP' 324), nowhere in this work or in any other does Chaucer mention the Norman Conquest. Yet although Chaucer likely conversed with his own parents in English, the language that he spoke with his wife (raised in the English court but of Hainault origin) and probably children was French.

In rejecting French as a literary vehicle Chaucer rejected the history that had previously made French both elite and prestigious. In deciding to write as if English were already a tongue that could bestow the same immortality on an insular author that Latin had given to Virgil, Chaucer undercut the classical tradition that had formed the core of his education, had formed *him*. The breathtaking panache of the words with which he closes his courtly poem *Troilus and Criseyde* can be appreciated only with this radical departure in mind:

> Go, litel bok, go, litel myn tragedye . . .
> And kis the steppes where as thow seest pace
> Virgile, Ovide, Omer, Lucan, and Stace. (5. 1786–92)

Chaucer had reaped economic benefits from his knowledge of Latin, but through works like the *Canterbury Tales* he also sabotaged that classical tradition, stealing some of its status to bestow upon a vernacular that had for the past three centuries not seemed capable of being literary. Chaucer transformed a subaltern language into a readable one.

Given that Chaucer mastered a tradition only to reject its foundational claim to exclusivity, it is ironic that he should be regarded as the most canonical of authors. Chaucer's fifteenth-century followers, poets like Hoccleve and Lydgate, happily discovered in him a founding father whose sophisticated English they could harness to their own nationalistic aspirations. The problem with the doctrine of Chaucer's supreme Englishness, so popular during the Age of Empire, is that it has little basis in Chaucer's literary record. Although the frame of the *Canterbury Tales* unfolds in England, it does not seem 'a place for which we are encouraged to feel a particular affection, as a beloved land or heritage-site'.[2] Even the Canterbury Pilgrims are, on the whole, a motley and unidealized group.

Postcolonial criticism holds that writers and texts ought to be seen as part of history, not as transcending it. What this means in practical terms for the contemporary study of Chaucer is that it is often necessary for a disenchantment to be performed, rather like the clap in the 'Franklin's Tale' that dispels the visions of swirling 'revel' from the room to allow other, more quotidian kinds of magic to proceed (1203–4). Chaucer was a medieval poet, a limited and fallible human being. His works call into being an intoxicatingly imperfect series of worlds. It is difficult to reduce these wide expanses to a jingoistic paean or harness them to some xenophobic nationalism, though that never stopped later writers from trying.

The medieval and the postcolonial

Postcolonial critique is fundamentally about refusing to judge the non-Western and the non-modern by contemporary Eurocentric standards. 'The problem of getting beyond Eurocentric histories', Dipesh Chakrabarty has observed, 'remains a shared problem across geographic boundaries.'[3] Isn't it somewhat perverse to find an entry for postcolonial criticism neatly tucked into an undertaking as official, Eurocentric, and Anglophilic as an Oxford Guide to Chaucer, founding father of the English literary tradition? Yet I wonder if such labels as 'Eurocentric' should be hurled so cavalierly at the Middle Ages, especially given that neither Europe nor England existed as the unified entities we now imagine are designated by the words. Neither Europe nor England is timeless; nor are they the inevitable culmination of evolutionary processes, as if they were modernity itself. They are, in other words, one or two centres among many others, composed in turn of multiple centres of their own.

The historian Robert Bartlett has written at great length of how Europe had to 'Europeanize' itself in order to be able to imagine a kind of transnational community.[4] This long and not unresisted process of internal harmonization meant that peoples finding themselves suddenly annexed to expanding realms had to give up their 'barbarous' ways, had to learn (in Uppinder Mehan's words) that they inhabited 'the margin of someone else's center.'[5] Mediterranean culture displaced and absorbed other modes of being; the West slowly Latinized. England was meanwhile involved in a process of self-colonization, Anglicizing its inhabitants in an effort to produce a nation united in culture, custom, and ardour.[6] The once circumscribed kingdom of England ambitiously began to imagine itself as coterminous with the British Isles, thereby appropriating more and more of the land to itself.

Postcolonial critique tends to concentrate on the 'middle spaces' which open up when a dominant culture's demand to recentre the world around itself is resisted. When London is granted no primacy over Dublin, Norwich, or Cornwall, when Rome (or sometimes, in Chaucer's day, Avignon) is accorded no innate superiority over local shrines and 'provincial' rituals (or over Constantinople, Cairo, Beijing), the world begins to spin along multiple axes, the music of the spheres is traded for a noise that cannot be anticipated in advance. This conceptualization eliminates the binarism between subordinated peripheries and dominating metropoles, offering a multiplicity of centres instead. It also checks the tendency to think of that which is located at some important centre as being more advanced, while that at the supposed fringe is primitive, uncouth. An ambition of postcolonial theory is to grant to all cultures a coevalness, a temporal equality that disallows careless labels like 'backward' and 'undeveloped'.

Postcolonial London

A poet who composed verse that tends to be aesthetically rich rather than socially provocative, Chaucer was not all that interested in absolutes. Neither imperialist writer nor postcolonial intellectual, he evinces some traits of both. It is useful to keep in mind that Chaucer inhabited a heterogeneous and difficult world, starting with the city of his birth. The riotous 'Cook's Tale', Chaucer's sole narrative set entirely in contemporary London, begins with an interjection of Flemish, the proverb 'Sooth pley, quaad pley' ('A true jest is a bad jest', 4357). Perhaps the Cook is revealing a surprising cosmopolitanism. With a population reaching as many as 50,000 inhabitants, the late fourteenth-century metropolis was a polyglot place. Chaucer's family home was on Thames Street in the Vintry Ward, close enough to the water to see ships sailing to and from Scandinavia, Iberia, the Mediterranean. This wealthy merchant neighbourhood was the residence of many Italian families involved, like Chaucer's father, in the international wine trade. Chaucer's knowledge of Italian served him well later in life as he undertook state business in Genoa and Florence. Other languages that he would have heard in a stroll through London include Flemish, Greek, French, German.

But London, 'oure citee' according to the Cook (4365), also offered an urban landscape in which sudden ethnic violence could claim the lives of non-natives. During the Peasants' Revolt the gate above which Chaucer lived was used by rebels to storm the city. The insurgents vented their wrath not only against detested superiors like the archbishop of Canterbury (whom they executed), but against any foreigner they could find. When a group of terrified Flemings took refuge inside the parish church where Chaucer had worshipped as a child, the building was besieged and its occupants decapitated. Thames Street was the dumping ground for forty headless corpses. Chaucer sold the family house there a week later. The Cook's Flemish proverb takes on a darker resonance in light of this massacre, especially given that Chaucer's only recorded reaction to the bloody episode is a joking allusion in the 'Nun's Priest's Tale', where a barnyard frolic is compared to the noise of the angry mob who 'wolden any Flemyng kille' (3396). 'The fact that the Cook knows some Flemish', David Wallace writes, 'does not mean that he is a friend of Flemings.'[7] The same might be said of Geoffrey Chaucer, who never acknowledges that innocent blood and violated corpses on his boyhood street are at least worth memorializing.

Chaucer's London was a culturally energetic place where diverse languages rubbed against each other, a geography of sheer possibility. It was also the location of great cruelty and intolerance. Differences in class, geographic origin, ethnicity, and race ensured that fractured segments of the population found themselves competing with some groups and placidly coexisting with others—sometimes in alternation, sometimes with sudden changes, new alliances, shedding of blood. Few of the specificities of this history find their way into Chaucer's texts, but they may (more positively) lie behind his endemic ambivalence and love of multiplicity and openness (for more on London, see Chapter 4).

It is often Chaucer's profoundest silences that illuminate what his poetry *does* contain.

From English writer to island writer

Although England's Jewish population had been expelled in 1290, the 'Prioress's Tale' makes them present in the *Canterbury Tales*. Other groups extant on Chaucer's island, however, find themselves strangely missing from the worlds imagined in his texts. These are the denizens of what England eventually came to label its Celtic fringe, the areas to the north and west of the kingdom populated by non-English speakers. Chaucer lived in a kingdom bounded by and expanding into lands possessed by peoples with distinctive histories and substantial internal heterogeneity. Oddly, although his works range geographically from Africa to Italy to the Mongol empire, from heaven (the ascent to the spheres that closes *Troilus and Criseyde*) all the way to hell (the hapless summoner's destination at the end of the 'Friar's Tale'), nearby Wales, Scotland, and Ireland are almost entirely absent.

As an adolescent Chaucer was attached to the household of Prince Lionel, second in line for the crown. Count of Ulster and the king's viceroy, Lionel had inherited about half of Ireland through marriage (although many of its residents, needless to say, insisted that it did not belong to any Englishman to inherit). During his stay on the island in 1366 he presided over a parliament in Kilkenny that issued a statute forbidding English settlers from going native, from adopting Irish language, customs, or dress. Even if he never set foot in Ireland, Chaucer was certainly aware throughout his life of the ongoing project of subjugating and Anglicizing its population, partly through the promulgation of the very language in which he was about to start composing poetry. Chaucer would also have been well aware of the colonial history of England in Wales, the site of sporadic but intense resistance long after its official conquest had ended in the previous century. He would have been frequently reminded of the fluctuating enmity and alliances that English nobles forged with Scotland, especially because his patron John of Gaunt became so embroiled in Scottish politics.

The project of turning 'an archipelago shared unequally . . . between four countries and peoples' into a 'virtually unitary and exclusive orbit of power', begun in Anglo-Saxon days, was most visible years before Chaucer was writing.[8] Yet the marginalization of the Celtic population and the privileging of London's English (both as dialect and as metropolitan culture) over regional differences were ongoing throughout the fourteenth century. John Bowers has written that Chaucer participated in the 'internal colonialism' of England by promulgating the superiority of 'London/Westminster' over the rest of the country, especially the north. The Canterbury pilgrims hail from various regions of England but find themselves in a London suburb speaking London English. Those who would in life have been bilingual never utter a word of French. By making London everywhere, Chaucer silently promulgates a reductive kind of Englishness.[9] Hand-in-hand with this internal colonialism, Chaucer quietly erases the outward push of England's imperialism on the island by either relegating it to an ancient past or passing over it in silence. Chaucer's single Arthurian narrative, the 'Wife of Bath's Tale', implies that this genre so intimately tied to Welsh nationalism is quaint and outdated, as insubstantial as the disappearing elves and fairies that populate its prologue:

> In th'olde dayes of the Kyng Arthour,
> Of which that Britons speken greet honour,
> Al was this land fulfild of fayerye.
> The elf-queene, with hir joly compaignye,
> Daunced ful ofte in many a grene mede. (857–61)

The Britons (i.e. the Welsh) are aligned with the 'olde dayes' of the island, 'manye hundred yeres ago' (863).[10] The present, empty of such fantastic content ('now kan no man se none elves mo', 864), belongs to friars like the Canterbury pilgrim Huberd ('GP' 269), mendicants who divide the land among themselves to farm its revenue (865–77). Such men might from time to time sprinkle their conversation with some urbane French to impress the ladies ('*je vous dy sanz doute*' declares the unctuous protagonist of the 'Summoner's Tale', 1838), but they, like the Britons' world once the friars purge its content and set up their 'lymytaciouns', are thoroughly and unthinkingly English. Chaucer's only other Celtic narrative, the Breton *lai* told by the Franklin, completely ignores the non-English inhabitants with whom the writer shares the island by unfolding in Brittany rather than proximate Wales. The setting seems especially perverse given that the names of the protagonists (Aurelius, Arveragus, and perhaps Dorigen) are taken from Geoffrey of Monmouth's *History of the Kings of Britain*, a profoundly influential text that provided the island a rich, pre-English history—and a text that was integral to contemporary Welsh nationalism. When the knight Arveragus travels abroad to hone his chivalry, he goes to 'Engelond, that cleped was eek Briteyne' (810), silently granting as ancient fact an equivalence for which only England would argue. Like all the Canterbury tales set abroad, moreover, the 'speech and customs are thoroughly anglicized', as if the Bretons were Londoners and all the world were England.[11]

What would happen, though, if Chaucer were considered as one island writer among many, a notable British poet rather than the foundational English one? Think of how different 'Chaucer's England' would seem if he were studied alongside fellow writers of the archipelago he inhabited, writers as internationally minded and as insular as he, writers who did not cohabit some happy multicultural expanse but whose work is intimately entwined through the conflicts, violences, and pleasures that transmuted their cultures via mutual contact. To read a Welsh romance like *Peredur vab Efrawc*, with its notoriously resistant relationship to 'mainstream' romance tradition and its ambivalence towards acculturation, alongside Chaucer's 'Knight's Tale' might enable the meditation on conquest and order which animates both to take on new complexities, to transform the questions we readers ask of each. The multiple endings of Chaucer's *Troilus and Criseyde* resonate differently when read with Robert Henryson's Middle Scots rewriting of the poem, where Creisseid dies an abject leper. After all, Henryson asks with a witty scepticism that anticipates the postcolonial mode of interrogating texts, 'Quha wait gig all that Chauceir wrait was trew?' ('Who knows if everything Chaucer wrote was true?').

Chaucer's orientalism

Although he spent most of his days in domestic civil service, Chaucer was also frequently chosen for important diplomatic missions abroad. His travels brought him to France, Flanders, Italy, Spain. England was religiously homogeneous (even if its

Christianity was prone to troubling internal diversity), but France had many areas in which Ashkenazic Jews dwelled alongside Christian neighbours, and some cities in Spain had populations of Sephardic Jews, Muslims, and a diverse array of Christians living at times in peace, at times in deadly conflict. It may well be that Chaucer first noticed differences in human skin pigmentation as he stood as a boy at a quay by the Thames; it could also be that he did not behold living men and women (as opposed to the caricatured Jews and Muslims of manuscript illustration) with skin not as pale as his own until he travelled to Genoa with its international slave trade or to Castile with its proximity to Muslim Granada. The Revolt of 1381 had targeted unassimilated domestic foreigners, but the non-English abroad were enduring objects of xenophobia throughout the period, especially if they were not Christian. Crusading against infidels remained a highly regarded activity, allowing John of Gaunt (for whom Chaucer wrote the *Book of the Duchess*) to organize a pontifically sanctioned expedition against Castile in 1386. Henry Bolingbroke, future king of the realm, had attempted to join his fellow Englishmen in a crusade to northern Africa in 1390. Prevented by the suspicious French from crossing their country with an army, he executed a campaign against the pagans of Prussia instead. Chaucer's Knight, not surprisingly, has fought frequently in 'hethenesse' ('GP' 49). His battles in places like Turkey, Morocco, and Spain reveal the same piety as his decision to visit the bones of Thomas Becket at Canterbury.

The Chaucer canon may be devoid of proximate others (the Welsh, Scots, Irish), yet his writing examines at some length geographically distant figures of cultural alterity. The 'Squire's Tale' is set in the Mongol empire, the exotic East. Its narrative brims with such fabulous riches that it seems unable to come to its own point: 'I sholde to the knotte condescende', the Squire reminds himself after a particularly poetic flight (407); he seems well aware that his story could expand infinitely. Structurally the 'Squire's Tale' mimics the Orient itself, imagined by the West as a place of superabundance. Before being either abandoned by Chaucer or skilfully interrupted by the Franklin, the Squire manages to stock his Eastern tale with lavish feasts, talking animals, nubile maidens, a horse made of brass, a magic mirror, ring, sword, sumptuous garments, a quotidian, abounding opulence. There are even suggestions of forbidden sexuality. Canacee, the requisite beautiful princess, appears destined to be won in a tournament by her brother Cambalo (667–9). The Squire is the youngest of the Canterbury pilgrims, the one most filled with longing and desire ('GP' 97–8). It is at once ironic and fitting, then, that his narrative derives from an ancient genre renowned for being replete with longing and desire.

Edward Said famously argued that Western culture has never really known the realm that it christened its Orient, preferring instead to populate its vast geographies with elaborate and intractable imaginings. Said labels this propensity *orientalism*, arguing that it renders the East timeless *and* primal, enthralling *and* barbaric, an intricate twinning. Although Said has relatively little to say about the Middle Ages, medievalists have been quick to point out that the medieval period has often itself been treated in orientalizing fashion (timeless *and* primal, enthralling *and* barbaric, an intricate twinning). Medievalists have also frequently adapted Said's bifurcated conceptual scheme to their materials, especially when examining the relations between Latin Christianity and Islam during the crusades.[12]

The anti-Islamic rhetoric surrounding Pope Urban's call for the first crusade (1095) ensured that the word 'Saracen' would designate a monstrous figure, as dangerous and Christian-hating as he was perverse. The extreme otherness attached to the Saracen has provided abundant material for medievalists to critique how the Latin West represented religious and cultural difference. Largely this work has focused upon errors to be acknowledged and injustices to be excoriated, a revisionist account of the Middle Ages that does away with the Christian triumphalism that animates some scholarship. Norman Daniel's argument that the Saracen was depicted as utterly sensual (*luxuriosus*) and dangerous (*bellicosus*) pre-dates Said, but makes it abundantly clear that crusading polemic was orientalist in the extreme.[13]

Saracen monstrosity finds unforgettable expression in the *Canterbury Tales*. The 'Man of Law's Tale' imagines that, given the opportunity, a Syrian sultan would naturally desire a Christian over a Muslim princess. That the ruler of a 'Barbre nacioun' (281) is willing to convert his entire people and submit to the authority of the pope in order to obtain this matrimonial prize makes it clear that Custance, daughter of the Emperor of Rome, embodies a Westernness that is inherently superior to the Sultan's religion and culture. No possibility is acknowledged that religious conversion might be the inflicting by a dominant civilization of its 'practices, institutions, and cultures upon a subordinate, recipient civilization, whose own native practices, institutions, and cultures are concomitantly weakened through the invasive imposition'.[14] Resistance to the imperialism that the marriage represents is offered by the Sultan's mother. Unwavering in her love of her native religion, this far from maternal figure is described as a 'virago', 'serpent under femynynytee', and 'feyned womman' (359–62). The Sultaness is a monster because she violates gender, taking bloody action in a world that requires feminine passivity. These crimes against femininity are inextricable from her Easternness, from her embodying so strongly her supposedly aberrant culture: 'Unlike the somewhat European Sultan . . . the Sultaness rejects this "newe lawe" (337), and vows to uphold her culture's traditions and religion. Her credo to Mohammed and to the past manifests the essence of her culture . . . The Sultaness functions here as a sign for the East and its essential difference from Europe.'[15] Unlike properly docile Custance, who might shed a few tears when commanded to take ship for a 'straunge nacioun' but will nonetheless submit, the Sultaness acts. Her massacre of the Christians at the nuptial celebration demonstrates the impossibility of the East being anything but the immutably hostile East. Geraldine Heng writes that 'there should be little doubt that what Constance accomplishes in her story is the enactment of a successful crusade'— especially desirable in a literary register, because the actual reclamation of Jerusalem seemed by the fourteenth century an impossible dream.[16]

The 'Man of Law's Tale' reveals a typically fourteenth-century sensibility that finds crusading still viable and the destruction of Islam to be desired. Like the gleeful destruction of the Jews narrated in the 'Prioress's Tale', however, this negative representation of Muslims cannot stand as some definitive summary of Chaucer's individual feelings about the permissibility of such violence. These are two tales among many, fragments that do not aspire to a whole. Both are distanced through potentially fallible narrators. Nor is the treatment of English 'others' in the *Canterbury Tales* much better. Pilgrims of low social class like the Miller and Cook are grotesques, drunkards with bristly warts and ulcerating sores. The fabliaux are full of coarse humour at the expense of characters who do not have access to wealth and prestige. Aleyn and John, the two northerners of the 'Reeve's Tale', are ridiculed simply because their regional English sounds funny to London ears. 'Swa werkes ay the wanges in his heed', John declares of the manciple's aching teeth; the effect of John's northern dialect is to make the *wanges* of its readers likewise ache through these 'hilariously' provincial pronunciations (4030).

Chaucer's renditions of cultural difference, internal and external, do not necessarily lack nuance. Emelye, the exotic Amazon who has been captured by the Greek duke Theseus, speaks only once during the 'Knight's Tale', the longest of the *Canterbury Tales*. In a scene absent from Chaucer's source, Emelye prays to the goddess Diana that she not be transformed into a wife for one of the two knights who are duelling for her:

> Chaste goddesse, wel wostow that I
> Desire to ben a mayden al my lyf,
> Ne nevere wol I be no love ne wyf. (2304–6)

She prays to remain an Amazon, to remain unassimilated into the chivalric, Western milieu. Her prayer goes unanswered, but that does not mean that its passionate desire does not continue to resound throughout the tale. The constriction of possibility for Emelye in the tale told by the Knight, moreover, is answered by an opening up of possibilities by his son: 'The father is the one who has had real experience in wars against the East . . . The Squire lacks such experience, and he is perhaps dangerously open and sympathetic to the cultural difference of the East.'[17] Even the wicked Sultaness of the 'Man of Law's Tale' becomes a bit more complex when it is borne in mind that Syria in the poem most resembles Britain, not Rome (it is in Britain, after all, that another 'wicked' stepmother, Donegild, refuses Christian colonization). Arguing for what she calls 'contrapuntal histories', Patricia Ingham writes that this supposedly orientalist narrative is less about strict East versus West dualities than about categories of difference that become 'multiple, unstable, and liable to shifts across time and space'.[18] Perhaps David Wallace has said it best: 'Chaucer, like Boccaccio, explicitly rejects the Dantean option of writing a text with pretensions to universal knowledge.'[19] Works like the *Legend of Good Women,* the *House of Fame,* and the *Canterbury Tales* are not theological allegories, are not Dante's *Divine Comedy* in English. They are imperfect pieces of a reality too large to reduce to a harmonious world.

Remembrance and loss

In this closing section I would like to turn to a function that medieval studies (as well as any discipline focused on the past) has always shared with postcolonial theory: memorialization of that which might otherwise be forgotten. We live in a frightening and dangerous world, mainly because we human beings are so frightening and dangerous. But we are also creatures of history, both formed by the past and desirous of the past. Postcolonial critique refuses to see history as inert, and turns to what has gone before in order to remember it differently, less absolutely and less singularly—a way of seeing that isn't so much relativism as *perspectivism*.

In the tale told by the Prioress, a schoolboy decides to memorize a Latin hymn to Mary, an endeavour that necessitates neglecting his primer.[20] In the religiously plural Asia that the 'litel clergeon' inhabits, the 'litel scole of Cristen folk . . . in which ther were | Children an heep' (495–7) performs an important differentiating function. That the children are 'ycomen of Cristen blood' (497) may hint at a biological dimension to their community. Yet it is the 'litel scole' that imparts to the young pupils the culture and history that will ensure they know their difference from the 'Hebrayk peple' (560) of the 'Juerie', as well as from the Muslims who apparently govern the land. In choosing the hymn over his primer, the young boy's act of rebellion is not all that subversive: his passion serves to remind the Christians of his unnamed city and the Christians of the Canterbury pilgrimage that a shared and timeless inheritance, codified in the song's Latin words, separates them from the rest of the world, renders them a people with an exclusive history, specially chosen and protected by God. The clergeon's worry over punishment at school is misplaced, for it is the nearby Jews through whose neighbourhood he passes twice a day who will harm him, not his teachers. These very same Jews will, by the end of the tale, be tied to horses, dragged through the streets, and then hanged.

The ardour of the 'litel clergeon' for the Latin words which he does not fully understand is supposed to be admirable. Precocious sanctity *should* inspire exactly the kind of reverential awe that greets the ending of the 'Prioress's Tale' ('Whan seyd was al this miracle, every man | As sobre was that wonder was to se', 'PST', 691–2). Yet what happens when the ears through which the echoing hymn is heard are not Christian, but Jewish? *Alma redemptoris* ('nourishing [mother] of the redeemer'), the opening line of the clergeon's song, means little to a people whose sacred language is not Latin and whose messiah has not arrived. Cried 'ful murily' twice a day in passing through the ghetto (553), the hymn becomes an act of violence, announcing to its unwilling auditors that their religion, culture, and very identity have been superseded. Postcolonial criticism encourages us to pay attention to how communities come into being and who is excluded. It asks us to listen with the other's ear and interrogate what is at stake when a body of knowledge is created, codified, promulgated as universal and peerless. The culmination of the 'Prioress's Tale' is the eradication of its Jews, leaving its narrative as empty of 'Hebrayk peple' at its close as the English nation was in Chaucer's day. What history is being remembered here, and what is being forgotten?

Though the action is set in ancient Asia, the Jews of the 'Prioress's Tale' are not as distant as they seem. England expelled its Jewish population in 1290, but rather than thus ridding itself of antisemitism, the Jew who was no longer anywhere came to be everywhere. Jews were central to post-expulsion 'English religious devotion and national identity', an absent presence around which community solidified.[21] Once Jews no longer lived in England, their eradication was repeatedly performed figuratively, a repetition that demonstrates that violence committed long in the past can still trouble and haunt for many years, seeming to have happened, in the Prioress's words, 'but a litel while ago' (686). The Prioress ends her tale with an apostrophe to another boy martyr, Hugh of Lincoln, 'slayn also | With cursed Jewes' (684–5). Young Hugh's corpse had been discovered in a well almost 150 years earlier, but to an England that owed its sense of cohesiveness to the absence of its Jews, that death possessed an enduring vividness. The ideological uses to which his corpse was put can obscure the fact that a boy named Hugh really did perish, probably an accidental drowning, likely at the home of a Jewish friend. Because this death, all the more terrible because it claimed a child, was believed to be an act of murder, other innocents likewise lost their lives. According to Matthew Paris, the ringleader of the group of Jews who had supposedly crucified the boy as part of a secret ritual was tied to a horse, dragged, and hanged—exactly the punishment repeated on the Prioress's Jews. King Edward himself took a special interest in punishing the supposed malefactors; eighteen more Jews were eventually hanged as co-conspirators.[22]

Hugh of Lincoln's death and the violence that exploded around it hearken back to the first recorded accusation that Jews routinely kill Christian children, and the first attempt to create a boy martyr for communal reverence. When a boy named William was found dead in the woods outside Norwich in 1144, the grisly murder was blamed upon the local Jewish population.[23] In this first instance of the blood libel, the accusation that Jews commit murder as part of their religious rituals, enough citizens of the city were sceptical of the charge not to attack their accused neighbours. Yet the boy's corpse was eventually interred in the cathedral and worshipped as a saint. Again, I would like to point out what is obvious but often overlooked in the scholarship attempting to analyse the significance of this episode: a young boy dies horribly (gagged, stripped, tortured), and a demand is made that other innocents forfeit their lives in order to give some meaning—*any* meaning—to this utterly senseless act. This makes William's fate similar not only to Hugh's, but also to that of another boy who died under terrible circumstances, this time at his own mother's hand. Unlike William, Hugh, and the nameless 'litel clergeon,' however, this boy was Jewish.

Besieged by crusaders who, on their way to the Holy Land, decided that they ought not to spare God's domestic enemies, a group of Jews found themselves trapped inside the archbishop's palace at Mainz. Realizing that barred doors offered only some few moments of safety, these Jews chose to take their own lives rather than be forcefully baptized or hacked by Christian swords. Two surviving Hebrew chronicles narrate the martyrdoms of 1096. A chilling scene centres upon a mother named Rachel, who declares to her companions that her four children must pre-decease her so that the 'uncircumcised ones' will not convert them to their 'pseudo-faith'. As her friend takes a knife to her youngest boy and her two girls are cut in turn, Rachel realizes that her older son, Aaron, ought not to have witnessed his siblings' deaths because he is too young to face his own demise with resolve. 'Mother, Mother, do not slaughter me!' Aaron wails, then cowers beneath a bureau. Rachel 'lifted her voice and called to her son: "Aaron, Aaron, where are you? I shall not have pity or mercy on you either." She pulled him by the leg from under the bureau, where he had hidden, and sacrificed him before the sublime and exalted God.'[24] It is difficult not to see in Rachel a shocking coldness. As she announces to hidden, terrified Aaron exactly what fate she will inflict upon him, as she drags him by the leg from the only spot of safety he could find in this room flowing with blood, as Aaron pleads with his mother not to be cut open like his siblings, her actions seem inhuman—and that is exactly the point of the episode. Rachel's heroism resides for the chronicler in her ability to transcend human emotion and maternal attachment. Aaron is young and weak and human in order to ensure that his mother becomes timeless, a sublime example rather than a mere historical fact. Aaron, in other words, exists in that innocent space between infant insensibility and the adult ability to choose self-obliteration; he is able to feel the pain of martyrdom but horrifically unable to desire it. Aaron suffers so that his parents and his community accrue the glory of *kidush hashem* ('sanctification of the divine name'). The story in which he figures is not ultimately about him at all, but about his mother, Rachel's, sacrifice.

The Jewish choice of mass martyrdom over conversion shocked their Christian antagonists. Based upon the pioneering work of Israel J. Yuval, however, John McCulloh has argued that the fantasy that Jews ritually murder Christian children arose in the aftermath of the Rhineland Jews' choice of death for themselves and for their own offspring.[25] I would go even further and argue that this spectacular choice to take one's life 'in the sanctification of God's name' and the flow of blood which resulted from these actions resulted in an enduring Christian fascination with Jews and sanguinary ritual. The violence that connects the 'litel clergeon' to Hugh of Lincoln, William of Norwich, and Aaron of Mainz also binds together Christian and Jewish boys who did not and could not choose their own martyrdom. When childhood becomes the orientalized space of Edenic purity, existing only so that adult ideologies can assert themselves, then lives are lost once again. Chaucer's eerily bloodless narrative of the 'litel clergeon' can hide in its conventionality the fact that behind its piety a flow of blood emanates from a boy who, when faced by an inflexible demand to suffer and die for an ideology he knows imperfectly, can answer back only the very human 'Mother, Mother, do not slaughter me!' If there is a historical voice that resonates after death in the 'Prioress's Tale', it is indeed an innocent one, but it is also a hybrid one, speaking not just in Latin and in English but in Hebrew.

In the gruesome but literary demise of the 'litel clergeon' can be witnessed the historical deaths of three boys, two Christians and a Jew, whose furthest thought was martyrdom. I do not think that this knowledge makes the 'Prioress's Tale' unreadable, but it does unalterably transform the text. In the process it also illustrates well what postcolonial critique ultimately aims to do: not simply to offer one more interpretation among many, but to alter profoundly the grounds upon which interpretation is conducted.

FURTHER READING

Ashcroft, Bill, Gareth Griffiths, and Helen Tiffin (eds.), *The Post-Colonial Studies Reader* (London: Routledge, 1995). An excellent overview of the field. Excerpts from seminal essays and books with good geographical range.

Biddick, Kathleen, *The Shock of Medievalism* (Durham, NC: Duke University Press, 1998). Argues for the complicity of medieval studies as a discipline with imperialism.

Cohen, Jeffrey Jerome (ed.), *The Postcolonial Middle Ages* (New York: Palgrave, 2000). A collection of fourteen essays mapping the interactions between postcolonial theory and medieval studies.

Delany, Sheila (ed.), *Chaucer and the Jews: Sources, Contexts, Meanings* (New York: Routledge, 2002). A variety of approaches to what has been called England's 'internal other', the Jews. Materials presented here have received much recent critical attention in Chaucer studies.

Heng, Geraldine, *Empire of Magic: Medieval Romance and the Politics of Cultural Fantasy* (New York: Columbia University Press, 2003). Traces the imperialism animating a fundamental medieval genre that profoundly influenced Chaucer, romance.

Holsinger, Bruce W., 'Medieval Studies, Postcolonial Studies, and the Genealogies of Critique', *Speculum*, 77 (2002), 1195–1227. Demonstrates the deep continuity between medieval and postcolonial studies.

Ingham, Patricia Clare, and Michelle R. Warren (eds.), *Postcolonial Moves: Medieval through Modern* (New York: Palgrave Macmillan, 2003). A wide-ranging look at postcolonialism, modernity, and the past.

Lynch, Kathryn L. (ed.), *Chaucer's Cultural Geography* (New York: Routledge, 2002). Gathers a variety of recent and classic scholarship on Chaucer's relation to the wide world of cultural difference. Especially good material on Chaucer and orientalism; useful bibliography.

Tomasch, Sylvia, and Sealy Gilles (eds.), *Text and Territory: Geographical Imagination in the European Middle Ages* (Philadelphia: University of Pennsylvania Press, 1998). Collects essays examining the relation between geographical and other kinds of difference (racial, sexual, and so forth).

Wallace, David (ed.), *The Cambridge History of Medieval English Literature* (Cambridge: Cambridge University Press, 1999). Though not explicitly a postcolonial project, this volume's interest in cross-cultural readings and sheer diversity is exemplary.

NOTES

1. Homi K. Bhabha, *The Location of Culture* (New York: Routledge, 1994), 171.
2. Derek Pearsall, 'Chaucer and Englishness', in Kathryn L. Lynch (ed.), *Chaucer's Cultural Geography* (New York: Routledge, 2002), 291.

3. Dipesh Chakrabarty, *Provincializing Europe: Postcolonial Thought and Historical Difference* (Princeton: Princeton University Press, 2000), 17.

4. Robert Bartlett, *The Making of Europe: Conquest, Colonization and Cultural Change, 950–1350* (Princeton: Princeton University Press, 1993).

5. Uppinder Mehan and David Townsend, '"Nation" and the Gaze of the Other in Eighth-Century Northumbria', *Comparative Literature*, 53 (2001), 1.

6. R. R. Davies, *The First English Empire: Power and Identities in the British Isles, 1093–1343* (Oxford: Oxford University Press, 2000); John Gillingham, *The English in the Twelfth Century: Imperialism, National Identity and Political Values* (Woodbridge: Brewer, 2000).

7. *Chaucerian Polity: Absolute Lineages and Associational Forms in England and Italy* (Stanford, Calif.: Stanford University Press, 1997), 167.

8. Davies, *The First English Empire*, 83.

9. John Bowers, 'Chaucer after Smithfield: From Postcolonial Writer to Imperialist Author', in Jeffrey Cohen (ed.), *The Postcolonial Middle Ages* (New York: Palgrave, 2000), 53–66.

10. On Arthur, Welsh nationalism, and the complexities of postcolonial identities, see Patricia Clare Ingham, *Sovereign Fantasies: Arthurian Romance and the Making of Britain* (Philadelphia: University of Pennsylvania Press, 2001) and Michelle R. Warren, *History on the Edge: Excalibur and the Borders of Britain, 1100–1300* (Minneapolis: University of Minnesota Press, 2000).

11. Bowers, 'Chaucer after Smithfield', 56.

12. Edward Said, *Orientalism* (1978; repr. London: Penguin, 1995).

13. Norman Daniel, *Islam and the West: The Making of an Image* (Edinburgh: Edinburgh University Press, 1960).

14. Geraldine Heng, *Empire of Magic: Medieval Romance and the Politics of Cultural Fantasy* (New York: Columbia University Press, 2003), 183.

15. Kathleen Davis, 'Time behind the Veil: The Media, the Middle Ages, and Orientalism Now', in Cohen (ed.), *The Postcolonial Middle Ages*, 116.

16. Heng, *Empire of Magic*, 189.

17. Kathryn L. Lynch, 'East Meets West in Chaucer's Squire's and Franklin's Tales', in Lynch (ed.), *Chaucer's Cultural Geography*, 86.

18. 'Contrapuntal Histories', in Patricia Clare Ingham and Michelle R. Warren (eds.), *Postcolonial Moves: Medieval through Modern* (New York: Palgrave Macmillan, 2003), 66.

19. *Chaucerian Polity*, 163.

20. The bibliography on this tale is vast, but some recent work I found helpful to this argument includes Louise Olga Aranye Fradenburg, 'Criticism, Anti-Semitism, and the "Prioress's Tale"', *Exemplaria*, 1 (1989), 69–115; Michael Calabrese, 'Performing the Prioress: "Conscience" and Responsibility in Studies of Chaucer's "Prioress's Tale"', *Texas Studies in Literature and Language*, 44 (2002), 66–91; and Lee Patterson, '"The Living Witness of our Redemption": Martyrdom and Imitation in Chaucer's "Prioress's Tale"', *Journal of Medieval and Early Modern Studies*, 31 (2001), 507–60.

21. Sylvia Tomasch, 'Postcolonial Chaucer and the Virtual Jew', in Cohen (ed.), *The Postcolonial Middle Ages*, 244.

22. Gavin I. Langmuir, 'The Knight's Tale of Young Hugh of Lincoln', *Speculum*, 47 (1972), 459–82.

23. John M. McCulloh, 'Jewish Ritual Murder: William of Norwich, Thomas of Monmouth, and the Early Dissemination of the Myth', *Speculum*, 72 (1997), 698–740; Jeffrey J. Cohen, 'The Flow of Blood in Medieval Norwich', *Speculum*, 78 (2004), 26–65.

24. The chronicle is translated by Robert Chazan in *European Jewry and the First Crusade* (Berkeley: University of California Press, 1987), 238–9. Patterson explores its resonance with the 'Prioress's Tale' in 'The Living Witness of our Redemption'.

25. McCulloh, 'Jewish Ritual Murder', 699–700, 738–9.

27 | **Psychoanalytic criticism**

Patricia Clare Ingham

Against common sense

Whatever the differences among various psychoanalytic thinkers of the last century—from the movement's famous founder, Sigmund Freud, to the French analyst and interpreter of Freud, Jacques Lacan, the object relations theorist Melanie Klein, the feminist psychoanalyst and theorist Julia Kristeva, or the cultural theorist and interpreter of Lacan, Slavoj Žižek—all begin from the following premiss: no matter how full of conscious intent they may be, people do not always know exactly what it is that they are up to. Psychoanalytic theory and criticism presume an uncommon (not at all commonsensical) view of the individual and of the knowledge a person has about others and about themselves. One of the strengths of psychoanalytic criticism is its forceful push against common sense, specifically against interpretative methods that understand texts primarily in terms of the explicit and straightforward claims made in or through them. To this end psychoanalytic critics stress the omissions, exclusions, excesses, oversimplifications, and contradictions in Geoffrey Chaucer's work or throughout the history of his critical reception. The resulting criticism reconsiders conventional views of medieval culture and history to offer rich, often counter-intuitive, histories of the complications of language, desire, and scholarly method, both in Chaucer's time and for our own.

This chapter offers one account of the uncommon wisdom of psychoanalytic criticism about Chaucer over the past twenty years. Like many scholars in the humanities, Chaucerians have recently faced a number of methodological, historiographic, and political questions regarding the relevance and significance of humanistic study at this particular historical moment. Some of these questions address the continued pertinence of older texts, interest in which has sometimes been thought of as an amusing, if irrelevant, antiquarianism with limited value for the contemporary world. What does it mean to study Chaucer in the midst of the current global economy, amid debates about the globalization of literature and its effect upon the production of knowledge and university curricula more generally? What is the status of a long-lived field like Chaucer studies in the midst of competing demands for space and funds, and the proliferation of 'new' disciplines and subdisciplines?

I will be arguing here that the self-consciousness of psychoanalytic criticism has made its practitioners particularly well suited to address such questions important to the future of the field. I will argue, furthermore, that far from being (as has sometimes been charged) an inert, ahistorical method that violates medieval historical 'difference' from modernity, psychoanalytic criticism has helped to reinvigorate the historical and narratological methods with which it is frequently paired. Psychoanalytic critics have framed crucial discussions about desire and knowledge—the libidinal and epistemological arrangements that drive us—thereby addressing and at times reorienting some of the most significant methodological questions today. Such criticism combines a close attention to the formal characteristics of Chaucer's language and the material conditions surrounding his texts with a willingness to venture outside the concerns that that language or those texts self-evidently proclaim.

We begin with a necessary summary of some concepts that are key to psychoanalytic approaches, specifically the uncommon view of the speaking subject of psychoanalysis. In the interests of conceptual precision, psychoanalytic criticism deploys a technical vocabulary that cannot easily be dismissed as 'jargon'. While I will be referring to specialized terms from time to time, I will illustrate the fundamental insights of a psychoanalytic method by way of examples taken from Chaucer's poetry. Psychoanalytic criticism, as we will see, presses upon the contradictions, ambivalence, and ambiguities that particular texts register, pushing against the flattening effect of common sense.

An uncommon subject

As is well known, many manuscripts of the *Canterbury Tales* include a 'Retraction' within which Chaucer abjures nearly all of his most famous works. Linked with the sober sermon that precedes it, the 'Parson's Tale', this particular 'Retraction' raises a double contradiction: on the face of it the tone and content of the piece seem an awkward addition to the larger work of the *Canterbury Tales*, especially given the extensive readerly pleasures of the tales themselves. And the text of the 'Retraction' mirrors this tension. Chaucer begins with a prayer to his readers asking that they ascribe any goodness found in his 'litel tretys' to the wit and goodness of Christ, reminding them that all texts can move us towards the goodness of God ('Al that is writen is writen for oure doctrine'). In the next sentence, however, the speaker immediately denies the goodness of much of his work, turning instead to beseech mercy and forgiveness for his guilt at having written it. He goes on in detail: 'namely of my translacions and enditynges of worldly vanitees, the whiche I revoke in my retracciouns: | as is the book of Troilus; the book also of Fame . . . the book of the Duchesse . . . the tales of Caunterbury, thilke that sownen into synne. . . and many another book, if they were in my remembrance, and many a song and many a leccherous lay, that Crist for his grete mercy foryeve me the synne' ('CR' 1081–7).

Given its contradictory impulses, the 'Retraction' manifests an ambivalent poetic voice. The speaker seems alternately sanguine and forlorn. For the most part, however, critics have identified Chaucer on one side of this ambivalence or the other. Some critics have, for example, located Chaucer's 'real' voice in the plea for mercy, as a response to the penitential sermon of the Parson that precedes it, a deliberate application of the theme of pilgrimage to the speaker's own life. Another common view of the 'Retraction' is that Chaucer deployed it not sincerely so much as self-consciously, a standard literary convention that would help to establish his canon of works as a poet. These views each emphasize one side of things, dealing with the text's contradictions by asserting Chaucer as either devout pilgrim or masterful poet. And these two 'Chaucers' seem distinctly at odds with one another.

Psychoanalytic critics question this opposition. What would it mean to see Chaucer as simultaneously located in both elements of his 'Retraction'? After all, Chaucer's 'Retraction' preserves his texts, taking time to list all his best works *in the act of* repudiating them. And in the midst of this repudiation, the speaker's own pleasure in language emerges in a characteristically beautiful Chaucerian phrase: 'and many a song and many a leccherous lay'. A beautiful poetic modulation, the line highlights the elegant pleasures of poetry at the very moment that the reader is urged to forswear them. Common sense would insist that Chaucer is either doing one thing or the other, but not both. Alternately, common sense might presume that if Chaucer is both recommending his poetry and repudiating it, this is a conscious aim on his part, another of his masterful displays of irony (displays of irony, after all, testify to Chaucer's conscious and controlled linguistic and narrative technique).

Psychoanalytic critics presume, in contrast, that the speaking subject is never entirely in conscious control of his words, no matter how well crafted they may be. Such critics would reframe the apparent oppositions to read the text's ambivalence. Psychoanalysis, in other words, takes both linguistic modes of Chaucer's 'Retraction' seriously as signs of desire. What might these modes tell us about Chaucer and about the texts that he wrote? Might we thus come to understand something about Chaucer as a writer, something that he may not himself entirely have understood? In fact, psychoanalytic theory has a specific term for the combination of repudiation and preservation that Chaucer's text displays. In psychoanalytic terms, Chaucer here *disavows* the pleasures of his text, denying them while also retaining them. Instead of Chaucer the penitent pilgrim or masterful poet, the ambivalence in this 'Retraction' suggests that the poet's alienation from his texts exists, paradoxically, alongside his ambition for them, his pleasures in them.

As the subject of a complex desire, Chaucer remains immersed in a larger linguistic and cultural milieu, the contexts, traditions, and languages presented in other chapters of this Guide. While interested in those contexts, psychoanalytic critics attend to aspects of language that are structural and fundamental, positing a subject whose psychic and social identity is mediated through such structures of language, a speaking subject literally *subjected* to language. This is in part because any speaking subject articulates and understands herself through the strictures of the first-person pronoun, in the grammatical position of 'I'. This articulation produces an identity, a psychic and literary 'I' who speaks, but at a cost. As an 'I', the subject mediates and manages the fiction that her identity is not contradictory, ambivalent, alienated, and split, but always unified, singular, coherent. This fiction of unity and coherence requires the psychic repression (and not infrequently the social suppression) of all those impulses, drives, and desires that seem at odds with it. Something is always left out, silenced, unable to be spoken directly. Furthermore, the articulation of desire in language structures a split in the subject, an alienation that marks the frustration of the subject's desire to be entirely seen, known, satisfied completely, immediately, effortlessly.

The psychic and cultural power of the grammatical 'I' entrances us with the fantasy that the subject commonly knows, and can clearly say, exactly and entirely what it is that she wants. The attractions of this fantasy, as well as its limitations, bring us back to our example. Chaucer's direct address, his use of the first-person pronoun (especially, but not only, in his 'Retraction') often strikes students as something of a relief, a momentary glimpse into the 'real' voice of the famously elusive poet. But this sense of immediacy fades under psychoanalytic scrutiny. It becomes instead a phantasmal effect of the first-person pronoun, an 'I' that silently claims a fiction that it can never deliver: to give us unmediated access to Chaucer's unified, coherent, and authentic desires (it is important here to note that when psychoanalytic critics speak of 'fantasy', they do not mean (as is commonly understood) 'lie' or 'myth'—as my own students' experience shows, and, as I hope to make clearer below, fantasies like that of the grammatical 'I' have very real effects upon the world).

Psychoanalytic critics would thus argue that when Chaucer writes concisely 'I revoke my poems' he is (both consciously and unconsciously) managing various ambivalences and contradictions in his position as a writer and, more fundamentally, as a unified 'I' who (apparently) desires only one thing. For even as 'I revoke' is written, the subtleties of Chaucer's language imply that something else remains also true, something more difficult to articulate as concisely. When Chaucer speaks as an 'I' who revokes his poems, the grammatical structure of his phrase covers over the contradictions in that desire. Those contradictions do not simply disappear; they re-emerge elsewhere in the text. Psychoanalytic critics would not, therefore, be surprised that it is a singularly complicated matter to describe what it is that Chaucer's 'Retraction' tells us about Chaucer as a poet, or about the cultural position of his text. And they would also note that the grammatical structure of language that produces Chaucer as an 'I' who writes produces as well the contemporary reader's desire for the poet as a unified, coherent, unambivalent self, a self that the grammar of criticism marks as a singular, readily knowable, object.

Uncommon language and culture: the Symbolic Order

Jacques Lacan, the French theorist and rereader of Freud who claimed that 'the unconscious is structured like a language', termed this structure of language (which includes the various power relations, authorities, and hierarchies signified by and through it) the *Symbolic Order*.[1] The Symbolic is the realm of sign and meaning-making systems, and includes symbol systems that structure and define identity, including the arrangements of gender and sexuality, race, ethnicity, and class. There is, in other words, a great deal to which we submit when we submit to the structures of language. Gender, for example, is a part of that linguistic identity, evinced forcefully through the third-person pronouns, but also (to take Lacan's famous example) in the ways that the placement of the nouns 'men' and 'women' on the doors of public lavatories force us to recognize, even organize, our selves as, first and foremost, gendered.[2] We must subject ourselves—that is, subject the organization of our identities, drives, and desires in the intimate yet entirely social fact of personal hygiene—to one such designation or the other (such insights suggest one reason why psychoanalytic tactics have been important to feminist critics of Chaucer). Furthermore, Lacan forcefully emphasizes that desire involves the desire to be desired by someone else; our desire, in other words, is the desire for the desire of an 'other'. This means that the 'other'—the object of our desire, the persons we address by and through our desires, whose desire we seek—will know us in some ways that we do not, or cannot, know ourselves. The speaking subject of psychoanalysis thus remains structured by and through a double kind of 'alterity' or 'otherness': the other 'outside' (analyst, lover, enemy, father, friend, and so forth) to whom we address our desire; the 'other' within, the difference of ourselves to ourselves, or the ways that we are, in Julia Kristeva's words, 'strangers to ourselves'.[3] Lacan has also given us a term for this dynamic structure of the other within as well as without the subject: *extimité*, a word that evokes both 'intimate alterity'—otherness within—and 'exterior intimacy'—intimacies external to us, strangeness that is nonetheless quite close.[4]

The implications for historicism are immense. The notion of the Symbolic Order has helped illuminate the subject *in* history, giving us a way to approach a particular subject situated amid the ideologies and trends of his or her time. Further, the textured picture of the *intimate* relation of subject to other opens the way for a reconsideration of differences—whether gendered, raced, historical, textual, or linguistic—and the psychic and social processes by which absolute differences (and the categorical hierarchies they often signify) are defined. Psychoanalytic Chaucerians have shown us, for one thing, that far from being 'other' to medieval studies, psychoanalysis might better be understood as *extime* with it, sharing uncanny intimacies over a longer history than we might expect (the theorists Jacques Lacan, Julia Kristeva, and Slavoj Žižek have each written on the traditions of medieval courtly love, Lacan extensively, crucially insisting that modern subjectivity remains structured by its erotic contours[5]). For another thing, critics have analysed long-standing medievalisms, including the intimate relation of 'medieval' to 'modern', as witnessed in the traditional use of the Middle Ages to conjure (for good or ill) everything that modernity is not. And psycho-analytic critics of Chaucer analyse the psychic and political stakes in fantasies of unity and coherence. Such fantasies underlie nostalgic desires for a complete recovery, not only of the identity of a particular poet, but of medieval times more generally. Explicitly critiquing the exegetical method that read Chaucer as giving voice to the Middle Ages as a unified 'Age of Faith' (see Chapters 9 and 19), psychoanalytic critics interrogate any unified, and overly homogenized, view of a subject, a culture, or a past. In its interest in what criticism and culture *repress*, specifically in the formal ways that texts conceal as well as reveal their interests, psychoanalytic criticism frequently com-bines with other criticism that also relies on close, counter-intuitive readings, such as deconstructive or narratological approaches. In its interest in those persons who suffer more explicitly because of the repressions and suppressions of culture, psychoanalysis has been instrumental to feminist, queer, postcolonial, and materialist accounts of Chaucer, his reception, and his milieu.

Uncommon histories

Given its rich insights, it is not surprising that psychoanalytic criticism of the past twenty years has gained a purchase upon historical modes of scholarship. Yet at the outset it is also important to understand the difference psychoanalysis makes to the forms of historicism its practitioners deploy. Not satisfied to 'recover' the past 'in its own terms', as if such a thing were even possible, psychoanalytic criticism opens beyond the explicit terms raised by any text since, as Paul Strohm has put it, 'certain matters cannot be pursued in a text's own terms'.[6] Chaucer, famously, refused to wade in explicitly on the political controversies of his day. Psychoanalytic readings of his texts, alongside other approaches, have nonetheless made legible sensitivity to the dynamics of power and authority; to issues of patronage; to the politics of race, gender, sexuality, or class; to the poignancy and pleasures of the subject in/of desire amid the complexities of particular times.

Psychoanalysis has been useful in examining the unconscious content in the jokes and gibes that circulate throughout the *Canterbury Tales*, reading, for instance, the satirical, yet aggressive, relation of the 'Miller's Tale' to the Knight's, or the former's 'dirty jokes'. Elsewhere seemingly trivial jokes are seen to do significant cultural work, as in Strohm's reading[7] of a joke the Pardoner tells at the expense of gluttonous cooks ('Thise cookes, how they stampe, and streyne, and grynde, | And turnen substaunce into accident | To fulfille al thy likerous talent!', 'ParT' 538–40). Relating the play on 'substance' and 'accident' to late medieval controversies of Eucharistic theology (specifically, to the relation of the substance of the body of Christ to the accidents of bread and wine), Strohm argues that when Chaucer's text muffles those controversies in the vulgar joke voiced by the Pardoner, it channels aggressions, in a roundabout way, towards those at whom the Pardoner's joke also takes aim, specifically Lollards, who would challenge Eucharistic orthodoxy. That is, while the text may seem to direct us towards a characterological reading of the scornful, aggressive Pardoner, both the Pardoner (a character) and his joke (a form that invites relaxed enjoyment from its readers) function to *screen* (in the paradoxical double sense of both 'hide from view' and 'display') the text's own unconscious yet utterly serious aggression towards heretical Lollards.

As the previous example suggests, psychoanalytic readers understand history to consist as much in what one (the poet or the critic) does *not know* one is saying as well as in one's intentional references. They thus interrogate the limits of history's claim to report 'what actually happened', questioning the politics of what counts as historically real, of whose history matters. Read in the context of both literary history and psychoanalysis the 'Wife of Bath's Tale' emerges not as the reactionary wish-fulfilment of the Wife herself, but as an example of the at times revolutionary power of medieval romance for imagining the world otherwise. Considered as a 'group fantasy', Chaucer's Arthurian romance deploys the enchantment of Arthur's 'olde dayes' ('WBT' 857) to critique the commodifying realism of the Wife's mercantile present. Building upon this account, my own analysis of the 'Wife of Bath's Tale' situates Chaucer's text amid the controversial fantasies of Arthurian sovereignty, historical romances purveying divergent political, regional, and cultural projects.[8]

Criticism of the 'Prioress's Tale' shows the difference that psychoanalysis makes to understanding the material effects of fantasy. Louise Fradenburg uses psychoanalytic theories of *abjection* (a particular dynamic of *repression* and *projection* that allows a subject to resist, without dismantling, the authority of the other) to read the excessive description of the murder of the little 'clergeon' by the Jews. When Chaucer's text subtly links the Prioress's own self-presentation to that of the innocent 'clergeon', it suggests her unconscious identification with him in his linguistic insufficiency and his subsequent victimization. At the same time, Chaucer's text makes legible the ways in which the Prioress represses her own anger at a Church demanding humble obedience (and not creative ambition) from its 'children'. Projecting that anger onto Christianity's racial other, the Jew, the Prioress's fury erupts in the horrific fantasy of a victimized innocent, throat slit and dumped in a privy. The psychosocial dynamics of antisemitic fantasies in Chaucer's text reframe the long-standing debate about the tale's antisemitism, showing its pertinence to the exacerbation of those concerns in fourteenth-century Europe.[9]

In these accounts 'fantasy', or 'imagination', emerges not as the opposite of historical fact, or as a false consciousness aimed at avoiding the material world, but as dreamings with particular force and effect in history. Fantasies work both subjectively (for particular subjects) as well as culturally (for encoding broader beliefs of a group), circulating tropes and traditions specific (but hardly unique) to medieval textuality and culture. And Chaucerians interlace psychoanalysis with these specificities, contributing to the refinement of psychoanalytic concepts with regard to particular cultural or historical scenes. Thus, Sarah Stanbury reads the representation of Griselda in the 'Clerk's Tale' to reveal features specific to premodern spectatorship. Griselda's representation, in contradistinction to psychoanalytic accounts of the oppressive nature of 'the male gaze' from twentieth-century feminist film theory, shows the conditions under which gazing can destabilize rather than secure standard definitions of gender identity. In another example, Elizabeth Scala argues that the Man of Law's repetitive (yet also strangely circumlocutory) references to incest as an inappropriate subject for narration in the introduction to his tale (77–89) draw attention to silence, compulsion, and repression as necessary conditions of tale-telling. Chaucer's text thus forces us to see that narrative, whether literary or historicist, is never entirely under the control of the person who utters it.[10]

These insights dovetail with historicist projects increasingly important since the advent of postcolonial and multicultural critiques of dominant history. They raise the omissions, silences, compulsions, repetitions, and repressions of a text or an archive not as the absence or 'lack' of history, but as an intimate part of it. But in its critique of what Lacan terms the *sujet supposé à savoir* (literally 'the subject supposed to know', the authoritative, interpreting agent) psychoanalysis also cautions critics and readers against the assumption that our answer to those silences or our versions of those repressions and compulsions constitute the final word.

Analyses of 'lack' and 'loss' have been an especially important, and perhaps the most insistently historiographic, thread within the field under discussion over the past twenty years. Sustained attention to the losses (psychic, social, historical) that Chaucer's poetry commemorates and negotiates constitutes one of the greatest contributions in this area. Psychoanalytic theories of mourning, of the relation of loss to language and to gender, have helped critics reconsider the elegy structure of the *Book of the Duchess*, or Troilus' loss of Criseyde. One enormous contribution of this work has been interrogating the extent to which historical losses are figured as feminine ones, both in Chaucer's texts and in criticism about them. To what extent does the dead Blanche in the *Book of the Duchess* bear the burden of death and loss for an entire culture suffering the trauma of the plague? Critics argue that such fantasies of woman as (a general) lost object render historical women invisible, pressing gender difference into service for the psychic mastery of the (male) subject who can manage loss or trauma by mourning the fantasy woman that he loses. To take another example: if Criseyde's infidelity, and not the war that literally kills him, is understood as Troilus' most consequential and traumatic loss, we are less well able to consider the complications of Criseyde's desire to survive, despite the fact that Chaucer's text attends repeatedly and poignantly to her. These readings have thus pointed to the larger project of recovering or memorializing that constitutes historical method generally. They have argued that the cultural effect of this structure produces a historicism unable to think of women as themselves cultural subjects.

Most recently, Chaucerians have joined with colleagues in French medieval studies to engage 'lack' from another angle, emphasizing the fascinations that nonetheless circulate even through pain and sacrifice. Psychoanalytic treatments of fantasy emphasize the limitations that fantasy places on pleasure, explicating the power of *enjoyment* as, paradoxically, 'beyond the pleasure principle'. That is, subjects tend to seek out not only (or even mainly) satisfaction and fulfilment, but the dissatisfactions of limitation, frustration, painful repetition. These treatments take seriously the satisfaction of desire itself, offering rich analyses of the pleasurable difficulties, the unpleasant pleasures, of *jouissance* (literally orgasm, but as Louise Fradenburg points out, both bodily enjoyment and its avoidance[11]) as 'pleasure in unpleasure' in medieval texts and traditions. Readings of investments in impossible situations, repeated trauma, loss, and pain, have offered detailed accounts of courtly love, chivalric brotherhood, hagiography, tragedy, or history. This aspect of psychoanalytic theory has been especially useful in examining the arrangements of medieval masculinity. It emerges as a fruitful tool for thinking about the conjunctions as well as the tensions between medieval erotic and spiritual discourses. If in earlier decades psychoanalytic approaches to Chaucer focused primarily upon the poet's courtly texts, this turn to sacrifice has resulted in more direct attention towards religious and hagiographical works, where critics continue to explore the interplay between the devotional and the profane.

Considerations of medieval enjoyment and our enjoyments as medievalists may well drive future directions in the field. This is precisely where the self-consciousness of psychoanalytic method intervenes to remind us that difference, whether between persons or historical periods, is never absolute. In so far as we enjoy them, in so far as our thinking remains indebted (in ways not always acknowledged) to Chaucer's time, Chaucer's texts continue to be *extime* to our own time. Dynamic transactions between contemporary readers and Chaucer's text are thus, and of necessity, sites for important temporal crossings. Reading Chaucer psychoanalytically means simultaneously taking account of the specificity of medieval texts and cultures while considering matters in terms resonant for our own day.

Considering the 'Knight's Tale'

In this final section, a psychoanalytic reading of Chaucer's 'Knight's Tale', I wish to begin by making some temporal crossings of my own. This is in part because, from time to time during the past two years, my students and I have been struck by the acute resonance of the 'Knight's Tale' following the events of 11 September 2001. I mean particularly the tale's extraordinary rendering of the horrors of violence, war, death, and of the narrator's linguistic insufficiency in the face of devastation. I refer as well to Theseus' entreaty, at the end of the tale, to 'make a virtue of necessity' (3042). As readers have long noted, the tale focuses on the challenges that destruction and death pose to those in power, concerns that have recently felt extraordinarily pressing. Furthermore, Fradenburg has recently emphasized the tale's representation of 'sacrificial desire' as a fundamental structure of medieval knighthood.[12] 'Sacrificial desire', the willingness and desire of subjects to suffer or die for a goal rendered in the highest ethical terms, resonates perhaps grimly with current political and military arrangements.

Drawing on these concerns, I wish here to engage the specific suppressions and repressions legible in Chaucer's text. Critics have long noted that the treatment of the figure of Emelye ranks among the most crucial differences between Chaucer's tale and his source, Boccaccio's *Teseida*. Unlike his source, Chaucer begins his story after Theseus' battles with the Amazons are over, thus suppressing both the prior history of Emelye and Hippolyta and impressive images of them as female warriors. Furthermore, Chaucer transfers many of the poem's most important philosophical concerns, articulated by Emilia in Boccaccio's version, to the male characters Theseus, Arcite, and Egeus. Critics have also observed that in his depiction of Emelye in the garden, and in her plea before the goddess Diana, Chaucer poignantly renders the limitations placed on Emelye's freedom. Such textual suppressions and elaborations amount, as John Ganim has argued, to a repression of effective female agency in the plot of Chaucer's poem.[13]

Repression marks a starting not an ending point for psychoanalytic critics, hinting at something that cannot be commonly, easily, straightforwardly known or said. What follows, then, is not a straightforward account of Chaucer's tale, but a reading of the uncommon way the 'Knight's Tale' negotiates constraint and loss by way of gender. On one level, Chaucer's textual omissions emphasize the losses suffered by and the constraint placed upon Emelye as a result of the political, social, military situation in which she is caught. Furthermore, the text's repeated representations of mourning females (seen early on in the train of Argive widows who beg Theseus for a proper burial for bodies that Creon has tyrannously dishonoured) suggest the tale's investment in a gendering of loss. Crucially, the text will portray Emelye's mourning of Arcite at a particularly significant moment, amid a self-conscious and even awkward insertion of the Knight's own voice as a speaking subject, as narrator of his tale. This means, as I will explain below, that Chaucer's text unconsciously acknowledges the affective responsibility (and thus power) that women like Emelye bear for self-sacrificial men like the Knight who desire to tell about them, and for the cultures that produce those gendered arrangements.

On its face Chaucer's tale gives ample evidence of the victimization of men as well as women in war. Theseus' initial meeting with the Argive widows itself, of course, alludes to the bodies of dead soldiers. As it happens the text will move, almost immediately, to one of the most striking images of male victimization in the poem, cousins Palamon and Arcite poised together in battle array, on the edge between life and death:

> And so bifel that in the taas they founde,
> Thurgh-girt with many a grevous bloody wounde,
> Two yonge knyghtes liggynge by and by,
> Bothe in oon armes, wroght ful richely,

Of whiche two Arcita highte that oon,
And that oother knyght highte Palamon.
Nat fully quyke, ne fully dede they were,
But by hir cote-armures and by hir gere
The heraudes knewe hem best in special
As they that weren of the blood roial
Of Thebes, and of sustren two yborn. (1009–19)

The description has long fascinated readers. The horror of mangled bodies disguised in a heap of bloody corpses is rendered in places with remarkably gentle language. The tenderness here subtly diverts our attention from the horror of death at the same time that it marks death as soft, gentle: two young knights lie 'by and by', a figuration that evokes the intimacies of the bedroom as much as it does the sacrifices of the grave. Furthermore, in contrast to the grisly enumeration of lesions, lacerations, and dis-memberment we will later witness at the Temple of Mars (1995–2040), or the gruesome biology of Arcite's death (2743–60), this description foregrounds death in war as a scene of satisfying union, not bodily mutilation. Indeed the gentle tone marks the scene of knightly togetherness with a fond poignancy often reserved for lovers. Fradenburg reads the softer pleasures of this description to signal psychic enjoyments in pain and loss, enjoyments that attract subjects to the sacrificial structure of knight-hood. I wish to consider what such enjoyments have to do with the text's emphasis upon female loss and mourning.

Battle emerges in this scene as a site of contraries: affection and aggression, brotherly intimacies amid carnage, familiar cousins rendered strange under a massive pile of flesh. The twinning resemblance between the cousins provides an eerie reminder of death, the great equalizer. War does not distinguish; death is indifferent to the particu-larity of male subjects, leaving a mass of battlefield carnage. Poised on death's edge, these two knights seem uncannily alike, bereft of individuation, of the particular dif-ferences and personal specificities that grant them separate identities. In fact, the con-fluences between Palamon and Arcite are so deeply woven here that this description has prompted a number of critics to wonder if these two characters are really different from each other at all.

The combined horror and fascination of this scene of doubling resonates with Freud's account of 'the Uncanny', a narrative effect crossing the familiar with the strange. Crucial to this effect is the emergence of the doppelgänger, the double. For Freud this 'invention of doubling' functions as a 'preservation against extinction'; he links fantasies of doubleness to 'all those strivings of the ego which adverse external circumstances have crushed and all our suppressed acts of volition which nourish in us the illusion of free will'.[14] That is, doubles hint at the wilful acts of the subject crushed by external authorities and circumstances. They hint as well at the subject's acts of self-regulation, at his willingness to submit to the authority of the super-ego, the ideal version of self (embedded in the fiction of the 'I') that grants the subject an illusory experience of coherence, control, free will. Doubles, in other words, raise an undercurrent of compulsion, repetition, and constraint thereby troubling conventional accounts of freedom and agency.

This is to say that the doubling in Chaucer's description (unconsciously) hints at the compulsions that drive the cousins to be in combat, as well as at the external forces (war, death) that threaten violently to annihilate the two as subjects. These are issues at stake for chivalric (or military) culture as a whole, a historical apparatus devoted to producing (and organizing into groups) warriors who desire such risks and sacrifices, interested, too, in the *group* threat that wartime annihilation poses to chivalry as a whole. That is to say, chivalric culture needs to produce subjects who desire to uphold their obligations through battlefield sacrifice despite the horrifying facts of the battlefield. Chivalric culture needs subjects who consider it a privilege to endure such horrors for their feudal lord. Precisely *as* doubles Palamon and Arcite allude to warrior desire for the traumatic experiences of combat as a compulsion, a site of pressures both interior and exterior to the subject. Unfreedom remains at issue throughout the tale. And I argue that in suppressing Emelye's role the text attempts to resolve irresolvable issues of unfreedom.

Difference (in this case the differences of gender) compensates for anxieties of powerlessness. No one in this tale, in fact, has the control or agency that some characters seem at first to have. Yet at key moments the text conjoins unfreedom with females: for one thing, the constraint under which Palamon and Arcite suffer is immediately recast from the register of war to that of love. Competing love for Emelye, rather than either their wartime imprisonment or their risks of bodily harm, now constitutes the primary pressures bearing down upon Palamon and Arcite. As an allusion to the tradition of courtly love, the textual shift is conventional enough. Yet we should also note that as part of the courtly love tradition, the figure of the unattainable woman is a structure important to Lacan's psychoanalytic account of modern subjectivity.

It is thus perhaps not coincidental that the most traumatic death of all, Arcite's unexpected death, occurs at the moment when he has won Emelye's hand. Instead of those satisfactions, death chaotically interrupts Theseus' otherwise well-ordered state festivities, causing all to cry and weep at their unanticipated loss. The turn of events reminds the reader that even the most prodigious of soldiers and conquerors is powerless before death. Theseus nonetheless attempts to command the scene:

> Shrighte Emelye, and howleth Palamon,
> And Theseus his suster took anon
> Swownynge, and baar hire fro the corps away.
> What helpeth it to tarien forth the day
> To tellen how she weep bothe eve and morwe?
> For in swich cas wommen have swich sorwe,
> What that hir housbondes ben from hem ago,
> That for the moore part they sorwen so,
> Or ellis fallen in swich maladye
> That at the laste certeinly they dye. (2817–26)

The passage presents a range of responses to the fact of death: Emelye, who shrieks and weeps ceaselessly; Palamon, who howls and then falls silent; Theseus, who apparently subordinates his grief in the compassionate care of his excessively grieving 'suster', an Amazon woman he previously conquered. The narratorial voice of Chaucer's Knight moves immediately to contextualize Emelye's hapless mourning as an attribute of her gendered difference from him: 'Wommen have swich sorwe', he tells us, and are 'fallen in swiche maladye' that 'at the laste certeinly they dye'. Women's sadness becomes a means to death. As such women's weeping remains outside the consolations of language: an account of it will help neither the woman who suffers it nor those who hear it second-hand. 'What good does it do', the Knight asks rhetorically, 'to spend the day telling of woman's weeping?'

Yet while the narrative voice professes that rehearsing Emelye's sorrow is either impossible or unnecessary or both, the text structurally and specifically offers evidence to belie such a claim. Immediately before his narration of the piteous Emelye, Chaucer's Knight registers his own verbal insufficiencies when confronted by such senseless tragedy:

> [Arcite's] spirit chaunged hous and wente ther,
> As I cam nevere, I kan nat tellen wher.
> Therfore I stynte; I nam no divinistre;
> Of soules fynde I nat in this registre,
> Ne me ne list thilke opinions to telle
> Of hem, though that they writen wher they dwelle.
> Arcite is coold, ther Mars his soule gye!
> Now wol I speken forth of Emelye. (2809–16)

In this important aside Chaucer's Knight records his own limitations as narrator. His story is halted. He cannot, or will not, parse the meaning of Arcite's fate. This is the speaking subject subjected to language, the subject who cannot command through explanation the meaning of such an event. The excessive emphasis upon the first-person pronoun here urges a psychoanalytic insight: the repetition (why so many in such a short passage?) of the 'I' directs us to the speaker's anxiety about his ability to manage a coherent sense of self, to say nothing of a singular and coherent response, in the face of death's horror. It thus raises the possibility of the dissolution of the speaking subject, marking a speaking subject *not* in command of his words. A psychoanalytic interest here draws attention to what has been suppressed and repressed, to what cannot be said forthrightly, straightforwardly.

What remains hidden, I am arguing, are the ways in which here, as earlier, considerations of gender compensate for anxieties specific to the subject. Because the next words imply that one can move out of debilitating confusion by describing the piteous shrieks of a woman, indeed by describing loss, constraint, and linguistic insufficiency as attributes of a mourning female. In what seems a remarkably sudden shift in tone and content the narrator moves quickly to an apparently more comforting subject, describing a female in need of comforting. Despite his fears of the annihilation of his voice, the futility of his narration, the image of Emelye's weeping has, in fact, helped the speaker a good deal. Her shrieks are not, thus, the opposite of his linguistic poverty. Her difference to him is far from absolute. In fact, read psychoanalytically, the text reveals her shrieking to be *extime* to his speaking. It is the means whereby he moves beyond his silence before the unpredictable fact of death. That is, despite the speaker's declaration of the futility of narrating Emelye's weeping, he moves back into his narrative precisely by describing her sadness. The narrator relies on Emelye (the unconscious and thus unacknowledged symptom of his own limitation) to rescue him from a premature end to his story. He uses her position as his 'other' to embody the loss he hopes to escape.

Uncommon wisdom

In moments like these Chaucer's 'Knight's Tale' offers plenty of reasons to resist what was once read as wisdom, specifically Theseus' entreaty that we 'make a virtue of necessity' (3042). In displaying the complex negotiations through which subjects manage their responses to loss and death, the tale allows us to read Theseus' remark, too, as such a response, one ultimately indebted to both the victimization of soldiers like Arcite and the shrieks of women like Emelye. The 'Knight's Tale' can thus caution us to be wary of the extent to which cultures use images of victimization not merely to register horror at injustice, but to achieve a sense of identity, coherence, even competence in the face of massive suffering. We might, thus, wonder whether Theseus' remark alludes not only to a philosophical consolation specific to the Middle Ages but also to the psychic transformations required for and produced by cultures specific to times of war and devastation. For the 'Knight's Tale' makes clear that subjects are asked to refigure the losses and risks of war as virtue, indeed, as the highest virtue. Transforming necessity into virtue marks a primary means whereby cultures justify their wars and attract their soldiers to them. But read with an eye for its textual repressions and cultural suppressions, Chaucer's text can also inspire us to consider whose shrieks of mourning remain embedded invisibly in our sacrifices.

These are issues that reverberate both then and now. For one thing, Theseus' commendation to 'make a virtue of necessity' strikes at the present moment as at best a hollow answer, and at worst a horrifying kind of realpolitik. And given that the sacrificial desires of the 11 September hijackers have been claimed as evidence of their 'medieval' culture, one could argue that texts like the 'Knight's Tale' remain *extime* to current political discourse. The attractions of the Middle Ages for our present have implications for a thoughtful understanding of the projects of both historicism and of ethics. This is not only because medieval texts offer considerable wisdom, though of course they do, but because our current desires to be readers of Chaucer, our current projects as his readers at this particular moment, might harbour ambitions for ourselves as well. If we allow such textual and temporal crossings, they can help to redefine what counts as the relevance of then to now. Psychoanalytic criticism becomes, then, not a means of escaping history, but of reconsidering the breadth and range of what the medieval past might continue to mean.

FURTHER READING

Dinshaw, Carolyn, 'Eunuch Hermeneutics', in her *Chaucer's Sexual Poetics* (Madison: University of Wisconsin Press, 1989), 156–84, 256–78. This influential chapter interrogates Chaucer's Pardoner and the various lacks from which he suffers from the vantage of Lacanian psychoanalysis. It displays the links between psychoanalytic, feminist, and queer readings.

Fradenburg, Louise O. Aranye, *Sacrifice your Love: Psychoanalysis, Historicism, Chaucer* (Minneapolis, University of Minnesota Press, 2002). An important recent book designed to affect psychoanalytic theory as much as Chaucer studies. Fradenburg rethinks both Chaucer's texts and critical historicism in light of a new understanding of the pleasure and desire of sacrifice. She develops the 'history of the signifier', a crucial way of reading change in the Symbolic Order.

Fradenburg, Louise O. Aranye, 'Voice Memorial: Loss and Reparation in Chaucer's Poetry', *Exemplaria*, 2 (1990), 169–202. One of the most important psychoanalytic essays in late medieval English studies. Deploying Freud, Lacan, and Kristeva to understand the losses Chaucer's poetry commemorates and negotiates, Fradenburg's essay originates the psychoanalytic study of this material, tracing its implications for what she terms a 'compassionate historicism'.

Leicester, H. Marshall, 'Newer Currents of Psychoanalytic Criticism and the Difference "It" Makes: Gender and Desire in the "Miller's Tale"', *English Literary History*, 61 (1994), 473–99. Offering a useful introduction to psychoanalytic theory, this essay reads the 'dirty jokes' in the 'Miller's Tale' in light of the unconscious to suggest that the investments of the medieval fabliau can push beyond the anti-feminist reference usually presumed to be its limit.

Margherita, Gayle, *The Romance of Origins: Language and Sexual Difference in Middle English Literature* (Philadelphia: University of Pennsylvania Press, 1994). An important account of the medieval and medievalist project of recovering historical losses in terms of gender figurations. Margherita analyses both medieval and contemporary critical cultures.

Scala, Elizabeth, 'Canacee and the Chaucer Canon: Incest and Other Unnarratables', *Chaucer Review*, 30 (1995), 15–39. An account of the 'unnarratables' found in the 'Squire's Tale' and in the 'Man of Law's Introduction'. Scala finds alternatives to the brand of straightforward historicism usually associated with the Knight and long used to organize readings of the *Canterbury Tales*.

Stanbury, Sarah, 'Regimes of the Visual in Premodern England: Gaze, Body, and Chaucer's "Clerk's Tale"', *New Literary History*, 28 (1997), 261–89. Stanbury's work engages medieval discourses on visibility and spectatorship with psychoanalytic accounts of the 'gaze' found in twentieth-century feminist film theory. Here she suggests that 'premodern regimes of the visible' have a potentially destabilizing effect upon orthodox gender identities.

Strohm, Paul, 'Chaucer's Lollard Joke: History and the Textual Unconscious', *Studies in the Age of Chaucer*, 17 (1995), 23–42. An influential essay detailing the implications of psychoanalysis for historicist readings of medieval texts. Strohm argues that the 'fullest understanding of a text must include attention to what it represses, to the gaps, traces, and other derivatives of a textual unconscious'.

NOTES

1. Lacan, *Feminine Sexuality: Jacques Lacan and the École Freudienne*, ed. Juliet Mitchell and Jacqueline Rose (London: Macmillan, 1982).

2. Lacan, 'The Agency of the Letter in the Unconscious or Reason since Freud', *Écrits*, ed. and trans. Alan Sheridan (New York: Norton, 1977).

3. Julia Kristeva, *Strangers to Ourselves*, trans. Leon S. Roudiez (New York: Harvester, 1991).

4. *The Seminar of Jacques Lacan*, book VII: *The Ethics of Psychoanalysis, 1959–1960*, ed. Jacques-Alain Miller, trans. Dennis Porter (New York: Norton, 1992). See also Jeffrey Jerome Cohen, *Of Giants: Sex, Monsters, and the Middle Ages* (Minneapolis: University of Minnesota Press, 1999).

5. See Sarah Kay, *Subjectivity in Troubadour Poetry* (Cambridge: Cambridge University Press, 1990).

6. 'Chaucer's Lollard Joke: History and the Textual Unconscious', *Studies in the Age of Chaucer*, 17 (1995), 24.

7. Ibid.

8. Louise Fradenburg, ' "Fulfild of fairye": The Social Meaning of Fantasy in the "Wife of Bath's Prologue and Tale" ', in Peter G. Beidler (ed.), *Geoffrey Chaucer: The 'Wife of Bath's Prologue and Tale'* (Boston: St Martin's Press, 1996), 205–20; Patricia Clare Ingham, 'Pastoral Histories: Utopia, Conquest, and the "Wife of Bath's Tale" ', *Texas Studies in Literature and Language*, 44 (2002), 34–46.

9. Louise Fradenburg, 'Criticism, Anti-Semitism, and the "Prioress's Tale" ', *Exemplaria*, 1 (1989), 69–115.

10. Sarah Stanbury, 'Regimes of the Visual in Premodern England: Gaze, Body, and Chaucer's "Clerk's Tale" ', *New Literary History*, 28 (1997), 261–89; Elizabeth Scala, 'Canacee and the Chaucer Canon: Incest and Other Unnarratables', *Chaucer Review*, 30 (1995), 15–39.

11. *Sacrifice your Love: Psychoanalysis, Historicism, Chaucer* (Minneapolis: University of Minnesota Press, 2002), 6–7.

12. Ibid. 155–75.

13. John Ganim, 'Chaucerian Ritual and Patriarchal Romance', *Chaucer Yearbook*, 1 (1992), 65–86. See also Robert M. Stein, 'The Conquest of Femenye: Desire, Power, and Narrative in Chaucer's "Knight's Tale" ', in James J. Paxson and Cynthia A. Gravlee (eds.), *Desiring Discourse* (Selinsgrove, Pa.: Susquehanna University Press, 1998), 188–205.

14. Sigmund Freud, 'The Uncanny', in his *On Creativity and the Unconscious: Papers on the Psychology of Art, Literature, Love, Religion* (New York: Harper, 1958), 141–2.

Part IV

Afterlife

28 | Editing Chaucer

Elizabeth Scala

Every modern reader of Chaucer's poetry encounters his works in printed form. Where Chaucer lived in a late medieval manuscript culture that could not yet imagine, let alone witness, the advent of print, modern students typically encounter Chaucer in a material form markedly different from the one with which he worked. The technology of the printing press, introduced into England by William Caxton in 1476, made possible a more rapid production of uniform copies of a text with its movable type. Today ever more sophisticated versions of that technology make possible the mass distribution and consumption of identical texts and contribute to the widest readership Chaucer has ever known. To get from the individually hand-copied manuscripts of Chaucer's own late medieval textual culture to the mass-produced print runs of our own has involved an enormous amount of detailed labour by the often under-appreciated textual editor. These textual editors carefully (re)construct the contents, presentation, and form of Chaucer's poetry from the mass of evidence left behind. This chapter will narrate a textual history of Chaucer's works, focusing principally upon the *Canterbury Tales*, by describing the original form and condition of medieval poetry that is largely hidden from readers by modern editorial programmes. It will also explain the *necessary* way in which such editorialization obfuscates the multiplicity of the medieval manuscript in order to render the works in it readable. In its closing, the chapter will address the postmodern return to the multiplicity of medieval textuality in the form of digitized facsimiles and electronic editions. I devote my remarks to the *Canterbury Tales* as Chaucer's best-known and most often taught work. It is also the most textually complex and difficult of Chaucer's works to edit, an unfinished tale collection that exists in no fewer than eighty-two varying manuscript copies, which had yet to receive anything like final authorial revision.[1]

Textual notes ignored here

Students will find the kinds of Chaucer editions used in university classrooms more elaborate than those produced for the casual reader. Often including frontmatter that discusses language, phonology, biographical, and historical information, Chaucer's *Tales* will also be accompanied by a glossary, an index, and explanatory and textual notes. It is not difficult to see how these materials assist post-medieval readers of Chaucer's Middle English language by making the literary, cultural, and linguistic aspects of the text more accessible. The *Riverside Chaucer*'s explanatory notes, for example, seek to cover basic information that relates to generic features, source material, cultural allusions, and idiomatic expressions of the works. One feature of this helpful academic apparatus tends to be less used than others. The textual notes (in the *Riverside*, occupying pages 1117–1210) offer no such obvious profit and are rarely noticed by student readers. Indeed, few readers of any kind but the most professionally specialized ever have cause to consult these notes, which consist largely of a bunch of seemingly cryptic abbreviations for various manuscript texts and groupings.

However obscure and seldom used, the textual notes convey the very material essence of Chaucer's poems. Arguably far more important than biographical, introductory, or explanatory materials typically included in an edition, the textual notes signal the editorial negotiations—the choice of verbal forms, spellings, punctuation, and so forth—that determine the text one is reading. In order to appreciate this kind of work and its role in guaranteeing the stability of the printed copy of the *Canterbury Tales* before us, we must consider in more detail the very different circumstances of Chaucer's late medieval manuscript culture, the fragmentary and unfinished condition of Chaucer's poem, and the mysterious whereabouts of the author's copy of his last work. Where are Chaucer's 'foul papers'—that is, those latest copies of his tales with corrections, substitutions, jottings, and markings in his own hand?

Reading different translations of the *Canterbury Tales*, which are available in modern English verse and prose forms, can make clearer the precarious status of Chaucer's texts. One detects immediately the difference between translations, which can vary widely in terms of word choice, diction, euphemism, sentence structure, as well as metrics. One need only look at two widely available modern translations of the 'Miller's Tale' to make the point, where Nicholas's infamous courting gesture towards Alison, 'prively he caughte hire by the queynte' (3276), is described very differently. In a crude and vulgar idiom, David Wright's Oxford translation leaves no room for confusion: 'on the quiet [he] caught her by the cunt'.[2] Kent and Constance Hieatt's rendering is more polite and evasive: 'privily he grabbed her where he shouldn't'.[3] Reading these modernized versions of Chaucer's poem, one may readily see, differs significantly from reading 'Chaucer', who has cleverly taken a Middle English adjective, 'queynte' (meaning curious, elegant, pleasing) and made it into a substantive noun (elegant or pleasing thing). The original Middle English poem offers an authentic and historical experience, a 'real' Chaucer that translation corrupts and changes.

The original Chaucer and Chaucer's 'originals'

The problem of translation might suggest a return to the 'original' from which the translations were made. But this 'original' Chaucer is ephemeral and illusory. The texts of Chaucer's *Canterbury Tales* in Middle English vary from one edition to the next much like the translations (if not so flagrantly). These editions do not present a single authorial text handed down from the writer's pen but a composite work, reconstructed on the basis of one of a number of editorial principles. Common sense might dictate here a return to what Chaucer himself wrote, a look at a holograph manuscript (a manuscript written in the author's own handwriting) or the foul papers found in his study. Such a turn is by no means a simple gesture. While many medieval manuscripts of Chaucer's *Tales* have survived the centuries since their copying, no manuscript of any kind from Chaucer's own lifetime exists.

Thus, there is no 'original' text, no 'real' Chaucer to which modern readers might turn. Instead, Chaucer's tales are preserved in more than eighty witnesses: manuscripts of the entire poem, single tales included in other miscellanies, fragments of the poem circulating on their own, and two early printed editions that are generally accorded the status of manuscripts. These two very special editions, Caxton's first and second edition of the *Tales*, were based on manuscripts that subsequently did not survive. But as many as six of the earliest printed editions may bear witness to lost manuscripts. The *Canterbury Tales* that students now read is a reconstructed text, one that has to be reconstituted by editorial methods to have *any* existence at all.

If no direct line can be traced from Chaucer's hand to the extant manuscripts of his poem, the matter is further complicated by the unfinished nature of the literary work itself. At the time of Chaucer's death in 1400 he had yet to complete the *Canterbury Tales*. Moreover, his method of composition makes for some uncertainty. Chaucer's tales do not emerge from a stable narrative order; rather, the frame narrative of the poem thematizes a number of ordering principles. The 'General Prologue' arranges the pilgrim narrators in a fictitiously random order according to the Chaucerian narrator's memory while it simultaneously raises the possibility of social, moral, and competitive hierarchies. Before Chaucer finished writing a tale for each of the pilgrims that he describes in the 'General Prologue' (the Plowman and the five Guildsmen have no tales), he added to their number by inventing a Canon and his Yeoman who join the pilgrimage at 'Boghtoun under Blee' ('CYP' 556). We not only lack a number of pilgrims' tales, then, we also have the excess of the 'Canon's Yeoman's Tale' to boot. The intended number of tales has also been called into question. In the 'General Prologue' the Host, Harry Bailly, demands that each pilgrim tell four tales: two on the way to Canterbury and two on the return journey (791–4). This plan is different from the one alluded to at the end of the outward journey; in the 'Parson's Prologue' the Host announces that 'Now lakketh us no tales mo than oon' (16). Yet even if a one-way, one-tale-per-pilgrim plan were by now in operation, we still lack more than one tale as the missing Plowman's and Guildsmen's tales attest. Chaucer was certainly not composing the tales in the order in which they would appear. Added to the pilgrims described in the 'General Prologue', some of whom tell a tale, we also have the Chaucerian narrator, who reports the tales of the other pilgrims and is himself the only pilgrim who tells two different tales, 'Sir Thopas' and the 'Tale of Melibee', the Host having terminated his first story because of its 'drasty rhymyng' which is 'nat worth a toord!' ('TST' 930). These shifting and changeable plans, coupled with a few unfinished tales (like the Cook's and the Squire's) and some intentionally interrupted tales ('Sir Thopas' and the 'Monk's Tale') make for an unusually unstable literary text. When combined with the instability of the pre-print origin of the *Canterbury Tales*, the state of the poem posits a textual puzzle of acute complexity.

If a return to Chaucer's 'original' text is impossible, we must look to the manuscript witnesses of Chaucer's poem. What relation do these manuscripts bear to the lost holograph or Chaucerian foul papers scattered about his desk at the time of his death? While the mystery of Chaucer's own copy of the tales (copied in his own hand or by a professional like 'Adam, his owne scriveyn'[4]), or his marked-up and revised papers, continually lingers over scholars of the *Canterbury Tales*, the state of the oldest copies of the poem have been investigated for what light they might shed on the work's earliest situation. From where did the manuscripts that survive, the extant copies of the *Canterbury Tales*, emerge? What relation do they bear to each other, to the earliest imprints of the poem, and to Chaucer's own copy? These are the questions that beset the textual scholar and drive the investigation of the *Canterbury Tales* manuscripts.

Of the surviving manuscripts of the *Canterbury Tales*, fifty-five appear to be entire copies of the poem, although some have suffered damage, while twenty-eight are partial copies. The two most important manuscripts of the *Canterbury Tales* are the Ellesmere manuscript, now owned by the Huntington Library in San Marino, California (a manuscript named from its former owner, the earl of Ellesmere) and the Hengwrt manuscript (named after the residence of Colonel Robert Baughan, its seventeenth-century owner, who lived at Hengwrt in Wales), now in the National Library of Wales in Aberystwyth.[5] These are the oldest surviving manuscripts of the *Canterbury Tales*, copied in the quarter-century immediately following Chaucer's death. They offer the best evidence as to what Chaucer 'originally' wrote. All modern editions are based upon either Ellesmere or Hengwrt, and no matter which of these is chosen the other is heavily consulted for its variant readings. These two manuscripts carry pre-eminent status in the field of Chaucer studies, but it was not always so. It was only in the very late nineteenth century, with the publication of Walter W. Skeat's six-volume edition of the *Works of Geoffrey Chaucer* (1894), that Ellesmere gained pre-eminent textual status.[6] After Skeat, all editions of the *Canterbury Tales* were based on Ellesmere, including the editions by F. N. Robinson (1933, 1957) on which the *Riverside Chaucer* (1987) is based. Hengwrt, however, fared very differently, most likely because of its less refined state. Hengwrt has no such decorative features as Ellesmere and is, instead, marred with a grease stain on its opening page. It would not be until the editorial work of John

Matthews Manly and Edith Rickert that Hengwrt would begin to gain its proper status, and not until the production of the *Variorum Edition of the Works of Geoffrey Chaucer* (still in progress) that it would eclipse Ellesmere in stature (although such a claim might still be contested in some quarters, see below). Hengwrt, with 'its more accurate representation of a flexible, idiomatic and successful metrical practice, and in its freedom from editorialisation . . . [as well as] in numerous readings of a substantive and significant nature', offers a clearly superior text to Ellesmere.[7] Perhaps the next logical step for textual editors of printed editions is an edition of the *Canterbury Tales* based much more closely on Hengwrt. However, the defects in Hengwrt, no matter how authentically 'Chaucerian' they may be, may always prevent that manuscript from superseding Ellesmere. Hengwrt suffers from a lack of some texts that appear in Ellesmere, the latter half of the 'Parson's Tale' and the 'Canon's Yeoman's Prologue and Tale'. Moreover, it also offers a less appealing order for the tales. This situation, however, provides an interesting historical picture of textual production around 1400. Derek Pearsall's discussion of Hengwrt in his introductory volume *The Canterbury Tales* suggests the hurried nature of the manuscript's production:

The changes in ink, the spaces left for matter known to exist but not immediately available, the fudging of the lay-out to hide errors in such calculations, all indicate that the copyist was dealing with exemplars that were arriving on his desk in fragmentary form and unpredictable sequence. The hustle and bustle of the writing-shop, as Chaucer's literary executors, having presumably scoured the poet's study for the *Canterbury Tales* papers, now tried to bring out as a matter of urgency the first copy of the whole text of the long-awaited masterpiece, could hardly be more vividly conveyed.[8]

That Hengwrt and Ellesmere share the same scribe somewhat complicates matters but may offer further illumination. Hengwrt appears to have been copied from the materials that could be immediately gathered. The scribe then copied Ellesmere after a more careful inventory and editorial preparation could be made of the contents of Chaucer's poem.

Our modern editions of Chaucer also lend stability to another aspect of the poem that relates to the status of the manuscripts: tale order. A casual glance at the table of contents for the *Riverside*'s presentation of the *Canterbury Tales* calls attention to the dominance of the poem's fragmentary form. Dispersed into ten unlinked fragments— small groups of tales that are connected by short dramatic episodes recalling the pilgrimage frame and storytelling contest—the *Canterbury Tales* displays its unfinished nature. While tale order within the fragments remains stable from manuscript to manuscript (with the omission of some tales or, more often, linking material), the order of the fragments themselves is by no means certain. Our best manuscripts, Ellesmere and Hengwrt, offer two different tale orders. The varying disposition of tales in the fifty-odd complete or nearly complete manuscripts of the poem clearly indicates that Chaucer's plan was still evolving and that no order had yet been firmly set. Even more particularly, such disposition speaks to the efforts of Chaucer's fifteenth-century editors in dealing with the lack of 'final' arrangement.

The initial position of the first fragment, which consists of the 'General Prologue', Knight's, Miller's, Reeve's, and Cook's Tales, cannot be doubted. Its clearly written links and dramatic connections between tales, as well as its description of an extensive round-trip journey and four-tale-per-pilgrim programme, argue for its late development in Chaucer's still-evolving plan for the *Canterbury Tales*. The 'Parson's Prologue', as I have already mentioned, completes Fragment X by calling for the only tale yet lacking and thus an end to the poem. With these boundaries in place (and indeed they are attested as such in the vast majority of manuscripts), we have the general shape of the pilgrimage framework secured. But, as has often been noted, Fragments I and X secure the boundaries of quite different poems. Reading 'teleologically' from 'General Prologue' to 'Parson's Tale', one finds the capacious four-tale and two-part journey giving way to a single-tale, linear trip for the pilgrims. This shrinking of the itinerary of the 'General Prologue' has been generally understood as Chaucer's own modification of his initial and over-enthusiastic idea. However, Charles Owen, among others, has argued convincingly that the more expansive plan of the 'General Prologue' was, in fact, a later development.[9] The ending so concretely provided for the *Canterbury Tales* by the 'Parson's Prologue and Tale' is thus a conclusory gesture that has been entirely superseded by a more openly competitive and dramatic one. At the time of his death Chaucer was not drawing the poem towards its close but expanding and further enlivening his multi-voiced tale collection. This situation itself only further dramatizes the unfinished and so hypothetical nature of the poem's textual status.

Chaucer in print

Chaucer's *Canterbury Tales* has been in print almost continuously since its publication in Caxton's first edition in 1478. Caxton's two editions provide important witnesses to the condition of Chaucer's poem before the advent of print. Although printed editions, they are typically accorded manuscript status by textual scholars. The fifteenth and sixteenth centuries saw a number of writers emulate and imitate Chaucer (for example, Lydgate, Dunbar, Henryson, Spenser, and Shakespeare), through which period a number of editions of the *Canterbury Tales*, usually in collected editions of Chaucer's *Works*, appears: Pynson's (1492), Wynkyn de Worde's (1498), Pynson's second (1526), Thynne's (1532), Thynne's second (1542), Thynne's third (1545), Stow's (1561), Speght's first (1598), second (1602), and third (1687). These early editions are based largely on Caxton's (in so far as each is a revision of the previous editor's text) with some 'emendation'—the changing of lines or working away from the base text—in the light of information from another manuscript source.[10] Textual scholars argue about the manuscripts that may have been used in these editorial revisions. Thynne's son Francis claims that his father owned twenty-five Chaucer manuscripts and one, particularly, of the *Canterbury Tales* that shows the sign of direct examination by Chaucer by being marked 'examinatur Chaucer' in the margin.[11] And Stow's edition (often described as 'a mere reprint of Thynne with a supplement') has been reclaimed as one that took into consideration the large number of manuscripts that passed through its antiquarian editor's hands.[12] For some scholars of the early Chaucer imprints, hope for manuscript evidence springs eternal on the promise of such information.

The eighteenth-century texts of the *Canterbury Tales*, Urry's (1721) and Tyrwhitt's (1775), still follow in this tradition. By 1602 we can see problem after problem reaching back to Caxton's print shop. In Pearsall's words, 'Unfortunately, the tradition of the printed texts was by now so degenerate that no attempt to improve a text set up from a printed copy could do more than tinker with its defects.'[13] But these editions raise issues other than questions of the 'accuracy' of the *Tales*. Beginning with Pynson's 1526 edition, in which the *Canterbury Tales* forms Part 3 of the *Works*, the blackletter books of the Renaissance are marketed as omnibus editions of the renowned author's works. Thus begins the collecting of Chaucer's works, which eventually includes materials known not to be Chaucer's. These are advertised, like Stow's 1561 Chaucer, as 'newly printed with diuers addicions, whiche were neuer in print before'. The Chaucer canon would eventually accumulate works by Usk, Henryson, and Lydgate, among many others, and the issue of authorship would be muddied by Stow's attribution.

This accretion to the Chaucer canon was not unintentional, nor was it entirely random. Pearsall notes the sixteenth-century booksellers' reprints of Thynne that reproduced his text line by line but augmented Chaucer's canon by adding anonymous works that seem 'Chaucerian' as well as works known to be written by another author but which are associated with Chaucer.[14] These editions are not so much attempts to authenticate Chaucer's text as to canonize the poet by reproducing some of the literary offspring for which he was responsible. Speght's edition still operates within the 'tradition of reprint-with-augmentation',[15] while it also includes a list of hard words that make it the first edition with a glossary. It remains the standard until Urry's edition in 1721. The attribution of an emerging editorial apparatus to Speght can be more easily seen in the 1687 imprint, whose title page claims to present a text that has 'lately been Compar'd with the best Manuscripts'. While 'the claim to have consulted manuscripts is false', Pearsall concludes, 'it is an interesting sign of the times, and of the interest in antiquity, that it should have been made'.[16] Already in 1687 we see the appeal of a return to the manuscripts, but this return is markedly different from those urged in other periods. In the blackletter editions of Chaucer, manuscripts are sought for the texts they might add to the Chaucer canon, and consulted to an extent for their spelling and orthography, which these editors sought most to regularize. For more on the early editors of Chaucer, see Chapters 29 and 30.

Critical editions

Developing this tradition further, John Urry assembles more than fourteen manuscripts and a number of Caxton texts for collation, the process of line-by-line comparison. Like the 1687 Speght, the eighteenth-century editions of Chaucer are generally consulting manuscripts to deal with issues of orthography, spelling, and metrics (metre and rhyme), where the desire is to regularize Chaucer's poetry. The manuscripts are not studied in any genetic or historical way, with an eye to their relations to each other (whether one of the manuscripts is a direct copy of another and therefore not an independent witness to what Chaucer may have originally written), as they will be in a later period. Instead, Urry treats the manuscripts as equal authorities. With the variation in the English language between Chaucer's Middle Ages and Urry's Augustan age, it is clear why the eighteenth-century editor felt the need to regularize spelling and syllabic pattern so as to produce recognizably good poetry for his readers. But critically, Urry's text was almost universally despised, both at the time of its publication and through the early twentieth century, for its questionable addition of words and syllables not found in the manuscripts it purports to follow. Urry's work is important to the history of the textual tradition of the *Tales* for the very Augustan tastes and sensibilities to which it bears witness, as well as the glossary (much used by his successor Thomas Tyrwhitt) and the 'Life of Chaucer' by John Dart prefacing the text. What we might say of Urry is that his rhetorical recourse to the manuscripts of the *Tales* far exceeds the authority he sought in them. His choices for emendation were far too subjective, nor were they defended (and therefore marked) in his text.

Like almost every other reader of Urry's text, Thomas Tyrwhitt is no admirer of its scholarship. Tyrwhitt improves on Urry's treatment of the manuscripts by trying to avoid all previous editions. In the preface to his edition (1775) he writes, 'The first object of this publication was to give the text of THE CANTERBURY TALES as correct as the MSS. within reach of the Editor would enable him to make it.'[17] Tyrwhitt consulted twenty-six manuscripts and gives a full list of them. Foremost are Harley 7335, Cambridge Dd.4.24, and Harley 7334, which Skeat will later call 'faulty and treacherous'.[18] Harley 7334 enjoys an undeservedly high reputation during the mid-nineteenth century that perhaps begins here. Tyrwhitt has great respect for manuscripts but limited access to them. He claims to have disregarded any previous edition of Chaucer, showing preference for the manuscripts themselves, 'except the two [editions] by Caxton, each of which may now be considered as a Manuscript' (Preface, p. i). For Tyrwhitt, a manuscript of good authority would be a full (or nearly full) copy of the *Canterbury Tales* with neat handwriting, not exactly what we recognize as an authoritative text today. But Tyrwhitt shares with modern editorial principles the assumption that all editorial contributions should be clearly marked, and in this he shows real scholarly qualities. It is not that he does not make subjective editorial decisions in his edition, but rather that he makes no attempt to conceal them.

In practice, however, Tyrwhitt allows the edited texts he so clearly abjured as inferior to the manuscripts themselves to affect his work. His collation papers show that he worked against the Speght 1687 edition by using its pages as the copy-text from which he collated the manuscripts. Similarly, he used the pages of a 1602 Speght as the base for the printer's copy, to which he added his corrections from his collation (a similar charge will be levelled against Manly and Rickert for using Skeat's *Student's Chaucer* as the basis for collation for their large-scale edition). Tyrwhitt's principal contribution to the project of editing the *Canterbury Tales* can be seen in his 'Essay on Language and Versification' in his edition that continues Urry's work. But if Urry believed that Chaucer must be *made* metrically regular, then Tyrwhitt believed Chaucer to *be* metrically regular. It is the reader who fails to understand Chaucer's pronunciation and syllabic values. He argues for the pronunciation of -*es* and -*ed*, as well as final -*e*. His work on the order of the tales anticipates modern scholarship, and his commentary on the *Tales* is extensive and learned, betraying a vast reading of the unedited manuscripts in the British Museum.[19]

It is not until the mid- to late nineteenth century—a relatively recent date in the history of the *Canterbury Tales*'s textual tradition—that the clearly discernible signs of modern scholarship are seen and the contents of the Chaucer canon finally settled. Those signs are detectable by a more rigorous comparison of manuscript witnesses. Here lies the distinction between the kind of authority accorded manuscripts in the Augustan age and the philological investigations (involving the historical study of words and their origins) carried out in this period. Earlier editors consulted manuscripts in a more or less haphazard way and offered an eclectic text, which was typically based on the taste of the editor and his familiarity with the manuscripts and the language in them. From German philologists, however, manuscript study became 'scientific' through the genetic study of texts. Textual relations were discerned on the basis of shared errors so that manuscripts that derived directly from others could be eliminated from the pool of witnesses. This science of 'recension' led to the use of genealogical trees ('stemma', producing a science of 'stemmatics') to explain manuscript relations and to establish the authority of certain manuscripts—and not necessarily the prettiest or the neatest—over others. Recension made the choice of manuscripts and their hierarchical relations clearer, but it was by no means foolproof. Many of the manuscripts do not reveal direct relations to the others and are subject to 'contamination' from different manuscript sources. In other words, for a manuscript tradition as extensive as that of the *Canterbury Tales*, no clear and unitary line of descent emerges.

The historically driven and nationalist efforts of Frederick James Furnivall, founder of learned organizations such as the Chaucer Society, the Philological Society, the Early English Text Society (EETS), and the *New English Dictionary* (now known as the *Oxford English Dictionary*), drive modern textual scholarship of the *Canterbury Tales*. In 1868–77 the Chaucer Society printed *A Six-Text Print of Chaucer's 'Canterbury Tales' in Parallel Columns*. These volumes 'diplomatically' reproduce the information of Ellesmere, Hengwrt, Cambridge Gg, Corpus 198, Lansdowne 851, and Petworth manuscripts, side by side in aligned columns. In subsequent years Furnivall also transcribed Cambridge Dd and Harley 7334, so that his work is often known as the *Eight-Text Edition* as well. Furnivall's work here, as well as his efforts to get established scholars like Walter Skeat and Richard Morris to edit ancient English texts for the EETS, resulted in the eventual publication of Skeat's edition of *The Complete Works of Geoffrey Chaucer* (1894). Through these editions, EETS also provided the material for the *New English Dictionary*'s historical record of word usage. While Furnivall is no editor in the strict sense of the term, he 'was a keen student of the manuscripts' whose choice of Ellesmere and Hengwrt for the *Six-Text* edition was at the time 'a triumph of judgment' that rescues him from the charge of being 'an inspired textual amateur'.[20] Furnivall's claim to editorial fame was, as he himself admits, to pave the way for other scholars, notably Walter W. Skeat and his Oxford Chaucer. Skeat's 'complete' edition includes for the first time Chaucer's prose works, produces an extensive glossary and set of explanatory notes, and reliably settles the boundaries of the canon.

Skeat's text is the first to choose the attractive and beautifully illustrated Ellesmere manuscript as its copy-text, basing editorial decisions on the authenticity of the readings in that manuscript. His choice of Ellesmere displaced a number of other manuscripts, particularly Harley 7334, that had recently enjoyed a prominence that was textually undeserved. 'A handsome volume that contains a text of deceptive smoothness and fluency',[21] easily found in the Bodleian Library, Oxford, the Harley manuscript provided the base text for the edition of Thomas Wright (1847–51), which was reprinted by Robert Bell (1854–6) and Robert Blackwood (1890). The manuscript seems to have had some undue influence that no one really intended. When Skeat first edits Chaucer in 1878, he revises the edition of Robert Bell and reprints the *Tales* from Bell (and thus Wright). Harley 7334 was given further authority when F. J. Child, the eminent Harvard scholar, used Wright's edition for his *Observations on the Language of Chaucer* (1862). While Child and Skeat level criticism at Wright, whose edition Child called 'essentially a reprint of Harleian MS 7334',[22] they also canonize the manuscript to some degree by working from his text. Skeat's Ellesmere-based edition redirected attention to a more worthy authority, where it has firmly remained.

'Literary' complications and the order of the tales

The manuscripts of the *Canterbury Tales* are also complicated by the question of tale order. While the pilgrimage framework posits a geographical logic to the poem's narrative, the place references in the fragments, even in the best manuscripts, do not tally with the well-known itinerary of the pilgrimage journey from London to Kent. In many of the dramatic links between tales within a fragment, Chaucer orients the group in relation to locale and in astrological time. A well-known instance occurs in the Prologue to the 'Monk's Tale' in Fragment VII when Harry Bailly notes, 'Loo,

Rouchestre stant heer faste by!' (1926). Rochester lies roughly halfway between London and Canterbury and should have been passed by the pilgrims well before this point. In fact, a geographic location well to the east of Rochester, Sittingbourne, had been mentioned as early as Fragment III. Henry Bradshaw used the geographic information in the links to argue for a repositioning of the *Tales* fragments into what he concluded must have been the order in which Chaucer intended to arrange them before he died. Bradshaw's proposed rearrangement, commonly referred to as the 'Bradshaw shift', moves the tales of Fragment VII (Shipman–Prioress–Thopas–Melibee–Monk–Nun's Priest) forward to follow Fragment II ('Man of Law's Tale') and connects them by renaming them fragments B^1 and B^2 respectively. Bradshaw follows these two B-groups with the tales in Fragment VI (Physician–Pardoner). A number of editions, most notably Skeat, adopted the new order created by the Bradshaw shift, referred to as 'the Chaucer Society order', after the learned society for which Skeat laboured. It has now been largely discredited as an expression of Chaucer's final intentions. Similarly, the arguments for recension as an editorial method to determine Chaucer's 'original' text and the privilege accorded to final 'authorial' intentions have generally given way to a 'best-text' editing method which was established by classicists in the same period. Best-text method demands the choice of a base manuscript, ideally the 'best text' of a particular work, from which an editor deviates only in cases of clearly discernible error. In all other cases, and when in doubt, the editor retains the reading of the base manuscript. The assumption underlying this method holds that a modern editor could not improve on Ellesmere or Hengwrt and should not intervene unless a mistake in copying could be proven. More fascinating than any notion of final intent are the myriad ways the *Canterbury Tales* was still evolving when Chaucer was forced to stop writing, presumably by his death. The order reproduced by the standard *Riverside Chaucer* is that of Ellesmere, with some additional materials in brackets and explained in the notes. The Ellesmere editor was clearly a superior judge as to aesthetic and thematic order for the tales, and may have even been working with materials provided by Chaucer's son Thomas, who wanted a deluxe manuscript of his father's *Canterbury Tales* produced soon after his death.

Ellesmere's dominance of the textual tradition in modern scholarship may soon be reaching a terminus due to the increasing attention paid to Hengwrt, a postmodern interest in rival textual traditions and the 'local' particularities of the manuscripts themselves, and the possibilities offered for textual and critical investigation by the digital age. In 1997 the Huntington Library produced a full-colour, photographic-quality facsimile of Ellesmere, a publishing venture that now seems almost impossible to imagine. This full-size, high-quality reproduction was marketed largely to libraries in two forms: a leather-bound copy (for $10,000) and an unbound, boxed copy (for $8,000). A smaller, monochromatic facsimile was designed for individuals and sold for $275. This supreme act of manuscript reproduction appears to be the last of a dying kind. The expense of such products has been outmoded by the relatively inexpensive costs of digitization. Not that manuscript facsimiles will not continue to be produced. In 2002 the EETS advertised a facsimile of Thomas Hoccleve's autograph manuscript of his poetry in the Supplementary Series. But the excessive cost of the library editions of the 1997 Ellesmere Chaucer has been replaced by electronic manuscript projects.

Hengwrt

Despite its less attractive appearance—including grease-stained pages and rat-nibbled corners—Hengwrt has emerged as a superior manuscript of the *Canterbury Tales*. First published in Furnivall's parallel texts in 1868 and in facsimile for the *Variorum Chaucer* in 1979, Hengwrt has drawn increasing attention since John M. Manly and Edith Rickert's collection and study of all *Canterbury Tales* manuscripts, published in 1940. What happened between the very end of the nineteenth century, when Skeat published his edition of Chaucer's *Works*, and 1940, when Manly and Rickert's eight-volume *Text of the Canterbury Tales, Studied on the Basis of All Known Manuscripts* appeared? How, in this short space of time, can the progressive study of manuscripts have changed so much?

Manly and Rickert, who were colleagues at the University of Chicago, began planning for a new and quantitatively different edition of the *Canterbury Tales*. Their edition would attempt to determine what Chaucer's autograph manuscript might have looked like by reconstructing genealogically the ancestor of the surviving copies of the *Canterbury Tales*. For this project, begun in 1924, Manly and Rickert had to undertake the Herculean task of tracking down all manuscripts known to exist as well as those whose survival was unsure. With the then 'modern' technology of the photostat, Manly and Rickert could make copies of the manuscripts (to reduce damage) for a collation of the entire collection of witnesses. Yet procuring the manuscripts themselves was no easy task. Many manuscripts were still in private collections. A number of British peers had to be approached to allow Manly and Rickert access to their libraries. With the help of Sir William McCormick (a British administrator of university grants) and Sir Frederic Kenyon, director of the British Museum, access was granted to the American scholars. Many owners sent their manuscripts to the British Museum for examination and photostatting. A full narrative of these endeavours can be found in the prolegomena to the Manly–Rickert edition (i. 1–9). In addition, the editors searched for copies of the *Canterbury Tales* mentioned in wills, library book lists, and sale catalogues but whose whereabouts were uncertain. In this project they uncovered a number of manuscripts and pages, including the Merthyr fragment (related to Hengwrt), and settled the number of known surviving copies of the *Canterbury Tales* to this day. In analysing *all* the information available, rather than a selected or convenient portion of it as all others had before them, they sought to determine, as far as such determination was possible from the materials that survived into the present, what

Chaucer actually wrote. The very thought remains tantalizing and its logic seductive. With the mystery of the manuscripts' location solved and the relics procured, the textual puzzle could then be worked upon. Playing the part of sleuth and cryptographer (both of which Manly and Rickert occupied for the US War Department in a code-breaking capacity), they hoped to solve the greatest literary puzzle of all: fitting the pieces of the *Canterbury Tales* together as Chaucer had intended.

While Manly and Rickert's efforts have revealed much information about the nature of the production of the extant manuscripts, it brought them, however, to no such end. The final result of the collation of all known manuscripts was that they descended from no common ancestor. Chaucer had put parts of the poem into circulation as independent fragments, and each tale had therefore to be treated as an independent text with a distinct textual history. This independent textual history of each fragment meant that the manuscripts resisted the classification necessary to produce a text by recension. Yet where Manly and Rickert may have failed to reproduce the text they sought to recover, they did further our understanding of the relations of the extant manuscripts. Foremost among their discoveries is the superiority of Hengwrt as a witness. Additionally, an older grouping of the manuscripts based largely on the geography of the pilgrimage and the ordering of fragments has since given way to Manly and Rickert's constant Groups a, b, c, and d, which are based on the type of exemplar from which each manuscript family descends.[23]

The Manly–Rickert edition is the logical extension of Skeat's, the first critical edition that took the evidence of a truly best set of manuscripts to determine its readings. Manly–Rickert takes *all* the evidence to determine its readings, yet its readings are hardly what is of most value. Like the many editions of Chaucer discussed earlier, Manly–Rickert's least important component is in fact its text. But the rest of their eight volumes include an extensive description of each manuscript, an essay on illumination and decoration, a list of recorded manuscripts whose whereabouts are undetermined, and a complete corpus of variants for the entire manuscript tradition of the *Canterbury Tales*. Here Manly–Rickert records every reading in every manuscript, a compilation of information that resembles the work of Furnivall and Skeat. These findings have been useful to scholars of the *Canterbury Tales*, most notably those working on the *Variorum Chaucer* Project. This project begins with a facsimile of the Hengwrt manuscript, upon which its best-text edition is based, and produces each of the *Canterbury Tales* individually, with full critical annotations in the footnotes to the text (for details of the *Variorum Chaucer*, see Chapter 35).

Chaucer in the age of computing

In 2002 *The Hengwrt Chaucer: Digital Facsimile* appeared on CD-ROM. If one might expect a rival edition of Chaucer's *Canterbury Tales* based on Hengwrt to challenge the

Riverside Canterbury Tales—a teaching and scholarly text born out of the *Variorum Chaucer* Project—such an expectation may be confounded by a new interest in digitization rather than printed text. I and others would argue that digital texts cannot replace a unitary and stable printed text in the undergraduate classroom. A unitary and stable text must needs be the point of introduction to the many provocative questions of division and instability in Chaucer's poem and its manuscript tradition. But those very issues and our contemporary fascination with them may sound the death knell for any new printed edition of Chaucer's *Tales* of *Riverside*'s scope and stature.

Hengwrt's digitization had been preceded by some electronic initiatives that promise to expand and renew manuscript study. Most notably, the Canterbury Tales Project, led by Peter Robinson, has resulted in CD-ROM editions of the 'General Prologue' (2000) and the 'Wife of Bath's Prologue' (1996). These electronic editions present digitizations of all the manuscripts accompanied by transcriptions; a collation program; a spelling database; and several search engines. The benefit of computer technology in the field of textual studies seems clear, and the Canterbury Tales Project would present the manuscripts to the largest possible audience in their most 'unedited' form. These electronic editions, in addition to a renewed interest in manuscript culture, may provide the greatest hope for the continuation of the diminishing field of textual scholarship. Martha Driver notes that new research has already emerged from the electronic *Canterbury Tales*, 'particularly about erasures in the margins of the Hengwrt manuscript, for example'.[24] Even the dating of Hengwrt is now under reconsideration, and research may prove it dates from Chaucer's own lifetime.[25] The electronic edition, created for scholarly use but increasingly adapted to the classroom, presents us with a true record of the unfinished nature of the *Canterbury Tales* and the provisional arrangement of its parts. The future promises further refinement and innovation in a renewed study of the Chaucer manuscripts and early editions.

FURTHER READING

Bowers, John (ed.), *The Canterbury Tales: Fifteenth-Century Continuations and Additions* (Kalamazoo, Mich.: Medieval Institute Publications, 1992). Teaching text of the tales appended to various early manuscripts and prints of the *Canterbury Tales*: Lydgate's *Siege of Thebes*, the 'Ploughman's Tale', 'Cook's Tale', and the 'Tale of Beryn'. Does not include the 'Tale of Gamelyn'.

Damico, Helen (ed.), *Medieval Scholarship: Biographical Studies on the Formation of a Discipline, ii: Literature and Philology* (New York: Garland, 1998). Biographical essays on important medievalist scholars, including a number of Chaucerians and their editions: Furnivall, Skeat, Kittredge, and Manly and Rickert.

Dane, Joseph, *Who is Buried in Chaucer's Tomb? Studies in the Reception of Chaucer's Book* (East Lansing: Michigan State University Press, 1998). A collection of chapters treating issues of reception and reproduction in relation to editorial and print history.

Greetham, David, *Textual Scholarship: An Introduction* (New York: Garland, 1994). Basic introduction to problems and pursuits of textual scholarship.

Hammond, Eleanor Prescott, *Chaucer: A Bibliographical Manual* (New York: Macmillan, 1908). Excellent, if dated, commentary on manuscripts, editions (scholarly and otherwise), and versions (adult, children's, popular) of Chaucer's texts up to the early twentieth century.

Machan, Tim William, *Textual Criticism and Middle English Texts* (Charlottesville: University Press of Virginia, 1994). Recent and most sophisticated introduction to the relation of the interpretation of literary texts and their textual situations.

Matthews, David, *The Making of Middle English, 1765–1910* (Minneapolis: University of Minnesota Press, 1999). History of Middle English scholarship and politics of editing, especially the establishment of the Middle English canon via a movement from 'antiquarianism' to professional study.

Prendergast, Thomas, and Barbara Kline (eds.), *Rewriting Chaucer: Culture, Authority, and the Idea of the Authentic Text, 1400–1602* (Columbus: Ohio State University Press, 1999). Essay collection examining the reproduction of the idea of 'a' Chaucerian text in medieval (scribal), early modern, and print cultures.

Ruggiers, Paul (ed.), *Editing Chaucer: The Great Tradition* (Norman, Okla.: Pilgrim Books, 1984). Chapters by various scholars on landmark editions of Chaucer: Caxton, Thynne, Stow, Speght, Urry, Tyrwhitt, Wright, Furnivall, Skeat, Root, Manly and Rickert, and Robinson.

Stevens, Martin, and Daniel Woodward (eds.), *The Ellesmere Chaucer: Essays in Interpretation* (San Marino, Calif.: Huntington Library; Tokyo: Yushodo, 1997). Recent collection of essays on the Ellesmere manuscript of the *Canterbury Tales* by leading scholars in field. Published as accompaniment to the New Ellesmere Facsimile.

NOTES

1. The precise number of 'manuscripts' of the *Canterbury Tales* is a matter of some debate. Ralph Hanna's textual notes to the *Tales* in the *Riverside Chaucer* clarify the issue of the exact count of manuscript witnesses nicely: 'There are eighty-two (or if the Morgan fragment of the "Pardoner's Tale" is considered separately, eighty-three) manuscripts of the Tales, either complete or fragmentary. . . . The Tales exist not only in the manuscripts but in six early prints, all of which potentially have manuscript status' (p. 1118). However, most editors accord only Caxton's two imprints, for reasons to be explained presently, with manuscript status.

2. Geoffrey Chaucer, *The Canterbury Tales*, trans. David Wright (Oxford: Oxford University Press, 1985), 83.

3. Geoffrey Chaucer, *The Canterbury Tales*, ed. and trans. A. Kent Hieatt and Constance Hieatt (New York: Bantam Books, 1964), 155.

4. See the *Riverside Chaucer*, 650.

5. For the provenance of these manuscripts and particularly the origin of the name of the Hengwrt manuscript, see John M. Manly and Edith Rickert, *The Text of the Canterbury Tales, Studied on the Basis of All Known Manuscripts*, 8 vols. (Chicago: University of Chicago Press, 1940), i. 282.

6. A seventh volume, *Chaucerian and Other Pieces*, was published in 1897. Skeat's edition is most respected for its scholarly commentary and its efforts to stabilize the contents of the Chaucer canon.

7. Derek Pearsall, *The Canterbury Tales* (1985; repr. London: Routledge, 1995), 8.

8. Ibid. 12–13.

9. See Charles A. Owen, *Pilgrimage and Storytelling: The Dialectic of 'Ernest' and 'Game'* (Norman: University of Oklahoma Press, 1977), esp. 10–47; Elizabeth Scala, 'The Deconstructure of the *Canterbury Tales*', *Journal x*, 4 (2000), 171–90.

10. James E. Blodgett, 'William Thynne', in Paul Ruggiers (ed.), *Editing Chaucer: The Great Tradition* (Norman, Okla.: Pilgrim Books, 1984), 46–7.

11. Ibid. 39–40.

12. Anne Hudson, 'John Stow', in Ruggiers (ed.), *Editing Chaucer*, 53.

13. Derek Pearsall, 'Thomas Speght', in Ruggiers (ed.), *Editing Chaucer*, 87.

14. Ibid. 71.

15. Ibid.

16. Ibid. 91.

17. Thomas Tyrwhitt, Preface, in *The Poetical Works of Geoffrey Chaucer* (1775; repr. 1852), p. i.

18. W. W. Skeat, *The Chaucer Canon* (Oxford: Clarendon Press, 1900), 28.

19. See Barry Windeatt's discussion in Ruggiers (ed.), *Editing Chaucer*, esp. 137–40.

20. Donald C. Baker, 'Frederick James Furnivall', in Ruggiers (ed.), *Editing Chaucer*, 166.

21. Thomas W. Ross, 'Thomas Wright', in Ruggiers (ed.), *Editing Chaucer*, 148.

22. Quoted by Skeat, *Chaucer Canon*, 23.

23. For further discussion and elaboration on these groups, see Roy Vance Ramsey, *The Manly–Rickert Text of the 'Canterbury Tales'* (Lewiston, NY: Edwin Mellen, 1994), esp. 205–62.

24. 'Medieval Manuscripts and Electronic Media: Observations on Future Possibilities', in Derek Pearsall (ed.), *New Directions in Later Medieval Manuscript Studies: Essays from the 1998 Harvard Conference* (Woodbridge: Brewer, 2000), 59.

25. See N. F. Blake, 'A New Approach to the Witnesses and Text of the *Canterbury Tales*', in Pearsall (ed.), *New Directions*, 29–40.

| # Reception: fifteenth to seventeenth centuries

John J. Thompson

Premodern and early modern Chaucers

The period under discussion in this chapter extends from the years of the deposition of Richard II and the Lancastrian usurpation of 'England's empty throne' through the post-Reformation Elizabethan period and into the seventeenth century. It runs from the time when Chaucer's works, biography, and reputation first became objects of fascination and discovery for a range of fifteenth-century poets and readers, listeners, and commentators, such as Thomas Hoccleve and John Lydgate, and for early printers such as Caxton, through to the time of Spenser and the editorial labours of Thynne, Stow, and Speght. The period also represents four of the six reception stages Caroline Spurgeon identified long ago.[1]

Spurgeon's first stage consisted of a series of eulogies to Chaucer from his immediate fifteenth-century successors, an evolutionary phase followed by a period of gradual dispersal, and, Spurgeon argues, diminution, of Chaucer's name and reputation among a geographically and socially broad audience, especially when the technological innovation associated with the advent of English printing allows 'the Chaucer tradition' in sixteenth-century manuscripts and prints to be annexed in distinctive ways either by English reformed sensibilities or by Scottish writers. This then allows her third phase to run from what is characterized as the golden age of Spenser's Chaucer set against 'the common opinion that Chaucer's style was rough and unpolished, his language obsolete, and his metre halting',[2] a view that eventually came to dominate her fourth phase and the beginnings of the Chaucer translated versions, while her fifth era takes us to the editorial work of Tyrwhitt, who attempts to rescue what might pass for an authentic Chaucer text and canon.

James Simpson's recent articulation of a particular kind of institutionalized periodization that would apparently seal off the Middle Ages (admittedly in innovative and challenging fashion) as part of the grand narrative of literary history, can be mapped onto Spurgeon's lead in identifying discrete phases in Chaucer reception history as part of a much larger and gradual evolutionary process.[3] It is difficult, admittedly, for twenty-first century medievalists to attempt to break free from these particular types of scholarly mindset. But it is important to try to do so, largely because of the inevitable smoothing of some of the ruts and potholes along the way that must accompany any such journeys through literary history of the kinds variously advocated by Spurgeon or Simpson. In one of the liveliest recent accounts of Chaucer and his early readers, for example, Seth Lerer reiterates what has long been the current critical orthodoxy when he states that 'Chaucer—as author, as laureate and as father of English poetry—is a construction of his later fifteenth-century scribes, readers and poetic imitators.'[4] He then follows Spurgeon in arguing for an account of literary history that sees Chaucer transformed, in a later evolutionary phase, from 'a remembered literary presence guiding literary making to a dead *auctor* valued for his exemplarity'.[5] Lerer takes this reading along a particularly dangerous route in his next book, where he argues (over-ingeniously, in my view) for the Tudor recovery of the subtleties of Chaucer's art following a fallow period marked by fifteenth-century dullness and childish miscomprehension.[6] Stephanie Trigg's recent monograph on reading Chaucer from medieval to postmodern, on the other hand, is much more adventurous and not afraid of confronting multiple reading strategies and having them speak to each other across the ages. In negotiating the concerns for periodization that have dictated the shape of previous studies, Trigg sets up what is, in the end, a synchronic version of literary history driven by the politics of intentionalism and the polemic of feminist ideology. She reads different reception moments across history in relation to one another, insisting that, whatever their other differences, such moments and contexts reflect the same homosocial impulse to read Chaucer 'congenially', according to a masculinist 'clerical' discourse now increasingly being challenged, she thinks, by recent global trends in cultural, postcolonial, and gender studies.[7]

Part of the task of this chapter will be to search for other ways of deconstructing the apparently settled picture of Chaucer's early reception we have inherited from Spurgeon. Trigg's provocative engagement with literary history suggests there is now much to be gained from experimenting with both synchronic and diachronic historicized readings. One would hope that any such future enterprise would set as a goal the more patient pursuit of the historical uncertainties it seeks to clarify by stressing the specificity of individual interpretative and reinterpretative acts at different levels in the processes of literary production and reception. As such, early manuscript copyists sometimes had important and overlapping roles to play as both writers and active readers, critics, and receivers. In addition to Chaucer's imaginatively expressed worries over scribal miswriting and mismetring in *Troilus and Criseyde* (5. 1793–8), the lines in 'Chaucers Wordes unto Adam, his Owne Scriveyn' rapidly spring to mind at this point, words that suggest the dangers of scholarly complacency when, in order to make the evidence work harder in reception studies, one certainly needs to devise new strategies for privileging the polyvocal quality of the huge variety of Chaucer criticisms, references, and allusions so impressively marshalled and monumentalized by Spurgeon.

It therefore seems important to chart the simultaneous ebbing and flowing of Chaucer's reception and reputation, and the haphazard nature of canon formation in a predominantly manuscript culture that also witnessed the technological breakthrough from script to print, the ideological confusions of the English Reformations, and, linked to all of this, the supposed transition from 'medieval' to 'Renaissance' in English literary history. This is a tall order and one can hardly hope to be definitive or exhaustive in the course of a single short chapter. But it is possible to trace the basic contours of the terrain in prospect. In such a complex writing, reading, listening, and hearing culture, for example, we find that texts by Chaucer, or associated with his name, or linked in some other way with his traditions of fictional writing, are not always valued in biographical, authorial, or, strictly speaking, canonical terms. They are instead often appropriated for different purposes and audiences, as reusable aspects of a polite European literary court culture, occasionally also imbued with a strong sense of being, somehow, quintessentially 'English' and of transcendent cultural value. An important aspect of this discussion will be the teasing out and historicizing of several different but often related reception strands and Chaucer identities that, together, make up the thoroughly amorphous and occasionally contradictory and puzzling 'Chaucer traditions' in the centuries following his death.[8]

Chaucer as author and canon formation

The literary-critical truism that Chaucer's voice within his fiction has multiple and often inconsistent and unstable characteristics makes the canon formation processes operating within the 'Chaucer traditions' fascinating to trace. Viewed from a teleological, author-based perspective, Chaucer's prescient genius would appear to have initiated practically everything in this respect, particularly the strenuous efforts of later editors, printers, and modern scholars to create their author by compiling, or reassembling, or at times interrogating, the textual evidence for his life and works with varying degrees of success.[9]

Chaucer was, of course, only too aware that his texts would have some kind of afterlife and that parts of the larger design of his major works would perforce remain incomplete. The metropolitan afterlife his writings enjoyed began in the poet's own lifetime, with the immediate effects witnessed in the Chaucer borrowings found in works by Clanvowe and Usk, dating from the 1380s and 1390s. Similarly, Chaucer's cross-references and intertextual allusions basically promote the idea that his fiction should be read in the context of a larger poetic corpus, perhaps signalling his awareness, as an author of a growing body of works, of some early 'broadening' of interest in his verse, to borrow the apt descriptive term deployed by Paul Strohm in his discussion of Chaucer's audience.[10] Notable examples include the autobiographical cross-referencing in the linking passage preceding the 'Man of Law's Tale' ('MLI' 45–89) or the prose 'Retraction' following the 'Parson's Tale' and the description of other earlier works in the two variant prologues associated with the *Legend of Good Women*. They serve as possible forerunners of the 'complete works' mentality also underlying the production of the extraordinary manuscript survival now known as Cambridge

University Library MS Gg.4.27, or of the desire since Caxton to print the *Works of Geoffrey Chaucer*, an author-centred view of his œuvre that in all subsequent printings, by Wynkyn de Worde, Richard Pynson, William Thynne, John Stow, and Thomas Speght, holds to the shape of a formed poetic canon.

There is an almost irresistible temptation in Chaucer reception studies to focus on this important and well-documented development to the exclusion of everything else. But it is worth pausing to reflect that the Chaucer passages alluded to above might also have fuelled other different and sometimes quite contradictory images of Chaucer's poetical reputation. Without sharing modern scholarly enthusiasms for grappling with post-Romantic notions of authorship, textual authority, and canon, one can still relatively easily relocate within such contradictory images our strong sense of Chaucer as an Anglophone love-poet. He was the courtly poet of his age, it seems, and therefore, presumably, someone with a name and reputation around which fifteenth-century compilers were prepared to assemble similar verse of a courtly caste as and when it became available, and if it appealed to them. In other words, these remote and anonymous figures may have attempted to undertake the task without any particularly strong bibliographical sense that they were also compiling strongly author-centred anthologies. Such an imagined setting can then be used to explain the likely origins of the 'Oxford group' textual clusters and manuscripts, particularly productions like Bodleian Library MSS Fairfax 16, Bodley 638, and Tanner 346 and their immediate antecedents, the sources for which may not necessarily have come directly from Chaucer's desk.[11]

Indeed, Chaucer scholars often find themselves having to negotiate a series of other unpalatable details in discussing fifteenth-century reading tastes and the uncertain transmission and reception processes that affected Chaucer texts in the years immediately following the poet's death. Firstly, apart from the exceptional cases quoted above, relatively few 'Chaucer' anthologies containing significant clusters of his shorter poems actually survive. Where they do, it is clear that not all of the extant verse was actually written by Chaucer and that not all of it is love-poetry, or 'courtly', even by the most generous stretch of the imagination. The original book compilers usually also palpably fail to valorize Chaucer's clearly authentic writings over those of his contemporaries and later imitators. Sometimes, in fact, the point of an entire collection seems to be to promote Hoccleve or Lydgate's verse and reputation. Often, Chaucer's verse is ascribed to him by just one or two late, and perhaps not always entirely reliable, copyists or readers. Sometimes it is not ascribed at all. In short, then, it would seem that hardly any fifteenth-century compilers and early readers (apart from a few of the earliest Chaucer editor–printers and their late fifteenth-century collaborators doggedly working on various *Canterbury Tales* projects) seem to have cared much about either identifying or 'building' the Chaucer canon.[12]

Worth noting at this point is the survival of other more amorphous 'offshoot' miscellanies from later in the century into which poems belonging to similar early and probably metropolitan 'Chaucer' textual traditions evidently leaked. Examples include the 'Findern' manuscript (Cambridge University Library MS Ff.1.6), Trinity College, Cambridge, MS R.3.19, and related manuscripts associated with the so-called 'Hammond' scribe, or many of the diverse manuscripts associated with the collecting and copying activities of London readers, such as John Shirley in the fifteenth century and John Stow in the next century.[13] Shirley and Stow both seem to have had particular interests in recovering, or inventing, the circumstances in which items associated with Chaucer's name and reputation were first written and enjoyed. Many more members of Chaucer's early audiences were probably 'silent' readers. They remain silent in almost every sense of the word since they have left no marks on their books as a discernible record of their reading practices. One can now only rather desperately deduce from such silences that they were probably very often content to enjoy vicariously the games and politics of love played out in variously imagined polite narrative and lyric settings, or to learn dutifully from the short poems on moral and devotional themes that often circulated with Chaucer works of a similar caste. Such mainly anonymous and largely unrecoverable reading and listening interests from the period are important for a number of reasons. For one thing, they act as a corrective to the notion that nearly every fifteenth-century Chaucer reader was a literary agent of some kind, who shared some of Shirley and Stow's presumed bibliographical obsessions. More importantly, they might be regarded as providing a precedent for the imagined literary interests of the 'gentil' readership that the early printers strenuously attempted to woo, in the prefaces of Caxton's printed works, for example, or in the expansive Tudor editorial projects where Chaucer's 'complete works' were reprinted in forms designed to appeal to the good taste of purchasers.

Another major strand that presumably alerted later readers to Chaucer's personality and interests late in life is represented by the 'Retraction' following the 'Parson's Tale'. At this late point in the *Canterbury Tales*, readers are imaginatively invited to witness Chaucer in penitential authorial mode, apparently rehearsing details of his earlier life and career for the purposes of denying all, or almost all, of his named poetical achievements. Here we have Chaucer the totally orthodox and religious poet who wrote 'ful many a lyne' in praise of the Virgin, an image of the poet that both Thomas Hoccleve and John Lydgate promoted in their religious verse.[14] It is also an image that was variously pressed into service in the earliest visual representations of the poet, in the Ellesmere manuscript of the *Canterbury Tales* and in an early copy of Hoccleve's *Regement of Princes* (see Figure I.1) and its imitators. The iconic value of the orthodox Christian writer that was so created seems to have suited Lancastrian purposes well, since some significant intellectual and practical investment was apparently also made in closing down or curbing the symbolic potential of signs, images, or texts inimical to the ruling order. Although ultimately contested (in reformed Tudor eyes, at least) by the emergence of a more strident and ideologically sounder proto-Protestant Chaucer, it is not difficult to find some grounds in the poet's fictional writings for reinventing him in this conservative and orthodox fashion. Chaucer did indeed write a fair few lines in praise of the Virgin, some of which (the *Invocacio ad Mariam*) ended up in the

'Second Nun's Prologue', while other lines on the same topic became the short poem known as 'An ABC'. Arguably, 'An ABC' is one of Chaucer's earliest poems. Having lurked around the edges of Chaucer's poetical identity for some time, it was one of the last items to be admitted to the printed Chaucer canon, only finally securing its place there in Thomas Speght's second Chaucer edition of 1602.[15]

Unlike Troilus in the eighth sphere, Chaucer in the 'Retraction' stops short of rue-fully laughing at the folly of a life spent largely in the service of love. But when his canon of writings is listed at the end of the *Canterbury Tales*, it is only for most of the items to be dismissed by him almost immediately as of little or no importance in the larger Christian scheme of things. It is indeed fortunate that several early readers actually read against the text of the 'Retraction' at this point, demonstrating by their actions as book compilers and scribes an awareness that Chaucer had in truth bequeathed them a substantial and important poetical legacy, one that, where pos-sible, they should seek to preserve and augment. Because of the multifarious remote and strangely decontextualized ways in which Chaucer's name and reputation is some-times evoked in individual works and books as a result—and sometimes not—one should certainly never begin with the assumption that author-centred or canonical interests can be taken for granted in the work of every scribe who copies Chaucer texts, every copyist or printer who adds another Chaucer poem to a pre-existing collection, or every reader who ascribes works to the father of English poetry.

Scholars who care to look at the surviving manuscripts with this thought in mind will find plenty of other poetical identities presented to them regarding the writer they will also often see revered as England's master poet: classical Chaucers, philosophical Chaucers, moral Chaucers, pious Chaucers, Lollard Chaucers, reformed Chaucers, bawdy Chaucers, proverbial Chaucers, Scotticized Chaucers, misogynist Chaucers, and Chaucers who are every woman's friend. The successful recovery of such multiple and overlapping Chaucer versions in this earlier period usually depends on painstaking codicological analysis of scattered and often undatable marginalia, annotation, and other textual minutiae that, of themselves, will often create a complex and thoroughly puzzling picture of possible scribal motivation for copying material or attributing works to Chaucer. The survival of so much material of this nature suggests that the singularity of Chaucer's achievement as England's first laureate poet was widely recog-nized, and that Chaucer's own interest, one presumes, in the possible afterlives of his texts was also shared by a good number of later readers.

Chaucer the father and England's laureate poet

Chaucer's fatherly reputation as England's first laureate poet belongs to apparently secure yet largely retrospective processes of identity formation that have been recently much discussed. Such early valorization links his achievement directly to the works of other contemporary or near-contemporary writers such as Thomas Usk, John Gower, Thomas Hoccleve, and John Lydgate. There are important differences in the terms by which Chaucer is complimented by these writers and others as a still-living poet and then after his death. Usk in the *Testament of Love* (c.1387?) has the God of Love describe Chaucer as 'the noble philosophical poete in Englissh'. Without actually declaring him a laureate, Usk makes it clear that Chaucer is the pre-eminent living English poet of the day: 'Certaynly, his noble sayenges can I not amende: In goodnes of gentyl manlyche speche without any maner of nycite of starieres [*sic*; read "storiers"] ymagynacion in wytte and in good reason of sentence he passeth al other makers.'[16] The lines were written in the knowledge that Chaucer had earlier bestowed the epithet 'philosophical' on his fellow poet (Radulphus) Strode, to whom, jointly with 'moral' Gower, Chaucer dedicates *Troilus and Criseyde* (5. 1856–7). John Gower, in turn, has Venus greet Chaucer in the early recension of the *Confessio amantis* as 'mi disciple and mi poete' and speaks of a land filled with his verse 'whereof to him in special | Aboue alle other I am most holde'.[17] The mutuality and reciprocal exchange of such complimentary gestures took place within a select group of living poets, thinkers, and writers and would have had to change in character and tone when members of the group stopped writing for some reason. Chaucer's death silenced his contribution in the coterie setting of the burgeoning English vernacular literary scene but immediately gave licence to other fifteenth-century admirers and their associates to create and manage an image of the dead poet on basically their own terms.

In the case of both Thomas Hoccleve and John Lydgate, the dead laureate is created and managed as the absent father of English poetry who engaged deeply and proleptically with the literary concerns and professional preoccupations of his later admirer–poets. In the *Regement of Princes*, this means that Hoccleve quite naturally becomes the quasi-legalistic petitioner acting rhetorically in the court of heaven on behalf of Chaucer, described here as the great Marian poet. Elsewhere Hoccleve adapts his role as courtly petitioner to fit the more imaginative secular concerns expressed in some of his shorter verse in a comparable manner to the adaptations of the public voice in some of Chaucer's shorter verse: his 'Envoys' to Bukton and Scogan, for example, or his 'Complaint to his Purse', or, indeed, in 'Truth', 'Gentilesse', or 'Lak of Stedfastnesse'. Once one discovers the shifting presence of this rhetorical style in many places in Chaucer and Hoccleve's verse, it is easy to speculate that both poets must have always been closely identified with such discourses precisely because they held public office. In Hoccleve's case, we know much about his professional duties and other varied activities both inside and outside the office of the Privy Seal. Recalling Chaucer to mind and becoming his petitioner with fondness and respect, therefore, coincidentally becomes a means of helping Hoccleve play out in his 'public poetry' the drama of a metropolitan life spent finding and enhancing his own poetical voice.

John Lydgate similarly made a shrewd investment in Chaucer's posthumous invention. His many allusions to and imitations of Chaucer's works and reputation are matched by an evident desire to bear witness to the pre-eminence and quality of

Chaucer's linguistic and literary achievements as laureate poet, achievements that he sometimes defines according to classical models and precedents. Lydgate's Chaucer is the first founder and embellisher of our language, but he is also a completely pious and conventional religious poet. Lydgate thus embraced the opportunity offered by his 1426 verse translation of Guillaume de Deguilleville's *Pèlerinage de la vie humaine* for Thomas Montagu, earl of Salisbury (the second husband of Chaucer's granddaughter), to heap fulsome compliments on Chaucer's 'An ABC'. His paean of praise for Chaucer nostalgically conjures up the Deschamps-like memory of the 'grant translateur' who is now dead and absent, rather than the father of English poetry whose work will presumably live on for ever. Lydgate's image is of a devout poet who once translated 'ful many a line' (to borrow Hoccleve's term again) in praise of the Virgin from de Deguilleville, 'word by word, as in substaunce . . . fful devoutly, in sentence' (19757–9[18]). In making such a precise claim for Chaucer's translation skills, Lydgate seems determined to ignore his radical linguistic and metrical experimentation, transforming the dead master into a religious poet who was not unlike Lydgate himself. Indeed, in the next few lines he announces his plan to 'ympen thys Oryson'; in other words he intends to graft the Chaucer lyric into his own text:

> My purpos to determine,
> That yt shal enlwmyne
> Thys lytyl book, Rud off [rude of] making
> Wyth som clause off hys wrytyng. (19781–4)

Lydgate's plan for his commission represents a second occasion when a compiler with sympathies for the Lancastrian cause planned to graft lines from Chaucer into the service of some greater good. In Henry Scogan's 'Moral Balade' the courtier and royal tutor to whom Chaucer's 'Envoy' to Scogan was dedicated finally returned the compliment by reportedly sending his royal charges (the sons of Henry IV) a short moral poem recommending virtue. Scogan's poem quotes within itself Chaucer's 'Gentilesse' in its entirety. The whole point of such an exercise would seem to have been to memorialize the dead poet and, simultaneously, redeploy Chaucer's text and reputation as a monumental source of moral and religious guidance. In each of these cases, an important additional motivating factor would seem to be to 'enlwmyne' (enhance through display) both Scogan's and Lydgate's own prestigious Lancastrian commissions.

One is left wondering what other local considerations may conceivably have influenced the principles of selection in those few other mainly anonymous cases where we know that individual fifteenth-century writers and book compilers were charged with selecting for copying certain moral and courtly extracts from *Troilus and Criseyde*; the *Canterbury Tales* (including, notably, the 'Clerk's Tale', the 'Monk's Tale', and the 'Melibee', all of which Lydgate specifically commended in the *Fall of Princes*, 1. 346–50), or one or two free-standing amatory, moral, or religious items from the larger textual clusters in which Chaucer's shorter poems once circulated. Furthermore, the juxtaposition of selected Chaucer extracts and short items alongside poems by Hoccleve and Lydgate in several different manuscript settings is striking and suggestive. It may well testify to the original success of the promotional activities practised by both these 'Lancastrian' poets and their associates, at court, in Westminster Hall, in other professional circles, and in the London book trade. Hoccleve and Lydgate certainly made some strenuous effort in their own writings to enhance Chaucer's prestige and fatherly reputation as the laureate poet who (in addition to his other qualities) wrote and spoke publicly and well on religious, moral, and sententious themes.

Reformation Chaucers and 'Canterbury Tales'

By the time they reach the 'Retraction' at the end of the *Canterbury Tales*, most modern readers will be only too aware of the contingent and unfinished nature of Chaucer's experimental fiction. Still partly a matter for educated guesswork is the question of how much more obviously the incompleteness of the *Canterbury Tales* would matter to fifteenth-century readers and listeners operating in a manuscript culture, without the stabilizing influence and apparatus of a modern printed edition. Modern bibliographical responses to questions of textual incompleteness are based largely on quasi-scientific, but ultimately subjective, analyses of the various textual histories that can be recovered from the extant manuscripts and the differing traditions of tale ordering preserved there.

The editors of the Ellesmere manuscript of the *Tales* seem to have responded positively and energetically to this potentially unsettling and chaotic situation. They obviously felt some responsibility for completing, or, at least, rounding out as best they could for him, Chaucer's celebration of robust living and fine loving on the road to Canterbury and 'enlwmyning' their completed book accordingly. These are important details since, arguably, the ambitious and overlapping Ellesmere–Hengwrt project may even have begun in Chaucer's lifetime, with Hoccleve included among the team of metropolitan copyists working on the task (for more on these two manuscripts, see Chapter 28).

Other early editors, copyists, and printers, all working to their own agendas slightly later than the Hengwrt–Ellesmere copyists, and sometimes, perhaps, in the light of their impressive editorial achievement, occasionally made further efforts to smooth out (by erasure, rewriting, or textual interpolation) some of the most obvious remaining gaps, or perceived flaws of one kind or another, in Chaucer's fiction. The text of the *Canterbury Tales* in British Library MS Harley 7333, for example, is associated with the Austinian canons at Leicester Abbey and has been emended, one assumes, according to the prevailing standards of correctness operating in such a milieu: as a result, there is some useful evidence in this manuscript of perceived examples of obscenity, heresy, and anticlerical sentiments in Chaucer's fiction being cancelled or censored by closely supervised scribal rewriting. A more personal response to the *Canterbury Tales* can be gleaned from the Bibliothèque Nationale, Paris, MS fonds anglais 39, the manuscript made for Jean d'Angoulême, brother of Charles d'Orléans and, similarly to his brother, someone with plenty of opportunities for polite English leisure time pursuits since he was an aristocratic prisoner in England for a number of years. Tales are rearranged at will in his manuscript, with one of the notes in Jean's hand making reference to the 'Squire's Tale' remnant that survives in this copy as 'valde absurda' ('really absurd'), and Jean's copy of a radically truncated 'Monk's Tale' (a truly transistorized version) is referred to as 'valde dolorosa' ('really melancholy').

There were many other early readers and copyists who also acted as Chaucer's earliest editors. In the course of this work, linking passages were written and erased and 'new' *Canterbury Tales* enter the canon: the 'Tale of Gamelyn' displaces the unfinished 'Cook's Tale', and, in just one manuscript, the 'Tale of Beryn' is presented as the first tale told on the homeward journey (by the Merchant). In the *Siege of Thebes*, John Lydgate also seems to have imaginatively taken advantage of the long empty miles on the rest of the road back from Canterbury to London in order to write an image of himself and his telling of the Thebes story into Chaucer's fiction. That this tendency to consider the *Canterbury Tales* slightly apart from the rest of Chaucer's works was widespread is suggested by the manner in which by 1535, in some circles at least, the idea of telling a 'Canterbury tale' had become synonymous with indulging oneself in telling idle and worthless stories. With the advent of printing, the wholesale introduction of apocryphal material into the *Canterbury Tales* and the rest of the Chaucer canon also gathered apace.

From its earliest appearance in manuscript form, the *Canterbury Tales* seems to have become recognized as a special kind of text that invited editorial intervention and audience participation in its (re)construction. In 1542–3 the *Canterbury Tales* prints are also singled out for specific attention, apart from the rest of Chaucer's works, in *An Acte for thaduauncement of true Religion and for thabolisshment of the contrarie* (1542–3). Momentarily attempting to establish what constituted forbidden books in Henrician reformed eyes, the Tudor statute expressly declares:

> Provided allso that all bokes in Englishe printed before the yere of our Lorde a thousande fyve hundred and fourtie intytled the Kings Hieghnes proclamacions iniunctions, translacions of the Pater noster, the Aue Maria and the Crede, the psalters prymers prayer statutes and lawes of the Realme, Cronycles Canterburye tales Chaucers bokes Gowers bokes and stories of mennes lieues, shall not be comprehended in the prohibicion of this acte.[19]

One is here left to wonder just what constituted the 'Canterburye tales' in the eyes of the Tudor legislators. The answer is probably related to the reception history of William Thynne's printed Chaucer; in 1542, acting in complex relation with the Tudor royal household and the Henrician reforms, Thynne had reprinted his 1532 edition of Chaucer's collected works, adding the robustly anti-papal 'Plowman's Tale' immediately after the *Canterbury Tales*. By the time of his 1550(?) reprint, Thynne had inserted the 'Plowman's Tale' within the pilgrimage frame, just before the 'Parson's Tale' (Thynne had supposedly earlier tried to incorporate another virulently anticlerical piece, the 'Pilgrim's Tale', into his first Chaucer edition). By the 1540s, therefore, Thynne was actively incorporating a proto-Protestant strand into Chaucer's voice, and he was doing so in a manner that was apparently sensitive to the current prevailing temper of the Henrician court. It is hardly surprising that the reformed voices in Thynne's Chaucer continue to be heard in later printings: it is still heard in John Stow's 1561 print, where, along with other apocryphal material, Lydgate's *Siege of Thebes* is added at the end of the volume, and in Thomas Speght's reprintings of Stow (1598; revised and reprinted in 1602), and in subsequent prints right up until the time of Tyrwhitt, in 1775, who famously castigates the 'editorial' work that produced earlier printed Chaucers.

One must exercise a degree of caution in interpreting this evidence since it remains impossible to say just when, how, or even if, Chaucer had been thoroughly 'Protestantized' for his English readers by Thynne, Stow, or Speght. An interesting test case in this context is the manner in which Chaucer's Marian text 'An ABC' was brought in from the cold in Thomas Speght's second Chaucer edition (1602). It is slightly surprising that this apparently authentic Chaucer text had to wait so long for its first printing. Given the harsh monovocal tone of religious intolerance that seems to have dominated the official record of England's past for long stretches of time in Henrician England, one might readily enough assume that 'An ABC' was so redolent of pre-Reformation religious orthodoxy that it could have been easily lost from the sixteenth-century reformist record of the Chaucer canon. Its salvation may well have been its impeccable textual pedigree. Speght's text of 'An ABC' was taken from the Chaucer manuscript that most nearly approximates an attempt to compile a 'complete works' anthology, Cambridge University Library MS Gg.4.27. Equally astonishing in this context is the manner in which 'An ABC' is joined in the 1602 print by another late arrival in the Chaucer canon, Jack Upland's *Complaint against Friars*. The Jack Upland text was taken from the second edition of John Foxe's *Actes and Monumentes*, a version that claimed for Chaucer the strident reformed voice that can be detected in the text. It was Foxe who described Chaucer as 'a right Wiclevian', a posthumous reputation as a Wycliffite that has clung to the poet (in one form or another) ever since.[20]

Endings as beginnings: Chaucer absences

Tyrwhitt's now famous characterization of the apocryphal additions in the 1561 Stow Chaucer as 'a heap of rubbish'[21] represents his awareness of one kind of Chaucer absence: the absence of an authoritative reading text drawn from the genuine Chaucer archive which Tyrwhitt expresses his determination to return to in his 1775 edition. He shares this determination with the modern scholars who have since powerfully redeployed the surviving documentary evidence to frame their accounts of both the life of the poet and the text of his works. Chaucer's ending also marks the beginning of the recording of an English literary history in which the father of English poetry plays a central role, but where he has obviously had to be reinvented by later writers. Ironically, it is also at this point, or shortly afterwards, that much of Chaucer's personal archive was presumably considered obsolete and thus written out of literary history.

Related to these kinds of seemingly inevitable absences and losses are the intriguing early moments of resistance to or the suppression of material one might otherwise have expected to find in abundance in the more general Chaucer archive. The failure by John Shirley, John Stow, and others to annotate properly all the Chaucer manuscripts they are known to have checked, for example, when one knows that they knew some of these contained authentic Chaucer poems presented anonymously in these contexts, is an intriguing prospect. Of a different order is the manner in which the passage containing Gower's complimentary reference to his disciple–friend Chaucer in the first recension of the *Confessio amantis* seems to have been later actively repressed, presumably because the passage seemed redundant and outdated once Chaucer had died. Similarly, in nearly all the relevant extant manuscripts we have the general failure to survive of the 'Hoccleve' Chaucer portrait required as a crucial visual aid for Hoccleve's encomium to the dead poet in the *Regement of Princes* (Figure I.1). Such an absence significantly reduces the point of the passage, practically rendering Hoccleve's original idea obsolete as a result. More disastrously yet for real reading experiences of Chaucer is the complete absence of any sign of 'An ABC' from the remaining manuscripts of Lydgate's Deguilleville translation, an absence that sits very oddly beside Lydgate's effusive praise of the dead Chaucer immediately preceding the embarrassing blank space in all the relevant copies. This constitutes a hole in the Chaucer archive that even John Stow, with his penchant for textual patch and repair, was not prepared to fill when he consulted Lydgate's defective text a century or more later. It was perhaps due to the unfavourable ideological climate of the day that Stow did nothing. Prior to its appearance in the 1602 Speght Chaucer, however, Stow had clearly known about 'An ABC' in several different manuscript copies. He may even have nudged Speght in their general direction, yet it still seems a striking and notable omission that he failed to include Chaucer's inoffensive Marian item in one of his own Chaucer printings.

These examples from across a broad historical period are matched by other kinds of absences from the record that can be associated with attempts to reconfigure Chaucer's texts and reputation. As seems to have been the case with both the Hoccleve and Lydgate examples discussed above, many complimentary references to the father of English poetry have the effect of profiling Chaucer as a decorative addition, rather than as a poet living on for ever through his verse. The main focus in such passages is often not Chaucer but a reconfigured version of Chaucer that will enhance the achievement, profile, and burgeoning reputation of the later writer in question. Into this category might fall Spenser's Chaucer in the *Shepheardes Calendar*, where English and classical literary history and traditions are rewritten, creatively confused, and possibly even inverted, in a particularly interesting way. In this new, unfamiliar setting, Spenser has inherited the poetical mantle from Chaucer and is now the contemporary English Virgil. Chaucer is known as Tityrus, the name that once belonged to Virgil. By a neat twist of history, the excellence of the classical poet is adjudged in terms of the high standard originally set by the remote first English Virgil (Chaucer–Tityrus), now long dead and absent but imaginatively granted a reception history that antedated Virgil.

Later poet–translators were also acutely aware of their great Chaucer legacy but felt compelled to restore it to present-day readers through various acts of translation. They argue consistently that such translation activities are necessary because of the great antiquity and difficulty of Chaucer's language and metre. Thus, yet another new departure is suggested in *Fables Ancient and Modern* (1700), where John Dryden actively writes Chaucer back into the English literary present in which he is fully participating as a living poet. With Spenser, the story is entirely different. The great English poet is dead and is imagined as a greater and more antique monumental presence than Virgil. As a result, in the *Shepheardes Calendar*, Chaucer has been graciously consigned to (or even beyond) the remotest possible imagined reaches of English literary history.

FURTHER READING

Brewer, D. S. (ed.), *Chaucer: The Critical Heritage*, 2 vols. (London: Routledge & Kegan Paul, 1978). With a focus on the heritage of Chaucer criticism, Brewer outlines 'a unique index to the course of English criticism and literary theory' (p. 1) in what he sees as incorporating a general tradition of neo-classical, Romantic, and Victorian premises about literature and society that had mid-sixteenth-century origins and became dominant with Dryden. Volume i covers the period 1385–1837.

Griffiths, Jeremy, and Derek Pearsall (eds.), *Book Production and Publishing in Britain 1375–1475* (Cambridge: Cambridge University Press, 1989). Particularly relevant because it takes into account recent work and new discoveries in the field of Chaucer manuscript studies: on the role and social status of book-owners in book production and the book trade, the manuscripts of the major English poetic texts, and issues of production and choice of text in anthologies and miscellanies.

Lerer, Seth, *Chaucer and his Readers: Imagining the Author in Late-Medieval England* (Princeton: Princeton University Press, 1993). A provocative study of the reception and revoicing of Chaucer's poetry in the fifteenth and early sixteenth centuries that stresses how Chaucer's creation as an author and the invention of English literary history are the greatest achievement of C. S. Lewis's 'drab age', though largely dictated by the vocabulary of literary imitation and the dynamics of reader response already present in Chaucer's verse.

Morse, Ruth, and Barry Windeatt (eds.), *Chaucer Traditions: Studies in Honour of Derek Brewer* (Cambridge: Cambridge University Press, 1990). A coherently organized collection of essays that serves as a companion volume to volume i of Brewer's *Chaucer: The Critical Heritage*, at least in so far as it analyses a variety of critical responses to Chaucer or 'Chaucer traditions' that extend from the beginnings of Chaucer's influence on his contemporaries as far as his impact on writers active in the late seventeenth century.

Pinti, Daniel J. (ed.), *Writing after Chaucer: Essential Readings in Chaucer and the Fifteenth Century* (New York: Garland, 1998). Largely reprints of recent significant essays that examine how fifteenth-century scribes, commentators, poets, and editors shaped and defined the Chaucer canon, thus determining how Chaucer was initially received, his reputations defined, and his works transmitted to later eras.

Prendergast, Thomas A., and Barbara Kline (eds.), *Rewriting Chaucer: Culture, Authority, and the Idea of the Authentic Text 1400–1602* (Columbus: Ohio State University Press, 1999). A series of commissioned essays that examines the cultural and aesthetic implications of revoicing Chaucer as part of the late medieval and early modern reception of the Chaucer canon.

Ruggiers, Paul G. (ed.), *Editing Chaucer: The Great Tradition* (Norman, Okla: Pilgrim Books, 1984). A collection of essays that examines the textual practices of Chaucer editors from Caxton to R. K. Root. The partly biographical essays on Chaucer's earliest editor–printers survey their awareness and utilization of the manuscript and textual traditions that laid the foundation for establishing the canon of Chaucer's works and establish an appropriate historical context and socio-literary milieu within which it is possible to imagine such editorial activities taking place.

Spurgeon, Caroline F. E. (ed.), *Five Hundred Years of Chaucer Criticism and Allusion 1357–1900*, 3 vols. (Cambridge: Cambridge University Press, 1925). Spurgeon's monumental work offers a collection of observations regarding Chaucer and his works. Her work aims for completeness in its coverage of the earliest period of Chaucer criticism and allusion.

Trigg, Stephanie, *Congenial Souls: Reading Chaucer from Medieval to Postmodern* (Minneapolis: University of Minnesota Press, 2002). A polemical study of Chaucer's 600-year reception history that seeks to uncover how attempts by Chaucer's readers to recuperate their author's writings and his past create an elite transhistorical community of 'congenial souls', all claiming familiarity with their author while attempting to reshape him in their likeness, a homosocial process, in Trigg's view, and one that is as interesting for what it often unconsciously seeks to repress as for what it makes manifest.

NOTES

1. Caroline F. E. Spurgeon (ed.), *Five Hundred Years of Chaucer Criticism and Allusion 1357–1900*, 3 vols. (Cambridge: Cambridge University Press, 1925), vol. i, p. x.

2. Ibid., vol. i, p. xxv.

3. James Simpson, *Reform and Cultural Revolution, The Oxford English Literary History*, ii: *1350–1547* (Oxford: Oxford University Press, 2002).

4. Seth Lerer, *Chaucer and his Readers: Imagining the Author in Late-Medieval England* (Princeton: Princeton University Press, 1993), 3.

5. Ibid. 19.

6. Lerer, *Courtly Letters in the Age of Henry VIII* (Cambridge: Cambridge University Press, 1997).

7. Stephanie Trigg, *Congenial Souls: Reading Chaucer from Medieval to Postmodern* (Minneapolis: University of Minnesota Press, 2002).

8. For a judicious overview of the mainstream traditions that sees them as more evolutionary and less amorphous than the account offered here, see Barry Windeatt, 'Chaucer Traditions', in Ruth Morse and Barry Windeatt (eds.), *Chaucer Traditions: Studies in Honour of Derek Brewer* (Cambridge: Cambridge University Press, 1990), 1–20. The older idea of a singular 'Chaucer tradition' belongs more appropriately to the era of Spurgeon and Brusendorff; see Aage Brusendorff, *The Chaucer Tradition* (Oxford: Oxford University Press, 1925).

9. For materials used to construct both early and modern Chaucer biographies, see Derek Pearsall, *The Life of Geoffrey Chaucer: A Critical Biography* (Oxford: Blackwell, 1992), and Pearsall's account of audience and reception in *The Canterbury Tales* (London: George Allen & Unwin, 1985), esp. 294–320.

10. See the chapter 'Chaucer's Audience' in Strohm, *Social Chaucer* (Cambridge, Mass.: Harvard University Press, 1989), 47–83.

11. Julia Boffey and John J. Thompson, 'Anthologies and Miscellanies: Production and Choice of Texts', in Jeremy Griffiths and Derek Pearsall (eds.), *Book Production and Publishing in Britain 1375–1475* (Cambridge: Cambridge University Press, 1989), 279–315.

12. Paul G. Ruggiers (ed.), *Editing Chaucer: The Great Tradition* (Norman, Okla.: Pilgrim Books, 1984); see also the useful survey in Stephen Partridge, 'Questions of Evidence: Manuscripts and the Early History of Chaucer's Works', in Daniel J. Pinti (ed.), *Writing after Chaucer: Essential Readings in Chaucer and the Fifteenth Century* (New York: Garland, 1998), 1–26.

13. See Boffey and Thompson, 'Anthologies and Miscellanies'.

14. John J. Thompson, 'After Chaucer: Resituating Middle English Poetry in the Late Medieval and Early Modern Period', in Derek Pearsall (ed.), *New Directions in Later Medieval Manuscript Studies: Essays from the 1998 Harvard Conference* (York: York Medieval Press, 2000), 183–99.

15. Ibid. 195–8; John J. Thompson, 'Chaucer's "An ABC" in and out of context', *Poetica* (Tokyo), 37 (1993), 38–48.

16. D. S. Brewer (ed.), *Chaucer: The Critical Heritage*, 2 vols. (London: Routledge & Kegan Paul, 1978), i. 43.

17. Ibid. i. 43.

18. Ibid. i. 51.

19. Ibid. i. 98.

20. Ibid. i. 108.

21. See Barry Wineatt, 'Thomas Tyrwhitt', in Ruggiers (ed.), *Editing Chaucer*, p. 142.

30

Reception: eighteenth and nineteenth centuries

David Matthews

Chaucer at the end of the nineteenth century

The organized study of Middle English as a university discipline and, within it, Chaucer studies, only came into being in the last third of the nineteenth century. The term 'Middle English' itself came into general currency in the 1870s, when the study of Middle English literature began in the universities of Britain, those of the newly unified Germany, and in some parts of the United States, particularly Harvard University. Consequently, a great deal of Middle English writing was only read and studied for the first time at the end of the nineteenth century. The work of Chaucer was in a different position as it already had a long critical history, involving considerable appreciation as well as a great deal of misunderstanding and error. The poet immediately took his place as a central, canonical author in the new university study of Middle English.

Much of the new prominence of Chaucer was due to the work of Frederick Furnivall, who established the Chaucer Society in London in 1868 to advance publication of the poet's works by public subscription. In direct association with Furnivall and the Chaucer Society, W. W. Skeat produced *The Complete Works of Geoffrey Chaucer* in 1894–7, a monumental seven-volume publication which unequivocally aimed to be the definitive edition for which Chaucerians had been waiting. In 1898 the Globe edition of Chaucer appeared under the editorship of A. W. Pollard and others, a cheaper one-volume work which enlarged the potential readership. In the same period a series of scholarly breakthroughs transformed the ways in which Chaucer was read. The understanding of how Chaucer's verse should be pronounced was fundamentally altered by the phonological researches of Alexander Ellis in his work *On Early English Pronunciation* (1869–89). Many post-Chaucerian texts that had been spuriously attributed to Chaucer in the sixteenth century were removed from the canon in this period, and searches of archives refined Chaucerian biography. Furnivall also brought to prominence two previously unknown manuscripts, Hengwrt and Ellesmere, on which all modern *Canterbury Tales* editions are based.

The late Victorian Chaucerians were also keen to promote Chaucer beyond the bounds of university scholarship. Furnivall himself did not have a university post and did not draw a clear line between scholarship and popular appreciation. At the end of the Victorian period there were dozens of cheap editions of the poet's work in circulation; there were also many translations, some in verse aimed at sophisticated readers, some in prose and aimed at children. In 1896 the prestigious Kelmscott Press operated by the artist Edward Burne-Jones and the writer and designer William Morris issued the lavishly printed and illustrated Kelmscott Chaucer, clearly aimed at the wealthy, art-buying upper-middle class. In short, at the end of the nineteenth century Chaucer's poetry (particularly the *Canterbury Tales*) was available as never before and the poet was being read as never before.

At the beginning of the period surveyed in this chapter, by contrast, and when John Dryden took him up at the end of the seventeenth century, Chaucer, once celebrated in Tudor times as a national English poet, was as little read as he ever has been in the history of his reception. His work was scarcely available and his reputation at the nadir of a century-long decline. This chapter surveys the ways in which Chaucer was taken from this position in 1700 to one of apparent adulation as an English classic by 1900. It examines the attempts made in the period, by scholars and poets in particular, to establish Chaucer as having classic status comparable to that of Shakespeare and Milton. The chapter looks at the reshapings of Chaucer's poetic persona in the period and the connection of his writing and persona to ideas about the nation and its national literature. First, John Dryden's discussion of Chaucer will be examined and then the poet's fortunes in the later eighteenth century. Examination of the changing ideas about the poet, increasingly influenced by academic scholarship in the nineteenth century, brings the chapter to a close.

The period surveyed does not involve a uniform and unproblematic rise in understanding of Chaucer. Some things do not change a great deal in the period: the idea that Chaucer is the father of English poetry is constantly reiterated (often with the implication that no other Middle English verse need be bothered with). The emphasis on Chaucer's supposed realism, seen to best advantage in the *Canterbury Tales*, is also constant throughout. Views of Chaucer's biography and understanding of what he actually wrote changed a great deal, on the other hand, and for the better. However, tolerance for Chaucer's perceived immorality diminished, so that, despite academic acceptance, there is still some resistance to his work in the nineteenth century. Even such a proponent as Skeat (who had originally trained for the Church) argued that such bawdy tales as those of the Miller or Wife of Bath 'can hardly be defended'.[1] Another facet of Chaucer reception is the much better understanding of Chaucer's medieval context in the nineteenth century than in the eighteenth. But this too comes at a cost, as the conclusion of this chapter will show.

Chaucer and Dryden

The language of Chaucer was evidently becoming difficult to read by the end of the sixteenth century. In the seventeenth, there were no editions of the poet's work (other than a reprint of a Tudor edition in 1687) and by 1700 there was little to help the aspiring reader of Chaucer. Medieval culture in general had become very unfashionable and Middle English, in particular, was barely known and poorly understood. Most Middle English literature was not easily available and what there was—cheap, reduced versions of the romances of *Guy of Warwick* and *Bevis of Hampton*, for example—was thought of as popular literature for children or the lower classes. The tales of these legendary heroes were now bywords for extravagant, unbelievable fictions. Chaucer's standing was certainly higher than this, but in popular usage the term 'Canterbury tale' had become a general idiom meaning 'tall story'. The archaic and consequently difficult character of Chaucer's language is proverbial in late seventeenth-century commentary:

> Age has Rusted what the *Poet* writ,

Joseph Addison wrote in 1694,

> Worn out his Language, and obscur'd his Wit:
> In vain he jests in his unpolish'd strain
> And tries to make his Readers laugh in vain.[2]

At the beginning of the eighteenth century there were nevertheless some stirrings of interest in late medieval English culture. The fourteenth-century *Mandeville's Travels* was popular in the years either side of 1700, when its tales of incredible travels and fabulous beasts were in vogue. The fortunes of Chaucer, too, were on the rise, but for the opposite reason. Chaucer would be promoted as a realist, a poet who copied nature. Mandeville, to eighteenth-century taste, was truly 'medieval' but Chaucer was about to be seen as an incipient modern. The most significant early promoter of Chaucer in this respect was the poet John Dryden.

Dryden had been poet laureate for more than thirty years and was the most distinguished poet in England when he produced *Fables Ancient and Modern, Translated into Verse, from Homer, Ovid, Boccace, & Chaucer. With Original Poems* in 1700. The title's implications are clear: Chaucer belongs in exalted company, in a lineage that stretches back to the classical greats Homer and Ovid and which takes in the eminent fourteenth-century Italian poet Boccaccio. The *Original Poems* refer to Dryden's own work, suggesting just as clearly that he was placing *himself* in this lineage. Dryden translated the 'Knight's Tale', the 'Nun's Priest's Tale', and the 'Wife of Bath's Tale' (discussed in detail in Chapter 32), explaining in his preface, in words that suggest a strong sense of national ownership of the poet, that he wanted to promote Chaucer for 'the Honour of my Native Country'. Having tackled Ovid, he wrote, he resolved to translate Chaucer because he saw resemblances between Ovid and 'our old *English* Poet'. Comparing the two, Dryden refers to Chaucer as 'the Modern Author', creating a strong sense of an opposition between classical and modern, with no sense of the Middle Ages having come between.[3]

Dryden develops a number of ideas that were not new in 1700 but which received a new impetus from the laureate's promotion of them. 'From *Chaucer*', Dryden writes, 'the Purity of the *English* Tongue began', reiterating the notion first current among Chaucer's fifteenth-century English successors that the poet was responsible for extending and beautifying the hitherto barbarous English language (1450). Dryden was not the first to call Chaucer 'the Father of *English* Poetry'—it was a fifteenth-century label—but the authority he gave the idea helped establish it as a commonplace of Chaucer criticism (1452). Chaucer's role extends beyond that of a poet; he becomes a kind of moral philosopher, 'a perpetual Fountain of good Sense; learn'd in all Sciences', who 'speaks properly on all Subjects' (1452). His role is paralleled by Dryden with that of Homer for the Greeks and Virgil for the Romans, making it clear that Dryden is here setting up an origin, a foundational figure in the form of a fatherly, almost heroic, poet, for a national poetry—a poetry of which he himself happens to be the current pre-eminent practitioner.

Chaucer, Dryden wrote, 'follow'd Nature every where; but was never so bold to go beyond her' (1452). By 'Nature' Dryden means reality; Chaucer's great virtue is that he painted from life, depicting accurately what he saw around him. This, in the conventional view of Dryden's time and for most of the eighteenth century, was what classical writers had also done and what was most to be applauded in poetry. It was also the failing of most medieval writing (such as the romances of Guy and Bevis) that it did not copy nature. In this view, Chaucer is considered as being a quite different kind of writer from other English medieval poets, and his *Canterbury Tales* becomes his most important, because most 'realistic', work. In the *Tales* all 'the various Manners and Humours (as we now call them) of the whole *English* Nation, in his Age' were encompassed. 'Not a single Character has escap'd him', Dryden wrote, leading up to his famous statement: 'here is God's Plenty. We have our Fore-fathers and Great Grand-dames all before us, as they were in *Chaucer*'s Days; their general Characters are still remaining in Mankind, and even in *England*' (1455). There is once again a strong sense of lineage here, not now looking back to a distant classical heritage but to the medieval forebears of Dryden's own contemporaries.

Despite his concern to link Chaucer back to the classical writers and forward to the moderns and in that way to 'de-medievalize' him, Dryden is of course aware that Chaucer is a medieval poet. And like Addison or any other seventeenth-century critic, he believes that medieval writing has its inevitable defects, from which even Chaucer must suffer. It was not known at the time that the unstressed final -*e* in Chaucer's verse was on occasion pronounced and consequently Dryden thought that metrically Chaucer's verse was inferior to modern productions. The father of English poetry was therefore 'a rough Diamond, and must first be polish'd e'er he shines'. This licenses Dryden to depart from literal translation (he tells us) and to 'improve' in places. He does so 'embolden'd, because (if I may be permitted to say it of my self) I found I had a Soul congenial to his, and that I had been conversant in the same Studies' (1457). The lineage in which Chaucer is situated in relation to classical poets is therefore also one in which Dryden locates himself, adopting the role of inheritor of a tradition begun by Chaucer but linked to Ovid and Homer.

Alongside these concerns with Chaucer's place in a pan-European tradition of literature, Dryden also acknowledges a need to make Chaucer morally acceptable. In choosing his three tales to translate, he states that he avoided anything that might give offence on moral grounds, explaining (with just a hint of regret) that he has not translated the tales of the Miller, Reeve, Shipman, Merchant, or Summoner, nor the 'Wife of Bath's Prologue'. Dryden's successor Alexander Pope was less scrupulous about avoiding the bawdy tales and produced a translation of the 'Merchant's Tale' in 1709 (see Chapter 32). But by the century's end Chaucerian morality was an increasing concern for many readers.

When Dryden died not long after the appearance of his Chaucer translations, he was buried in Westminster Abbey, not far from the tomb of Chaucer. Grieving fellow poets commended Dryden's success in the translations and played on the poet's own claim to have reanimated Chaucer's spirit:

> New Cloath'd by You, how *Chaucer* we esteem,

wrote the poet Henry Hall,

> When You've new Polish'd it, how bright the Jem!
> And lo, the Sacred Shade for thee make's room,
> Tho' Souls so like, should take but up one tomb.

An anonymous poet wrote,

> *Chaucer* shall again with Joy be Read,
> Whose Language with his Master lay for Dead.[4]

Dryden's own idea of Chaucer's need for 'polish' was echoed by others, as in Samuel Wesley's 'An Epistle to a Friend Concerning Poetry' (1700):

> Of CHAUCER's verse we scarce the *Measures* know,
> So *rough* the *Lines*, and so *unequal* flow;
> Whether by Injury of *Time* defac'd,
> Or *careless* at the *first*, and writ in *haste*;
> Or *coursly*, like old *Ennius*, he design'd
> What After-days have *polish'd* and *refin'd*.[5]

Fellow poets and critics seem to value Chaucer just as Dryden had done: more for his representations of the national character in the past than for his actual verse, which is universally regarded as deficient. Wesley allows the possibility that, like a dilapidated medieval building, Chaucer's verse has been 'defac'd' by the passage of time and so could be patched up, much as Addison had seen Chaucer's poetry as 'Rusted'. But Wesley is finally undecided: perhaps the verse was simply not done properly in the first place. Many were inclined to this view that there was something wrong with Chaucerian verse from the beginning.

Despite these evident defects, however, from the time of Dryden onwards the consensus grew that Chaucer was the first English poet, an idea restated many times in the eighteenth and nineteenth centuries. In 1721 the first new edition of Chaucer's works since 1602 appeared, undertaken by John Urry. It is obviously a major new stage in the dignifying of Chaucer and indicative of a fresh concern in the early eighteenth century to monumentalize him by putting his works in folio format and according him the same treatment given to classical writers. The edition contains a 'Life of Chaucer' by John Dart, which presents the poet as having been as serious and sober an eighteenth-century gentleman as any reader could wish. Chaucer's immorality, according to Dart, belongs to the early part of his life, and later 'the gay Gentleman gave way to the grave Philosopher and pious Divine'. Chaucer was 'a great Scholar, a pleasant Wit, a candid Critick, a sociable Companion, a stedfast Friend, a grave Philosopher, a temperate Œconomist and a pious Christian'.[6]

Despite these claims for the poet, Urry's edition was a failure, to become regarded as the worst of all Chaucer editions. It did not win many new readers, nor much fresh respect for Chaucer. It was Dryden's translations and his essay that had the biggest impact in the early eighteenth century.

Thomas Warton and the Romantic revival

Sixty years after Dryden a major revival of interest in English medieval culture had grown from tentative early beginnings. After decades in which classical ideas dominated notions of literary taste, by the 1770s a new generation of antiquarian scholars was turning to medieval literature to unearth ballads and romances in Middle English, a largely unknown literature which allowed a greater focus on a native and national tradition. These antiquarians provided the impetus for what, a century later, would become organized as 'medieval studies'.

One of the key works in this revival was Thomas Warton's huge *History of English Poetry* (1774–81), a three-volume work chiefly concerned with romance but which inevitably dealt with Chaucer. He was 'a poet with whom the history of our poetry is by many supposed to have commenced', Warton wrote, arguing that Chaucer was a 'man of the world' whereas previously poets had been reclusive.[7] Chaucer's position out in the world was important in the eighteenth-century view of him, enabling him 'to give . . . an accurate picture of antient manners'.[8] So Warton follows Dryden in seeing Chaucer as an observer and realist, 'painting familiar manners with humour and propriety'. And, again like Dryden, he finds Chaucer transcending his time: 'he surpasses his predecessors in an infinite proportion . . . his genius was universal, and adapted to themes of unbounded variety'. This universality operated despite the times in which Chaucer lived, 'which compelled him to struggle with a barbarous language, and a national want of taste'.[9] Chaucer has 'the lustre and dignity of a true poet', instanced above all by his universality.

Warton also had something new to say. Chaucer paints reality; but 'his merit was not less in . . . moving the passions, and in representing the beautiful or the grand objects of nature with grace and sublimity'.[10] Warton's Chaucer is not simply a realist but also a poet of the emotions, a proto-Romantic whose sympathetic relation to nature—here the natural world rather than Dryden's 'Nature'—would be important in the nineteenth century.

This new emphasis is not, however, evident in the important new Chaucer edition that appeared at the same time Warton was writing. The Oxford-trained classicist Thomas Tyrwhitt produced his landmark edition of the *Canterbury Tales* in 1775. It was often reprinted or plundered in the nineteenth century, when it remained highly influential. It set Chaucer scholarship in new directions: Tyrwhitt argued that the final -*e* in Chaucer's language must be pronounced, a breakthrough that showed Dryden had been wrong about Chaucer's metrical deficiency; he reordered the *Tales* and rejected most of the spurious additions of the previous two centuries; he also used a range of manuscripts rather than relying on one or two. Showing little interest in the nascent romantic sentiment that motivated Warton to study medieval literature, Tyrwhitt looked to put the study of Chaucer on what he regarded as a proper footing. If readers paid attention to his arguments, they would now be able to read Chaucer aloud in a way that had not been possible for hundreds of years. They still, presumably, read the Middle English with what was essentially a modern pronunciation, but the poetry would have sounded more regular and the remaining difficulties of Chaucer's language would have been at least in part addressed by Tyrwhitt's extensive explanatory notes and glossary. There is no great literary-critical content in Tyrwhitt's edition; he is more interested in issues of language and does not echo Dryden or Warton in their commendation of Chaucerian realism. Instead (showing little concern over Chaucerian immorality), he argues that in his serious tales Chaucer 'often follows his author with the servility of a mere translator, and in consequence his narration is jejune and constrained'. In the comic tales by contrast Chaucer borrows less, 'and gives the whole the air and colour of an original; a sure sign, that his genius rather led him to compositions of the latter kind'.[11] Tyrwhitt, the first serious modern Chaucer scholar, recognized Chaucer's *comic* bent.

There were increasing numbers of readers, nevertheless, who found precisely the comic elements offensive, as is reflected in translations that proliferate by the end of the eighteenth century. Initially, after Dryden, poets enjoyed the bawdy potential of translating Chaucer, as Pope had done. In a saucy version of the 'Miller's Tale' written by Samuel Cobb around 1712 and reprinted several times, Absolon, at the denouement of the tale, 'curs'd the Hour, and rail'd against the Stars, | That he was born to kiss my Lady's Arse'.[12] As late as 1774 Warton defended the 'Miller's Tale' on the grounds of its 'compliance with the prevailing manners of an unpolished age'.[13] But when Cobb's 'Miller's Tale' was reprinted in a collection of translations of the *Canterbury Tales* by various hands anthologized by George Ogle in 1741, offending words were replaced by dashes, and in 1795 the Yorkshire rector William Lipscomb's modernized and supposedly complete *Canterbury Tales* omitted the Miller's and Reeve's Tales altogether (for more on eighteenth-century translation, see Chapter 32).

In justifying his censorship, Lipscomb referred to 'the grossness and indelicacy of the times in which Chaucer lived'.[14] Warton had used the same argument to reverse effect: the coarseness of his times should *excuse* Chaucer from such coarseness as he displays. To this extent, Warton has to concede that Chaucer *is* a man of the fourteenth century, circumscribed by his times. Elsewhere, however, he wants to argue that Chaucer is universal. Lipscomb wants to *make* Chaucer more universal by cutting out his more obviously fourteenth-century aspects. Either way, although Chaucer is seen as a 'native genius', eighteenth-century readers are equivocal about the barbarous Middle Ages in which, as if by some oversight, Chaucer lived. The result is a Chaucer not only purged of things the eighteenth century regretted he had ever written, but also rendered into a particularly eighteenth-century idiom. Warton himself memorably complained of Pope's translation of the *House of Fame* that it was 'like giving Corinthian pillars to a Gothic palace'.[15] By the end of the eighteenth century Chaucer translations were showing signs of the new Romantic fashions rather than classical influence. Lipscomb's own translation of the 'Nun's Priest's Tale' turns Chaucer's beast fable, set in a poor widow's simple farmyard, into a kind of Wordsworthian pastoral in which Chaucer's poem is initially barely recognizable:

> Time's snowy honours sprinkled on her head,
> Her peaceful life an aged widow led;
> A lofty grove, her humble cot behind,
> Fenc'd off the rudeness of the western wind:
> In front a limpid stream meand'ring flow'd,
> And breath'd gay health around the neat abode.[16]

At the end of the eighteenth century Chaucer had been translated often and edited rather less. Dryden's and Tyrwhitt's essays, and Warton's notes, formed the major substantial critical material on his work. Despite the acclaim contained in these writings, Chaucer was a long way from being appreciated in the wider culture.

Chaucer, nineteenth-century man of the world

The researches in medieval art, architecture, literature, and history that continued after the 1760s led to a widespread taste for Gothicism and the medieval, resulting in such famous neo-Gothic architectural monuments as the Houses of Parliament at Westminster (1837–60). Where literature was concerned the emphasis was on romances and ballads of chivalry, which appealed partly because of their extravagant and fantastic character. Chaucer—who in 'Sir Thopas' roundly mocked the romances and who was traditionally valued for his realism—was consequently a little awkwardly placed in relation to this revival. Nevertheless, in the new climate of acceptance for medieval culture in the early years of the nineteenth century Chaucer's work was increasingly widely available. In 1792–5 Robert Anderson published *A Complete Edition of the Poets of*

Great Britain in thirteen volumes. The first poet in the anthology was Chaucer, and this was the typical pattern followed in numerous cheap, small-format multi-volume anthologies of English poetry of the nineteenth century: Robert Southey's *Select Works of the British Poets* (1831); the *Aldine Edition of the British Poets* published by William Pickering in 1845; the 1866 reissue of the *Aldine Edition* under the editorship of the important Chaucerian Richard Morris; and the *Annotated Edition of the English Poets* edited by Robert Bell in 1854–6. There was little editorial work involved in these volumes; each simply plundered Tyrwhitt's text of the *Tales* (usually unacknowledged), and Urry's or an even earlier printed edition for Chaucer's other works.

In the period of Britain's rise as the first industrialized nation and world power, the anthologies bolster Britain's claims to a distinguished literary heritage. Basing that heritage on Chaucer, they radically truncate the medieval tradition. For the anthology editors, Chaucer is the only medieval English poet that anyone needs to know about, 'the first English versifier who wrote poetically', as Robert Anderson put it, strongly implying that no earlier medieval poet was worth considering.[17] Anderson ignored the fifteenth century, skipping from Chaucer to the early sixteenth, implicitly adopting the long-established attitude in which Chaucer was considered as first of the moderns rather than the last of the medievals. Robert Southey later underlined this sense of Chaucer's place, commenting that 'his proper station is in the first class, with Spenser, and Shakspeare, and Milton'.[18] Leaping from Chaucer to Wyatt and Howard or linking Chaucer to the late Tudor period, the anthologies elide Hoccleve, Lydgate, and the so-called Scottish Chaucerians, creating an absence in British literary history that has only recently begun to be redressed in medieval scholarship.

The anthologies were usually the initiative of booksellers rather than scholars, who were generally critical of them. In the first half of the nineteenth century there was still no complete edition of Chaucer that had any scholarly support despite an increasing sense that one should be produced. Obviously, however, there were many readers among the burgeoning middle class who bought the anthologies without too much concern for the more specialized questions of text-editing. What was happening was a shift in the study of Chaucer from the exclusive control of the small, poetically literate elite implied by an expensive folio edition such as Urry's, to the middle-class scholar and general reader who seized on Tyrwhitt's *Canterbury Tales* and its many copies. In the second half of the century there were concerted and successful efforts to establish the academic study of Chaucer, but the line between popular and academic appropriations was not always clear. Many of the scholars were equally concerned with popularizing Chaucer (Skeat, for example, having completed his major edition, went on to translate much of Chaucer's verse).

Other Middle English literature (and particularly the romances) was increasingly studied in the later nineteenth century. But despite attempts to popularize it (again by the indefatigable Furnivall), Middle English, with some exceptions such as Malory's *Morte D'Arthur*, became largely the preserve of scholars. The history of the study of

Chaucer was quite different from that of the rest of Middle English literature. The attempts to popularize Chaucer were more sustained and more successful. One consequence was the persistence of popular ideas, long after scholars questioned them. In 1803 the radical William Godwin produced a speculative, inaccurate biography of Chaucer which repeats some spurious traditions. Chaucer's nearness to nobility, particularly in the shape of John of Gaunt, duke of Lancaster, is constantly emphasized. In Godwin's view Edward III was Chaucer's 'patron and personal friend'; he took the poet under his wing, 'desiring to relieve the cares of empire by his conversation, to listen to his remarks, to have his hours of relaxation enlivened by the sallies of the poet, and probably to be the first hearer of his productions'.[19] This idealized picture of harmonious interaction between art and aristocracy evidently remained appealing to many in the nineteenth century, receiving dramatic illustration in Ford Madox Brown's 1851 painting *Chaucer at the Court of Edward III* (see Fig. IV.1). Brown, who read Godwin's book as part of his preparation for this large canvas, depicts Chaucer as towering above the viewer, reading from a book at the centre of the court to king and nobles who listen with rapt attention. (A smaller version is in the Tate Gallery, London.) Early designs (not completed) show that Brown conceived of the painting as a triptych with other English poets on the outer panels, so that Chaucer was enshrined in the company of Spenser, Shakespeare, and Milton.

By depicting Chaucer's supposed aristocratic connections and eminence at court Brown reiterates notions he found in Godwin but which go back to Tudor times. His original three-part design reinforced the more recent shaping of a lineage in English poetic tradition linking Chaucer to Shakespeare and other English poetic greats. But Brown also has something new to show: the way in which he depicts Chaucer's medieval setting would have been completely alien to the eighteenth century. Brown's medieval court is wildly colourful, his people gay, happy, and very far from the ravages of warfare or plague. There is no embarrassment about the Middle Ages here, no apology for the times which eighteenth-century commentators had tended to label rude and barbarous. This idyllic fourteenth century was a frequent feature of nineteenth-century medievalism; for many Victorians the fourteenth century was *the* medieval century, just as Chaucer was *the* medieval poet. However, Brown's (and Godwin's) idea of Chaucer as essentially a court poet generally receives less emphasis later in the nineteenth century. Victorian writers (and their American counterparts, increasingly important in the period) saw Chaucer less as a highly dignified 'true poet', successor of Homer, Virgil, and Ovid, and precursor of Shakespeare, and more as an ordinary man (if an exceptional poet), a man of the people. His essential Englishness is emphasized rather than his links with the classics, and the rather remote philosopher–poet becomes a more human figure, often described (partly on the basis of an overly literal reading of Chaucer's own self-representation in the *Canterbury Tales*) as modest and quiet. 'The father of English poetry was essentially a modest man', the essayist and journal editor Leigh Hunt wrote; 'he sits quietly in a corner.' Adolphus William Ward notes 'one very pleasing quality in Chaucer must have been his modesty'. Chaucer's

Fig. IV.1 *Chaucer at the Court of Edward III*. Painting by Ford Madox Brown, 1851. Oil on canvas (Art Gallery of New South Wales).

virtues are related to his simplicity: his verse has 'a simple pathos and feminine gentleness' for Henry David Thoreau, while for James Russell Lowell in 1870, 'he was a good man, genial, sincere, hearty, temperate of mind'.[20]

This simplicity tends to be related to what remains Chaucer's great virtue in the critics' eyes: his realism. Sitting quietly in his corner, as Leigh Hunt described him, Chaucer is 'looking down for the most part and meditating; at other times eyeing everything that passes, and sympathising with everything'. He 'gave not merely stories', as Lowell put it, 'but lively *pictures* of real life'. 'He is the first great painter of character, because he is the first great observer of it among European writers', Ward argues.[21] When a French critic, E. G. Sandras, proposed in 1859 the importance of *literary* sources to Chaucer as opposed to plain observation of real life, Frederick Furnivall was indignant. Sandras, for example, pointed to the French poet Guillaume Machaut as a source for the hunt in the *Book of the Duchess*. For Furnivall, 'the notion of going to a Frenchman to learn the way over a hurdle or a hedge is, of course, supremely ludicrous . . . If [Chaucer] couldn't describe a lovely woman when he saw her, except in French phrases (as M. Sandras imagines), he surely could, in English words, a bit of our greenwood life. Hang it!'[22]

These words show Furnivall's commitment to ideas of Chaucerian observation and realism but also point to another favourite nineteenth-century theme, that of Chaucer's love of nature. Chaucer is now less the poet of 'Nature' and more a nature-poet, describing rural England as no one had done before. 'Such pure and genuine and childlike love of Nature is hardly to be found in any poet', wrote Thoreau in 1843, drawing a comparison with Wordsworth.[23] 'Nature' in this sense was emerging as an enthusiasm just as industrialism threatened; the natural world and Chaucer's relation to it became the object of Victorian nostalgia for a pre-industrial Britain. In Ford Madox Brown's painting the focus is on the court setting, but in the background a distant ploughman and his team are at work: nobles listen to poetry and peasants work the fields, each knowing his place. From the Pre-Raphaelites, with whom he was friendly, Brown had taken a dreamlike, idealized vision of the Middle Ages, and for many this vision of the fourteenth century was an increasingly appealing antithesis to industrial Britain with its class conflicts. The socialist writer William Morris frequently fixed on that century and had it in mind in the prologue to his long poem *The Earthly Paradise* (1868–70), when he urged readers:

> Forget six counties overhung with smoke,
> Forget the snorting steam and piston stroke,
> Forget the spreading of the hideous town;
> Think rather of the pack-horse on the down,
> And dream of London, small, and white, and clean,
> The clear Thames bordered by its gardens green . . .[24]

As he did elsewhere in his work, Morris chose to focus not on such notable elements of the fourteenth century as plague, famine, rebellion, and protracted warfare but on the idea of an organic, harmonious, pre-industrial, and naturally socialist community.

Morris was aware of the less attractive side of the fourteenth century but still maintained, as he put it in his essay 'Feudal England' in 1887, that Chaucer's was 'a sunny world even amidst its violence and passing troubles, like those of a happy child'.[25]

The idea that Chaucer 'invented' English literature and even the English language became a standard of nineteenth-century thinking. 'English Literature begins with Chaucer', as the poet Arthur Hugh Clough put it in 1852.[26] Some writers were prepared to go even further. In a work of popular scholarship entitled *Chaucer's England*, Matthew Browne (the pseudonym of the minor poet William Brighty Rands) proposed that there was 'a sense in which it may be said that the history of England begins about the time of Chaucer, or in his century'. In the time of Chaucer 'Every thing is alive . . . and we feel that we are in England.'[27] Once more this is an example of someone prepared to overlook the crises of the fourteenth century to see it as the sunny birthplace of Englishness. Chaucer has a great deal to do with this: 'who is an English man more English than Chaucer?', Browne asked.[28]

Nevertheless, despite this new prominence and the notice of critics, the translations of Chaucer that continued to appear in the nineteenth century were often motivated by the desire to bring an unread poet to more people, as R. H. Horne suggested when he presented his versions in 1841, saying 'that although he is one of the great poets for all time, his works are comparatively unknown to the world. Even in his own country, only a very small class of his countrymen ever read his poems.'[29] Remarking on Horne's book, the critic Walter Pater was supposed to have said, 'Of course . . . I have heard of the *Canterbury Tales*, but I did not know that they were considered of sufficient importance to be modernised.'[30] In 1873 John W. Hales wrote that 'Chaucer is in many respects a lesser Shakespeare', meaning this as a compliment but inevitably highlighting the medieval poet's secondary status.[31] It was partly frustration that drove Frederick Furnivall to establish the Chaucer Society in 1868 to further the study of a poet he regarded as underappreciated.

Despite the strong tradition, going back to Dryden, of regarding Chaucer as 'timeless', Chaucer was increasingly resituated as essentially a medieval poet as more was learned about medieval culture. The stigma of barbarism attached to the Middle Ages in the eighteenth century had lost its force and Chaucer's medieval character was by now a great virtue. As Morris's and Thoreau's words above suggest, the period was now viewed by many as the innocent childhood of modernity. While this helped free the Middle Ages of the tag of barbarism it still meant that the period was distinguished from modernity by something it lacked: in Victorian eyes, the Middle Ages are not quite grown up. For many, Chaucer was irrevocably *limited* by his medievalness and could *only* be secondary. Probably the most famous of all nineteenth-century judgements on Chaucer was that of the poet and critic Matthew Arnold in his essay 'The Study of Poetry' (1880). Arnold was full of praise for Chaucer, whom he sees, as had so many before him, as forming a break with the medieval past. He is superior to the medieval romancers and, although his language is difficult, 'He will be read, as time goes on, far more generally than he is read now.'[32] Arnold reiterates Dryden's praise of the poet and hails Chaucer, again, as the father of English poetry, locating him in a tradition that now runs from Spenser, Shakespeare, and Milton to Keats.

Chaucer's place in English poetic tradition appears, then, to be triumphantly reasserted by the era's most important critic. But Arnold then makes the bald assertion that 'Chaucer is not one of the great classics.'[33] While he was a poet superior to those who preceded him and were contemporary with him, something is 'wanting' in Chaucer's verse. 'And there is no doubt what that something is', Arnold continues. 'It is . . . the high and excellent seriousness which Aristotle assigns as one of the grand virtues of poetry.'[34] In 1700 one of Dryden's ways of putting Chaucer forward was to compare the 'modern' Chaucer favourably with the classical poet Ovid. In eighteenth-century England there was then a shift away from Latin towards a more vernacularly based education. But the criteria of classical literary theory, as Arnold's comment shows, were still important in the nineteenth century. By those criteria, Chaucer was still found wanting.

At the end of the nineteenth century weight of numbers strongly suggests that Chaucer was vastly more important than ever before, with editions, translations, criticism, and commentary (both popular and academic) appearing in unprecedented volume, especially in the last third of the century. This picture must be adjusted by the knowledge that for a number of critics, including perhaps the most influential of them, Chaucer was still secondary and not a great classic, irrevocably medieval. Despite the massive efforts of those associated with the Chaucer Society—especially Skeat, Furnivall, and Richard Morris—they themselves were never satisfied that Chaucer was being sufficiently read or receiving due recognition. In some ways that sense of Chaucerian secondariness remains a feature of Chaucer studies beyond this period. Nevertheless, the 1890s very obviously are the high point of Chaucerian reception to that time, with the appearance of Skeat's edition, the Globe edition, the Kelmscott Press edition, and the availability of numerous translations. Chaucer was present as never before, for richer and poorer alike. Whatever the merits of Arnold's criticism, he was certainly right in his prediction that Chaucer would be read 'far more generally than he is read now' as Chaucer studies, thanks to the efforts of nineteenth-century scholars, took off in the twentieth century.

FURTHER READING

Bowden, Betsy (ed.), *Eighteenth-Century Modernizations from the 'Canterbury Tales'* (Woodbridge: Brewer, 1991). An edition of eighteenth-century versions of the *Tales*.

Brewer, Derek (ed.), *Chaucer: The Critical Heritage*, 2 vols. (London: Routledge & Kegan Paul, 1978). Extensive anthology of Chaucer criticism, adding some material not in the earlier anthology of Spurgeon.

Dane, Joseph A., *Who is Buried in Chaucer's Tomb? Studies in the Reception of Chaucer's Book* (East Lansing: Michigan State University Press, 1998). Contains two chapters on eighteenth-century editions of Chaucer.

Ellis, Steve, *Chaucer at Large: The Poet in the Modern Imagination* (Minneapolis: University of Minnesota Press, 2000). Discusses the modern non-academic reception of Chaucer, including William Morris's impact.

Matthews, David, *The Making of Middle English, 1765–1910* (Minneapolis: University of Minnesota Press, 1999). Discusses the wider context of the growth of Middle English studies, with one chapter devoted to Chaucer.

Patterson, Lee, 'Historical Criticism and the Development of Chaucer Studies', in his *Negotiating the Past: The Historical Understanding of Medieval Literature* (Madison: University of Wisconsin Press, 1987), 3–39. Discusses the eighteenth- and nineteenth-century origins of modern Chaucer criticism.

Ruggiers, Paul (ed.), *Editing Chaucer: The Great Tradition* (Norman, Okla.: Pilgrim Press, 1984). Contains chapters analysing the editions of John Urry, Thomas Tyrwhitt, and Walter Skeat.

Spurgeon, Caroline F. E. (ed.), *Five Hundred Years of Chaucer Criticism and Allusion, 1357–1900*, 3 vols. (Cambridge: Cambridge University Press, 1925). The essential anthology of Chaucer criticism.

Trigg, Stephanie, *Congenial Souls: Reading Chaucer from Medieval to Postmodern* (Minneapolis: University of Minnesota Press, 2002). Discusses scholarly Chaucer reception, particularly by Dryden and Furnivall.

Utz, Richard J., *Chaucer and the Discourse of German Philology: A History of Reception and an Annotated Bibliography of Studies, 1793–1948* (Turnhout: Brepols, 2002). Provides a detailed history of Chaucer reception in Germany.

NOTES

1. Walter W. Skeat (ed.), *The Complete Works of Geoffrey Chaucer*, 7 vols. (1894–7), vol. i, p. liii.

2. Quoted in Caroline F. E. Spurgeon (ed.), *Five Hundred Years of Chaucer Criticism and Allusion, 1357–1900*, 3 vols. (Cambridge: Cambridge University Press, 1925), i. 266; hereafter 'Spurgeon'.

3. John Dryden, Preface to *Fables Ancient and Modern* (1700), in *The Poems of John Dryden*, ed. James Kinsley, 4 vols. (Oxford: Clarendon Press, 1958), iv. 1445.

4. Henry Hall, 'To the Memory of John Dryden' (1700); Anon., 'To Dr Samuel Garth, occasioned by the Much Lamented Death of John Dryden, Esq.' (1700); Spurgeon, i. 286, 287.

5. Spurgeon, i. 289.

6. Ibid. i. 359.

7. Thomas Warton, *The History of English Poetry*, 3 vols. (London, 1774–81), i. 341; quoted in Derek Brewer (ed.), *Chaucer: The Critical Heritage*, 2 vols. (London: Routledge & Kegan Paul, 1978), i. 226; hereafter 'Brewer'.

8. *History of English Poetry*, i. 435; Spurgeon, i. 440; Brewer, i. 229.

9. *History of English Poetry*, i. 457; Spurgeon, i. 441; Brewer, i. 230.

10. *History of English Poetry*, i. 457; Spurgeon, i. 440; Brewer, i. 230.

11. Thomas Tyrwhitt, *The Canterbury Tales of Chaucer*, 5 vols. (London, 1775–8), i. 143.

12. Samuel Cobb, *The Miller's Tale, from Chaucer* (London, 1725), 19.

13. *History of English Poetry*, i. 423.

14. William Lipscomb, *The Canterbury Tales of Chaucer Completed in a Modern Version*, 3 vols. (Oxford, 1795), vol. i, p. vii.

15. *History of English Poetry*, i. 396; Spurgeon, i. 440.

16. Betsy Bowden (ed.), *Eighteenth-Century Modernizations from the 'Canterbury Tales'* (Woodbridge: Brewer, 1991), 228.

17. Robert Anderson, *A Complete Edition of the Poets of Great Britain*, 13 vols. (London, 1792–5), i. 3.

18. Robert Southey, *Selected Works of the British Poets: From Chaucer to Jonson* (1831); Spurgeon, ii. 183.

19. *Life of Geoffrey Chaucer, the Early English Poet*, 2 vols. (1803), i, 389, 395.

20. Hunt, in Spurgeon, ii/2. 271, and Brewer, ii. 74; Ward, in Spurgeon, ii/2. 124, and Brewer, ii. 208; Thoreau, in Spurgeon, ii/2. 251, and Brewer, ii. 54; Lowell, in Spurgeon, ii/3. 111, and Brewer, ii. 148.

21. Hunt, in Spurgeon, ii/2. 271, and Brewer, ii. 74; Lowell, in Spurgeon, ii/3. 109, and Brewer, ii. 138; Ward, in Spurgeon, ii/3. 125.

22. Frederick J. Furnivall, *Trial-Forewords to my 'Parallel-Text Edition of Chaucer's Minor Poems'* (1871), 49–50. For Sandras, see Spurgeon, iii/5. 71.

23. Spurgeon, ii/2. 251; Brewer, ii. 55.

24. Spurgeon, ii/3. 96.

25. Ibid. ii/3. 137; Brewer, ii. 226.

26. Spurgeon, ii/3. 8.

27. Matthew Browne, *Chaucer's England*, 2 vols. (1869), i. 52.

28. Ibid. i. 47.

29. R. H. Horne, *The Poems of Geoffrey Chaucer, Modernized* (1841), p. v.

30. Spurgeon, ii/3. 74.

31. Ibid. ii/3. 115.

32. Ibid. ii/3. 126; Brewer, ii. 217.

33. Spurgeon, ii/3. 128; Brewer, ii. 219.

34. Spurgeon, ii/3. 129; Brewer, ii. 219.

31 | Reception: twentieth and twenty-first centuries

Stephanie Trigg

Throughout the course of the twentieth century, many writers and thinkers challenged the idea of historical and cultural continuity with the past. Given such rapid rates of social, political, and cultural change, how could the past speak to a present with which it seemed to share so few cultural and social values? Responses to Chaucer in the twentieth century dramatize a range of possible answers to this question. The history of Chaucer's reception in this period is a story about the changing institutions of literary study and the changing ideas about cultural heritage, as much as it is the story of particular readings of his poetry. We can draw a sharp contrast between professional Chaucer criticism and its remarkable proliferation of specialist critical discourses, and the more general reception of Chaucer outside the academy, where the specific understanding of Chaucerian poems is channelled along quite narrow, even predictable, courses. In the later decades of the century the cultural importance of Chaucer and other writers of the traditional canon of English literary studies came under vehement attack from a range of cultural minorities and socially marginalized groups, offering powerful critiques of the cultural hegemony such traditions seem to entail and propagate on behalf of a privileged group: white, male, middle-class, and English. In the global culture of the late twentieth and early twenty-first centuries, the signifier 'Chaucer' has thus become a deeply contested sign.

This chapter focuses on written discourse on Chaucer produced outside the academy, directed to a more general readership, and I begin by examining the concept of the general reader, and the important and growing split between academic and non-academic criticism, using some of the theoretical frameworks suggested by the French sociologist Pierre Bourdieu. I will then look at the work of three influential 'general readers' of Chaucer: Virginia Woolf, G. K. Chesterton, and Harold Bloom, before considering the role of Chaucer in the 'culture wars' of the late twentieth century. I will then consider the role of 'Chaucer' as an important social and cultural signifier, as the object of revisionary writing in fiction and poetry, and as a representative of English literary heritage. Moving beyond the literary field, I will then consider some of the more general uses to which Chaucer is put in the broader sphere of global culture.

Chaucer and the general reader

From the perspective of academic and professional writing on Chaucer, the twentieth century was a period of rich growth in the critical study of his work. As English literary studies gradually became established as an academic discipline in the late nineteenth and early twentieth centuries, Chaucer studies found two secure footholds in the syllabus. As an appealing writer of Middle English texts, Chaucer became an important object of linguistic analysis, as Old and Middle English studies tried to match the rigours of Greek and Latin philology; while in the increasingly professional discourses of literary studies, his life and works became the object of historical, biographical, and critical study. As a canonical author, Chaucer was well placed to flourish amid the growth of critical theory from the 1970s, and its renewed interest in political, philosophical, and linguistic approaches to the study of literary texts, approaches that were best tested against a range of familiar, that is, canonical, literary texts. While some Chaucerians resisted these changes, and fretted about the diversity of new critical modes, and their perceived threat to the traditional understanding of medieval literature, most were reassured when they realized that little harm was actually being 'done' to Chaucer; that, indeed, his canonical status was being affirmed by the multiplicity of interpretative strategies being developed around or tested on his works.

From a broader perspective, however, it is possible to see a rather different pattern, one that forces a divide between the academic or professional study of Chaucer, in all its sophisticated variety, and the more general reception of his work across a wider range of discursive and cultural fields, from biographical studies to the poetic and fictional reimaginings of Chaucer and his poetry: the reception that is the subject of this chapter. This division does not depend upon a simple opposition between those inside and outside the academy: one of the most influential writers on Chaucer for this less specialized readership, Harold Bloom, holds professorial positions at Yale and New York universities. Chaucer's many biographers, too, are often university academics. For the purposes of this chapter, however, I am drawing a distinction between critical responses published with a professional audience in mind and those that are written for a more general audience. That category itself is far from stable or self-evident, however, and so this is a subsidiary theme of the chapter as a whole: the changes in the construction of the 'general reader' of literature in the twentieth century.

In making this distinction and in focusing on this secondary issue, I am drawing on the work of Pierre Bourdieu. Bourdieu's anthropological approach to culture has been very significant for literary critics concerned with the broader roles literature and its institutions play in our society. Such a perspective allows us to shift our attention away from the highly contested Chaucer scholarship within the academy, in order to consider the broader cultural and social uses of Chaucer, and the interplay between the social and the personal in our interest in reading Chaucer.

Bourdieu makes an important distinction between economic, symbolic, and cultural capital, as different ways of accruing social prestige. In the field of Chaucer studies, for example, economic capital is almost entirely the preserve of the publishers who sell texts, editions, translations, and other studies on Chaucer, though it is also true that professional medievalists need to keep publishing and teaching to maintain their employment. The reputations and rewards they earn for their work within the university system are examples of what Bourdieu calls symbolic capital, like the awards and prizes earned by famous authors. Even more diffuse, and more intangible, however, is the cultural capital to be accumulated by those who read and write on Chaucer, and other canonical literary texts.

Cultural capital is concerned with the dissemination and control of cultural knowledge, including the frameworks and institutions in which members of a society acquire this knowledge, which is often relatively restricted in its circulation. Bourdieu argues that 'a work of art has meaning and interest only for someone who possesses the cultural competence, that is, the code, into which it is encoded'.[1] In other words, when we read Chaucer, we read his texts through a particular framework, or code, whether it is one concerned with canonical literary texts, or with medieval literature, or even with a very generalized understanding of 'culture' or 'heritage'. So, as we examine the forms of cultural capital that can be generated around the site of Chaucer, we will also be considering the terms of the 'encoding' by which Chaucer is mediated for such readers, and by which such readers are constituted as a general readership.

These categories—inside and outside the academy—are not set up here as mutually exclusive ones: there is much productive exchange between the two spheres. But as the professionalization of literary studies became more and more acute over the course of the twentieth century, the more general reception of Chaucer developed its own distinctive course, as the following discussion will show.

As the push to include literary studies into the syllabus of the universities of Cambridge, Oxford, and London developed momentum, one of the arguments mounted against its inclusion was that English literature was already part of the cultural heritage of the nation, and could never require specialist instruction or training that would be comparable to philology or classical languages. Terry Eagleton provides a useful caricature of this view: 'English was an upstart, amateurish affair as academic subjects went . . . since every English gentleman read his own literature in his spare time anyway, what was the point of submitting it to systematic study?'[2] Chaucer was an important figure in this conception of the national literature, through his traditional position as father of English poetry, though the greater difficulty of his language and the alterity of the medieval made him more obviously 'examinable' than the writings of Jane Austen, for example. One of the shifts we will track across the century, however, is a growing perception of Chaucer's linguistic difficulty, the painful sense that to read his poetry might in fact require the assistance of experts. This higher degree of difficulty, as we might say, while it eased Chaucer's entry into the university, makes it harder for the general reader to acquire cultural capital through Chaucer. But at the same time it also increases the value of that capital.

Virginia Woolf, G. K. Chesterton, and Harold Bloom

In the 1920s Woolf writes about Chaucer from a perspective that takes for granted that his poetry is perfectly accessible to the 'common reader' (this is in fact the title of her two collections of essays, *The Common Reader*, published in 1925 and 1932). Woolf never attended university, and was deeply conscious of the forms of social exclusion that kept higher education predominantly under male control, but she read and wrote confidently about English and other literary traditions. It might be possible, then, to see her essays as a forceful challenge to the growing enclosure of literary studies within the university. Woolf's essay 'The Pastons and Chaucer' reveals not a syllable of anxiety about Chaucer's readability, nor the specialist knowledge that might be able to contribute other insights to the study of his poetry.

Woolf's Chaucer is a poet of Englishness and the English landscape, but in accordance with much early twentieth-century literary criticism, she is also interested in the potential of literature to embody broader qualities, whether these are transcendent or spiritual insights or, more generally, a kind of ethical understanding. This was a commonly held view at this time, that poetry could enhance the cultural life and imaginative response of its readers; it could both represent and celebrate human life in all its variety. Woolf writes, 'Chaucer was a poet; but he never flinched from the life that was being lived at the moment before his eyes.'[3] And further:

Chaucer lets us go our ways doing the ordinary things with the ordinary people. His morality lies in the way men and women behave to each other. We see them eating, drinking, laughing, and making love, and come to feel without a word being said what their standards are and so are steeped through and through with their morality. There can be no more forcible preaching than this where all actions and passions are represented, and instead of being solemnly exhorted we are left to stray and stare and make out a meaning for ourselves. (p. 18)

This passage is typical of Woolf's essay and, indeed, typical of much 'general' criticism of Chaucer, in that it draws large descriptive characterizations of Chaucer's works, considered as the œuvre of a distinct personality. In her brief preface to *The Common Reader*, Woolf appeals to Samuel Johnson's understanding of 'the common reader', and comments: 'The common reader . . . is guided by an instinct to create for himself . . . some kind of whole—a portrait of a man, a sketch of an age, a theory of the art of writing' (p. 1). In contrast, one of the most distinctive features of professional Chaucer criticism over the last twenty years or so has been a growing distaste for such generalizing pronouncements, in the context of an increased consciousness that the 'common reader' is a problematic category, and is probably not common at all, but an ideological mask for a reader who is normatively privileged, white, and English. One of the major tenets of late twentieth-century literary theory has been that literary texts will find different con-stituencies, depending on variations in age, class, gender, sexuality, and ethnicity. The 'identity politics' of such insights have come under sustained critique from a variety of quarters, and need not detain us here, but they do explain the increasing suspicion of such canonical pronouncements from within academic literary studies.

However, one of the very empowering aspects of Woolf's reading of Chaucer is that she naturalizes the act of reading Chaucer, showing that his poetry is really about quite ordinary things, presented in a way that allows us to bring our own valued responses to the text: 'we are left to stray and stare and make out a meaning for ourselves'. And while her preface modestly cedes place to 'the critic and the scholar', better educated than the common reader, nevertheless her discussion of Chaucer emphasizes the poet's ability to offer his own profound critical discussion of life in such a way as to silence any commentary: 'And so, when we shut Chaucer, we feel that without a word being said the criticism is complete; what we are saying, thinking, reading, doing, has been commented upon' (p.18). Any further literary criticism, in effect, has been displaced as redundant.

G. K. Chesterton uses a similar strategy in his very influential book *Chaucer*, pub-lished in 1932. He tells us repeatedly that he is no Chaucer scholar, though this never inhibits him from the broadest generalizations and pronouncements. Much of this kind of criticism has an aphoristic quality, an important rhetorical feature that works to draw the reader into a kind of 'common-sense' view of the matter. This is very much Chesterton's tone: 'The whole point, so far as I am concerned, is that it is as easy for an ordinary Englishman to enjoy Chaucer as to enjoy Dickens.'[4] Moreover, 'the book would have served its purpose if anyone had learned, even by getting as far as this page, that what matters is not books on Chaucer, but Chaucer' (p. 11). Chesterton also voices resistance to the modernist craving for novelty:

It has only been for a short time, a recent and disturbed time of transition, that each writer has been expected to write a new theory of all things, or draw a new wild map of the world. The old writers were content to write of the old world, but to write of it with an imaginative freshness which made it in each case look like a new world. (p. 31)

Chesterton is concerned with more than aesthetic issues, though, and writes at length of Chaucer's religious sensibility, affirming his Catholicism: 'between the black robes of Gower and the grey gown of Langland, he stands clothed in scarlet like all the house-hold of love; and emblazoned with the Sacred Heart' (p. 275). But Chaucer is also 'the most human of human beings' (p. 293). This is a common theme of Chesterton's book, that Chaucer provides special insight into and tolerance of fallible human nature.

Despite the immense popularity of Chesterton's book, the tradition of general criti-cism of Chaucer has not been an extensive one in the twentieth century: response to Chaucer beyond the academy is increasingly deflected into the imaginative re-creation of his life, voice, his personalities, or his characters in works of biography, fiction, or poetry, in ways that often draw on Chesterton's insights.

But there is one important critical figure who does inherit a voice from Chesterton and Woolf, and other commentators from earlier centuries: the controversial American critic Harold Bloom. Associated with the Yale school of literary theory and deconstruction in the 1970s, Bloom has been a very influential writer, not least through his study of literary tradition in *The Anxiety of Influence*.[5] More recently, Bloom has revived the reading position of the 'general reader', often in defence of the traditional canon of English literature. The titles of his recent works indicate his interests: *Genius: A Mosaic of One Hundred Exemplary Creative Minds* and *The Western Canon: The Books and Schools of the Ages*.

In his writings on Chaucer, Bloom constructs his own tradition as a critic: 'I still prefer the Catholic storyteller–polemicist G. K. Chesterton to all other critics of Chaucer, since he has the surest sense of Chaucer's greatness.'[6] Elsewhere he singles out E. Talbot Donaldson, Jill Mann, and Donald Howard, the author of the imaginative biography *Chaucer: His Life, his Works, his World*.

Bloom's method is comparative in that he tends to ignore the historical contexts in which Chaucer wrote and places him instead in the company of the other great writers of 'genius', or the Western tradition. Needless to say, the Chaucer who emerges here is not a poet concerned with social critique, or with the construction of gendered identity, or with fourteenth-century court politics. As we might expect of an American writer, Bloom is also less concerned than Woolf, Chesterton, and other writers with Chaucer's exemplary Englishness, and more with a generalized sense of what makes Chaucer great, and how he fits into the canon of selected writers:

Like his direct precursors—Dante and Boccaccio—his great originality emerges most strongly in both his characters and his own voice, his mastery of tone and figuration. Like Dante, he invented two modes for the representation of the self, and he has something of the same relation to Shakespeare that Dante had to Petrarch, the difference being the unbelievable fecundity of Shakespeare, which transcended even what John Dryden meant when he said of the *Canterbury Tales:* 'Here is God's plenty'.[7]

Bloom's avowed concern in this discussion is with character, and so he compares the Wife of Bath to Shakespeare's Falstaff, and the Pardoner to Iago. Bloom's comparisons here, as elsewhere in *The Western Canon* and *Genius*, imply an extraordinary familiarity with the canon he commends to our attention: it is a broad allusiveness that instructs with its insights while also assuming in his readers a comparable knowledge of, or at least a shared wish to belong to, that tradition, to share its cultural capital. In tracing such genealogies, and in making such comparisons across different languages and literary traditions, Bloom is also deploying the classical trope of the heavenly company of poets, whose shared affinity transcends differences of language and time. Dryden certainly appeals to this trope to put himself into Chaucer's company, just as Chaucer does when he bids *Troilus and Criseyde*, his 'litel bok', to kiss the steps where Virgil, Ovid, Homer, Lucan, and Statius pass up and down (5. 1786–92). For discussions of Chaucer and Dryden, see Chapters 30 and 32.

Woolf and Chesterton write for an audience familiar with English literary tradition, but not necessarily trained in academic study. This audience has almost certainly diminished, or has at least aged, through the twentieth century. Since the huge growth in secondary and tertiary education after the Second World War, however, a different kind of general reader has emerged, one whose knowledge of Chaucer, for better or worse, has been mediated to some degree by pedagogical and critical tradition, either through university study, or through university-educated teachers in secondary school. Through the institutional constraints of the syllabus, Chaucer has thus been securely encoded or framed as part of the canon of English literature.

Chaucer and the canon

Like many critics, Harold Bloom has ferociously resisted the broadening of the canon of literary study to include the writing of previously marginalized groups on the grounds of 'political correctness' or identity politics, though Bloom prefers the phrase 'cultural justice':

Reading Chaucer or his few rivals in literature since the ancients—Dante, Cervantes, Shakespeare—can have the happy result of restoring perspectives that all of us may be tempted to lose as we face the onslaught of instant masterpieces that threatens us at this moment when cultural justice is at work, enforcing the exile of aesthetic considerations.[8]

His position had become even more intemperate several years later: 'We do not accept tables and chairs whose legs fall off, no matter who carpentered them, but we urge the young to study mediocre writings, with no legs to sustain them'.[9]

This is frequently the converse side of the confident pronouncements of the 'general' or 'common' reader, that they tend to confirm the traditional canon, resisting or dismissing critiques of the canon as representing white, middle-class male cultural supremacy, to the exclusion of the texts (and, by implication, the experiences and perspectives) of women, the working classes, and racial and ethnic minorities. It seems to be a natural tendency of such criticism to affirm the status quo, in favour of a so-called 'common-sense' view of literary or aesthetic quality as a cultural given. This tendency also affects the *kind* of criticism written under its umbrella.

In such debates Chaucer holds an indisputable place at the chronological head of the traditional English canon. This is a mixed blessing, of course, as while it means 'Chaucer' and Chaucer studies benefit from these acts of cultural 'consecration', to use Bourdieu's term, there is sometimes an implicit thematic flow-on from this elevation, to assume that Chaucer's work itself somehow embodies traditional or conservative views. Of course, this is one of the most hotly contested topics within professional Chaucer criticism. Where Chaucer is discussed in critical terms outside the academy, however, it is often in terms very reminiscent of Chesterton and Bloom.

Not surprisingly, the *Canterbury Tales* is the work that features most prominently in such discussions, with its diverse range of characters and appealing stories. It would be much harder to construct a general humane Chaucer out of the more arcane materials of the *House of Fame*, for example, or even the complex narrative of *Troilus and Criseyde*. Because the *Canterbury Tales* features such a wide range of characters, this text lends itself to those many accounts of Chaucer that praise his comprehensive understanding and sympathy with humanity, in terms very reminiscent of Ben Jonson's praise of Shakespeare, as 'not of an age, but for all time'.

This perception of the timeless and universal quality of Chaucer's poetry has been crucial for his canonical status in the twentieth century and his prominence in the school and university curriculum. Chaucer's language, too, presents just the right degree of difficulty to justify bringing his texts into a disciplinary regime, in the teaching of Middle English language skills, although the relation between Chaucer's linguistic alterity and his immediate accessibility in human terms has always been a problematic and mysterious one. Student guides to Chaucer must spend a little time carefully negotiating his language; but the general reader is assumed to have that knowledge already. As Anthony Burgess writes, in praise of the *Riverside Chaucer*, 'The reading of Chaucer is made into an exquisite pleasure not a philological chore.'[10] This scholarly edition of Chaucer is thus for Burgess 'the best edition of Chaucer in existence' because it has been able to present Chaucer's poetry in an aesthetically pleasing way. The edition promises the cultural capital of reading Chaucer, without any of the hard work associated with university scholarship. The scholars work in the service of readers who, Burgess implies, might have been frightened by the 'chore'-like aspect of reading Chaucer at school. Even the choice of Anthony Burgess, better known as a novelist (most famously, as the author of *Clockwork Orange*), as the blurb writer for the edition sends a clear signal that expertise in Chaucer studies is not restricted to the professional caste.

The days when close familiarity with the poetry of Chaucer and the plays of Shakespeare was assumed naturally to be a part of a 'standard' cultural literacy are numbered, displaced by a much wider range of global concerns. Chaucerians may regret the passing of those days when Chaucer rested securely in the compulsory part of the syllabus. However, if we cast our net more broadly, beyond the canons of literary study, we see Chaucer's works enjoying an astonishingly broad afterlife, in the worlds of cinema, television, fiction, and poetry.

Rewriting Chaucer

We turn now to consider Chaucer in the many reinventions of his writing in modern fiction and poetry. This is a surprisingly broad field, too large to be considered in all its detail here, so I will focus on a few representative texts and the critical commentary they have recently begun to attract. Although there is a long tradition of considering Chaucer's afterlife in later English literature, in the works of Hoccleve and Lydgate, for example, and from later periods, in the works of Spenser, Shakespeare, Dryden, Pope, and Wordsworth, extending into discussion of the poetry of T. S. Eliot and other writers, it is only very recently that the vast amount of popular fiction that refers to Chaucer has received any substantial commentary, beyond the tracking of various allusions. In addition to Steve Ellis's comprehensive study of such examples in his *Chaucer at Large*, there is a very suggestive discussion in Peter Conrad's study of 1995, *To Be Continued: Four Stories and their Survival*. Conrad isolates four key stories that have generated a number of revisitations in literature and film: Chaucer's tales of Canterbury; the stories of Romeo and Juliet, and Lear, from Shakespeare; and the myth of Prometheus as figured through Milton and Percy and Mary Shelley.

Like many commentators who equate Chaucer's canonical status with the timeless insights his work seems to hold, Conrad finds a structural feature in Chaucer's inability to bring his pilgrims to Canterbury, as an indication that 'the collective life is chaotically continuous and resists control'.[11] In fact, he goes further, and identifies in the *Canterbury Tales* the condition of possibility for all English writing:

the *Canterbury Tales* is an inevitable starting-point. All of English literature is a continuation of Chaucer's anarchic miscellany, precisely because the digest of tales he has assembled is so discontinuous. (p. 7)

Literary history is a prison, from which the individual escapes by his wilful, devious misinterpretation of the stories he inherits. (p. 8)

Conrad is something of a Bloomian here, in his insistence that literary history is constituted by individual responses to tradition, although in his readings of various twentieth-century reprises of Chaucer, he is more concerned than Bloom with the question of modernism's response to medieval alterity. Literature is not just a series of individual trajectories and responses to tradition, but rather a vehicle or expression of cultural commentary, an inevitable rewriting of what has gone before. T. S. Eliot's *The Waste Land*, for example, with its famous opening negation of Chaucer's spring fecundity—'April is the cruellest month'—typifies modernism's version of literary history as 'an anthology of quotations, contextless and disconnected' (p. 14). Instead of Chaucer's company, headed to Canterbury on their 'orderly itinerary', the inhabitants of Eliot's poem, after the First World War, are 'victims of diaspora, vagrants in a middle Europe where all maps are provisional' (p. 14).

Conrad stresses the impossibility of any text having the last word, describing William S. Burroughs's postmodernist *The Western Lands*, with its own Chaucerian citations, as a 'postscript' to 'Eliot's decidedly terminal poem' (p. 15). Conrad also tracks the trajectory of cruel spring to Australia, in the poetry of Les A. Murray, who both rewrites spring into the southern hemisphere's August, and translates the modernist, urban angst of Eliot into a form of renewed pastoral:

August is the winter's death.
He dries the rotted June rain in the earth.
Stiffens fat roots, ignites within the peach tree
Flower and seed.[12]

Conrad's central fictional example of the continuation of Chaucer is Margaret Atwood's *A Handmaid's Tale*, an example of what Steve Ellis calls the 'professional' or 'vocational' response to Chaucer, in which the telling of a tale becomes a vehicle for the protagonist's own history, often with little or no other reference to Chaucer.[13] Conrad and Ellis disagree on the import of Atwood's dystopia as a response to Chaucer, especially on the question of the male appropriation of female voices and on the relation between repression and resistance. And Conrad is surely guilty of dramatic exaggeration here: 'Atwood's novel is a reflection on the link between literature and human freedom and a tribute to the subversiveness of Chaucer, who practically invented that freedom by bending the rules of a prescriptive, legalistic literary culture' (p. 32). Conrad thus disagrees with Chesterton, who argued that the *Tales* presented a world inaccessible or alien to modernity through its religiosity, but crucial for my purposes is the tendency shared by both Conrad and Chesterton to make this kind of sweeping generalization. Whatever we think of Chaucer's attitude to dominant religious or political authority—and modern scholarly opinion is deeply divided on the matter—it must be absurd to think that Chaucer, in any sense, might have invented 'human freedom'. Where Conrad writes as a non-Chaucerian general reader, Ellis's study is located more securely within medieval, or at least, medievalism studies, and is correspondingly much less essayistic, and more deeply and closely informed about the texts it discusses. *Chaucer at Large* ranges widely across poetic, cinematic, fictional, and other performative versions of Chaucer, and is essential reading for anyone making a more comprehensive study of this topic.

Poetic reprises of Chaucer's poetry are pretty much restricted to versions of or responses to the famous opening of the 'General Prologue', although there is also a very specialized, restricted tradition of writing mock Middle English in the twentieth century (I discuss several instances in my *Congenial Souls*[14]). Perhaps one of the most endearing is the Prologue by 'Jeff Chaucer' for the 'Cardiffe Citie Tales', celebrating the English football finals being held in that city:

When that Aprill with his lager bitter
The footballe fanne hath pierced to the roote,
And bathed every crowde in swich sweet licour
Of which anger engendered is the floure,
When Zephirus reek with his beery breathe,
And inspired hath every ground and heathe . . .[15]

Overall, however, Chaucerian poems are far outnumbered by novelistic supplements or borrowings. In addition to works like *The Handmaid's Tale* that work across or around the intersection between personal narrative and social or professional identity (Peter Ackroyd's recent *Clerkenwell Tales* is another example), another important cluster of texts takes Chaucer as a character in historical fiction and writes around him. This group of writers tends to do their historical research quite carefully, and works with standard biographical or critical studies of Chaucer. One of the most popular of these is Anya Seton's *Katherine* of 1954, the story of Chaucer's sister-in-law Katherine Swynford, who became the third wife of John of Gaunt. Chaucer and his wife, Philippa, appear as minor characters in this novel, in a rather matter-of-fact marriage: Chaucer's first and only real love in this novel is Blanche of Lancaster, so that his elegy for her, the *Book of the Duchess*, is a heartfelt and personal tribute. Seton's novel draws on a dominant trend in Chaucer scholarship, in the first part of the century, which read much of Chaucer's poetry as autobiographical, or as making quite precise, if coded, references to figures in fourteenth-century political and social life.

A more recent emphasis in Chauceriana also follows an important trend in contemporary research, setting Chaucer in a European context. Chaucer appears as an important touchstone for medieval English culture in Europe in Barbara Tuchman's best-selling popular history *A Distant Mirror: The Calamitous Fourteenth Century* (1978). Tuchman's book is structured around the life of Enguerrand de Coucy, who spent substantial periods of time in England, but her central concern is to explore the period itself: 'a violent, tormented, bewildered, suffering and disintegrating age'. And further, 'if our last decade or two of collapsing assumptions has been a period of unusual discomfort, it is reassuring to know that the human species has lived through worse before'.[16] In fact, Tuchman cites Dryden's commentary on Chaucer's pilgrims as her epigraph: 'For mankind is ever the same and nothing is lost out of nature, though everything is altered.'[17]

This interesting pairing of assumptions—that human nature is stable and immutable, but that the medieval period was particularly gruesome (matched only by our own times)—is shared by many crime fiction novels set in medieval England and Europe that play off the similarities and differences between medieval and modern against each other. The trend was inaugurated by Ellis Peters's *Cadfael* series, and spectacularly internationalized by Umberto Eco's *Name of the Rose*, but there are many examples set in fourteenth-century England (inspired, perhaps, by the success of Tuchman's history) that also feature Chaucer. In Candace Robb's Owen Archer mysteries, for example, set with great historical precision in York, Chaucer appears as a rather shadowy minor figure, a spy on the king's business overseas.

Most often, the pilgrimage storytelling frame is used to gather a collection of tales. Two examples will serve here: the murder mysteries of Paul Doherty (*A Haunt of Murder, An Ancient Evil, A Tournament of Murders, Ghostly Murders, A Tapestry of Murders, The Hangman's Hymn*) are framed as alternative Canterbury Tales, also told by Chaucer's pilgrims; while the 'pilgrims' in Karen King-Aribisala's *Kicking Tongues* exchange life narratives on a bus journey to Abuja, the capital of Nigeria, stories that dramatize political and cultural tensions in a postcolonial setting, and framed by their own 'General Prologue'.

'Chaucer' can be rewritten, then, in many ways; as a character, as a poet, as a silent, virtually anonymous originator of a story collection, or as a very specific personality or guide to English heritage culture. Unsurprisingly, perhaps, given the dominance of the *Canterbury Tales* in the school syllabus, this is the text that inspires the most revisitations, while its spring opening, and the general idea of the storytelling competition, are referred to with the greatest frequency.

Australian Chaucer

This very selective understanding of Chaucer is repeated and even accentuated in the broader reception of Chaucer beyond the academic and the literary fields. To 'google' Chaucer internationally throws up countless thousands of 'hits', but to restrict the search to Australian web sites, as I did recently, gives us an instructive insight into this rather more ephemeral understanding of Chaucer, and his reach across global culture.

None of the sites I found was thematized as distinctively Australian, or foregrounded any specifically national or postcolonial understanding of Chaucer, though this is a fascinating area of study. It might also be revealing to repeat this experiment in countries with a highly developed sense of postcolonial culture, such as India; or in countries that have developed their own distinctive traditions of Chaucer scholarship, such as Japan. Similarly, a search that was confined to languages other than English might identify different patterns of reception. On the Australian pages, however, the poet is presented as part of a curiously globalized version of English culture, accessible to all (in line with the concerns of this chapter, I exclude more specialized university web sites featuring subjects or courses on Chaucer, or bookshops simply advertising sales).

Many of these citations make only the vaguest allusions to Chaucer's poetry, and as we might expect the *Canterbury Tales* is the key text here. The naming of the specialist wine shop Chaucer Cellars in Glen Iris, Melbourne, signifies good cheer and bonhomie, like the now defunct but once very popular Chaucer's wedding reception and banquet venue in the Melbourne suburb of Canterbury. As in many cities, 'Chaucer' also signifies a vague notion of Englishness in the minds of town planners: there are eleven 'Chaucer' streets (differentiated by postcode) in suburban Melbourne, for example (the same as for Shakespeare). Chaucer and Swynford also feature evocatively as names of horses in one racing stud. These examples are typical of a relatively arbitrary 'heritage Chaucer', like the roses developed by David Austin in England and equally popular in Australia, one group of which is named after various characters in English literature, including Chaucer, Wife of Bath, Prioress, and Reeve.

Not surprisingly, the educated middle classes make more precise use of Chaucerian references, and these tend to be channelled along ethical interests and concerns. An Anglican parish priest in Ararat, in central Victoria, refers to Absalom the parish clerk, and in another sermon cites Chaucer's Parson as the model for his priest: 'each rectory needs a parson something like Chaucer's poor parson, who stands out as so authentic, loveable, loving and lovely, among the multifarious, colourful, bawdy, devout, rag-tag-and-bobtail company of pilgrims on their way to Canterbury so long ago'.[18] Other references reflect the strands of moral criticism of the characters that used to dominate school or university study of Chaucer. The brother of Sir Robert Douglas, knight of the Order of Malta and a judge of the Queensland Supreme Court, structures his eulogy for his brother around the idealized qualities of Chaucer's knight: 'chivalry', 'truth and honour', 'freedom', 'courtesy', and 'worthiness'.

An address to the University of Melbourne law students entitled 'The Role of a Clerk of the House of Representatives' begins with the image of the Clerk from the 'General Prologue' as a kind of ethical and professional model. The scholarly Clerk also makes an appearance in the motto of Macquarie University in North Sydney: 'and gladly teche' ('GP' 308). Elsewhere I have discussed the first chancellor's suggestion of this motto, and his presumption of the community's familiarity with Chaucer and the traditional pleasure of completing a well-known quotation. The choice of the motto exemplifies Chaucer's status as a cultural icon, while also taking for granted a deep familiarity with Chaucer's work.[19]

Similarly, a story in the *Sydney Morning Herald* about the New South Wales rugby league club Canterbury and their breaches of the salary cap for players draws an extended analogy from Chaucer. Roy Masters summarizes the 'Pardoner's Tale' for his readers, and draws a parallel between the three *riotours* and the three key officials of the club, and their mutual enmity. The article concludes with the National Rugby League wanting the matter ended, Masters parodying the relevant final lines of the 'Pardoner's Tale' (962–8): 'No more, we've all had quite enough . . . Let's laugh again and keep the ball in play. They kissed, and we continued on our way.'[20]

Chaucer's familiar reputation for bawdiness and liveliness persists, too, on the web page of a bookshop in Geelong, the second largest city in Victoria, which summarizes the 'Miller's Tale' under the heading 'Tut, tut, Mr Chaucer', concluding

there is no doubt Mr C gave the English language such richly descriptive but rude words as 'fart', 'arse' and 'piss', and there is equally no doubt that he was the first Englishman to write a 'dirty story', but in so doing Mr C undoubtedly alleviated the tedium of English study for many generations of schoolkids. Tut, tut (and thankyou), Mr C.[21]

In its misleading (if common) claims about Chaucer's influence on the development of the English language and its possibilities for bawdy narratives, this web site rehearses some very familiar aspects of Chaucer's reception.

While these informal sites and references are often deeply contingent on very immediate, local needs, they all bear witness to the strength of a powerful formation in traditional views of Chaucer, even though that influence is very generalized. If most of these references are mediated through the idea of a Chaucer made attractive and 'relevant' within the secondary education system, this itself harks back to Dryden's idea of Chaucer's persistent and timeless understanding of human nature. This position was strongly mediated through William Blake's 'Descriptive Catalogue' of his own illustration of the Canterbury pilgrimage, and his comments that Chaucer's characters represent unchanging types: 'The characters of Chaucer's Pilgrims are the characters which compose all ages and nations . . . they are the physiognomies or lineaments of universal human life, beyond which Nature never steps. Names alter, things never alter.'[22] This view was influentially promoted for the twentieth century by Chesterton, and so, for example, when the Australian artist Bill Clements produced his own illustrations, a set of ten images of the Canterbury pilgrims, he introduced the pictures with a quotation from Chesterton: 'He is not only the father of all our poets, but the grandfather of all our hundred million novelists.'[23]

My last citation is perhaps the most typical of all. A brief summary of Chaucer on the 'Poetry in Motion' home page concludes with a pithy condensation of some of these familiar views about Chaucer:

Geoffrey Chaucer expanded the reputation of English as a great literary language. William Shakespeare wrote many of his plays to show a sign of Geoffrey Chaucer's comic spirit. John Dryden, a modern interpreter of The Canterbury Tales, named Chaucer as the 'Father of English poetry.' Chaucer will always be remembered for his wisdom, humour and humanity.[24]

Conclusion

Web pages are by nature ephemeral: by the time this book appears in print, many of these web sites may no longer be maintained, but they help us to register Chaucer's life outside the academy, even if that life is so heavily mediated by the *Canterbury Tales* as a compendium of moral examples (positive or negative), or by the unexamined recycling of Chestertonian and Drydenian views about Chaucer's linguistic, literary, and humanistic paternity.

It is only very recently that people have started to play with these ideas. Brian Helgeland's film *A Knight's Tale* breaks with many of these conventions in its affection-ate portrait of Chaucer as a compulsive gambler and inspired forger. The film has also generated some examples of a genre that Dryden could certainly not have imagined, even though he took his own liberties with Chaucer in his translations. In 'slash fiction', typically posted on the Internet, fans of a film or novel write supplementary stories, usually with a gay theme, either implicitly or explicitly sexual, about the main characters. Several such sites linked to the film feature a number of homosexual scenes between Chaucer and Sir Ulrich, the main character, or his squires, written by movie fans who may or may not know anything about the historical Chaucer at all (for more on Helgeland's *A Knight's Tale*, see Chapter 33).

Such writing depends on its transgressive potential, but at some level Helgeland's rewriting of Chaucer, and the slash fiction it has prompted, may signify a growing impatience and reluctance with the standard trajectories of Chaucerian reception. The time may well be ripe for a new wave of Chaucerian reinvention. Contemporary students of Chaucer may become inspired to reinvent the poet in different ways in their own poetry, fiction, and film; perhaps by focusing on poems other than the *Canterbury Tales* for inspiration, or by drawing on more recent academic criticism that is concerned with the politics of gender, class, and ethnicity in Chaucer's poetry, or, indeed, the high level of textual and interpretative uncertainty in Chaucer's texts. The broadly humanist reception of Chaucer still has a great deal to commend it; reading Chaucer for his insights into the human character, however, is only one of the many things we can do with Chaucer and his writings.

FURTHER READING

Biddick, Kathleen, *The Shock of Medievalism* (Durham, NC: Duke University Press, 1998). A somewhat uneven collection of essays, but includes the provocative 'Bede's Blush: Postcards from Bali, Bombay, Palo Alto', which sketches out some possibilities for the history of medieval studies in postcolonial contexts.

Brewer, D. S. (ed.), *Chaucer: The Critical Heritage*, 2 vols. (London: Routledge & Kegan Paul, 1978). An essential compendium of historical responses to Chaucer's writing.

Burrow, J. A. (ed.), *Geoffrey Chaucer: A Critical Anthology* (Harmondsworth: Penguin, 1969). Another anthology of writings on Chaucer from the fourteenth to the twentieth centuries, specializing in non-academic criticism and commentary. Burrow's introductions provide a useful guide to the changing dynamics of response to Chaucer.

Ellis, Steve, *Chaucer at Large: The Poet in the Modern Imagination* (Minneapolis: University of Minnesota Press, 2000). Will be the standard account of modern Chaucerian response across many different media for years to come. In addition to modern Chaucerian literature, it discusses Chaucer on film, in translation, on radio, and for children.

Guillory, John, *Cultural Capital: The Problem of Literary Canon Formation* (Chicago: University of Chicago Press, 1993). One of the most powerful interventions into the debates about the literary canon in the 1980s and 1990s. Guillory makes no special mention of Chaucer, but discusses 'identity politics' in the context of challenges to the traditional literary canon.

Mead, Jenna, '. . . The Anti-Imperial Approaches to Chaucer (Are there Those?): An Essay in Identifying Strategies', *Southern Review*, 27 (1994), 403–17. Takes issue with Gayatri Spivak's suggestion that Chaucer studies should give way to a broader understanding of the literary canon, and considers some versions of Chaucerian reception in Australia.

Trigg, Stephanie, *Congenial Souls: Reading Chaucer from Medieval to Postmodern* (Minneapolis: University of Minnesota Press, 2002). Examines the history and development of the trope of Chaucerian community, and the idea of speaking and writing in a Chaucerian voice, from the fourteenth to the twentieth century. It includes longer discussions of Woolf and Chesterton, and of Chaucerian pedagogy.

NOTES

1. Randal Johnson, Introduction to Pierre Bourdieu, *The Field of Cultural Production: Essays on Art and Literature*, ed. and trans. Randal Johnson (London: Polity Press, 1993), 7.
2. Terry Eagleton, *Literary Theory: An Introduction*, rev. edn. (1983; Oxford: Blackwell, 1996), 29.

3. Virginia Woolf, *The Common Reader*, First Series, ed. and introd. Andrew McNeillie (London: Hogarth Press, 1984), 15.

4. G. K. Chesterton, *Chaucer* (London: Faber, 1932), 10.

5. *The Anxiety of Influence: A Theory of Poetry* (New York: Oxford University Press, 1973).

6. Harold Bloom, *Genius: A Mosaic of One Hundred Exemplary Creative Minds* (New York: Warner Books, 2002), 104.

7. Harold Bloom, *The Western Canon: The Books and Schools of the Ages* (New York: Harcourt Brace, 1994), 107.

8. Ibid. 105.

9. *Genius*, p. xvii.

10. Anthony Burgess, back cover, *The Riverside Chaucer*, ed. Larry Benson, 3rd edn. (Oxford: Oxford University Press, 1988).

11. Peter Conrad, *To Be Continued: Four Stories and their Survival* (Oxford: Clarendon Press, 1995), 2.

12. Quoted ibid. 19.

13. Steve Ellis, *Chaucer at Large: The Poet in the Modern Imagination* (Minneapolis: University of Minnesota Press, 2000), 86.

14. Stephanie Trigg, *Congenial Souls: Reading Chaucer from Medieval to Postmodern* (Minneapolis: University of Minnesota Press, 2002).

15. <http://www.footballpoets.org/p.asp?Id=221>.

16. Barbara W. Tuchman, *A Distant Mirror: The Calamitous Fourteenth Century* (Harmondsworth: Penguin, 1978), p. xv.

17. Tuchman's epigraph comes from Dryden's preface to his *Fables Ancient and Modern*, in *The Poems of John Dryden*, ed. James Kinsley, 4 vols. (Oxford: Clarendon Press, 1958), iv. 1455. Tuchman has modernized the spelling.

18. Fr. Andrew Neaum, 'A Povre Persoun of a Toun', Fourth Sunday in Lent, 30 March 2003: <http://www4.tpgi.com.au/users/aneaum/pewsheets/Fourth_Sunday_in_Lent-30th_March_2003.htm>.

19. *Congenial Souls*, 19.

20. <http://www.smh.com.au/articles/2002/08/30/1030508102307.html>.

21. <http://www.gspp.com.au/tuttut_mrc.htm>.

22. William Blake, 'A Descriptive Catalogue of Pictures, Poetical and Historical Inventions, Painted by William Blake', quoted in J. A. Burrow (ed.), *Geoffrey Chaucer: A Critical Anthology* (Harmondsworth: Penguin, 1969), 77.

23. <http://users.dragnet.com.au/~clements/chaucer.html>. The quotation from Chesterton's *Chaucer* is from p. 34.

24. <http://www.nambourshs.qld.edu/inform/faculties/ccx/thinkquest/poetry/page14.html>.

32 | Translations

Malcolm Andrew

This chapter provides a largely chronological account of translations from Chaucer's work. It concentrates on modernizations—translations from Chaucer's English into more modern forms of the language. Imitations, adaptations, and translations into other languages are mentioned more briefly. The chronological organization of this chapter should serve to facilitate appreciation of how responses to Chaucer's work and perceptions of it have changed over a period of several hundreds of years. Abundant evidence of such responses and perceptions is provided by two collections of relevant materials, those of Caroline Spurgeon (1925) and of Derek Brewer (1978), to which references are supplied throughout.[1]

The first translations

Towards the end of the sixteenth century readers were finding Chaucer increasingly difficult to understand. Thus the anonymous author of *The Arte of English Poesie* (1589)—generally identified as Richard or George Puttenham—states that the language of Chaucer and his contemporaries 'is now out of vse with vs'.[2] It is, therefore, no coincidence that the first edition of Chaucer equipped with a glossary, that of Thomas Speght, appears around this time (1598). Almost twenty years earlier (1579), Edmund Spenser had deemed it necessary to provide a 'glosse' at the end of each month of his *Shepheardes Calender*. Here he offers a range of explanatory materials, and glosses many of the archaic words he uses—most of which occur in Chaucer, and include relatively familiar words such as 'ay' and 'elde'.

During the sixteenth and seventeenth centuries numerous writers published works based on Chaucer. These include a ballad (1566), a poem (1612), and several plays (1599, 1606, *c*.1610) inspired by *Troilus and Criseyde*, a play (*c*.1608) based on the 'Franklin's Tale', and a ballad (1612) which tells the story of the 'Wife of Bath's Tale'.[3] The two earliest translations from Chaucer appear in the 1630s, both of them partial versions of *Troilus and Criseyde*. The first three of Chaucer's five books are rendered into English verse by Jonathan Sidnam (*c*.1630), the first two into Latin verse by Sir Francis Kynaston (1634). While the former remained unpublished and barely known until the appearance of a modern edition,[4] the latter was published, achieved a good deal of acclaim, and was still remembered nearly two hundred years later.[5] In prefatory verses attached to Kynaston's translation, various writers give their opinions as to its significance. These include assertions to the effect that Chaucer had become incomprehensible, that it will now be possible to read his work without a dictionary, and that this version will replace the original.[6] However surprising (or even perverse) such views may seem to a reader in the twenty-first century, they clearly indicate that Chaucer was regarded with respect, as an author whose work was worth preserving.

Respect for Chaucer is also expressed by many of the most significant poets, writers, and literary commentators of the period, from John Skelton to Samuel Pepys.[7] In the *Shepheardes Calender*, Spenser represents himself as a successor to Chaucer, whom he relates to Virgil. These views are endorsed by the commentator Edward Kirke.[8] In the *Faerie Queene*, Spenser translates some lines from the 'Franklin's Tale' (3. 1. 25. 7–9; compare 'FrT' 764–6) and refers to Chaucer as the 'well of English vndefyled' in his continuation of the 'Squire's Tale' (4. 2. 32. 8). The same tale is mentioned by Milton in *Il Penseroso* (109–15). The only negative views of Chaucer expressed during this period—other than those regarding the relatively uncivilized time in which he lived and the difficulties of understanding his language—concern the (supposed) roughness and uncertainty of his metre, and his tendency to include indelicate words and happenings in some of his works. This last characteristic—censured, for instance, by Sir John Harington in 1591[9]—proves especially contentious in relation to subsequent translations.

Dryden

Arguably the most significant single publication in the history of translations from Chaucer appears in 1700. This is John Dryden's *Fables Ancient and Modern*, which was published a few months before his death, and consists mainly of translations from Homer, Ovid, Boccaccio, and Chaucer. It includes four renditions of works by Chaucer: *Palamon and Arcite*, based on the 'Knight's Tale'; 'The Cock and the Fox', based on the 'Nun's Priest's Tale'; 'The Wife of Bath her Tale'; and 'The Character of a Good Parson', a substantially expanded version of the portrait of the Parson in the 'General Prologue'. The selection of texts is striking: while Sidnam and Kynaston translate *Troilus and Criseyde*, Dryden's translations are all from the *Canterbury Tales*. This implied change of priorities establishes a trend that lasts throughout the eighteenth century.

In his preface to *Fables Ancient and Modern*, Dryden provides a generous and perceptive critical appreciation of the *Canterbury Tales*, and an account both of his decision regarding which texts to translate and of the method he employed as a translator. He makes a careful and explicit statement about his choice of texts for translation:

I have confin'd my Choice to such Tales of *Chaucer*, as savour nothing of Immodesty. If I had desir'd more to please than to instruct, the *Reve*, the *Miller*, the *Shipman*, the *Merchant*, the *Sumner*, and above all, the *Wife of Bathe*, in the Prologue to her Tale, would have procur'd me as many Friends and Readers, as there are *Beaux* and Ladies of Pleasure in the Town. But I will no more offend against Good Manners: I am sensible as I ought to be of the Scandal I have given by my loose Writings; and make what Reparation I am able, by this Publick Acknowledgment.[10]

While Dryden is plainly here justifying himself to his audience and attempting to divert potential censure, his statement on 'immodesty' and the choice of Chaucerian texts for translation remain relevant to the process of translating Chaucer well into the twentieth century.

The preface also provides an insight into Dryden's view of his own procedures as a translator. He justifies these in the case of Chaucer by contending that 'his Sense is scarce to be understood',[11] supporting this assertion by reference to a passage he has just quoted in the original ('GP' 725–42). Present-day readers may well find it surprising that someone of Dryden's intelligence and sophistication could make such a claim with regard to a relatively straightforward passage from Chaucer. Views like his were, however, generally accepted at the time—though they were rejected during the early nineteenth century (a change in attitude the significance of which will be considered in due course). Dryden goes on to state that Chaucer 'is a rough Diamond, and must first be polish'd e'er he shines'; thus, he continues:

I have not ty'd my self to a Literal Translation; but have often omitted what I judg'd unnecessary, or not of Dignity enough to appear in the Company of better Thoughts. I have presum'd farther in some Places, and added somewhat of my own where I thought my Author was deficient, and had not given his Thoughts their true Lustre, for want of Words in the Beginning of our Language.[12]

Some twenty years earlier, in his preface to a translation of Ovid's *Epistles*, Dryden had offered a basic theory of translation. He argued that all translations conform to one of three types: 'Metaphrase' ('turning an Authour word by word, and Line by Line, from one Language into another'); 'Paraphrase' ('Translation with Latitude, where the Authour is kept in view by the Translator . . . but his words are not so strictly follow'd as his sense, and that too is admitted to be amplyfied, but not alter'd'); and 'Imitation' ('where the Translator . . . assumes the liberty not only to vary from the words and sence, but to forsake them both as he sees occasion . . . taking only some general hints from the Original').[13] The views expressed in both prefaces have substantial significance for the understanding of Dryden's translations from Chaucer.

It is probable that Dryden would have regarded these as examples of 'paraphrase'— though this perhaps shades into 'imitation' in the final part of 'The Character of a Good Parson'. The main techniques he uses in composing a 'paraphrase' are immediately apparent when a passage from Chaucer is compared with Dryden's version of it. An extract from the initial description of Emelye in the 'Knight's Tale' provides a good example:

> This maked Emelye have remembraunce
> To doon honour to May, and for to ryse.

Yclothed was she fressh, for to devyse:
Hir yelow heer was broyded in a tresse
Bihynde hir bak, a yerde long, I gesse.
And in the gardyn, at the sonne upriste,
She walketh up and doun, and as hire liste
She gadereth floures, party white and rede,
To make a subtil gerland for hire hede;
And as an aungel hevenysshly she soong. (1046–55)

In Dryden's *Palamon and Arcite* this is rendered:

In this Remembrance *Emily* e'er Day
Arose, and dress'd her self in rich Array;
Fresh as the Month, and as the Morning fair:
Adown her Shoulders fell her length of Hair:
A Ribband did the braided Tresses bind,
The rest was loose, and wanton'd in the Wind:
Aurora had but newly chas'd the Night,
And purpl'd o'er the Sky with blushing Light,
When to the Garden-walk she took her way,
To sport and trip along in Cool of Day,
And offer Maiden Vows in honour of the *May*.
　At ev'ry Turn, she made a little Stand,
And thrust among the Thorns her Lilly Hand
To draw the Rose, and ev'ry Rose she drew
She shook the Stalk, and brush'd away the Dew:
Then party-colour'd Flow'rs of white and red
She wove, to make a Garland for her Head:
This done, she sung and caroll'd out so clear,
That Men and Angels might rejoice to hear.
Ev'n wondring *Philomel* forgot to sing;
And learn'd from Her to welcome in the Spring. (1. 180–200)

The most striking aspect of the second passage is the extent to which Chaucer's work has been transformed, and has become Dryden's.

The technique of 'paraphrase' has, therefore, effected transformation. This is achieved by a variety of procedures. Dryden has expanded the passage from ten lines to twenty-one—something which he does sparingly in this poem, the length of which (2,441 lines) exceeds that of the original (2,250 lines) relatively slightly. He avoids line-by-line translation (the characteristic procedure of 'metaphrase'), and clearly feels free to modify the sequence of thought: thus the idea of honouring May, which comes at the beginning of the passage in Chaucer, is held back by Dryden until the middle of the passage, where it serves to complete a description of Emily's appearance. He exercises similar freedom with Chaucer's vocabulary, retaining some key words but omitting others. The fifth line in Chaucer's passage is virtually ignored: perhaps its tone struck Dryden as unduly informal and 'not of dignity enough'. Only two of Chaucer's rhyme-words ('rede' and 'hede') are retained. The greater length of Dryden's passage arises from descriptive expansion, especially in the lines on picking flowers.

With the exception of the last two lines on the nightingale, these are all based on suggestions in Chaucer. They do, however, contribute to what I have termed the transformation of Chaucer—through the typically Augustan qualities of balance and order, the distinct implication of sensuality, and various traces of the social norms endorsed in the poetry of Dryden's day (as in terms like 'sport' and 'trip'). The allusion to how Emily's hair 'wanton'd in the Wind' may well echo the 'wanton ringlets' of Milton's Eve (*Paradise Lost*, 4. 306). While Chaucer's Emelye is described in less suggestive terms, and could not be imagined 'sporting' or 'tripping', it is conspicuous that Dryden's Emily cannot be said to sing like an angel. Thus the simple strength of the lovely final line in the passage from Chaucer is dissipated in Dryden's rather weak couplet.

This suggests one of the fundamental differences between Chaucer and Dryden as poets. While the relevant parts of the *Canterbury Tales* are written in an essentially natural style, using a relaxed couplet, informal syntax, and idiomatic expression, Dryden's heroic couplets are far more formal, encouraging and facilitating balance, antithesis, and epigrammatic comment. It is, therefore, surprising neither that some of the best lines in *Palamon and Arcite* have an utterly un-Chaucerian quality, nor that Dryden seems uncomfortable with the informal tone of expressions such as 'a yerde longe, I gesse'. It might seem rather less predictable that Dryden's renditions of Chaucer's great set-piece descriptions, especially that of the temple of Mars, should be somewhat disappointing. The essential reason for this is, I think, that whereas Chaucer's description of the temple works cumulatively, moving swiftly from one stark and troubling image to another, Dryden's elaborations diminish the starkness and dissipate the momentum. His representation of Emily continues, throughout, to reflect the style and values espoused in the poetry of his own time, as his repeated allusions to her as 'charming' or 'beauteous' (for example, 1. 521; 3. 661, 789) suggest.

Similar characteristics may be observed in Dryden's other translations from Chaucer. Each of these is longer than the poem on which it is based: 'The Cock and the Fox' and 'The Wife of Bath her Tale' extend, respectively, to 821 and 546 lines, compared to the 626 and 408 lines of their respective originals. Thus the degree of expansion in these two poems somewhat exceeds that in *Palamon and Arcite*. It is greater still in 'The Character of a Good Parson', in which 52 lines from the 'General Prologue' (477–528) inspire a total of 140 lines, of which the first 105 constitute an elaborated translation, and the remainder an addition not based on Chaucer. Here, as in the other three poems, Chaucer's work is totally transformed by Dryden.

Dryden's translations from Chaucer were generally well received, most commentators maintaining that he had improved upon the originals.[14] If one consequence of his success was to establish his translations as standard versions for more than a century, a second, and more significant, was to encourage others to make their own translations of Chaucer. The first—and the foremost—of these was Alexander Pope.

Pope

At the beginning of his career (*c.*1704–11), Pope wrote two imitations of Chaucer and two translations from his work. The contrast between the two imitations could hardly be greater. One, published among his *Imitations of English Poets*, and entitled simply 'Chaucer', is a slight and somewhat obscene story of twenty-six lines, written in a feeble imitation of Middle English.[15] The other, *The Temple of Fame*, is a serious and substantial poem (524 lines), inspired by the third book of Chaucer's *House of Fame*. The translations are 'January and May', a version of the 'Merchant's Tale', and 'The Wife of Bath her Prologue'. It has also been asserted by some commentators, from the eighteenth century onward, that Pope was the author of translations from the 'Reeve's Tale' and from the 'General Prologue' (1–714), attributed to Thomas Betterton—texts of which are included in the anthology edited by Betsy Bowden.[16] Whether or not Pope should be credited with these translations, the most striking aspect of his choice of texts to translate is that it includes some of those which Dryden identified, in his preface to *Fables Ancient and Modern*, as texts he would have translated had he been bold enough to do so. This constitutes one of several parallels and contrasts between the translations of Dryden and of Pope. On the one hand, these are often discussed together, and were written in the same style within a period of less than fifteen years; and Pope clearly followed in Dryden's footsteps as a translator of Chaucer. On the other hand, their respective translations are among the last works of Dryden and among the first of Pope; there is (as has already been noted) a marked contrast between their choice of texts; and, while Dryden's translations are longer than the relevant originals, Pope's are shorter.

Unlike Dryden, Pope offers no account of his practices as a translator. These can, however, be inferred from a comparison of his translations with the originals: his treatment, in 'January and May', of a passage from near the end of the 'Merchant's Tale' will serve as an example. This passage describes how May, walking with her husband, January—who is not only old and jealous, but also (temporarily) blind—in their private garden, makes signals to her prospective lover, Damyan. In Chaucer it reads:

> And with that word she saugh wher Damyan
> Sat in the bussh, and coughen she bigan,
> And with hir fynger signes made she
> That Damyan sholde clymbe upon a tree
> That charged was with fruyt, and up he wente.
> For verraily he knew al hire entente,
> And every signe that she koude make,
> Wel bet than Januarie, hir owene make,
> For in a lettre she hadde toold hym al
> Of this matere, how he werchen shal.
> And thus I lete hym sitte upon the pyrie,
> And Januarie and May romynge myrie. (2207–18)

This is rendered by Pope:

> Thus while she spoke, a sidelong Glance she cast,
> Where *Damian* kneeling, worshipp'd as she past.
> She saw him watch the Motions of her Eye,
> And singled out a Pear-Tree planted nigh:
> 'Twas charg'd with Fruit that made a goodly Show,
> And hung with dangling Pears was ev'ry Bough.
> Thither th' obsequious Squire address'd his Pace,
> And climbing, in the Summit took his Place:
> The Knight and Lady walk'd beneath in View,
> Where let us leave them, and our Tale pursue. (599–608)

Pope has slightly but significantly reduced the length of this passage, as he does that of the poem as a whole (from 1,174 to 820 lines). He achieves this compression mainly by cutting some passages and some explanatory comments: thus, here he omits the passing explanation about May's letter. This still leaves scope for some elaboration—in the present passage, about the appearance of the tree and the fruit. While that addition is not out of place, the notion of the opportunistic and worldly Damian kneeling and worshipping May seems incongruous. Like Dryden, Pope transforms the setting and social norms of the original into contemporary terms: phrases such as 'goodly Show' and 'the Motions of her Eye' reflect the world of Augustan poetry. He also evinces conspicuous independence from Chaucer's vocabulary, to an even greater extent than that evinced by Dryden: in this passage, none of the rhyme-words and hardly any of what might be considered the key words survive in Pope's version.

The abbreviation of the 'Merchant's Tale' and the 'Wife of Bath's Prologue' is achieved in part (as has already been mentioned) by the omission of some passages. These include virtually all lines containing any material that could be considered obscene, such as the repulsive description of May enduring January's lovemaking in the 'Merchant's Tale' (1821–57) and the Wife of Bath's entertaining account of the various uses of sexual organs ('WBP' 115–34). Thus, paradoxically, while Pope translates some of the tales that Dryden had feared to translate, he omits the very passages that made these texts contentious. Such omissions have a profound effect on the two poems: both lose much of their complexity and subtlety. While 'January and May' remains a lively and engaging poem, Pope's version of the 'Wife of Bath's Prologue' seems flat and trivial by comparison with the original. The omission of such material also sets a precedent that is to prove highly significant: Pope produces what are, in effect, the first expurgated versions of Chaucer.

Other eighteenth-century translations

The study of the other translations from Chaucer written during the eighteenth century is greatly facilitated by Bowden's splendid anthology. This contains over thirty modernizations of Chaucer by some seventeen different writers. The influence of Dryden and Pope is ubiquitous. All the translations are from the *Canterbury Tales*, all tend to modernize social norms, and almost all are written in heroic couplets. While the most frequently translated texts are fabliaux—the tales of the Miller, the Reeve, and the Shipman appearing in three versions each—there are also translations of more decorous works, including the tales of the Clerk, the Squire, and the Man of Law. While some expand the originals (like Dryden), others abbreviate them (like Pope)—sometimes substantially.

When George Ogle set out to compile a complete translation of the *Canterbury Tales*, he made use of various currently available translations, despite the significant differences between them. His three-volume collection, published in 1741, includes the established versions of the 'Knight's Tale' and the 'Wife of Bath's Tale' by Dryden, the 'Merchant's Tale' and the 'Wife of Bath's Prologue' by Pope, and several other previously published translations, among them his own translation of the 'Clerk's Tale' (first published in 1739). Ogle did, however, translate various linking passages, including the prologues to several tales. This is significant, since it would, for the first time, have provided the reader of a translation from Chaucer with a sense of the interlinked nature of the *Canterbury Tales*.

Ogle did not live to fulfil his apparent intention of producing a complete translation of the *Canterbury Tales*. This task was taken up half a century later by William Lipscomb, whose collection, published in 1795, was entitled *The Canterbury Tales, Completed in a Modern Version*. Lipscomb made various important revisions to Ogle's volume, many of which were based on the first truly scholarly edition of Chaucer, that of the *Canterbury Tales* edited by Thomas Tyrwhitt (1775). These included the removal of the spurious 'Tale of Gamelyn' (a translation of which appeared as the 'Cook's Tale' in Ogle), and modifications to the order of the tales and to some of the links. Lipscomb included his own version of the 'Pardoner's Prologue and Tale' (first published in 1792) and provided translations of eleven more tales, including the 'Tale of Melibee'. The *Canterbury Tales* was, however, not literally 'completed'. Lipscomb omitted not only the 'Parson's Tale' (which had never yet been translated) on the grounds that it was dull, but also the tales of the Miller and the Reeve (which had been included by Ogle) on the grounds of obscenity. His procedure as a translator is fairly consistent: he abbreviates the tales (generally to between 60 and 80 per cent of their original length), and removes anything even remotely offensive. Thus Lipscomb's translations are free not just from obscenity but also from bad manners: even the Host becomes unfailingly civil.

Wordsworth

The translations of William Wordsworth, written in 1801–2, inaugurate a fundamental shift in the dominant approach to translating Chaucer. They comprise versions of the 'Prioress's Tale' and the 'Manciple's Tale', a passage from *Troilus and Criseyde* (5. 519–686), and Clanvowe's the *Cuckoo and the Nightingale* (which was still regularly attributed to Chaucer). The translation of the 'Prioress's Tale' was revised for publication in Wordsworth's volume *The River Duddon* (1820). In terms of Dryden's categories, this translation is clearly a 'metaphrase': it follows the original closely—line by line and word by word. Wordsworth's method may be illustrated by comparing a stanza from his version of *Troilus and Criseyde*—which was not published until considerably later (see below)—with the original. Chaucer's account of the sense of loss experienced by Troilus after the departure of Criseyde includes the following stanza:

> Therwith he caste on Pandarus his yë,
> With chaunged face, and pitous to biholde;
> And whan he myghte his tyme aright aspie,
> Ay as he rood to Pandarus he tolde
> His newe sorwe and ek his joies olde,
> So pitously and with so ded an hewe
> That every wight myghte on his sorwe rewe. (5. 554–60)

Wordsworth renders this:

> Therewith he cast on Pandarus an eye,
> With changèd face, and piteous to behold;
> And when he might his time aright espy,
> Aye as he rode, to Pandarus he told
> Both his new sorrow and his joys of old,
> So piteously, and with so dead a hue,
> That every wight might on his sorrow rue.[17]

Wordsworth retains most of Chaucer's vocabulary and all of his rhyme-words (about three-quarters of which are retained in this, as in his other translations)—in striking contrast to the approach of Dryden and Pope. The closeness of his translation leads him to adopt a semi-archaic diction, in which he feels no need to alter words such as 'aright' and 'wight'. This stanza is quoted by Marvin Mudrick to exemplify the inadequacy of Wordsworth's translations—based, in his view, on 'bogus principles'—by comparison with those of Dryden and Pope.[18]

Though Mudrick's criticism may seem rather extreme and less than entirely fair, it may also prove thought-provoking. Dryden did, in fact, clearly acknowledge the validity of 'metaphrase' as a mode of translation, though he chose not to use it himself. Various considerations would have led Wordsworth to regard 'metaphrase' as the appropriate mode for his own translations from Chaucer. The advances in scholarly understanding of Chaucer's language and metre had undermined the view of him as a 'rough diamond', expressed with such confidence by Dryden. The notion that his language was virtually incomprehensible, also endorsed by Dryden, was increasingly rejected by knowledgeable readers, including Wordsworth himself, so that by 1823 Leigh Hunt could refer to 'the imaginary difficulties of Chaucer's language'.[19] Meanwhile, attitudes to Dryden's translations were changing. Whereas throughout the eighteenth century his *Palamon and Arcite* had been regarded almost unanimously as superior to the 'Knight's Tale', opinion during the nineteenth century first became divided, and then swung emphatically in favour of Chaucer.[20] This reflects a growing respect not just for Chaucer, but also for the Middle Ages. The consequence of such views was a preference for 'metaphrase' over 'paraphrase', and a conviction that the modernization of attitudes, characteristic of eighteenth-century translations of Chaucer, was inappropriate.

Other nineteenth-century translations

Somewhat as the translations of Dryden and Pope inspired Ogle's collection (1740), Wordsworth's translation of the 'Prioress's Tale' was the inspiration for the collection edited by R. H. Horne (1841). The contents of this volume are notably eclectic. They include versions of the 'General Prologue' and six of the *Canterbury Tales*, extracts from *Troilus and Criseyde* and the *Legend of Good Women*, and complete translations of *Anelida and Arcite* and the *Complaint of Mars and Venus* (treated as a single work). This volume combines two previously unpublished translations by Wordsworth (the spurious *Cuckoo and the Nightingale* and the extracts from *Troilus and Criseyde*) with commissioned work by translators including Elizabeth Barrett (*Anelida*) and Leigh Hunt (the tales of the Squire, the Friar, and the Manciple), as well as less celebrated writers such as Thomas Powell, Robert Bell, and Horne himself. While the contents are various, the approach to translation is clearly based on the principles established by Wordsworth, which are endorsed by Horne in his introduction to the volume. The translations are, in the main, true to these principles: most are close, reasonably accurate, and fairly competent—though often dull. Even Elizabeth Barrett and Leigh Hunt struggle with the demands of close translation. These prove especially awkward in relation to any material considered obscene. Surviving correspondence indicates that Wordsworth was persuaded not to permit the inclusion of his translation of the 'Manciple's Tale', on the ground that the subject matter is 'somewhat too indelicate'.[21] In the event, his translation was replaced by that of Leigh Hunt—which is not only markedly inferior, but also handles the most contentious passage (248–56) with far less assurance. The same letter indicates that Wordsworth disapproved of the inclusion of the 'Reeve's Tale' (in Horne's translation). This might seem strange, given the allusion in the *Prelude* (3. 276–9) to his enjoyment of this poem as a young man, or those in the *Journal* of Dorothy Wordsworth to her reading aloud to William from works including the 'Miller's Tale'.[22] While this implicit contradiction doubtless indicates that Wordsworth became more conservative as he grew older, it would also seem to reflect a double standard: a disjunction between what is deemed acceptable, on the one hand, for private reading by educated people and, on the other, for presentation to a general readership through publication.

If so, it strikes a chord that echoes through the nineteenth century—and does not die away until well into the twentieth. A few years before the publication of Horne's collection, Charles Cowden Clarke published a two-volume anthology, *The Riches of Chaucer* (1835), with a notably revealing subtitle: 'in which his impurities have been expunged; his spelling modernized; his rhythm accentuated; and his obsolete terms explained'. Clarke offers a selection from the *Canterbury Tales* and substantial extracts from other works, including *Troilus and Criseyde*, the *Book of the Duchess*, and the *House of Fame*. The text constitutes a strange hybrid between an edition and a translation, with modernized spelling, minimal alterations to the syntax, indications of the stress, and glosses at the foot of the page. Even though he omits the fabliaux, Clarke thoroughly expurgates his text, removing any lines or words that could cause the least offence to the most sensitive reader. This is, truly, a bowdlerized Chaucer.

While Horne's anthology was not well received and his projected second volume never appeared, Clarke's was revised and reprinted several times, and was still in print at the end of the century. Various other modernized versions appear during the remainder of the century, including the *Canterbury Tales from Chaucer* of John Saunders (1845; revised edition 1889) and *The Canterbury Tales and the Faerie Queene, with Other Poems by Chaucer and Spenser* of D. Laing Purves (1870). Interestingly enough, anonymous reviews of both Horne and Saunders (possibly by the same writer) contend that modernization of Chaucer is unnecessary.[23] The typical response of the translator to such assertions may be found in Leigh Hunt's preface to his own modernization of the 'Pardoner's Tale' (1855): that the essential purpose of modernizations is to encourage the reading of the original.[24] It is, perhaps, not surprising that both arguments have been repeated ever since. Meanwhile, nineteenth-century modernizers were attempting to cater for two further groups of potential readers: children and the general public. The first adaptation of Chaucer for children was produced by Cowden Clarke as early as 1833. His *Tales from Chaucer in Prose*, modelled on the *Tales from Shakespear* of Charles and Mary Lamb (1807), provided paraphrases of several tales. He was followed by Mrs H. R. (Mary) Haweis, whose *Chaucer for Children: A Golden Key* (1877) also offered prose versions of several tales, along with some of the lyrics. Haweis went on to produce a *Chaucer for Schools* (1881) and *Tales from Chaucer* (1889)—the latter an inexpensive volume aimed at the general reader. In each case, Chaucer is freely adapted and heavily expurgated.

While such authors were attempting to foster a new readership among the young and the general populace within the English-speaking public, Chaucer was being translated into two other languages, French and German. In the preface to his *Fables Ancient and Modern*, Dryden reports that '*Mademoiselle de Scudery* . . . is at this time translating *Chaucer* into modern *French*';[25] unfortunately, no trace of this translation has been found. The earliest surviving translations of Chaucer into French appeared during the early nineteenth century. A rather poor three-volume translation of the *Canterbury Tales* by the chevalier de Chatelain was published in 1857–61. The French had to wait until 1908 for an authoritative version of the *Canterbury Tales*, prepared by a group of scholars including Louis Cazamian and Emile Legouis.[26] The Germans fared considerably better. The earliest translation into German appeared around 1800. In the middle of the century the scholar Wilhelm Hertzberg produced first a version of the 'Clerk's Tale' (1856), and then a close and reliable translation of the *Canterbury Tales*, complete except for the 'Tale of Melibee' and the 'Parson's Tale' (1866). Another scholar, John Koch, published a parallel text edition of the *Parliament of Fowls* and some lyrics (1880). This was followed by a translation intended to comprise the complete works, by Adolf von Düring—of which three volumes, containing versions of the *House of Fame*, the *Legend of Good Women*, the *Parliament of Fowls*, and the *Canterbury Tales* appeared (1883–6).[27]

Developments in the twentieth century

These German translators anticipated a significant trend: during the twentieth century, translation from Chaucer, which had previously been carried out largely by poets, increasingly became the preserve of scholars. Their work was greatly facilitated by the publication, at the end of the nineteenth century, of the first authoritative edition of the complete works of Chaucer, that of Walter W. Skeat (1894). In the early years of the twentieth century, while French scholars were at work on their translation of the *Canterbury Tales*, Skeat himself produced several small volumes of translation from Chaucer for the King's Classics series (1904–8). These include the *House of Fame*, the *Parliament of Fowls*, the *Legend of Good Women*, and several of the *Canterbury Tales*. Skeat's renditions are broadly in the manner pioneered by Wordsworth: close, line-by-line translations in an archaic style. While the accuracy of these versions and the provision of line-numbers reflect an increasingly scholarly approach to translation, the issue of obscenity remains a problem. Skeat avoids the fabliaux, but still finds it necessary to cut offending lines from texts such as the tales of the Pardoner and the Nun's Priest. The contemporaneous version of the *Canterbury Tales* prepared for the Everyman's Library by Arthur Burrell (1908) is significant essentially in that it provided an almost complete text at a modest price. Burrell's translations are close and conspicuously archaic. His introduction expresses anxiety about the issue of obscenity, to which he responds in a novel manner—by silently omitting the 'Cook's Tale' and leaving the fabliaux untranslated, with the assertion that these poems 'are so broad, so plain-spoken, that no amount of editing or alteration will make them suitable for the twentieth century' (pp. vii–viii). A few years later the complete works of Chaucer appear for the first time in an English translation, that of John S. P. Tatlock and Percy Mackaye, published in the United States. This was produced in two versions: first in verse, as *The Complete Works of Geoffrey Chaucer* (1912), and then in prose, as *The Modern Reader's Chaucer* (1914). Both are expurgated.

   The remainder of the century brings a conspicuous increase in the freedom and variety of translations into modern English. A modernized version of *Troilus and*

Criseyde appears as a separate volume for the first time in the close and somewhat archaic verse translation of George Philip Krapp (1932). Several further verse translations follow in due course, notably those of Margaret Stanley-Wrench (1965) and Nevill Coghill (1971). While both avoid the archaisms of Krapp, the style adopted by Coghill is markedly more formal and elevated than that used by Stanley-Wrench. The recent modernization of *Troilus and Criseyde*—the accurate and scholarly version by Barry Windeatt (1998)—is, notably, in prose. Modernized versions of the *Canterbury Tales* are more various and more numerous: some in verse, others in prose; some selective, others complete. The best-known and most successful is the verse translation of Nevill Coghill, first published in 1951, and still in print. Other significant modernizations include the verse translations of Frank Ernest Hill (1934) and David Wright (1985), and the prose translations of R. M. Lumiansky (1948) and David Wright (1964). A collection of Chaucer's *Love Visions* (1983) contains verse translations, by Brian Stone, of the *Book of the Duchess*, the *House of Fame*, the *Parliament of Fowls*, and the *Legend of Good Women*. Two more varied selections of verse translations take contrasting approaches: Theodore Morrison's *Portable Chaucer* (1949) offering a wide selection of excerpts and translations (often slightly abbreviated), while Nevill Coghill's *Choice of Chaucer's Verse* (1972) provides a briefer selection with texts and translations arranged in parallel. In general, prose translations tend to be closer and more accurate than verse translations—where the translator has to contend with the exigencies of rhyme and rhythm. By the time Hill's version of the *Canterbury Tales* was published in 1934, it had become possible to provide an essentially unexpurgated modernization—though translators continue to evince some uncertainty in their handling of Chaucer's 'bawdy' (for instance, in the rendition of words such as 'swive' and 'queynt'). Such matters are generally judged well by Coghill, whose version of the *Canterbury Tales* also has the virtue of great fluency—which Steve Ellis relates to its origins in a series of radio broadcasts on the BBC Third Programme in the late 1940s.[28] Coghill was also involved in adaptations of the *Canterbury Tales* for television and as a musical, both of which stressed its festive qualities. The film of the *Canterbury Tales* made by Pier Paolo Pasolini (1972), released in both English and Italian versions, concentrates exclusively on bawdy elements—incidentally demonstrating what a poor prophet Arthur Burrell proved to be. (For more on this, see Chapter 33.)

For this reason, it would seem unwise to offer any prediction about likely future trends. Even the current position seems somewhat elusive and paradoxical. It can, of course, be stated with confidence that Chaucer's reputation as a major English poet seems secure. This may be attested by the ever-increasing range of languages into which his work has now been translated—including Italian, Spanish, Dutch, Swedish, Danish, Finnish, Russian, Polish, Czech, Romanian, Bulgarian, Chinese, Japanese, Hebrew, and Esperanto. The position regarding translations into modern English does, however, have its oddities. In the early twentieth century, verse and prose translations of Chaucer's complete works were published; they have never been replaced. Modern English versions of most, but not all, of his work are currently available; but, though publishers must be aware that these are widely used by students as 'cribs', most of them do not contain line-numbers for ease of reference. A majority of these translations are produced by professional academics—a group of people who regularly express unease about the future for the study of Chaucer at university level in the English-speaking world. The reasons for this unease (at least in the United Kingdom) include the decline in the teaching of Chaucer and of foreign languages at secondary school level, and the liberalization of the university curriculum. While this situation presumably increases the need for modernizations of Chaucer, most university teachers of English are adamantly opposed to teaching Chaucer in translation—though they would regularly use translations for teaching texts studied for comparative purposes. A witty and perceptive account of these issues is provided by Peter G. Beidler. In the process, he stresses the essential and obvious reason for the reluctance to teach Chaucer from translations: the inevitable loss of complexity and subtlety that occurs whenever his work is translated. Beidler's comments on the translation of the opening lines of the 'General Prologue' demonstrate that it is extremely difficult to produce an adequate version in modern English. Some of the other examples he cites, all from well-known and respectable translations of Chaucer, range from the inept to the ludicrous.[29]

Yet, with an unbroken tradition stretching back over 300 years, translations of Chaucer are clearly here to stay. This being the case, it seems to me that concerned members of the scholarly community should address the fundamental questions of who these translations are for, and what kind of translations should they be. The answer to the first question is, I think, obvious: translations of Chaucer serve both the general reader and the student. The answer to the second would then involve a judgement as to whether these two distinct groups of readers are best served by the same translations. My own view is that they are not—and that the current uncertainty about translations of Chaucer results in part from a failure to distinguish between the needs of these two groups of readers. The distinction between the requirements of these two groups might be encapsulated in the traditional contrast between the spirit and the letter: while the main concern of the general reader would be to have a readable translation, reasonably true to the spirit of the original, the student needs accuracy. It is instructive to relate this argument to some of the most significant current and recent offerings. Nevill Coghill's verse translations of the *Canterbury Tales* and *Troilus and Criseyde*, published by Penguin, seem better suited to the general reader than the student. Barry Windeatt's prose translation of *Troilus and Criseyde*, published in the Oxford World's Classics series, makes an ideal student 'crib'. It might, therefore, seem curious that the translation of the *Canterbury Tales* in this series, the verse translation by David Wright, is more suitable for the general reader—particularly since Wright's earlier prose translation would serve students better. The early twenty-first century would, perhaps, benefit from complementary translations of Chaucer's complete works—both in verse, for the general reader, and in prose, specifically for students. Both would be of interest to the growing body of scholars and students approaching translation as a subject for academic study.

FURTHER READING

Beidler, Peter G., 'Chaucer and the Trots: What to Do about those Modern English Translations', *Chaucer Review*, 19 (1985), 290–301. Beidler's informal and engaging article considers what happens when students read Chaucer in translation rather than in the original.

Bowden, Betsy (ed.), *Eighteenth-Century Modernizations from the 'Canterbury Tales'* (Cambridge: Brewer, 1991). This remarkable collection of texts facilitates study of the eighteenth-century translations of Chaucer prepared by writers other than Dryden and Pope. It includes a helpful introduction and full supporting material.

Brewer, Derek, 'Modernising the Medieval: Eighteenth-Century Translations of Chaucer', in Marie-Françoise Alamichel and Derek Brewer (eds.), *The Middle Ages after the Middle Ages in the English-Speaking World* (Cambridge: Brewer, 1997), 103–20. Brewer's essay provides a helpful account of translations of Chaucer from Dryden to the end of the eighteenth century.

Brewer, Derek (ed.), *Chaucer: The Critical Heritage*, 2 vols. (London: Routledge & Kegan Paul, 1978). This collection of responses to and comments on Chaucer's work complements that of Spurgeon (see below).

Ellis, Steve, *Chaucer at Large: The Poet in the Modern Imagination* (Minneapolis: University of Minnesota Press, 2000). This unusual and original study considers the reception of Chaucer and responses to his work during the twentieth century; includes a chapter on translations.

Graver, Bruce E. (ed.), *Translations of Chaucer and Virgil by William Wordsworth*, The Cornell Wordsworth (Ithaca, NY: Cornell University Press, 1998). This edition provides scholarly texts of Wordsworth's translations from Chaucer, supported by full annotation and a thorough introduction.

Matthews, David, 'Infantilizing the Father: Chaucer Translations and Moral Regulation', *Studies in the Age of Chaucer*, 22 (2000), 93–114. This stimulating article relates the notion of Chaucer as the father of English poetry to bowdlerized versions of his work, intended both for children and for the general populace.

Mudrick, Marvin, 'Chaucer as Librettist', *Philological Quarterly*, 38 (1959), 21–9. Mudrick's challenging article contends that Dryden and Pope are the only writers who have produced successful translations of Chaucer.

Spurgeon, Caroline F. E. (ed.), *Five Hundred Years of Chaucer Criticism and Allusion, 1357–1900*, 3 vols. (Cambridge: Cambridge University Press, 1925; first pub. Chaucer Society, 2nd ser., vols. 48–50, 52–6; London: Trübner, 1908–17). This work provides an invaluable collection of responses to and comments on Chaucer's work; compare Brewer (ed.), *Chaucer: The Critical Heritage*, above.

NOTES

1. Caroline F. E. Spurgeon (ed.), *Five Hundred Years of Chaucer Criticism and Allusion, 1357–1900*, 3 vols. (Cambridge: Cambridge University Press, 1925), hereafter 'Spurgeon'; Derek Brewer (ed.), *Chaucer: The Critical Heritage*, 2 vols. (London: Routledge & Kegan Paul, 1978), hereafter 'Brewer'.
2. Spurgeon, i. 125–6; compare Brewer i. 126–7.
3. See Spurgeon, iii. 34–62.
4. *A Seventeenth-Century Modernisation of the First Three Books of Chaucer's 'Troilus and Criseyde'*, ed. Herbert G. Wright (Berne: Francke, 1960).
5. See e.g. Spurgeon, ii/1. 159.
6. See ibid. i. 207–15.

7. See ibid. i. 68–271; Brewer, i. 81–160.

8. Spurgeon, i. 117–18; Brewer, i. 117–18.

9. Spurgeon, i. 134; Brewer, i. 129–30.

10. *The Poems of John Dryden*, ed. James Kinsley (Oxford: Clarendon Press, 1958), 1455–6.

11. Ibid. 1456.

12. Ibid. 1457.

13. Ibid. 182.

14. See Spurgeon, i. 286–90.

15. *The Poems of Alexander Pope*, ed. John Butt (London: Methuen, 1963), 9–10.

16. Betsy Bowden (ed.), *Eighteenth-Century Modernizations from the 'Canterbury Tales'* (Cambridge: Brewer, 1991).

17. *Translations of Chaucer and Virgil by William Wordsworth*, ed. Bruce E. Graver (Ithaca, NY: Cornell University Press, 1998), 57.

18. Marvin Mudrick, 'Chaucer as Librettist', *Philological Quarterly*, 38 (1959), 25.

19. See Spurgeon, i. 504, ii/1. 144–5; compare ii/1. 91–2, 126, 139–40.

20. See e.g. ibid. i. 480–1, ii/1. 56, 70, 102–3, 124–5.

21. See ibid. ii/1. 242.

22. Ibid. ii/1. 2–3.

23. See ibid. ii/1. 241, 275.

24. See ibid. ii/2. 22–3.

25. *Poems*, 1459.

26. See Spurgeon, iii, app. B.

27. See ibid. iii, app. C.

28. Steve Ellis, *Chaucer at Large: The Poet in the Modern Imagination* (Minneapolis: University of Minnesota Press, 2000), 115–16.

29. Peter G. Beidler, 'Chaucer and the Trots: What to Do about those Modern English Translations', *Chaucer Review*, 19 (1985), 290–301.

| # Chaucer in performance

Kevin J. Harty

In memory of Julian N. Wasserman,
'gladly wolde he lerne and gladly teche'

The dramatic nature of so many of Chaucer's works, especially of the *Canterbury Tales*, should have guaranteed the poet a continuing presence on the modern stage and screen. But while many other medieval figures and works have repeatedly appeared on stage or screen in post-medieval times, Chaucer and his works have not. Opera's great medieval love-story is that of Tristan and Isolde, not that of Troilus and Criseyde. We have no animated version of the *Parliament of Fowls*, no television mini-series of the *Legend of Good Women* from the BBC or Channel 4 in Britain, or from PBS or HBO in America—and what we do have of Chaucer in performance is not always that noteworthy.

Chaucer on stage

The *Canterbury Tales* did become a general source for elaborate outdoor stage pageants in the early twentieth century at the hands of Percy Mackaye (1875–1956), and through the efforts of Charles Douville Coburn and his Coburn Players, who travelled for almost a decade throughout the American Northeast staging their outdoor productions at colleges and universities and open-air theatres, often to rave reviews. The Coburn Players were one of several theatrical groups who offered a stage alternative to Broadway and stock productions, in some cases for performers who had had less than successful careers in these more traditional dramatic venues.

Coburn's idea was to stage texts taught in colleges and universities at the same colleges and universities. By doing so during the late spring and summer, Coburn hoped to attract as his audience not only college and university students and faculty, but public secondary school teachers as well. Initially, Coburn staged productions of Shakespeare, but in 1909 he obtained exclusive rights to stage Percy Mackaye's *The Canterbury Pilgrims* in an arrangement that benefited both Coburn and Mackaye.

Mackaye's *The Canterbury Pilgrims: A Comedy* was first performed in 1903. It imagines further interactions among Chaucer's pilgrims on their way to Canterbury and adds to their number King Richard II, John of Gaunt, the duke of Gloucester, the archbishop of Canterbury, the Lollard religious reformer John Wyclif, Johanna the marchioness of Kent, and De Vere, duke of Ireland and King Richard's favourite. *Theatre Magazine* favourably reviewed a 1909 outdoor production of *The Canterbury Pilgrims* in Gloucester, Massachusetts, finding it 'charmingly poetical', 'fresh', and technically skilful. The more than appreciative audience was supposedly to have included President Taft, until legislative matters prevented him from leaving Washington.[1]

Chaucer has come to the stage more recently in two separate versions of selected *Canterbury Tales*. Phil Woods's 1980 *Canterbury Tales: Chaucer Made Modern* became a set piece in the repertory of Micky O'Donoughue's London-based New Vic Theatre. As the play opens, the Reverend Barrington Pardoner gathers some of his neighbours together for 'the six-hundredth anniversary Geoffrey Chaucer Story Telling Competition'. As part of the competition, the neighbours re-enact the tales of the Pardoner, the Franklin, the Reeve, the Nun's Priest, the Wife of Bath, and the Miller with a sustained emphasis on the comic, the bawdy, and the outrageous. The production continues to tour throughout Great Britain and North America, where it has become a fixture on college and university campuses.

Arnold Wengrow's 1988 *Canterbury Tales*, which has been staged across the United States, retells the tales of the Wife of Bath, the Merchant, the Miller, the Reeve, the Pardoner, and the Nun's Priest. An appendix to the printed script includes the tale of the Franklin, which stage directions indicate can be substituted for any of the other six tales in a production. Unlike Woods, Wengrow seems content simply to stage tales both comic and serious, taking his lead from his source rather than pitching his script more broadly for laughs.

Markedly less true to its source is Britain's Modernising Theatre Company's *Chaucer in the Sky with Diamonds*, which was produced at London's Riverside Theatre in January 1988. The production, which met with critical scorn for being racist, sexist, crude, and simply inept, is set in a contemporary railway station as the train to Canterbury is cancelled. It purports to stage the tales of the Miller, Wife of Bath, Franklin, Shipman, and Parson by updating them with references to, among other things, rap music and *Star Trek*.

Chaucer receives decidedly better treatment in Nick Revell's play *Love and Other Fairy Tales*, based on the tale of the Wife of Bath. The play, which premiered at London's Southwark Playhouse in 2001, turns the Wife's discourse on the woes of marriage and her story of a rapist knight into a cautionary tale on spousal abuse, while still managing, unlike *Chaucer in the Sky with Diamonds*, to respect its source.[2]

Chaucer, Caryl Churchill, and John Guare

The most intriguing Chaucerian presence on the modern stage comes, however, in a more unexpected text, Caryl Churchill's *Top Girls* (1982). The play's first scene is a brilliant *coup de théâtre*, a celebratory dinner party attended by notable women—each a 'top girl' in her own right—from the ninth to the twentieth centuries. Present at table—though late in arriving—is Chaucer's Griselda, who recounts her treatment at the hands of Walter to an increasingly astonished and appalled on-stage sisterhood.

Griselda's story was immensely popular in medieval times. Chaucer has the Clerk tell her tale, and his rendering is indebted to versions of the tale by Petrarch and Boccaccio and finds analogues in an Italian novella by Giovanni Sercambi and a number of French works. But the medieval perspective on the tale has not always been accepted in post-medieval times. The modern world is likely to find nothing admirable about the tale of what appears to be a victim of spousal abuse. And it becomes clear in Churchill's play that the central character, Marlene, as she assumes her corporate directorship, has learned nothing from the 'her-stories' of her invited guests from across the centuries, including Griselda, each of whom remained true to herself despite being marginalized by history in general and by the men in their lives in particular.

In contrast, Marlene's price for success is to abandon any ideas of sisterhood, motherhood, or the feminine. She ignores her mother, fights with her sister, and dismisses her daughter without a second thought, all to achieve corporate success. Churchill's play is a feminist critique of the wrong kind of feminism, which the playwright sees typified by then British prime minister Margaret Thatcher, who at one point in the play is called 'Hitlerina'.

John Guare's 1999 *Chaucer in Rome* is a sequel to his 1971 *The House of Blue Leaves*. In the earlier play the pope is coming to New York; in the later, New York is, in a sense, coming to the pope, as millions of pilgrims, including a family of New Yorkers, descend upon Rome for the millennial Holy Year Jubilee. The central character in the later play is an American painter in Rome, Matt, who can no longer paint because the special paints he mixes are carcinogenic. (In the earlier play Matt's father, then a soldier absent without leave, hopes to blow up the pope; here the father comes to Rome to find his son, who has, in a sense, gone AWOL from the family.) In search of a new medium of artistic expression, Matt decides to masquerade as a priest, hear pilgrims' confessions, video- and audio-tape them, and then incorporate them into pieces of performance art. Like so many latter-day Chaucerian pilgrims, the people Matt encounters seem to be seeking a quick and easy way into heaven, with results more often tragic than comic for themselves and for Matt and his friends and family.

Canterbury Tales: the musicals

The *Canterbury Tales* have also found a home—albeit an at times uneasy one—on the modern stage thanks to the musical stage comedy. The first version of what would become the best-known musical stage version of the *Canterbury Tales* was a production by the John Ford Society of Exeter College at the Oxford Playhouse in October 1964. This production, based on Nevill Coghill's modern translation of the *Tales*, was the work of the actor and broadcaster Martin Starkie. The production was part of the college's celebration of its 650th anniversary. At the same time, the composers John Hawkins and Richard Hill produced a musical recording, again using some of Coghill's translations. When the authors of the separate projects applied for permission to use Coghill's text, the two projects became one musical comedy, which, with further fine-tuning, premiered in London at the Phoenix Theatre in March 1968.

Originally comprising only four tales (those of the Miller, Reeve, Merchant, and Wife of Bath), the London West End production at times introduced materials either from the Nun's Priest's or the Pardoner's Tales. The premiere production in London coincided with the virtual abolition of stage censorship, and the musical was able to exploit with great success the bawdier aspects of its source. Indeed, the musical was so popular that it played for almost five years in London, while road companies took the show, with either four or five tales, literally to the four corners of the earth.

Today the show seems more juvenile than bawdy, but in their time songs such as 'I Have a Noble Cock', 'Hymen, Hymen', and 'I Am All A-Blaze' were not typical theatre fare, and theatregoers flocked to the show. The American production proved less popular, playing in New York on Broadway for only 120 performances, although it also went briefly on tour. An Australian production had more success, opening in August 1969 in Melbourne, then playing throughout the country for more than two years, and finally spawning a 1976 sequel, *More Canterbury Tales*, which promptly flopped. In 1996 a scaled-down version of the original musical was staged in London to little critical notice under the title *Love, Lust and Marriage*.

In the United States, Jan Steen and David Secter presented *Get Thee to Canterbury: A Medieval Happenynge* at the Sheridan Square Playhouse in 1969, a musical production that ran for fewer than two dozen performances and presented stage versions of the tales of the Wife of Bath, the Reeve, the Miller, and the Merchant. The highlight of the production was a flying Chaucer, who hovered over the dramatic proceedings on stage.

The musical stage versions of the *Canterbury Tales* showcase the supposedly naughty Chaucer. The results are decidedly mixed, and even the original version of the musical would probably not hold up today. What was risqué in the 1960s is fairly tame by contemporary standards, and these musical versions of the *Canterbury Tales* lack the spectacular staging effects such as crashing chandeliers and whirling helicopters that audiences have increasingly come to expect.

Chaucer as ballet

Britain's Ballet Rambert first choreographed Chaucer's 'General Prologue' in 1951 as part of the Festival of Britain. Although the major events were held in London on the South Bank of the Thames, the festival was a national celebration with the aim of providing some respite from the aftermath of the Second World War by celebrating the nation's achievements in the arts, industry, and science. The ballet, with choreography by David Paltenghi, consisted of one act in twelve scenes based on characters from Chaucer's Prologue.

In 1999–2000 the company mounted a full-length ballet, *God's Plenty*, choreographed by Christopher Bruce, its title taken from John Dryden's seventeenth-century tribute to the *Canterbury Tales*: ''Tis sufficient to say, according to the proverb, that here is God's plenty.'[3] The 1999–2000 production staged the tales of the Wife of Bath, Knight, Man of Law, and Miller separated by appearances from an actor playing Chaucer reading from the text of the *Tales* and prefaced by a prologue meant to place Chaucer's great work in its historical and social contexts.[4]

Chaucer as opera

Chaucer's *Canterbury Tales* has twice loosely inspired operas, although these are now largely forgotten. In 1884 Sir Charles Villiers Stanford's *The Canterbury Pilgrims*, with a libretto by Gilbert à Beckett, was staged to general critical acclaim at London's Drury Lane Opera House.[5] Irish by birth, Stanford (1852–1924) was perhaps the most popular and one of the most prolific musicians of his day; his musical output included ten operas. The scenario of *The Canterbury Pilgrims* is built around the love of Hubert, a London apprentice, and Cicely, the young daughter of Geoffrey, owner of the Tabard Inn, who opposes their marriage. When Geoffrey sends Cicely to her maiden aunt in Kent in the company of a group of pilgrims, numerous sub-plots develop. In the end, however, true love wins out. The score, like that of many of his operas, shows Stanford's continuing debt to Wagner, and the whole project capitalized on the Victorian interest in, if not obsession with, all things medieval.

A second opera with the same title as Stanford's was scored by the equally prolific American composer Reginald de Koven (1859–1920) with a libretto by Percy Mackaye based on the script of his pageant play discussed above. The opera premiered in New York in 1917 at the Metropolitan Opera House and was given six more performances, five in New York and one in Philadelphia. Originally intended to be part of the Met's continuing repertory, the opera's premiere had the misfortune to feature a conductor and principal singers who were German, just as a wave of anti-German sentiment swept across the United States.[6]

Mackaye's libretto calls for Chaucer to be travelling in disguise with a group of pilgrims from London to Canterbury. While en route, the Wife of Bath falls in love with Chaucer, who in turn falls in love with the Prioress, here a secular woman who has taken no vows but who nonetheless holds an ecclesiastical position. Not one to suffer rejection lightly, the Wife plots to win Chaucer's affection by setting up a wager that requires the poet to marry her if she can steal the Prioress's brooch from her. When the Wife is successful, Chaucer appeals to King Richard II for aid. The king promptly decrees that the Wife can marry, but that she must marry the Miller rather than Chaucer, who himself is then united with the Prioress. Long-quieted anti-German sentiment notwithstanding, given the rather bizarre elements of its plot, it is little wonder that de Koven's opera has not been revived. Stanford's has suffered a similar fate, the Irish composer's reputation having also long gone into eclipse.

Opera's great medieval love-story is, as I indicated above, that of Tristan and Isolde. Chaucer's *Troilus and Criseyde* was, however, turned into an opera by the British composer Sir William Walton (1902–93) with a libretto by Christopher Hassall. Hassall's original inspiration for his version of Chaucer's poem was a comment by the critic C. S. Lewis about Chaucer's heroine:

Chaucer has so emphasized the ruling passion of his heroine, that we cannot mistake it. It is Fear—fear of loneliness, of old age, of death, of love, and of hostility; of everything, indeed, that can be feared. And from this Fear springs the only positive passion which can be permanent in such a nature; the pitiable longing, more childlike than womanly, for protection, for some strong and stable thing that will hide her away and take the burden from her shoulders.[7]

Walton and Hassall began work on the opera in 1948; it finally premiered at London's Covent Garden in 1954. The opera was revised and shortened in 1963 and again in 1972–6 to accommodate a greater range of singers for the female title role.

The opera opens in the Trojan citadel ten years after the war with the Greeks has begun, and the opera's debt to Chaucer's poem is clear in the first two acts. In Act 3, however, Hassall strikes out on his own. Calkas, the traitorous Trojan high priest, stabs Troilus in the back, for which treachery he is returned to Troy in chains. As further punishment, Cressida is ordered to remain among the Greeks as a prostitute, but she instead picks up the dead Troilus' sword and kills herself. Walton's opera remains popular; it continues to be staged, albeit somewhat infrequently, around the world.

Chaucer as choral piece: Dyson's *The Canterbury Pilgrims*

Literally, on another note, the major work of Sir George Dyson (1882–1964), *The Canterbury Pilgrims*, sets Chaucer's 'General Prologue' to music in a piece for chorus, orchestra, and three singers (soprano, tenor, and baritone). Dyson's first choral work, *In Honour of the City* (1928), set the Scottish Chaucerian William Dunbar's (1465?–1513?) verse to music and paved the way for the Chaucer piece, which Dyson composed in two parts. The choral piece proper (1930) sets to music the verses that open the 'General Prologue' and moves quickly to the portraits of the Knight, Squire, Prioress, Clerk, Haberdasher and his colleagues, Merchant, Sergeant of the Law, Franklin, Shipman, Physician, Wife of Bath, and Parson. The work concludes with an *envoi* in which the company agree to entertain themselves on the way to Canterbury in a game of storytelling. In 1943 Dyson added an orchestral overture, *At the Tabard Inn*, to his original work. The overture resets Chaucer's opening lines in the 'General Prologue' in a piece for trumpet, oboe, and clarinet.

Dyson's popularity has waxed and waned over the years. Until 1945 he was celebrated as a leading proponent of traditional English music, but after the Second World War that traditionalism was no longer viewed so positively. Dyson's work was 'rediscovered' in the 1980s, and *The Canterbury Pilgrims* was given a major revival at London's Barbican Hall in 1996, in a concert that is available on compact disc. Despite the vagaries of Dyson's reputation, his importance lies in large part in the fact that he was the first modern composer to set Chaucer to music.

Chaucer on (and in) film: Pasolini's *I racconti di Canterbury*

In the early 1970s the Marxist Italian film director Pier Paolo Pasolini undertook what he would come to call his 'trilogia della vita' ('trilogy of life'), three cinematic adaptations of medieval texts. The first, *Il decamerone* (1971), based on the fourteenth-century Italian poet Giovanni Boccaccio's *The Decameron*, a collection of interrelated short tales that may have served as a model for Chaucer's *Canterbury Tales*, has generally been critically acclaimed by literary and film scholars alike as a masterly and enlightened reading of its medieval source. In contrast, the third, *Il fiore delle mille e una notte* (1974), based on an anonymous collection of tales in Arabic collectively known as *The Thousand and One Nights* and dating in part from at least the tenth century, has been less well received and dismissed as hopelessly jumbled and even downright pornographic.

The middle film, *I racconti di Canterbury* (1972), based on selections from Chaucer's *Canterbury Tales*, has escaped both the critical acclaim of the earlier Boccaccio film and the critical derision of the later *Arabian Nights*, although early critical reaction to the Chaucer film in the popular press was not always positive. *I racconti di Canterbury*, however, still deserves greater attention than it has received.[8] Despite its flaws, Pasolini's film presents an interesting commentary on the *Canterbury Tales* by a film-maker noted for his adaptations of literary texts from many periods (*Oedipus Rex*, *The Gospel According to Matthew*, *Medea*, *Salò*).

Pasolini, who, in addition to being a film-maker, was a poet, novelist, and respected literary critic, carefully chooses which Chaucerian tales to film and in what order to present them. The script written by Pasolini himself contains the following selections from Chaucer: 'General Prologue', 'Merchant's Tale', 'Friar's Tale', 'Cook's Tale', 'Miller's Tale', 'Wife of Bath's Prologue', 'Steward's [that is Reeve's] Tale', 'Pardoner's Tale', and 'Summoner's Tale'.

I racconti di Canterbury is both medieval in content and modern in form and interpretation. For instance, Pasolini purposefully retains Chaucer's 'General Prologue' (itself basically a long-running monologue), but with almost no dialogue. The camera guides us as we encounter the pilgrims visually. We simply watch them as they come together early in the morning in the yard of an inn. Further, while the 'General Prologue' reflects a selected hierarchy, and the characters we meet are types, conflations of the vices and the virtues common to their trades or their stations in life, Pasolini eschews hierarchies and types. His camera introduces us to individuals as it pans across the yard of the Tabard Inn, and among those individuals is a slightly buffoonish-looking pilgrim and poet, Chaucer, played by Pasolini himself. In the film's opening sequence, neither vice nor virtue is readily apparent. If we are familiar with Chaucer's work, we may readily identify some of the characters we see on the screen by their outfits or their deportment, but Pasolini is interested from the start more in Chaucer himself than in the actual pilgrims, and that interest in Chaucer continues later in the film when his reappearance, instead of those of the pilgrims, is used to link the tales together.

Both Chaucer and Pasolini establish an initial narrative perspective, but with completely opposite results. In the 'General Prologue' Chaucer separates himself as narrator and pilgrim, whereas Pasolini seeks to unite himself as film-maker and actor. Pasolini's subsequent appearances in the film suggest his central concern, an examination of the relationships that exist among the artist, his art, and the world at large. Pasolini's appearance in the earlier *Il decamerone* as an assistant to the painter Giotto is static and basically secondary to the film's plot and theme; here Pasolini's role as Chaucer is central to the film and essential to its message.

Pasolini's most original cinematic note comes in his full-blown version of the 'Cook's Tale', based on what is only a prologue and a fragment in Chaucer. Peterkin has all the Chaucerian vices, but, because of Pasolini's eye for the comic, he remains sympathetic and engaging in ways that it would be hard to imagine had Chaucer fleshed out fully the 'Cook's Tale'. In Pasolini as in Chaucer, we are asked to make comparisons between, and judgements about, the characters we meet at various levels of narrative. Peterkin may be sympathetic, but others, such as January, clearly are less so.

Like Chaucer, Pasolini borrows freely from his source materials, paying homage to those before him, while presenting a generic mix in a work whose whole may be greater than the sum of its parts. For instance, Pasolini's extensive debts to painting in many of his films have been well documented: here the film-maker's 'Summoner's Tale' suggests it has sources in Bruegel and Bosch as much as it does in Chaucer. And the most original sequence in Pasolini's film, the expansion of Chaucer's brief allusion in the Cook's fragment to Peterkin into a full-length tale, is part of a stylistic homage to Charlie Chaplin underscored elsewhere in the film by Pasolini's casting of his daughter Josephine as the Merchant's May.

Whatever its limitations as a film, *I racconti di Canterbury* presents an intriguing visual response to Chaucer's verbal narrative that deserves more critical attention than it has received from both literary and film critics. And, in what is nothing less than a truly Chaucerian footnote to his entire medieval trilogy, soon after the trilogy was completed, Pasolini abjured all three films just as Chaucer famously retracted much of his work at the end of the *Canterbury Tales*. In his abjuration, Pasolini argued that it was impossible to make films about the past, idealized or otherwise, because the past had been irreparably corrupted by the present.

Chaucer on (and in) film: Brian Helgeland's *A Knight's Tale*

Brian Helgeland's 2001 film *A Knight's Tale* is one of a number of recent films that try to reimagine the past (medieval or otherwise) to meet present-day concerns, prejudices, and attitudes—another popular example is John Madden's 1998 *Shakespeare in Love*, which posits an Elizabethan England free of gender bias and prejudice. In Helgeland's film, William (played by Heath Ledger), the son of a thatcher, dreams of changing his destiny and becoming a knight, and thus, to use the film's oft-repeated catchphrase, 'changing his stars'. Such a rise from rags to riches and fame may sit comfortably with twenty-first-century audiences who see William as some kind of proto-individualist battling and ultimately besting the entrenched system, but we know that medieval society was rigidly class-bound, and that the barrier dividing peasant from even minor noble was unbreachable.

Perhaps the most interesting feature of *A Knight's Tale* is its indebtedness to Chaucer and his works. On one level, the tournament scenes suggest the panoply of the 'Knight's Tale', but more that is Chaucerian is going on in the film than simple literary allusion. Chaucer appears as a character in the film, though perhaps not a Chaucer we would readily recognize (see Figure IV.2). We first meet him after William has trained himself to compete in the lists in place of his dead master, Sir Ector. As William and his two companions set off for a tournament at Rouen, they encounter Chaucer (Paul Bettany)—stage directions in the script tell us he is 29 years old—walking down the road 'buck solid' naked; a compulsive gambler, the poet has literally lost the clothes off his back. When a clearly baffled William asks just who the naked man is, he replies 'Geoff Chaucer's the name; writing's the game.' The name means nothing to William, or to his fellow servants Roland and Wat, so Chaucer continues:

> I'm a writer . . .
> WAT: *A what?*
> CHAUCER: Writer. With ink and parchment? For a penny, I'll scribble all you want: summonses, warrants, decrees, edicts, patents of nobility. Even a poem or two. Perhaps you read my *Book of the Duchess*? It was allegorical.
> ROLAND: We won't hold that against you. That's something each man has to decide for himself.

Fig. IV.2 William (Heath Ledger, left) and Chaucer (Paul Bettany). Still from Brian Helgeland's film *A Knight's Tale* (2001).

We know the real Chaucer was probably in France (though doubtless not 'buck solid' naked) on a diplomatic mission in 1369 (when he would have been 29) and after he had written the *Book of the Duchess*.[9]

When William wins in swordplay but loses the tournament championship, Chaucer turns to Peter the Pardoner (Jonathan Slinger) and Simon the Summoner (Steve O'Donnell), his gambling nemeses, and threatens to unleash his verbal skills on them in a tirade whose in-joke is readily apparent to anyone who has read the *Canterbury Tales*: 'I'll eviscerate you in fiction. Every last pimple, every last flaw of character. You two will be "naked" for eternity.' And when William is unmasked as a fraud and put into the stocks, Chaucerian eloquence is once again put to good use arguing—perhaps in a nod to the hag's speech on *gentilesse* in the 'Wife of Bath's Tale' (1109–76)—that nobility is innate rather than inherited, although it is the intervention of the Black Prince that finally saves William.

The Chaucer of *A Knight's Tale*, like the film itself, is clearly a modern reimagining of things medieval. The film moves far beyond the mad irreverence towards things medieval found, say, in the 1975 farcical romp *Monty Python and the Holy Grail*. The cultural issues raised by *A Knight's Tale* are different. Director–screenwriter Helgeland seeks to reinvent the medieval (and Chaucer in the bargain) in order to make the medieval less distant from the modern and more acceptable to what we would like history to have been. The film's approach to the medieval is obviously anti-classist—and mildly anti-sexist as well: the heroine, Lady Jocelyn (Shannyn Sossamon), is, within limits, a fairly free spirit, and there is a feisty woman blacksmith (played by Laura Fraser) who is more or less self-sufficient and who is more technologically sophisticated than her male counterparts—her armour is lightweight and flexible. But, in the final analysis, *A Knight's Tale* is a harmless romp with a genuine affection for the medieval in general and for the Chaucerian (and for Chaucer himself) in particular.

Chaucer on film: minor appearances and allusions

Cinema's love-affair with the medieval begins at least as early as 1895, and, depending upon which films one chooses to include in a 'medieval' filmography, there are hundreds of films with recognizably medieval plots, settings, and themes. Chaucer has, however, not been a ready source for film-makers seeking medieval plotlines from which to borrow in contrast say to Robin Hood, King Arthur, and Joan of Arc, who each have been the subjects of many dozens of films.[10]

The title of Michael Powell and Emeric Pressburger's 1944 film *A Canterbury Tale* suggests something more Chaucerian than the film actually delivers. The film does open with a sequence in which Chaucer's pilgrims traverse the road to Canterbury. But, when the Squire releases his falcon, it flies aloft and morphs into a British Second

World War Spitfire. The film itself, set for the most part in a village just outside Canterbury, is, to say the least, a curiosity. The village finds itself home to increasing numbers of billeted English soldiers. To keep the distracting local girls indoors so that the soldiers will attend his lectures on the national heritage instead, a magistrate goes around pouring glue on the girls' heads. Most of the film is given over to unmasking the magistrate. When it was released, film censors were at a bit of a loss about what to make of *A Canterbury Tale*. It definitely seemed to them to be a bit of wartime propaganda, but for what, no one was clear.[11]

Less perplexing and more clearly indebted to the Chaucerian is John Huston's 1948 classic *The Treasure of the Sierra Madre*, which borrows a scene from Chaucer's 'Pardoner's Tale'. Chaucer's Pardoner tells an *exemplum* illustrating his favourite maxim that the root of all evil is greed. In that *exemplum* three riotous young men go out to seek and kill Death. Huston's film tells the story of Fred C. Dobbs (played by Humphrey Bogart), an American drifter in Mexico. When Dobbs sets off with two friends, Howard (Walter Huston) and Curtin (Tim Holt), to panhandle for gold in the mountains, the film's debt to Chaucer comes to the fore. Dobbs becomes increasingly paranoid while prospecting, convinced that his partners are out to cheat him. When they end up low on provisions, Howard and Curtin want to send Dobbs to town to get them, but he refuses. Later, when Howard goes off to help a sick Indian boy, Dobbs plots to do Curtin in, and almost succeeds in doing so, and to steal both his partners' gold. As the film progresses, Dobbs's greed and paranoia become one, and he is eventually, in an appropriately Chaucerian touch, undone by them, as bandits kill him and then unknowingly scatter the gold dust that all three prospectors have hoarded to the winds.

In a lesser way, Pasolini's *I racconti di Canterbury* suffered a fate similar to his *Decameron* film. It inspired shameless, basically soft-core imitations more interested in titillating audiences than in bringing literary classics to the screen. In the case of *Il decamerone*, there were many such imitations. For *I racconti di Canterbury*, there were (thankfully) only two, both released in 1972. Mino Guerrini's *Gli altri racconti di Canterbury* ('The Other Canterbury Tales') is an anthology of six unrelated bawdy tales, none, despite the film's title, derived from Chaucer. Lucio Dandolo's *I racconti di Canterbury N. 2* ('The Tales of Canterbury No. 2'—released in England as *The Lusty Wives of Canterbury*) presents six additional tales about cuckolded husbands and nymphomaniac nuns and clerics, again without any debt to Chaucer. And in what may be the film's most unintentionally funny note, it is clear from its dialogue that Dandolo thought that the tales he was presenting were based on tales originally written by someone named 'Canterbury'![12]

David Fincher's 1995 film *Se7en* employs a familiar enough narrative device when it pairs seasoned older homicide detective William Somerset (played by Morgan Freeman) with rookie partner David Mills (Brad Pitt) to solve a series of especially grisly murders based on the Seven Deadly Sins. Somerset is first to recognize the theological connections among the murders, and he turns to the shelves of the public library for help in solving them. Somerset consults Dante, Milton, and, of course, Chaucer, specifically the 'Parson's Tale'. He urges Mills to do the same, and in a wonderfully comic note that neatly marks the generation gap between them, Mills rushes out to buy Cliffs Notes for the *Inferno, Paradise Lost*, and the *Canterbury Tales,* instead of reading the works themselves.[13]

Chaucer on television

Chaucerian sightings on television do exist, but tapes of the actual shows and records of their episodes either do not survive or are not easily accessible. Materials in the library of the British Film Institute in London do, however, contain at least passing references to a number of televised versions of Chaucer.[14]

In 1951 the BBC broadcast a contemporary retelling of the 'Pardoner's Tale' set in Cambridge and Cornwall. In 1969 the BBC produced a seven-part series based on Chaucer's *Canterbury Tales* adapted for television by Nevill Coghill and Martin Starkie, featuring versions of the tales of the Knight, the Miller and Reeve, the Shipman and Nun's Priest, the Friar and Pardoner, the Wife of Bath and Clerk, the Merchant and Manciple, and the Canon's Yeoman and Franklin. In 1975 BBC2 broadcast *The Trinity Tales*, a six-part dramatic series in which rugby fans en route to Wembley for the cup final pass the time telling somewhat far-fetched tales. The individual episodes were entitled the 'Driver's Tale', 'Fryer's Tale', the 'Judy's Tale', 'Joiner's Tale', 'Wife of Batley's Tale', and 'Man of Law's Tale'. The 1980 television season in Britain included an animated version of selected Canterbury tales directed by Ralph Bakshi, and 1984 saw Thames Television's *Six Centuries of Verse: Chaucer to Ted Hughes*, in which noted stars of the British stage gave voice to selections from the English poetic canon.

In 1998 the BBC commissioned an animated series based on the *Tales*, which was produced in cooperation with Welsh Television Channel S4C and Moscow-based Christmas Films. The tales were first broadcast on BBC2 over the Christmas holidays at the end of 1998. They were subsequently shown on the HBO channel in the United States, and then released in a three-videotape set after they won a BAFTA award in Britain and an Emmy award in the United States.

Retold in modern English in voice-overs provided by well-known television, film, and stage actors, the series, adapted by Jonathan Myerson, begins with the tales of the Nun's Priest, Knight, and Wife of Bath as the pilgrims set out for Canterbury. In Part 2 the pilgrims arrive at Canterbury after having told the tales of the Merchant, Pardoner, and Franklin. In Part 3 they return to London while telling the tales of the Squire, Canon's Yeoman, and Miller and Reeve, the last two in overlapping versions better to emphasize the competition between them.

As part of its Autumn 2003 season, BBC1 featured a series of six one-hour versions of the *Tales*, commissioning its writers to come up with teledramas reflecting life in the new millennium. The series begins with the 'Miller's Tale', set in Kent, where the love triangle comprises a pub owner, his karaoke-singing wife, and a young man from out of town who claims to be a talent scout and who seemingly seduces the entire village. In the 'Wife of Bath's Tale' a 'mature' actress finds herself abandoned by her husband of some sixteen years and turns to her much younger co-star for love. In the 'Knight's Tale' two incarcerated friends fall in love with an inspirational teacher working in their prison. In the 'Sea Captain's [that is, Shipman's] Tale' the beautiful but spoiled wife of a wealthy godfather figure living in East London's Asian community finds herself hopelessly in debt because she is addicted to shopping; in an attempt to settle her debts, she seduces her husband's business partner. In the 'Pardoner's Tale' three ne'er-do-wells join in a search in contemporary Rochester for a missing teenage girl, where greed gets the better of them. In the final episode, the 'Man of Law's Tale', Constance, a young Nigerian refugee found washed up in a boat near Chatham, brings both chaos and serenity to the lives of three men whom she meets in London, one of whom follows her back to her homeland.

When they were broadcast, the BBC *Tales* received mixed reviews, perhaps unfairly so. They are not so much modernized versions of Chaucer as they are simply tales inspired by his work. In each case, writers have, admittedly with mixed results, borrowed a basic plot situation from Chaucer and built a teledrama around it in keeping with the BBC's intention of presenting a perspective on contemporary life inspired by Chaucer's similar exercise some 600 years earlier.[15]

Conclusion

The contemporary Italian cultural critic, novelist, and semiotician Umberto Eco once simply noted, 'it seems that people like the Middle Ages'.[16] Within the academy, Chaucer's reputation remains secure. But popular culture has not rushed to embrace Geoffrey Chaucer, and we might well ask why. Successive post-medieval cultures have readily embraced the medieval in general, but they have done so by embracing a view of the medieval that they find comfortable and by often ignoring Chaucer in the process.

Perhaps, from a post-medieval perspective, Chaucer remains too identifiably Catholic for a post-Reformation world, whereas other versions of the medieval have been received through Protestant lenses: the legend of King Arthur was synthesized by Malory, but it was further filtered through the Protestant world-views of Tennyson in England and of Twain in America; Joan of Arc was burned at the stake by the Catholic Church and clearly became the first Protestant in the eyes of George Bernard Shaw; Robin Hood, always a symbol of transgressive behaviour, is an anti-authoritarian figure comfortably at home in any era, despite the era's religion or politics. Dante's immense popularity in the modern period among both English and American writers may be because writers have concentrated on Dante as a person as much as they have on his works, especially the *Divine Comedy*. In Chaucer's case, there has been no such distinction between the man and his works, and the scarcity of examples of Chaucer in performance may be due not to any question concerning Chaucer's continued literary merit or worth but to the differences in his and our world-views, differences in the final analysis that are ultimately perhaps more religious than anything else.

FURTHER READING

Ellis, Steve, *Chaucer at Large: The Poet in the Modern Imagination* (Minneapolis: University of Minnesota Press, 2000). Study of Chaucer's modern legacy, including a chapter entitled 'Performance Chaucer'.

Green, Martin, 'The Dialectic of Adaptation: The *Canterbury Tales* of Pier Paolo Pasolini', *Literature/Film Quarterly*, 4/1 (Winter 1976), 46–53. One of the more insightful critical comparisons of Pasolini's film with its source in Chaucer.

Harty, Kevin J., *The Reel Middle Ages: American, Western and Eastern European, Middle Eastern and Asian Films about Medieval Europe* (Jefferson, NC: McFarland, 1999). Comprehensive guide to more than 500 films set in the Middle Ages, including films indebted to Chaucer.

Palmer, Charles, *George Dyson: Man and Music* (1984; London: Thames, 1996). A principal source of information about him.

Rodmell, Paul, *Charles Villiers Stanford* (Burlington, Vt.: Ashgate, 2002). This study, together with Jeremy Dibble, *Charles Villiers Stanford: Man and Music* (New York: Oxford University Press, 2002), suggests Stanford may once again be a source of critical interest.

WEB LINKS

Internet Movie Database. For general details about, and reader-submitted reviews of, most films and television series and programmes, this is perhaps the most useful web site: <http://www.imdb.com>.

NOTES

1. In gathering details about this early dramatic pageant and about later stage versions of the *Canterbury Tales*, I have relied on materials in the appropriate clippings files in the Theater Collection, New York Public Library, Lincoln Center, and in the Library of the Theatre Museum, Covent Garden, London.

2. Both scripts have apparently not been published. For reviews, see *Theatre Record* (London), 29 Jan. 1998, 117, and 22 Oct. 2001, 1405–6.

3. John Dryden, *Of Dramatic Poesy and Other Critical Essays*, ed. George Watson, 2 vols. (London: Dent, 1962), ii. 284.

4. For information about the 1951 ballet, which was given thirty-three performances in London, Harrogate, Canterbury, and Belfast, I am grateful to Jane Pritchard, the Rambert's archivist, for her kind assistance. The 1999–2000 ballet was given twenty-nine performances throughout England and Scotland from 15 Sept. 1999 to 20 Apr. 2000. Reviews of these performances, especially that at London's Sadler's Wells on 23–7 Nov. 1999, are readily available online.

5. For a review of Stanford's *The Canterbury Pilgrims*, see *The Times*, 29 Apr. 1884, 8.

6. On this anti-German sentiment, see the memoir by Mrs Reginald de Koven, *A Musician and his Wife* (New York: Harper, 1926), 228–33. For representative reviews of the opera, see *Current Opinion*, 62 (Apr. 1917), 254–5; *New York Times*, 9 Mar. 1917, 7; and *North American Review*, 205 (Apr. 1917), 616–19.

7. C. S. Lewis, *The Allegory of Love: A Study in Medieval Tradition* (1936; repr. New York: Oxford University Press, 1948), 185.

8. While much has been written about Pasolini's trilogy as a unit and about each of the three films separately, the most insightful reading of the Chaucer film remains Martin Green's 'The Dialectic of Adaptation: The *Canterbury Tales* of Pier Paolo Pasolini', *Literature/Film Quarterly*, 4/1 (Winter 1976), 46–53, upon which many of my following comments are based.

9. See e.g. Derek Pearsall, *The Life of Geoffrey Chaucer: A Critical Biography* (Oxford: Blackwell, 1992), 82–93.

10. Kevin J. Harty, *The Reel Middle Ages: American, Western and Eastern European, Middle Eastern and Asian Films about Medieval Europe* (Jefferson, NC: McFarland, 1999), catalogues more than 500 films set in the Middle Ages, including dozens of Robin Hood, King Arthur, and Joan of Arc films, but only three films indebted to Chaucer.

11. There is no published screenplay for *A Canterbury Tale*. The film is, however, available on videotape from Carlton Home Entertainment.

12. The screenplays for these two soft-core films have not been published, nor are the films themselves available on videotape or on DVD. For further information about them and about Pasolini's Chaucer film, however, see their respective entries in Harty, *The Reel Middle Ages*.

13. The screenplay for *Se7en* has not been published, but the film is readily available on videotape and on DVD from New Line Cinema.

14. The British Film Institute's online catalogue, SIFT, is only available to the public for in-house use.

15. Whether the BBC *Tales* will be rebroadcast, either in Great Britain or elsewhere, or made available on videotape and DVD is as yet unclear. For further details about the series, see *BBC TV Programme Info*, 36 (6–12 Sept. 2003) to 41 (11–17 Oct. 2003), and the BBC's web site: <http://www.bbc.co.uk/canterburytales/>. Reviews in the British press are readily available online.

16. Umberto Eco, *Travels in Hyperreality*, trans. William Weaver (San Diego: Harcourt Brace, 1990), 61.

34 Chaucer and his guides

Peter Brown

It is difficult to imagine the future of this book in its present form. Ten years from now its essays may have been reassembled countless times in bespoke course booklets printed on demand in short runs, or downloaded from the Internet as individual items made available through an institutional subscription or pay-as-you-read scheme. These trends already determine the kinds of book academic publishers produce: as in the present case, there is a move towards compendious volumes of multi-authored essays easily dismembered into smaller units for electronic delivery. Such books may assume conventional shapes in hardback and paperback versions, but are easily reconfigured for different kinds of output. CD-ROMs have not fulfilled their promise as the technology to supersede books, but the Internet is fast revolutionizing the production and consumption of academic texts. It is doing so not by replacing books—the reading of lengthy texts on screen is not a pleasant experience—but by complementing them. One symptom of this process is the website accompanying the present Guide.

Technological change is only one of several extraneous forces affecting the publication of books on Chaucer (and of academic books more generally). Another is the intensification of financial pressures as commercial publishers compete in a global marketplace, and university presses struggle to justify their existence as 'cost centres' in terms of profit and loss, rather than in terms of intellectual capital alone. One consequence is the decline of the single-author monograph, which rarely sells more than a few hundred copies and so is difficult to justify in financial terms, however original its content. A third factor is the pressure on academic authors to publish their research in order to uphold and extend their reputations and that of their departments, or to achieve tenure or promotion. In Britain research standing is determined through a quinquennial assessment exercise operated by a government agency, with the results tied to departmental funding. Research-active individuals are expected to produce four or five high-quality 'outputs' within the timespan of each review. A chapter in a companion or guide carrying the imprint of a distinguished press is a relatively reliable way of achieving one such publication. Finally, there is the issue of affordability: students are unable to buy multiple volumes of secondary reading, but are drawn to a single volume that promises authority and scope. Similarly, university libraries, obliged by reduced budgets to choose between a collection of new essays by diverse hands on a variety of topics and a single-author monograph, tend to choose the item that is of greater apparent benefit to their students.

The creation of books from constituent parts of separate authorship, or the reassembling of some of those parts in custom-built handbooks, has interesting similarities with the production of academic and literary texts in the later Middle Ages. Professional stationers—manuscript 'publishers' operating from a shop—produced booklets (complete texts, or sections of larger works) for rental. A scribe would then copy the booklet for use in a volume that reflected his (or his client's) particular interests, needs, or tastes—and what he could afford. These practices help to explain why the late medieval book often resembles a miscellany or anthology. But the comparison should not be pressed too far. As the preceding remarks indicate, the present-day situation is the result of a particular set of circumstances that do not precisely match those of the Middle Ages. It might also be noted that the production of medieval texts was a relatively slow and expensive process, involving much arduous copying by hand, whereas in today's print culture texts are created cheaply, at immense speed, and in large quantities; that the ability to read and write was confined in Chaucer's day to an elite of courtiers, lawyers, clerics, diplomats, and merchants, but today literacy is a birthright; and that university education in the late Middle Ages was the preserve of those destined for occupations in the Church, government, medicine, and teaching, and was not available to the population at large.

Nevertheless, the above observations give pause for thought about the appearance of texts such as this Oxford Guide. The form a book takes is determined not just by the policies of the publisher and editor, or the expertise and enthusiasm of the contributors, but also by the demands, expectations, and circumstances of the readership; by technological possibility; and by economic, cultural, and professional factors. That being the case, it is possible to see symptomatic changes over time in particular types of text such as 'the guide to Chaucer', and witness its birth and growth to maturity. This chapter is an attempt to write a 'guide to guides' in the hope that it will shed some light on the range, reception, reputation, and perception of Chaucer and his works. I will begin with some thoughts about the history of academic guides to Chaucer, look at one or two of the earliest examples, then widen the focus to include Chaucer guides intended for more general consumption, including those that divert attention away from what he wrote and towards 'the pilgrimage experience' and literary topography.

Academic guides to Chaucer

'Guide to Chaucer' is here used as a generic term covering any book on Chaucer with 'guide', 'introduction', or 'companion' in the title. It therefore excludes some publications with strong claims to be considered as guides, but my concern is not to be all-inclusive—rather to consider a sufficiently significant sample of the total output. Some fifty guides to Chaucer have been published, of which the earliest is Thomas Betterton's *Chaucer's Characters; or, The Introduction to the 'Canterbury Tales'* (1712). There is then a long gap until Henry Hope Reed's *Introduction to English Literature from Chaucer to Tennyson* (1855). Since it is a book of general literary history it may be discounted for present purposes. It is some twenty years later, with Frederick Gard Fleay's *Guide to Chaucer and Spenser* (1877)—of which more later—that the genre of academic guides to Chaucer really gets under way. Statistically speaking, there are some distinct trends and tendencies. Over time, Chaucer guides appear with increasing frequency. Clusters appear sporadically from Fleay through to J. G. Southworth's *Verses of Cadence: An Introduction to the Prosody of Chaucer and his Followers* (1954),[1] but from 1960 onwards, with the reprinting in a second edition of Derek Brewer's *An Introduction to Chaucer*,[2] there is no five-year span that does not see one or more new guides (eight in 1985–9, seven in 1995–9). The majority, some thirty-eight of the titles, have been produced in the last forty years: 76 per cent of the total output in the last 30 per cent of the genre's timespan.

These facts and figures invite observations and hypotheses. In general, there is a correlation between the increasing number of guides and the rise of English as a university discipline. As the subject has developed, and as Chaucer's writings have become embedded in the curriculum, so there has been a corresponding demand for ancillary texts. There are also particular explanations for different phases of the Chaucer guide phenomenon. It begins at a time when the great Victorian scholars such as Henry Bradshaw, Frederick J. Furnivall, W. W. Skeat, and Bernhard ten Brink were stimulating interest in Chaucer's life and works. In this phase the guides have a strong biographical and textual orientation, and are intended for use in school. One of the first guides with a university audience in mind is Robert K. Root's *The Poetry of Chaucer: A Guide to its Study and Appreciation* (1906),[3] with G. L. Kittredge's *Chaucer and his Poetry* (1915)[4] a close second. Little is produced in the remainder of the war years, or for some time thereafter. It is not until the 1930s that there is another spate of introductory studies, but this time with another kind of audience in mind: general readers. An example would be G. K. Chesterton's *Chaucer* (1932).[5] War again spells a pause in the production of guides to Chaucer. From the 1960s the exponential increase in the number and frequency of texts, which shows no sign of abating, is in Britain a symptom of the expansion in higher education consequent upon the government's acceptance of the recommendations of the Robbins Report (1963). At the same time Chaucer studies have become globalized under the banner of the New Chaucer Society. On both sides of the Atlantic there are recurrent anxieties about the place of Chaucer within the university curriculum, but he continues to enjoy a high profile in survey modules as well as in more specialized courses.

Thus, the conditions for publishers of guides to Chaucer are relatively favourable. Chaucer is a mainstream author; there is consanguinity between the smaller British market and the huge American one; Chaucer sells. An important factor in marketing guides to his works is the title of the book in question—its choice being a matter of great sensitivity and debate on the part of publishers and authors, since a wrong title can doom a book to oblivion. 'Companion' has never been popular: there are only seven examples from the past 150 years. R. S. Loomis's *A Mirror of Chaucer's World: A Pictorial Companion to Chaucer* (1965)[6] contained a set of supplementary, contextualizing documents in photographic reproduction. Beryl Rowland's *Companion to Chaucer Studies* of 1968,[7] with a second edition in 1979, provided a comprehensive collection of specially commissioned essays that surveyed the secondary material. *The Cambridge Chaucer Companion* (1986),[8] edited by Piero Boitani and Jill Mann, offered a smaller number of essays on topics selected to address current critical concerns and stir debate. What all 'companions' share is a certain latitude in their approach to the role of reader, which is seen as essentially collaborative. 'Introduction', by contrast, has been a title of choice since the early eighteenth century, and it remains the most common (there are twenty-three 'introductions to Chaucer'). However, it is now somewhat passé (there have been only two 'introductions to Chaucer' since 1986) because the term suggests a subaltern or prefatory status, with the contents of the book curtailed or at least concise. 'Guide' is less desiccated, more expansive, and is far and away the dominant current term (there have been thirteen 'guides to Chaucer' since 1987). Publishers favour its aura of authority, and the implication that it will provide purposeful direction, a rich fund of relevant and helpful knowledge, and a communicative mode of address carefully attuned to its intended audience.

In an overcrowded market guides to Chaucer have diversified as publishers have endeavoured to find different niches for their offspring. Four types of guide are current. There is the anthology of previously published essays, endorsed by a well-known editor who provides an agenda for the selection, such as Derek Pearsall's *Chaucer to Spenser: A Critical Reader* (1999).[9] Secondly, there is the conspectus attempting to cover the essentials of Chaucer's life, works, and critical reception, as in Gillian Rudd's *Complete Critical Guide to Geoffrey Chaucer* (2001).[10] Third is the 'issue-led' guide, such as Corinne Saunders's *Chaucer* (2001),[11] which foregrounds critical debate on certain chosen topics, excerpting the previously published writings of Chaucerians and providing those excerpts with overviews. Finally, there is the blockbuster: a large collection of original essays threatening to dwarf for sheer bulk the substantial volume of Chaucer's own writings. My *Companion to Chaucer* (2000)[12] ran to some 200,000 words; the present volume is half as long again. These and most other types of guide are not designed to be read from cover to cover, but as reference works. One of the most ambitious, scholarly, and enduring is the three-volume set of *Oxford Guides to Chaucer*[13] written by Helen Cooper (*Canterbury Tales*, 1989),[14] Barry Windeatt (*Troilus and Criseyde*, 1992), and A. J. Minnis (*Shorter Poems*, 1995).

The variety and sophistication of modern guides to Chaucer are a response also to the explosion of scholarship and criticism in Chaucer studies. By way of comparison and contrast it is instructive to look at a guide produced when the fuse for that explosion was being laid by Victorian researchers. Fleay's 1877 *Guide to Chaucer and Spenser* appeared in the Collins School and College Classics series alongside guides to Shakespeare, Milton, and Marlowe. Fleay is conscious of writing in a new genre for the edification of students, and of pulling together in a single, accessible format fragments of scattered material. He openly intervenes in controversy with the leading Chaucerians of the day (especially Furnivall), deploying evidence from metre and rhyme-schemes, source study, and the historical record to argue his own position on the corpus of Chaucer's works (Fleay includes the apocryphal *Dream of Chaucer* and *Cuckoo and the Nightingale*), Chaucer's date of birth (he upholds 1328), dates of composition, the order of the Canterbury tales, and Chaucer's biography, which included an unhappy marriage: 'Mrs Chaucer seems to have been cold, unsympathising, and shrewish.'[15] Much of this is directed at fellow members of the Chaucer Society; how intelligible it was to the 13-year-old pupils for whom it was ostensibly written is questionable. It probably went over their heads. However, the sections on Chaucer's life, sources, the pronunciation of his language, and the nature of his metre and rhyme could have been absorbed without engaging in the more polemical sections. And something of Fleay's characteristics as a teacher do come across: he draws on his experience as an erstwhile poet to map the process by which Chaucer tired of certain rhymes before moving on to new ones (p. 32)—a highly speculative and dubious basis on which to date poems; and he sees himself as a scholar in the vanguard of pedagogical practice, having been the first to introduce English literature 'as a specific subject of education in our grammar schools' some twenty years earlier (p. 10)—a claim in need of further investigation.

Fleay, who taught in northern England, appends a manifesto arguing how English literature, and especially its earlier examples, could profitably replace Latin and Greek classics (the cause of 'lassitude and disgust') in the school curriculum, and also counterbalance the then current emphasis on teaching the natural sciences. His approach is part of a more general debate then raging, but his inflections sound remarkably progressive: for example, he advocates studying not just key authors, but periods of literature in their cultural contexts ('contemporary politics, manners, and historical events', p. 122); the lives of contemporaries; whole not excerpted works; texts rather than literary history; and non-canonical writing. He deplores the spoon-feeding of facts, preferring instead to encourage in students the practice of forming independent judgements based on careful evaluation of the available evidence. Literature is for Fleay a nexus of cultural and historical forces, 'the best preparation for the higher study of mankind' (p. 124). Such principles are ones with which a modern author of a Chaucer guide, such as Catherine Richardson (*Chaucer: A Beginner's Guide*, 2001),[16] would have little cause to quarrel.

The common reader

In the 1920s and 1930s there was a reaction against academic and scholastic authors of literary guides to Chaucer. Instead, the arbiters of taste and judgement in matters literary were to be readers themselves—here construed as being outside educational establishments—and suitably helped by a different type of guide-writer. Virginia Woolf felt the need for such guides thanks to her own experiences, as a woman, of being excluded from the male-dominated mysteries of literary scholarship. To describe the kind of person for whom she was writing, Woolf borrowed from Samuel Johnson's *Life of Gray* the term 'common reader', a species he associated with the exercise of common sense, a lack of prejudice, and freedom from 'the dogmatism of learning'. Woolf's presentation of Chaucer occurs in her *The Common Reader* (1925)[17] account of Sir John Paston—as a member of the Norfolk gentry a somewhat uncommon reader—encountering Chaucer's works in the fifteenth century as he struggled with familial, social, and financial problems. A more sustained, and still powerful, example of writing in the same vein is G. K. Chesterton's *Chaucer*, published in 1932, with a second edition in 1948. Making a virtue of his amateurism—'this book . . . is intended to be simple . . . It makes no claims to specialism'—[18] he advances in the opening chapter a vigorous claim for the greatness of Chaucer, and in so doing reclaims him from the professionals and 'the clinging curse of all the criticism of Chaucer; the fact that while the poet is always large and humorous, the critics are often small and serious' (20). (For more on Woolf and Chesterton, see Chapter 31.)

The non-academic impulses of Woolf and Chesterton are pronounced, and have specific contexts both in the politics of their day and also in the formation of their own credos. However, the writing of books on Chaucer designed to make him available to a general reader has a longer history. By way of example, there are the dialogues on Chaucer in *Conversations on Some of the Old Poets* (1845) by the American poet James Russell Lowell, and *Chaucer* by Adolphus William Ward, a professor at Owens College, Manchester, which appeared in 1879 as part of Macmillan's English Men of Letters series. It was still being reprinted in 1936. Ward recognizes the authority both of the Chaucer Society under Furnivall, and of Fleay, and tries to steer a mid-course between them. Quite unreflectively, and with considerable panache, he derives Chaucer's character from the impression left by his poetry. Thus we learn that he was modest, enjoyed a settled and contented faith 'as far removed from self-torturing unrest as from childish credulity',[19] kept his political views to himself, had an unhappy marriage (evident in his attacks on women), and demonstrated splendid Victorian virtues in his attitude towards work and career—'a man of practical good sense, desirous of suitable employment and of a sufficient income' (p. 156). In literary matters he was a passionate reader, loved nature, 'his chief joy and solace' (p. 162), and spoke for England 'not only as the first great poet of his own nation, but as a great poet for all times' (p. 168). He was also the first English love-poet, had a creative temperament characterized by vivacity and joyousness, and exercised a keen sense of the ridiculous through the power of satire. He is 'the first great painter of character' among modern European writers (p. 151), strongly appreciative of dramatic situations, and sensitive to pathos. The secret of his genius is vitality: 'in his poetry there is *life*' (p. 188).

Ward's allusion to Furnivall is significant, because the founder of the Early English Text Society (1864) and Chaucer Society (1868) insisted on the importance of making Chaucer's writings accessible to all. Through his activities with the Working Men's College in London (founded in 1854) he promoted the education of those—chiefly men, but also women—denied access to a university education. His impulses were both socialist and nationalist as he encouraged, through the study of medieval literature, ideals of companionship and equality. He himself, though educated at University College London, and Cambridge, was an enthusiastic amateur, a gadfly to professional scholars who delighted in differentiating himself from them, and from wealthy dilettantes. He sought to demystify the study of medieval literature, urging his followers to edit manuscripts (to the consternation of archivists and librarians). He envisaged a community of readers who, by engaging directly with the writings of Chaucer, would sharpen their sense of Englishness, and recognize in him a moral guide.

Furnivall's project was controversial, and it remains so, but there can be little doubt of its widespread impact both in establishing Chaucer as a canonical writer within the emergent university discipline of English literature, and in securing for his works a wider range of general readers. One instance of the latter effect takes the form of an illustrated volume published in 1885, written by Elizabeth Robbins Pennell (then developing her writing career as a contributor to *Century* and *Atlantic* magazines) and with drawings by her husband, Joseph, who was to become an important and influential illustrator (see Figure IV.3). *A Canterbury Pilgrimage* describes their progress on a Coventry Rotary Convertible tandem through Kent in the summer of 1884. A significant document in the history of cycling, it is also informed by a good working knowledge of the *Canterbury Tales* and one of its medieval sequels, the prologue to the *Tale of Beryn* (discussed below). And while the Pennells are not quite the English working people Furnivall had in mind as the beneficiaries of his enthusiasm—they were Americans from Philadelphia on a honeymoon trip—they share his democratic instincts, observing with sympathy the bedraggled labourers on their latter-day pilgrimage from the east end of London to the hop fields of Kent. They do so in the personae of Chaucerian pilgrims, with an air of detached amusement, a sharp eye for detail, and with due attention to the key landmarks of Chaucer's poem:

What we wanted was in all reverence to follow, as far as it was possible, the road taken by the famous company of bygone days, setting out from the hostelrie where these lordings lay one night and held counsel, making stations by the way at the few places they mention by name, and ending it, as they did, at the shrine of the 'holy, blissful martyr', in the Canterbury cathedral.[20]

Elizabeth Pennell describes the places sanctioned by Chaucer—Deptford, Greenwich, the Watering of St Thomas, Rochester, Boughton, and Harbledown—with much more

The Pilgrims are Chased by Dogs.

Fig. IV.3 A bicycle ride along the pilgrims' route to Canterbury. Illustration by Joseph Pennell in Joseph and Elizabeth Robbins Pennell, *A Canterbury Pilgrimage* (1885).

attention to detail than he deemed necessary or desirable. The narrative is structured according to three days of travel, in a way that reflects the scholarly controversies then raging about the time it would have taken to travel from London to Canterbury on horseback, which stories were told on which days (including those of the return trip), and the correct ordering of the tales according to topographical markers in the text. Those debates are reflected in the prefatory material of a fifteenth-century text edited by Furnivall and W. G. Stone for the Early English Text Society and published in 1887, the *Tale of Beryn*. Its prologue, here called 'A Prologue of the Merry Adventure of the Pardoner with a Tapster at Canterbury', had been issued earlier to members of the society and Elizabeth Pennell had read it. The prologue describes the arrival of Chaucer's pilgrims in Canterbury and thereby furnished allusions and phrases for the Pennells' own experiences. Like their predecessors, they stay overnight in a local hostelry, having 'ordeyned' their dinner wisely, and meet a fellow pilgrim (also a cyclist) with whom they exchange stories and resolve to visit the cathedral 'in company' the following day. Before setting out, they 'cast on fresher gowns', and join a throng of pilgrims sporting 'signs of Canterbury' (not pilgrim badges, but red guide books). They then identify the remains of the Chequer of the Hoop where the Beryn pilgrims stayed. In the cathedral choir, the site of St Thomas's shrine, Pennell reports: 'we deposited our sixpences, our modest offerings in place of "silver broch and ryngis" ' (p. 74).

The common non-reader

To Furnivall may be traced the origins of a radical impulse to make Chaucer's writings accessible to all. It culminated in the work of Woolf and Chesterton, to be largely replaced either by the more specialized study of Chaucer at degree level (itself no longer the preserve of an elite), or by versions of Chaucer produced for entertainment. The writings of Woolf and Chesterton are in any case hard acts to follow. As influential and authoritative writers of fiction in their own right, they offer particular insights denied to more mundane critics. Unlike an academic guide to Chaucer, which is always painfully aware of its dependence upon Chaucer's writings, Woolf's essay, or Chesterton's book, is complete in itself however much it might exhort its reader to experience Chaucer's works direct. To this extent their authors' project is self-contradictory, for it asserts the desirability of reading Chaucer while at the same time rendering it unnecessary by writing studies that give Chaucer in a nutshell. Their guides are surrogates, unlike academic guides which are essentially ancillary.

But far from their being a dead end in the popularizing of Chaucer, Woolf and Chesterton belong in a tradition of authors who write for the non-reader of Chaucer's works. In this case there is a particular strategy often used to replace the chore of reading him with the illusion of being brought closer to an understanding of his works—an account of the pilgrimage to Canterbury. The Pennells' book works in this way, remaking the pilgrimage for its nineteenth-century audience while creating frissons of recognition as the authors visit the very places mentioned by their admired poet. Whether authors of guides to the Canterbury pilgrimage target the antiquary, hiker, cyclist (armchair or otherwise), religious devotee, or patriot, few can resist the temptation of suggesting that the enactment of a latter-day pilgrimage (or reading about one such enactment) provides authentic and privileged access to the *Canterbury Tales*.

H. Snowden Ward's *The Canterbury Pilgrimages* (1904), also follows Chaucer's itinerary. The book is one of the Pilgrimage Series, published by A. & C. Black, that identifies regions with the names and works of famous writers (*The Scott Country, The Hardy Country*). To that extent it is laying claim to the pilgrimage route through Kent as 'Chaucer country'. It begins with a loss-and-absence trope, focusing on the martyrdom of Thomas Becket and the disappearance of the 'worship' of him. For these 'disasters' Chaucer provides a remedy, for he is the poet of hope (that is, springtime), 'whose puppets move serenely under the very shadow of impending doom'. That doom—the Reformation—is not named as such, and is in any case insignificant, a mere detail in the larger scheme of things from Ward's conservative (or Anglo-Catholic) viewpoint. The evidence lies in Chaucer's own creations:

He helps us to see how eternal and how indifferent to incidents are nature and human nature. He shows us that his monk and his pardoner, his wife of Bath and his prioress, his gentle knight and his poor parson are people we meet today under other names. And he preaches the resurrection and the life: not only for individuals, but for ideas, for thoughts, and for aspirations.[21]

The first half of this lengthy book is devoted to the first tragedy Ward bemoans—the life and murder of Becket, coupled with accounts of the miracles, canonization, and cult of St Thomas. Thereafter, it provides an account of the *Canterbury Tales* organized according to four days of travel. It begins with a biographical sketch, and proceeds to treat Chaucer's tales as historical documents capable of yielding information about the journey to Canterbury. Along the way it includes lengthy quotations from his writings, line illustrations of the pilgrims from the Ellesmere manuscript, numerous photographs of existing artefacts and buildings, and frequent digressions on cultural contexts, especially of the religious variety. As a portmanteau guide to the *Canterbury Tales*, and as a substitute for actually reading them, it works moderately well, but comes unstuck in trying to pursue its central conceit, the futility of which becomes increasingly apparent: 'It is impossible to connect the tales [of the first day] with any definite part of the day or way' (p. 237); or, more wistfully: 'the Wife's tale must have been early in the third day' (p. 257). And there are clear signs of frustration when nothing in the *Tales* indicates that Chaucer's pilgrims took any notice at all of Faversham Abbey, which is, for Ward, an important site which he cannot refrain from describing in detail (pp. 277–8). He adopts an 'as if' approach in the mingling of Chaucer's pilgrims—disingenuously represented as historical figures—with the verifiable remains of the road. Harry Bailly 'must have seen the Kentish crowd surging past his door' (pp. 239–40). The reader willy-nilly becomes a participant: 'leaving Chartham we climb the height of Chartham Hill' (p. 266).

Homes and haunts

The ways in which Ward approaches Chaucer reflect a form of literary topography popular in the nineteenth century and still flourishing today. It is predicated on the idea of a visit to a place hallowed by association, and undertaken in the belief that the experience will create a closer communion with the writer and his or her works. William Howitt's *Homes and Haunts of the Most Eminent British Poets* was first published in 1847 and ran to many subsequent editions. Its opening essay is on Chaucer, who is both exemplary and difficult, a test case for the entire enterprise. With all poets, Time 'lays waste their homes and annihilates the traces of their haunts with an active and relentless hand'.[22] So little is known of Chaucer's life, claims Howitt, that he seems a mercurial, fugitive figure, difficult to pin down to a particular place. This is to the advantage of those places that would lay claim to him, and is part of his allure for Howitt. His essay is in effect a guide to those places with which Chaucer might conceivably be linked.

One strong contender is Woodstock, where the king held court on numerous occasions. Chaucer would have attended him, and so must have had a house there, which 'became his favourite abode. It was a square stone house near the park gate, and long retained the name of Chaucer's house' (p. 4). What is more, 'Many of the rural descriptions in his works have been traced to this favourite scene of his walks and studies' and it is at Woodstock that Chaucer wrote the *Canterbury Tales*. Unfortunately, 'Every trace of it has been long swept away' (p. 4). Another claim is based on Donnington Castle, in Berkshire, known to have been owned by Chaucer's son Thomas. 'Evelyn tells us there was an oak in the park which tradition asserted to have been planted by Chaucer, and which was still called Chaucer's Oak' (p. 5). The castle was in Howitt's day (inevitably) a ruin.

Such connections may strike us as tenuous and specious, but in a sense that is not the point. What we are dealing with here is the sanctioning of place by virtue of its association with a writer presumed to have lived there, a place which is supposed to have prompted the thoughts, feelings, and descriptions that eventuated in great poetry. It is an attempt to get nearer to the mysteries of the creative process, while idolizing the individual through whom they were channelled. Paradoxically, as Howitt turns from the supposed facts of Chaucer's biography to allusions to place in his fiction, so the tangible referents become more substantial, solid, and complete. He describes the Tabard Inn, then still functioning as the Talbot, in some detail, registering surprise at its longevity. Evidently it housed a real relic of Chaucer's imaginary journey: 'a large table, said to be the one at which the pilgrims were entertained' (p. 7). Appropriately enough, Howitt's own pilgrimage ends at Chaucer's tomb in Westminster Abbey, an object that Time has not neglected to ravage. Indeed Time, as much as Chaucer himself, is Howitt's main protagonist. A large part of the appeal of the places he describes stems from their state of ruin or absence, which stirs nostalgia in the contemplation of change and decay, and romantic feelings of desolation and sadness, but—in this case, at least—redress is at hand. Chaucer's pilgrims are 'the very quintessence of human nature. They live yet, fresh and vivid, passionate and strong, as they did on the way to the tomb of St Thomas' (p. 9). 'Dan Chaucer' has triumphed over the depredations of Time, and will do so for a thousand years yet.

Howitt's essay, which could be supplemented with others, is an example of a more general cultural process whereby a mystique accumulates around a place associated with a writer. Its origins have been traced to the mid-eighteenth century, and to the creation of Poets' Corner in Westminster Abbey, although there are some seventeenth-century precursors among Warwickshire antiquaries eager to claim various locales in their county for Shakespeare. Those attracted by the mystique are offered the role of enthusiasts seeking personal epiphanies: they are pilgrims visiting literary shrines in order to express their devotion to an author able to effect miraculous, life-changing experiences. The literary pilgrim hopes to make contact with the spirit of the writer which haunts the designated place. As we have seen, Chaucer's spirit is particularly elusive, but at the same time he offers a lifeline—a pilgrimage to Canterbury—that would seem to fulfil the enthusiast's most ardent needs. Yet the route from London to Canterbury is not strictly a 'literary place' at all, but something less stable and tangible, requiring a process of movement in the course of which places named by Chaucer might be glimpsed only in passing, and even then through the distorting lens of a fiction. Worse, the place that is the object of the pilgrimage has little authorial sanction except as a destination: Chaucer's pilgrims never arrive, and there is precious little historical evidence to associate Chaucer and Canterbury. His 'presence' there is less a haunting than a chimera of the imagination.

Such details and qualms are of little consequence to modern guide culture. Within the redundant medieval parish church of St Margaret's, Canterbury, 'The "Canterbury Tales" Visitor Attraction' (subtitled with unconscious irony 'Medieval Misadventures') offers its customers a half-hour simulation of Chaucer's pilgrimage. After imbibing some information about the key historical event that brought the pilgrimage, and the *Canterbury Tales*, into existence—Becket's murder—the visitor becomes a latter-day pilgrim, following a path that winds through a London street and out into the Kent countryside. Movement is controlled by the headset each visitor wears, through which come medieval music, commentary, and the voices of well-known actors and celebrities. Periodically a halt is called so that the traveller can witness brief presentations—done by automata in front of a stage set—of five tales (Knight's, Miller's, Wife of Bath's, Nun's Priest's, Pardoner's). The pilgrimage ends at the shrine of St Thomas, but the journey continues through a medieval market street, which in turn disgorges into a modern gift shop where, according to the current publicity leaflet, 'A superb range of Canterbury merchandise is available.'

If 'The "Canterbury Tales" Visitor Attraction' works, it does so by providing participants with something they can feel on their pulses as direct contact with the medieval past (the sights, the smells, the sounds) and one of its great authors ('England's finest poet', no less). Ironically, for this illusion of authenticity of place and time to succeed it has to do so through a dizzying set of dislocations: from twenty-first century to twelfth (Becket's death), to fourteenth (the time of the pilgrimage); from historical fact to literary fiction; from pilgrimage framework to narrative world, and back again, five times—all within the space of thirty minutes. What the visitor encounters at the core of this process is a form of hyper-reality always in danger of becoming caricature and so defeating its own purpose (the Summoner's carbuncles, a tooth extracted without anaesthetic, the bawdy pantomime of the 'Miller's Tale'). For anyone with a modicum of historical or literary knowledge the experience produces cultural vertigo, not to say sensory nausea: the place is super-saturated in visual information, the ear constantly assailed by the voices of half-recognized 'personalities', the nose challenged by the ersatz stench of leather and dung. The prevailing feeling is not of liberation (of know-ledge, of imagination) but of claustrophobia—of being trapped, powerless, in a phan-tasmagoric world. Reviewing the Visitor Attraction (or 'Canterbury Pilgrims Way' as it then was) under the headline 'Disney Comes to Chaucertown', Sebastian Faulks found the attachment to 'authenticity' 'neurotic'. He commented:

A man on children's television [Mark Curry, a former presenter of *Blue Peter*] is the model for a dummy who is the adjunct to a non-existent scene in a medieval religious poem, none of whose words you hear, in a deconsecrated church adjacent to the site of the martyrdom of an actual archbishop . . . Surely English history is a strange thing.[23]

Even stranger than Faulks suspected: hidden behind the stage sets of the Visitor Attraction are the tomb and monument of Canterbury's great antiquary, William Somner (1606–69), who dedicated his life to researching and writing about the material remains of the city as evidence of actual, not virtual, history. But Faulks was in any case well placed to know about the malleability of the past. A few years after writing his review he published his critically acclaimed *Birdsong* (1993),[24] a fictional-ized account of trench combat in the First World War interwoven with the story of a love affair.

Conclusion

It is inevitable that academics and intellectuals will want to disparage what they see as travesties of the literature and historical processes they cherish and strive to under-stand. Yet the durability and widespread impact of populist and commercial versions of Chaucer give pause for thought. 'The "Canterbury Tales" Visitor Attraction' has now existed for close on twenty years—a reasonably long run as these things go—and while easy to castigate as a dumbing down of medieval culture and Chaucer's works, it will also have intrigued some visitors enough to make them want to know more. And although the media it uses are technologically advanced and highly distinctive, its general rationale and content are securely in the tradition of textual guides to Chaucer for non-readers of his works. Moreover, the whole idea of a make-believe pilgrimage—did the proprietors of the 'Visitor Attraction' but know it—would not have seemed strange to Chaucer's contemporaries, who used a variety of devices to substitute for the real thing: a person delegated to undertake the pilgrimage on behalf of someone unable or unwilling to do so; books that described in vivid detail pilgrimage journeys and their destinations, thus enabling the pious, sedentary reader to undertake a virtual pilgrimage as an act of meditation; and mazes, trodden by the devout, that represented in symbolic form the process, obstacles, and achievement of pilgrimage. True, medieval pilgrimage was supposedly a pious affair, rather than the secularized commercial activity of the 'Visitor Attraction', but—as is clear from the *Canterbury Tales*—religious motivation was not necessarily dominant, and the commercial aspects of medieval pilgrimage were real enough to be the subject of scorn among Lollard reformers.

To reflect on some of these points, and bring the present chapter to a close, we might glance again at the very earliest text that can claim to be a guide to Chaucer—the prologue to the *Tale of Beryn*. It was written by a person familiar with Chaucer's works, who knew that sections of his audience would enjoy the knowing references to the characteristic behaviour of the pilgrims. Yet a working knowledge of the *Canterbury Tales* is not a prerequisite: the prologue stands on its own merits, at once sophisticated and popular in its appeal, straddling the specialist and non-specialist categories of 'guide'. Like the latter, it takes up the theme of pilgrimage, and encourages its audience to participate in that conceit, pretending to complete the *Canterbury Tales* by describing how the pilgrims enter the city, lodge at a pilgrim inn, visit the cathedral and shrine of St Thomas (making appropriate offerings and purchases of souvenir badges), dine, and inspect other significant sites such as the city gates and defences. Its commercial orientation is quite clear. Written in all probability to attract pilgrims to the city and cathedral for the 1420 jubilee of Becket's martyrdom, its author may have been a 'cathedral guide' in his own right—a monk–custodian of the shrine used to the ways of pilgrim visitors, and conscious of their economic importance. The inn at which his pilgrims stay (thereby encouraging their real-life counterparts to do the same) is named as the Chequer of the Hoop, built by Prior Chillenden and owned by the cathedral as means of taking advantage of the pilgrim trade (a substantial part of the original building remains, at the south end of Mercery Lane, and is now used as shops). Similarly, the *Beryn* author describes the expensive gifts—silver rings and brooches—that devout pilgrims liked to leave at the shrine—using them as models for what others should also do. All of this is done, as it were, under the aegis of Chaucer, which makes the *Beryn* prologue one of the earliest instances of a linkage between a writer and a place. Canterbury, only twenty years after the poet's death, had already acquired its 'Chaucer aura'.

The *Beryn* prologue and tale exist in only one manuscript (Duke of Northumberland's Library, Alnwick, MS 455), bound in with a copy of the *Canterbury Tales*, the order of which seems eccentric to a modern reader. It is a reminder that the medieval book, not unlike a modern web site, was a living document, prone to expansion, contraction, or revision according to the needs and wishes of its owner and users. Indeed, Chaucer's own, accretive mode of composition is in part a reflection of that mode of book production. The *Canterbury Tales* grew as a series of narratives, some incomplete, some still in need of revision, that circulated individually or in small clusters before the poet's death, and which were collected together in more or less coherent (but different) sequences only afterwards. It is hardly surprising that his work continues to have the incomplete, interactive feel of work in progress. That in turn helps to explain why Chaucer guides down to the present day have little compunction about becoming involved in the continuation of what he left unfinished. After all, his own pilgrimage is given much of its dynamic by two guides—Harry Bailly as Host, and Chaucer as pilgrim—so the lure of assuming the role of guide, once the post falls vacant, is almost irresistible.

FURTHER READING

Baldick, Chris, *The Social Mission of English Criticism, 1848–1932*, Oxford English Monographs (Oxford: Clarendon Press, 1983). A historical examination of the social function of literary criticism, and of the origins and development of English literature as a school, college, and university discipline.

Benzie, William, *Dr F. J. Furnivall: Victorian Scholar Adventurer* (Norman, Okla.: Pilgrim Books, 1983). The standard biography of the eccentric and energetic radical who promoted the study of medieval literature for all readers.

Bowers, John M. (ed.), *The Canterbury Tales: Fifteenth-Century Continuations and Additions* (Kalamazoo: Medieval Institute Publications, 1992). Includes a modern and accessible edition of the prologue to the *Tale of Beryn*.

Ellis, Steve, *Chaucer at Large: The Poet in the Modern Imagination* (Minneapolis: University of Minnesota Press, 2000). A comprehensive study of the modern, non-academic reception of Chaucer (for example, through films, children's literature, novels). See especially chapters 2 ('Popular Chaucer') and 5 ('English Chaucer').

Griffiths, Jeremy, and Derek Pearsall (eds.), *Book Production and Publishing in Britain 1375–1475* (Cambridge: Cambridge University Press, 1989). Fifteen original essays introducing different aspects of book production and consumption. See especially the essay by Julia Boffey and John J. Thompson, 'Anthologies and Miscellanies: Production and Choice of Texts', 279–315.

Marsh, Kate (ed.), *Writers and their Houses: A Guide to Writers' Houses of England, Scotland, Wales and Ireland* (London: Hamish Hamilton, 1993). A fascinating modern example of the 'homes and haunts' approach, with perceptive essays by well-known modern writers on their favourite literary places.

Ousby, Ian, *The Englishman's England: Taste, Travel and the Rise of Tourism* (Cambridge: Cambridge University Press, 1990). See the first chapter, 'Literary Shrines and Literary Pilgrims: The Writer as Tourist Attraction', which traces the origins of the 'literary place' phenomenon.

Rainsford, Dominic, *Literature, Identity, and the English Channel: Narrow Seas Expanded* (Basingstoke: Palgrave, 2002). An exemplary study, using minor or unknown works, as well as more famous authors, to map the cultural formation of a place.

Trigg, Stephanie, *Congenial Souls: Reading Chaucer from Medieval to Postmodern* (Minneapolis: University of Minnesota Press, 2002). An account of readers' responses to Chaucer from the fifteenth to the late twentieth centuries. Includes a survey of modern academic guides, and discussions of Furnivall, Woolf, Chesterton, and the 'common reader'.

Zacher, Chris, *Curiosity and Pilgrimage: The Literature of Discovery in Fourteenth Century England* (Baltimore: Johns Hopkins University Press, 1976). Thought-provoking account of the varied motivations for pilgrimage, and its literary representations.

NOTES

1. (Oxford: Blackwell).
2. First pub. as *An Introduction to Chaucer* (Harlow: Longman, 1984); repr. as A New *Introduction to Chaucer* (Harlow: Longman, 1988).
3. (London: Constable).
4. (Cambridge, Mass.: Harvard University Press).
5. (London: Faber).
6. (Princeton: Princeton University Press).
7. (Toronto: Oxford University Press, 1968; 2nd edn. 1979).
8. (Cambridge: Cambridge University Press).
9. (Oxford: Blackwell).
10. (New York: Routledge).
11. (Oxford: Blackwell).
12. (Oxford: Blackwell).
13. (Oxford: Clarendon Press).
14. (2nd edn. 1996).
15. F. G. Fleay, *Guide to Chaucer and Spenser* (London: Collins, 1877), 41.
16. (London: Hodder & Stoughton).
17. *The Common Reader*, First Series, ed. and introd. Andrew McNeillie (London: Hogarth Press, 1984).
18. G. K. Chesterton, *Chaucer* (London: Faber, 1932), 9.
19. A. W. Ward, *Chaucer* (1879; repr. London: Macmillan, 1936), 149.
20. *A Canterbury Pilgrimage. Ridden, Written, and Illustrated by Joseph and Elizabeth Robbins Pennell* (London: Seeley, 1885), 11–12.
21. H. Snowden Ward, *The Canterbury Pilgrimages*, Pilgrimage Series (London: Black, 1904), p. xii.
22. William Howitt, *Homes and Haunts of the Most Eminent British Poets*, 3rd edn. (London: Routledge, 1873), 1.
23. *The Independent*, 11 June 1988, 13.
24. (London: Hutchinson).

Part V

Study resources

Printed resources

Mark Allen

This chapter identifies major printed resources for the study of Chaucer, works widely available in academic libraries. The brief introductions to the categories below offer historical perspective and in some cases indicate how these resources have developed. Most of them are rooted in the apparatus accompanying early editions of Chaucer's works, and many have ancestors among the volumes published by the original Chaucer Society between 1868 and 1925 to encourage the study of Chaucer. Reflecting changes in Chaucer scholarship, the works listed have largely replaced the Chaucer Society publications, and, in turn, online resources are replacing some of them. The goals of research are many and varied, however, and different goals require different tools; so this list and its annotations clarify the value (and sometimes the limitations) of a selection of the best available printed resources.

The student's beginning point in any research project should be a good, recent edition of Chaucer's works (Section 3), where introductory and explanatory notes provide fundamental information and indicate what topics have been discussed by scholars and critics. Bibliographies and other resources below will help students understand what has been accomplished in the study of Chaucer and what yet needs to be done. Scholarly essays about Chaucer are published in a wide variety of professional academic journals, but two are dedicated to the study of his works and his age: *The Chaucer Review* (first published in 1966) and *Studies in the Age of Chaucer* (1979). A third, *The Chaucer Yearbook*, published five volumes, 1992–8.

1 Bibliographies

Chaucer studies are well served by a variety of reference bibliographies. Students are advised to use several different kinds to discover their various uses. The sheer volume of Chaucer scholarship has prompted increasingly specialized bibliographies since the 1920s, when academic bibliographies began to appear annually. Until then, members of the close-knit world of Chaucer scholarship relied largely upon personal reading and word of mouth—aided by library catalogues and early, hit-and-miss indexes to periodical literature.

In the 1920s the English Association at Oxford, the Modern Humanities Research Association at Cambridge, and the Modern Language Association of America began to compile annual topical bibliographies of literary scholarship that sought to be complete. But the quantity increased exponentially over the decades, and in 1978 the newly formed New Chaucer Society took as one of its responsibilities the reporting and annotating all that was written about Chaucer in each year. This annual bibliography (1.1.1 below) continues today in both printed and electronic forms, augmented by cumulative, selective, and specialized bibliographies.

1.1 Annual bibliographies

Best for recent criticism and keeping up to date. None is absolutely complete, so check them all for thorough research. The titles of these bibliographies have changed over time; the most recent titles are used below.

1 'An Annotated Chaucer Bibliography, 1975– ', *Studies in the Age of Chaucer*, The New Chaucer Society (Notre Dame, Ind.: University of Notre Dame Press). The best resource for Chaucer studies from 1975 to the present; available annually in the journal *Studies in the Age of Chaucer*. Each entry includes a brief summary of the book or article; a separate list identifies the book reviews produced in a given year. Also freely available online: <<http://uchaucer.utsa.edu>>.

2 'English Literature/1100–1499. Middle English period: Chaucer, Geoffrey (1340/5–1400)', *MLA International Bibliography* (New York: Modern Language Association of America, 1922–). This annual listing covers 1921 to the present, with 1963 to the present also available electronically in many libraries. Early lists concentrated on books and articles published in the United States.

3 'Middle English: Chaucer', *Year's Work in English Studies* (Oxford: English Association, 1921–). This commentary on (rather than listing of) annual publications briefly evaluates the works it mentions and occasionally discusses trends, but its discursive format makes it difficult to locate specific items efficiently. Covers 1919 to the present.

4 'Middle English and Fifteenth Century: Geoffrey Chaucer', *Annual Bibliography of English Language and Literature* (Cambridge: Modern Humanities Research Association, 1921–). This annual listing covers 1920 to the present; also available electronically in many libraries.

1.2 Cumulative bibliographies

Best for studying critical trends and traditions, and for in-depth research of a given topic. They are listed here in reverse chronological order since they build upon one another.

1 Bowers, Bege K., and Mark Allen (eds.), *Annotated Chaucer Bibliography, 1986–1996* (Notre Dame, Ind.: University of Notre Dame Press, 2002). Compiles the entries, annotations, and book reviews from eleven years of 'An Annotated Chaucer Bibliography' (1.1.1), extensively cross-referenced within topical categories. Includes author and subject indexes.

2 Baird-Lange, Lorrayne Y., and Hildegard Schnuttgen, *A Bibliography of Chaucer, 1974–1985* (Hamden, Conn.: Archon Books, 1988). Lists ten years of Chaucer studies, arranged by topic

and cross-listed. Includes book reviews, and author and subject indexes. The introduction surveys critical trends.

3 Baird, Lorrayne Y., *A Bibliography of Chaucer, 1964–1973* (Boston: G. K. Hall, 1977). Lists ten years of Chaucer studies, arranged by topic and cross-listed. Includes book reviews, and author and subject indexes.

4 Crawford, William R., *Bibliography of Chaucer, 1954–63* (Seattle: University of Washington Press, 1967). Lists ten years of Chaucer studies, arranged by topic; some entries annotated. Includes book reviews. The index includes authors and some subjects; the introduction surveys critical trends.

5 Griffith, Dudley David, *Bibliography of Chaucer, 1908–1953* (Seattle: University of Washington Press, 1955). Lists fifty-five years of Chaucer studies, arranged by topic; most entries annotated very briefly. Includes book reviews; the index includes authors and some subjects.

6 Hammond, Eleanor Prescott, *Chaucer: A Bibliographical Manual* (1908; repr. New York: Peter Smith, 1933). The first comprehensive Chaucer bibliography; a major work, although unorthodox in its arrangement. Describes, summarizes, and comments upon Chaucer scholarship from its beginnings to 1908, surveying the development of Chaucer's biography, his canon, and its chronology; the manuscripts, editions, and modernizations of his works; and the history of opinions on his language and versification. The index of authors and topics is helpful but not thorough.

1.3 Selective bibliographies

Best for quick reference and for surveying critical trends.

1 Allen, Mark, and John H. Fisher, *The Essential Chaucer: An Annotated Bibliography of Major Modern Studies* (Boston: G. K. Hall; London: Mansell, 1987). Annotated entries arranged topically, cross-listed, and indexed. Also freely available online at <<http://colfa.utsa.edu/chaucer>>.

2 Leyerle, John, and Anne Quick, *Chaucer: A Bibliographical Introduction* (Toronto: University of Toronto Press, 1986). Arranged topically, cross-listed, and indexed. Especially good for backgrounds.

3 Morris, Lynn King, *Chaucer Source and Analogue Criticism: A Cross-Referenced Guide*, Garland Reference Library in the Humanities, 454 (New York: Garland, 1985). Alphabetical bibliography pertains to source study of Chaucer's works, indexed to ease access and student use. See Section 5 below.

1.4 Bibliographies of individual works

Best for focused study and for researching the history of individual topics.

1 *The Chaucer Bibliographies*, ed. Thomas Hahn (Toronto: University of Toronto Press). Eighteen volumes are projected in this series, with those published to date listed below. In each, detailed annotations are arranged chronologically within broad categories. Each volume also includes an introductory survey of criticism and an author and subject index.

(*a*) *Chaucer's 'General Prologue' to the 'Canterbury Tales': An Annotated Bibliography, 1900–1984*, by Caroline D. Eckhardt (1990).

(b) *Chaucer's 'Knight's Tale': An Annotated Bibliography, 1900–1985*, by Monica McAlpine (1991).

(c) *Chaucer's Miller's, Reeve's, and Cook's Tales* [an annotated bibliography, 1900–92], ed. T. L. Burton and Rosemary Greentree (1997).

(d) *Chaucer's 'Wife of Bath's Prologue' and 'Tale': An Annotated Bibliography, 1900 to 1995*, ed. Peter G. Beidler and Elizabeth M. Biebel (1998).

(e) *Chaucer's 'Pardoner's Prologue' and 'Tale': An Annotated Bibliography, 1900–1995*, by Marilyn Sutton (2000).

(f) *Chaucer's Lyrics and 'Anelida and Arcite': An Annotated Bibliography, 1900–1980*, by Russell A. Peck (1983).

(g) *Chaucer's 'Romaunt of the Rose' and 'Boece', 'Treatise on the Astrolabe', 'Equatorie of the Planetis', Lost Works, and Chaucerian Apocrypha: An Annotated Bibliography, 1900–1985*, by Russell A. Peck (1988).

2 The bibliographical index in each volume of the Variorum Chaucer (3.4 below) provides an extensive bibliography dedicated to a single work.

2 Dictionaries and reference works

Chaucer study has had a significant role in the development of lexical reference works. The earliest Chaucer glossary (and the first known English–English wordlist) appeared in *Grammatica Anglicana* (1594) by P.G. (probably Paul Greaves), although the list of hard words in the 1598 edition of Chaucer by Thomas Speght has had much more sustained influence—used by dictionary-makers well into the eighteenth century.

Prompted by Frederick J. Furnivall, the founder of the Chaucer Society, work on a comprehensive 'glossarial concordance' to Chaucer began in 1872—really the beginning of Middle English lexicography—although it was 1927 before John S. P. Tatlock and Arthur G. Kennedy produced the first complete Chaucer concordance (2.1.5). Furnivall had long been involved in the *Oxford English Dictionary*, and early work on the Chaucer concordance played a role in the development of the *Middle English Dictionary* (2.1.3). Although Chaucer's linguistic innovation has been recently challenged (see 4.3.1), his works are near the roots of English dictionary-making.

2.1 Dictionaries and concordances

1 Benson, Larry D., *A Glossarial Concordance to the 'Riverside Chaucer'*, 2 vols., Garland Reference Library of the Humanities, 1699 (New York: Garland, 1993). A comprehensive list of Chaucer's words (except function words, such as 'the', 'of', 'and'), arranged alphabetically by *MED*-preferred spelling. Each entry includes a brief definition, parts of speech, references to parallel *MED* and *OED* entries, spelling frequencies of the word, and a list of the word's occurrences with line numbers and quotations. The indexes in volume ii help to locate entries obscured by spelling variation.

2 Davis, Norman, Douglas Gray, Patricia Ingham, and Anne Wallace-Hadrill (eds.), *A Chaucer Glossary* (Oxford: Clarendon Press, 1979). A dictionary of Chaucer's unfamiliar words for the

beginning student; entries include parts of speech, brief definitions, indications of etymology, and line references to Chaucer's works. For more complex definitions, the student should consult the *MED* below.

3 Kurath, Hans, Sherman M. Kuhn, Robert E. Lewis, *et al.* (eds.), *The Middle English Dictionary*, multiple vols. (Ann Arbor: University of Michigan, 1952–2001) (*MED*). Comprehensive, authoritative dictionary of Middle English, based on historical principles, with each definition accompanied by illustrative quotations arranged chronologically. Also indicates parts of speech, pronunciation, and etymology.

4 Oizumi, Akio (ed.), programmed by Kunihiro Miki, *A Complete Concordance to the Works of Geoffrey Chaucer*, 12 vols. (Hildesheim: Olms-Weidmann, 1991–4). More extensive than other Chaucer concordances and more confusing to use as a result. Includes every instance of every word and lists them in several ways: alphabetical concordances, word frequency, reverse word order, etc. Volumes i–ix concord individual works by Chaucer separately; volume x integrates these into a single wordlist. Volumes xi–xii analyse individual works by rhyme-words and provide a single integrated rhyme index. A lexical concordance to Chaucer's works is projected for volume xiii (5 parts).

5 Tatlock, John S. P., and Arthur G. Kennedy, *A Concordance to the Complete Works of Chaucer and to the 'Romaunt of the Rose'* (1927; repr. Gloucester, Mass.: Peter Smith, 1963). An easy-to-use concordance to Chaucer's works, with all significant words arranged in normalized spelling and their occurrences listed by line number. Based on the outdated (1913) Globe edition of Chaucer, but widely available in libraries.

2.2 Encyclopedias and reference

1 De Weever, Jacqueline, *Chaucer Name Dictionary: A Guide to Astrological, Biblical, Historical, Literary, and Mythological Names in the Works of Geoffrey Chaucer*, Garland Reference Library of the Humanities, 709 (New York: Garland, 1988). Alphabetical listing of all personal and planetary names in Chaucer's works. Entries identify the named figure, explain its background, and comment on Chaucer's various uses of the name and its implications.

2 Gray, Douglas (ed.), *The Oxford Companion to Chaucer* (Oxford: Oxford University Press, 2003). A one-volume encyclopedia, with contributions from a team of scholars, covering Chaucer's life and times, works and themes, genre terms, language and metre, critical legacy, and select topics that pertain to his sources and contemporaries. Entries range from succinct identifications to essay-length studies, some with selective bibliographies.

3 Magoun, Francis P., Jr., *A Chaucer Gazetteer* (Chicago: University of Chicago Press; Stockholm: Almqvist & Wiksell, 1961). Alphabetical listing of all place names in Chaucer's works. Individual entries identify and locate the places, give etymologies of the names, briefly discuss Chaucer's uses of them, and provide line references.

4 *New Catholic Encyclopedia*, 2nd edn., 15 vols. (1967; repr. with suppl. vols., Detroit: Gale, in association with the Catholic University of America, 2003). Comprehensive information about Church institutions, history, theology and philosophy, and major personnel. Entries include definitions and history, with attention to biblical and classical roots, patristic and medieval understandings, and modern developments. The first edition (1907–14) is also freely available online at <<http://www.newadvent.org/cathen/>>.

5 Rossignol, Rosalyn, *Chaucer: A to Z. The Essential Reference to his Life and Works* (New York: Facts

on File, 1999). For beginning students, a one-volume quick look-up of Chaucerian names and places, topics, and individual works.

6 Strayer, Joseph R. (ed.), *The Dictionary of the Middle Ages*, 13 vols. (New York: Charles Scribner's Sons, 1981–9). An encyclopedia rather than a dictionary: 5,000 articles on cultural, literary, historical, and artistic topics, covering the medieval European, Arabic, Byzantine, and Jewish traditions. Cross-listed and extensively indexed (volume xiii).

3 Editions of Chaucer's works

Chaucer's works have been continuously in print since the first English printer, William Caxton, began publishing them in 1477–8—the longest sustained legacy of any author in English. For editions earlier than the modern ones listed below, see Ruggiers's collection (7.2).

1 *The Riverside Chaucer*, gen. ed. Larry D. Benson, 3rd edn. (Boston: Houghton Mifflin, 1987; Oxford: Oxford University Press, 1988). The standard edition of Chaucer's works, compiled by a team of contributors, with an excellent text and very useful introductions, glosses, and notes.

2 *The Complete Poetry and Prose of Geoffrey Chaucer*, ed. John H. Fisher, 2nd edn. (Fort Worth, Tex.: Holt, Rinehart, and Winston, 1989). Useful introductions and bibliography accompany a readable text. The only edition of Chaucer's works to include *Equatorie of the Planetis*.

3 *The Complete Works of Geoffrey Chaucer, Edited from Numerous Manuscripts*, ed. Walter, W. Skeat, 7 vols. (Oxford: Clarendon Press, 1894–7). A monumental work of scholarship, and the first edition of Chaucer's works to be based on comparison of manuscripts, with valuable notes and glossary. Volume vii is the best available collection of poems once attributed to Chaucer (Chaucerian apocrypha).

4 *The Variorum Chaucer*, gen. eds. Paul G. Ruggiers and Daniel J. Ransom (Norman: University of Oklahoma Press). Eight volumes, in 46 parts, are projected for this series; 12 parts already published, indicated by dates below. Each edition includes an authoritative survey of critical discussion, textual commentary, tables of variants, and explanatory notes. When a Variorum volume is available, use it for serious study, especially its notes and critical introduction.

Vol. i, *The Canterbury Tales: A Facsimile and Transcription of the Hengwrt Manuscript, with Variants from the Ellesmere Manuscript*, introd. Donald C. Baker, A. I. Doyle, and M. B. Parkes (1979). Photographic reproduction of the Hengwrt Manuscript, the base text for the Variorum edition, with an authoritative palaeographical and codicological description of the manuscript.

Vol. ii, *The Canterbury Tales* (25 parts projected).
Parts 1A and 1B, *The General Prologue*, ed. Malcolm Andrew, Daniel J. Ransom, Lynne Hunt Levy, *et al.* (1993).
Part 3, *The Miller's Tale*, ed. Thomas W. Ross (1983).
Part 7, *The Summoner's Tale*, ed. John F. Plummer III (1995).
Part 9, *The Nun's Priest's Tale*, ed. Derek Pearsall (1984).
Part 10, *The Manciple's Tale*, ed. Donald C. Baker (1984).
Part 12, *The Squire's Tale*, ed. Donald C. Baker (1990).
Part 17, *The Physician's Tale*, ed. Helen Storm Corsa (1987).
Part 20, *The Prioress's Tale*, ed. Beverly Boyd (1987).

Vol. iii, *Troilus and Criseyde* (3 parts projected).

Vol. iv, *The Vision Poems* (4 parts projected).

Vol. v, *The Minor Poems* (2 parts projected).
Part 1, *The Minor Poems*, ed. George B. Pace and Alfred David (1982).

Vol. vi, *The Prose Treatises* (2 parts projected).
Part 1, *A Treatise on the Astrolabe*, ed. Sigmund Eisner (2002).

Vol. vii, *The Romaunt of the Rose*, ed. Charles Dahlberg (1999).

Vol. viii, *History of the Printed Editions*.

5 Manly, John M., and Edith Rickert (eds.), *The Text of the Canterbury Tales: Studied on the Basis of All Known Manuscripts*, 8 vols. (Chicago: University of Chicago Press, 1940). Authoritative description and discussion of the manuscripts of the *Tales* and their variants. Daunting for beginning students. The electronic *Canterbury Tales* project seeks to replace this standard work.

4 Language and metre

The works below have important eighteenth- and nineteenth-century predecessors, but perspectives have changed over time. Early commentators thought Chaucer's metre rough, for example, largely because they did not understand that final *-e* changed in the history of English pronunciation; that is, that syllables pronounced in Chaucer's day became silent in later tradition, creating the illusion of metrical unevenness. Similarly, Chaucer's place in the development of standard English and its vocabulary has been unclear or mistaken because accurate descriptions of Middle English dialects and spellings were not possible until a sufficient number of manuscripts were edited and analysed.

Progress has been made, but many Middle English manuscripts and texts still await proper editing, and others may come to light. Computer processing and analysis have speeded up things, but reliable e-texts are most often those of 'major' authors like Chaucer, while linguistic understanding depends as much on mundane data as it does on literary masterpieces. No comprehensive grammar of Chaucer's language exists, and aspects of his metre remain very much in debate. Much work remains to be done.

4.1 Linguistic context

1 Baugh, Albert C., and Thomas Cable, *A History of the English Language*, 5th edn. (Upper Saddle River, NJ: Prentice-Hall, 2002; 1st edn. 1935). A readable narrative account of the development of English, useful for the frames of reference it provides and for its generally reliable details.

2 Blake, Norman (ed.), *The Cambridge History of the English Language*, gen. ed. Richard M. Hogg, ii: *1066–1476* (Cambridge: Cambridge University Press, 1992). Authoritative (and often technical) description of the linguistic features that characterize Middle English. Topics include phonology

and morphology, dialects, syntax, vocabulary and semantics, literary language, and proper names.

4.2 Pronunciation

1 *The Chaucer Studio Recordings*, cassette and/or CD-ROM audio recordings of most of Chaucer's works, recorded by Chaucer teachers and students, and marketed at very reasonable prices. Contact information: <<http://english.byu.edu/Chaucer>>.

2 Kökeritz, Helga, *A Guide to Chaucer's Pronunciation* (rev. edn. 1961; repr. Medieval Reprints for Teaching, 3, Toronto: University of Toronto Press, 1978; 1st edn. 1954). For beginning students, a description of how to pronounce Chaucer's English, with nine practice passages in phonetic transcription. Originally published with an audio recording.

4.3 Vocabulary

1 Cannon, Christopher, *The Making of Chaucer's English: A Study of Words*, Cambridge Studies in Medieval Literature, 39 (Cambridge: Cambridge University Press, 1998). Shows that Chaucer creates the illusion of lexical innovation even though his vocabulary is in fact traditional. An alphabetical list identifies where Chaucer's words first occur in written English and in Chaucer's works.

2 Elliott, Ralph W. V., *Chaucer's English*, The Language Library (London: André Deutsch, 1974). Surveys issues of Chaucer's pronunciation, grammar, and prosody, and discusses his vocabulary at length. Assesses prose and poetry, colloquialisms and slang, oaths and proper names, technical and literary language, etc. Includes indexes of words and subjects.

4.4 Grammar and syntax

1 Burnley, J. D., *The Language of Chaucer* (Basingstoke: Macmillan, 1988); first pub. as *A Guide to Chaucer's Language* (1983). Brief description of Chaucer's grammar, arranged by parts of speech, and followed by discussion of Chaucer's verb tenses, techniques of negation, and devices of cohesion. Assesses Chaucer's linguistic diversity—grammatical, lexical, and stylistic.

2 Kerkhof, Jelle, *Studies in the Language of Geoffrey Chaucer*, 2nd edn. (Leiden: Leiden University Press, 1982; 1st edn. 1966). Comprehensive description of Chaucer's parts of speech and their grammatical uses, arranged as a linguistic handbook, with representative examples from Chaucer's works.

3 Roscow, G. H., *Syntax and Style in Chaucer's Poetry*, Chaucer Studies, 6 (Cambridge: Brewer; Totowa, NJ: Rowman & Littlefield, 1981). Examines Chaucer's syntax for the ways it creates emphasis and immediacy, considering word order, idioms, repetition and ellipsis, and coordination and subordination, with frequent attention to pronouns and relative clauses.

4 Sandved, Arthur O., *Introduction to Chaucerian English*, Chaucer Studies, 11 (Woodbridge: Brewer, 1985). Linguistic description of the major features of Chaucer's grammar and pronunciation.

4.5 Metre and rhyme

1 Duffell, Martin J., ' "The Craft so Long to Lerne": Chaucer's Invention of Iambic Pentameter', *Chaucer Review*, 34 (2000), 269–88. Explains how Chaucer developed the iambic pentameter line, clarifying its relations with French, Italian, and English precedents.

2 Masui, Michio (ed.), *A New Rime Index to the 'Canterbury Tales'* (Tokyo: Shinozaki Shorin, 1988). Alphabetical index of rhyme- words in the *Tales*; includes accompanying lines of verse or prose context for each occurrence of the word. For rhyme indexes to works in addition to the *Tales*, see Oizumi (2.1.4 above).

3 Robinson, Ian, *Chaucer's Prosody: A Study of the Middle English Verse Tradition* (Cambridge: Cambridge University Press, 1971). A readable commentary on Chaucer's metre, stress, and rhythms, their roots, and their legacy. Emphasizes that Chaucer's poetry is not metrically lock-step and not scanned the same by all critics; yet it is related to iambic pentameter.

5 Sources, analogues, and influences

Chaucer's sources are works he borrowed from directly when creating his poetry and prose, while the analogues are works close enough to Chaucer's own to indicate how he may have shaped traditional material when precise sources are unknown. The 'major influences' listed below inspired a wide array of Chaucer's references, allusions, plots, and characters. Like other early writers, Chaucer did not create the illusion that his work leapt purely from his own imagination; he made it clear that he was adapting his predecessors, and he often did so in ways that draw attention to this creative relationship.

Early editors began to identify the sources of Chaucer's plots and particular passages. The first compilations of such material were published as *Originals and Analogues of Some of Chaucer's 'Canterbury Tales'* by the Chaucer Society (1872–88), but some have been challenged and new sources have been discovered. Still, almost all critical approaches to Chaucer are informed by source-and-analogue study, because comparison of Chaucer's works with such materials reliably indicates the directions of his intention. See also Morris's bibliography (1.3.3).

5.1 Sources and analogues

1 Bryan, W. F., and Germaine Dempster (eds.), *Sources and Analogues of Chaucer's 'Canterbury Tales'* (1941; repr. London: Routledge & Kegan Paul; New York: Humanities Press, 1958). Collects the major sources and close analogues of the *Canterbury Tales*, with chapters dedicated to the links and each individual tale. Foreign-language materials are not translated, but summaries in modern English accompany them. For the 'Knight's Tale', use with Havely (5.1.3).

2 Correale, Robert M., and Mary Hamel (eds.), *Sources and Analogues of the 'Canterbury Tales'*, 2 vols. (Cambridge: Brewer, 2002– .) Updated replacement of Bryan and Dempster (5.1.1), with additions and modifications, and facing-page English translations of all foreign-language texts. Volume i includes chapters on the links, the Reeve's, Cook's, Friar's, Clerk's, Squire's, and Franklin's Tales, the 'Pardoner's Prologue and Tale', 'Melibee', the Monk's and Nun's Priest's Tales, the 'Second Nun's Prologue and Tale', and the 'Parson's Tale'. Volume ii forthcoming for the remainder.

3 Havely, N. R. (ed. and trans.), *Chaucer's Boccaccio: Sources for 'Troilus' and the Knight's and Franklin's Tales*, Chaucer Studies, 3 (Cambridge: Brewer; Totowa, NJ: Rowman & Littlefield, 1980). Modern English translations of Boccaccio's *Filostrato* (complete), *Teseida* (excerpts), and *Filocolo* (excerpts), accompanied by translated excerpts from Troy stories by Benoît de Sainte-Maure and Guido delle Colonne.

4 Windeatt, B. A. (ed. and trans.), *Chaucer's Dream Poetry: Sources and Analogues*, Chaucer Studies, 7 (Cambridge: Brewer; Totowa, NJ: Rowman & Littlefield, 1982). Translates into modern English the major sources and analogues of the *Book of the Duchess*, *Parliament of Fowls*, *House of Fame*, and the Prologue to the *Legend of Good Women*, most excerpted but several complete. Identifies parallels in plot or phrasing between Chaucer's works and those that inspired him.

5.2 Major influences

1 *The Holy Bible*, with notes and preface by Richard Challoner (New York: Douay House, 1941). Known as the Douay–Reims Bible, this modern English version is a close translation of the Catholic Latin Bible that Chaucer knew—the Vulgate Bible of St Jerome.

2 Boethius, *Consolation of Philosophy*, trans. Richard Green (Mineola, NY: Dover, 2002; 1st edn. 1962). A pervasive philosophical influence on Chaucer, which he translated and glossed in his *Boece*. Green's translation includes succinct summaries of each of Boethius' five books.

3 Guillaume de Lorris and Jean de Meun, *The Romance of the Rose*, trans. Charles Dahlberg (Hanover, NH: University Press of New England, 1983; 1st edn. 1971). A pervasive influence on Chaucer's art throughout his career, and a work Chaucer tells us he translated (*LGW* (G) 255), although only a partial translation survives.

4 Robert E. Lewis (gen. ed.), The Chaucer Library, 7 vols. to date (Athens: University of Georgia Press, except where indicated below). The series publishes works that Chaucer knew and used, providing original texts with facing-page translations (one exception), textual notes, and extensive commentaries.

(*a*) *Jankyn's Book of Wikked Wyves, i: The Primary Texts*, ed. Ralph Hanna III and Traugott Lawler, using materials collected by Karl Young and Robert A. Pratt (1997). Walter Map's *Dissuasio*, Theophrastus' *De nuptiis*, and portions of St Jerome's *Adversus Jovinianum*—that is, inspiration for much of the 'Wife of Bath's Prologue' and portions of the Merchant's and Franklin's Tales.

(*b*) Somer, John, *The Kalendarium of John Somer*, ed. Linne R. Mooney (1998). A work that Chaucer tells us he knew (*TA*, Prologue, 81–6), and one he perhaps used when calculating astrological details for his poetry.

(*c*) Lotario dei Segni (Pope Innocent III), *De miseria condicionis humane*, ed. Robert E. Lewis (1978; repr. London: Scolar Press, 1980). Inspired portions of the 'Man of Law's Prologue and Tale' and the 'Pardoner's Tale', and a work that Chaucer tells us he translated under the title *Of the Wreched Engendrynge of Mankynde* (*LGW* (G) 414).

(d) Machaut, Guillaume de, *'Le Jugement du Roy de Behaigne' and 'Remede de Fortune'*, ed. James I. Wimsatt and William W. Kibler, with music ed. Rebecca A. Baltzer (1988). Inspired much of the *Book of the Duchess* and portions of *Troilus and Criseyde* and Chaucer's complaints.

(e) Nicholas of Lynn, *The Kalendarium of Nicholas of Lynn*, ed. Sigmund Eisner, trans. Gary Mac Eoin and Sigmund Eisner (1980). Chaucer's reference work for the astrological calculations in the *Tales*, and a work that Chaucer tells us he knew (*TA*, Prologue, 81–6).

(f) Statius (Publius Papinus), *The Medieval Achilleid of Statius. Edited with Introduction, Variant Readings, and Glosses*, ed. Paul M. Clogan (Leiden: Brill, 1968). Influenced Chaucer's knowledge of the Troy story. A portion of the common medieval school textbook the *Liber Catonianus*. Latin only; not translated.

(g) *Summa virtutum de remediis anime*, ed. Siegfried Wenzel (1984). Source for the *remedia* sections of the 'Parson's Tale'.

6 Chaucer's life

Biography is itself a literary form with its own historical developments. No comprehensive history of Chaucer biographies has been written, but his recent biographers have acknowledged the historical contingencies of their depictions, and confront these contingencies directly. Hammond (1.2.6 above, pp. 1–49) discusses the early landmarks in the biography of Chaucer, and in their introduction, Crow and Olson (6.2) summarize the scholarly pursuit of Chaucer's life-records.

1 Brewer, Derek, *The World of Chaucer* (Woodbridge: Brewer, 2000); rev. repr. of *Chaucer and his World* (1977, 1992). A readable account of Chaucer's life and historical context, illustrated with some 120 colour and black-and-white photographs, mostly manuscript illuminations.

2 Crow, Martin M., and Clair C. Olson (eds.), from materials compiled by John M. Manly and Edith Rickert, with the assistance of Lilian J. Redstone *et al.*, *Chaucer Life-Records* (Oxford: Clarendon Press, 1966). An anthology of nearly 500 historical records from Chaucer's lifetime, most mentioning him by name, edited for scholarly use in their original languages.

3 Howard, Donald, *Chaucer and the Medieval World* (London: Weidenfeld & Nicolson, 1987); pub. in Canada and the United States as *Chaucer: His Life, his Works, his World* (Toronto: Fitzhenry and Whiteside; New York: E. P. Dutton, 1987). An interpretative or psychological biography of Chaucer that builds a sense of his character and personality from historical records of his life, his writings, and knowledge of his intellectual and historical contexts.

4 Pearsall, Derek, *The Life of Geoffrey Chaucer: A Critical Biography*, Blackwell Critical Biographies, 1 (Oxford: Blackwell, 1992). The best available literary biography of Chaucer, notable for its balanced integration of biographical details, historical context, and perspective on Chaucer's works. Includes an illustrated chapter on portraits of Chaucer.

7 Reception and reputation

Part IV of this volume discusses the 'Afterlife' of Chaucer in detail. The compilations below provide the groundwork for such studies.

1 Brewer, Derek (ed.), *Geoffrey Chaucer: The Critical Heritage*, The Critical Heritage Series, 2 vols. (1978; repr. London and New York: Routledge, 1995). Complements Spurgeon (7.3); a compendium of 155 assessments of Chaucer's works that documents the critical appreciation of Chaucer between 1385 and 1933. Excerpts are lengthier than Spurgeon's, and the index almost as good. Provides brief biographies for each critic included.

2 Ruggiers, Paul (ed.), *Editing Chaucer: The Great Tradition* (Norman, Okla.: Pilgrim Books, 1984). Thirteen essays by various scholars describe the career and assess the methods and contributions of Chaucer's editors. Covers the fifteenth to the early twentieth centuries.

3 Spurgeon, Caroline F. E., *Five Hundred Years of Chaucer Criticism and Allusion 1357–1900*, 7 vols., Chaucer Society Publications, 2nd ser., 48–50, 52–6 (London: K. Paul, Trench, Trübner, and Oxford University Press, 1908–17; repr. 3 vols., Cambridge: Cambridge University Press, 1925; New York: Russell & Russell, 1960). Excerpts allusions to, references to, and discussions of Chaucer from his lifetime through the nineteenth century, although selective after 1800 and highly selective after 1868. Chronological arrangement and excellent indexing help to make this monument of scholarship crucial to exploring the critical history of responses to Chaucer.

36 | **Electronic resources**

Philippa Semper

Electronic study resources have come a long way in the last ten years. As the power and availability of the personal computer has improved, so the range of educational aids has increased a hundredfold; the days are past when tutors were armed with only the text and perhaps a tape or video recorder, and when students' only vital possession was a well-worn library card.

It is no longer necessary to explain the workings of the Internet to students or academics; it enables resources for teaching and learning innumerable subjects, concepts, and bodies of information to be quickly shared by people living thousands of miles apart. Chaucer's poetic compliment to Rosemounde—'Madame, ye ben of al beaute shryne | As fer as cercled is the mapamounde' (1–2)—could easily be updated to 'as fer as cercled is the World Wide Web'. In fact, the 'worlds' represented by the medieval *mappa mundi* (a coloured map of the world filled with text and images) and the modern Web have a certain amount in common. Both are repositories for apparently encyclopedic quantities of information which can be read and understood in various ways for differing purposes. Both are shaped by the interests, priorities, and practical circumstances of those who create (or even fund) them. The contents of any web site are as selective as those of the *mappa mundi*, reflecting factors such as the quantity of web space available and the hardware and software specifications of the server. In addition, the choice of material to appear on its pages, whether new or recycled from elsewhere, also answers to the perceived need that underlies the creation of the site in the first place. It is this unavoidable selectivity—even among such an apparent breadth of content—that requires students, teachers, and webmasters alike to develop ways of analysing and evaluating the sites they visit, recommend, or create. Similar qualifications apply to other electronic resources, from film versions of Chaucerian tales to digitized manuscript facsimiles, from databases to CD-ROMs containing image archives and other study aids. In all of these, the tendency may be to forget the selection process, hidden, as it often remains, behind the pleasures of technological wizardry and the evident usefulness of the resource.

Habitual web users often assume that it is now possible to find out more or less anything, since the trick is to know how (rather than where) to look. 'I don't know, but I know someone who does' has metamorphosed into 'I don't know, but I know a search engine that can help me find out'. In many respects this is a liberating change, yet there are several caveats to bear in mind.

Firstly, there is what we might call 'the transference of authority'. The idea that if time and money have been put into publishing something, then it is probably worth reading, can lend a printed text an appearance of authority. This appearance is not always merited in the case of conventionally printed texts, but it is still less likely to be merited in the case of web pages. Because the Web itself is a form of publishing, the unwary surfer often awards the material credence beyond what it deserves. The process of publishing on the Web is now so straightforward that most people could manage it given a couple of hours of trial and effort or training, and so rapid that many web sites now contain their writers' daily journals (or 'blogs'). Web users need to judge the quality of the pages they access, rather than assuming that they are authoritative, well edited, and largely correct in what they present.

Secondly, perhaps because of the unconscious influence of the computer through which the Web is accessed, material acquired in this way is frequently treated as though it is somehow 'scientifically' true: less subjective, more reliable than material made use of elsewhere. Yet however technologically impressive a site—or the Internet itself—may be, its content remains as liable to human error and personal opinion as if its author were using pen and ink.

Thirdly, because of the sheer quantity of sites now available through the World Wide Web, there is an increasing temptation to assume that the Web contains 'all that there is to know' about something. Even if theoretically possible, this is certainly not the case at present. Search any single topic, and it quickly becomes clear that a limited amount of information is circulating, and that often the same information is being reused, reworked, or linked to by many different sites. What is available is the sum of what has interested or been available to web site providers so far.

Using web-based resources: searches

Web sites may have one or more of a series of objectives, such as: to provide new material (images, information, ideas, analysis) in a form that is easily available to a wide audience; to provide links to material that exists elsewhere on the Web; and to provide opportunities for interaction and communication about this material. Many sites now attempt to fulfil all of these objectives at once. While the ever-increasing range and quality of resources will continue to transform the ways in which we create and disseminate knowledge, the exponential increase in 'casual' publication on the Web requires serious users to develop skills for evaluating resources. Web-based resources concerned with Geoffrey Chaucer and his works now number in the hundreds of thousands. It is vital that users are able to sift through the listings provided by search engines to identify reliable sites.

It is advisable always to use a combination of different resources in order to verify content; comparisons can help in the identification of discrepancies, gaps, or errors. Such a combination should include traditional library-based resources and other media in addition to those available online. Searching the Web should form only one part of a research process that includes planning, consultation, and discussion as well as the location of resources of all kinds.

For those without much previous experience of the Web, a good starting point is the Virtual Training Suite for English Studies (see item 52 at the end of this chapter) created by the Resource Discovery Network (RDN). Although not Chaucer-specific, this free online tutorial is designed to 'help students, lecturers and researchers improve their Internet information literacy and IT skills' and includes 'quizzes and interactive exercises to lighten the learning experience'.

For those more familiar with the Web, there are some basic processes and points of information that can help to begin with. For example, sites can be considered in terms of the people responsible for their production and maintenance, as well as the validity of their content. Sites with .edu as an element in their URL (Universal Resource Locator: the web site address used to access a site) belong to educational institutions in the United States or in one of several other countries (.edu.au in Australia, for example); higher education institutions in the UK have .ac.uk as part of their URLs. Such web sites are most likely to be reliable and useful to students. Other places to check are the 'about this site' or 'contact us' pages.

Commercial web sites (those containing the element .com or .co in the URL) are less likely to answer to either the depth of interest or the academic standards required of students in higher education programmes. There are also 'personal interest' web sites on Chaucer, provided by enthusiastic individuals. These must be carefully assessed by any student considering making use of their material; some represent useful, product-ive, and inspiring approaches to Chaucer and to electronic resources, while others create or reproduce errors and oversimplifications.

It is also useful to look for a 'last updated' comment on the home page of a web site, as this gives a clue to how recently the site has been provided with new material, checked for broken links, and cleared of redundant pages. Since ideas, discoveries, and critical comment can rapidly become outdated in academic contexts, this is a critical indicator of whether a site is a lively and useful work in progress or simply a remnant of some past course of study or research interest now left to decay.

With only a little usage it becomes obvious that the techniques for web research cannot be divorced from the resources themselves. In the case of Chaucer, a sensible approach is to locate four or five wide-ranging, current, scholarly sites and keep their locations to hand by adding them to the 'favourites' or 'bookmarks' lists pro-vided by web browsers. These sites can then form the first port of call for any more specific search. Research into particular areas of Chaucer's life and work can be focused by putting more specific search terms into a search engine. For example, putting 'Chaucer' into the search engine Google currently results in nearly 300,000

URLs; searching on 'Chaucer' and 'Parliament of Fowls' narrows it down to just over a thousand.

It is well worth checking the criteria any search engine uses to list its findings; most show the closest matches first, and often the pages are no longer entirely relevant to the original query beyond the first twenty or thirty listings. Many search engines now provide the option to search for images or news stories concerning a particular subject as well. The decision about precisely what is of interest should be made before the search begins to avoid working through an excessively long set of results. Also available are meta-search engines, which supply results to a single enquiry from several different search engines. Some meta-search engines are more serviceable than others; a comprehensive introduction to the pros and cons can be found on the University of California at Berkeley Library pages (50).

Time can be saved by consulting appropriate portals and metapages before resorting to the search engine. A portal acts as a doorway into sites collected together according to certain criteria, while a metapage can be used beside other sites concerned with the same subject; in addition to providing links, it may carry reviews of their content and value. The Humbul Humanities Hub (4) provides a portal with subject categories such as English Studies, History, and Manuscript Studies, all of which can be searched using whatever term(s) are required (try 'Chaucer' to begin with!). It is constantly updated and is an excellent starting place for research. The Chaucer MetaPage (9), a communal project developed by a number of Chaucer scholars, reviews the web sites it links to under 'Chaucer pages' and under 'Bibliographies'. Part of the Chaucer MetaPage's project is the Electronic *Canterbury Tales* (26) provided by Daniel T. Kline, which collects reliable links, assesses their contents, and presents new material. Many of this site's subject headings link to other trustworthy sources on the Web, such as the Harvard Geoffrey Chaucer page (43) for details of Chaucer's life. It even provides a Chaucer 'in/ and popular culture' page where you can check for the existence of films, coffee shops—even care homes!—that are somehow connected to Chaucer. For further popular, but sometimes admirable, resources, type 'Chaucer' into the BBC's educational web site BBCi (40). An excellent portal is the Labyrinth Resources for Medieval Studies site (7), supported by the Georgetown University Medieval Studies program. This lists a range of web sites, of which many are online texts. Chaucer resources are to be found under the subject heading 'English, Middle'. Michael Hanley's Chaucer Scriptorium (3) has a wide range of links to bibliographies, reference resources, and images, including a very useful 'Links related to Chaucer and Medieval Studies' page. Similarly, Jane Zatta's site (6), designed primarily for the use of her own students, lists links under the headings 'Context', 'Tales and Background', and 'Other Chaucer and Medieval Resources'. For a wide range of resources, the medieval section of Jack Lynch's site (5) is always worth consulting.

Learning to navigate sites is of primary importance. At base, of course, there is always the 'Back' button on the browser, which can help a web surfer work through a maze of URLs. Another way to a site that has been visited and then lost is by using Explorer's

'History' button, which lists links to the sites visited in alphabetical order under the headings 'Today', each day of the previous week when the Web was used, 'Last Week', and '2 Weeks Ago', and also allows searches for a particular subject among all the pages viewed regardless of date. Sites often have indexes if the number of pages is large or the cross-referencing likely to be complex. These can operate in whatever manner the designer chooses, but the most helpful arrange links to their pages in alphabetical order and allow searches. For example, the index of the Harvard Geoffrey Chaucer site (43) provides links to all its 'Texts and General Subjects'.

Using web-based resources: content

A useful web site may offer new material in a variety of guises, or provide access to printed material in electronic form. This may include primary texts that are now difficult to find or out of print, or have never before been published. It may provide links to other electronic resources—textual, visual, or aural—and point to discussion lists or other forms of online forums that will be useful for the researcher. For students of Chaucer all of these categories of data and material are available at numerous sites.

New critical material

New material containing critical comment is surprisingly hard to find on the Web. Numerous sites offer links to critical essays, but the majority of these have already been published elsewhere. Luminarium's Geoffrey Chaucer page (8), for example, has a section entitled 'Essays on Chaucer', but, with the exception of the student essays listed, almost all the links are to articles already published elsewhere, whether in hard copy now digitized, or by means of electronic journals. This is typical; many web sites content themselves with lists and links to pre-existing resources rather than creating new ones. A notable exception is the Harvard Geoffrey Chaucer page (43), which frequently provides concise, informative, and insightful essays (that are not available elsewhere) on its numerous Chaucer-related texts, authors, and subjects.

The online student essay itself should be treated with great caution; students may benefit from reading the essays of others, but it is safer to avoid such essays unless they come specially recommended. When they appear on the Web with a marker's comments, some dangers are allayed, but not all institutions or tutors mark in the same way and marking scales may be differently calibrated from institution to institution. Ultimately, most students are unlikely to consider the work of their peers essential reading for essay preparation, and there is little reason to change this opinion simply because such work is mounted on the Web. Luminarium (8) offers a timely warning against plagiarism of such essays and papers: like books and journals, they are copyright to their authors and must be properly cited when quoted.

E-journals and online bibliographies

For critical work on Chaucer and many other medieval matters, electronic journals are the most easily accessible sources, although many require a subscription. Higher education institutions often pay this, so students can access the appropriate journal through a university terminal or by use of a username and password. One of the key publications for Chaucer research, the *Chaucer Review* (39), is available online from volume 34 (2000) onwards, and can be viewed in HTML or PDF format, that is, either through a web browser such as Internet Explorer or Mozilla, or via Adobe's free Acrobat Reader software (49). Institutions may subscribe to a journal service like JSTOR (38), an online archive whose holdings include scholarly journals such as *English Literary History* (which can also be subscribed to individually, 36) and *Speculum*. JSTOR allows searches by title, author, or keywords in the full text, with a choice of sorting priorities; articles accessed can be read on screen or printed out. Other web sites give listings for electronic journals; one of the most complete and easily accessible is that provided on the scholarly publications page of the Labyrinth site (37). There are also online libraries such as *Questia* (51), although these also require a subscription that is unlikely to be paid by a university or college.

A specific bibliography should usually be compiled before electronic journals are consulted. Further, students should always utilize the electronic catalogues of their own libraries in order to discover what is near at hand, in addition to the online catalogues of other academic institutions, including copyright collections such as those of the Bodleian Library in Oxford (16) and the British Library in London (17).

Numerous web sites offer their own searchable bibliographies. The *On-Line Chaucer Bibliography* (13), maintained by Mark Allen and also published each year in the non-electronic journal *Studies in the Age of Chaucer*, allows searching by author, title, subject, or expert keyword, and provides advice on effective search terms. Mark Allen and John Fisher's 1900–84 annotated *Essential Chaucer* bibliography (14) is available electronically after first publication in hard copy in 1987, although it has to be searched through its subject headings rather than through a dedicated search facility. Thirty volumes of the *Chaucer Review* (15) are available in its annotated bibliography, which can be searched through the index or by using the 'find in page' facility of a browser on the single page of 798 entries. The Harvard Geoffrey Chaucer page offers Derek Brewer's *Thirty-Year Working Bibliography for Chaucer and Middle English Literature 1970–2000* (11), which has a rather broader scope (although it too must be searched through subject headings) and also recommends those bibliographies gathered together at the Chaucer MetaPage website. Of these, Alan Baragona's Chaucer page (1) is particularly useful, with a wide range of resources including a number of other bibliographies listed.

David Wilson-Okamura of East Carolina University has a carefully annotated list of online resources, including bibliographies, at <http://www.geoffreychaucer.org> (12).

A non-commercial site which aims to 'sift and sort' online Chaucerian materials, it also offers categories such as 'reception' dealing with less well represented but increasingly important areas of Chaucer studies.

Primary Texts

Online texts—both editions and translations—can be of assistance to those looking for copies of Chaucer's works, or for other medieval literary works with which to compare his writing. Some of these, such as the Canterbury Tales Project's recent release of Caxton's *Canterbury Tales*: The British Library Copies (18), are exceptionally easy to work with, supplying digitized images of manuscripts or incunabula and making the most of hyperlinks and pop-up glosses to give the richest possible reading experience. Others are supplied without much, or any, critical apparatus. The latter often represent editions that are now out of copyright and have been scanned in without any further attention. It can be difficult to trace where and when these editions originated and who was initially responsible for them. This situation is not particularly helpful, but it is better to have access to a text than not to have it at all; the online solution gets around the problem of expensive or out-of-print editions and translations, while offering the chance to compare different readings with ease.

Online texts may be provided as part of wider resource projects. The *On-Line Reference Book for Medieval Studies* (*The ORB*) (24), 'an academic site, written and maintained by medieval scholars for the benefit of their fellow instructors and serious students', is a good example, providing an array of electronic texts with an extraordinarily detailed listing of web resources. The *Internet Medieval Sourcebook* (27) has a comprehensive listing (once again, Chaucer is found under the subheading 'Middle English') together with an exemplary display of information about its texts, including sources, copyright conditions, and citation details.

Another key resource is the Corpus of Middle English Verse and Prose (21), a fully searchable site. The Electronic Literature Foundation's *Canterbury Tales* (23) allows both a reading through the text in one of a number of different forms, and a specific search for whatever words interest you most: typing 'miller' into the search box, for example, will bring you a list of all the lines of the *Canterbury Tales* that have the word 'miller' in them, referenced by tale number and line number within that tale. The publications of the Canterbury Tales Project (25) also provide this function. The 'Electronic *Canterbury Tales*' (26) has an annotated list of online texts, with comment on the suitability of each one for different academic and non-academic purposes, as does the 'Texts of Chaucer's Works Online page' from the Chaucer MetaPage site (19). For any electronic text, the University of Virginia's Electronic Text Centre (28) is a good place to start.

Historical contexts

In addition to work focused upon Chaucer himself, a range of resources can help with the related issues of historical and cultural context. Some are specifically grouped around Chaucer, as in the Harvard Geoffrey Chaucer site (43), which discusses issues such as pilgrimage and courtly love. Others are concerned with the fourteenth and fifteenth centuries more generally, or with their political, aesthetic, or military endeavours. Luminarium's page 'Additional Sources for Medieval England' (42) gathers together a long list and can provide a link for most areas of medieval life and history.

For a rapid glance at the general context for Chaucer's writing, timelines are extremely useful; a first port of call should be the wide-ranging TimeRef Medieval History Timeline (44), which includes month-by-month events, brief bibliographies of key figures, and even details of medieval locations, including castles, abbeys, and cathedrals, with three-dimensional reconstructions.

Several sites host sets of images, creating a vivid sense of the visual and aesthetic contexts of Chaucerian texts. For example, geoffreychaucer.org (2) and the Chaucer Scriptorium (3) include image sections among their pages, with annotated links. Medieval maps can be viewed through the online cartographic index of late medieval maps (41).

Online reference works

One of the most obvious, and yet potentially most troublesome, uses of the Web is as a vehicle for encyclopedias of all kinds. For rapid access to bite-sized information on Chaucerian topics, it can hardly be bettered. Some encyclopedias are more reliable than others, however. The *Catholic Encyclopaedia* dates from 1908, but its preface is included so that readers can be aware of its particular agenda and nuances. The *On-Line Reference Book for Medieval Studies* (10) incorporates a scholarly encyclopedia. Less easy to judge are those entries contained by, for example, the online encyclopedia *Wikipedia*, which is under a constant process of construction by a large number of online contributors. In some cases, the encyclopedic 'information' is, quite simply, out of date. Users should beware of the Chaucer entry in *Infoplease*, despite the link to it from Luminarium (8), since its bibliography section contains nothing more recent than 1989 and makes the claim that 'the best editions of Chaucer's works are those of F. N. Robinson (1933) and W. W. Skeat (7 vol., 1894–97); of *The Canterbury Tales*, that of J. M. Manly and E. Rickert (8 vol., 1940)'.[1] A student convinced that these works remain 'the best editions' would be seriously disadvantaged. Similarly, there remains much of interest in the 1907–21 edition of the *Cambridge History of English and American Literature* (to which several sites have links), yet there is also a great deal that is now outdated.

Language resources

Students encountering Middle English for the first time may wish for assistance in reading the language. The Harvard Geoffrey Chaucer site (43) has sections for 'Teach Yourself Chaucer' and 'Chaucer's Language', and also hosts the Middle English Glossarial Database (32). Edwin Duncan supplies a basic Chaucer glossary (29), which marks up the most common words. Teresa Reed has a quick guide to Middle English pronunciation (33), while Melinda Menzer includes material on Chaucer's work in her site on the Great Vowel Shift (31). Most practical of all, the *Middle English Dictionary* (35) online allows a range of searches and provides links to several lines for each example of a word it cites, allowing a much wider sense of the contexts in which any single word acquires a range of meanings. A visit to the Chaucer Studio (34) provides further access to the sounds of Chaucerian texts, as do the Chaucer MetaPage audio files (30).

Discussion lists

Many discussion lists are archived on the Web, and some of these form a valuable resource. Although browsing through the archived messages can be productive, it is often quicker to put very specific search terms into a search engine that will automatically pick up relevant postings to the list. Subscription to discussion lists is a possibility; the Chaucer Discussion List (45) is an obvious choice, but there are others with a wider range, such as the Medtextl Discussion Group (47). Members of such groups often dislike being petitioned for help with student essays, and only those interested in participating in a wide-ranging and high-level discussion should subscribe. The *Medieval Review* emails electronic reviews of recent books to its subscribers, providing a means of keeping up to date with critical material. For all such lists, subscribers should ensure that they have sufficient mailbox space to accommodate the messages that will arrive as a result. These messages remain the intellectual property of their authors and must be properly cited if quoted in essays or papers.

Online forums

There are increasing opportunities for more direct interaction using the Web. The Chaucer MetaPage (9) promotes a Metamentors scheme to provide advice for both teachers and learners in matters Chaucerian. Metamentors even offer 'distance learning by grouping students into on-line classes (on a listserv), or into groups that focus on one issue for a set period of time, or into individual tutorials'.[2] This is in addition to any other educational programmes students may be following. Here the special functions and facilities of the Web come into their own; it is impossible to imagine such an international exchange of teaching and learning without it. For a more informal environment in which to discuss Chaucer and his works, try requesting a chat room, message board, or mailing list in the 'authors' section of Catherton.com (46), or use a search engine to find one of the several bizarrely Chaucer-related chat rooms.

A further way of using the Web to make contact with others is through sites that link into a community of scholars. Membership of these is often primarily for teachers and scholars, such as the New Chaucer Society (48), but their web pages also give information about their conferences and journals. These demonstrate the way in which the Web facilitates the distribution and dissemination of material and ideas in other media.

Teaching and learning

Many web sites are designed as study resources for higher education modules and programmes. Such sites are likely to contain high-quality and factually reliable materials that university students and instructors will find of particular use. Most obvious is the Harvard Geoffrey Chaucer website (43), which 'provides materials for Harvard University's Chaucer classes in the Core Program, the English Department, and the Division of Continuing Education', but which also notes that 'others . . . are welcome to use it'. The site, which has primarily focused on the *Canterbury Tales* to date, offers a virtual cornucopia of high-quality resources, including glossed Middle English texts, translations of Chaucerian analogues, selected works by other writers, critical articles, graphics, and general information on the Middle Ages. The Chaucer MetaPage (9) is an initiative of 'a group of medievalists interested in promoting Chaucer studies on the WWW'. Launched at the 33rd International Congress of Medieval Studies, it aims to organize and provide navigation aides for Chaucer resources on the Web, and to work towards enhancing and extending those resources. For teachers of Chaucer, *The On-Line Reference Book* (10) includes a useful 'Resources for Teaching' section, and Dan Kline maintains an invaluable section of the Chaucer MetaPage (9) entitled 'Online Assistance for Teachers and Students of Chaucer and the Later Middle Ages'.

Non web-based electronic resources

A number of important electronic resources, particularly digitized manuscripts, are available on DVD or CD-ROM. Until recently, the large file-size of high-resolution images has precluded their distribution over the Internet. Often producers or copyright holders are bound by financial constraints to ensure that the dissemination of their materials earns revenue. Consequently, licensing agreements vary from allowing single users to view a CD-ROM, to enabling an institution to publish content across its intranet from a networked CD. A range of regulations governing 'legitimate use' may permit use for 'personal research', or allow resources to be used in the classroom. It is exceedingly rare for copyright holders or publishers to allow users to republish (electronically or in print) the resources contained in a CD.

Such resources, however, can profoundly enrich the study experience. The CD-ROM of the *Book of the Duchess*, published by the University of Calgary Press in hypertext in 1997, includes audio files of the complete poem being read in Middle English, pop-up notes and glossary, and useful editions of source texts for comparison. The work of the Canterbury Tales Project (25), based at the Centre for Technology and the Arts at De Montfort University, has thus far published CD-ROMs of the 'Wife of Bath's Prologue', the 'General Prologue', and a Hengwrt Chaucer digital facsimile, with several other tales scheduled to follow soon. This is a highly labour-intensive initiative involving the transcription of all manuscripts and early printed books of the *Canterbury Tales* into computer-readable form. Each publication is a truly encyclopedic hypertext edition, enabling students and scholars to compare all known early textual versions of the *Canterbury Tales*.

All of these electronic resources have much to offer in assisting students, scholars, and teachers in the study of Chaucer and his works. Like non-electronic books and articles, they represent the interests and labour of many different people, and we have much to be grateful for in their efforts. Such resources will continue to grow and develop, even as we learn to understand 'information' and our own responses to it in different (even as yet unimaginable) ways.

WEB LINKS

Portals and metapages
1 Baragona's Chaucer Page: <http://academics.vmi.edu/english/chaucer.html>.
2 geoffreychaucer.org: <http://geoffreychaucer.org/>.
3 Hanley's Chaucer Scriptorium: <http://www.wsu.edu:8080/~hanly/chaucer/chaucer.html>.
4 Humbul Humanities Hub (English Studies): <http://www.humbul.ac.uk/english/>.
5 Jack Lynch, Literary Resources—Medieval: <http://andromeda.rutgers.edu/~jlynch/Lit/medieval.html>.
6 Jane Zatta, Chaucer: *The Canterbury Tales* Portal: <http://www.siue.edu/CHAUCER/>.
7 The Labyrinth: Resources for Medieval Studies: <http://labyrinth.georgetown.edu/>.
8 Luminarium Geoffrey Chaucer Page: <http://www.luminarium.org/medlit/chaucer.htm>.
9 The Chaucer MetaPage: <http://www.unc.edu/depts/chaucer/>.
10 *The ORB (On-Line Reference Book for Medieval Studies)*: <http://www.the-orb.net/>.

Bibliographies
11 Derek Brewer's *Thirty-Year Working Bibliography for Chaucer and Middle English Literature 1970–2000*: <http://www.courses.fas.harvard.edu/~chaucer/bibliography/b-1-intr.htm>.
12 geoffreychaucer.org Bibliography Page: <http://www.geoffreychaucer.org/bibliography/>.
13 *On-Line Chaucer Bibliography*: <http://ncs.rutgers.edu/biblio.htm>.
14 *The Essential Chaucer (Annotated Bibliography of Chaucer Studies 1900–1984)*: <http://colfa.utsa.edu/chaucer/>.

15 *The Chaucer Review: An Indexed Bibliography Vols. 1–30*: <http://www3.baylor.edu/~Chaucer_Bibliography/>.

Library catalogues online

16 Oxford Libraries Information System Catalogue: <http://www.lib.ox.ac.uk/olis/>.
17 The British Library Public Catalogue: <http://blpc.bl.uk/>.

Primary texts online

18 Caxton's *Canterbury Tales*: The British Library Copies: <http://www.cta.dmu.ac.uk/Caxtons/>.
19 Chaucer MetaPage Listing: Texts of Chaucer's Works Online: <http://www.unc.edu/depts/chaucer/chtexts.htm>.
20 Chaucertext: An Online Archive for Electronic Chaucer Scholarship: <http://www.winthrop.edu/chaucertext/>.
21 Corpus of Middle English Verse and Prose: <http://www.hti.umich.edu/c/cme/>.
22 Edwin Duncan, *An Electronic Edition of the 'General Prologue' to Geoffrey Chaucer's 'Canterbury Tales'*: <http://www.towson.edu/~duncan/chaucer/indexn.htm>.
23 Electronic Literature Foundation *The Canterbury Tales*: <http://www.canterburytales.org/canterbury_tales.html>.
24 *On-Line Reference Book* Text Library: <http://www.the-orb.net/libindex.html>.
25 The Canterbury Tales Project: <http://www.cta.dmu.ac.uk/projects/ctp>.
26 The Electronic *Canterbury Tales*: <http://hosting.uaa.alaska.edu/afdtk/ect_etexts.htm>.
27 *The Internet Medieval Sourcebook*: <http://www.fordham.edu/halsall/sbook.html>.
28 University of Virginia Electronic Text Centre: <http://etext.lib.virginia.edu/>.

Language resources

29 A Basic Chaucer Glossary: <http://www.towson.edu/%7Eduncan/glossary.html>.
30 Chaucer MetaPage Audio Files: <http://academics.vmi.edu/english/audio/audio_index.html>.
31 Melinda Menzer, *The Great Vowel Shift*: <http://alpha.furman.edu/~mmenzer/gvs/>.
32 Middle English Glossarial Database: <http://www.courses.fas.harvard.edu/~chaucer/tools/>.
33 Teresa Reed's Middle English Pronunciation Guidelines: <http://www.jsu.edu/depart/english/treed/chpronounce.htm>.
34 The Chaucer Studio: <http://english.byu.edu/chaucer/>.
35 *The Middle English Dictionary Online*: <http://ets.umdl.umich.edu/m/med/>.

Online journals and journal archives

36 *English Literary History*: <http://muse.jhu.edu/journals/elh/>.
37 Labyrinth Scholarly publications (links to online journals): <http://www.georgetown.edu/labyrinth/professional/pubs/scholarly_pubs.html>.
38 Jstor: The Scholarly Journal Archive: <http://www.jstor.org/>.
39 *The Chaucer Review*: <http://muse.jhu.edu/journals/cr/>.

Information on historical contexts

40 BBCi History Page: <http://www.bbc.co.uk/history/>.
41 Late Medieval Maps 1300–1500: <http://www.henry-davis.com/MAPS/LMwebpages/LM1.html>.
42 Luminarium Additional Sources for Medieval England: <http://www.luminarium.org/medlit/medresource.htm>.

43 The Harvard Geoffrey Chaucer Page: <http://www.courses.fas.harvard.edu/~chaucer/>.
44 TimeRef Medieval History Timelines: <http://www.btinternet.com/~timeref/index.htm>.

Discussion lists and forums

45 Archives of the Chaucer Discussion Group: <http://listserv.uic.edu/archives/chaucer.html>.
46 Catherton.com: A Guide to Artists, Authors, Directors and Musicians—Chaucer page: <http://www.catharton.com/authors/76.htm>.
47 Medtextl Discussion Group Database: <http://www.mun.ca/mst/medtext/>.
48 The New Chaucer Society: <http://www.artsci.wustl.edu/~chaucer/>.

Other useful sites

49 Adobe Acrobat Reader—free download: <http://www.adobe.com>.
50 Meta-Search Engines (Information from library at University of California, Berkeley): <http://www.lib.berkeley.edu/TeachingLib/Guides/Internet/MetaSearch.html>.
51 Questia: <http://www.questia.com/popularSearches/geoffrey_chaucer.jsp>.
52 Resource Discovery Network's Virtual Training Suite for English Studies: <http://www.vts.rdn.ac.uk/tutorial/engstud>.

NOTES

1. <http://www.infoplease.com/ce6/people/A0864398.html>, 18 Jan. 2003.
2. <http://www.unc.edu/depts/chaucer/mentors.htm>, 8 Aug. 2003.

Postscript

Julian Wasserman †

In his landmark 1980 volume *Approaches to Teaching Chaucer's 'Canterbury Tales'*, Joseph Gibaldi captured the anxieties of many of his academic colleagues:

on the one hand, no other literary figure continues to generate more enthusiasm and dedication in teachers and students alike than Geoffrey Chaucer does. On the other hand, because of the decline of the study of both language and history in contemporary American education—and the corresponding decline in contemporary American life of linguistic and historical interest or even awareness—no other major English author is in as much danger of having his work either completely eliminated from the standard curriculum or so watered down and 'simplified' as to be eliminated in all but name only.[1]

Yet the fears voiced by Gibaldi have been no more realized than *hende* Nicholas's prediction of the second flood in the 'Miller's Tale'. As even a brief perusal of almost any contemporary bibliography will demonstrate, academic Chaucer is alive and well in the twenty-first century with record production of Chaucer scholarship in a daunting variety of forms and methodologies. In particular, the dire predictions of the 1980s suggesting the demise of Chaucer and medieval studies in the face of the wave of newer methodologies have proved largely unfounded. In part such fears came from the adoption of bodies of critical theory in Early Modern or Renaissance studies that saw the 'logocentric' premodern Middle Ages as a straw man or mythological counterpoint to the currentness of the then new regime in reading texts, if in fact there be texts at all. One might think of some of the early work of Stanley Fish in this regard. Similarly, Jacques Derrida's positing that the notion of separating signifier from signified began with the Enlightenment again implied a positivist, logocentric Middle Ages that stood in symbolic counterpoint to deconstructive postmodernism. Such constructions of the Middle Ages, not unlike the superstition-riddled dark ages of Enlightenment polemics, proved to be just that—constructions, parts of a new set of arbitrary dualities or oppositions, favouring one half of the dualism (in this case the postmodern) against its complement, 'the medieval'. Indeed, seeing history as linear and progressive made postmodernism simply another step away from the Middle Ages, a movement that threatened to leave Chaucer and the rest of the medieval canon one phase remoter from the present. Yet viewing cultural history as a series of antithetical pendulum-like movements may suggest that the postmodern turn away from 'the modern' may be a return to many of the medieval tropes originally discarded by the Renaissance.

One reason for anxiety among Chaucerians was the rejection, or at least interrogation, of the notion of periodicity by some new critical modes, the traditional division of English literature into distinct periods. Such an approach had been part of what made the Middle Ages, and hence Chaucer, special, or at least an area of specialization. A worrying implication was the overhaul of the curriculum in which medieval literature was an essential (or often required) component. Even today the question of the extent to which the supposed 'alterity' of the medieval should be stressed is subject for debate. Another implication was the broadening of the canon, which effectively meant the elimination of some traditionally taught authors in favour of the newly included ones.

Despite such fears, Chaucer studies have proved to be fertile ground for these 'newer' approaches, as this Guide shows, from deconstruction to Marxist, feminist, and psycho-analytical readings, and to gender studies and queer studies. Certainly postmodern-ism's fundamental assertion of the radical instability of the text is embodied in the complicated manuscript tradition inherent in the hand-copied texts of the medieval period. And if to read a text is to rewrite it, are not such reader-response rewritings all the more evident when the read text is in Middle English rather than modern English? As Chaucerians have been quick to point out, Chaucer's poem to 'Adam, his Owne Scriveyn' or his plea that his text of *Troilus and Criseyde* be not mismetred by some future scribe (5. 1793–6), can be read as paralleling postmodern anxieties about the instabilities of texts. Moreover, the problems of finding or creating a stable text among or from the eighty-plus pre-1500 manuscripts or printed texts that bear witness to the *Canterbury Tales* raise many of the same issues inherent in the postmodern perception of textual instability. Indeed, the fragmentation or fluidity of text has been compared by Dan Kline to the fluid nature of the Web itself on his 'Electronic *Canterbury Tales*' web site.[2] Thus, far from becoming antiquated, marginalized work unsuitable for con-temporary critical approaches, Chaucer has proved to be an important arena in which contemporary critical discourse has taken place. Pre-college and undergraduate readers searching for a helpful survey of such approaches to Chaucer might well consult Peter Beidler's casebook on the 'Wife of Bath's Prologue and Tale', or Steve Ellis's Longman Critical Reader.[3] Among other things the 1980s saw the founding of *Exemplaria*, a journal devoted exclusively to modern theoretical approaches in the field of medieval and Renaissance studies. Of *Exemplaria*'s fifteen-year output, a good deal of space has been devoted to Chaucer, including several special issues. At the same time, a measure of how successfully Chaucer studies have weathered the critical threats of the 1980s is the fact that the type of approach for which *Exemplaria* was founded has now become an essential part of mainstream Chaucer studies in journals such as *Studies in the Age of Chaucer* or the *Chaucer Review*, the former being founded after Gibaldi's declaration of the uncertain future of Chaucer studies in the academy.

The same evolution is evident in the Chaucer classroom. Rather than, as Gibaldi feared, sliding into obscurity in the face of a changing culture and profession, Chaucer studies have, like most disciplines, benefited from the fact that the artificially constructed dualism between theory and literature classes has for the most part withered away, so that instead of a course devoted exclusively to deconstruction or psychoanalytic approaches to literature, one is as likely to encounter these methodologies taught among the several approaches to Chaucer in a given class.

At the same time, there is a long and rich tradition of readers—academic and non-academic alike—enjoying in Chaucer the drama of universally recognized human types with virtues and vices familiar to every age. Florence Ridley, in the introduction to the Gibaldi volume, paraphrasing Beryl Rowland's earlier assessment, finds part of Chaucer's eternal popularity in 'what we today might call a constant of mammalian motivation'.[4] What was true for Beryl Rowland and Florence Ridley is no less true today. A little over twenty years later Harold Bloom, in a fascinating study of human genius, still turns to Chaucer for such qualities.[5] In this, Bloom certainly captures much of what we value Chaucer for today. Chaucer's seeming pluralism, or at least his remarkable ability to maintain core values while withholding absolute judgement, have much appeal in increasingly pluralistic societies.

Ambiguity, or rather a richness and complexity that refuse to be reduced to simple threads, has meant that Chaucer has continued to appeal and be taken up by a multitude of varying and often contradictory constituencies. In both America and Britain, Chaucer can be invoked as a conservative staple, a subject that is a traditional part of the purer education of a golden age and a better time, one that must be conserved at all costs in the face of changing values and popular culture. At same time, Chaucer is often invoked as a touchstone by liberals fighting censorship, for example by Senator Patrick Leahy on 24 July 1995 at the Senate Judiciary Hearings on child pornography and the Internet. Chaucer continues to be invoked as an emblem of Empire and a colonial educational regime at the same time as he is, elsewhere, regarded as a democratic leveller who could bring together a high-born prioress and a miller as verbal compeers in the same company. Today he is also written of and taught as a proto-feminist who takes care to voice women (and powerful ones at that), or the masculinist author of rape tales.

From where do such Chaucers spring? Despite the much-vaunted Chaucerian universals of human nature, there is a sense in which, like politics, all Chaucer is local Chaucer. That is, there are many Chaucers because Chaucer has taken on the contours of the places in which he is taught and read. What one finds, then, is that Chaucer, even in Middle English, is Chaucer with a local accent. Accordingly, one must consider what might be called the continental drift that has increasingly separated British and American perceptions of the poet among those who pass through their very different educational systems. One might thus project two very different responses to Chaucer on the part of middle-aged graduates of these systems. Chaucer for the average middle-class Briton might well elicit a groan and a remembrance of school exams. British Chaucer, as he is conceived by many graduates of the educational system, is inextricably a part of high-stakes testing that determines fate and income. Master Geoffrey is matter to be mastered. More generally, Chaucer has been in this system part of a nationalistic programme of self-identity, a poet valued for his 'Englishness' and hence—no matter the 'naughty bits'—part of a conservative cultural agenda.

For American liberals education is potentially a great equalizer (in the context of civil rights), not a means of plucking the clever out of the herd. Thus, emphasis on pedagogy in American Chaucerians is not merely an act of self-preservation or of obligation to 'quyte' Master Geoffrey for a good tale or two but a political act, a redistribution of intellectual wealth. There is a long tradition of romanticizing the classroom, evident in cinema from the 1950s' *Blackboard Jungle* to the 1990s' *Dangerous Minds*. This is also a theme with an equally long television history: *Room 222*, *Mr. Novak*, *The White Shadow*, and the current *Boston Public*. So the pedagogical movement in Chaucer studies has a complex context, which has in turn added to the growing differences between British Chaucerians and their American cousins.

American Chaucer teachers report the ubiquitous party-goer who upon the mention of Chaucer feels compelled to recite as many lines of the 'General Prologue' as can be recalled. The 'Prologue' evokes a far-off place, a remove that is physical as well as temporal. Chaucer is both exotic, in terms of sound—at least to American ears—and comfortably familiar in terms of content. While British notions of Chaucer might be sourced in the Spenserian proclamation of Chaucer as the 'well of English undefiled' (*Faerie Queene*, 4. 2. 32)—perhaps even a purity lost or a declining purity that must be defended—American Chaucer is perhaps best embodied in the Chaucer evoked by Washington Irving in *Bracebridge Hall*, in which Irving wistfully imagines the pilgrims gathering outside the Tabard Inn, expressing a desire to join in their classless camaraderie as an equal. For Irving, as for his late twentieth- and twenty-first-century heirs, Chaucer is posited as democrat, someone who could mix knight with miller. For Irving, Chaucer further combines a sense of European culture and heritage with what even the nineteenth-century writer imagined as frontier conditions (or at least rustic living). The same amalgam is arguably attractive to modern Americans, who find in the Middle Ages primitivism and culture laid side by side, a combination that remains an important part of the American self-image.

NOTES

1. *Approaches to Teaching Chaucer's 'Canterbury Tales'* (New York: MLA, 1980), p. ix.
2. See Ch. 36, item 26.
3. Peter G. Beidler (ed.), *The Wife of Bath: Complete, Authoritative Text with . . . Essays from Five Contemporary Critical Perspectives* (Basingstoke: Macmillan, 1996); Steve Ellis (ed.), *Chaucer: The 'Canterbury Tales'* (London: Longman, 1998).
4. 'Introduction: The Challenge of Teaching the *Canterbury Tales*', in Gibaldi (ed.), *Approaches*, p. xii.
5. See Harold Bloom, *The Western Canon: The Books and School of the Ages* (New York: Harcourt Brace, 1994), ch. 4.

Chronology

Chaucer's major works

The precise dating of all of Chaucer's works is problematic. The most securely dated is the *Book of the Duchess*, an elegy for Blanche, duchess of Lancaster, who died in 1368 or 1369, but even here a few scholars have claimed that the poem was not written at Blanche's death but for one of the annual commemorations held to observe that death. The *House of Fame*, which shows a powerful response to the Italian poet Dante, is generally held to follow Chaucer's two trips to Italy in the 1370s. We are on more secure ground at least in knowing the *order* of Chaucer's works, thanks to the 'bibliographies' he himself gives in the introduction to the 'Man of Law's Tale' and particularly the Prologue to the *Legend of Good Women*, a poem that lists the first five items below as preceding the *Legend* (F 332, 417–25; G 264–5, 405–13). This Prologue also lists various lost works, as well as noting Chaucer's translation of the *Romance of the Rose*; its reference to Chaucer's stories of Palamon and Arcite and the life of St Cecilia indicates that early versions of some of the *Canterbury Tales* (the 'Knight's Tale' and 'Second Nun's Tale' respectively) were already in existence. Other features that have helped determine the generally accepted chronology below are studies of Chaucer's stylistic development and the pattern of influences from other authors, as well as references to his works in works by other writers like Usk and Deschamps (though the latter works cannot themselves be securely dated).

1368–9	*Book of the Duchess*
*c.*1378	*House of Fame*
*c.*1380	*Parliament of Fowls*
*c.*1385–6	*Troilus and Criseyde* finished
*c.*1385–6	*Boece* finished
*c.*1386	*Legend of Good Women*
*c.*1386–1400	*Canterbury Tales*
*c.*1391	*Treatise on the Astrolabe*

Chaucer's life and career: an outline chronology

Early 1340s	Chaucer born, probably in London
1357	Page in the household of the Countess of Ulster
1359–60	Captured during wars in France and ransomed by the Crown
1366	Diplomatic mission to Spain
By 1366	Marriage to Philippa de Roet
1367	Receives life annuity from Edward III; *Valettus* and esquire in his service
1372–3	First mission on Crown business to Italy
1374–86	Controller of customs in the port of London
1374–*c*.1386	Holds lease on dwelling over city gate at Aldgate
1378	Second mission to Italy
1380	Cecily Chaumpaigne's release to Chaucer concerning her *raptus*
1380	Lewis Chaucer born
1385–9	Justice of the Peace for Kent
1386	Testifies aged 'forty years and more' in legal case involving the Scrope family
1386	MP for county of Kent
By 1387	Philippa Chaucer dies
1389–91	Clerk of the King's Works
1390	Robbed three times between 3 and 6 September
1394	Granted royal annuity of £20
1399	Further annuity from Henry IV
1399	Takes lease on house in the grounds of Westminster Abbey
1400	Death and burial in what has since become Poets' Corner, Westminster Abbey

Index

A

Aaron of Mainz 460
'ABC, An' 90, 117, 308, 336, 502, 504, 507, 508
Ackroyd, Peter 537–8
Addison, Joseph 514, 515
Aers, David 36, 246, 247, 366
Alan of Lisle 214, 264, 299
Albertanus of Brescia 259, 265, 308, 341
alchemy 77, 186–7
Alfred the Great 160
allegory 347
Allen, Mark 612
altri racconti di Canterbury, Gli 571
*An Acte for thaduauncement of true Religion and for
thabolisshment of the contrarie* 506
Ancrene Wisse 281
Anderson, Robert 519–20
Anelida and Arcite 116, 243, 297
Anglo-Norman 293, 294, 304
Anne, queen 40, 120, 122, 295, 427
antisemitism 195, 357, 469
Aquinas, Saint Thomas 217
Aquitaine 52, 54, 55
Arian heresy 88
Ariès and Béjin 248
Aristotle 44, 157
Arnold, Matthew 355, 356, 402, 524–5
Arnoldus of Villanova 187
Arundel, Archbishop Thomas 40, 117, 282
astrology 176–81, 182
astronomy 174–6
At the Tabard Inn 566
Atwood, Margaret 537
Auchinleck manuscript 204, 286
auctor 274
Augustine, Saint 165–6, 190, 220, 347:
Bible exegesis 166, 347
Confessions 227
De doctrina Christiana 166, 190, 347
sex and 220
Austin, David 539
Australia 539–41
author:
make-up of 10
neglect of 21
relevance of 10
author-narrator:
naive, self-effacing 243
postmodernism and 401
relationship between 2, 296–7
as simpleton 2
see also under names of works
author/author-function 20–3
authorship, multiple 577
Avignon 319
Ayenbite of Inwit 281

B

Bacon, Roger 185
Bakhtin, Mikhail 36–7, 199, 384–6, 391, 392,
393, 396–8
Bakshi, Ralph 572
Bale, John 327
ballet 564
Ballet Rambert 564
Barnett, Allen 433
Barrett, Elizabeth 553
Barthes, Roland 9–10
Bartlett, Robert 451
Baughan, Colonel Robert 484
BBC 1, 572–3
Beauchamp, Sir William 17, 429
Beckett, Gilbert à 564
beggars 33
Beidler, Peter G. 557, 622

Bell, Robert 490, 520
Bennett, L. A. W. 329
Benson, C. David 365–6
Berkeley, Lord Thomas 275
Bersuire, Pierre 190, 258, 319
Bessermann, Lawrence 340, 346, 348
Betherum, Dorothy 297
Betterton, Thomas 549, 578
Bevis of Hampton 286, 287
Bible:
    accessability 93, 116, 279
    canon established 335
    Chaucer and 332–49
    composition of 334–5
    exegesis 166, 347
    familiarity of 333
    glosses 338, 343–6
    interpretation of 167, 335–8, 344, 349
    language of 84, 116, 117
    patristic exegesis 348
    Sodom and Gomorrah 218
    translation of 167, 338–9
    vernacular 117
bibliographies 595–98, 612–13
biography:
    future of 23
    as narrative 19–20
    readings based on 9
    see also under Chaucer, Geoffrey
Black Death 12, 29–30, 34
Blackwood, Robert 490
Blake, William 540–1
Blamires, Alcuin 36, 346
Blanche, Duchess of Lancaster 12, 14, 57, 166,
    168, 298, 538
Bloch, R. H. 248
Bloom, Harold 529, 533, 534, 623
Boccaccio, Giovanni 221, 269, 292, 293, 318,
    319:
    Dante and 314
    Decameron 316, 320, 325–6, 566
    on English people 59
    Filocolo 25
    Filostrato 14, 261, 322
    Florence and 74
    Latin writings 323
    Teseida 14, 184, 261, 323, 325, 410, 411, 412,
        472
Bodel, Jean 288
Boece 116, 161, 164, 165, 242, 308
Boethius 13, 219, 262–3, 305, 411:
    Consolation of Philosophy 61–3, 159–60, 160–4,
        171, 347
Boitani, Piero 116

Boitani and Mann 579
Bolingbroke, Henry, duke of Hereford 40, 41 *see
    also* Henry IV
Book of the Duchess:
    author-narrator 2, 118, 235
    Bible and 340
    Blanche of Lancaster and 14, 166, 168
    CD-ROM 617
    Ceyx and Alcione story 260
    date 625
    John of Gaunt and 166, 168, 295
    language 146
    literalism and 168
    London and 71
    poetic status 268–9
    Roman de la Rose and 292
    Seton and 538
    sources 295, 298–9, 300, 523
Book of Vices and Virtues 216, 275
Booth, Wayne C. 119
Bourdieu, Pierre 529, 530, 534
Bowden, Betsy 549, 550–1
Bowers, John 453
Bracton, Henry 29
Bradshaw, Henry 491
Brantingham, Bishop of Exeter 39
Brembre, Nicholas 14, 69, 70, 78
Brétigny, Treaty of 55
Breton lay 293
Brewer, Derek 240, 544, 578
Brown, Ford Madox 521, 522, 523
Browne, Matthew 524
Bruce, Christopher 564
Bukton, Sir Peter 14, 17, 121, 122
Burgess, Anthony 535
Burley, Sir Simon 14, 39
Burne-Jones, Sir Edward 513
Burnley, David 240
Burrell, Arthur 555, 556
Burroughs, William S. 536
Burrows, John 366
Bury St Edmunds 35
Butler, Judith 437, 438–9

C

Cadden, Joan 218
Caie, Graham 119
Cambridge Chaucer Companion 579
Cambridge Corpus Christi manuscript 61, 113,
    114, 123, 124, 202–3, 204
Cambridge Dd.4.24 manuscript 488, 490
Cambridge University Library MS Gg.4.27
    499–500, 507

Camille, Michael 194, 199
Cannon, Christopher 9, 11, 18–19, 419
'Canon's Yeoman's Tale':
　alchemy and 186–7
　London and 77
Canterbury Tales Project 494, 613, 617
Canterbury Tales:
　apocryphal material 506
　Augustinian reading 166
　author-narrator 2, 236, 256
　Bailly, Harry *see* Host
　Boethius and 116
　Canon's Yeoman 483
　carnival 389–91
　CD-ROM 493–4
　Chaucer the pilgrim 2, 35, 76, 236, 364,
　　484
　Clerk 231
　Cook 76, 77, 78, 202
　Dante and 320
　digital text 494
　dissident voices in 37
　divine judgement and 3
　Doctor of Physic 181–2, 185
　editions 481–96, 483, 613, 614
　films of 556, 566–8, 570–1
　Friar 345
　Guildsmen 232
　Host 76, 94, 219, 231, 283:
　　Cook and 77, 78
　　literary opinions of 275–6, 287
　　as Lord of Misrule 389–90
　　marriage of 386–8
　　Pardoner and 126, 219
　　on 'Physician's Tale' 424–5
　itinerary 585
　Knight 27, 101–2, 105, 230, 232
　links between tales 490
　London and 74, 76–9, 77
　Man of Law 230
　Manciple 76
　manuscripts surviving 484–6
　'marriage group' 247, 360, 432
　Merchant 230
　Miller 76, 280
　Monk 76, 230, 232
　multiple voices in 403
　narrative framework 424
　narrator 118
　Nun's Priest 278–9
　order of tales 485–6, 490–1
　Pardoner 76, 87, 94, 126, 202, 279:
　　appearance 231
　　sexuality 213, 219, 432, 433, 434

Parson 86–7, 92, 94, 220–1, 276, 279, 282–3,
　340, 346
　performance in 230
　plan for tales 483, 486
　Plowman 232
　printed editions 486–7
　Prioress 76, 119, 202, 230, 241–2, 284
　questions in unanswered 170–1
　reading of and listening to 118
　'Retraction' 20, 82–3, 118, 274, 348, 464–5,
　　501, 502
　Second Nun 94
　social relations in 13, 35–8
　Squire 105
　staging of 560–1, 563
　stolen parchment and 17
　Summoner 28, 435
　Tabard Inn 74, 586
　television version 1, 572–3
　as term for 'tall tales' 506, 514
　textual problems 483–6
　translations of 482, 551, 557 *see also under*
　　names of tales
　unfinished state of 483, 484, 485, 486, 491
　Wife of Bath 29, 83, 106, 107:
　　ambiguity of 374
　　assertiveness 32
　　authors and 106
　　Bible and 344–5
　　birthmarks 177
　　body 375, 377, 378, 381
　　character 373–4
　　chivalry and 107
　　Church and 83, 344–5
　　clothing 231
　　feminism and 371, 375–6, 377, 378, 380–2
　　genitalia 380
　　manuscript illustration of 202
　　marriages 28
　　as monster 379–80
　　orality and 373–6, 377
　　quotations and 106, 123–24
　　religion and 285
　　sexuality 178, 209–11, 217, 220, 432
　　sound and 376–8, 378, 381
　　as talking 'queynte' 380
　　voice of 373–5, 376
　　women's rights and 345, 372
　Yeoman 77, 102
　see also Ellesmere manuscript; 'General
　　Prologue'; Hengwrt manuscript; St
　　Margaret's, Canterbury, 'Canterbury
　　Tales' Visitor Attraction *and under names
　　of Tales*

Capellanus, Andreas 100
'Cardiff Citie Tales' 537
carnivalesque, the:
  body and 393, 394
  enactment of, twentieth century 396–8
  medieval culture and 386–9
  pilgrimage and 388–9
  as safety valve 385–6, 390
Castiglione, Baldesar 97
Castile 54
Cato 259
Caxton, William 124, 314, 481, 600:
  editions of *Tales* 483, 486, 488, 613
CD-ROMs 493–4, 576, 607, 616, 617
censorship 281, 282, 518–19, 554, 555, 563
Chakrabarty, Dipesh 450
Chandos Herald 293
Chaplin, Charlie 567
Chaplin, Josephine 567
character study 359
characters (Chaucer's):
  carriage of 231
  descriptions of 230–1
  identifying with 227
  interiority 233–5
  modernity of 224
  self-definition 228–9
  subjectivity of 237
characters: literary 224–5
charity 87
Chartier, Roger 10, 14, 21
Chatelain, chevalier de 554
Chaucer, Agnes (mother) 12
Chaucer Cellars 539
Chaucer, Elizabeth (daughter?) 13
Chaucer, Geoffrey:
  Aldgate residence 14, 15
  annuities made to 14, 15, 16, 57
  apocryphal material relating to 506, 507
  audience 119–24
  autobiographical cross-referencing of 499
  bawdiness 540, 550, 551, 553, 563 *see also*
    censorship
  biblical poetics of 346–9
  biography 9–23, 513, 521, 529, 605, 610, 626
  as bureaucrat 58
  burial 15
  canonical status 449–50, 498, 499–502
  capture in France 13, 56
  Catholicism and 573
  chronology 626
  class and 457
  classical background 255–69
  Clerk of the King's Works 15, 40, 74

as compiler 274–5
as conservative 36
as court poet 119, 120, 122
as courtier 58
cultural importance of 528
cultural uses of 529
customs controller 14, 15, 39
Dante and 3, 320–2
darker side of 2, 3
dating of works 625
death 16
as decorative addition 508
diplomatic missions 13, 454
education 159, 449
'elusiveness' 3
endings 404
English canon and 534–5
English language and 116
Englishness 63–4, 521
family home 451
as father of English poetry 63, 235, 503, 513,
  515, 516, 524
as fictional character 11, 538
fiction's allusions to 536
as first modern 520
foreign travel 13–14, 56, 315, 317, 452
foreigners and 455 *see also* orientalism
French background 292–311
French poetry and 295–8
gentil status of 16
historical references absent in 12
Hundred Years War and 13, 38, 56
identity of 235–6
Italian journeys 13–14, 315, 317–18, 328, 625
Italian period 328
John of Gaunt and 9, 12, 13, 17, 57, 120, 121
as JP 19–20
as king's man 16
language 130–56, 513, 514, 518, 530, 535, 601
as laureate poet 502–5
listeners 118, 119
literary life 9, 235
as 'local' author 623
as Londoner 58
as love poet 242–5
manuscripts, copies of 21–3:
  accuracy of 126, 127, 276–7
marketing of 579
marriage 13, 56, 580, 581
medical interests 182
medieval audience 119–24
metamorphosis and 260
metre 149–56
misreading of works, sensitivity to 428

MP 15
obscenity 553
official posts 12, 15, 17, 70, 74
order of works 625
as 'ordinary man' 521
orientalism 454–7
Peasants' Revolt and 9, 37, 70
pharmacological knowledge 182
places and 586–8
poetic forms introduced by 307
poetic status 268–9
poetical followers 204–5
politics and 16, 45–7
popular culture and 21, 573
popularization of 521, 584
protestantization of 506–7
ransomed 13, 38, 56
rape case 2, 11, 14–15, 18, 418–19
readers of 117, 118, 119–21
as reader 259–60
reconfigured version of works of 508
reputation 327–9, 498, 500
rewriting 535–9, 541, 544
robbed 15
royal connections 12, 14
school boredom and 1
school syllabuses and 16
scribal miscopying and 23, 498
scribes, distrust of 126, 127
self-fictionalization 402, 405
seriousness 525
social pessimism 396
social status 16
sources 13, 15, 255, 289, 361–2, 603–5 see also
    under names of works
as squire 120
stage versions 560–5
study of 512, 520, 521, 529, 557, 578, 621–24,
    624
as subversive 36
three-period division of works of 15, 359
translations 482, 509, 513, 514, 516, 519,
    544–57
as translator 274–5, 307–8, 504 see also Roman
    de la Rose
uncompleted works 403–4, 505
US–UK education systems and 4, 623–4
as vernacular writer 273, 281
Virgin Mary and 501–2
women, attitude to 11
see also under names of works
Chaucer, John (father) 12, 13, 70
Chaucer, Philippa (wife) 10, 13, 14, 17, 57,
    538

Chaucer, Robert (grandfather) 66
Chaucer, Thomas (son) 13, 17, 586
Chaucer criticism:
  development:
    early 327–9
    post-Victorian 356–62
    post-Second World War 362–5
    later twentieth century 365–6
  professional 528, 529
Chaucer Review 595, 612, 622
Chaucer Society 489, 512, 524, 580, 581, 582,
    595, 603
Chaucer Yearbook 595
'Chaucers Wordes unto Adam, his Owne
    Scryveyn' 23, 428, 498, 622
Chaumpaigne, Cecily 2, 11, 18–19, 418, 427,
    428, 429
Chesterton, G. K. 532, 533, 534, 537, 541, 578,
    581, 584
Chestre, Sir Thomas 286
Child, F. J. 490
children, adaptations for 554
Chillenden, Prior 589
Chrétian de Troyes 100, 246, 302
chivalry:
    Chaucer's modernity and 105–10
    definition 97–8
    origins 98–101
    origins of term 97–8
Church, the:
    Bible and 334, 335–6
    corruption in 83, 86
    diversity in 348–9
    early fathers 347
    internalization 81
    Lollardy and 93, 282, 338–9
    magic and 185–6
    sexuality and 221
Churchill, Caryl 562
Cicero 259, 264, 299
Clanchy, Michael 115
Clanvowe, Sir John 14, 17, 122, 295, 297, 429,
    499, 552
Clarke, Charles Cowden 554
classical background 255–69:
    authority 264–7
    settings 261–4
    see also under names of writers
Claudian 320
Clements, Bill 541
clerical hierarchy 28–9
'Clerk's Tale':
    Griselda 46–7, 247, 303–4, 338, 377, 445, 470,
    562

influences on 303–4
people, the 45, 46–7
Clifford, Sir Lewis 14, 17
Clifton, Nicholas 425, 427, 429
clothing 230–1
Clough, Arthur Hugh 524
Cobb, Samuel 518
Coburn, Charles Douville 560
Coburn Players 560
codices 125
Coghill, Nevill 556, 557, 563, 572
Cohen, Jeffrey 379
Colet, John 339
commerce 440, 441, 442, 443, 445
'common reader' 531–2, 581–4
'Companion' 579
Companion to Chaucer 579
'Complaint of Chaucer to his Purse' 45, 503
'Complaint of Mars' 406
'Complaint of Venus' 275, 307
concordances 598–9
conjugality 444–6
Conrad, Peter 536, 537
Constantine the African 212
Constitutions 117–18
'Cook's Tale':
    completed version 126
    London and 77–79
    omitted from *Tales* 555
    Perkyn 78, 79
Cooper, Helen 186, 579
courtly love 103, 214, 293, 361, 391–2, 394:
    ambiguity of 240
    importance of 239–40
    invention of 100
    terminology 240–1
Cox, Catherine 371
Crane, Susan 371–2
Crow and Olson 9
crusades 99, 100, 300, 456
Curry, Walter Clyde 183
Cursor mundi 287, 288, 290

D

Dandolo, Lucio 571
Dante Alighieri 13, 228, 296, 318, 320, 324, 325–6:
    Convivio 37, 106
    De vulgari eloquentia 116
    Divine Comedy 3, 116, 241, 257, 269, 314, 318, 320–2, 322
    Inferno 321
    Paradiso 321, 322

popularity of 573–4
Purgatorio 107, 314, 321, 322
Vita nuova 322
Dares the Phrygian 257, 261, 268
Dart, John 488, 517
Daudin, Jean 319
David, Alfred 343
deconstruction 369, 623 *see also*
    postmodernism
Delany, Sheila 35–36, 349
Denis de Rougemont 246
Derrida, Jacques 621
Deschamps, Eustache 2, 241, 295, 296, 299, 302, 310, 311
devotional literature 280–5
dictionaries 598–9
Dictys the Cretan 257, 261, 268
Dido, Queen of Carthage 266–7
Dinshaw, Carolyn 11, 364, 365, 366, 428, 429, 434
dits amoureux 292, 295, 297
Dives and Pauper 194
Doherty, Paul 538
Dolan, Terry 20
Dollimore, Jonathan 439
Domesday Book 34
Donaldson, E. T. 21, 297, 362, 363, 364, 533
Donnington Castle 586
Dor, Juliette 20
Douglas, Sir Robert 540
Douglas, Gavin 247, 267
dramatic theory 359, 360
dream poems:
    Dante and 320
    French influence on 292, 297, 298–9
    metafictional identity of 405–6
    narrator 235, 256
    see also under names of poems
Driver, Martha 494
Dryden, John 327, 328, 509, 513–17, 518, 519, 524–5, 533, 538, 540, 545–8, 549, 552–3, 554, 564
Duke of Northumberland's Library, Alnwick, MS 455 589
Dunbar, William 275, 565
Düring, Adolf von 555
DVD 616
Dyson, Sir George 565–6

E

-*e*, unstressed 515, 518
e-journals 612
Eagleton, Terry 530

Early English Text Society (EETS) 490, 582
Eco, Umberto 168, 538, 573
economic change 30–2
Edelman, Lee 439
editing Chaucer 481–94 *see also* printed editions; textual history
editions 600–1
Edmund, St 41–3, 191
Edward II, king 39
Edward III, king:
  Chaucer and 12, 14, 120, 521, 522
  Hundred Years War and 38, 52
  Perrers and 74
Edward, the Black Prince 38, 39, 56, 58
Edward the Confessor, king 43, 191
Edwards, R. R. 246
Eleanor, queen 52
Electronic Literature Foundation 613
Elias, Norbert 99
Eliot, T. S. 11, 536
Elizabeth I, queen 160
Ellesmere manuscript 484, 485, 489, 490, 491, 501:
  Chaucer's portrait 21, 205
  illustrations 21, 201, 204, 585
  pilgrims' portraits 125
  readers of 119
  scribe of 485
  tale order in 485
  unfinished works and 505
Ellis, Alexander 512
Ellis, Steve 536, 537, 556, 622
England:
  Britain and 54, 452–4
  continent and 54
  cosmopolitan 293–5
English: as university discipline 578, 582
English language:
  education and 294
  French-derived terms 306–7
  law suits and 294
  literary 116, 117, 255, 313
  as marginal 255
  rhyme 307
English Literary History 612
Englishness 51, 63–4
estates satire 232, 358, 366
Eton Roundels 337
Europe, map of 53
Evans and Johnson 381
exchange 442–3
exegetical criticism 363–4, 364–5
Exemplaria 622

F

fabliau 292, 302–3
Faulks, Sebastian 588
feminism 226, 229:
  beginnings of 369
  French 369, 370
  in readings of Chaucer 371–3
  respectability of 372
feminization 213–14
Ferster, Judith 308
Fèvre, Le, Jean 299
film 566–72
Fincher, David 571–2
'Findern manuscript' 501
Fish, Stanley 621
Flanders 54, 57
Fleay, Frederick Gard 578, 580, 581
Flemish language 60
Fletcher, Alan 20
Florence 318
'forein' 62
Foucault, Michel 21, 225–6, 433
Foxe, John: *Actes and Monumentes* 507
Fradenburg, Louise 104, 469, 471–2, 473
Francis of Assisi, Saint 344
'Franklin's Tale' 107–8, 216, 454:
  Arveragus 107, 108, 109, 110, 217, 247, 454
  astrology 176
  Aurelius 108, 454
  Dorigen 108, 109, 110, 217, 247, 454
  romance and 288, 293, 300
  source 325
French background 292–311, 319–20
  Anglo-Norman and Continental 293, 304
  Chaucer's translations 307–8
French language 59, 60, 64, 116, 119, 272, 275, 306–7, 449:
  translations of Chaucer into French 554, 555
Freud, Sigmund 225, 467
friars 86, 167, 344
'Friar's Tale' 190
Froissart, Jean 12, 295, 297, 299:
  Chaucer, comparisons with 58
  Chroniques 58
  Paradis d'amour 295, 298
Furnivall, F. J. 328, 489, 490, 492, 493, 512, 520, 523, 524, 525, 581, 582, 584, 598

G

Galen 257
Ganim, John 391, 472
Garter, Order of 100

Gaunt, John of *see* John of Gaunt
Gawain-manuscript 204
gay: term 436
gender 370, 371–2
'General Prologue' of the *Canterbury Tales*:
  ballet 564
  CD-ROM 494, 617
  choral version 565–6
  Clerk 540
  clothing 230–1
  Doctor of Physic 181
  faces 231
  Franklin 182
  Friar 85, 86
  Guildsmen 36, 75–6
  Host 28, 60, 75
  Knight 27
  London and 74
  Manciple 75
  Merchant 28, 31, 75
  Miller 201
  order of pilgrims in 483
  Pardoner 75, 219
  Parson 27, 76, 83–4, 545, 548
  performance and 230
  Plowman 27, 83–4
  Prioress 75
  Reeve 28
  Sergeant of the Law 75
  Squire 39
  translation of 557
  Wyclif and 167–8
  see also under names of Tales
general reader 529–31, 533, 534, 578
Genoese 315
gentilesse 97, 106, 107, 422, 570
'Gentilesse' 503, 504
Geoffrey of Monmouth 454
George, Saint 43
Georgetown University Medieval Studies
    program 610
Georgianna, Linda 356, 357
German language 554–5
Germany 512
Get Thee to Canterbury 563
Gibaldi, Joseph 621, 622, 623
Giles of Rome 41
Globe edition of Chaucer 512, 525
God's Plenty 564
Godwin, William 328, 521
Goffman, Irving 229
Goldberg, Jonathan 416
Good Parliament 39
Goodwin, Amy W. 304

Gothic art 191
Gower, John 14, 17, 35, 47:
  Cinkante Ballades 293
  Confessio amantis 35, 45, 205, 273, 281,
    508
  copying, supervision of 276
  love and 240
  Mirour de l'Omme 30, 34, 45, 293, 316
  Peasants' Revolt and 70, 426
  sexuality in 219
  Tripartite Chronicle 44
  Vox clamantis 36
Grammatica Anglicana 598
Grandson, de *see* Oton de Grandson
Great Schism 84
Great Vowel Shift 132
Greaves, Paul 598
Greek authors 256–7
Greenblatt, Stephen 416
Gregory the Great, Pope 194
Gualtero dei Bardi 316
Guare, John 562
Guerrini, Mino 571
'guide' as term 579
guides to Chaucer 576–90
  academic 577–80
  history of 577–80
Guido delle Colonne 268
Guillaume de Deguilleville 116–17, 504
Guillaume de Lorris 116, 239, 244, 245, 309, 310
Guillaume de Machaut 235, 293, 294, 295, 296,
    297, 298, 299, 300, 404, 523
Guy of Warwick 286, 287, 301

H

Haidu, Peter 98
Hales, Sir Robert 28
Hales, John W. 524
Hall, Henry 516
Halpern, Richard 355
'Hammond' scribe 501
Hansen, Elaine Tuttle 366, 372
Harington, Sir John 545
Harley manuscripts 205, 488, 490, 505
Harvard University 610, 611, 614
Haskins, Charles Homer 227
Hassall, Christopher 565
Havelock the Dane 286
Haweis, Mary 554
Hawkins, John 563
Hawkwood, John 101, 105, 317, 318
Helgeland, Brian 541, 568
Heng, Geraldine 456

Hengwrt manuscript 484–5, 489, 490, 491:
  dating 494
  digitization 494
  hurried nature of 485
  scribe 485
  superiority of 492, 493
  tale order 485
Henry, duke of Lancaster 56, 293
Henry III, king 52, 55
Henry IV, king 15, 40, 45
Henry V, king 55
Henryson, Robert 454
heresy 282
Hertzberg, Wilhelm 555
heterosexuality 432–3, 436, 438
Hieatt, Kent and Constance 482
Higden, Ranulf 294
higher education, expansion of 578
Hill, Frank Ernest 556
Hill, Richard 563
historicism 416–17, 418
Hoccleve, Thomas 14, 273, 500, 501, 504, 505, 520:
  Chaucer's portrait and 22
  Chaucer's reputation and 204–5
  London and 71
  Regement of Princes 21, 22, 501, 508
Hoffman, Richard L. 184
Holcot, Robert 170
Holland, John 429
Homer 266, 268, 515
homosexuality 218–19
Horne, R. H. 524, 553, 554
horoscopes 176–9
House of Fame:
  Aeneas 267
  author-narrator 2, 235, 406
  classical authors 265–6
  dating 625
  Dido 267
  Italian influence 320–1
  language 146
  London and 71–2, 77
  'nacioun' in 61
  Philippa Chaucer and 10
  questions raised by 170
  translation of 519, 549, 555
  uncompleted? 404
Howard, Donald 329, 533
Howitt, William 586–7
Hugh of Lincoln 459, 460
humanism 362, 364
Hundred Years War:
  financing 31, 315, 317
  free companies and 101
  nationality and 50
Hunt, Leigh 521, 552, 553, 554
Huntingdon Library 491
Huppé, B. F. 35, 190, 347, 348
Huston, John 571

I

iambic pentameter 150–5, 307
iconographic traditions 191–5
identity 226
individual 225, 226:
  group identity and 232
  interior life 228
Ingham, Patricia 457
Innocent III, Pope 163, 228, 407
Internet 576, 608
Internet Medieval Sourcebook 613
'Introduction' as term 579
Iraq 397
Ireland 54, 59, 453
Irigaray, Luce 370
irony 35, 36, 240, 340, 341, 401
Irving, Washington 624
Isabella, queen 40, 43
Islam 306
Italian background 313–29:
  English in Italy 317–19
  financiers 315
Italian language 272, 314, 452

J

Jacquerie 169
Japan 4, 539
Jean d'Angoulême 506
Jean de Meun 116, 165, 170, 219, 239, 244–5, 293, 308, 309, 310
Jean II, king 54, 55
Jerome, Saint 265, 345
Jerusalem 317
Jews 195, 452, 455, 458–61, 469
John of Gaunt:
  Aquitaine and 55
  Chaucer and 9, 12, 13, 17, 57, 120, 121
  criticisms of 39
  daughter's consensual rape 425, 429
  death 40
  French language and 295
  house 67, 71
  London and 71
  marriage, political claims arising from 57

as patron? 9, 14
 Swynford and 57
John XXII, Pope 319
John of Northampton 69, 78
John of Salisbury 185
John the Baptist, St 43, 191
Johnson, Samuel 208, 531, 581
Jones, Terry 20, 101, 105
Jordan, Robert 191
JSTOR 612
Julian of Norwich 228, 281

K

Kaeuper, Richard 100, 105, 107
Kaye, Joel 443
Keen, Maurice 101
Kelly, H. A. 248
Kelmscott Press 513
Kempe, Margery 123, 228
Kendrick, Laura 390
Kennedy, Arthur G. 598
Kenyon, Sir Frederic 492
King Horn 286, 287
King-Aribisala, Karen 538
kingship:
 ascending concept 44–5
 descending concept 40–4
Kirke, Edward 545
Kiser, Lisa 349
Kittredge, G. L. 247, 295, 358–60, 364, 365, 578
Kline, Daniel T. 610, 622
Knapp, Peggy 32, 37
Knight, Stephen 37, 38
knights 98–100
'Knight's Tale':
 Arcite 74, 102, 103, 161, 180, 181, 182, 183, 184, 262, 263, 410, 411, 472–3, 474
 astronomy 179–81
 Boethius and 161
 chivalry and 102–3
 doubling 473–4
 Emelye 74, 161, 180–1, 262, 263, 410, 412, 457, 472, 474, 475, 476, 547, 548
 film version 568–70
 gender 472
 hierarchy and 37
 London and 72, 73
 narrator 475
 Palamon 74, 102, 103, 161, 180, 181, 262, 410, 411, 472–3, 475
 postmodernity and 410
 psychoanalytical reading of 471–6
 setting 261

source 14, 261, 262, 323, 325
 temples 258, 260, 412
 Theseus, Duke 47, 102, 161, 181, 183, 263, 410, 411, 413, 471, 472, 474, 475, 476
 translations of 545, 546–7, 548
Koch, John 555
Kolve, V. A. 79, 196, 198, 302
Koven, Reginald de 564
Krapp, George Phelp 556
Kristeva, Julia 467
Kruger, Steven 433–4
Kynaston, Sir Francis 544–5

L

Lacan, Jacques 225, 369, 370, 375, 467, 474
laity 27–8
'Lak of Stedfastnesse' 503
Lambeth Council 85
Lancaster, Blanche, Duchess of *see* Blanche, Duchess of Lancaster
Langland, William 47, 66:
 Piers Plowman 30, 34, 67, 71, 229, 273, 275, 281
 religion and 83
Lateran Council, Fourth 85, 228
Latin 59, 60, 115–1, 257, 272, 278, 294, 313–14, 449
Laurent de Premierfait 326
law, language of 59
Lawlor, John 298
Lay Folks' Catechism 85
Lay Folks' Massbook 88
Leahy, Senator Patrick 623
Legend of Good Women:
 astrology and 177–8
 author-narrator 235, 427
 Chaucer's works mentioned in 499, 625
 De contemptu mundi and 163
 French literature and 297
 Hypermnestra 178, 179
 London and 72
 love and 243
 narrator 118
 Ovid and 258, 311
 Philomela story 260
 postmodernism and 404–5
 Prologue 274, 283, 402
 questions raised by 170
 as reparation 296
 sources 299, 323
 Virgil and 311
 women, crimes against 427–8
Leibniz, Gottfried Wilhelm von 160

Leicester Abbey 505
Leicester, H. Marshall Jr 229
Lenaghan, R. T. 121, 122
'Lenvoy de Chaucer a Bukton' 121, 503
'Lenvoy de Chaucer a Scogan' 121, 503
Lerer, Seth 498
lesbianism 218, 436
letters 294
Lewis, C. S. 239, 241, 244, 246, 361–2, 565
Leyser, Henrietta 123
Libelle of Englyshe Polycye 59, 316
libraries, university 576
Lionel, duke of Clarence 56
Lipscomb, William 518, 551
literacy 92, 93, 115–19, 123, 203:
    vernacular 117, 118, 203
literalism 167–8
literary characters 224–5
Livre Griseldis 303, 304
Livy 259
Lochrie, Karma 372
'Lollard knights' 122, 168
Lollardy:
    Bible and 93, 282, 314
    Chaucer and 82, 94, 282–3
    lay reader and 282–3
    pilgrimage and 589
    preaching and 278
    public debate and 344
    significance of 93
    see also Wyclif, John
Lombard, Peter 338, 444
Lombards 315, 318
London:
    bridge 67
    Chaucer and 66, 70, 78
    churches 67
    citizenship 66
    conflict 69
    English language 130
    foundation 73
    government of 67–9
    guilds 69
    influence on Chaucer 66, 77
    Inns of Court 67
    languages and 58, 64
    Liber albus 68
    Lombard merchants 316
    map of 68
    multicultural 59–60
    Peasants' Revolt and 69, 452
    pillory 69
    plague 66
    population 66, 451
    post-colonial 451
    street life 67
    walls 67
Loomis, R. S. 579
Lords Appellant 12, 39–40, 164
Lounsbury, Thomas 356–7, 358
love:
    language of 239–42
    terms for 240, 241, 242
Love, Lust and Marriage 563
Love, Nicholas 282
Lowell, James Russell 328, 581
Lowes, John Livingston 183, 328, 360
Lumiansky, R. M. 556
Lunacharsky, Anatoly 385
Lusty Wives of Canterbury, The 571
Lydgate, John 193, 323, 328, 500, 501, 503–4,
    506, 507, 520
Lyotard, Jean-François 401

M

McCormick, Sir William 492
McCulloh, John 460
McEwan, Ian 4
McFarlane, K. B. 122
Mackaye, Percy 560, 561, 564–5
Macrobius 13
magic 185–6, 406, 409, 422
magic realism 406–9
Magnus, Albertus 218
'Man of Law's Tale' 150, 232, 273, 313, 407–8,
    456–7, 625:
    Custance 178–9, 217, 242, 305, 408, 456
    Donegild 212
    'love' in 242
    psychoanalysis 470
    sexuality in 212
    Trevet's *Chronicle* and 304–6, 407–8
'Manciple's Tale' 46, 260, 552, 553
Mandeville, John 205:
    Travels 315, 514
Manly, John M. 358, 363, 484–5, 489, 491, 493,
    614
Mann, Jill 179, 213, 358, 366, 533, 579
Mannyng, Robert 278
manuscripts:
    copying 124–7, 276, 498
    production 124, 577
manuscripts, Chaucer's: procuring 492
marginal images 198–201
Marie de France 275, 286, 288, 293, 303
marketplace 439, 443, 445
marriage 245–9, 432, 435

Mary, Virgin 89–90
Masters, Roy 540
Maurice, F. D. 19
Maximus, Valerius 259, 265, 294
May: love and 396
May Day 397
medicine 181–5
Mehan, Uppinder 451
Melbourne 539
Menagier de Paris 304
mentality 226–9
'Merchant's Tale':
  Bible and 336, 340–1, 395
  Damyan 197, 198, 214–15, 343, 549
  diction 364
  fabliau and 293
  garden in 196–8, 309
  influences on 302
  January 196, 197, 198, 209, 218, 247, 336,
    340, 341, 395
  May 196, 197, 198, 214–15, 247, 336,
    341
  translation of 549–50
Merciless Parliament 15, 39
Merthyr fragment 492
Messahala 275
metre 149–56, 515, 518, 601, 603
Meunier et les ii clers, Le 302
Middle Ages:
  alterity of 622
  attitudes to 523, 524, 622
Middle English:
  adjectives 144–5
  Chaucer's 130
  dialects 130
  morphology 141–9
  nouns 141–2
  pronouns 142–4
  sound-spelling correspondences 131–8
  stress 138–41, 153–5
  study of 512, 520–1
  verbs 145–9
Middle English Dictionary 598
Miller, Lucasta 23
'Miller's Tale':
  Absolon 199, 215, 219, 280, 333
  Alison 199, 215, 332, 333, 347, 472
  astrolabe in 176
  bawdiness 540
  Bible and 332–4
  indecency of decried 513
  John 187, 199, 280, 332, 333, 334
  literalism and 168
  Nicholas 199, 215, 332, 333, 347, 482

Peasants' Revolt and 37
  translation of 518, 551
Milton, John 9, 545, 548
Minnis, A. J. 349, 579
misericords 386, 387
Modernising Theatre Company 561
modernism 401, 402
money 440, 441, 442–6
Mongol empire 455
'Monk's Tale' 46, 163, 221, 310, 323, 490–1,
  506
Montagu, Sir John 14
Montagu, Thomas, earl of Salisbury 504
Montrose, Louis 416
More Canterbury Tales 563
Morel, Richard 429
Morey, James H. 349
Morris, Richard 490, 520, 525
Morris, William 19, 20, 513, 523–4
Morrison, Theodore 556
MS fonds anglais 506
Mudrick, Marvin 552
Murray, Les A. 536–7
Muscatine, Charles 239, 241, 245, 346, 347,
  362–3, 364
Myerson, Jonathan 572
Mystery plays 279–80, 333
mystics, female 228

N

'Nacioun' 51, 60–3
nationhood:
  cultural identity
    56–63
  Hundred Years War and 50, 51, 52–6
Neville, Sir William 429
New Chaucer Society 578, 596
New Criticism 347, 356, 362, 363, 364
New English Dictionary 490
new historicism:
  deconstruction and 417
  negotiation and 229–30
  symbolic significance of events 416
  textuality and 416, 417
Niccolò da Lucca 316
Nicholas of Lyra 338
Nine Worthies 100–1
Noah 332, 333–4
Noah 280
nominalism 168–71
non-readers 584–5
Noonan, J. T. 248
North, J. D. 180

'Nun's Priest's Tale':
  Bible and 341–2, 343
  Chauntecleer 182, 194, 213, 341, 342
  London and 70
  Peasants' Revolt and 9, 37, 70, 78
  Pertelote 182, 213, 342
  philosophy and 162–3
  Reynart cycle and 303
  translation of 519, 545

O

Ockham, William of 168
O'Donoughue, Micky 561
Ogle, George 518, 551, 553
Olson, P. A. 36
On-Line Chaucer Bibliography 612
On-Line Reference Book for Medieval Studies 613, 614
opera 564–5
Ordinance of Labourers 33
Oresme, Nicholas 170
orientalism 448, 454–7
Orléans, Charles d' 506
Ormesby Psalter 200, 201
Oton de Grandson 12, 295, 297, 307
Ovid 13, 177, 244, 255, 256, 257–9, 260–1, 266, 298, 309, 311, 362, 525
Owen, Charles 486
Oxford English Dictionary 598

P

Pagula, William of 85
Paltenghi, David 564
'Pardoner's Tale':
  Black Death and 30, 193
  carving of 191–4
  confession and 229
  echo of 4
  iconography of 191–4
  Masters and 540
  performance and 230
  preaching and 278
  teaching function 281
  television version 572
  translation of 551, 554, 555
  Treasure of the Sierra Madre and 572
Paris, Matthew 316, 458
Parliament 17
Parliament of Fowls:
  author-narrator 235
  carnivalesque and 391–6
  Chaucer's elusiveness and 3
  chivalry and 110
  Cicero and 259
  Complaint of Nature and 214
  garden 321
  love dispute in 239
  social pessimism 395
  sources 299
  translation of 555
'Parson's Tale':
  astrology and 176
  conservativeness of 37–8
  marriage and 247
  salvation and 47
  tree image in 195
Partner, Nancy 208–9
Pasolini, Pier Paolo 556, 566–7
Paston, Sir John 581
Pater, Walter 524
Patience 282
Patterson, Lee 102, 103, 363, 365, 416, 417, 443
Paul, Saint 216, 218, 220, 345, 346
Payer, Pierre 216
Pearsall, Derek 10, 11, 14, 15, 18, 20, 119, 365, 485, 579
Peasants' Revolt:
  account of 34–5
  carnivalesqe element in 384, 388
  Chaucer's mention of 37, 70
  Flemings attacked 59, 452
  foreigners as targets 59, 452, 455
  killings 28
  lawyers as target 425
  London 69
  rape and 426, 427, 429
  women and 426–7
Pennell, Elizabeth Robbins 582, 583, 584–5
Pennell, Joseph 582, 583, 584–5
Pepys, Samuel 545
performance 229–33
Perrers, Alice 39, 74
Peters, Ellis 538
Petrarch, Francesco 318, 319:
  'author's book' 21
  Canzoniere 322
  Griselda story 303, 304, 320, 338
  love poetry tradition 244
  meeting with Chaucer possible 14
  Rime 243
  sonnet 265, 322
Petworth manuscript 489
P.G. (Paul Greaves?) 598
Philipot, Sir John 67, 70, 75, 429
Philippa, queen 56–7, 58

Philippe de Mézières 30, 295, 303, 304, 320
philosophy:
    Augustinianism 165–6
    Boethius 159–65
    religion and 158–9
    term 158
'Physician's Tale' 46, 184–5
    Apius 184, 341, 423, 424
    Bible and 341
    Claudius 423, 424
    commentaries on 424–5
    Legend of Good Women and 425
    rape and 422–4
    source 310
    Virginia 184–5, 422–3, 425
    Virginius 184, 424
Pickering, William 520
pilgrimage 92, 388–9, 589
planetary influences 176, 179–81, 182
Plato 168–9, 187, 257
'Plowman's Tale' 506
poetic technique 356
Pole, Sir Michael de la 39
politics 38–40 *see also* kingship
poll tax 34, 39
Pollard, A. W. 512
Pope, Alexander 516, 518, 519, 549–50
population 29, 30, 35, 230
Portugal 54
post-colonial criticism:
    historical context and 450
    medieval world and 450–1
    practice 448
    remembrance and 458–61
    social justice and 448
postmodernism:
    belatedness 400–1
    Chaucer and 400–6
    Chaucer anticipates 2, 3, 4
    closure and 404
    future of 413
    intertextuality 402, 406
    meta-narrative's death and 3
    modernism and 401, 402
    playfulness 402
    self and 225
    subject and 225, 237
    text, instability of 622
Powell, Michael 570–1
Praz, Mario 328
pre-industrial Britain, nostalgia for
    523
Pre-Raphaelites 523
preaching 278–9

Pressburger, Emeric 570–1
Prestre ki abevete, Du 302
printed editions:
    early 486
    eighteenth century 487, 488–9
    nineteenth century 489
    recension 489, 491, 493
    regularization 488
    sixteenth century 488, 489
    see also textual history
printing 115, 124, 481, 497
'Prioress's Tale' 195, 232, 284, 285, 340, 452, 457, 458–9, 461:
    psychoanalysis and 469
    translations of 552
pronunciation 512, 515
Prudentius 170
psychoanalytic criticism:
    common sense and 463–4
    fantasies 469, 471
    historicism 468–71
    jokes 468–9
    lack and loss 470–1, 472–3, 475, 476
    repression 468, 472
    self-consciousness 464
    Symbolic Order 467–8
    unconscious 468, 469
publishers 530, 576–7
Purves, D. Laing 554
Puttenham, Richard or George 544
Pynson, Richard 487, 500

Q

queer: term 436, 436–7
queer theory 370, 371, 435–7
    historicization 439
    performativity 437, 438–9

R

racconti di Canterbury, I 571
Rachel of Mainz 460
Rands, William Brighty 524
rape:
    class and 106, 423, 426, 429
    consensual 421–2
    invisibility of 426–7
    marital 217
    meaning 418, 419
    representations of 420–4
    revolt and 424–6
reading, portrayals of 113, 118
realism 356, 358, 409, 513, 514, 515, 523

reception 606:
- fifteenth to seventeenth century 497–509
- eighteenth and nineteenth centuries 512–25
- twentieth and twenty-first centuries 528–42

Reed, Henry Hope 578
'Reeve's Tale' 143, 146, 216, 302, 457, 549, 551
religion 81–94:
- Chaucer and 82–3, 344, 359
- confession 85, 228–9, 234, 237, 277, 281
- Creed 88, 90
- debates about 81
- Mass 87, 88–9, 167, 277
- purgatory 91–2
- sermons 85–6
- sins, forgiveness of 91–2
- vernacular 82, 92–3, 284–5
- see also Church

Renaissance 226
Renaud de Louen 308
Resource Discovery Network 609
resources:
- electronic 607–19
- printed 595–606

Revell, Nick 561
Rex, Richard 93
Reynard stories 194
rhyme 149–50, 151, 603
Richard II, king:
- Boethius and 160
- Chaucer and 12, 16, 120
- French culture and 294, 295
- Hundred Years War and 54, 55
- kingship and 41–4
- opposition to 308
- Peasants' Revolt and 34, 427
- rape law 420, 421, 422, 425, 429
- tyranny and 40, 46
- Wyclif and 168

Richardson, Catherine 580
Rickert, Edith 358, 485, 489, 491, 493, 614
Ridley, Florence 623
Riverside Chaucer 482, 484, 485, 491, 494, 535
Robb, Candace 538
Robbins Report 578
Robertson, D. W. Jr 35, 165–6, 190, 243, 346, 347–8, 355, 364–5
Robertson, Kellie 19
Robinson, F. N. 484, 614
Robinson, Peter 494
Rochester 491
Roet, Katherine de 13
Rogers, W. E. 36
roman antique 293

Roman de la Rose:
- Chaucer and 309–11
- influence of 244, 292, 299, 300, 301, 321
- multiple attitudes in 292
- translation of 116, 283, 308
- see also Romance of the Rose

Roman de Renart 303
Roman de Troie 301
romance:
- English 285–7
- French 300–1
- origin of 293
- post-romance 409–13

Romance of the Rose:
- garden 197
- illustrations of 204
- sexuality in 209
- translation of 116, 283, 308
- see also Roman de la Rose

Romantic movement 517–19
Root, Robert K. 578
Rowe, D. W. 240, 246
Rowland, Beryl 579, 623
Rudd, Gillian 579
Rykener, John/Eleanor 434

S

Saddam Hussein 397
Said, Edward 448, 455, 456
St Albans 35
St Margaret's, Canterbury: 'Canterbury Tales' Visitor Attraction 587–8, 588
saints, communion of 90–1
Salter, Elizabeth 365
Sandras, E. G. 523
Saracens 456
Saunders, Corinne 579
Saunders, John 554
Saussure, Ferdinand de 225
Scala, Elizabeth 470
Scalby, John 17
Scattergood, John 122
Schweitzer, Edward C. 183
science 174–88
Scogan, Henry 14, 17, 121, 122, 503
Scotland 54, 59, 453
Scottish Chaucerians 520
Scrope-Grosvenor trial 15, 230
Se7en 571–2
'Second Nun's Tale' 91, 217, 220
Secter, David 563
Sedgwick, Eve Kosofsky 438
self 224–6, 227, 229

Seneca 259
Sercambi, Giovanni 562
Seton, Anya 538
sexuality:
    active and passive 214–15, 219
    burden of 220–21
    Chaucer studies and 432–5
    concept of in Chaucer 209–11
    debt concept 217, 444
    effeminacy 219
    heresy and 435
    modernity of concept 208
    money and 439, 440
    nature and 218–20
    ownership of 216–18
    pleasure of 221
    proto-capitalism 439–44
    sexualities 212–14
    term 208
    see also queer theory
Shakespeare, William 359, 521, 587
'Shipman's Tale' 60, 126, 218, 439–44, 551
Shirley, John 501, 508
Sidnam, Jonathan 544–5
Simpson, James 497, 498
Sittingbourne 491
Six Centuries of Verse: Chaucer to Ted Hughes 572
Skeat, Walter W. 484, 489, 490, 491, 492, 493,
    512, 513, 525, 555, 614
Skelton, John 545
Skute, Larry 36
society:
    change in 30
    Chaucer and 35–7
    class 29
    conflict in 32–5
    gender 29
    the three orders 26–7
    real structure 27
sodomy 218
Somner, William 588
Southampton 315, 316, 317
Southey, Robert 520
Southwark 67
Southworth, J. G. 578
Spain 455
'Spanish record' 13
Spearing, A. C. 365
Speculum 612
Speght, Thomas 327, 487, 489, 500, 507, 508,
    544, 598
Spenser, Edmund 508–9, 544, 545, 624
Spurgeon, Caroline 497, 498, 544
'Squire's Tale' 185, 301, 406, 455, 506, 545

Stallybrass and White 386
Stanbury, Sarah 470
Stanford, Sir Charles Villiers 564, 565
Stanley-Wrench, Margaret 556
Starkie, Martin 563, 572
Statius 261, 298
Statute of Labourers 33
Steen, Jan 563
Stone, Brian 556
Stone, W. G. 584
Stow, John 486, 487, 500, 501, 507, 508
Straw, Jack 70, 78
stress 138–41, 153–5
Strode, Ralph 14, 17, 70, 75, 170, 259, 503
Strohm, Paul 9, 11, 14, 16, 17, 20, 76, 102, 121,
    390–1
Studies in the Age of Chaucer 595, 622
Stury, Sir Richard 14, 17
subject 225, 226, 227, 228
Sudbury, Simon 28
Suetonius 259
'Summoner's Tale' 344, 454
sumptuary laws 33, 36, 230
Swanson, R. N. 87
Swinburne, Algenon 328
Swynford, Katherine 13, 57, 537
syllabuses 359

T

Tale of Beryn 360, 506, 582, 584, 589
Tale of Gamelyn 286, 506, 551
'Tale of Melibee' 46, 205, 236, 265, 287, 308–9,
    341
Tatlock, J. S. P. 425, 598
Tatlock and Mackaye 555
'tail'–'tally' pun 440
taxation 39, 98
television 572–3
tetrameter verse 150
text-image studies 201–3
textual history:
    absences 507–9
    apocryphal material 506, 507
    editorial changes, early 505–6, 507
    modern scholarship 489–90
    original Chaucer 483–6
    regularizing 488
    textual notes ignored 481–2
    variations in texts 483
    see also printed editions and under names of
        manuscripts
Thatcher, Margaret 562
Theatre Magazine 561

Theophrastus 265
Thoreau, James Russell 523, 524
Thoresby, Archbishop John 85
Thorpe, William 388–9
Thousand and One Nights 566
Thynne, Francis 486–7
Thynne, William 486, 487, 500, 506–7
Tolkein, J. R. R. 361
tournaments 99–100, 103
towns 30
translations, Chaucer's 116–17, 518, 524
Treasure of the Sierra Madre 571
Treatise on the Astrolabe 13, 176, 182,
    274–5
Trevet, Nicholas 165, 304–6, 308, 407
Trevisa, John 275, 315
Trigg, Stephanie 355, 360, 498
Trinity College, Cambridge, MS R.3.19 501
Trinity Tales, The 572
Troilus and Criseyde:
    Augustinian reading of 166
    author-narrator 163–4, 204, 236, 256, 274,
        297, 364
    Bible and 340
    Boccaccio and 14, 261, 265, 322, 323
    Boethius and 61, 62–3, 116, 161–62
    chivalry and 103–5
    Criseyde 73, 74, 103, 104, 203, 221, 233–4,
        263, 364, 405, 470
    Dante and 320, 321–2, 324–5
    dedicatees 70, 170, 503
    Diomede 104, 203, 234
    figurative rape 11
    fourteenth-century reputation and 15
    frontispiece, Cambridge Corpus Christi
        manuscript 61, 113, 114, 123, 124,
        202–3, 204
    interiority 233–4
    Lollius 265, 266, 268, 274
    London and 72, 73–4, 77
    love of God 347, 348
    narrator 118, 161
    opera 565
    Pandarus 73–4, 104, 159, 183
    poetic status of 268
    as psychological novel 364
    romance and 300, 301
    Romance of the Rose and 362
    scribal miscopying 498, 622
    setting 261
    sexuality in 212–13, 219–20, 221
    source 14, 261, 265
    tournament 74
    translations 544, 552, 555–6, 557

Troilus 74, 103, 104, 161–62, 183, 203, 240,
    263–4
Troy 257
troubadours 100, 228, 241, 244, 361
Troy 257
'Truth' 164, 503
Tuchman, Barbara 538
Tyler, Wat 388
tyranny 44–5, 46
Tyrwhitt, Thomas 487, 488–9, 497, 507, 518,
    519, 520.551

U

United States of America 512, 624
universities 302, 317
Upland, Jack 507
Urban II, Pope 99, 456
Urry, John 487, 488, 489, 517, 520
Usk, Thomas 14, 297, 499, 503

V

Vache, Sir Philip de la 14, 17, 121, 122, 164
Variorum Edition of the Works of Geoffrey Chaucer
    485, 493
Venice 317
Vere, Sir Aubrey de 39
Vere, Robert de, earl of Oxford 39, 45
Vernon manuscript 204
versification 275–6
Vinsauf, Geoffrey 36
Virgil 13, 255, 256, 265, 266–7, 268, 509, 515:
    Aeneid 257, 266, 311, 320
Virtual Training Suite for English Studies 609
Visconti, Bernabò 14, 46, 318, 323
visual culture 190–205

W

Walden, Roger 40
Wales 54, 59, 453–4
Wallace, David 3, 45, 47, 74, 75, 76, 329, 452,
    457
Walsingham, Thomas 44, 45, 425, 426
Walton, Sir William 565
Walworth, William 70
Ward, Adolphus William 521–3, 581–2, 585, 586
Ward, H. Snowden 585
Warton, Joseph 327
Wasserman, Julian N. 560
Watson, Nicholas 117–18
Waugh, W. T. 122

Wengrow, Arnold 561
Wesley, Samuel 516
West, Sir Thomas 425, 429
Westminster 67, 72, 73
Wharton, Thomas 517–18, 519
Whethamstede, Abbot John 319
White, Hugh 219
Whiting, B. J. 359
'Wife of Bath's Tale':
    anti-feminist literature and 345
    CD-ROM 617
    chivalry and 105–6
    gentilesse speech 570
    Gower and 273
    Lollardy and 346
    psychoanalysis and 469
    rape 420, 421–2
    romance and 301
    staging of 561
    translations of 545, 549, 550
    women and romances 289
William I, count of Hainault 57
William of Norwich 459, 460
Wilton Diptych 41–4, 191
Wimbledon, Thomas of 26, 27
Windeatt, Barry 338, 556, 557, 579
'Womanly Noblesse' 307
women:
    authoritative speakers 309–10
    books and 123
    Chaucer's portrayal of 366
    in marriage 247–8
    opportunities, post-plague 31–2
    representation impossible 370
    romances and 288–9
    as writers 284
Wonderful Parliament 39
Woods, Phil 561

Woodstock 586
Woolf, Virginia 531–2, 534, 581, 584
woollen cloth 31
Worde, Wynkyn de 500
Wordsworth, Dorothy 553
Wordsworth, William 551–3
World Wide Web 607, 608–16:
    bibliographies 612–13, 617–18
    critical material 611
    discussion lists 615, 619
    e-journals 612, 618
    forums 615–16, 619
    historical context 614, 618
    language 615
    library catalogues on-line 618
    metapages 610, 617
    portals 610, 617
    reference works 614
    study resouces 616
    texts 613, 618
Wright, David 482, 556, 557
Wright, Thomas 490
Wyclif, John:
    Bible and 93, 116, 117, 167, 282, 338
    Chaucer and 82, 167
    impact of 338–9
    literalism and 167
    see also Lollardy
Wykeham, Bishop of Winchester 39

Y

Yeager, Robert 20
Yuval, Israel J. 460

Z

Žižec, Slavoj 109–10, 467